G000292814

STREET ATLAS
South Hampshire

Contents

III   *Key to map symbols*

IV   *Key to map pages*

VI   *Administrative and post code boundaries*

1   *Street maps*

215   *Town maps of Andover and Basingstoke*

216   *Town maps of Farnborough and Newbury*

217   *Index of hospitals, railway stations, schools, shopping centres, street names and universities*

PHILIP'S

First edition published 1991
Fourth edition published 1994
First colour edition published 1998
Reprinted 1998, 1999, 2000 twice by

George Philip Ltd, a division of
Octopus Publishing Group Ltd
2-4 Heron Quays, London E14 4JP

ISBN 0-540-07476-4 (hardback)
ISBN 0-540-07477-2 (spiral)

To the best of the Publishers' knowledge, the information in this atlas was
correct at the time of going to press. No responsibility can be accepted
for any errors or their consequences.

The representation in this atlas of a road, track or path is no evidence
of the existence of a right of way.

**The mapping between pages 1 and 216 (inclusive) in this atlas is
derived from Ordnance Survey® OSCAR® and Land-Line® data,
and Landranger® mapping.**

Ordnance Survey, OSCAR, Land-Line and Landranger are registered trade
marks of Ordnance Survey, the national mapping agency of Great Britain.

Printed and bound in Spain by Cayfosa

Digital Data

The exceptionally high-quality mapping
found in this book is available as digital
data in TIFF format, which is easily
convertible to other bit-mapped (raster)
image formats.

The index is also available in digital form
as a standard database table. It contains
all the details found in the printed index
together with the National Grid reference
for the map square in which each entry
is named and feature codes for places
of interest in eight categories such as
education and health.

For further information and to discuss
your requirements, please contact
Philip's on 020 7531 8440 or
george.philip@philips-maps.co.uk

Symbol	Meaning
	Motorway (with junction number)
	Primary route (dual carriageway and single)
	A road (dual carriageway and single)
	B road (dual carriageway and single)
	Minor road (dual carriageway and single)
	Other minor road
	Road under construction
	Pedestrianised area
	Railway
	Tramway, miniature railway
	Rural track, private road or narrow road in urban area
	Gate or obstruction to traffic (restrictions may not apply at all times or to all vehicles)
	Path, bridleway, byway open to all traffic, road used as a public path
	The representation in this atlas of a road, track or path is no evidence of the existence of a right of way
	Adjoining page indicators

Acad	**Academy**
Cemy	**Cemetery**
C Ctr	**Civic Centre**
CH	**Club House**
Coll	**College**
Ent	**Enterprise**
Ex H	**Exhibition Hall**
Ind Est	**Industrial Estate**
Inst	**Institute**
Ct	**Law Court**
L Ctr	**Leisure Centre**
LC	**Level Crossing**
Liby	**Library**
Mkt	**Market**
Meml	**Memorial**
Mon	**Monument**
Mus	**Museum**
Obsy	**Observatory**
Pal	**Royal Palace**
PH	**Public House**
Recn Gd	**Recreation Ground**
Resr	**Reservoir**
Ret Pk	**Retail Park**
Sch	**School**
Sh Ctr	**Shopping Centre**
Sta	**Station**
TH	**Town Hall/House**
Trad Est	**Trading Estate**
Univ	**University**
YH	**Youth Hostel**

Symbol	Meaning
	British Rail station
	Underground station
D	**Docklands Light Railway station**
	Private railway station
	Bus, coach station
	Ambulance station
	Coastguard station
	Fire station
	Police station
+	**Accident and Emergency entrance to hospital**
H	**Hospital**
+	**Church, place of worship**
i	**Information centre** (open all year)
P	**Parking**
PO	**Post Office**
Prim Sch	**Important buildings, schools, colleges, universities and hospitals**
	County and unitary authority boundaries
River Medway	**Water name**
	Stream
	River or canal (minor and major)
	Water
	Tidal water
	Woods
	Houses
House	**Non-Roman antiquity**
VILLA	**Roman antiquity**

- The dark grey border on the inside edge of some pages indicates that the mapping does not continue onto the adjacent page
- The small numbers around the edges of the maps identify the 1 kilometre National Grid lines

The scale of the maps is 5.52 cm to 1 km (3½ inches to 1 mile)

0 ¼ ½ ¾ 1 mile
0 250m 500m 750m 1 kilometre

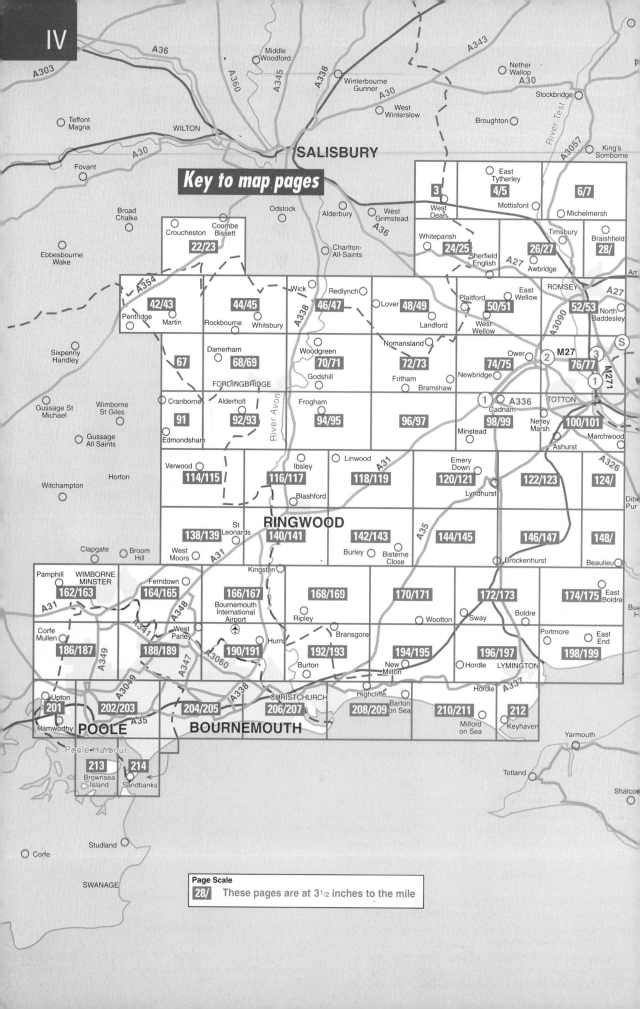

IV

Key to map pages

A303
A36
A360
A345
A338
A343

Middle Woodford
Teffont Magna
WILTON
Winterbourne Gunner
West Winterslow
Nether Wallop
Broughton
A30
Stockbridge
River Test
A3057
King's Somborne

Fovant
Odstock
Alderbury
West Grimstead
West Dean
SALISBURY
A36
A30

3
4/5
East Tytherley
Mottisfont
6/7
Michelmersh

Broad Chalke
Crouchestone
Coombe Bissett
22/23
Charlton-All-Saints
Whiteparish
24/25
Sherfield English
Timsbury
Braishfield
26/27
Awbridge
28/

Ebbesbourne Wake
A354
Pentridge
Martin
42/43
Rockbourne
Whitsbury
44/45
Wick
Redlynch
46/47
Lover
48/49
Landford
Plaitford
East Wellow
50/51
West Wellow
ROMSEY
A27
A3090
52/53
North Baddesley
A27
Am

Sixpenny Handley
67
Damerham
68/69
FORDINGBRIDGE
Woodgreen
70/71
Godshill
Nomansland
Fritham
Bramshaw
72/73
Ower
Newbridge
74/75
A336
1
Cadnam
98/99
M27
2
TOTTON
Netley Marsh
76/77
M271
3
S
1

Gussage St Michael
Wimborne St Giles
Cranborne
Alderholt
91
92/93
River Avon
Frogham
94/95
96/97
Minstead
100/101
Ashurst
Marchwood
A326

Gussage All Saints
Edmondsham
Verwood
Ibsley
Linwood
114/115
116/117
Blashford
118/119
A31
Emery Down
120/121
Lyndhurst
122/123
124/
Dib Pur

Witchampton
Horton
RINGWOOD
St Leonards
138/139
140/141
142/143
Burley
Bisterne Close
A35
144/145
Brockenhurst
146/147
148/
Beaulieu

Clapgate
Broom Hill
West Moors
A31
Kingston
162/163
Ferndown
164/165
166/167
Bournemouth International Airport
168/169
Ripley
170/171
Wootton
Sway
Boldre
172/173
Portmore
East End
174/175
East Boldre
Bu

Pamphill
WIMBORNE MINSTER
A31
Corfe Mullen
West Parley
A348
A347
A3060
186/187
188/189
190/191
Hurn
192/193
Burton
Bransgore
194/195
New Milton
Hordle
196/197
LYMINGTON
198/199
East End

Upton
201
Hamworthy
202/203
A35
204/205
CHRISTCHURCH
206/207
Highcliffe
208/209
Barton on Sea
Milford on Sea
210/211
212
Keyhaven
Hordle
A337
Yarmouth

POOLE
BOURNEMOUTH
Poole Harbour
213
Brownsea Island
214
Sandbanks
Totland
Totland
Shalco

Corfe
Studland
SWANAGE

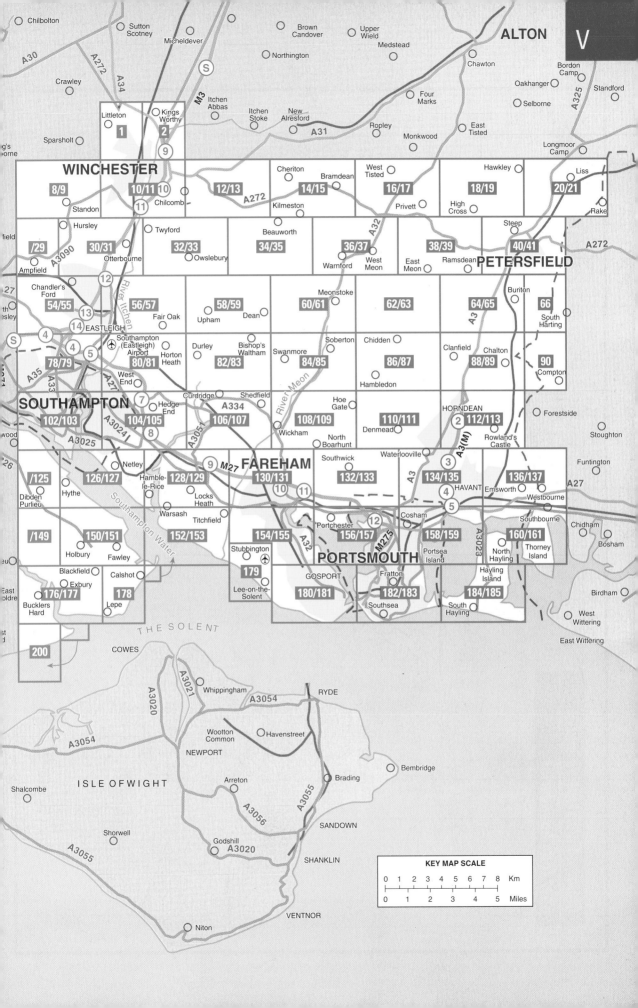

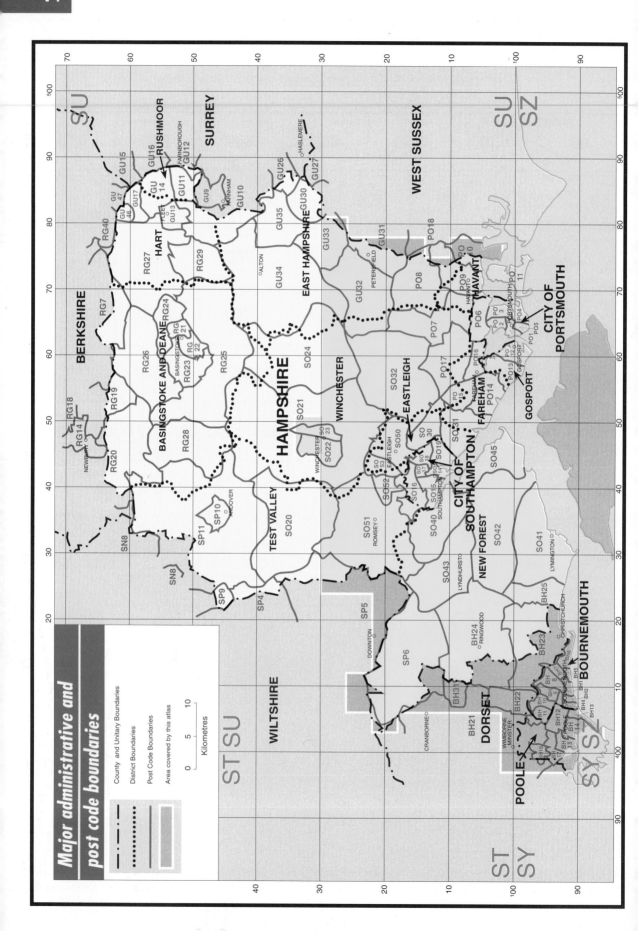

Major administrative and post code boundaries

County and Unitary Boundaries

District Boundaries

Post Code Boundaries

Area covered by this atlas

Kilometres

0   5   10

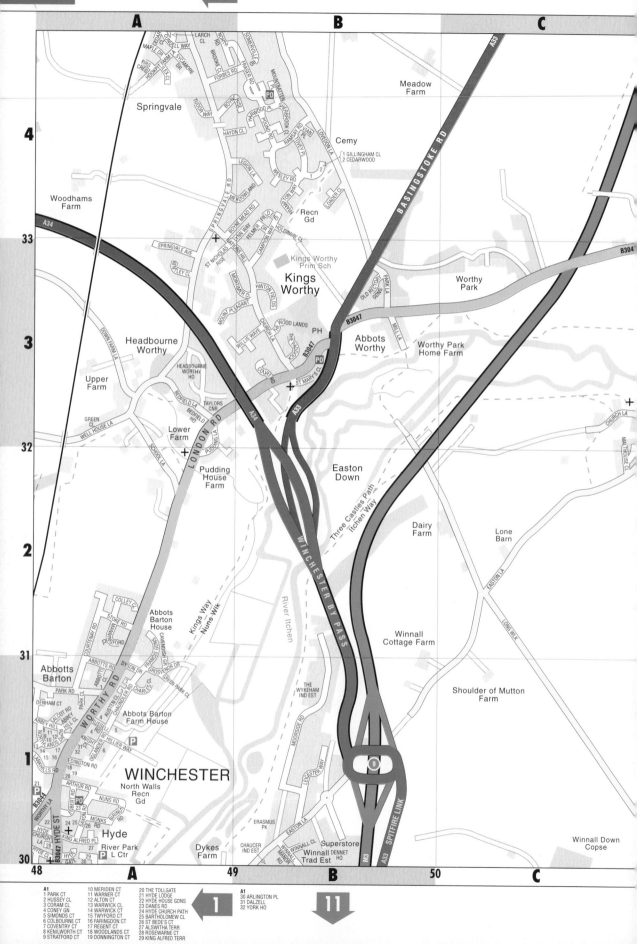

A   B   C

4

33

3

32

2

31

1

30

48   A   49   B   50   C

Springvale

Woodhams Farm

Meadow Farm

A34

BASINGSTOKE RD

B304

Cemy

1 GILLINGHAM CL
2 CEDARWOOD

Recn Gd

Kings Worthy Prim Sch

Kings Worthy

Worthy Park

B3047

PH

B3047

PO

Abbots Worthy

Worthy Park Home Farm

Headbourne Worthy

Upper Farm

Headbourne Worthy Ho

LONDON RD

A34

St Mary's CL

A33

Lower Farm

Pudding House Farm

Easton Down

Three Castles Path
Itchen Way

Dairy Farm

Lone Barn

WELL HOUSE LA

SCHOOL LA

WORTHY RD

WINCHESTER BY PASS

River Itchen

Kings Way

Nuns Wlk

Abbots Barton House

Abbots Barton Farm House

Winnall Cottage Farm

EASTON LA

LONG WLK

CHURCH LA

MALTHOUSE CL

Abbotts Barton

WINCHESTER

North Walls Recn Gd

P

THE WYKEHAM IND EST

MOORSIDE RD

LEICESTER WAY

9

Shoulder of Mutton Farm

SPITFIRE LINK

M3

A33

Hyde

River Park L Ctr

P

Dykes Farm

ERASMUS PK

EASTON LA

WINNALL CL

CHAUCER IND EST

Winnall Manor RD

DENNET HO

Superstore

Winnall Trad Est

Winnall Down Copse

B3047 HYDE ST

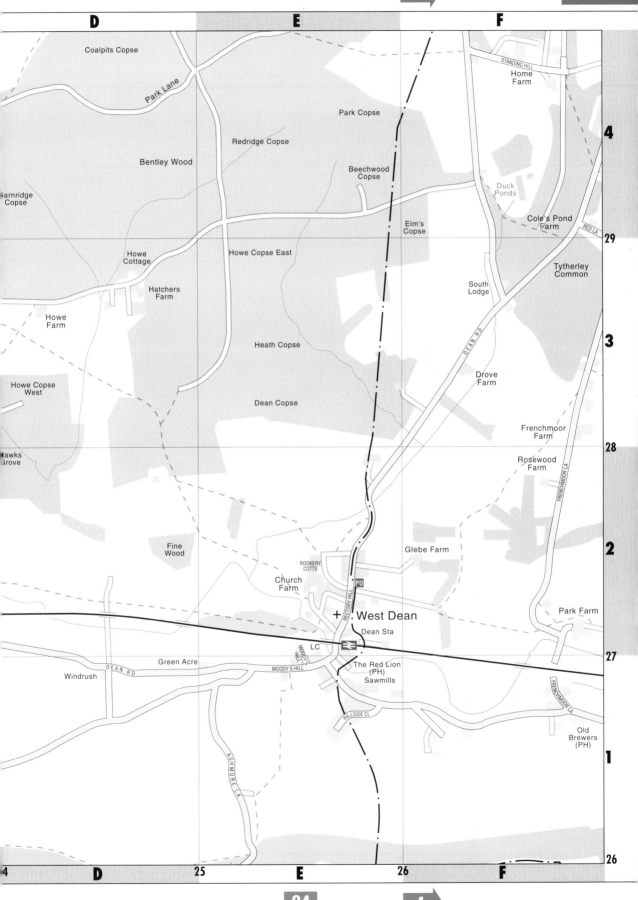

D

Coalpits Copse

Park Lane

Redridge Copse

Bentley Wood

Park Copse

Beechwood Copse

E

STANDING HILL

Home Farm

F

Duck Ponds

Cole's Pond Farm

RED LA

4

arnridge Copse

Elm's Copse

29

Howe Cottage

Howe Copse East

South Lodge

Tytherley Common

Hatchers Farm

Howe Farm

DEAN RD

Heath Copse

Drove Farm

3

Howe Copse West

Dean Copse

Frenchmoor Farm

Rosewood Farm

28

Hawks Grove

FRENCHMOOR LA

Fine Wood

Glebe Farm

2

ROOKERY COTTS

PO

Park Farm

Church Farm

RECTORY HILL

West Dean

Dean Sta

27

LC

Green Acre

DEAN RD

MOODY'S HILL

The Red Lion (PH)

Sawmills

FRENCHMOOR LA

Windrush

HILLSIDE CL

Old Brewers (PH)

1

ASHMORE LA

26

D

Redhills
Copse

Hackpits
Copse

B3084

Deborah
Copse

Pittleworth
Manor

Pittleworth
Farm

F

4

Little Bentley
Farm

Great Bentley
Farm

Holm Moor
Copse

Bentley
Firs

29

Blackpits Wood

The
Bungalow

Great
Copse

3

Lain Copse

Newlyns
Farm

BACK LA

Clapgate
Copse

Spearywell Wood

Snook's
Copse

28

Blackmoor Firs

Bushy
Copse

Culver
Leaze

Woodland
Walk   P

2

Cadbury
Farm

Spearywell

Dummer
Copse

Test Way

Mottisfont Abbey
(National Trust)

Gardens   Priory

27

KEEPERS LA

BENGER'S LA

OAKLEY RD

Abbey
Farm

Mottisfont

Drove Copse

HATT LA

PO

Glebe
Farm

The Monarch's Way

CHURCH LA

River Test

1

River Dun

Hatt Farm
Hatt Hill

Lockerley Endowed
CE Prim Sch

Dunbridge

The
School
Farm

LOCKERLEY RD

Butt's
Green

CLEEVE'S AVE

LC

LC

Test Way

River Dun

LOCKERLEY RD

PH
MILL RISE

DUNBRIDGE LA

Dunbridge
Sta

B3084

26

0   D   31   E   32   F

5

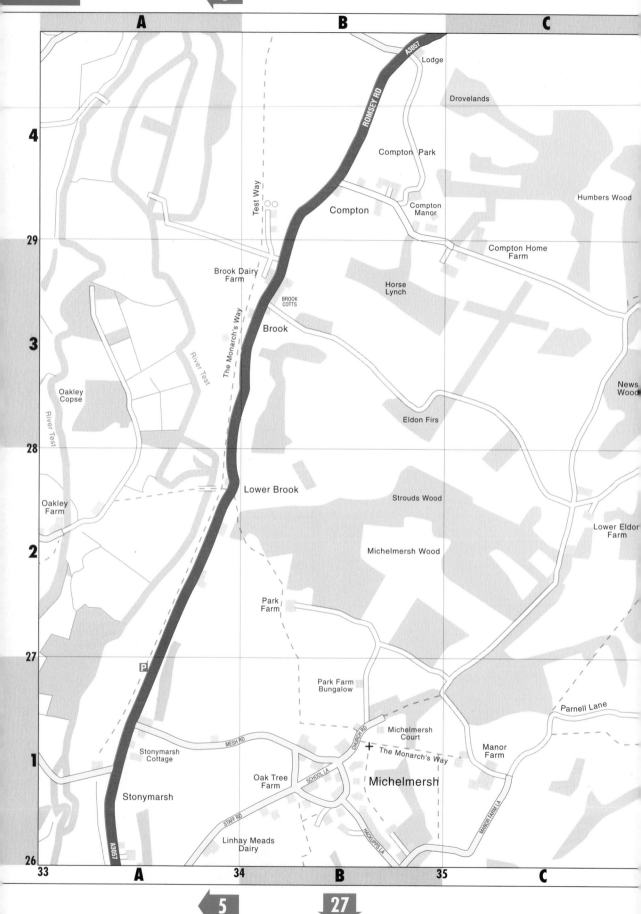

D

E

F

Charlwood Copse

Hoplands

Hoplands Cottages

Bourne Farm

FURZEDOWN RD

FURZEDOWN COTTS

Combe Bottom

4

Furzedown Farm

Luke Copse

29

FURZEDOWN HO

lumbers Wood

Dirty Mount

Parnholt Wood

ews Wood

ELDON RD

3

28

Bailey's Down

The Bungalow

Taunton Vale

Eldon House

+

Fishponds Farm

2

Bailey's Down Farm

PARNHOLT RD

Stubb's Copse

Farley House

27

Parnell La

Bull Grove Copse

Blue Haze Farm

The Monarch's Way

KINGS SOMBORNE RD

Windmill Cottages

FARLEY LA

1

Hall Place

Pitt Farm

BRAISHFIELD RD

Braishfield Manor

Fernhill Farm

Fern Hill La

PAYNES HAY RD

26

6

D

37

E

38

F

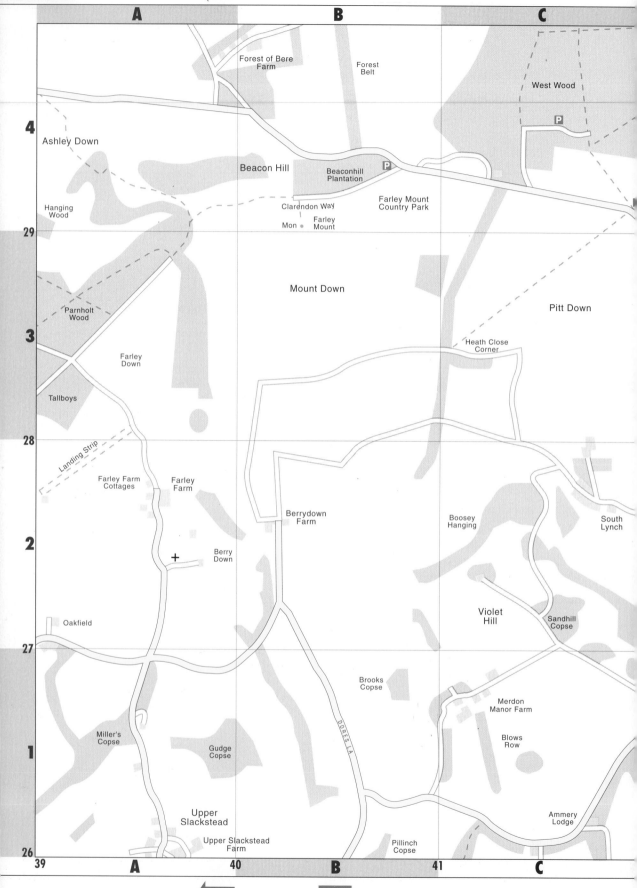

Forest of Bere
Farm

Forest
Belt

West Wood

4

Ashley Down

Beacon Hill

Beaconhill
Plantation

Hanging
Wood

Clarendon Way

Farley Mount
Country Park

29

Mon ●   Farley
Mount

Mount Down

Pitt Down

Parnholt
Wood

Heath Close
Corner

3

Farley
Down

Tallboys

28

Landing Strip

Farley Farm
Cottages

Farley
Farm

Berrydown
Farm

Boosey
Hanging

South
Lynch

2

＋   Berry
Down

Violet
Hill

Sandhill
Copse

Oakfield

27

Brooks
Copse

Merdon
Manor Farm

Miller's
Copse

Gudge
Copse

DORES LA

Blows
Row

1

Upper
Slackstead

Ammery
Lodge

26

Upper Slackstead
Farm

Pillinch
Copse

D

E

F

West Wood

Ashmore
Hill
Copse

Burrow
Copse

Crab Wood

Crabwood
Farm
House

Mast

4

P

Crabwood
House

Clarendon Way

SARUM RD

Pittdown
Plantation

29

Pitt Down

Enmill
House

3

Little
Pittdown
Plantation

Enmill
Barn

ENMILL LA

Vale Farm

Enmill
Farm

Pitt View

28

White House

A3090

Pages
Copse

Grovelands
Copse

Yew Tree

2

Stopham's
Copse

Pitt
Copse

FARLEY MOUNT RD

SPARSHOLT RD

MILLERS LA

Larkfarm
Plantation

Southlynch
Plantation

27

Standon
Farm

Juniper
Bank

Nan Trodd's
Hill

Standon

Down Farm

1

Merdon
Castle

Butcher's
Plantation

PORT LA

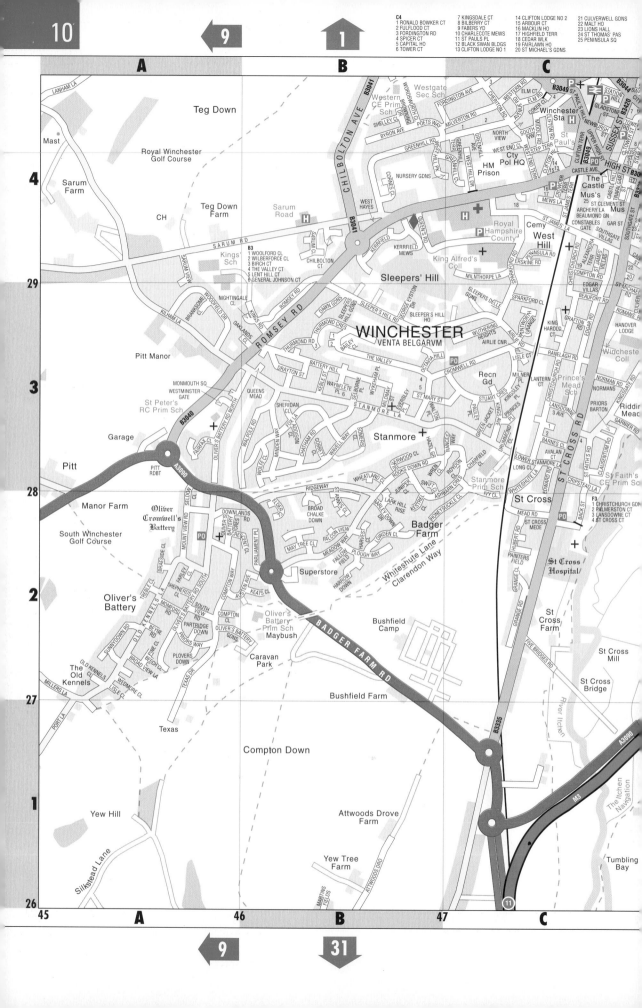

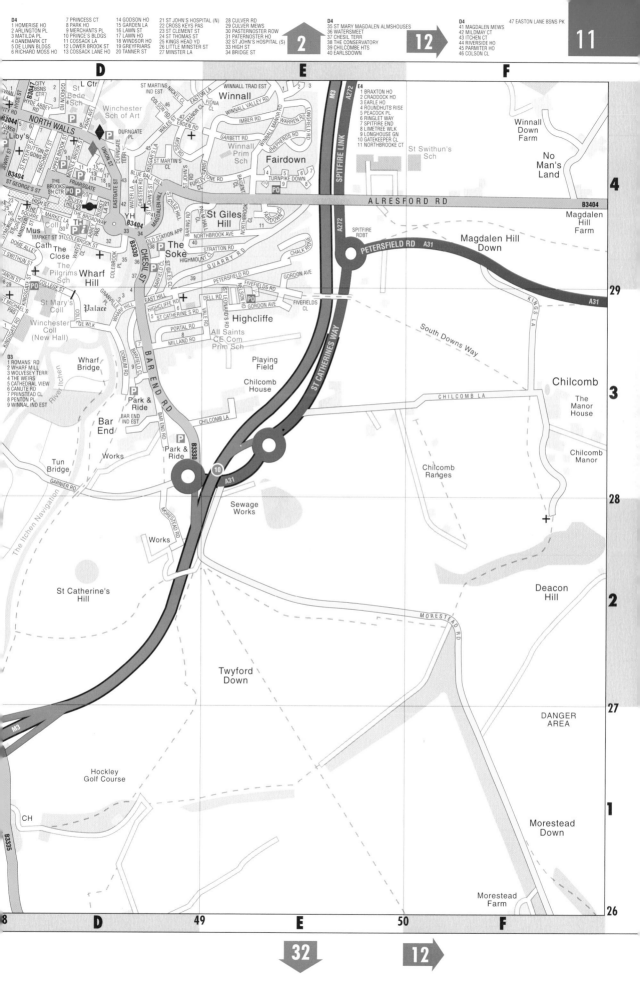

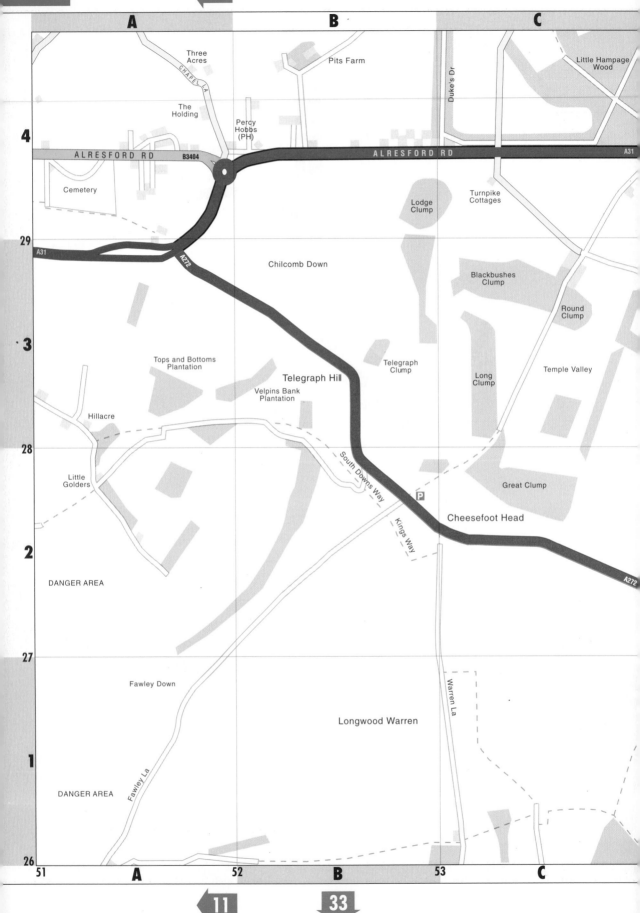

A   B   C

Three
Acres

CHAPEL LA

Pits Farm

Duke's Dr

Little Hampage
Wood

The
Holding

Percy
Hobbs
(PH)

4

ALRESFORD RD   B3404   ALRESFORD RD   A31

Cemetery

Lodge
Clump

Turnpike
Cottages

29

A31   A272

Chilcomb Down

Blackbushes
Clump

Round
Clump

3

Tops and Bottoms
Plantation

Telegraph
Clump

Temple Valley

Telegraph Hill

Velpins Bank
Plantation

Long
Clump

Hillacre

28

Little
Golders

South Downs Way

P

Great Clump

Cheesefoot Head

2

DANGER AREA

Kings Way

A272

27

Fawley Down

Warren La

Longwood Warren

1

Fawley La

DANGER AREA

26

51   A   52   B   53   C

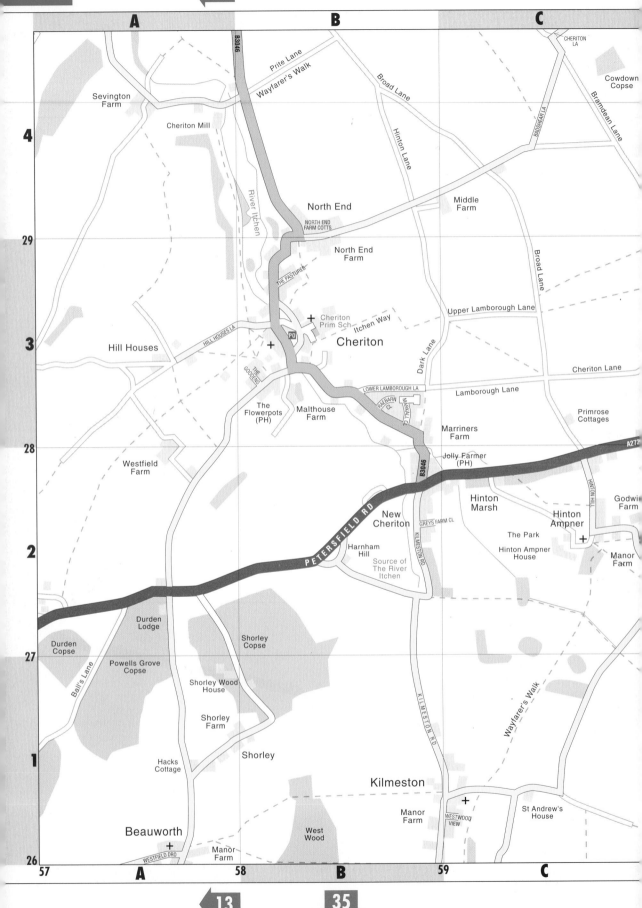

CHERITON LA

Cowdown
Copse

Brandean Lane

B3046

Sevington
Farm

BROSHEAR LA

Cheriton Mill

4

River Itchen

Prite Lane

Wayfarer's Walk

Broad Lane

Hinton Lane

North End

Middle
Farm

Broad Lane

NORTH END
FARM COTTS

29

THE PASTURES

North End
Farm

Upper Lamborough Lane

Cheriton
Prim Sch

Itchen Way

Hill Houses La

PO

Cheriton

Dark Lane

Cheriton Lane

3

Hill Houses

THE GODDENS

LOWER LAMBOROUGH LA

Lamborough Lane

RAEBARN CL

MARKAL CL

Primrose
Cottages

The Flowerpots
(PH)

Malthouse
Farm

Marriners
Farm

A272

28

Westfield
Farm

B3046

Jolly Farmer
(PH)

HINTON HILL

Godwi
Farm

PETERSFIELD RD

New
Cheriton

GREYS FARM CL

Hinton
Marsh

Hinton
Ampner

Manor
Farm

2

Harnham
Hill

Source of
The River
Itchen

KILMESTON RD

The Park

Hinton Ampner
House

Durden
Lodge

Shorley
Copse

Durden
Copse

Ball's Lane

Powells Grove
Copse

Shorley Wood
House

27

Wayfarer's Walk

Shorley
Farm

KILMESTON RD

1

Shorley

Hacks
Cottage

Kilmeston

Beauworth

Manor
Farm

WESTWOOD
VIEW

St Andrew's
House

West
Wood

WESTFIELD DRO

Manor
Farm

26

D
E
F

4

29

3

28

2

27

1

26

CHERITON LA

Common
Farm

Old Park
Wood

Tenant Woods

CHERITON ST

OLD PARK RD

Bullbeck
Copse

Cheriton Wood

Breach Plain
Cottages

Wood Farm
Cottages

Wood
Farm

Marriners
Farm

Alresford Lane

WOOD LA

Kelsey
Farm

Cheriton Lane

Kalamunnda
Farm

Woodlane
Farm

New
Cottages

Lacey's
Farm

West End
Farm

WOODLANE CL

A272

Bramdean

Woodcote Manor
House

WOODCOTE
COTTS

CHURCH LA

Manor
Farm

Bramdean
Manor

+

Bramdean
Farm

TITHELANDS LA

Hinton
Ampner

The Malthouse

Manor Farm

A272

Godwin's
Plantation

Humpty's Down

New Pond
Cottages

Joan's Acre

Broom
Wood

Brockwood
Park

Brockwood
Park Farm

Joan's Acre
Wood

DELL
COTTS

BROCKWOOD
BOTTOM

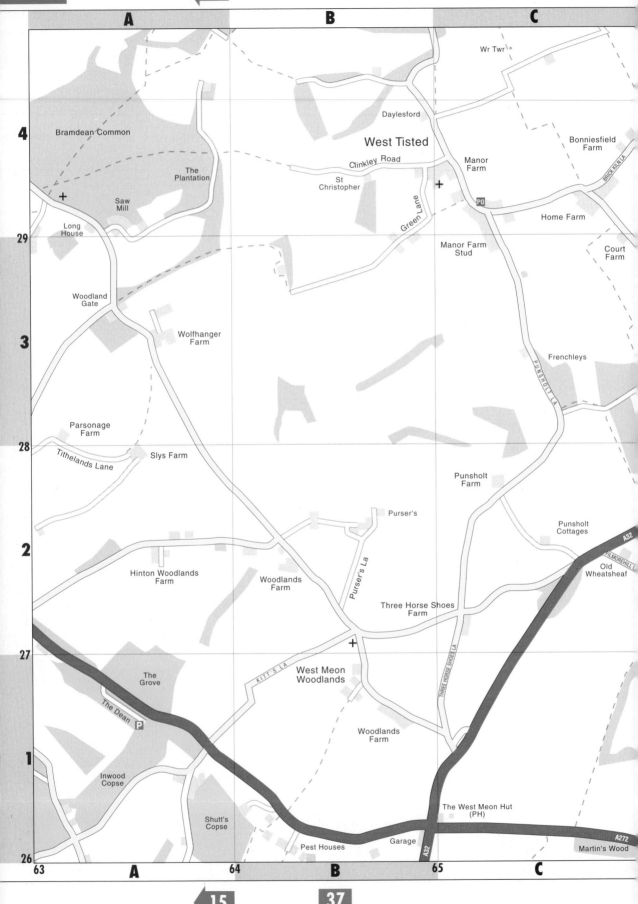

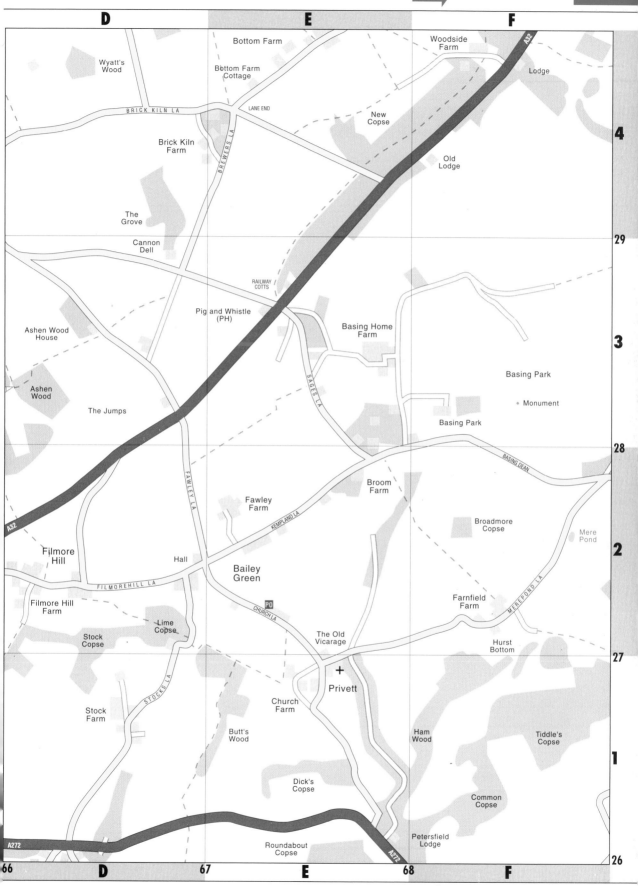

D   E   F

Wyatt's Wood

Bottom Farm

Bottom Farm Cottage

Woodside Farm

Lodge

A32

BRICK KILN LA

LANE END

New Copse

4

Brick Kiln Farm

BREWERS LA

Old Lodge

The Grove

29

Cannon Dell

RAILWAY COTTS

Pig and Whistle (PH)

Basing Home Farm

3

Ashen Wood House

SAGES LA

Basing Park

• Monument

Ashen Wood

The Jumps

Basing Park

28

FAWLEY LA

BASING DEAN

Fawley Farm

Broom Farm

Broadmore Copse

Mere Pond

KEMPLAND LA

2

Filmore Hill

Hall

Bailey Green

Farnfield Farm

MEREPOND LA

A32

FILMOREHILL LA

PO

Filmore Hill Farm

Lime Copse

CHURCH LA

The Old Vicarage

Hurst Bottom

27

Stock Copse

STOCKS LA

+

Privett

Stock Farm

Church Farm

Butt's Wood

Ham Wood

Tiddle's Copse

1

Dick's Copse

Common Copse

A272

Petersfield Lodge

A272

Roundabout Copse

26

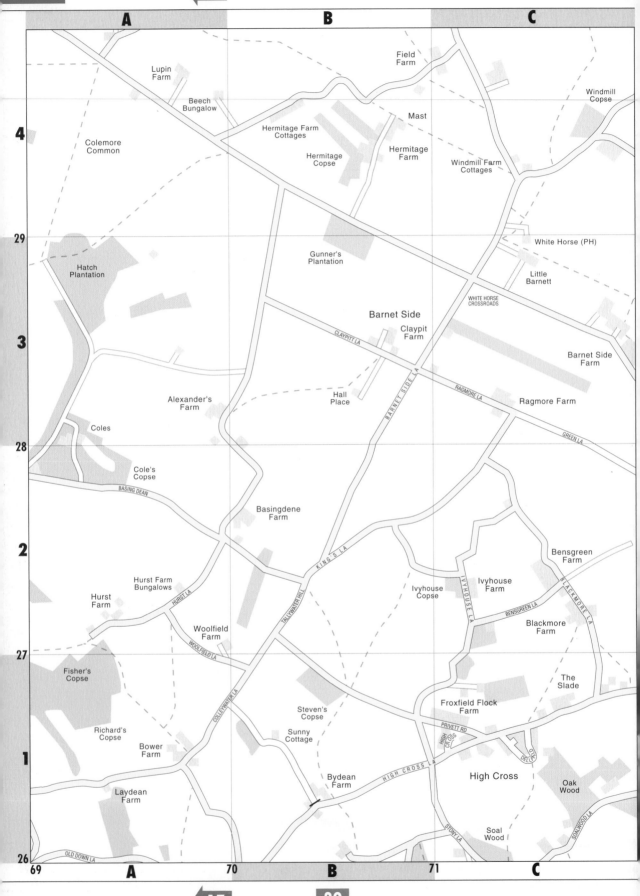

4

Lupin Farm

Beech Bungalow

Field Farm

Windmill Copse

Colemore Common

Hermitage Farm Cottages

Mast

Hermitage Copse

Hermitage Farm

Windmill Farm Cottages

29

Hatch Plantation

Gunner's Plantation

White Horse (PH)

Little Barnett

WHITE HORSE CROSSROADS

Barnet Side

Claypit Farm

3

CLAYPIT LA

Barnet Side Farm

Alexander's Farm

Hall Place

BARNET SIDE LA

RAGMORE LA

Ragmore Farm

Coles

GREEN LA

28

Cole's Copse

BASING DEAN

Basingdene Farm

2

Hurst Farm Bungalows

KING'S LA

IVYHOUSE LA

Ivyhouse Farm

Bensgreen Farm

BLACKMORE LA

Hurst Farm

HURST LA

Ivyhouse Copse

BENSGREEN LA

Blackmore Farm

Woolfield Farm

TALLYWATER HILL

27

WOOLFIELD LA

Fisher's Copse

The Slade

COLLEYWATER LA

Steven's Copse

Froxfield Flock Farm

PRIVETT RD

Richard's Copse

Sunny Cottage

HIGH CROSS

DELL RD

1

Bower Farm

Bydean Farm

HIGH CROSS LA

High Cross

Oak Wood

Laydean Farm

Soal Wood

SOALWOOD LA

STONY LA

26

OLD DOWN LA

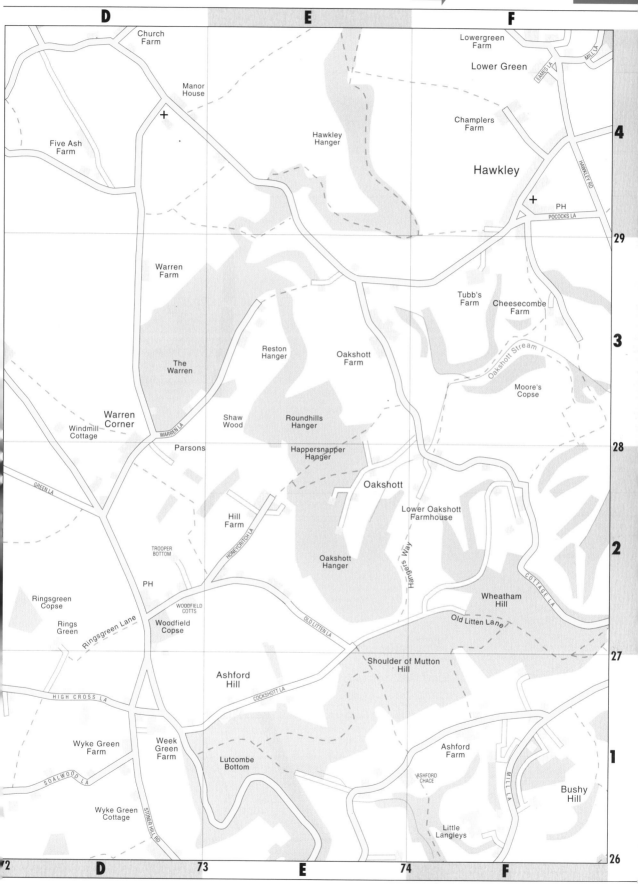

D

Church
Farm

Manor
House

Five Ash
Farm

✛

Lowergreen
Farm

Lower Green

Champlers
Farm

Hawkley

✛

PH

F

EAMES LA

MILL LA

HAWKLEY RD

POCOCKS LA

4

29

Hawkley
Hanger

Warren
Farm

Reston
Hanger

Oakshott
Farm

Tubb's
Farm

Cheesecombe
Farm

Oakshott Stream

Moore's
Copse

3

The
Warren

Warren
Corner

Windmill
Cottage

Parsons

WARREN LA

Shaw
Wood

Roundhills
Hanger

Happersnapper
Hanger

28

Oakshott

Lower Oakshott
Farmhouse

GREEN LA

Hill
Farm

HONEYCRITCH LA

TROOPER
BOTTOM

Oakshott
Hanger

Hangers Way

Wheatham
Hill

COTTAGE LA

2

PH

Ringsgreen
Copse

Rings
Green

Ringsgreen Lane

WOODFIELD
COTTS

Woodfield
Copse

OLD LITTEN LA

Old Litten Lane

27

HIGH CROSS LA

Ashford
Hill

COCKSHOTT LA

Shoulder of Mutton
Hill

Wyke Green
Farm

Week
Green
Farm

Lutcombe
Bottom

Ashford
Farm

ASHFORD
CHACE

MILL LA

1

SOALWOOD LA

STONER HILL RD

Wyke Green
Cottage

Little
Langleys

Bushy
Hill

26

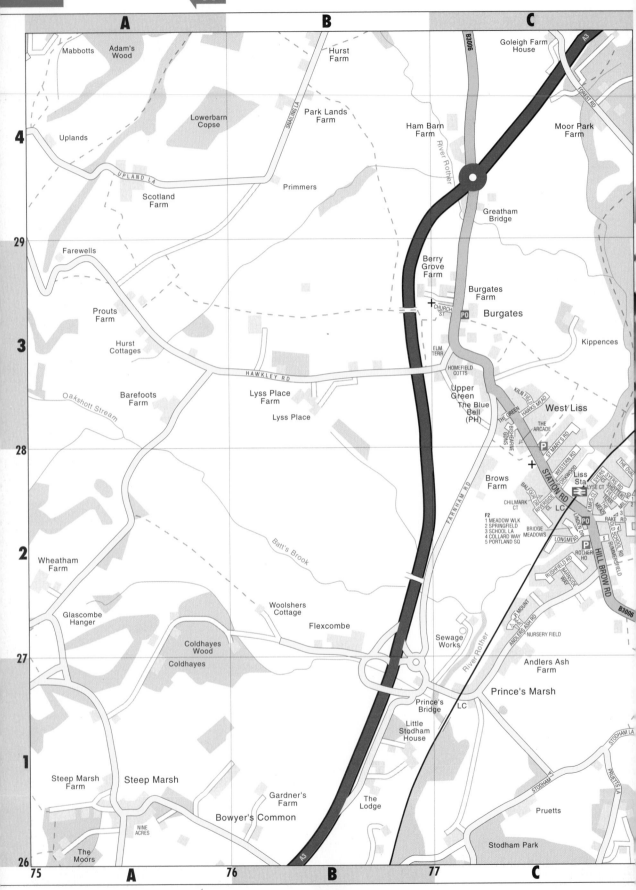

A   B   C

4

29

3

28

2

27

1

26

75   A   76   B   77   C

Mabbotts
Adam's Wood
Uplands
Lowerbarn Copse
Scotland Farm
UPLAND LA
Primmers
Farewells
Prouts Farm
Hurst Cottages
Barefoots Farm
Oakshott Stream
Lyss Place Farm
Lyss Place
Wheatham Farm
Glascombe Hanger
Coldhayes Wood
Coldhayes
Woolshers Cottage
Flexcombe
Batt's Brook
Steep Marsh Farm
Steep Marsh
Gardner's Farm
NINE ACRES
Bowyer's Common
The Moors

SMATLING LA
Hurst Farm
Park Lands Farm
Ham Barn Farm
River Rother
Greatham Bridge
Berry Grove Farm
Burgates Farm
CHURCH ST
PO
Burgates
ELM TERR
HOMEFIELD COTTS
HAWKLEY RD
Upper Green
The Blue Bell (PH)
Brows Farm
FARNHAM RD
Sewage Works
River Rother
Prince's Bridge
LC
Little Stodham House
The Lodge

B3006
Goleigh Farm House
A3
FOREST RD
Moor Park Farm
Kippences
KILN FIELD
HAWKS MEAD
West Liss
THE ARCADE
THE GREEN
BISHEARNE GDNS
ST MARY'S RD
WESTERN RD
CORNWOOD
P
STATION RD
BALFOUR RD
CHILMARK CT
RIVERSIDE CL
Liss Sta
LC
LINDEN RD
LIMES CL
THE MEAD
BRIDGE MEADOWS
F2
1 MEADOW WLK
2 SPRINGFIELD
3 SCHOOL LA
4 COLLARD WAY
5 PORTLAND SQ
LONGMEAD
RUSHFIELD RD
BADRISSE WAY
ROTHER HO
RAKE RD
SCHOOL LA
MILL RD
THE OVAL
HILL BROW RD
B3006
THE MOUNT
ANDLERS ASH RD
Nursery Field
Andlers Ash Farm
Prince's Marsh
STODHAM
STODHAM LA
PRUETTS LA
Pruetts
Stodham Park

D

Longmoor
Inclosure

Little Dean
Bottom

Warren
Hill

The Wylds

Wylds
Farm

The Lake

Langley

4

FOREST CNR
PINE
COTTS
BRIAR
WOOD
BERRYLANDS

WARREN RD

Langley Bridge
Farm

29

SHERWOOD CL

NEWFIELD
RD

PO
PINE WLK
TEMPLE RD
BEECHWOOD

The Temple
Inn
(PH)

Liss
Forest

The
Mint

Mangers

REEDS LA

Brewells
Farm

Little
Langley
Farm

Reeds

ROTHERBANK
FARM LA

FOREST RISE

MINT RD

LC

Home
Farm

Whangerei Nursery
Palmers Farm

Palmers

Newlands

3

DUCKMEAD LA

LC

LC

DUDLEY
TERR

WYLD GREEN LA

Wyld Green
Farm

Ciddy
Hall

ST PATRICK'S LA

BREWELLS LA

Rake CE
Prim Sch

THE
HOLLY
BANK
CT
WOODBOURNE
CL

KELSEY
CL
MILLBROOK
CL
SILVER BIRCH
CL
BEECH CL

East Liss

Rockpit
Cotts

B2070

28

MEADOW
WLK
GREENFIELDS
OAK TREE DR
MIDDLE
MEADOW
ST PATRICK'S CL

DESBOROUGH
CL
YEW TREE
CL

Liss

St Patrick's
Copse

RAKE
BSNS PK

The
Flying Bull
(PH)

Coldharbour Park
Farm

Rake

ROWAN
TREE CL
COPSE
CL
POTTERS
PL
PATRICK'S
PL

LONGACRE

RAKE RD

Little Barn

HIGHFIELD GDNS

High Firs
House

PRIMROSE LA

HILL RD

PO

WILLOW
RD
MOSS CL
CL
CHASE
CL
INWOOD RD
VINSON RD

THE
RIDINGS

HATCH LA

Highfield
Farm

SANDY LA

CANHOUSE LA

2

East
Hill
Liss
Inf & Jun
Schs

CARDEW
RD
DENNIS WAY

EAST HILL DR

HUNTSBOTTOM LA

Highfield
Wood

Pot
Well

B3006

HILL BROW RD

Hill
Side

WOODLANDS WAY

Black
Pond

27

STODHAM LA

EDGEWOOD
CT

Sussex Border Path

Rake
Common

MALTHOUSE RD

Rake
Hanger

Hill
Brow

B3006

PLANTATION RD

COMBE RD

Hambledon
Piece

1

Farther
Commons

PH

KNOWLES
MEADOW

Combe
Hill

Harting
Combe

LONDON RD

Clayton
Court

B2070

79

E

80

F

26

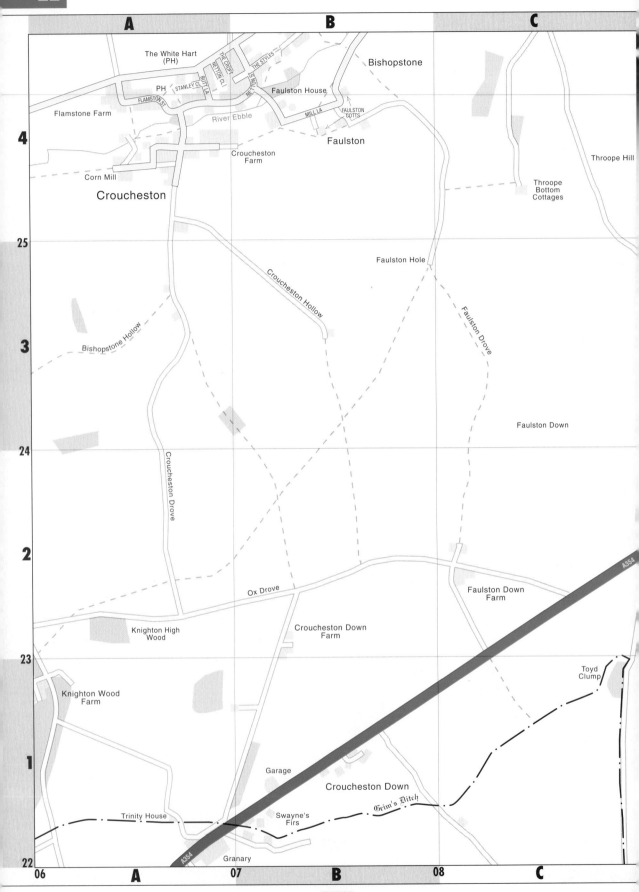

A B C

Bishopstone

The White Hart
(PH)

THE STYLES

THE CROFT

NETTON CL.

BUTT LA.

STANLEY CL.

PH

FLAMSTON ST.

MILL ST.

Faulston House

MILL LA.

FAULSTON
COTTS

Flamstone Farm

River Ebble

Faulston

Croucheston
Farm

Corn Mill

Throope Hill

Croucheston

Throope
Bottom
Cottages

4

Faulston Hole

25

Croucheston Hollow

Faulston Drove

Bishopstone Hollow

3

Faulston Down

24

Croucheston Drove

2

Ox Drove

Faulston Down
Farm

Knighton High
Wood

Croucheston Down
Farm

23

Toyd
Clump

Knighton Wood
Farm

A354

1

Garage

Croucheston Down

Grim's Ditch

Trinity House

Swayne's
Firs

22

Granary

A354

06

A

07

B

08

C

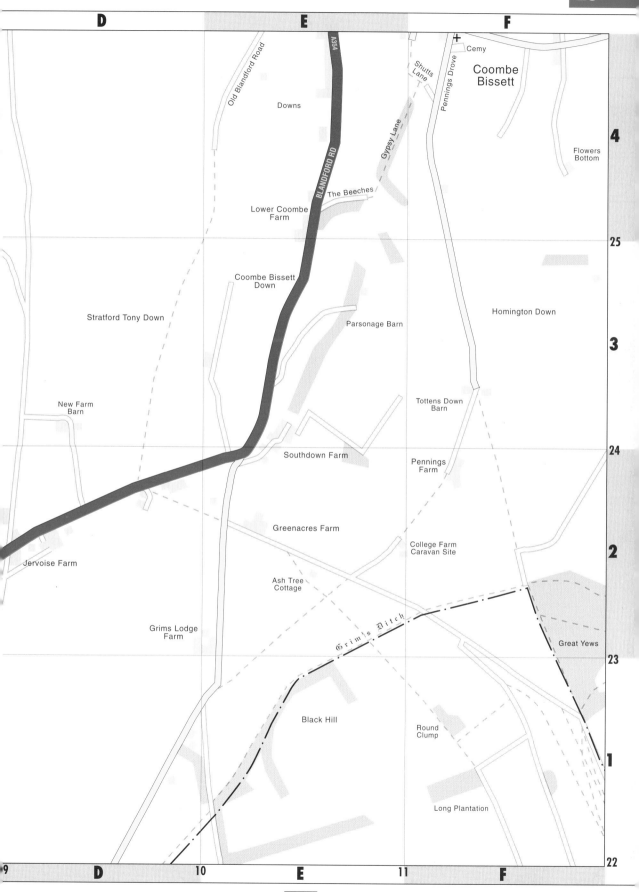

D   E   F

Old Blandford Road

A354

Downs

Shutts Lane

Pennings Drove

Cemy

Coombe Bissett

Gypsy Lane

Flowers Bottom

4

BLANDFORD RD

The Beeches

Lower Coombe Farm

25

Coombe Bissett Down

Stratford Tony Down

Homington Down

Parsonage Barn

3

New Farm Barn

Tottens Down Barn

Southdown Farm

Pennings Farm

24

Greenacres Farm

College Farm Caravan Site

2

Jervoise Farm

Ash Tree Cottage

Great Yews

Grims Lodge Farm

Grim's Ditch

23

Black Hill

Round Clump

1

Long Plantation

22

9   D   10   E   11   F

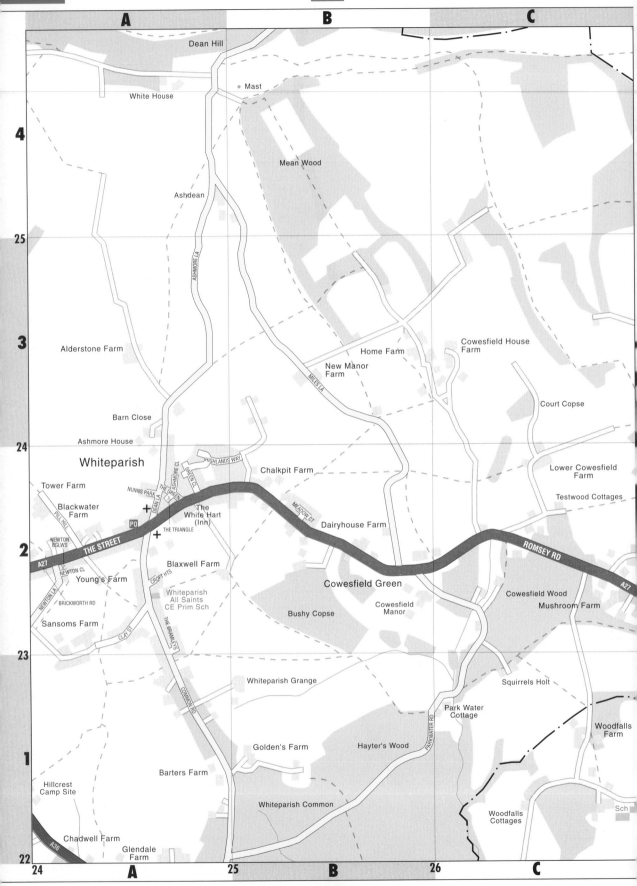

A B C

Dean Hill

White House

Mast

4

Mean Wood

Ashdean

25

ASHMORE LA

3

Alderstone Farm

Cowesfield House Farm

Home Farm

New Manor Farm

MILES LA

Court Copse

Barn Close

24

Ashmore House

Whiteparish

HIGHLANDS WAY

Chalkpit Farm

Lower Cowesfield Farm

Tower Farm

NUNNS PARK LA

ASHMORE CL

GREEN CL

THE GREEN

Testwood Cottages

Blackwater Farm

PILL HILL

DEAN LA

PO

The White Hart (Inn)

THE TRIANGLE

MEADOW CT

Dairyhouse Farm

ROMSEY RD

2

NEWTON BGLWS

A27

NEWTON CL

THE STREET

Blaxwell Farm

CROFT HTS

Cowesfield Green

Cowesfield Wood

A27

Young's Farm

NEWTON LA

BRICKWORTH RD

Whiteparish All Saints CE Prim Sch

THE BRAMLEYS

Bushy Copse

Cowesfield Manor

Mushroom Farm

Sansoms Farm

CLAY ST

23

Whiteparish Grange

Squirrels Holt

COMMON RD

Park Water Cottage

PARKWATER RD

Woodfalls Farm

1

Golden's Farm

Hayter's Wood

Hillcrest Camp Site

Barters Farm

Whiteparish Common

Woodfalls Cottages

Sch

A36

Chadwell Farm

Glendale Farm

22

24 A 25 B 26 C

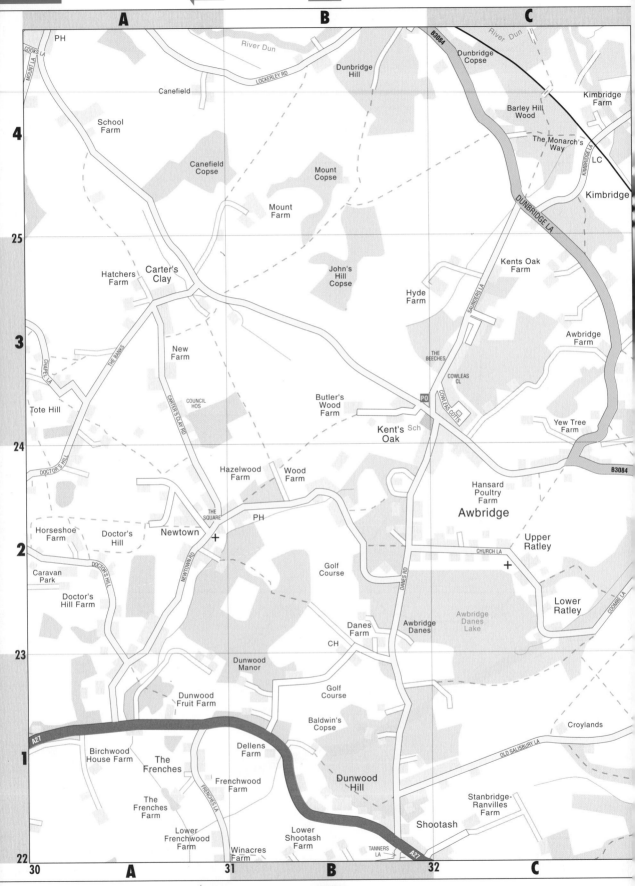

A

B

C

4

25

3

24

2

23

1

22

30

31

32

PH

COOKS LA

MOUNT LA

River Dun

LOCKERLEY RD

Canefield

Dunbridge Hill

B3084

Dunbridge Copse

River Dun

Kimbridge Farm

School Farm

Canefield Copse

Mount Copse

Barley Hill Wood

The Monarch's Way

KIMBRIDGE LA

LC

Kimbridge

Mount Farm

DUNBRIDGE LA

Hatchers Farm

Carter's Clay

John's Hill Copse

Kents Oak Farm

SAUNDERS LA

Hyde Farm

THE BANKS

CHAPEL LA

New Farm

CARTER'S CLAY RD

COUNCIL HOS

THE BEECHES

COWLEAS CL

Awbridge Farm

Tote Hill

Butler's Wood Farm

PO

COWLEAS COTTS

Yew Tree Farm

DOCTOR'S HILL

Kent's Oak

Sch

B3084

Hazelwood Farm

Wood Farm

Hansard Poultry Farm

Horseshoe Farm

Doctor's Hill

THE SQUARE

Newtown

PH

Awbridge

Upper Ratley

COOMBE LA

Caravan Park

DOCTORS HILL

NEWTOWN RD

Golf Course

CHURCH LA

Lower Ratley

Doctor's Hill Farm

DANES RD

Awbridge Danes

Awbridge Danes Lake

Danes Farm

CH

Dunwood Manor

Golf Course

Croylands

A27

Dunwood Fruit Farm

Baldwin's Copse

OLD SALISBURY LA

Birchwood House Farm

The Frenches

Dellens Farm

FRENCHES LA

Frenchwood Farm

Dunwood Hill

Stanbridge-Ranvilles Farm

The Frenches Farm

Lower Frenchwood Farm

Lower Shootash Farm

Shootash

Winacres Farm

TANNERS LA

A27

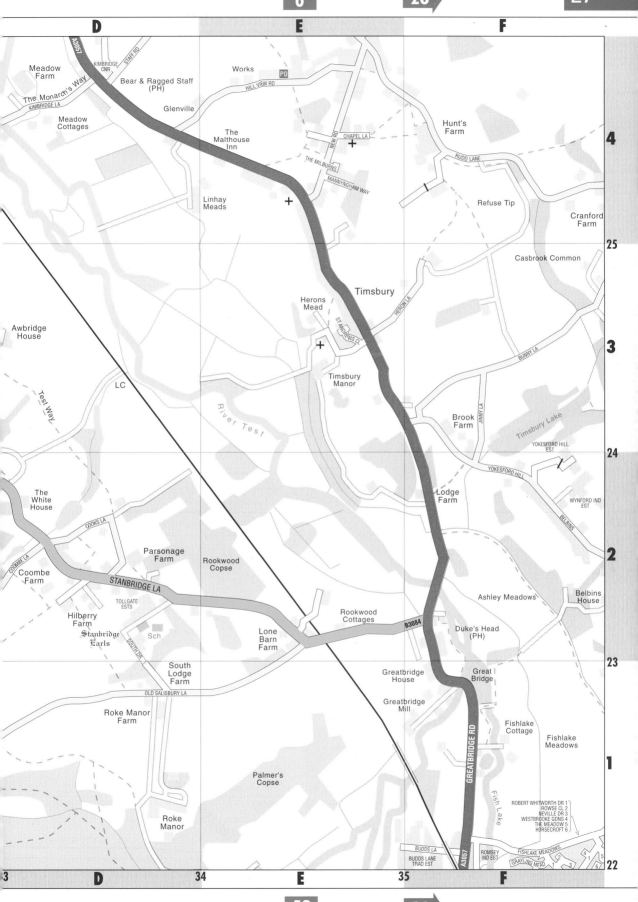

Meadow Farm

The Monarch's Way

KIMBRIDGE LA

Meadow Cottages

A3057

KIMBRIDGE CNR

STAFF RD

Bear & Ragged Staff (PH)

Glenville

Works

Hill View Rd

PO

The Malthouse Inn

Chapel La

New Rd

The Milburns

Mannyngham Way

Linhay Meads

Hunt's Farm

Rudd Lane

Refuse Tip

Cranford Farm

Casbrook Common

Awbridge House

Timsbury

Herons Mead

Heron La

St Andrews Cl

Test Way

LC

Timsbury Manor

River Test

Brook Farm

Jimmy La

Timsbury Lake

Yokesford Hill Est

The White House

Cooks La

Lodge Farm

Yokesford Hill

Wynford Ind Est

Belbins

Coombe La

Parsonage Farm

Rookwood Copse

Ashley Meadows

Belbins House

Coombe Farm

Stanbridge La

Tollgate Ests

Sch

South Dr

Hilberry Farm

Stanbridge Earls

Lone Barn Farm

Rookwood Cottages

B3084

Duke's Head (PH)

South Lodge Farm

Old Salisbury La

Greatbridge House

Greatbridge Mill

Great Bridge

Roke Manor Farm

Palmer's Copse

Greatbridge Rd

Fishlake Cottage

Fishlake Meadows

Fish Lake

Roke Manor

Robert Whitworth Dr 1
Rowse Cl 2
Neville Dr 3
Westbrooke Gdns 4
The Meadow 5
Horsecroft 6

Budds La

A3057

Budds Lane Trad Est

Romsey Ind Est

Grayling Mead

Fishlake Meadows

A **B** **C**

Malthouse Farm

PAYNES HAY RD

Merrie Meade Farm

Fern Hill Lane

ELDON RD

Paynes Hay Farm

4

Sharpes Farm

CHURCH LA

Braishfield

Hawkes Farm

Churchers Barn

DUMMER RD

The Monarch's Way

LOWER ST

NEWPORT LA

25

CHAPEL CL

The Newport Inn (PH)

HILL VIEW RD

P

PO

DORES LA

Pucknall

Pucknall Farm

COMMON HILL RD

BUNNY LA

Braishfield Prim Sch

KILN LA

Fairbourne Lake

The Wheatsheaf Inn (PH)

3

Round Copse

Fairbournes Farm

The Homestead

MEGANA WAY

Dog & Crook (PH)

24

Abbotswood Farm

BRAISHFIELD RD

Crookhill Farm

Sir Harold Hillier Gardens & Arboretum

Jermyns House

Outwood Lodge

The Bog

JERMYNS LA

BELBINS

Bracken Wood

2

SANDY LA

Works

Cemy

Nursery

A3090

Abbotswood

Abbotswood House

23

CUPERNHAM LA

ROMSEY

WOODLEY CLOSE FLATS

WOODLEY CL

Ganger Farm

South Holmes Copse

THE STRAIGHT MILE

Cupernham

GANGER FARM LA

WOODLEY WAY

Oxlease

BROOK WAY

WOODLEY LA

FOOTNER CL

ANDERSON CL

Woodley

Woodlands

CAVENDISH CL

STAPLEFORD DR

HORSESHOE DR

NORRIS CL

Ganger Wood

Crampmoor Farm

1

KINVER CL

OAKWOOD ABBOTS WOOD

SHORT HILL

DIBBEN WLK

GROVELY WAY

RICHMOND LA

WARREN

ANSTEY RD

SCHOOL RD

HUNTERS CL

NORTHLANDS RD

SOUTH CL

CRAMPMOOR LA

THE MEADOW

BRANSLEY CL

PINEWOOD CL

THE GREEN

THE COPSE

PEEL CL

1 GRANGE MEWS
2 COWSLIP WAY
3 HALTERWORTH LA
4 ST SWITHUN'S CL

Crampmoor

FISH LAKE MDWS

WOODLEY LA

LINCOLN CL

ADDISON CL

CEDAR LAWN

WINTERBOURNE RD

BEVERLEY GDNS

WINCHESTER RD

LC

GREEN LA

OXLEASE

HIGHFIELD

Cupernham Schs

WAVERLEY

RALPH LA

PO

FAIRVIEW DR

WESTERING

A3090

COLTSFOOT WLK

CANAL LN

SMITH'S FIELD

DURBAN CL

Cupernham CL

FAIRVIEW CL

WINCHESTER HILL

BRIAR WAY

SORREL CL

PRIMROSE WAY

CAMPION DR

BRAMBLE DR

COMFREY CL

CLOVER DR

22

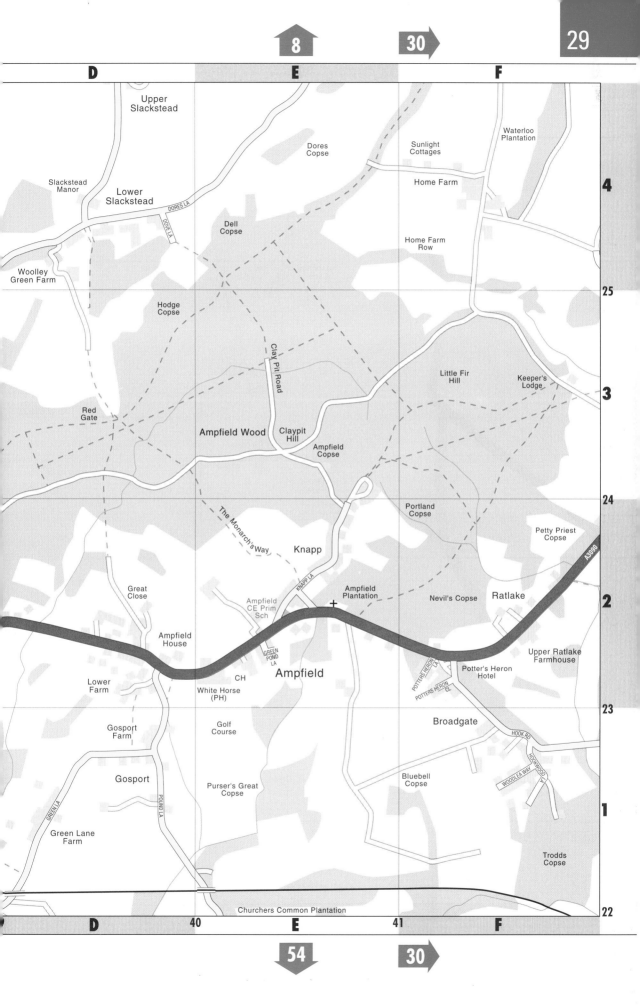

A B C

4

A3090

PORT LA

KEBLE CL

King's
Head
Inn

CATWAYS

Shawlands
Farm

HEATHCOTE PL

COLLINS LA

Hursley Park

Cemy

PO

Hursley

MEREDUN CL

SOUTH END CL

PELICAN CT

Parsonage
Farm

BUNSTEAD LA

The Monarch's Way

SILKSTEAD LA

Shepherds Lane

25

Bunstead

Upper Silkstead
Farm

POLES LA

Silkstead

3

B3043

Brooks Copse

Weedacre
Copse

Lower Silkstead
Farmhouse

P

Golf
Course

Hursley
Forest

Windmill Copse

24

A3090

Ladwell

Red
House

Strowdens
Copse

Freemantle
Copse

Kent's Copse

Wells Row

Cranbury Park

2

Field House

Cranbury
House

Hawstead
Farm

Home Farm

Great
Pond

Hocombe Plantation

23

Hocombe Upper
Plantation

ROTHVILLE PL

Hocombe

Hocombe Bridge

HOCOMBE RD

Castle
Copse

Upper
Pond

HOOK RD

Hook Water Cl

HOCOMBE PARK CL

ASHDOWN DR

Lower
Pond

The Cas

HOOK WATER RD

HURSLEY RD

HOCOMBE DR

CHARNWOOD GDNS

ASHDOWN CL

HEATHFIELD
CL

MAYTREE RD

RANDALL RD

HOOK CL HOOK CRES

HOCOMBE WOOD RD

TITHEWOOD CL

CHARNWOOD CRES

ASHDOWN RD

HEATHFIELD RD

WOODLANDS CL

COULTAS RD

CHARNWOOD CL

RICHMOND CL

WALNU

NICHOL RD

1

BEECHWOOD CRES

Beechwood

Hursley Ct 1
Ashton Pl 2
Hiltingbury Ct 3

CLEVELAND DR

SONY CL

ELM
CT

HAZEL CL

SYCAMORE AVE

Queen's Rd

LAKEWOOD RD

MALCOLM RD

SHERWOOD RD

WESTERN RD

MARLBOROUGH RD

KINGSWAY

THORNBURY WOOD

THE GLADE

2 3
4 Vanburgh Way
5 Chillington Gdns
6 Cranborne Gdns
7 Lauriston Dr
8 Ormesby Dr
9 Stratfield Dr
10 Albury Pl
11 Apsley Pl

PO Stewart
HO

Hiltingbury

GORDON RD

HILTINGBURY
CL

Caravan
Parks

FLEXFORD CL

BADDESLEY RD

AVEBURY GR

SCOTT

BRIDGE RISE

ROSEMOOR GR

6

HILTINGBURY RD

Recn
Gd

OAKWOOD
CT

HEATHERDENE
RD

THOROLD RD

GROSVENOR RD

FRESHWATER
CT

ST MARK

THORNBURY HTS

N MILLERS DALE

THE
WOODLANDS

MILLERS DALE

B3043

Cemy
Cuckoo
Bushes

PINE RD

Hiltingbury
Inf Sch

Hiltingbury
Jun Sch

PINE CRES

BEECH CL

PINE RD

OAKWOOD CL

OAKWOOD RD

MALCOLM RD

BROXBURN
CL

MALIBRES RD

WINCHESTER

22

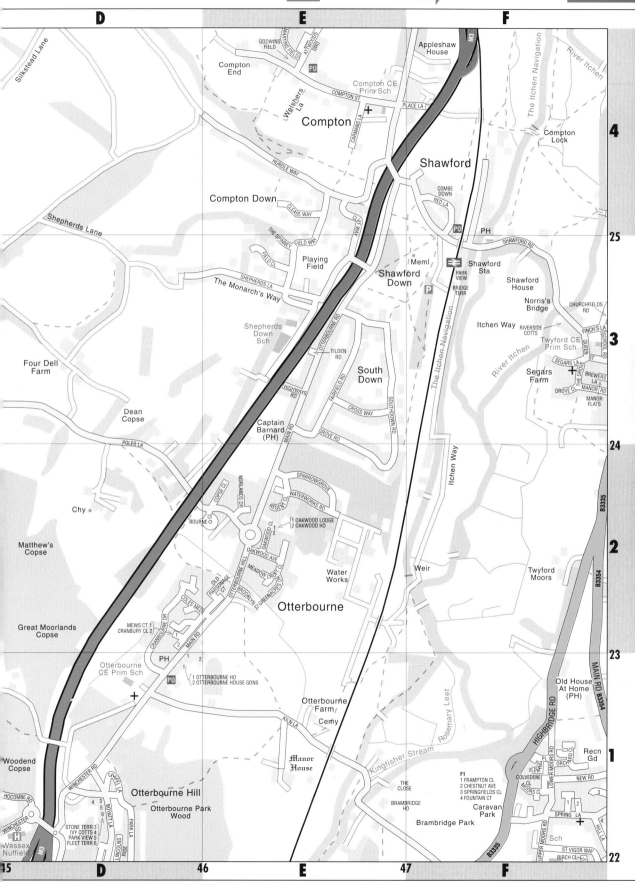

D
E
F

4

Silkstead Lane

GODWINS FIELD
MARTINS FIELDS
ATTWOODS DRO
PO
Appleshaw House
M3
The Itchen Navigation
River Itchen

Compton End
COMPTON ST
Compton CE Prim Sch
PLACE LA

Welshers La
Compton

Compton Lock

CARMANS LA

HURDLE WAY
Shawford

COMBE DOWN
RED LA

Compton Down

CLEASE WAY

THE SPINNEY
FIELD WY
FIELD CL
PO
PH
SHAWFORD RD

Shepherds Lane

SHEPHERDS LA
Playing Field

Meml

PARK VIEW
Shawford Sta
Shawford House

25

The Monarch's Way

Shawford Down

P
BRIDGE TERR

RIVERSIDE COTTS
Itchen Way
Norris's Bridge
CHURCHFIELDS RD

FINCH'S LA

OTTERBOURNE RD

Shepherds Down Sch

TILDEN RD

South Down

River Itchen

Itchen Way

Twyford CE Prim Sch

SCHOOL RD
QUEEN ST
THE DROVE
BREWERS LA

3

Four Dell Farm

FAIRFIELD RD

SEGARS LA
Segars Farm

DROVE CL
MANOR RD
MANOR FLATS

HIGHWAYS RD

CROSS WAY

SOUTHDOWN RD

Dean Copse

GROVE RD

Captain Barnard (PH)

MAIN RD

POLES LA

The Itchen Navigation

24

Chy

COPSE CL

NORLANDS DR

SPARROWGROVE
WATERWORKS RD

REGENT CL

1 OAKWOOD LODGE
2 OAKWOOD HO

Itchen Way

Twyford Moors

B3335

Matthew's Copse

BOURNE

OAKWOOD CL

OAKWOOD AVE

MEADOW CROFT CL
GREENACRES RD

Water Works

Weir

B3354

2

Great Moorlands Copse

OLD PARSONAGE CT
OTTERBOURNE HILL

COLES MEDE

BROOKLYN CL

Otterbourne

MEWS CT 1
CRANBURY CL 2

CRANBOURNE DR
MAIN RD

PH

23

Otterbourne CE Prim Sch

PO

1 OTTERBOURNE HO
2 OTTERBOURNE HOUSE GDNS

Otterbourne Farm

Cemy

Old House At Home (PH)

MAIN RD B3354

HIGHBRIDGE RD

KILN LA

Rosemary Leet

Woodend Copse

WINCHESTER RD
CAPEL LA

BOYATT LA
PARK LA

Otterbourne Hill

Manor House

Kingfisher Stream

THE CLOSE

F1
1 FRAMPTON CL
2 CHESTNUT AVE
3 SPRINGFIELDS CL
4 FOUNTAIN CT

LOWER MOORS CL
ORCHD CL
FLEM
COLVEDENE CL
NEW RD

Recn Gd

1

HOCOMBE RD

WINCHESTER RD
M3
Wessex Nuffield
H

STONE TERR 3
IVY COTTS 4
PARK VIEW 5
FLEET TERR 6

Otterbourne Park Wood

BRAMBRIDGE HO

Brambridge Park

Caravan Park

SPRING LA

UPPER MOORS RD
ST VIGOR WAY
BIRCH CL

Sch

HILL LA

B3335

22

45
D
46
E
47
F

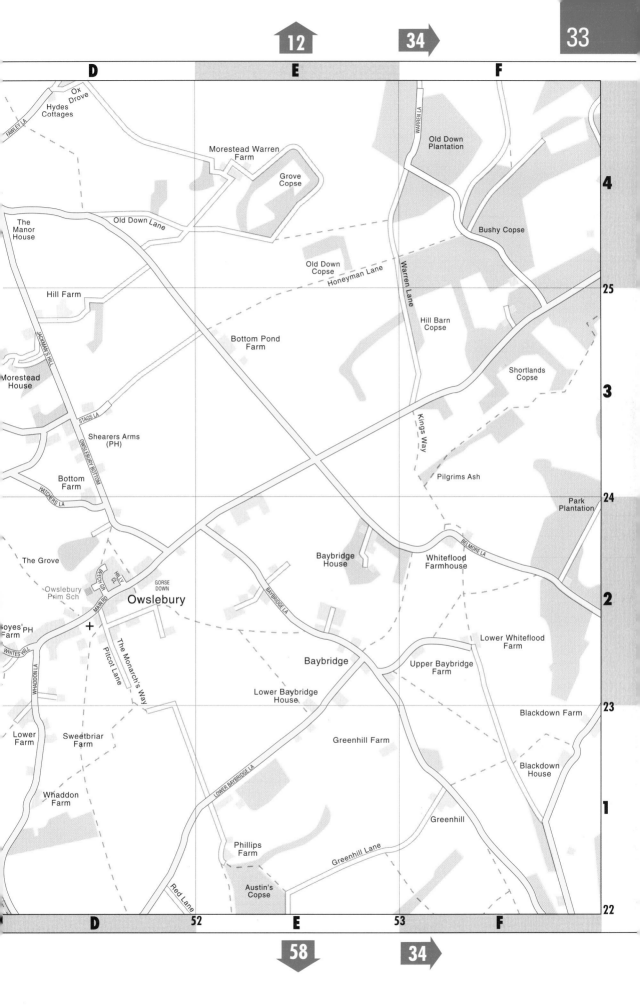

Ox Drove
Hydes Cottages
FAWLEY LA

Morestead Warren Farm

Grove Copse

WARREN LA

Old Down Plantation

The Manor House

Old Down Lane

Bushy Copse

Old Down Copse

Honeyman Lane

WARREN LANE

Hill Farm

Hill Barn Copse

JACKMAN'S HILL

Bottom Pond Farm

Morestead House

Shortlands Copse

STAGS LA

Kings Way

Shearers Arms (PH)

OWSLEBURY BOTTOM

HATCHER'S LA

Bottom Farm

Pilgrims Ash

Park Plantation

The Grove

BELMORE LA

Baybridge House

Whiteflood Farmhouse

BEECH GR
HILL CL

Owslebury Prim Sch

GORSE DOWN

Owslebury

MAIN RD

BAYBRIDGE LA

oyes' PH Farm

WHITES HILL

WHADDON LA

Pitcot Lane

The Monarch's Way

Lower Whiteflood Farm

Baybridge

Upper Baybridge Farm

Blackdown Farm

Lower Farm

Sweetbriar Farm

Lower Baybridge House

LOWER BAYBRIDGE LA

Greenhill Farm

Blackdown House

Whaddon Farm

Greenhill

Phillips Farm

Greenhill Lane

Red Lane

Austin's Copse

A
B
C

4

Piddles
Plantation

Ganderdown
wood

Honeyman
Farm

Stonywalls
Plantation

Lane End
Copse

Lane End
Down

Lane End

Lane End
Farm

Hamilton Far
Cottages

Hamilton Farm

WESTFIELD DRO

25

High
Stoke

Windmil
Farm

South Downs Way

HOLDEN LA

Greendowns

Loverdene

Lancen Cottages

The Milbury's
(Inn)

3

Forest
Copse

Millbarrow
Plantation

Douglas
Cottage

Glasspools Farm
House

May
Cottages

LONGWOOD DEAN LA

24

Longwood Dean
Farm

Rookery

Long
Wood

Dur Wood

Saltlane
Plantation

2

West
Lodge

SALT LA

Valley Walk

BELMORE LA

Durwood
Cottages

The Holt

23

High
Wood

Lime Wood

Stony Hard
Farm

The Holt
Lodge

Middle Preshaw

The Monarch's Way

Hazards
Copse

1

Well
Copse

Priest Wood

Lower Preshaw Lane

Linches
Rows

STAKES LA

Lower Preshaw
Farm

22

54
A
55
B
56
C

D **E** **F**

WESTFIELD DRO

Beauworth

West Wood

Yew Tree
Farm

Down Farm

4

Dean House

Dean Farm

College Down
Bungalow

25

College Down
Farm

Stanmore Farm

Millbarrow Farm

Kilmeston Down

College Down
Holding

3

𝔐ill
𝔅arrows

Millbarrow
Down

Wayfarer's Walk

South Downs Way

Wind Farm

24

Rooksgrove
Farm

Love Lane

Wyn Cottages

Lomer Farm

2

PRESHAW
EST

✠

The Monarch's Way

Preshaw
House

Wayfarer's Walk

Lomer Cottage

Rabbit Copse

23

Preshaw
Wood

Preshaw Down

WHITE WAY

1

Sailor's
Wood

Little Preshaw

Betty Mundy's
Cottage

Betty Mundy's
Bottom

22

7 **D** 58 **E** 59 **F**

A B C

4

Joan's Acre Wood

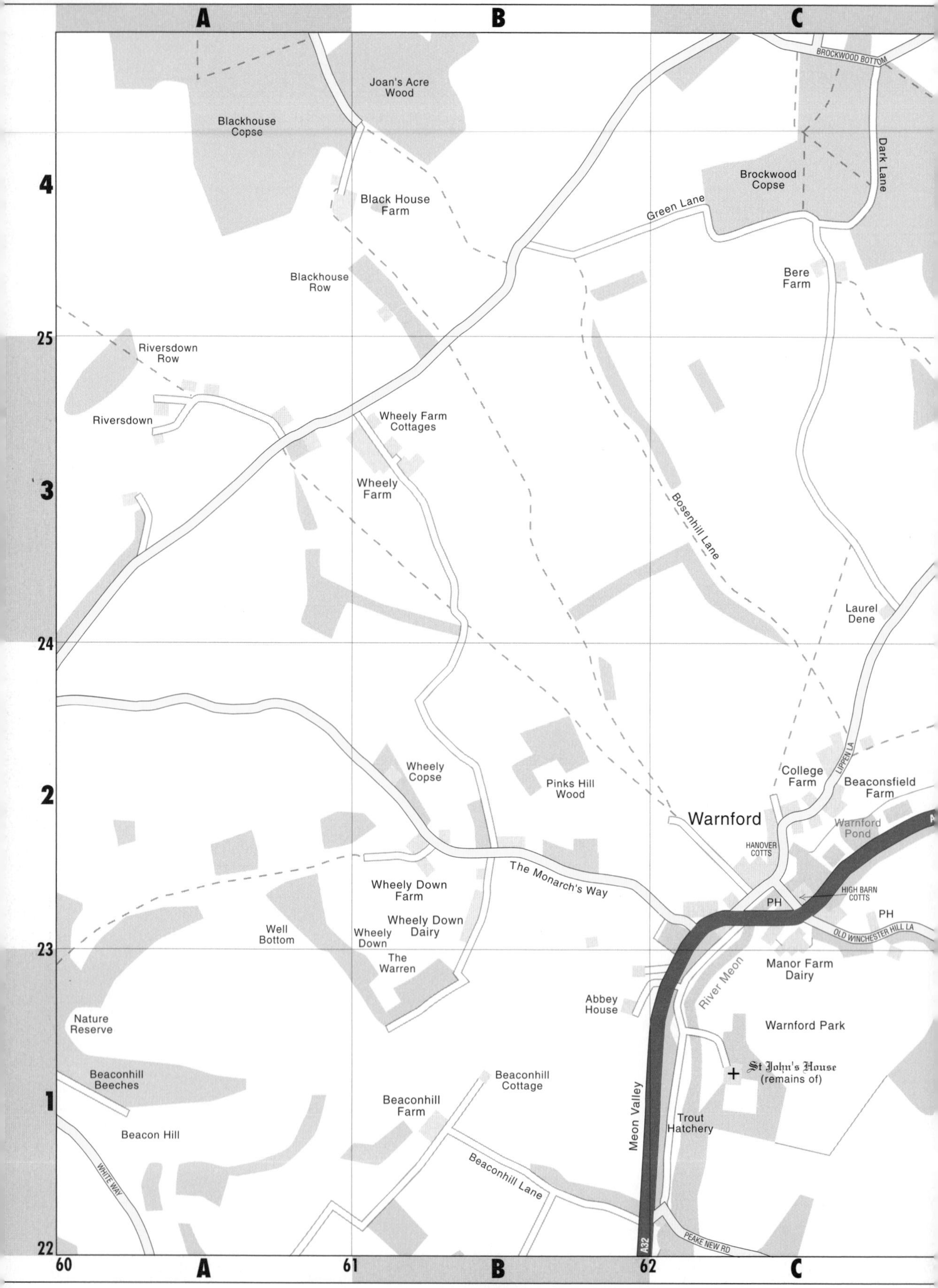

Blackhouse Copse

BROCKWOOD BOTTOM

Black House Farm

Green Lane

Brockwood Copse

Dark Lane

Blackhouse Row

Bere Farm

25

Riversdown Row

Riversdown

Wheely Farm Cottages

Bosenhill Lane

3

Wheely Farm

Laurel Dene

24

Wheely Copse

Pinks Hill Wood

College Farm

LIPPEN LA

Beaconsfield Farm

2

Warnford

Warnford Pond

HANOVER COTTS

The Monarch's Way

Wheely Down Farm

Wheely Down Dairy

PH

HIGH BARN COTTS

PH

OLD WINCHESTER HILL LA

Well Bottom

Wheely Down

The Warren

23

River Meon

Manor Farm Dairy

Abbey House

Nature Reserve

Warnford Park

Warnford Park

Meon Valley

St John's House (remains of)

Beaconhill Beeches

1

Beaconhill Cottage

Beaconhill Farm

Trout Hatchery

Beacon Hill

WHITE WAY

Beaconhill Lane

22

60 A 61 B 62 C

A32 PEAKE NEW RD

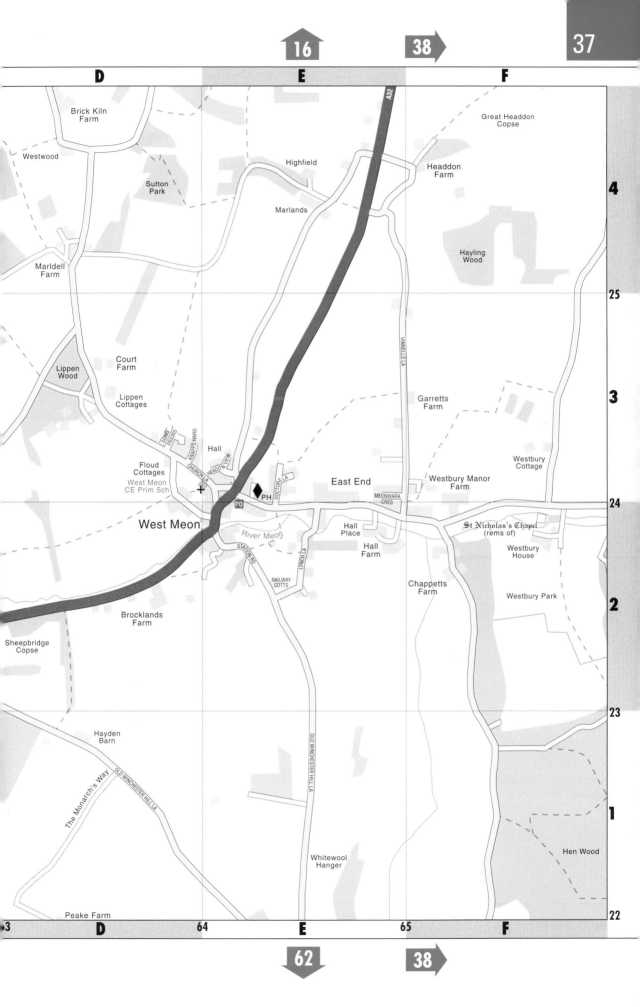

D E F

Brick Kiln Farm

Great Headdon Copse

Westwood

Highfield

Headdon Farm

Sutton Park

4

Marlands

Hayling Wood

Marldell Farm

25

Court Farm

Lippen Wood

VINNELLS LA

Lippen Cottages

Garretts Farm

3

Westbury Cottage

LONG PRIORS

KNAPPS HARD

Hall

HEADON VIEW

Fload Cottages

CHURCH LA

West Meon CE Prim Sch

DOCTORS LA

Westbury Manor Farm

West Meon

PO

PH

East End

MEONWARA CRES

24

River Meon

Hall Place

St Nicholas's Chapel (rems of)

STATION RD

Hall Farm

Westbury House

LYNCH LA

RAILWAY COTTS

Chappetts Farm

Westbury Park

2

Brocklands Farm

Sheepbridge Copse

23

Hayden Barn

The Monarch's Way

OLD WINCHESTER HILL LA

OLD WINCHESTER HILL LA

1

Hen Wood

Whitewool Hanger

Peake Farm

22

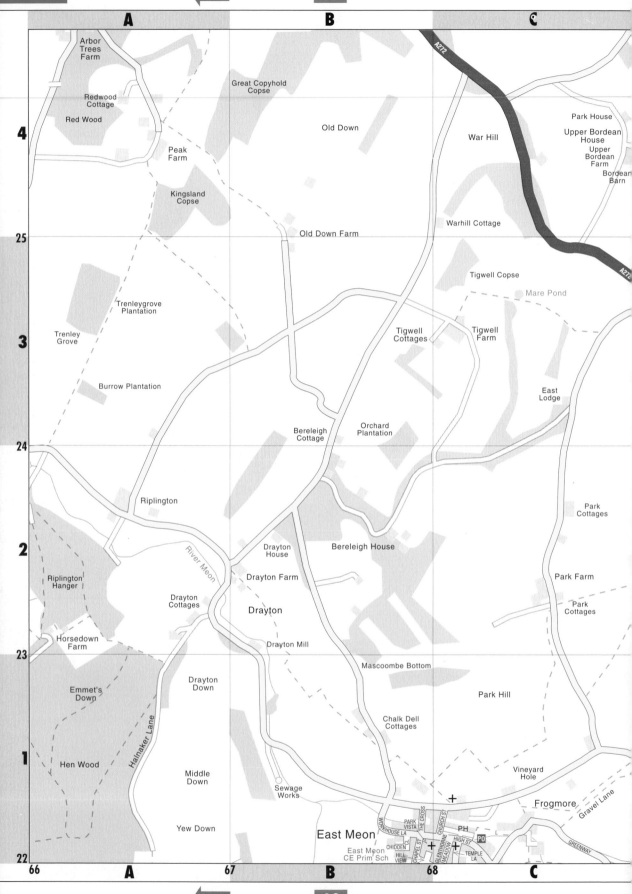

A B C

Arbor
Trees
Farm

Great Copyhold
Copse

A272

Park House

Redwood
Cottage

Old Down

War Hill

Upper Bordean
House

Red Wood

Upper
Bordean
Farm

4

Peak
Farm

Bordean
Barn

Kingsland
Copse

Warhill Cottage

25

Old Down Farm

Tigwell Copse

A272

Mare Pond

Trenleygrove
Plantation

Tigwell
Cottages

Tigwell
Farm

Trenley
Grove

3

East
Lodge

Burrow Plantation

Orchard
Plantation

Bereleigh
Cottage

24

Park
Cottages

Riplington

River Meon

2

Drayton
House

Bereleigh House

Park Farm

Riplington
Hanger

Drayton Farm

Park
Cottages

Drayton
Cottages

Drayton

Horsedown
Farm

Drayton Mill

23

Mascoombe Bottom

Emmet's
Down

Drayton
Down

Park Hill

Chalk Dell
Cottages

Hainaker Lane

1

Hen Wood

Middle
Down

Vineyard
Hole

Sewage
Works

Frogmore

Gravel Lane

Yew Down

East Meon

PARK
VISTA

THE CROSS

PH

PO

GREENWAY

East Meon
CE Prim Sch

CHIDDEN
CL

CHAPEL ST

HILL
VIEW

CHURCH ST

GLEBE
MEADOW

HIGH ST

TEMPLE
LA

22

66

A

67

B

68

C

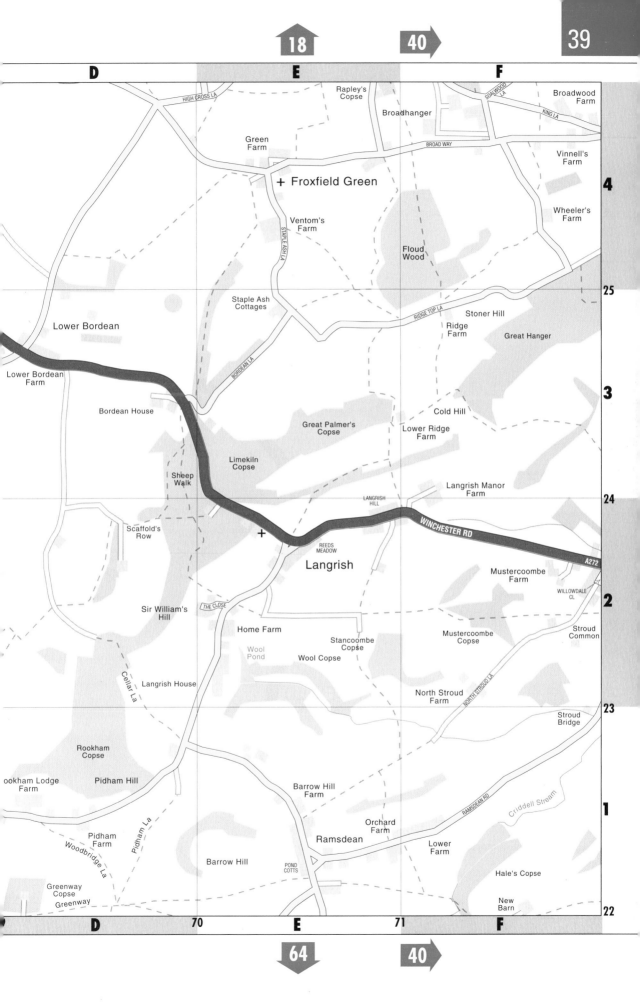

D
E
F

4

Rapley's Copse

Broadhanger

HIGH CROSS LA

Broadwood Farm

SOALWOOD LA

KING LA

Green Farm

BROAD WAY

Vinnell's Farm

+ Froxfield Green

Wheeler's Farm

Ventom's Farm

STAPLE ASH LA

Floud Wood

25

Staple Ash Cottages

Lower Bordean

RIDGE TOP LA

Stoner Hill

Ridge Farm

Great Hanger

Lower Bordean Farm

BORDEAN LA

3

Bordean House

Great Palmer's Copse

Cold Hill

Lower Ridge Farm

Limekiln Copse

Sheep Walk

Langrish Manor Farm

24

LANGRISH HILL

WINCHESTER RD

Scaffold's Row

+

REEDS MEADOW

A272

Langrish

Mustercoombe Farm

WILLOWDALE CL

Sir William's Hill

THE CLOSE

2

Home Farm

Mustercoombe Copse

Stroud Common

Wool Pond

Stancoombe Copse

Wool Copse

Langrish House

CELLAR LA

North Stroud Farm

NORTH STROUD LA

23

Stroud Bridge

Rookham Copse

Pidham Hill

Barrow Hill Farm

RAMSDEAN RD

Criddell Stream

1

ookham Lodge Farm

Orchard Farm

Pidham Farm

PIDHAM LA

Ramsdean

Lower Farm

WOODBRIDGE LA

Barrow Hill

POND COTTS

Hale's Copse

Greenway Copse
Greenway

New Barn

22

D
70
E
71
F

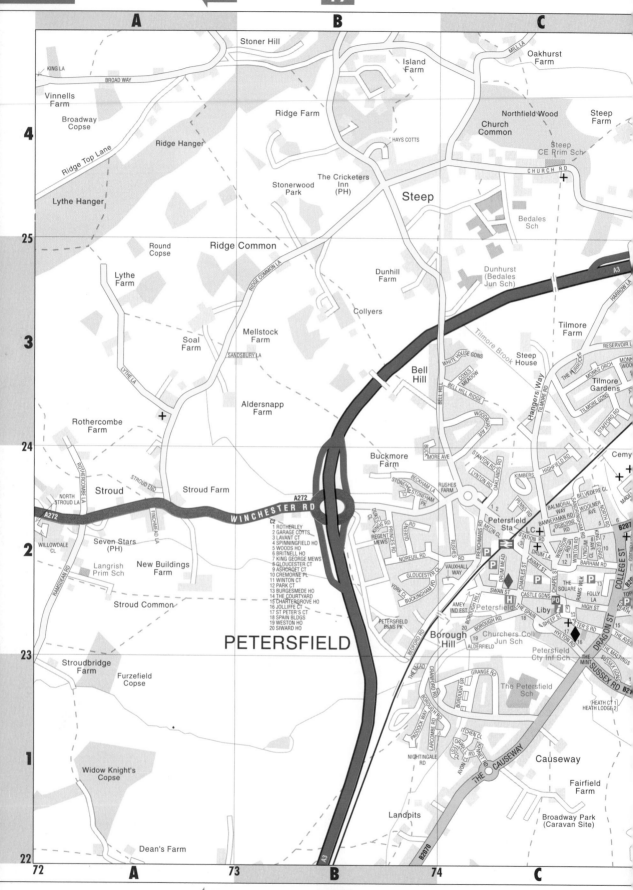

King La

Broad Way

Vinnells Farm

Broadway Copse

Ridge Top Lane

Ridge Hanger

Lythe Hanger

Stoner Hill

Island Farm

Ridge Farm

Stonerwood Park

The Cricketers Inn (PH)

HAYS COTTS

Steep

Oakhurst Farm

Northfield Wood

Church Common

Steep Farm

Steep CE Prim Sch

CHURCH RD

Bedales Sch

4

Round Copse

Lythe Farm

Soal Farm

Mellstock Farm

SANDSBURY LA

RIDGE COMMON LA

Ridge Common

Dunhill Farm

Collyers

Dunhurst (Bedales Jun Sch)

A3

25

3

LYTHE LA

Aldersnapp Farm

Bell Hill

White House Gdns

Coxes Meadow

Bell Hill Ridge

Bell Hill

Steep House

WOODMAN

Tilmore Brook

Hangers Way

Tilmore Farm

RESERVOIR L

Tilmore Gardens

THE MERRICKS

MONKS ORCH

MONK WOO

TILMORE GDNS

STAFFORD RD

Rothercombe Farm

Buckmore Farm

BUCKMORE AVE

STANTON RD

KINGS RD

OAKLANDS RD

HIGHFIELD RD

Cemy

ROTHERCOMBE LA

STROUD END

Stroud Farm

BECKHAM LA

RUSHES FARM

LYNTON RD

KIMBERS

PRINCE RD

BELVEDERE CL

24

NORTH STROUD LA

Stroud

A272

WINCHESTER RD

A272

FINCHDEAN LA

STONEHAM

DUKES CL

REGENT

PRINCES RD

NOREUIL RD

2

1

Petersfield Sta

BALMORAL WAY

BANNERMAN RD

OSBORNE RD

WOOLNER AVE

NORTH RD

SANDRINGHAM RD

KING GEORGE RD

BARHAM RD

B207

2

RAMSDEAN RD

WILLOWDALE CL

Seven Stars (PH)

Langrish Prim Sch

New Buildings Farm

C2
1 ROTHERLEY
2 GARAGE COTTS
3 LAVANT CT
4 SPINNINGFIELD HO
5 WOODS HO
6 BRITNELL HO
7 KING GEORGE MEWS
8 GLOUCESTER CT
9 ASHCROFT CT
10 CREMORNE PL
11 WINTON CT
12 PARK CT
13 BURGESMEDE HO
14 THE COURTYARD
15 CHARTERGROVE HO
16 JOLLIFFE CT
17 ST PETER'S CT
18 SPAIN BLDGS
19 WESTON HO
20 SIWARD HO

GLOUCESTER CL

YORK CL

BUCKINGHAM RD

Petersfield BSNS PK

VAUXHALL WAY

FRENCHMANS RD

MEON CL

CHARLES ST

LAVANT CL

WINDSOR RD

LC

THE SQUARE

DRUM MEAD

SWAN ST

CASTLE GDNS

PO

RAMS WLK

FOLLY LA

HIGH ST

Petersfield Liby

AMEY IND EST

Petersfield

BOROUGH RD

THE SPAIN

SHEEP ST

Churchers Coll Jun Sch

ALDERFIELD

Borough Hill

Petersfield Cty Inf Sch

DRAGON ST

COLLEGE ST

KING GEORGE

LINDUM CL

THE AVE

SUSSEX RD

B21

THE MINT

THE MALTINGS

PETERSFIELD

23

Stroudbridge Farm

Furzefield Copse

THE MEAD

BEDFORD RD

BOROUGH HILL

CRANFORD RD

BOROUGH GR

GRANGE RD

The Petersfield Sch

HEATH CT 1
HEATH LODGE 2

ITCHEN CL

LARCOOMB RD

PADDOCK WAY

BOROUGH RD

1

Widow Knight's Copse

NIGHTINGALE RD

ORMEL CL

AVON

EMMETT RD

THE CAUSEWAY

Landpits

Causeway

Fairfield Farm

Broadway Park (Caravan Site)

22

Dean's Farm

B2070

A3

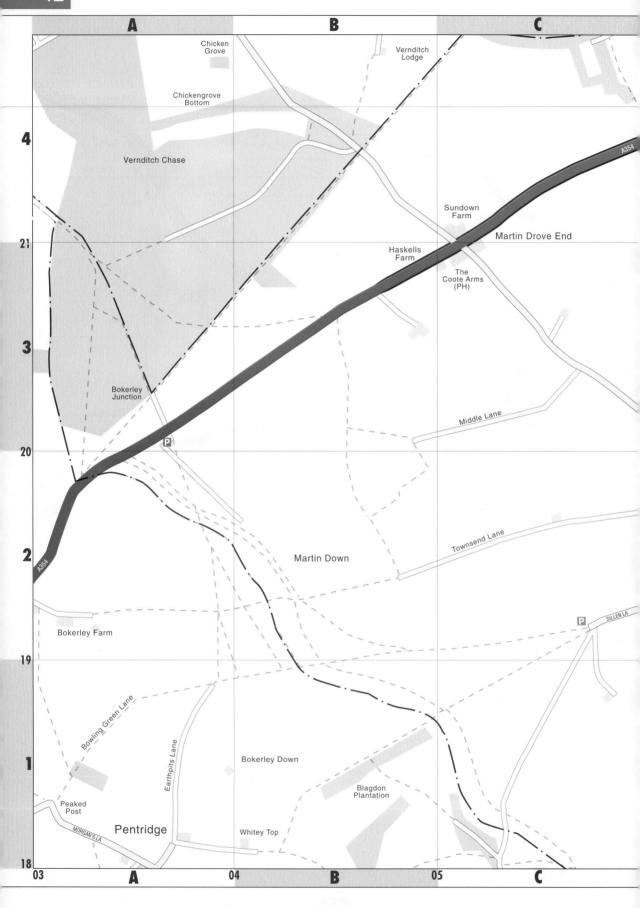

A   B   C

Chicken Grove

Chickengrove Bottom

Vernditch Lodge

Vernditch Chase

A354

Sundown Farm

Martin Drove End

Haskells Farm

The Coote Arms (PH)

4

21

Bokerley Junction

Middle Lane

P

3

20

Townsend Lane

Martin Down

2

A354

Bokerley Farm

P

SILLEN LA

19

Bowling Green Lane

Bokerley Down

Earthpits Lane

Blagdon Plantation

1

Peaked Post

Pentridge

MORGAN'S LA

Whitey Top

18

03   A   04   B   05   C

A   **B**   **C**

4

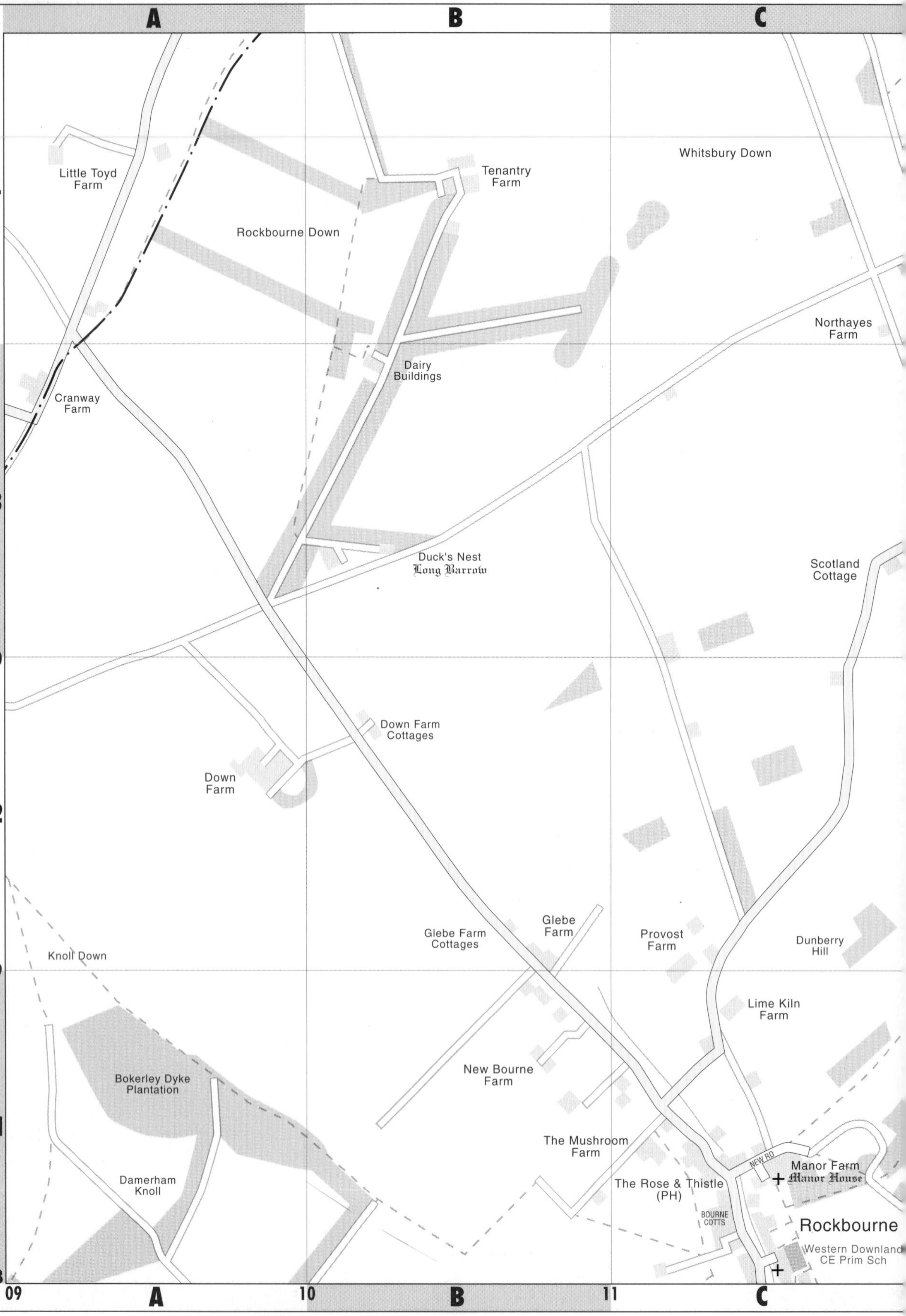

Little Toyd Farm

Tenantry Farm

Whitsbury Down

Rockbourne Down

21

Dairy Buildings

Northayes Farm

Cranway Farm

3

Duck's Nest
Long Barrow

Scotland Cottage

20

Down Farm Cottages

Down Farm

2

Glebe Farm Cottages

Glebe Farm

Provost Farm

Dunberry Hill

Knoll Down

19

Lime Kiln Farm

Bokerley Dyke Plantation

New Bourne Farm

1

The Mushroom Farm

NEW RD

Manor Farm
Manor House

Damerham Knoll

The Rose & Thistle (PH)

BOURNE COTTS

Rockbourne

Western Downland CE Prim Sch

18

09   **A**   10   **B**   11   **C**

Wick Down

Botley's Farm

Upper Wick Barn

Gallops

Gallows Hill

Jubilee Clump

Hulse's Clump

Well Bottom

Shoulder of Mutton Clump

Breamore Down

North Charford Drove

South Charford Drove

Giant's Grave
Long Barrow

Manor Farm

Whitsbury Castle Ditches
Fort

Long Steeple Lane

Down Farm

Manor House

Whitsbury Stud

Breamore Wood

Whitsbury

WELL HOUSE CL

Top Stud

Lower Farm

Glebe House Farm

Major's Farm

PO

Carpenter's Farm

THE CLOSE

Home Farm

LOWER GR

The Cart Wheel (PH)

Whitsbury Wood

Nippard's Farm

Lower Farm

Gravelhill Copse

The Rookery

ROOKERY LA

Upper Street

Roundhill Cross

Drove Barn

Whitsbury Common

Roundhill Farm

Topp's Farm House

WICK LA

45

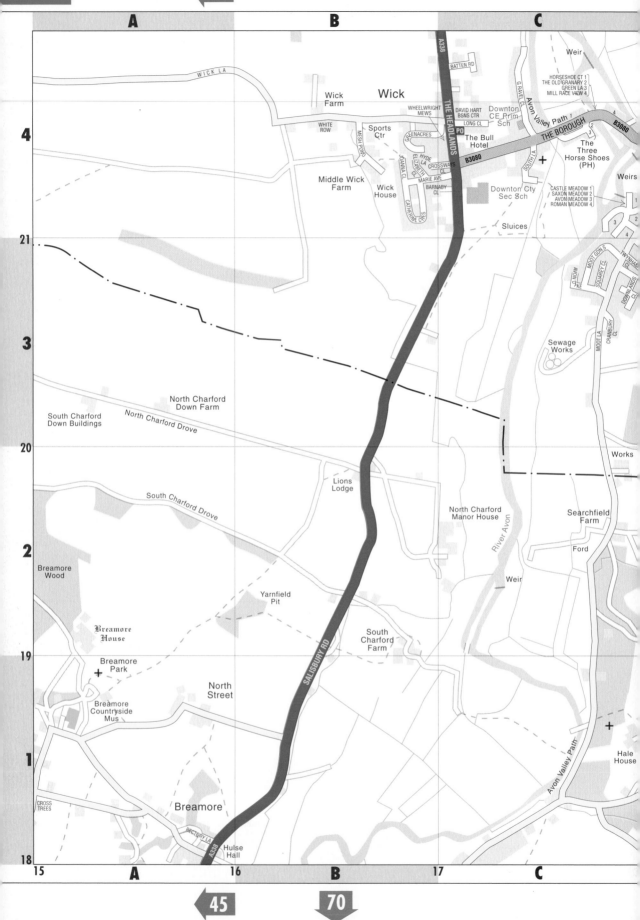

A   B   C

Titchborne
Farm

Mollcroft
Copse

MOOR LA

Great Sherwood
Copse

Redhills

Gill's Hole

Horse Pond
Copse

Wall Copse

East Copse

Thorn's
Copse

4

Lower Pensworth
Farm

Newhouse

Bagfield Copse

GROVE LA

Out Wood

21

GOGG'S LA

Appsy Copse

Homan's Copse

TIMBERLEY LA

Timbury Farm
House

Shearwood Copse

River Blackwater

Langley Wood

Round
Copse

3

Badger's
Copse

Lover

COLE'S LA

Witterns Hill
Farm

The
Forresters
Arms
(PH)

VICARAGE RD

CHURCH WLK

Langley Wood

Brickkiln
Cottages

Cole's
Copse

Bishops Wood

Golf
Course

CHURCH HILL

+

The
Mount

Ford

PO

SCHOOL RD

Redlynch
CE Sch

Hamptworth
Farm

20

BLACK LA

Moor Copse

HAMPTWORTH RD

Loosehanger Farm

Hamptworth
Lodge

2

Loosehanger Copse

Home
Farm

Pimlico
Firs

The Bog

19

Loosehanger Common

Pimlico
Bottom

1

Radnor Firs

LYBURN RD

Lyburn
Farm

B3080

Quar Hill
Plantation

Horse Common

Windyeats Farm

Cloven Hill Plantation

18

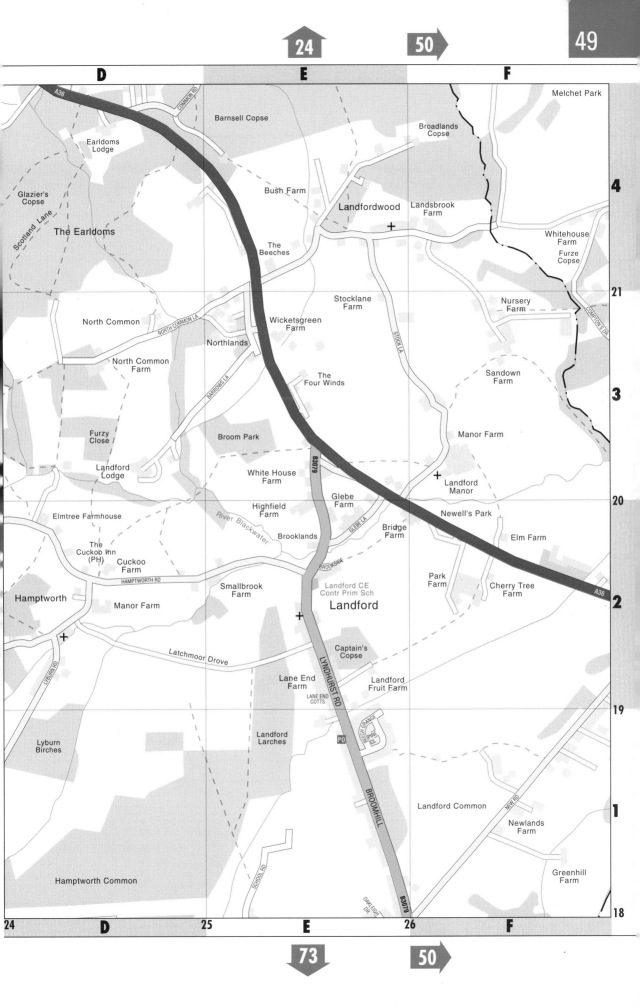

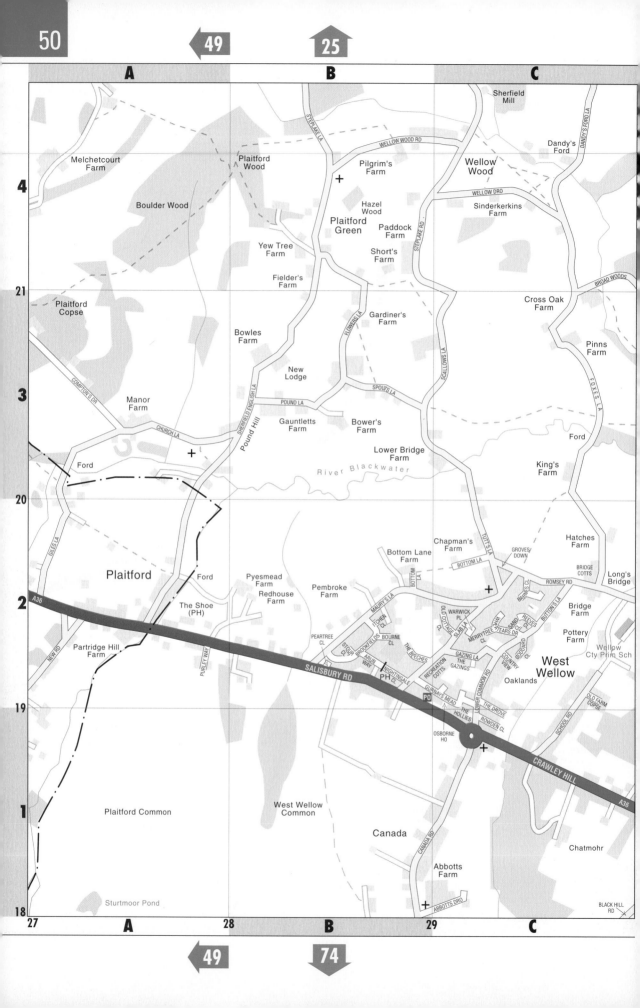

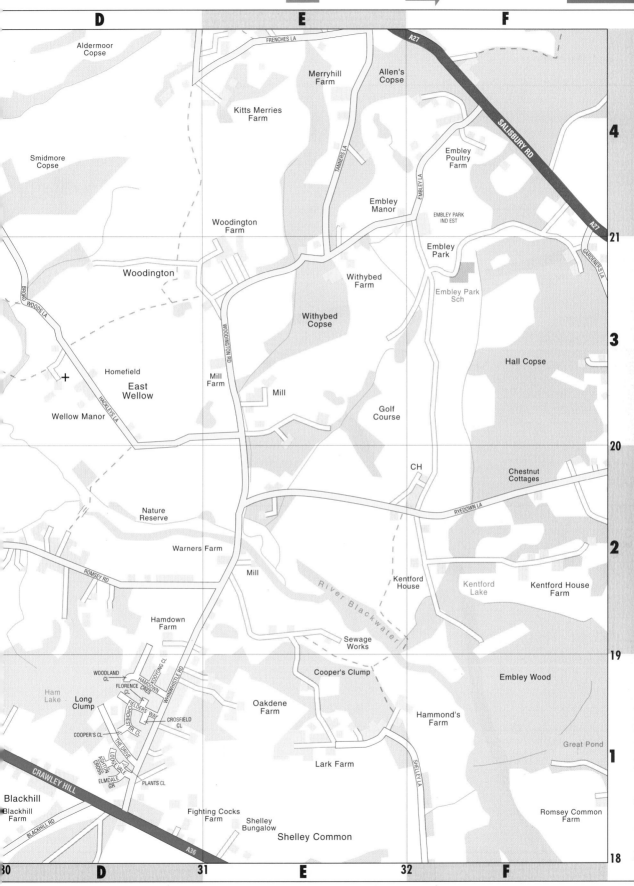

D E F

4
21
3
20
2
19
1
18

Aldermoor
Copse

FRENCHES LA

Merryhill
Farm

Allen's
Copse

A27

SALISBURY RD

Kitts Merries
Farm

Embley
Poultry
Farm

Smidmore
Copse

TANNERS LA

EMBLEY LA

Embley Manor

EMBLEY PARK
IND EST

Woodington
Farm

Embley
Park

GARDENERS LA

A27

Withybed
Farm

Embley Park
Sch

Woodington

Withybed
Copse

Hall Copse

BROAD WOODS LA

WOODINGTON RD

+

Homefield

East
Wellow

HACKLEYS LA

Mill
Farm

Mill

Golf
Course

Wellow Manor

CH

Chestnut
Cottages

Nature
Reserve

RYEDOWN LA

Warners Farm

Mill

Kentford
House

Kentford
Lake

Kentford House
Farm

ROMSEY RD

Hamdown
Farm

Sewage
Works

River Blackwater

WOODLAND
CL

COYLONG CL

HAMDOWN
CL

WHINWHISTLE RD

Cooper's Clump

Embley Wood

Ham
Lake

FLORENCE
CL

FIELDERS WAY

Long
Clump

CHICHESTER CL

CROSFIELD
CL

Oakdene
Farm

Hammond's
Farm

SHELLEY LA

COOPER'S CL

THE DRIVE

Great Pond

ASHTON
CROSS

LODGE DALE

Lark Farm

ELMDALE
GR

PLANTS CL

CRAWLEY HILL

A36

Blackhill

Blackhill
Farm

BLACKHILL RD

Fighting Cocks
Farm

Shelley
Bungalow

Shelley Common

Romsey Common
Farm

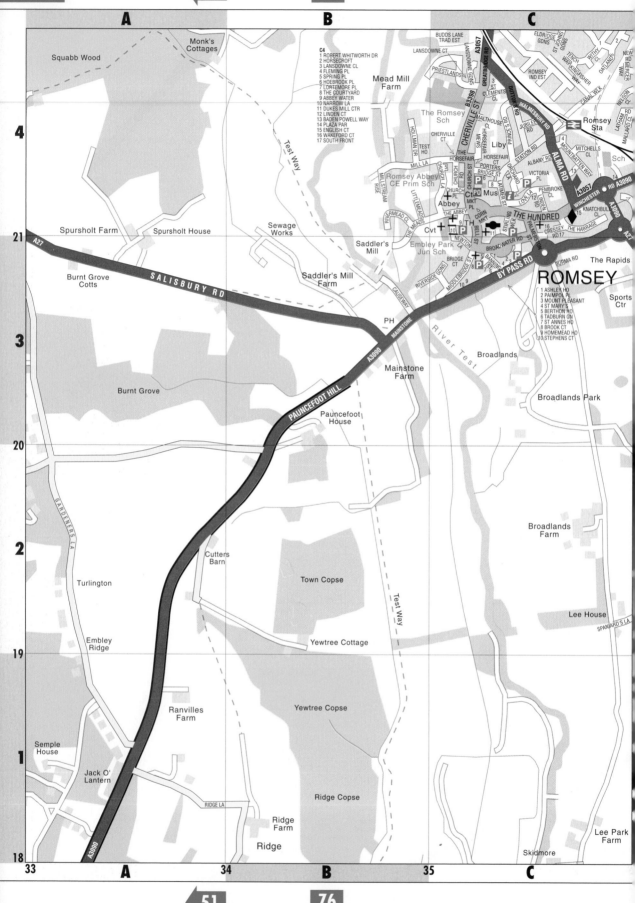

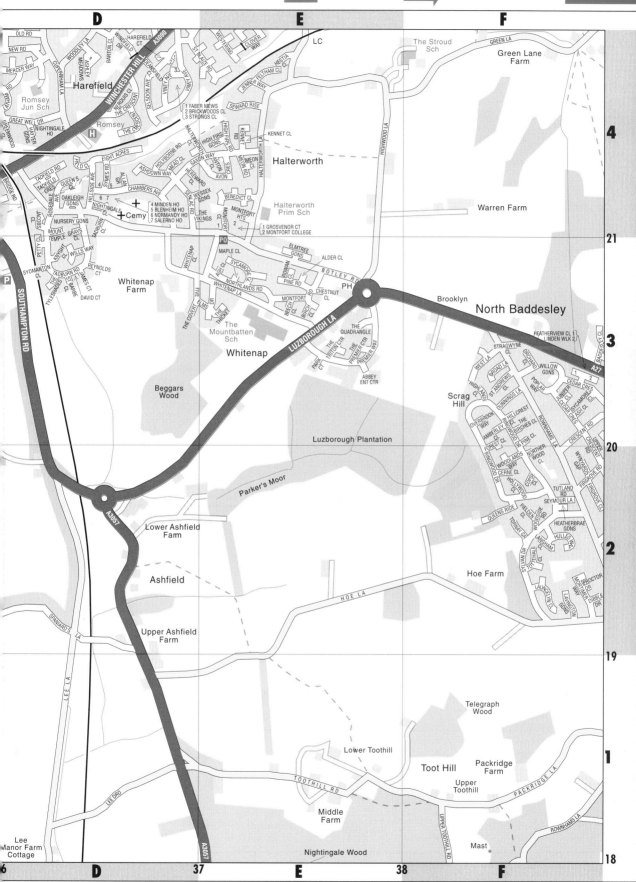

A   B   C

4

Broadgate Plantation
Woodend Copse
Thorn Hill
Green Acres
Newlands Copse
Bucket Corner
Castle Hill
KNIGHTWOOD RD
Baddesley Common
FLEXFORD RD
Knightwood Cotts
Sky's Wood

21

Lights Copse
Manor Farm
Tredgoulds Copse
FIELD VIEW
CRUSADER WAY
Manor House
SKY'S WOOD RD
GOOD ACRE DR
GOLDVINE DR

3

TEST VALLEY BSNS PK
Dirty Drive
Zion Hill Farm
Zionshill Copse
BADDESLEY CL
A27
BLENCOWE DR
WILD ARUM WAY
HEMLOCK CL
CELANDINE WAY

STREET END
SANDY LA
NUTBURN RD
EMER CL
WHITEBEAM WAY
CRESCENT RD
FIRGROVE RD
MERRY GDNS
CAMELIA CL
LABURNUM CL
SIX OAKS RD
EDWINA CL
Nutburn
CHAMBERLAYNE CT
GAINSBOROUGH CT
SANDY LA
Great Covert
ACORN GR
PRIMROSE CL
YORK CL
TEMPLARS WAY

20

SPRING GDNS
ROSSLYN CL
MIDDLE RD
PO
Ind Pk
SANDRINGHAM CL
BLENHEIM CL
TANSY MEADOW

Works
THE LAURELS
P
Liby
ROWNHAMS RD
CHURCH RD
BROWNHILL RD
BOTLEY RD
North Baddesley Jun & Inf Schs
Hogtrough Wood
CASTLE LA

THOMAS RD
ST CHRISTOPHERS RD
ENNEL CL
TANNERS RD
HEATH RD
NORTON WELCH CL
FLEMING AVE
ST BONIFACE CT
ST JOHN'S CT
FLEMING CT
Misslebrooks Copse
MISSLEBROOK LA

2

BROOK CL
BRACKEN CL
MEADOW CL
BRACKED RD
WINSTONE CRES
ST GEORGE'S CT
ST DAVID'S CT
ST PATRICK'S CT
CH
Austins Copse
HOE LA
Golf Range

ROWNHAMS LA

19

PACKRIDGE LA
Tanner's Brook
Calveslease Copse
Manor Farm
Chilworth Old Village
FOWLERS WLK
Chilworth
Hut Wood
WOODSIDE CRES
WOODSIDE

1

The Clump
CHILWORTH CL
PO
PH
CHILWORTH RD
THE ORCHARD
CSPCO LA

Rownhams Plantation
Home Copse
Chilworth Manor Hotel & Con Ctr
UNIVERSITY PARKWAY
CHILWORTH DRO
MANOR RD
ROMAN RD
GREEN LA

Kennels Farm
Science and Research Centre
VENTURE RD
ENTERPRISE RD
A27
M27

18

39   A   40   B   41   C

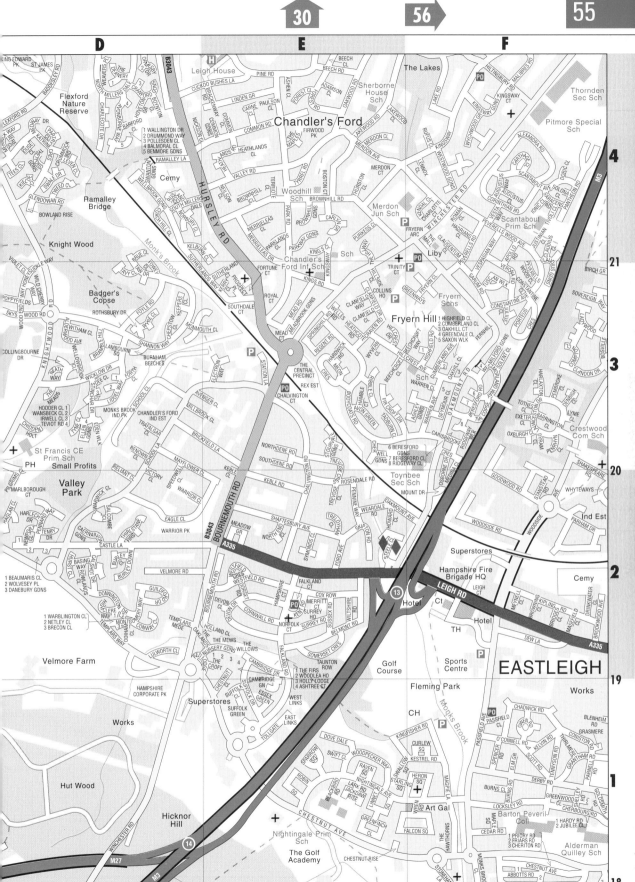

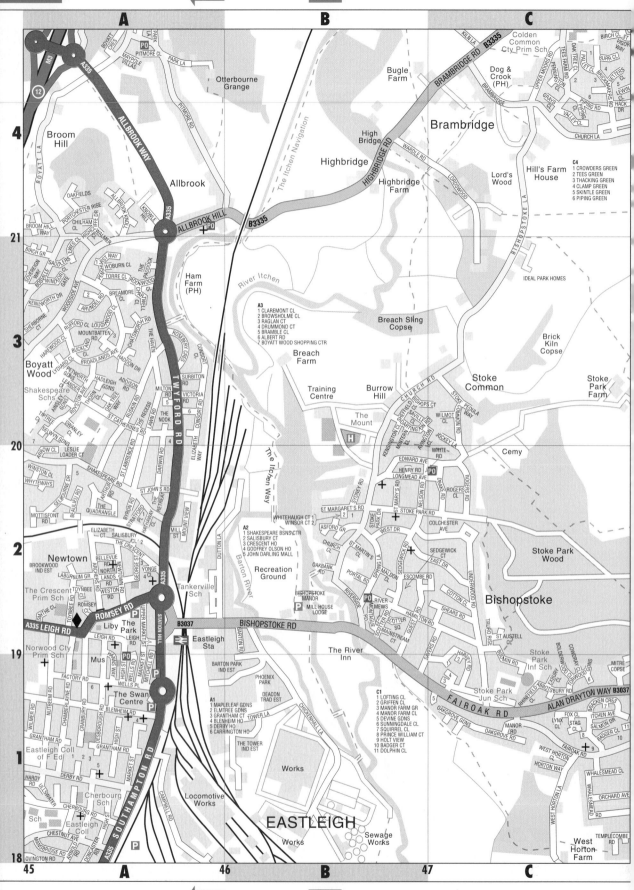

57 33

A
B
C
Rowhay Wood
Woodlock's Down Farm
Leybushes Copse
Greenhill Lane
LOWER BAYBRIDGE LA
WHADDON LA
THOMPSON'S LA
Marwell House
4
Red Lane
Kings Way
Summerlands
Hurst Farm
The Monarch's Way
Sladford's Copse
Roughay Farm
The Rookery
HURST LA
21
Woodcote Lane
White Hill
Rowhay Lane
Widlers Lane
SHOE LA
RED LA
Sweet Briar Cottage
WIDLERS LA
CHURCH ST
PH
B2177
Deeps Bushes Copse
3
Thistle Ridge Farm
Deeps Copse
Cawtes Copse
ELM CRES
OAK CL
West Hall
Upham
HATCHLEY LA
ROWHAY LA
Upham CE Prim Sch
Upham Copse
Bushy Copse
Pondside
Hatchley Lane
UPHAM ST
Deeps Farm
Popes Farm
20
POPES LA
Upham Farm
Stroudwood Farm
STROUDWOOD RD
New Farm
STAKES LA
Ashbourne Stables
WINCHESTER RD
PO
Lower Upham
2
B3037
HOYLE CL
Stroudwood
Alma Inn (PH)
Redlands Copse
Merry Orchard Farm
Woodman Inn (PH)
Kings Way
CROSS LA
MORTIMERS LA
Stroudwood Dairy Farm
Stakes Farm
Pond Farm
Torbay Farm
Oaklands Farm
Woolstreet Farm
Down Farm
B3037
19
Woodward Farm
ALMA LA
Woodley Farm
Meadowview
Golf Course
Coombs Farm
THE CRESCENT
SCIVIER'S LA
1
Wintershill Hall
Kimbers Copse
Moplands Copse
Oakdale Farm
Winters Hill
Wintershill Farm
Woodlands
Giles Farm
GREENWOOD LA
DURLEY HALL RD
B2177
WINTERS HILL
Job's Corner
Nursery
Wintershill
18
Durley Hall Farm
51
A
52
B
53
C

57 82

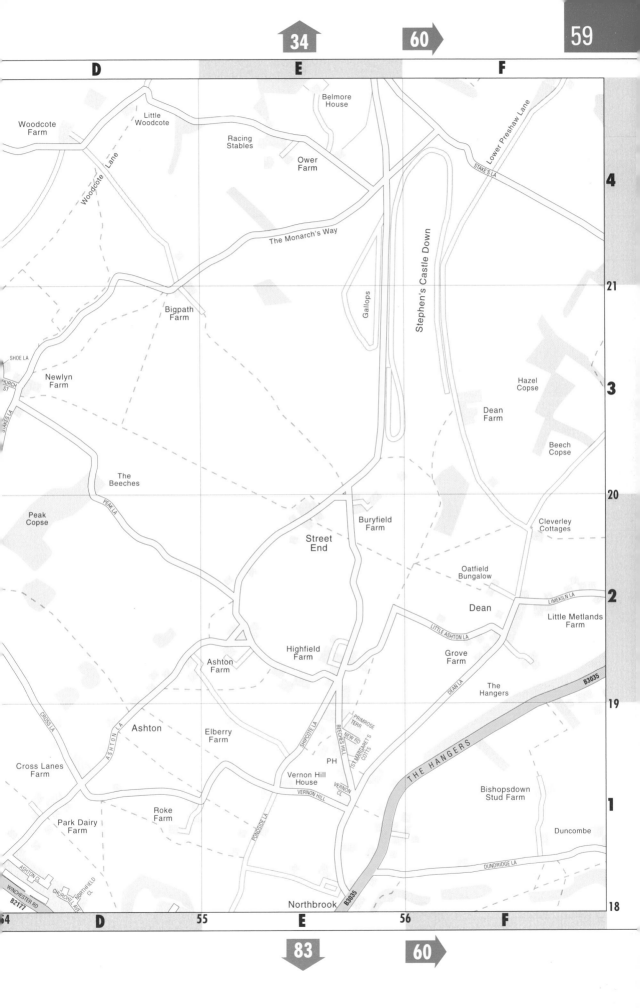

A **B** **C**

Sargeant's Copse

King's Copse

SAILORS LA

Downleaze Copse

Punch Bowl

4

Shellets Farm

Winters Down

LONE BARN LA

Littleton Copse

St Clair's Farm

Franklin Lane

STAKES LA

Corhampton Forest

21

Beacon Hill LA

Warners Cottage

Wyndham Lodge

CORHAMPTON LA

3

Bottom Copse

Franklin Farm

Corhampton Down

Wayfarer's Walk

Steynes Farm

Corhampton Lane Farm

B3035

Greenacres

Golf Course

20

Droxford Down

Club House

2

LIMEKILN LA

Hazel Holt

Sheep Pond LA

B3035

THE HANGERS

Hazel Holt Farm

Shepherds Down Farm

Galley Down

19

DUNDRIDGE LA

Shepherds Down

Peak Down

HACKETTS LA

Lycroft Farm

Wayfarer's Walk

1

Dundridge

Hampshire Bowman (PH)

PARK LA

Swanmore Barn Farm

Dundridge Farm

DAMSON HILL

Beechen Copse

Swanmore Park Farm

Fir Down

18

57 **A** **58** **B** **59** **C**

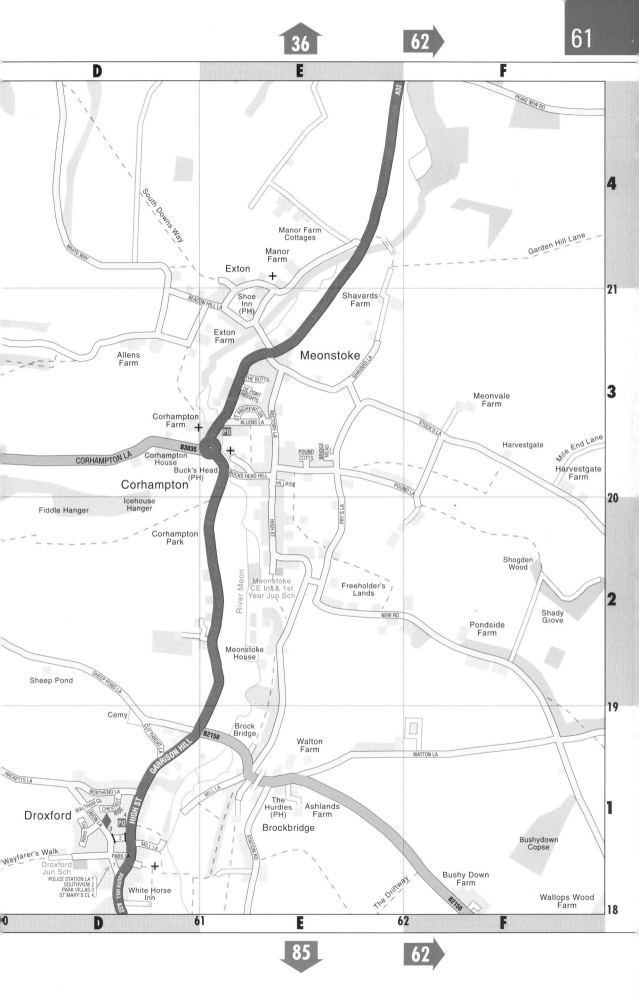

A **B** **C**

Peake New Rd

Peake Farm

Bullshead Copse

Old Winchester Hill La

Old Winchester Hill La

Hen Wood

Peake Wood

Whitewool Hanger

4

Whitewool Farm

Roll's Copse

South Downs Way

21

Old Winchester Hill

The Monarch's Way

Nature Reserve

3

Castle Cottages

Mile End Lane

20

Stocks Farm

Teglease Down

Stock's La

2

Little West End Farm

Teglease Copse

19

Westend Down

Teglease Farm

Sheepbarn Copse

1

Sheardley La

Little Sheardley Wood

Whiteleaf La

Stoke Wood

18

Wallops Wood Farm

63 **A** 64 **B** 65 **C**

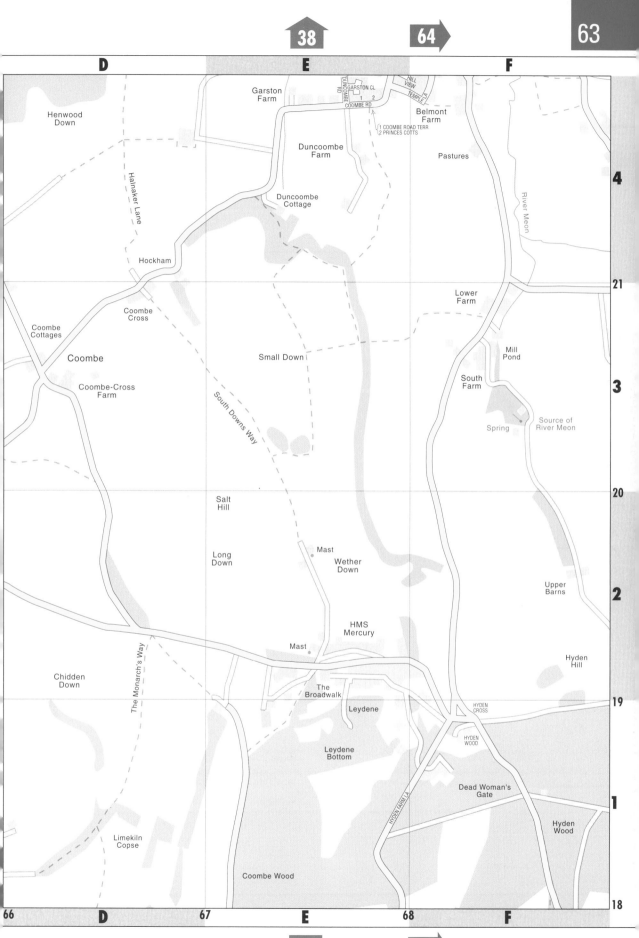

D · E · F

4

21

3

20

2

19

1

Henwood Down

Garston Farm

DUNCOOMBE RD

GARSTON CL
1 2

COOMBE RD

HILL VIEW

TEMPLE

Belmont Farm

1 COOMBE ROAD TERR
2 PRINCES COTTS

Duncoombe Farm

Pastures

Halnaker Lane

River Meon

Duncoombe Cottage

Hockham

Lower Farm

Coombe Cross

Coombe Cottages

Coombe

Small Down

South Farm

Mill Pond

South Downs Way

Spring

Source of River Meon

Coombe-Cross Farm

Salt Hill

Long Down

Mast

Wether Down

Upper Barns

The Monarch's Way

Mast

HMS Mercury

Hyden Hill

Chidden Down

The Broadwalk

Leydene

HYDEN CROSS

HYDEN WOOD

Leydene Bottom

HYDEN FARM LA

Dead Woman's Gate

Hyden Wood

Limekiln Copse

Coombe Wood

A **B** **C**

Nutcombe
Copse

Hill Hampton
Farm

Twentyways
Farm

Cumber's La

Hilhampton
Copse

4 Oxenbourne
Farm

LIMEKILN LA

Leythe House

Hopkiln

Harroway
Farm

Rakefield
Hanger

Browning's
Hill

Fishpond
Cottages

The Nore

Oxenbourne
Leythe

Ramsdean Down

21 Parsonage
Farm

Giants
Farm

Rake Bottom

Butser Hill

3 Preston
Farm

Limekiln La

Stonylands
Farm

HARVESTING LA

Radio Station
• Mast

P

20

South Downs Way

Queen Elizabeth
Country Park

2 Tegdown
Bottom

Hilhampton Down

Hilhampton
Bottom

Tegdown
Hill

19

NORTH LA

Nine Corner
Hanger

Oxenbourne
Down

A3

Blagdon
Farm

Newmans
Farm

Wascoombe Bottom

1

Blagden
Copse

Byden
Copse

P

Hyden Wood

Ditch Acre
Copse

Visitor
Ctr

18
Gravel Hill

A3

69 **A** **70** **B** **71** **C**

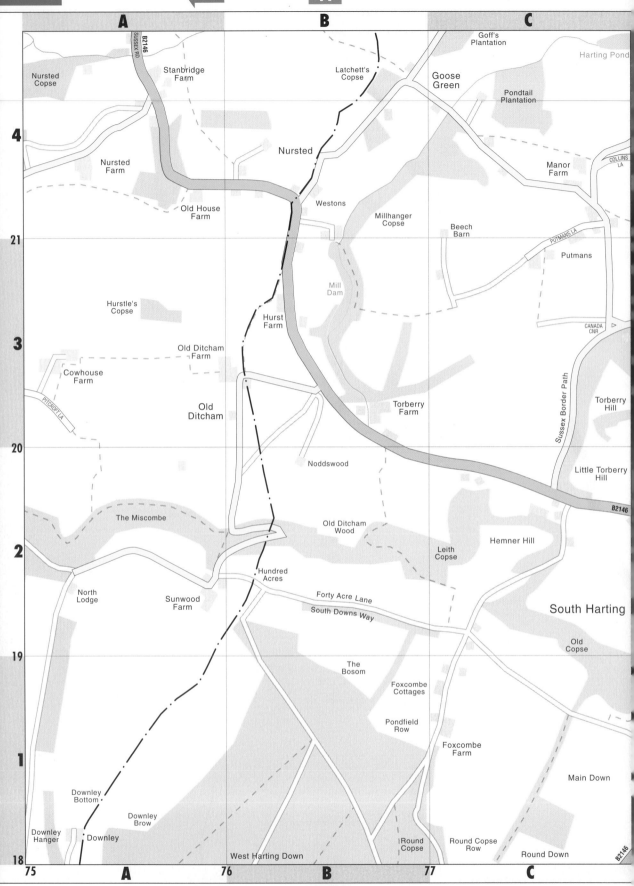

A B C

4

21

3

20

2

19

1

18

Nursted Copse

Stanbridge Farm

B2146

SUSSEX RD

Latchett's Copse

Goff's Plantation

Goose Green

Harting Pond

Pondtail Plantation

Nursted

Nursted Farm

Old House Farm

Westons

Millhanger Copse

Beech Barn

Manor Farm

COLLINS LA

PUTMANS LA

Putmans

Hurstle's Copse

Mill Dam

Hurst Farm

CANADA CNR

Cowhouse Farm

Old Ditcham Farm

PITCROFT LA

Old Ditcham

Torberry Farm

Sussex Border Path

Torberry Hill

Noddswood

Little Torberry Hill

B2146

The Miscombe

Old Ditcham Wood

Leith Copse

Hemner Hill

North Lodge

Sunwood Farm

Hundred Acres

Forty Acre Lane

South Downs Way

South Harting

Old Copse

The Bosom

Foxcombe Cottages

Pondfield Row

Foxcombe Farm

Main Down

Downley Bottom

Downley Brow

Downley Hanger

Downley

West Harting Down

Round Copse

Round Copse Row

Round Down

B2146

75 A 76 B 77 C

18

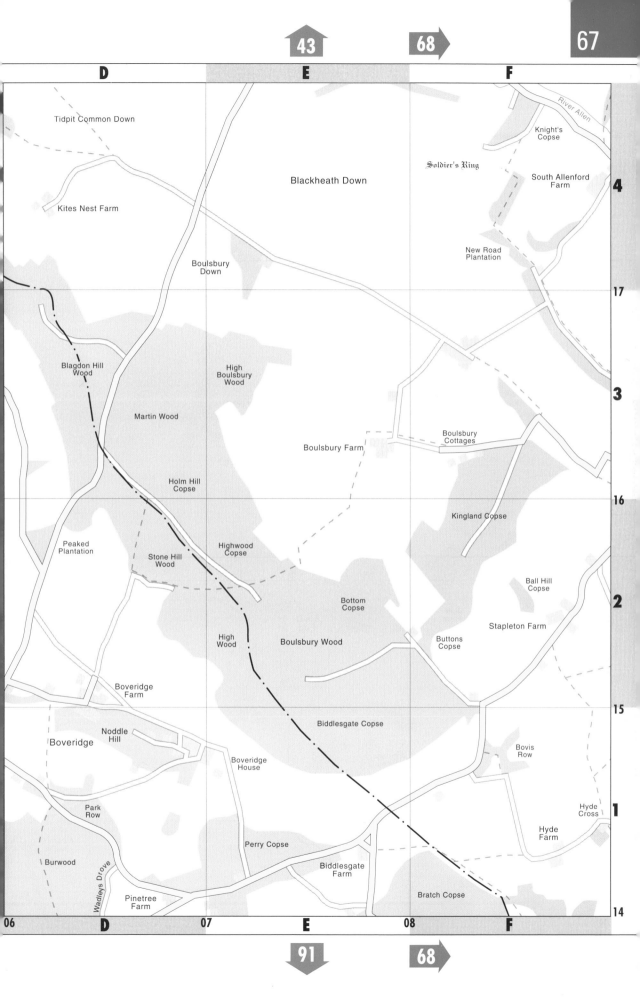

D
E
F

Tidpit Common Down

River Allen

Knight's Copse

Soldier's Ring

Blackheath Down

South Allenford Farm

4

Kites Nest Farm

New Road Plantation

Boulsbury Down

17

Blagdon Hill Wood

High Boulsbury Wood

3

Martin Wood

Boulsbury Cottages

Boulsbury Farm

Holm Hill Copse

16

Kingland Copse

Peaked Plantation

Highwood Copse

Stone Hill Wood

Ball Hill Copse

2

Bottom Copse

Stapleton Farm

High Wood

Boulsbury Wood

Buttons Copse

Boveridge Farm

15

Noddle Hill

Biddlesgate Copse

Boveridge

Bovis Row

Boveridge House

Park Row

Hyde Cross

1

Hyde Farm

Burwood

Wadleys Drove

Perry Copse

Biddlesgate Farm

Pinetree Farm

Bratch Copse

14

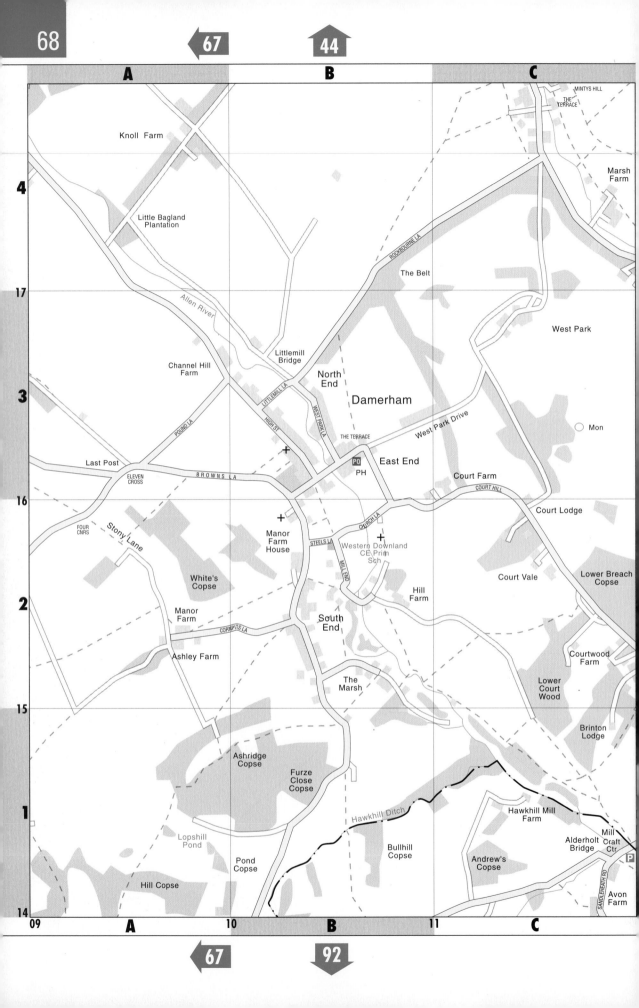

Whitsbury Common

Rockstead Copse

Whitsbury House

Whitsbury Cross

Kiln Wood

Outwick

4

Rockstead Farm

Radnall Wood

Flood Street

Whip's Hill Copse

17

ROMAN VILLA (remains of)

Brookheath

Clack Lane

Fryern Court Wood

Peas Ash Farm

Sagles Spring

Clack Barn

3

Sweatfords Water

Fryern Court Farm

Palmer's Copse

Fryern Court Rd

Mist Farm

Fryern Court

Allen's Farm

16

West Park Farm

Avon Vale Nurseries

Brickhill

Wilkins's Coomb

Sandle Dairy Farm

Avon Valley Path

Tinkers Cross

2

Hurley Farm

ARCH FARM IND EST

Fordingbridge Jun & Inf Schs

Puddleslosh Lane

Sandle Home Farm

Whitsbury Rd

Sandleheath

Marl Lane

15

CORONATION TERR

ELMS CL

SANDLEHEATH IND EST

Forres Sandle Manor

OLD BRICKYARD RD

PO

Thorps Farm

+

+

ALDERHOLT RD

Reeve's Copse

MANOR FARM RD

SANDLE COPSE

MAYFIELD RD

ELMWOOD AVE

DOWNWOOD CL

MARYFIELD CL

BRYMPTON CL

JUBILEE CL

JUBILEE RD

Ashford

STATION RD

ASHFORD CL

FERNDOWN CT

VICTORIA RD

GARENDON CT 1
MEADOW CL 2
OAKLANDS CL 3
WILSON CT 4
AVON CT 5
HOMEBRIDGE HO 6
THE HUNDRED 7

COTTAGE MEWS

1

Fordingbridge

THE OLD VINERIES

THE PANTILES

VICTORIA GDNS

BEECHWOOD

Hotel

FORDINGBRIDGE

Ashford Water

← 69
↑ 46

A
B
C

Breamore Marsh

Breamore CE Prim Sch

PO

A338

PH

Breamore

Marsh Farm

MARSH LA

Green's Farm

Arch Farm

Weir

Norton's Hole

Barn's Farm

Woodgreen

St Georges Cotts

PO

+ PH

HILL CLOSE EST

LOWER DENSOME WOOD

Higherend Farm

THE ALLEY

LOVE LA

GRACE LA

TRIMM'S DRO

HIGH ST

STEELS DRO

BROOK LA

LITTLE DRO

Woodgreen Common

+

Mill

4

THE SHALLOWS

The Shallows

Cemy

17

Godshill Inclosure

P

Upper Burgate

Castle Hill

FRYERN COURT RD

River Avon

BURGATE CROSS

Avon Valley Path

Godshill Wood

3

Burgate Cross Farm

Castle Hill

Weir

Armsley

16

Burgate Farm

Godshill Wood Farm

THE FAIRGATE CTR

Folds Farm

Burgate Court

P

Ford

Millers Ford Farm

PH

2

SALISBURY RD

The Burgate Sch

Burgate Manor Farm

Furze Close Copse

BURGATE E FIELDS

WAVERLEY RD

Lower Burgate

Frankenbury

SALISBURY RD

LANGLEY ROAD

STANBRIDGE ROAD

B3078

Roger Penny Way

Hall

PH

ROGER PENNY WAY

Godshill Green

15

HELSTY RD

Rookham Bottom

BRUYN RD

BRUYN CT

Sandy Balls

Holiday Centre

LINGCROSS LASCROFT DROM

FIELD WOODGREEN

WAY

THE PINES

+

PO

Godshill Farm

Hart Hill

+

Well Lane

Newgrounds

SALISBURY RD

Godshill

1

East Mills

Weir

AVON VIEW

Arniss Farm

Horseport

SOUTHAMPTON RD

Strawberry Farm

Ditchend Brook

B3078

BOURNE ST

A338

East Mill Farm

Criddlestyle

STUCKTON RD

St Johns Farm

BLISSFORD RD

14

15
A
16
B
17
C

← 69
↓ 94

D   E   F

Stricklands
Plantation

Hale
Purlieu

Millersford
Plantation

Turf Hill

4

ensome
Wood

Warren
Farm

P

Millersford
Copse

Warrenhouse
Copse

Turf Hill
Inclosure

Deadman Bottom

17

DENSOME
CNR

Cunninger
Bottom

B3078

Millersford
Bottom

P

DEADMAN HILL

ROGER PENNY WAY

P

3

Black Gutter

Stone Quarry
Bottom

Black Gutter
Bottom

Gravel Pit
Hill

16

Ditchend Brook

P

Leaden Hall

Cockley Bushes

2

Brune's
Purlieu

Ridge
Farm

Godshill Ridge

Little Cockley
Plain

Cockley Hill

Ashley Walk

Ashley Hole

P

Great Cockley
Plain

Lodge Hill

15

Ditchend
Bottom

Hive Garn
Bottom

Coopers Hill

Hive Gardens

Ditchend
Shade

Must Thorns
Bottom

Pitts Wood
Inclosure

Ashley Bottom

1

Forest Brook
Farm

Ditch End

Fernlea
Farm

Tickets Bury

Ashleycross
Hill

ASHLEY
CROSS

Burnt Balls

14

← 71   ▲ 48

A   B   C

B3080

Golden Cross
Jacob's Barrow

P

Pound
Bottom

Cloven Hill Plantation

Franchises
Common

Tinney's
Plantation

P

4

Rushy
Flat

Burnt Ground Wood

Franchises
Wood

Franchises
Lodge

17

B3080

Hope
Cottage

Firs Hill
Copse

B3078

ROGER PENNY WAY

Bramshaw
Telegraph

Tucker's
Hat

Picket
Corner

Studley
Head

3

Black Gutter

Claypitts Bottom

P

Bur
Bushes

Studley
Wood

Homy Ridge

16

B30

The Butts

2

Howen Bottom

Eyeworth Wood

Islands Thorns Inclosure

15

Crock Hill

Eyeworth
Pond

Latchmore Brook

1

Eyeworth
Lodge

P

Howen
Bushes

Fritham
Bridge

Fritham
Farm

The Royal Oak
(PH)

Fritham

14

Gorley Bushes

P

21   A   22   B   23   C

← 71   ▲ 96

LYBURN RD

A B C

4

Rockingham Arms
(PH)

CANADA RD

Black
Hill

P

PLANTATION RD

Canada
Common

Pitts
Farm

Swallow
Fields

BLACKHILL RD

Wicksmoor
Farmhouse

17

Penn
Common

Cooper's Lane

Hungerford
Farm

Furzley

FURZLEY LA

Furzley
Farm

Penn
Farm

3

Half Moon
Common

Mark's
Farm

Furzley
Common

Penn
Copse

Duck Hill

16

Stagbury
Hill

VICE LA

Porters
Farm

2

Blenmans
Farm

Cadnam Common

FURZLEY RD

Crock
Hill

Newbridge

NEWBRIDGE RD

B3079

Golf
Course

Warren's
House

15

Warren's
Park

Storm's
Farm

Cadnam River

CADNAM LA

PO

Golf
Course

Warren's
Farm

1

Brook
Hill

KENWAE LA

Cadnam
Green

Withers
Farm

BROOK DR

B3079

The
CH Bell Inn
Hotel

Brook

Manor
Farm

Springer's
Farm

Dairyhouse
Farm

Manor
Farm

M27

OLD
LYNDHURST
RD

A31

B3078

B3079

14

Ford

WITTENSFORD LA

27 A 28 B 29 C

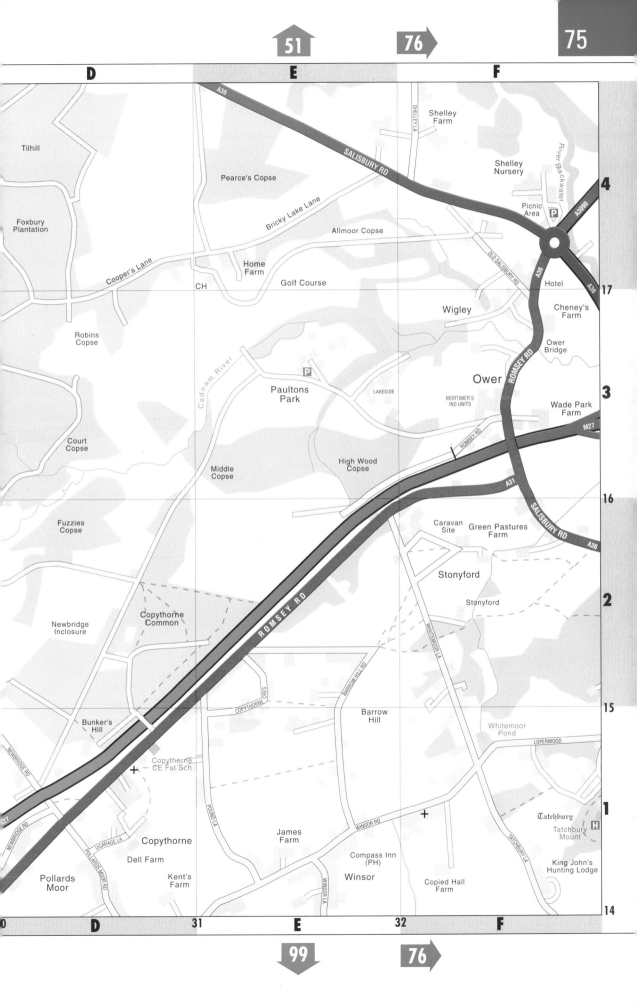

A   B   C

4

Moorcourt Copse

Longbridge Farm

Bowman's Farm

Test Way

Busheylease Farm

RIDGE LA

17

Moorcourt

Wade Hill Farm

Cadnam River

Wade Bridge

Wade Hill Drove

River Blackwater

HILL ST

Nursling House

3

M27

②

A326

Depot

Colbury House

Hillstreet

Broadlands Lake

River Test

Test Way

CHURCH LA

16

Brooke's Hill

Green La

The Laurels Farm

Wks

A36

Calmore Croft Farm

GREEN LA

Testwood House

Nursling Mill

MILL LA

Manor House Farm

2

Croft Farm

Sharves Hill

SALISBURY RD

Little Testwood Farm

TOTTON

Wks

River Test

Shorn Hill

PAULETTS LA

Loperwood

LOPERWOOD LA

15

Longbridge Ct

BRUNEL RD

NUTSEY CL

GRIFFIN IND PK

Loperwood

COOKS LA

EDDYSTONE RD

STEPHENSON RD

SOUTH HAMPSHIRE IND PK

CALMORE IND EST

WESTWOOD CT

TRINITY CT

Factory

NUTWOOD WAY

LULWORTH BSNS PK

FOREST WAY
H
HORSESHOE DR

Loperwood Farm
P
PO

Calmore

SNELLGROVE PL

COOKS LA

SNELLGROVE CL

BUCKLAND GDNS

WARREN PL

COPPICE RD

RANDALL CL

CALMORE DR

LONG CT

RIDGE CL

BY THE WOOD

SHELLEY RD

SHAKESPEARE DR

TENNYSON RD

STANLEY RD

SUTTON RD

ROYSTON CT

HUNTINGDON CL

Testwoodhouse Farm

Tatchbury Mount

Tatchbury

LOPERWOOD LA

CALMORE CRES

THE DRIVE

CALMORE RD

CHARMUS RD

Elizabeth Ho

RICHMOND CL

NUT

AMBERWOOD CL

ALLING CL

The Croft

The Paddock

BEECHDALE WLK

BIRCH

ARCHERS

THERONSWOOD

EWELL WAY

ALLERTON CL

CHEAM WAY

SUWA CRES

TESTWOOD AVE

HAMTUN GDNS

Testwood

GREENFIELDS CL

Testwood Sch

1

Calmore Inf & Jun Schs

DATFIELD GDNS 1
SEYMOUR CL 2
BOWATER CL 3
GREGORY GDNS 4

AIRTREE RD

FONTWELL CL

BEARSLANE

BRAKESHALL CL

MORTIMER CL

ROTHBURY CL

HAMTUN GDNS

GREENFIELDS AVE

THE REDFORDS

A36

HAMTUN CRES

Hazel Farm

WOODGREEN WLK

DANVELL CT

ST DAVID'S CL

THE STRIDE

INGLE GREEN

MELROSE CT

BROOK WLK

APPLETREE CL

FILTON CL

BOWATER WAY

TREAGORE RD

CORNFORTH RD

BLACKWATER MEWS

HALTONS

CHARNWOOD CL

KILNYARD

OAKFIELD CL

Hammond's Green

Oakfield Prim Sch

SHEPHERDS HEY RD

CALMORE DR

DANIELS WLK

A326

14

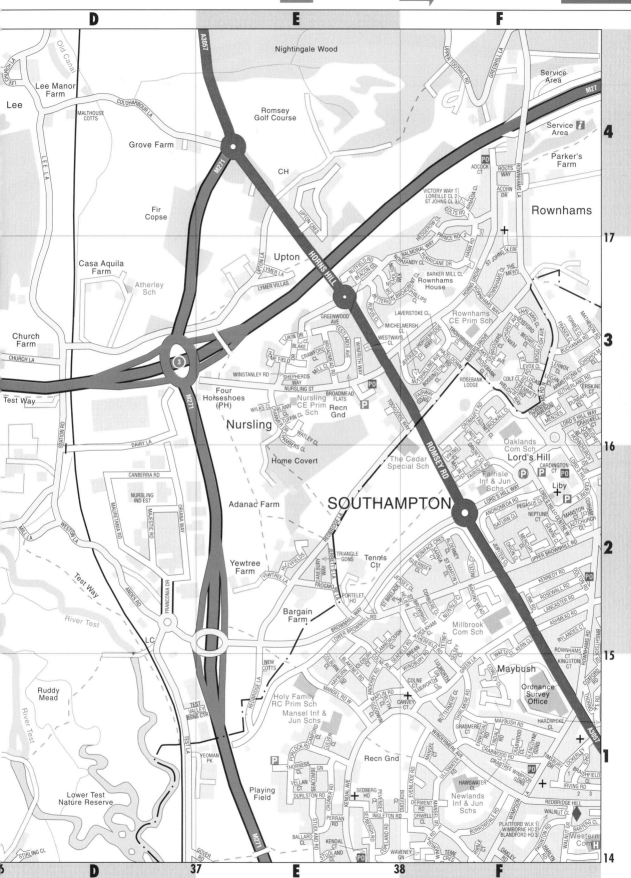

A B C

4

17

3

16

2

15

1

14

39 A 40 B 41 C

M27 · A27 · M27

Chilworth Common
Chilworth Tower
Dymer's Wood
Tanner's Brook
Lord's Wood
Castle Hill
Chilworth Common
Chilworth Ring

Heatherlands Rd · Pinelands Rd · Roman Rd · Pine Way · Little Toller · Fitzroy · Hadrian Way · Gene Way · Pine Wlk · Maple Beech Ho · Ling Dale · Linkwood Wlk · Pinehurst · Pine Ho · Linwood · Roman Dr · Pine Wlk · Bassett Heath Ave · The Ring · Julian · Links View Way · Saxholm Cl · Saxholm Dale · Saxholm Way · Saxholm · Bassett Dale · Beechmou · Birch Ho

Golf Course RD · CH · Bassett Row · Bassett Ave · Greenbank Cres · Ridgemount Ave · Ridgemount La 1 · Chelwood Gate 2 · Brampton Tower 3 · Brampton Manor 4 · Aromare Cres · Gables · Bassett Mews · Beechmou Rd · Chetwynd Rd

Matheson Rd · Sutherland Rd · Sinclair Jun Sch · Sinclair Inf Sch · Byron Rd · Goldcrest · Whinchat Cl · Wryneck Cl · Sandpiper · Firecrest · Hawfinch · Harrier · Wigeon Cl · Warbler Cl · Sheldrake · Tintagel Cl · Dunvegan Dr · Balmoral Cl · Dunster · Melville Cl · Oakwood Schs · Plover Cl · Osprey · Kestrel · Gannet Cl · Turnstone Gdns · Fulmar · Curlew Way · Oakwood Dr · Lordswood · Golf Course · Vectis Ct 1 · Redcourt 2 · Fairlea Grange 3 · Tower Gdns 4 · The Mount 5 · Canada Pl 6 · Bassett Wood Mews 7 · Vermont Sch · Holly Hill · Holly Hill Cl · The First · Little Oak Rd · Red Lodge Sch · Talbot Cl · Avington · Tudor Wood · Bassett Cl · Oaklands Way

Pembrey Cl · Kinloss · Northolt Gdns · Gatwick Gdns · Lewis Cl · Croydon Cl · Abercrombie Gdns · Petworth Gdns · Bransbury Cl · Purbrook · Salerno Rd · Taranto Rd · Lordswood Ct · Kelly Ct · Curzon Ct · Sports Centre · Redhill · Red Hill Way · Red Hill Cres · Boldrewood · Underwood · Overcliff · Wykeham Cl · Shawford Cl · Beaumont · Fernlea · Bassett Meadow · Boldrewood Con Ctr Univ

Caistor Cl · Tangmere Dr · Nightingale Ct · Chelveston Cres · Linden Rd · Peach Rd · Outer Circ · Aldermoor Rd · Myrtle Rd · Holly Oak Rd · Holly Oak Ct · Springford Rd · Langrish Rd · Shielden · Lyburn Rd · Wonston Rd · Greywell Ave · Bradley · Preston Rd · Stella Ct · The Polygon Sch (Annexe) · 1 Greywell Ct · 2 Pinelands Ct · 3 Lyburn Ct · Aldermoor Ct · Arnheim Cl · Dunkirk Rd · Lordswood Gdns · Lordswood Rd · Highclere Rd · Thornhill Cl · Rockleigh Rd · Oaktree · Pointout Cl · Pointout Rd · Sherwood · 1 Wellman Ct · 2 Glencarron Way · 3 Chestnut Lodge · Cutthor

Conford Rd · Olive Rd · Palm Rd · Wilton Rd · Mead Rd · Larch Rd · Rowan Cl · The Polygon · Tanner's Brook · Princess Anne · Arcadia Cl · Dale Valley Rd · Cemy · Holly Brook · Seymour · Malwood Ave · Hunton Cl · Seagarth · Schs · Winstone Bldgs · Burgess Rd · SOUTHAMPTON · Southampton Common · The Lake · Highfield · Coronation Ave · The Avenue

Aldermoor · Vine Rd · Coxford Rd · Elizabeth Ct · Birch Rd · Thornhill Rd · Ross Gdns · Sycamore Rd · Chestnut Rd · Warren Ave · Jessamine Rd · Tremona Rd · Elmwood Ct · Chalybeate · Southampton Gen · Shirley Warren · The Barton Ctr · Laundry Rd · Tardne Rd · Hollybrook · Dale Valley Gdns · Dale Valley Cl · Northbrook Ind Est · Norham Ave · Vincent · Seymour Cl · Pewsey Pl · Warwick Rd · Melrose Rd · Leicester Rd · Lincoln Rd · Luccombe · Shanklin Rd · Shanklin Cres · Malvern Bsns Ctr · Malvern Terr · Chester Rd · Bellemoor Sec Sch (Boys) · Pentire Ave · Queens Rd · Bellemoor Rd · Wilton Ave · Upper Shirley · Taunton Coll · Radway Rd

Coxford · Braishfield Cl · Irving · Redbridge Hill · William Macleod Way · A35 · Teburba Way · Romsey Rd · Percy Rd · King Edwards · Beech Ave · Beulah Rd · Clarendon Rd · Sydney Rd · The Mount · Bracken Pl · Holland Pl · Conv Old Shirley · Winchester Rd · Buckley Ct · Briarswood · Worthy · Anglesea Ct · Medina Rd · Hyde Cl · Salem · Wordsworth Inf Sch · Vaudrey St · Ludlow Rd · Didcot · St James's Park Rd · St James's Rd · Glayer Rd · Turners Oak Ct · Norcroft · Upper Shirley Ave · Bassome Rd · Colebrook Ave · Bourne Ave · Twyford Ave · James St · Brooksome · Wilton Cres · Parr Cl · Darlington Gdns · Cranbourne · Kineton Rd · Cemetery Lake · The Cowherds (PH)

Coxford · A3057 · Winchester Rd · Superstore

A1
1 UPTON HO
2 STURMINSTER HO
3 MAYBUSH CT
4 BROUGHTON CL
5 CHARMOUTH TERR
6 CHALFONT CT
7 ROMSEY LODGE
8 THE GRANGE
9 LAWSON CT
10 HUNTER CT
11 YARMOUTH GDNS
12 KINGSMEAD CT
13 RICHARDS CT
14 SHINWELL CT

D   E   F

4

17

3

16

15

1

14

Map labels (selection):

WINCHESTER RD · M3 · M27 · Home Wood · Fred Woolley House · North Stoneham · Golf Course · Park Farm · Park Pond · Shrubbery Pond · Stoneham Park · Hotel · CH · Crem · Bencraft Ct · Bassett Green · St George RC Sch (Boys) · STONEHAM LA · Monks Brook · Miniature Rly · Leisure Park · Doncaster Drove · CHERITON RD · TICHBORNE RD · WIDE LA · A335 · Southampton Airport (Parkway) Sta · Southampton (Eastleigh) Airport · MITCHELL WAY · ORION IND CTR · Works · 1 WESTFIELD CNR · 2 NORTHLEIGH CNR · STONEHAM WAY · STONEHAM CEMETERY RD · Cemy · Swaythling · MANSBRIDGE RD · White Swan (PH) · M27 · A27 · The Itchen Navigation · Mans Bridge

BASSETT GREEN RD · Bassett · Bassett Green · Stoneham Ct · Bassett Green Schs · BURGESS RD · Univ · Swaythling Sch · Cantell Sec Sch · Swaythling Sta · Market Bldgs · PH · A35 · A335 · FLEMING · Rayners Gdns · Montefiore Ho · South Stoneham Ho · Woodmill · Ellen Wren Ho · Bank Side · Friars Way · Connaught Hall · Alfred Rose Ct · 1 BROOKSIDE HO · 2 BROOKSIDE HO · 3 EDWINA HO · 4 BURMA HO · 5 LORD MOUNTBATTEN CL · 6 RONALD PUGH CT

Turner Sims Concert Hall · Nuffield Theatre · The Hartley Liby · Highfield Campus (Univ of Southampton) · Hampton Park · Highfield · Westwood Park · Liby · Holly Lodge · Portswood · The Broadway · Avenue Campus · HIGHFIELD LA · THOMAS LEWIS WAY · River Itchen · Queen Elizabeth Ct · Riverside Park · Bitterne Park Inf Sch · Bitterne Park Jun Sch · River View Ho · Homespinney Ho · Riverpark Ct · Bitterne Park Sec Sch · Bitterne Park · FOREST HILLS DR · WOODMILL LA · 1 PREMIER PAR · 2 GRENVILLE CT · Cobden Bridge · ST DENYS RD · A3035 · St Augustine Gdns

Index (bottom):

D1				E1	F1
1 KINGFISHER CT	10 LEIGH MANSIONS	20 SOVEREIGN CT	30 GUARDIAN CT	1 WESTMARCH CT	1 JULIAN CT
2 OMDURMAN CT	11 LATIMER CT	21 SANDRINGHAM CT	31 BARRINGTON CT	2 THE NEWLANDS	2 CAMELLIA CT
3 HIGHFIELD LODGE	12 COTSWOLD CT	22 BERMUDA CT	32 SOMBORNE CT	3 KENSINGTON CT	3 CASTLE HTS
4 BURLEY CT	13 PINEHURST	23 HAMILTON CT	33 CARRINGTON HO	4 MILL CT	4 CASTLE CT
5 CRANFORD HO	14 BROOKVALE CT	24 REGENT CT	34 SOBERTON HO	5 GROSVENOR LODGE	5 THE BROADWAY
6 OAKDENE	15 ABBOTTS CT	25 WINN MANSIONS	35 ADDIS SQ	6 RICHMOND HALL	6 PARKLANDS
7 ST ANNS CT	16 BENTLEY CT	26 CHELTENHAM CT	36 PORTSWOOD CTR	7 GROSVENOR HALL	
8 CHESTNUT CT	17 WICKHAM HO	27 TENNYSON CT	37 TENNYSON HO	8 GROSVENOR MEWS	
9 WESTBOURNE MANSIONS	18 AUTUMN PL	28 WESTWOOD MANSIONS	38 WICKHAM HO	9 SHAMROCK VILLAS	
	19 MELBURY CT	29 ELM CT	39 WESTRIDGE CT		

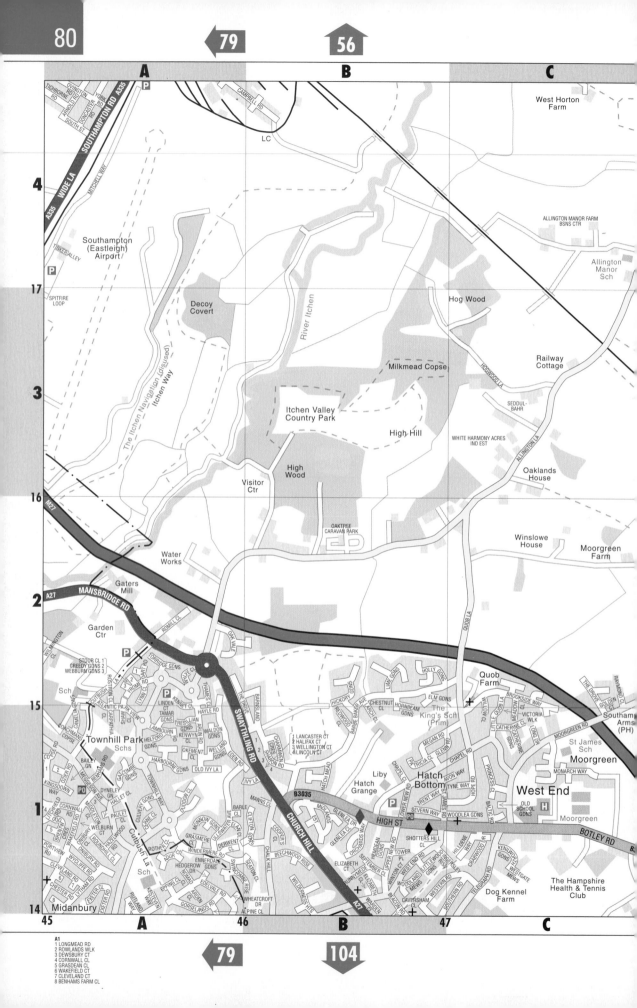

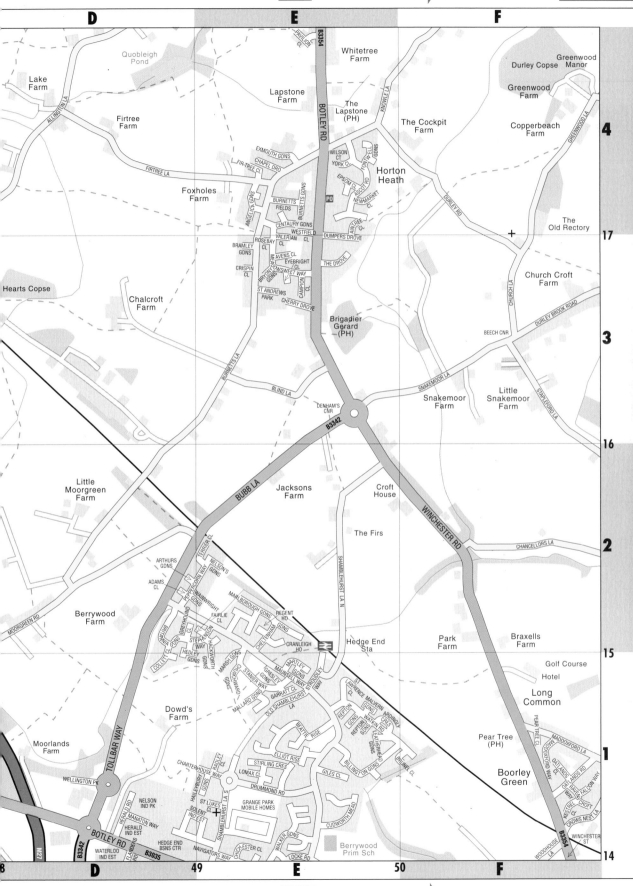

81
58

A   B   C

Laurel Farm

WINTERS HILL

Woodle Nursery

KINGS WAY

Trullingham Farm

Wintershill

PO

SCURRS LA

Robin Hood (PH)

Durley Street

THE DROVE

MANOR TERR

4

Greenwood

GREENWOOD LA

DURLEY LA

VICTORIA CT

MANOR RD

Durley Manor Farm

Tangier Farm

17

SNAKEMOOR LA

Perlins Farm

Durley CE Sch

Durley Lodge

Durley

KYTES LA

Broom Farm

Millstone Farm

MINCINGFIELD LA

Mincingfield Farm

3

Lower Farm

PARSONAGE LA

MILLWAY

Brownheath Park

Brown Heath

Mincingfield Terr

WHITE GATES

Farmer's Home (PH)

Stapleford Farmhouse

HEATHEN ST

Gregory Farm

GREGORY LA

Brokes Copse

16

STAPLEFORD LA

CHANCELLORS LA

Blundell's Copse

Brokes Farm

River Hamble

Harfields Bungalow

B30...

2

Hill Farm

Ford Lake

Netherhill Farm

MILL LA

Durley Mill

Calcot Farm

CALCOT LA

Calcot House

Harfields Farmhouse

15

NETHERHILL LA

Frogmill Farm

Breach Hill

Cricketer's Inn (PH)

CURDRIDGE LA

1

Maddoxford Farm

CROWS NEST LA

MADDOXFORD LA

Long Acres Farm

WANGFIELD LA

Wangfield Nursery

THE PLANTATION

CAPERS END LA

Hill Farm

BOTLEY RD

Curdridge Firs

LOCKHAMS RD

BORO...

Boorley Green

Holly Tree Farm

Lower Wangfield Farm

Parklands

Firs Farm

14

Boorley Green Farm

B3035

CHAPEL LA

51   A   52   B   53   C

81
106

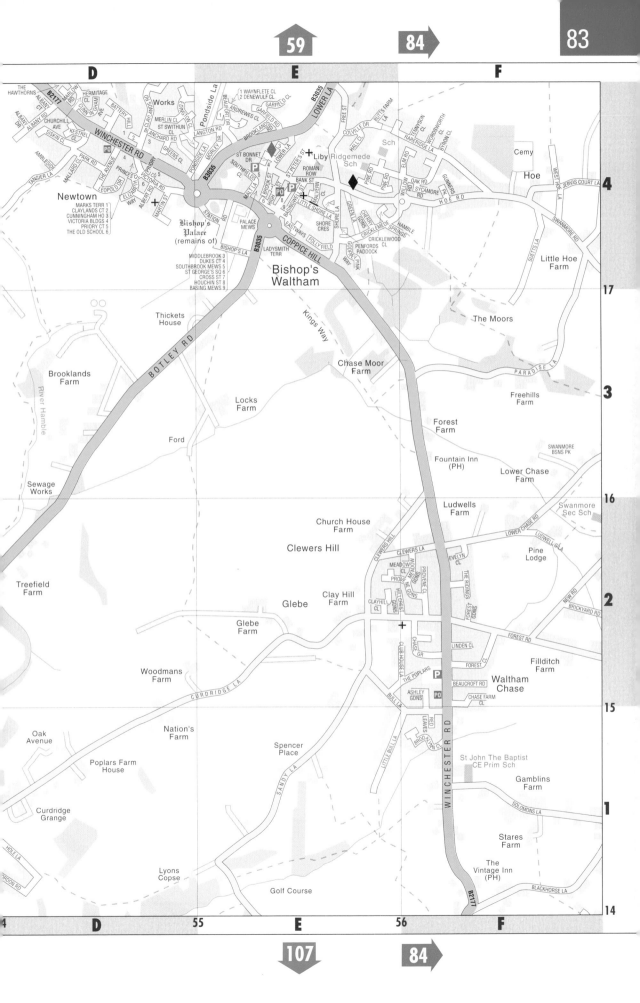

D   E   F

THE HAWTHORNS
B2177
Works
Pondside La
1 WAYNFLETE CL
2 DENEWULF CL
B3035
LOWER LA
FREE ST
BITTS FARM
Cemy
Hoe

ALBANY CT
ALBANY RD
CHURCHILL AVE
ST SWITHUN CL
HERMITAGE CL
BATTERY HILL
LONG LA
MERLIN CL
ANDREWES RD
BROOKLANDS RD
GARFIELD RD
COLVILLE DR
RAREIDGE LA
WORDSWORTH
BYRON CL
WEST AVE
JERVIS COURT LA

SISKIN CL
KESTREL CL
POMDSOUN LA
CLAY LA
BLANCHARD RD
LANGTON RD
MORLEY DR
PINE RD
OAK RD
SYCAMORE RD
GUNNERS PK
HOE RD
SWANMORE RD

WINCHESTER RD
PO
PARK RD
GREENS CL
VICTORIA RD
POMSIDE LA
ST BONNET DR
SOUTHFIELDS CL
P
St PETER'S ST
Liby
Ridgemede Sch
Sch
ELM RD
WILLOW
Little Hoe Farm

AMBLESIDE
MALLARD
TANGIER LA
THE AVENUE
PRINCES CL
ELIZABETH PRIORY
VICTORIA RD
ALBERT RD
MALL A
BROOK ST
HIGH ST
BANK ST
MALVERN
ROMAN ROW
CHERY GDNS
GREEN LA
SHORE LA
HAMBLE
CRICKLEMEDE SPRINGS

Newtown
MARKS TERR 1
CLAYLANDS CT 2
CUNNINGHAM HO 3
VICTORIA BLDGS 4
PRIORY CT 5
THE OLD SCHOOL 6
MARTIN ST
STATION RD
LITTLE SHORE LA
SHORE CRES
EASTWAYS
FOLLY FIELD
BASINGWELL ST
CRICKLEWOOD CL
PENFORDS PADDOCK
The Moors

Bishop's Palace
(remains of)
PALACE MEWS
BISHOP'S LA
LADYSMITH TERR
COPPICE HILL
Bishop's Waltham
MIDDLEBROOK 3
DUKES CT 4
SOUTHBROOK MEWS 5
ST GEORGE'S SQ 6
CROSS ST 7
HOUCHIN ST 8
BASING MEWS 9
PARADISE LA
Freehills Farm

Thickets House
BOTLEY RD
Kings Way
Chase Moor Farm

Brooklands Farm
River Hamble
Locks Farm
Ford
Forest Farm
Fountain Inn (PH)
SWANMORE BSNS PK

Sewage Works
Lower Chase Farm
Swanmore Sec Sch

Ludwells Farm
Church House Farm
LOWER CHASE RD
LUDWELL S LA

Clewers Hill
CLEWERS HILL
CLEWERS LA
EVELYN CL
Pine Lodge

Treefield Farm
MEADOW CL
MODEM GDNS
PROVENE GDNS
PROVENE CL
THE RIDINGS
FOREST GDNS
NEW RD
BRICKYARD RD

Glebe
Clay Hill Farm
CLAYHILL CL
HITCHEST
CHASE GR
LINDEN CL
FOREST
Fillditch Farm

Glebe Farm
CLUB HOUSE LA
THE POPLARS
P
FOREST RD
Waltham Chase

Woodmans Farm
CURDRIDGE LA
ASHLEY GDNS
PO
BEAUCROFT RD
CHASE FARM CL

Nation's Farm
BULL LA
RED LYNCH
BROOK CL
WINCHESTER RD
St John The Baptist CE Prim Sch

Oak Avenue
LITTLE BULL LA
SANDY LA
Spencer Place
LEAVES
Gamblins Farm
SOLOMONS LA

Poplars Farm House
Curdridge Grange
HOLE LA
RDOON RD
Lyons Copse
Golf Course
B2177
Stares Farm
The Vintage Inn (PH)
BLACKHORSE LA

D   55   E   56   F

A **B** **C**

4

Hill Top

DAMSON HILL

PARK LA

SWANMORE PARK HO

Swanmore Park

Upper Swanmore

Wyches Farm

GREEN LA

MAYHILL LA

Mayhill Copse

OXFORD LA

MIDLING HILL

JERVIS COURT LA

Jervis Court Farm

VICARAGE LA

Laurel Cottage

Mayhill Farm

Mayhill Stud Farm

Hampton Farm

MOORLANDS RD

SWANMORE RD

DONIGERS CL

DONIGERS DELL

HAMPTON HILL

WELL LA

SWANMORE RD

17

VICARAGE LA

CUT THROAT LA

Upper Hill Farm

3

LOWER CHASE RD

CHURCH RD

Swanmore CE Prim Sch

BROAD LA

FOXCOMBE CL

BUCKETTS FARM CL

MEON GDNS

CHURCH LA

CHURCH RD

DROXFORD RD

Hill Place

Bottom Copse

Swanmore

Hill Place

Hill Farm Orchards

+

PO

THE DROVE

Hill Grove

GREENWAYS

CORONATION RD

MYERS CL

UNION LA

OLD SPRING LA

CHAPEL RD

+

DODDS LA

Swanmore Sec Sch

LARKSPUR CL

CROFTON WAY

NEW RD

LEACOCK CL

BEVERLEY GDNS

ROWAN CL

SPRING LA

16

P

SPRING VALE

RUSSETT CL

Hunters Inn (PH)

Kings Way

COTT ST

Tudor Cottage

Oxford Cottages

COTT STREET LA

Cott Street Farm

The Bungalow

MARTIN CL

GLENDALE

MEON CUT WAY

PH Hillpound Farm

Hillpound

THE LAKES

Depot

BRICKYARD RD

ORCHARDLEA

HUNTERS CHASE

2

Forest Farm

FOREST RD

GRAVEL HILL

Longridge Farm

Dirty Copse

MISLINGFORD RD

Ragnals Copse

Holywell House

A32

15

Gravel Hill

Bishopsmore

Swanmore Golf Ctr

BISHOP'S WOOD RD

BISHOPS LA

Bishop's Inclosure

Bishopswood Farm

1

BLACKHORSE LA

SOLOMONS LA

HIGH ST

HEARNE GDNS

WINTERS RD

HOSPITAL RD

Shirrell Heath

Hawksnest Farm

NEWMANS HILL

River Meon

Soberton Mill

Timber Yard

PO

A32

BUDDEN'S LA

Mislingford

14

57 **A** **58** **B** **59** **C**

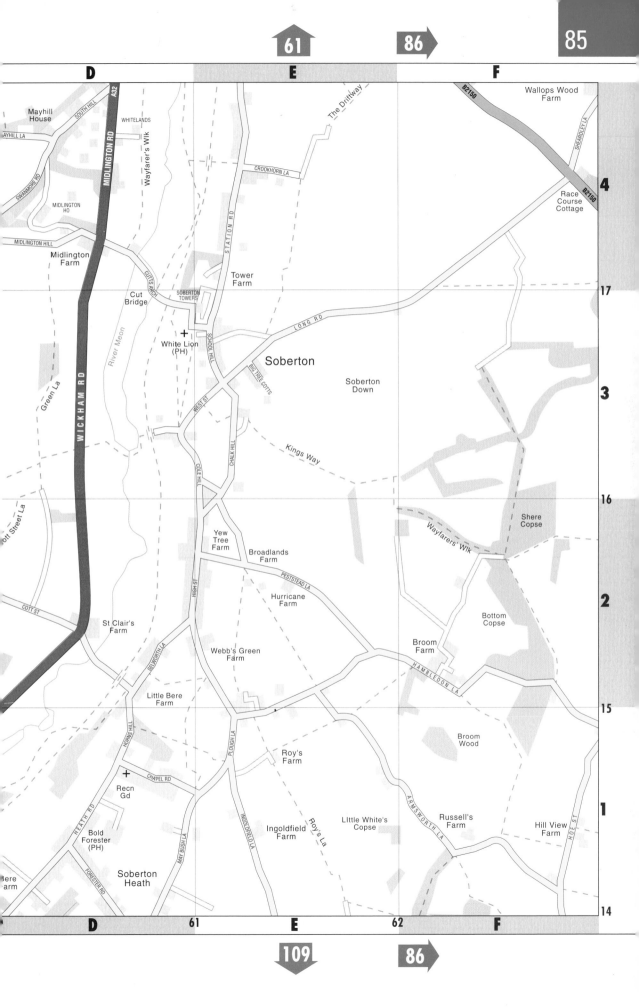

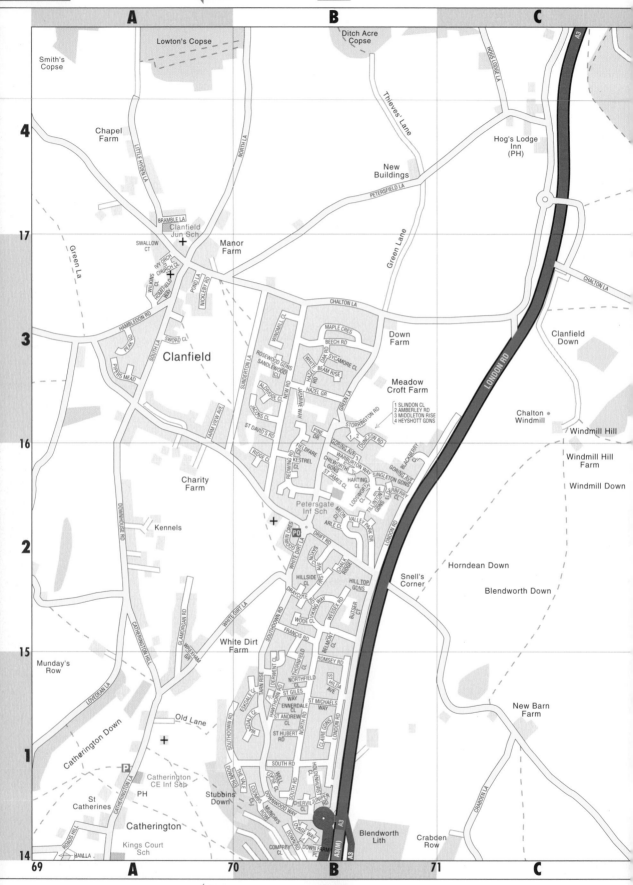

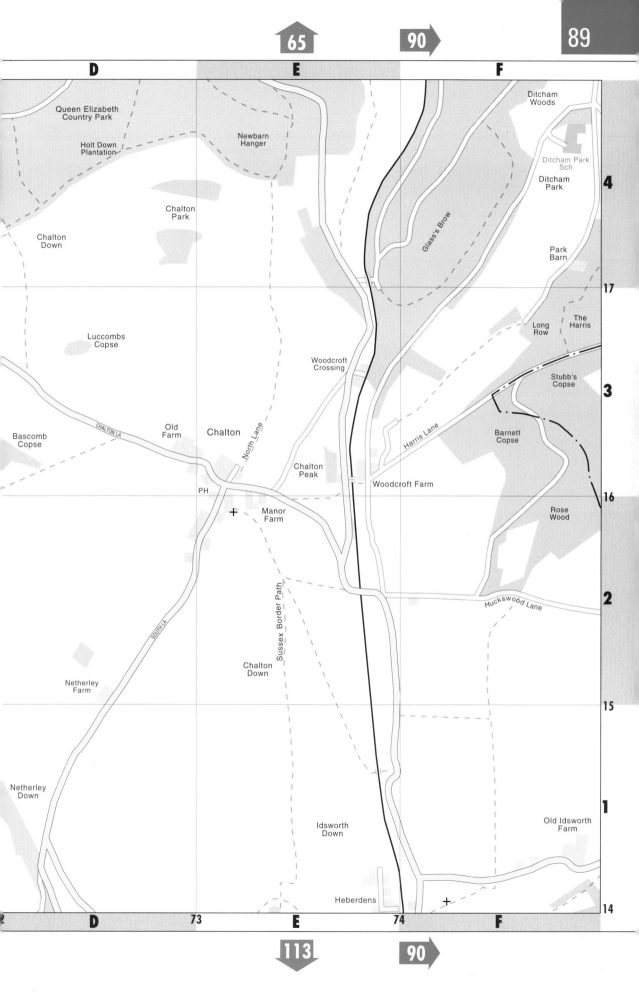

Queen Elizabeth Country Park

Holt Down Plantation

Newbarn Hanger

Ditcham Woods

Ditcham Park Sch

Ditcham Park

Chalton Park

Chalton Down

Glass's Brow

Park Barn

Luccombs Copse

Long Row

The Harris

Woodcroft Crossing

Stubb's Copse

CHALTON LA

Old Farm

Chalton

North Lane

Harris Lane

Barnett Copse

Bascomb Copse

Chalton Peak

Woodcroft Farm

PH

Rose Wood

Manor Farm

Sussex Border Path

SOUTH LA

Chalton Down

Huckswood Lane

Netherley Farm

Netherley Down

Idsworth Down

Old Idsworth Farm

Heberdens

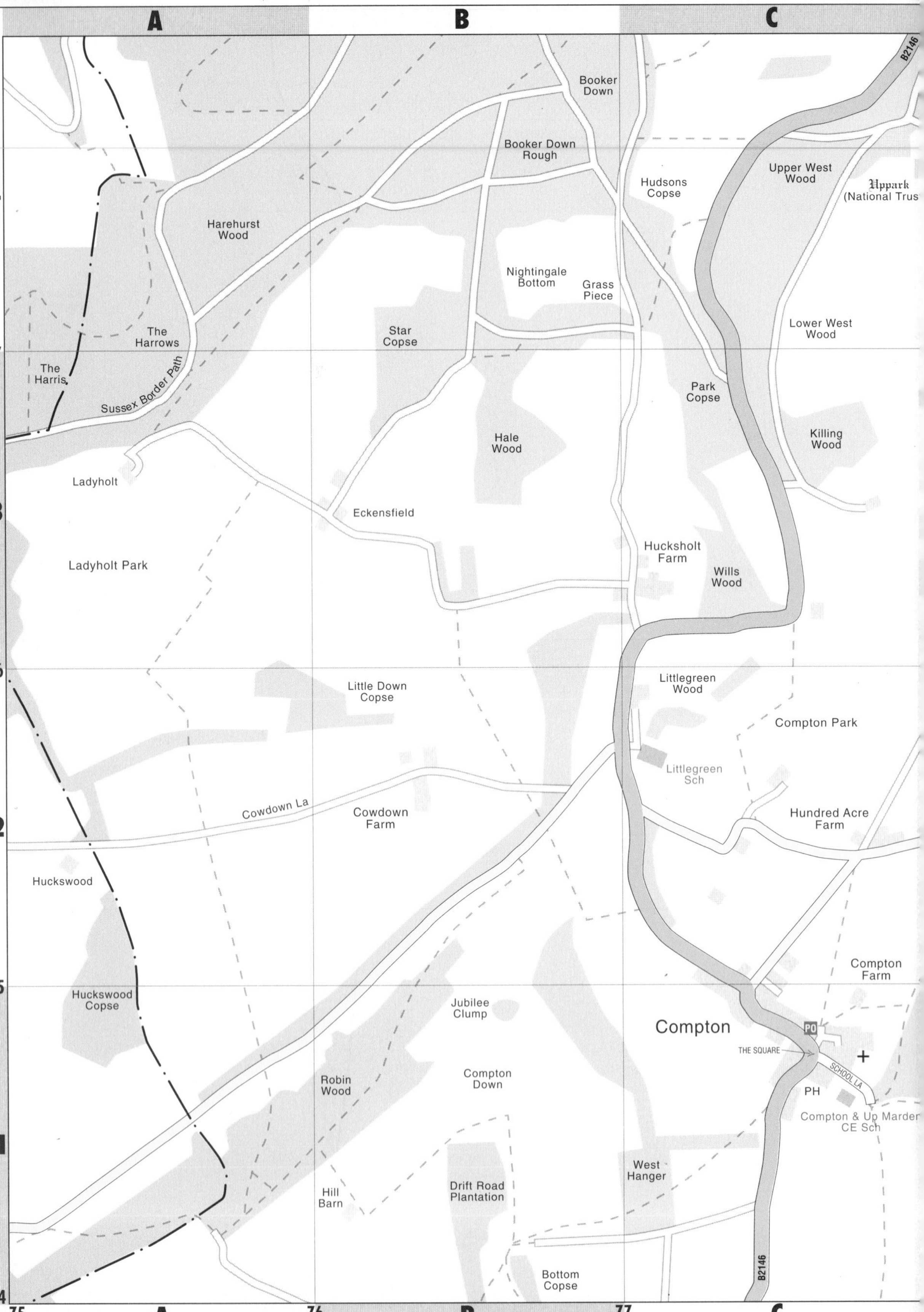

89
66

A **B** **C**

Booker Down

Booker Down Rough

Hudsons Copse

Upper West Wood

Uppark (National Trust)

Harehurst Wood

Nightingale Bottom

Grass Piece

Lower West Wood

4

The Harrows

Star Copse

Park Copse

Killing Wood

17

The Harris

Sussex Border Path

Hale Wood

Ladyholt

Eckensfield

Huscholt Farm

Wills Wood

3

Ladyholt Park

Littlegreen Wood

Compton Park

16

Little Down Copse

Littlegreen Sch

Cowdown La

Cowdown Farm

Hundred Acre Farm

2

Huckswood

15

Huckswood Copse

Jubilee Clump

Compton

THE SQUARE

PO

Compton Farm

SCHOOL LA

Robin Wood

Compton Down

PH

Compton & Up Marden CE Sch

1

West Hanger

Hill Barn

Drift Road Plantation

Bottom Copse

14

75 **A** 76 **B** 77 **C**

B2146

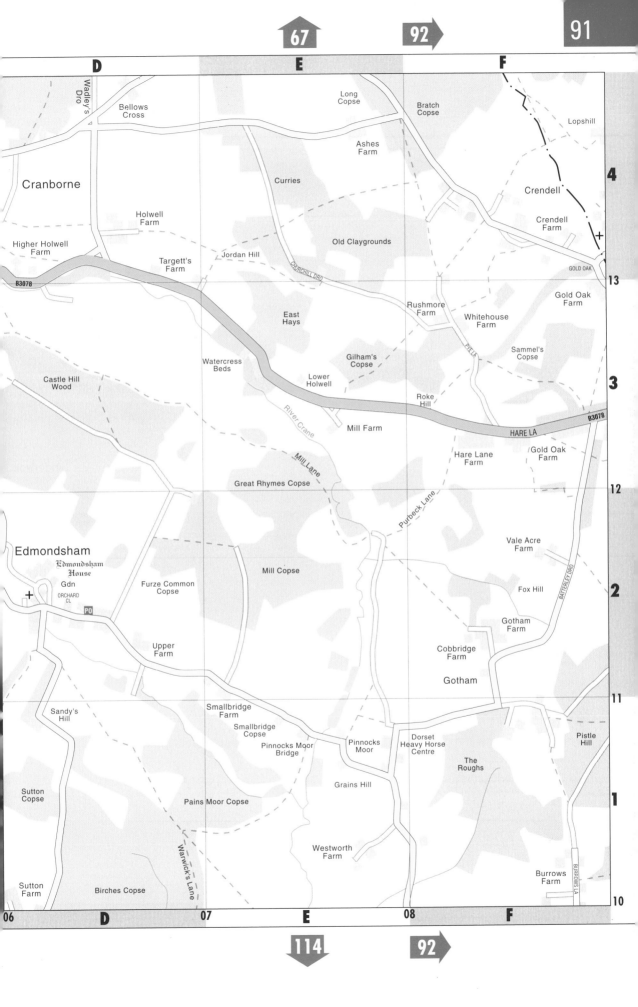

D
E
F

Wadley's Dro

Bellows Cross

Long Copse

Bratch Copse

Lopshill

Ashes Farm

Cranborne

Curries

Crendell

4

Holwell Farm

Crendell Farm

Higher Holwell Farm

Jordan Hill

Old Claygrounds

GOLD OAK

Targett's Farm

CHURCHILL DRO

B3078

13

Rushmore Farm

Gold Oak Farm

East Hays

Whitehouse Farm

Watercress Beds

Gilham's Copse

Sammel's Copse

PYE LA

Castle Hill Wood

Lower Holwell

Roke Hill

3

River Crane

Mill Farm

HARE LA

B3078

Hare Lane Farm

Gold Oak Farm

Mill Lane

Great Rhymes Copse

Purbeck Lane

12

Edmondsham

Vale Acre Farm

BATTERLEY DRO

Edmondsham House

Mill Copse

Fox Hill

2

Gdn

Furze Common Copse

ORCHARD CL

Gotham Farm

PO

Cobbridge Farm

Upper Farm

Gotham

Sandy's Hill

Smallbridge Farm

11

Pistle Hill

Smallbridge Copse

Dorset Heavy Horse Centre

Pinnocks Moor Bridge

Pinnocks Moor

Sutton Copse

Grains Hill

The Roughs

1

Pains Moor Copse

WARWICK'S LANE

Westworth Farm

Sutton Farm

Birches Copse

Burrows Farm

BURROWS LA

10

A   B   C

4

Higher Bullhill Farm

Pond Close

Cutts Copse

Lopshill Farm

CHEATER'S LA

Cheater's Gate

Lopshill Common

Alderholt Park

Lower Daggons

Hill Cottage Farm

Hart's Farm

High Wood

Park Farm

13

Hither Daggons Wood

Further Daggons Wood

Vicarage Farm

Churchill Arms (PH)

APPLE TREE RD

B3078

HIGHWOOD CL

STATION RD

PARK LA

DAGGONS RD

STATION RD

LIME TREE CL

PEAR TREE CL

3

Bittersweet Farm

OLD FORGE CL

ALDER DR

PINE RD

Daggons

PO

EARLSWOOD DR

OAK RD

B3078   CRANBORNE RD

CHURCHILL CL

ATTWOOD CL

RINGWOOD RD

Cripplestyle

BLACKWATER GR

Charing Cross

King Barrow

Alderholt

12

Sleepbrook Farm

Cross Roads Plantation

Ringwood Forest

2

Stanford Point

Alderholt Common

Cranborne Common

Telegraph Plantation

11

Sleep Brook

Sleep Bottom

Decoy Pond

Mast

1

Plumley Wood

Mount Ararat

10

09   A   10   B   11   C

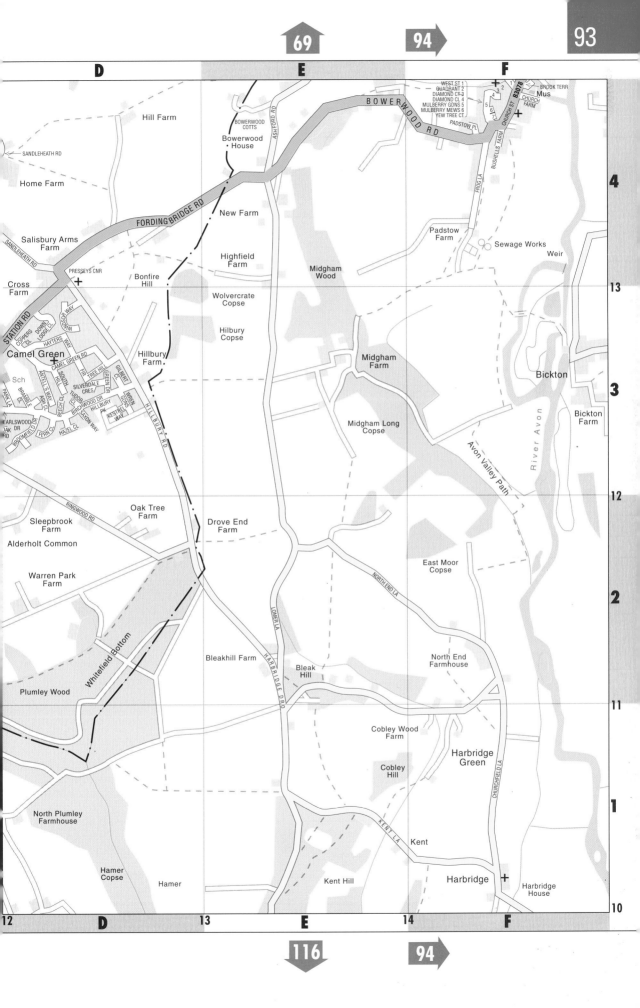

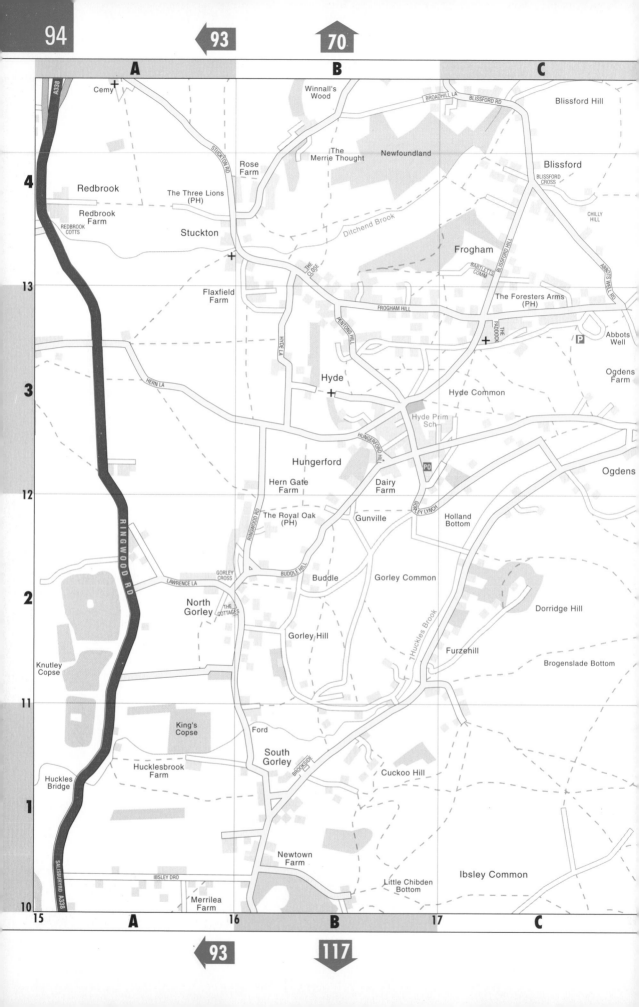

D   E   F

Long Bottom

Hampton Ridge

Amberwood
Inclosure

Alderhill Bottom

Gaze
Hill

Pitchers
Knowle

Alder
Hill

4

Alderhill
Inclosure

Thompson's Castle

13

Sloden Inclosure

Windmillhill
Pond

Latchmore Brook

Deadbuck
Hill

Windmill Hill

Latchmore Bottom

Watergreen Bottom

Latchmore
Shade

3

Ford

Hallickshole
Hill

P

Great
Witch

Little
Witch

Hasley Hole

Hasley Inclosure

12

Purlieu
Farm

Splash Bridge

Woodford Bottom

2

Broomy Inclosure

Ogden's Purlieu

Dockens Water

Broomy
Lodge

P

Nices Hill

11

Amberslade Bottom

High Corner
Wood

Broomy
Plain

North Hollow

Black
Barrow

Summerhill

High Corner
Inn
(PH)

Broomy Walk

1

Linwood
Bog

Linwood

P

Milkham Inclosure

10

8   D   19   E   20   F

A   B   C

Latchmore Brook

Whiteshoot
Bottom

Hiscocks
Hill

Fritham
Grange

Amberwood
Inclosure

4

Green
Pond

Queen North
Wood

North Bentley
Inclosure

Fritham Plain

Sloden
Inclosure

13

Freeworms
Hill

South Bentley
Inclosure

Rakes Brakes
Bottom

3

Dockens Water

Anses
Wood

Ragged Boys
Hill

Cadmans
Pool

Holly Hatch
Inclosure

12

Ocknell
Pond

Holly Hatch
Cottage

2

Ocknell Plain

Broomy
Lodge

11

Broomy
Bottom

Winding
Stonard

Spreading
Oak

Broomy Plain

Bratley Water

1

Slufters
Inclosure

Slufters
Bottom

A31

Fritham
Cross

10

21   22   23

D
E
F

Coppice of Linwood

The Butt

King's Garn Gutter
Inclosure

Brook Common

Lush's

Golf
Course

King's Garn Gutter

Skers
Farm

4

P
P

Janesmoor
Pond

Ford

Blackthorne's

Ford

Janesmoor
Plain

Blackthorn
Copse

13

Water
Tower

Upper
Canterton

P
P

Long Beech
Hill

Tom Pook's
Hill

Sir Walter Tyrrell
(PH)

Long Beech
Inclosure

Blackwool

Coalmeer Gutter

3

Stricknage
Wood

A31
12

Hotel

Stoney Cross

2

Ocknell
Inclosure

The
Grove

Bolderwood Walk

Stoney Cross
Plain

Asher's
Bottom

Highland Water

P

11

Fox
Hill

Ocknell
Arch

King's
Garn

1

Long Brook

Withybed Bottom

Mill Stream

Lucas
Castle

Stonard
Wood

Ringwood Ford
Bottom

Ringwood
Ford

Hart
Hill

10

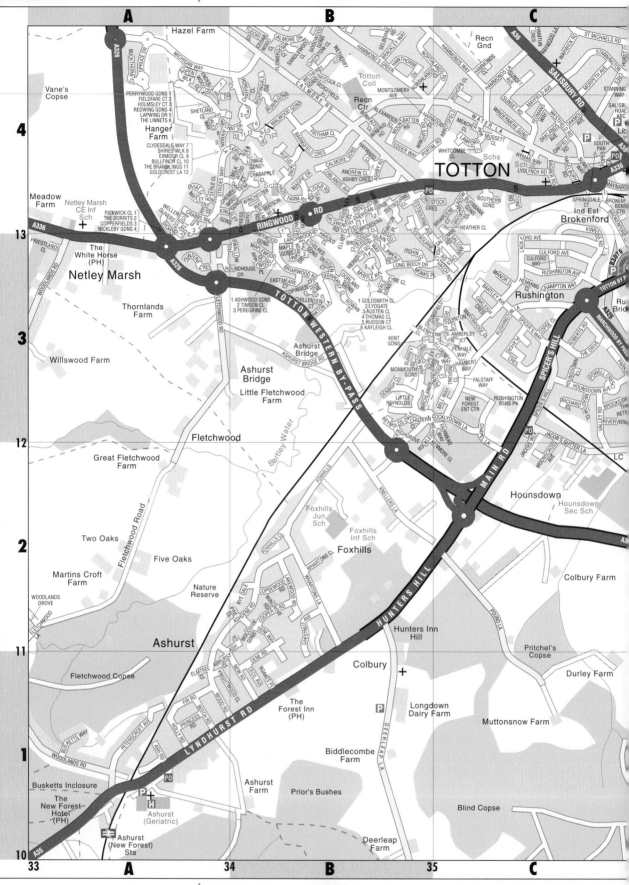

D **E** **F**

1 PEMBROKE CL
2 STIRLING CL

STIRLING CRES
YORK CL
ARUNDEL CT
STANNINGTON WAY
TESTWOOD PL

The Furlongs

Red Bridge

Redbridge

Wimpson

1 PAIGNTON RD
2 HARLYN RD

GOVER RD
WESTOVER RD
CONISTON RD
M271
REDBRIDGE TOWERS
STUDLAND RD
SEDBERGH RD
CHERWELL CRES
WINDRUSH
ISIS CL
CL

1 PARKLANDS
2 HANOVER HO

Salterns
Special
Sch

REDBRIDGE CAUSEWAY
REDBRIDGE FLYOVER A35
OLD REDBRIDGE RD
CUCKMERE LA

MARDALE RD 1
KENDAL CT 2
COLWELL CL 3

CHERWELL
HO

WHITSTONE
OAKLEY RD

4

COMMERCIAL RD
Totton
Sta

TATE RD
STA RD

REDBRIDGE RD

Recn
Gnd

Millbrook

TEBOURBA WAY

Tanner's
Brook

BEAUMONT
PL

Redbridge
Sta

1 TATE CT
2 RAILWAY COTTS
3 TATE MEWS
4 PAT BEAR CL
5 CLOVER NOOKE

ELING
VIEW

ALLINGTON RD
LEBANON RD
OAKRIDGE RD

MILLBROOK
TRAD EST

SECOND
AVE

MILLBROOK FLYOVER A3024

Schs

13

TOTTON BY PASS
B3076
WINSOR RD
P
PO

Works

5 ELINGFIELD CT
6 BRIDGEWAY CT
7 BANNISTER CT

Redbridge
Vehicle Depot

FIRST
AVE

AUCKLAND RD

TRINITY
IND EST

SOUTH
MILL
RD

MILLBROOK RD W A3024

EVER
GREENS

Eling
Wharf

FIRST
AVE

MANOR HOUSE AVE

THIRD AVE

WESTBURY RD

3

ROSE RD
Sch
BOOTHBY CL

The Anchor Inn
(PH)
Tide Mill

Toll

Mus

River Test

Luggy
Creek

Tanner's
Creek

MARIANNE CL
Recn
Gnd

Western
Ave

Wks

Bartley
Water

Cemy

Eling
The King Rufus
(PH)

Village
Bells
(PH)

ELING HILL
BURY LA
HOMEWAY
COTTS

Southampton Docks
Prince Charles
Container Port

Colbury Manor

12

JACOB'S GUTTER LA

Bury Brickfield Park
Caravan Site

Bury Brickfield
Cottages

Jacob's
Farm

MARCHWOOD RD

Newman's
Copse

2

A326

LC

Trotts

Bury
Farm

HAWKINS
CT

QUAYSIDE
WALK

TROTTS LA

Trotts Farm

BURY RD

Works

Cork's
Farm

Bull's Copse

MARCHWOOD BY PASS

LC

Recycling
Centre

NORMANDY WAY

ADMIRALTY
WAY

11

Golt's Copse

Tavell's Farm

Marchwood

CORK LA

Great Cole
Copse

The
Orchard Inn

BOLHINTON
AVE

PARK CL
PARK LA

MARSHFIELD
LC

TAVELL'S LA

Sch

Marchwood
Terr

PO

1

Langley
Lodge

Coffin's
Farm

Pooksgreen

STAPLEWOOD LA

POPLAR DR

Park's
Farm

LC

A326

Heron's Hill

Dumper's
Farm

LONG LA

LAKELAND
GDNS

10

D 37 **E** 38 **F**

SOUTHAMPTON

A4
1 REGENT'S GR
2 CARLISLE CT
3 LASHAM HO
4 COMPTON HO
5 BURLEY HO
6 REGENTS CT
7 LEIGHTON AVE
8 DENNISON CT
9 NORTH CT
10 CENTRE CT
11 SOUTH CT
12 WEST CT
13 OAKLEY HO
14 CLIFTON GDNS
15 CLIFTON CT
16 ASHDENE
17 ENDEAVOUR CL
18 MEDLEY PL
19 KELSTON CL
20 STANTON BLDGS

101 ◄

A4
21 STANTON ROAD IND EST
B4
1 BURLINGTON MANSIONS
2 WITHEWOOD MANSIONS
3 LUMSDEN MANSIONS
4 HATHERLEY MANSIONS

78

B3
1 MINSTER CT
2 TRINITY CT
3 PARK CT FLATS
4 SOMERSET CT
5 RICHMOND CT
6 CROSSLEY CT
7 CHERITON CT
8 HESKETH HO
9 NIGHTINGDALE CT
10 ROMSEY CT
11 ALMOND CT
12 FREEMANTLE BSNS CTR
13 BROOK CT
C4
1 AVENUE CT
2 CAVENDISH MWS
3 MAYCROFT CT
4 HULSE LODGE
5 CARLTON CT
6 ST MARGARETS HO
7 BARKSHIRE CT
8 HILDA CT
9 ROXAN CT
10 GWEN-RHIAN CT
11 OAKLEY HO
12 BEAULIEU HO
13 BANISTER CT
14 MAYFLOWER CT
15 ABBEY CT
16 BANISTER GRANGE
17 DORRICK CT
18 WOODLAND PL
19 FOXLEA
20 PAVILION CT
21 DURBAN CT
22 SILVERDALE CT
23 DORVAL HO
24 DORVAL MNR
25 OVERDELL CT
26 SHERFIELD HO

C2
1 SCULLARDS LA
2 WEST BARGATE
3 ALBION PL
4 FOREST VIEW
5 MADDISON CT
6 CASTLE LA
7 CEMENT TERR
8 CASTLE SQ
9 LANSDOWNE HILL
10 BIDDLESGATE CT
11 HAMTUN ST
12 IRONSIDE CT
13 SIMNEL ST
14 POSTERN CT
15 BLUE ANCHOR LA
16 ST MICHAEL'S SQ
17 CHURCH LA
18 ST MICHAEL'S ST
19 WESTGATE ST
20 VYSE LA
21 MERCHANTS WLK
22 CUCKOO LA
C3
1 UPPER BANISTER ST
2 HANDFORD CT
3 SOUTHAMPTON ST
4 WINCHESTER ST
5 VERNON WLK
6 SALISBURY ST
7 LOWER BANISTER ST
8 THORNERS CT
9 HEMSTEAD CT
10 DEVONSHIRE MANSIONS
11 OAKVILLE MANSIONS
12 MARLANDS SQ
13 FITZHUGH ST
14 WYNDHAM PL
15 SOUTHBROOK HILL
16 FOURPOSTS HILL
17 SPRING CT
18 TINTERN GR

101 ◄

125

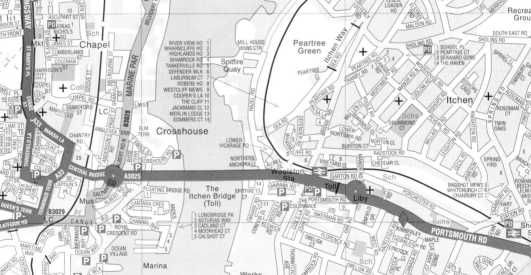

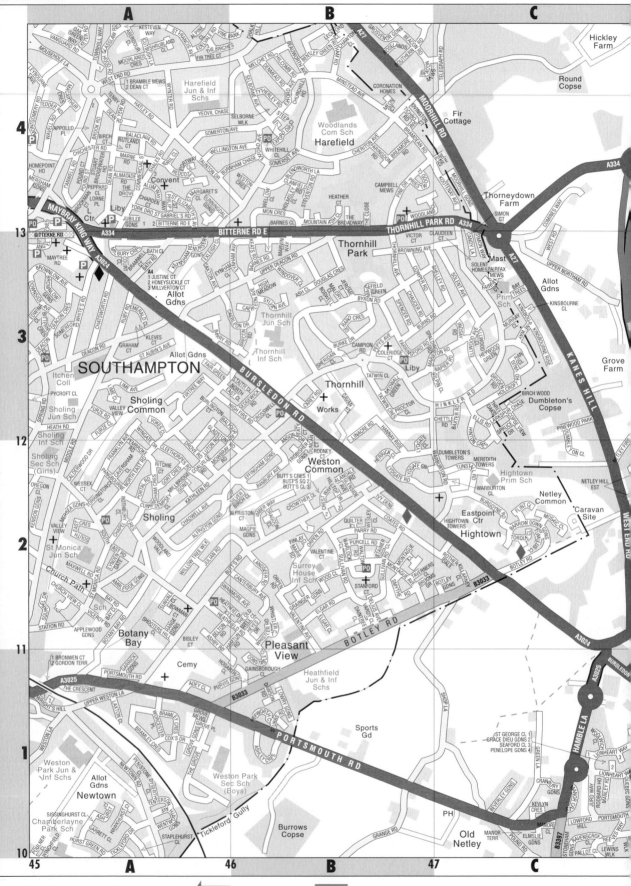

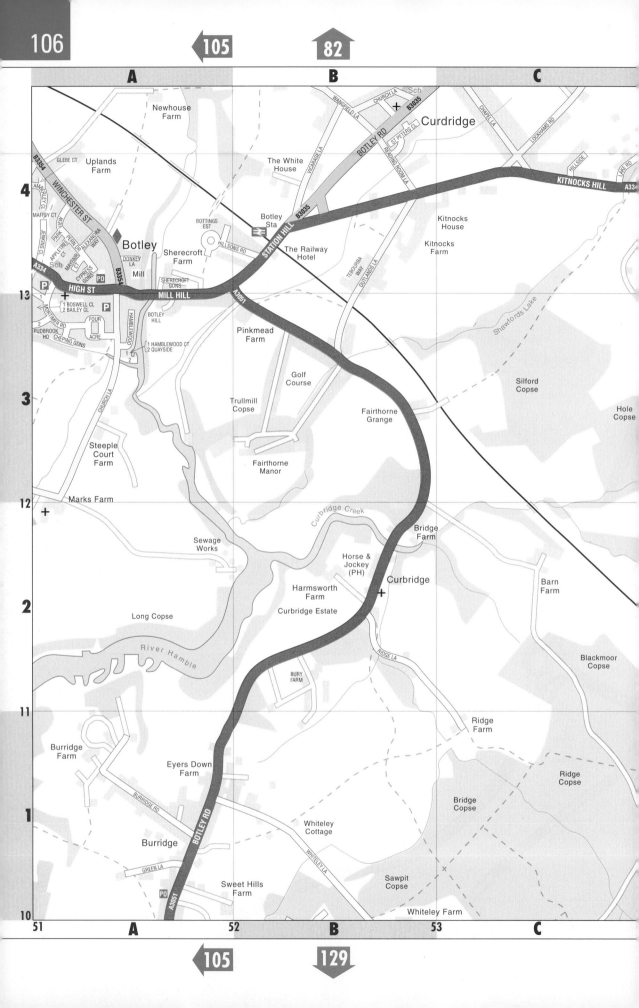

105

82

A   B   C

Newhouse
Farm

The White
House

Sch

B3035

Curdridge

CHURCH LA

WANGFIELD LA

VICARAGE LA

BOTLEY RD

ST PETERS CL

READING ROOM LA

CHAPEL LA

LOCKHAMS RD

B3354

GLEBE CT

Uplands
Farm

WINCHESTER ST

AMBERLEY CL

PARK
VIEW

PERI DR

MAFFEY CT

JENKINS CL

ALEXANDRA
WAY

MAYFORD

Botley

A334

APPLETREE CT

DONKEY
LA

CYPRESS
GDNS

Mill

Sch

P

B3354

PO

HIGH ST

P

1 BOSWELL CL
2 BAILEY CL

MORTIMER RD

PUDBROOK
HO

CHEPING GDNS

1
2

FOUR
ACRE

HAMBLEWOOD

HAMBLEWOOD

1
2

BOTLEY
HILL

1 HAMBLEWOOD CT
2 QUAYSIDE

Bottings
Est

HILLSONS RD

Sherecroft
Farm

SHERECROFT
GDNS

Botley
Sta

STATION HILL

B3035

The Railway
Hotel

Botley
Hill

MILL HILL

A3051

Pinkmead
Farm

Kitnocks
House

Kitnocks
Farm

KITNOCKS HILL

A334

HILLSIDE

LAKE RD

TEBOURBA WAY

OUTLANDS LA

Shawfords Lake

Silford
Copse

Hole
Copse

Golf
Course

Trullmill
Copse

Fairthorne
Grange

Steeple
Court
Farm

CHURCH LA

Fairthorne
Manor

Marks Farm

Curbridge Creek

Bridge
Farm

Sewage
Works

Horse &
Jockey
(PH)

Curbridge

Barn
Farm

Harmsworth
Farm

Curbridge Estate

Long Copse

River Hamble

BURY
FARM

RIDGE LA

Blackmoor
Copse

Ridge
Farm

Burridge
Farm

Eyers Down
Farm

BURRIDGE RD

BOTLEY RD

Whiteley
Cottage

Bridge
Copse

Ridge
Copse

Burridge

GREEN LA

WHITELEY LA

Sweet Hills
Farm

PO

A3051

Sawpit
Copse

Whiteley Farm

51   A   52   B   53   C

105   129

D E F

Row Ash

Rowash
Farm House

aglington
Farm

Ferny
Copse

HALL CT

Shedfield Grange

Country Club

Golf Course

Shedfield House

Shedfield Lodge

SANDY LA

Shedfield

THE OLD FORGE

MURRAY COTTS

ST ANNES LA

ST JOHNS LA

CHURCH RD

CAMDEN CL

PO

SLOANE PARK

Fairlands Montessori Sch

Shedfield Common

B2177

Sandy Hills House

SMITHS LA

GAMBLINS LA

HIGH ST

NIGHTINGALE CRES

UPPER CHURCH RD

Turkey Island

CULVERLANDS CL

CHURCH VIEW

PICKETT HILL

WINCHESTER RD

4

13

Hallcourt Wood

Biddenfield

Biddenfield High Wood

Blacklands Copse

Brook Wood

BIDDENFIELD LA

Tankerhill Copse

Redhill Copse

BLIND LA

3

Mansfield Lane

Mansfield Barn

Hangman's Copse

Cold Harbour Farm

LITTLE PARK MANSIONS

Meon Park

COLD HARBOUR CL

A334

12

Alder Moor

Marvane Cottage Farm

Park Place Farm

Park Place Pastoral Centre

HOLT CL

ELIZABETH CL

TANFIELD PARK

2

TITCHFIELD LA

Golf Course

Webb's Land Farm

TANFIELD LA

11

Dimmock's Moor

Quob Farm

Works

Mayles

Little Tapnage Farm

MAYLES LA

Ridge Copse

Sager's Down

Tapnage

River Meon

Fiddlers Green

1

Botley Wood

The Lodge

10

D 55 E 56 F

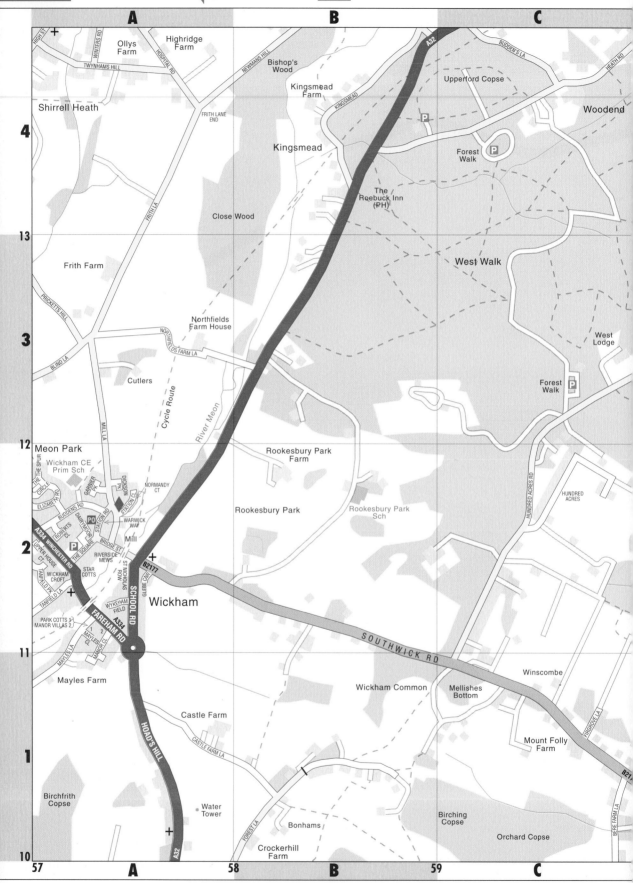

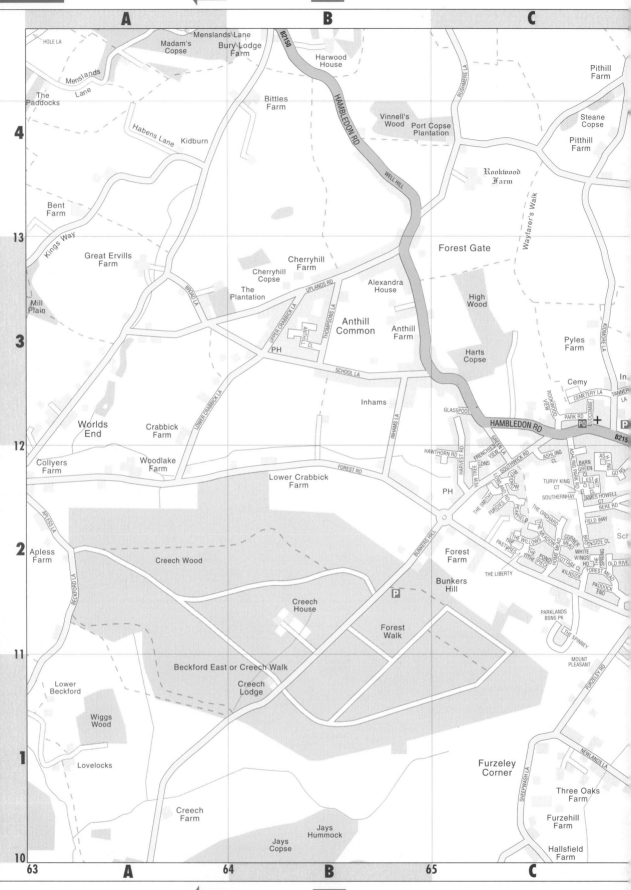

HOLE LA
The Paddocks
Mensland's Lane
Madam's Copse
Bury Lodge Farm
Menslands Lane
Harwood House
Pithill Farm

Habens Lane
Kidburn
Bittles Farm
Vinnell's Wood
Port Copse Plantation
Steane Copse
Pitthill Farm

4

Bent Farm
Rookwood Farm
Wayfarer's Walk

Kings Way
Great Ervills Farm
Cherryhill Copse
Cherryhill Farm
Forest Gate

13

Mill Plain
The Plantation
Uplands Rd
Alexandra House
High Wood
Pyles Farm
Cemy
In.
TANNER LA

Anthill Common
Anthill Farm
Harts Copse

3

PH
School La
Rookwood View
Cemetery La
Cemy

Worlds End
Crabbick Farm
Inhams
Glasspool
HAMBLEDON RD
PO
B215

Collyers Farm
Woodlake Farm
Lower Crabbick Farm
Forest Rd
Hawthorn Rd
Harvest Rd
Park Rd
Ludcombe

12

Apless Farm
Creech Wood
Bunkers Hill
PH
Forest Farm
The Smithy
The Liberty

2

Beckford La
Apless La
P
Creech House
P
Bunkers Hill
Forest Walk
Parklands Bsns Pk
The Spinney

Lower Beckford
Beckford East or Creech Walk
Creech Lodge
Mount Pleasant

11

Wiggs Wood
Furzeley Corner
Furzeley Rd
Newlands La

1

Lovelocks
Three Oaks Farm
Sheepwash La

Creech Farm
Jays Hummock
Furzehill Farm
Hallsfield Farm

10
Jays Copse

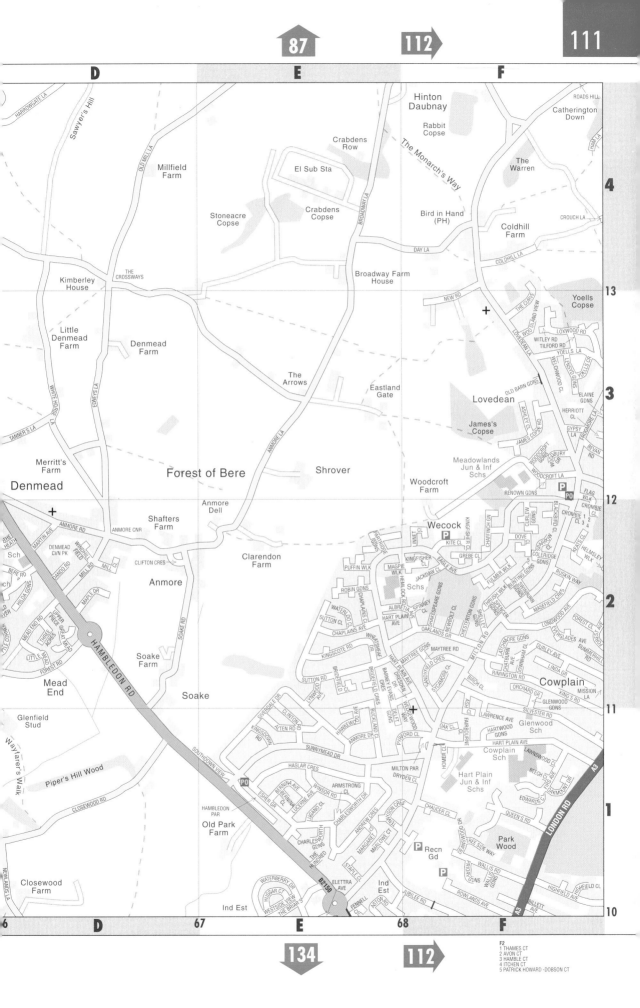

D
E
F

Hinton
Daubnay

ROADS HILL

Catherington
Down

HARROWGATE LA

Sawyer's Hill

Rabbit
Copse

The Monarch's Way

HAM LA

4

Millfield
Farm

OLD MILL LA

Millfield
Farm

El Sub Sta

Crabdens
Row

The
Warren

Stoneacre
Copse

Crabdens
Copse

BROADWAY LA

Bird in Hand
(PH)

Coldhill
Farm

CROUCH LA

DAY LA

COLDHILL LA

THE
CROSSWAYS

Broadway Farm
House

NEW RD

13

Kimberley
House

THE CURVE

Yoells
Copse

WITLEY RD
TILFORD RD

LOXWOOD RD

LOVEDEAN LA

OAKLAND VIEW

YOELLS LA

LINKSIDE

Little
Denmead
Farm

Denmead
Farm

Old Barn Gdns

Lovedean

ASHLEY CT

BIRCHWOOD CL

ELAINE
GDNS

HERRIOTT
CL

3

WHITE HORSE LA

EDNEY'S LA

The
Arrows

Eastland
Gate

James's
Copse

JAMES CLOSE

WOODCROFT RD

WOODCROFT LA

ASBURY
RD

BEVAN
RD

TANNER'S LA

Merritt's
Farm

Forest of Bere

Shrover

Woodcroft
Farm

Meadowlands
Jun & Inf
Schs

RENOWN GDNS

FLAG
WLK

CROMBIE
CL

12

Denmead

Shafters
Farm

Anmore
Dell

ANMORE LA

Wecock

KINGFISHER RD

PARTRIDGE
GDNS

KITE CL

CHAFFINCH GN

CURLEW
GDNS

BLACKBIRD CL

Crombie 1
CL 3 4
2
4

MARTIN AVE

ANMORE RD

ANMORE CNR

WINDMILL
FIELD

CLIFTON CRES

Clarendon
Farm

LINNET
CL

Kingfisher
CL

EAGLE AVE

GREBE CL

DOVE
CL

COLERIDGE
GDNS

HELMSLEY
WLK

2

Denmead
CVN PK

WINDMILL
RD

MILL RD

MILL CL

PUFFIN WLK

MAGPIE
WLK

JACKDAW CL

Schs

HEMLOCK RD

FULMER WLK

THRUSH CL

BUNTING GDNS

SWINBURN

SKELLY

MASEFIELD CRES

RUSKIN WAY

Anmore

Robin Gdns

ROBIN GDNS

CHAPLAINS CL

ALBRETTA

SPINNEY

SHAKESPEARE GDNS

NEWBOLT RD

CHESTERTON GR

FOREST CL

LONGWOOD AVE

Soake
Farm

WATERLOO
RD

SUTTON CL

CHAPLAINS AVE

HART PLAIN
AVE

OAKLANDS GR

MILTON GR

LATCHMORE GDNS

CHATBURN

DUNNINGHAM CL

DURLEY AVE

SUMMERHILL

EVERGLADES AVE

HAMBLEDON RD

SOAKE RD

KINGSCOTE RD

MAYTREE GDNS

MAYTREE RD

CANDYFIELD CRES

SYCAMORE CL

RIMINGTON RD

LINDA GR

Cowplain

Mead
End

Soake

SUTTON RD

BRIDFIELD
CL

BRIDFIELD CRES

BARNEY EVANS
CRES

BIRCH CL

ORCHARD GR

MISSION
LA

KING'S RD

11

Glenfield
Stud

SILVERDALE DR

CLINTON RD

ALTEN RD

LYNWOOD
AVE

ANMORE DR

PYRFORD CL

OAK CL

ASH

FAIRBOURNE

LAWRENCE AVE

HARTWOOD
GDNS

GLENWOOD
GDNS

SILVESTER
RD

Glenwood
Sch

Wayfarer's Walk

KINGSDOWN
RD

SUNNYMEAD DR

HOMER CL

WOODWARD
WAY

Cowplain
Sch

Hart Plain Ave

LAWNSWOOD CL

BEECH CL

OAKMOOR CL

Piper's Hill Wood

HASLAR CRES

MILTON PAR

DRYDEN CL

Hart Plain
Jun & Inf
Schs

EDWARDS

LONDON RD

A3

1

SOUTHDOWN VIEW

BERNINA AVE

BRETTINA

LUCERNE AVE

ARMSTRONG
CL

WINSOR RD

CHARLESWORTH DR

ANDREW CRES

MARLOWE CT

CHAUCER CL

QUEEN'S RD

Park
Wood

TREE SIDE WAY

CLOSEWOOD RD

HAMBLEDON
PAR

ESTHER GR

VICANO CL

CHARLESWORTH
GDNS

MARGARET
CL

TENNYSON CRES

Recn
Gd

WALLIS RD

PRIORY
GDNS

WALLIS
GDNS

Glenfield
Stud

Old Park
Farm

THE
HUNDRED

STAPLE
CL

GOODWOOD RD

HIGHFIELD AVE

Closewood
Farm

NEWLANDS LA

WATERBERRY DR

HUSSAR CT

WESTSIDE VIEW

THE BRIAR

B2150

ELETTRA
AVE

FENNELL

ASTON

JUBILEE RD

ROWLANDS AVE

BILLETT
RD

Ind Est

Ind Est

A3

10

F2
1 THAMES CT
2 AVON CT
3 HAMBLE CT
4 ITCHEN CT
5 PATRICK HOWARD -DOBSON CT

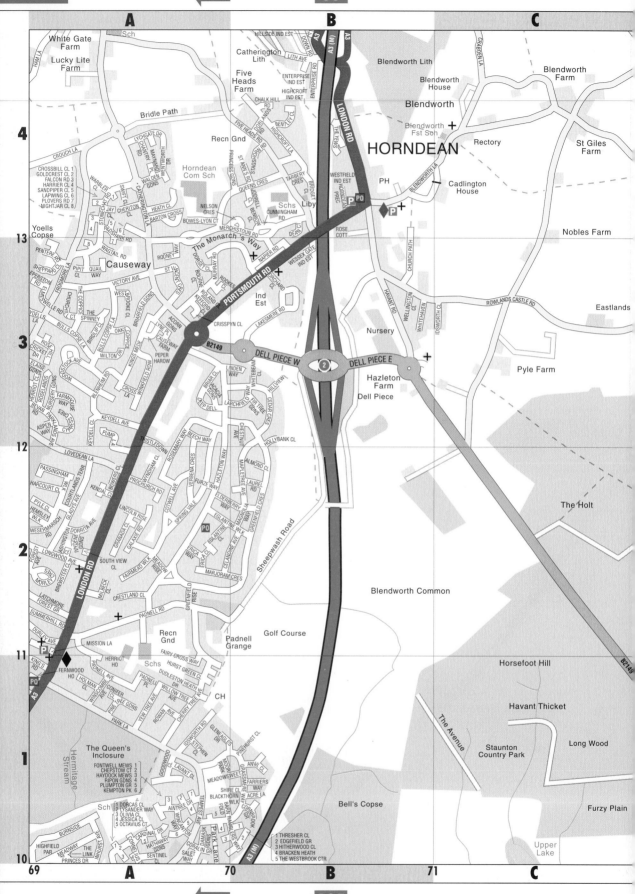

A B C

White Gate Farm
Lucky Lite Farm
Sch
HILLSIDE IND EST
Catherington Lith
LITH AVE
Blendworth Lith
Blendworth House
Blendworth Farm
Blendworth

Five Heads Farm
Enterprise IND EST
Highcroft IND EST
HORNDEAN
Rectory
St Giles Farm

Bridle Path
CHALK HILL RD
Recn Gnd
Blendworth Fst Sch
BLENDWORTH LA

4

Crossbill Cl 1
Goldcrest Cl 2
Falcon Rd 3
Harrier Cl 4
Sandpiper Cl 5
Lapwing Cl 6
Plovers Rd 7
Nightjar Cl 8
Horndean Com Sch
Cadlington House
PH
Nobles Farm

13
Yoells Copse
The Monarch's Way
PO
Rose Cott
Eastlands

Causeway
PORTSMOUTH RD
Ind Est
Nursery
Rowlands Castle Rd

3
B2149
DELL PIECE W
DELL PIECE E
Pyle Farm
Hazleton Farm
Dell Piece

12
Blendworth Common
The Holt

2
LONDON RD
PO
Golf Course

11
Recn Gnd
Padnell Grange
Horsefoot Hill
B2149
A3
PO
Fernwood
Schs
CH
Havant Thicket
Long Wood

1
The Queen's Inclosure
Hermitage Stream
The Avenue
Staunton Country Park

Fontwell Mews 1
Chepstow Ct 2
Haydock Mews 3
Ripon Gdns 4
Plumpton Gr 5
Kempton Pk 6
Furzy Plain

10
A3 (M)
Bell's Copse
Upper Lake

1 Thresher Cl
2 Edgefield Gr
3 Hitherwood Cl
4 Bracken Heath
5 The Westbrook Ctr

69 A 70 B 71 C

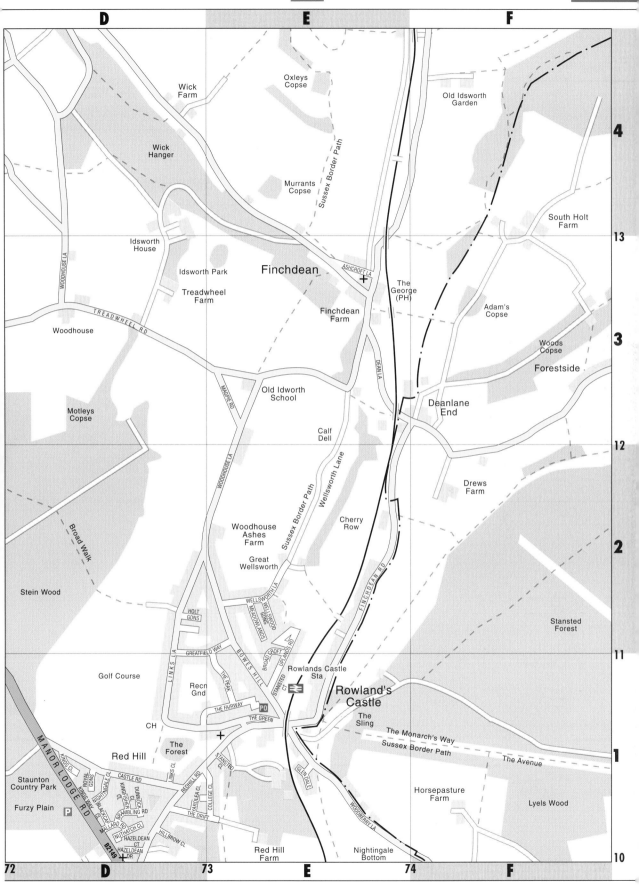

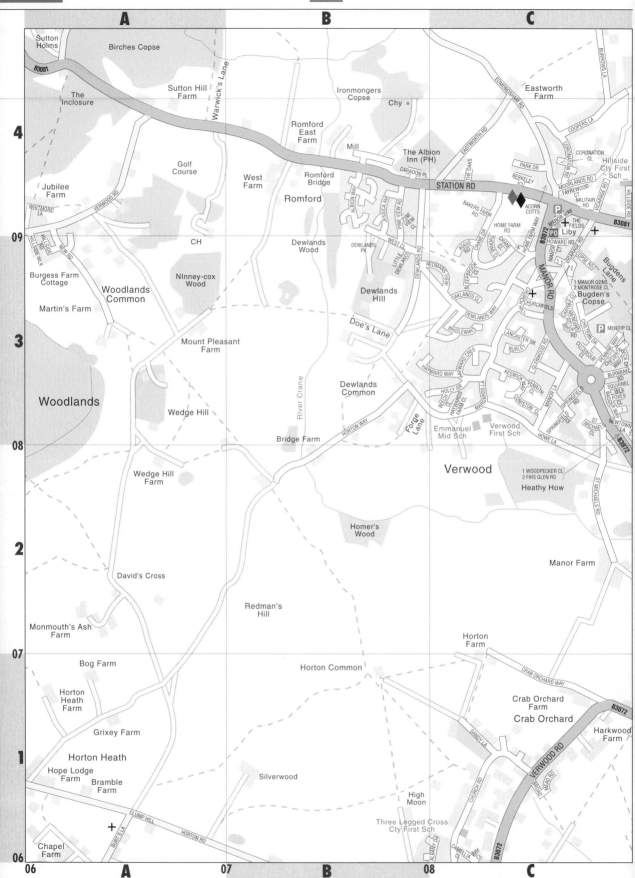

A   **B**   **C**

Sutton
Holms

Birches Copse

B3081

The
Inclosure

Sutton Hill
Farm

Warwick's Lane

Ironmongers
Copse

Chy

Eastworth
Farm

BURROWS LA

EDMONDSHAM RD

COOPERS LA

4

Jubilee
Farm

Golf
Course

West
Farm

Romford
East
Farm

Mill

The Albion
Inn (PH)

EASTWORTH RD

PARK DR

CORONATION

CORONATION
CL

Hillside
Cty First
Sch

VARAGE RD

HILLSIDE RD

WHITMORE
LA

VERWOOD RD

Romford
Bridge

Romford

CARADON PL

STATION RD

THE OAKS

BERKELEY
CL

MOORLANDS RD

FAYREWOOD
CT

MILITAIR
HO

B3081

HILLSIDE RD

NEW RD

HILLSIDE
WLK

HILL SIDE

ALBION WAY

JESSICA AVE

PINE VIEW RD

FINE
VIEW

BAKERS FARM
RD

HOME FARM
RD

ACORN
COTTS

P

MANOR WAY

THE
FIELDS

PO

Liby

MANOR WAY

09

CH

Dewlands
Wood

Dewlands
PK

WEST CL

LITTLE
DEWLANDS

DEWLANDS RD

REDMANS VIEW

SLEEPBROOK
CL

AGGIS
RD

CRANE DR

CRANE
CL

HOWARD RD

VICARAGE RD

COPSE RD

Bugdens
Lane

Burgess Farm
Cottage

Ninney-cox
Wood

Dewlands
Hill

OAKLANDS CL

CHURCHFIELD

1 MANOR GDNS
2 MONTROSE CL

Bugden's
Copse

Woodlands
Common

Martin's Farm

Doe's Lane

BRIDLEWAY

DEWLANDS WAY

HILL

2

3

Mount Pleasant
Farm

LANCASTER DR

BURLEY

KESWICK

PENRITH

GLENWOOD

MANOR LA

CHILTERN CL

CHEVIOT CL

PENNINE WAY

RECTORY RD

BURNBAKE
RD

Woodlands

Wedge Hill

HAYWARD WAY

HAYWARD CRES

HOLLY GR

BEECH

HAYWARDS
FARM CL

MARGARDS LA

CONISTON CL

SPRINGFIELD
RD

SPRINGFIELD
CL

ST
MICHAELS
CL

SQUIRREL
WLK

FOXES

BADGER WAY

NEWTOWN

River Crane

Dewlands
Common

Forge
Lane

HORTON WAY

Emmanuel
Mid Sch

Verwood
First Sch

HOWE LA

08

Bridge Farm

B3072

Wedge Hill
Farm

Verwood

Heathy How

1 WOODPECKER CL
2 FIRS GLEN RD

ST MICHAELS RD

Homer's
Wood

Manor Farm

2

David's Cross

Redman's
Hill

Monmouth's Ash
Farm

Horton
Farm

07

Bog Farm

Horton Common

CRAB ORCHARD WAY

B3072

Horton
Heath
Farm

Crab Orchard
Farm

Crab Orchard

Harkwood
Farm

Grixey Farm

SANDY LA

VERWOOD RD

1

Horton Heath

Hope Lodge
Farm

Bramble
Farm

Silverwood

High
Moon

CHURCH RD

MEAD RD

BROAD

CLUMP HILL

Chapel
Farm

BURT S LA

HORTON RD

Three Legged Cross
Cty First Sch

ALBANY DR

CAMELLIA
CL

RAY

B3072

06

A   B   C

4

09

3

08

2

07

1

06

12   A   13   B   14   C

Gravel Pit

Turmer
Hill

Harbridge
Farm

Avon Valley Path

Ibsley
Bridge

Weir

Turmer

Harbridge
Lodge

PH

Plumley
Farm

Lower
Turmer

Nea
Farm

SHEPHERDS LA

Turmer Brook

Mill Stream

Shepherds
Cottage

Home
Wood

SHEPHERDS HILL

Dog Kennel
Wood

Riverbank
Covert

Whitehoe
Cottages

CHESTNUT AVE

New Barn
Cottages

The Bothy

Old
Somerley

ELLINGHAM DR

New
Bridge

Ellingham
Farm

Ellingham

ELLINGHAM CROSS

ELLINGHAM DROVE

SALISBURY RD

NEA DR

Somerley
Park

Nursery
Cottages

Broad Close
Covert

Old Laundry
Cottage

Somerley

Park
Cottage

Gravel
Works

The Belt

Ringwood
Forest

DUNCOMBE DR

River Avon

Meadow
Lake

Blashford
Farm

Gravel
Pit

ASHLEY DR

Dockens Water

SALISBURY RD

Sunderton
Wood

Weir

Lifeland
Copse

Upper Hurst
Farm

B3081

VERWOOD RD

Duncombe
Lodge

Ashley
Farm

King Stream

Up
Mead

Gouldings
Farm

Hurst Old
Farm

B3081

Baker's
Hanging

Lin Brook

D
E
F

SALISBURY RD A338

Cottage
Plantation

Great Bottom

Whitefield
Plantation

Summerlug
Hill

Linwood
Bog

4

Ibsley Manor
Farm

NEW RD

PO

Digden
Bottom

CUFFNELLS CL

Mockbeggar
Farm

Ibsley

Hearns
Plantation

Cross Lanes
Farm

+

Mockbeggar

MOCKBEGGAR LA

CROSS LANES

Ibsley
House

09

Avon Valley Path

Newlands
Plantation

Dockens Water

Rodens
Bottom

Fir Walk

Gravel
Pit

Moyles Court
Sch
Ford

Big Whitemoor
Bottom

3

Rockford Common

Works

ELLINGHAM DROVE

New
Buildings

Little Whitemoor
Bottom

Alice Lisle Inn
(PH)

Rockford

08

Rockford
Green

Blashford Lakes
Study Ctr

Gravel
Pit

Waterslade

Ivy Lake

P

Bigsburn
Hill

Water Slade Bottom

IVY LA

Rockford
Farm

Rockford
Farm

Highwood

2

Highwood
Copse

LINFORD
HO

SNAILS LA

Bracken
Hill

Forest Edge
Farm

HIGHWOOD LA

Blashford

Linbrook
Almshouses

07

Depot

Highwood
Farm

LINBROOK
VIEW

Linford

WOOLMER LA

Northfield
Lake

Lin Brook

Linbank
Farm

SYCAMORE
CT

HEADLANDS
BSNS PK

IN BROOK RD

POULNER
MOBILE HOME
PK

COWPITTS LA

OLD
FARM CL

North
Poulner

Hangersley

+

1

Kingfisher
Lake

A338

NORTH POULNER RD

Poulner
Inf & Jun
Schs

SHAW
RD

LAWRENCE
RD

ST AUBYNS LA

Burcomb

Headlands
Adventure Ctr

WATERSIDE CL

MORANT RD

GIPSEY WAY

FORESTSIDE GDNS

ROSS
RD

CROFT RD

DENE CL

PADGET CL

Hangersley
Hill

+

Northfield RD

HOLM
CL

DENHOLM CL

BURCOMBE LA

HURST RD

EDWINA DR

BUTLERS LA

LINFORD RD

NARROW LA

Forest Corner
Farm

LINBROOK
CT

MEADOW CL

SEYMOUR RD

BROADSHARD LA

HAMPTON DR

WAKESTEAD

FAIRLIE PK

GORLEY RD

FAIRLIE

POULNER
PK

HAWKINS
CL

1 CHICHESTER RD
2 DRAKE CL
3 FROBISHER CL
4 GRENVILLE CL

SALISBURY RD

HIGHFIELD DR

06

5
D
16
E
17
F

Milkham
Inclosure

Amie's
Wood

Linwood

Webb's
Copse

Toms
Farm

4

Appleslade
Farm

Camping
& Caravan
Park

Linwood
Farm

The
Red Shoot Inn
(PH)

Linwood

King's
Garde

Amie's
Corner

Appleslade
Bottom

Lin Wood

Mount
Hill

09

Castle
Piece

Roe
Inclosure

Appleslade
Inclosure

Linford Brook

3

Red Shoot
Plain

Red Shoot
Wood

Buckherd
Bottom

Green
Ford

Greenford
Bottom

White
Hill

08

Great Linford
Inclosure

Pinnick
Wood

Collier's
Thorns

Handy
Cross

2

Linford Bottom

Akercombe
Bottom

Little Linford
Inclosure

Handy Cross Plain

Marrowbones
Hill

07

Ridley Plain

Linford

Picket
Bottom

Little
Wood

Harves
Slade

1

Brook
Farm

Old
Gate

Picket
Hill

Ridley
Bottom

Shobley

Ridley
Wood

Shobley
Bottom

Picket
Post

A31

06

D E F

A31

Linford Brook

Milkham
Bottom

Slufters
Inclosure

Bratley
Arch

Mogshade
Hill

Bratley
Inclosure

Bushy
Bratley

Bolderwood
Farm

Bratley
Plain

Sandy Ridge

Bratley
Wood

Deer
Sanctuary

Upper
Lazy
Bushes

Bushy
Bradley

Lazy
Bushes

Backley
Bottom

Smoky
Hole

Backley
Holmes

North Oakley
Inclosure

Bratley Water

Backley
Inclosure

Stinking
Edge
Wood

Blackensford
Bottom

Blackensford
Hill

Backley Plain

Blackensford
Lawn

Blackensford Brook

Soarley
Beeches

Beech Bed
Inclosure

Woolfield
Hill

Harvest
Slade
Bottom

Soarley
Bottom

Dogwood
Bottom

Woolfield
Cottage

Old
House

Mouse's
Cupboard

South Oakley
Inclosure

Burley
Outer Rails
Inclosure

Berry
Beeches

119
97

A **B** **C**

Acres Down House

Puckpits Inclosure

Wick Wood

4

Bolderwood Walk

Highland Water Inclosure

Bagshot Gutter

Coneygear Bottom

Cross

Woolsmoor Meads

09

Holm Hill

The Knowles

Holmhill Inclosure

Forest Walks

Deer Sanctuary

3

Highland Water

Bolderwood Cottage

08

Bolderwood Grounds

Wooson's Hill

Portuguese Fireplace

Millyford Bridge

Pound Hill

Holidays Hill

North Oakley Inclosure

Mark Ash Wood

Wooson's Hill Inclosure

2

Barrow Moor

Holidays Hill Inclosure

Dark Hat

07

Church Moor

Bolderwood Ornamental Dr

Warwickslade Cutting

Winding Shoot

Knightwood Oak

1

Knightwood Inclosure

Rhinefield Ornamental Dr

Hart Hill

A35

Eagle Oak

Anderwood Inclosure

06

24 **A** 25 **B** 26 **C**

121
99

A   **B**   **C**

Fox
Hill

Redbridge
Hill

Ironshill
Inclosure

Rushpole
Wood

Lodgehill
Inclosure

4

Whitebridge
Hill

Lodgehill
Cottage

Fair
Cross

Beaulieu River

Mallard
Wood

Dunces Arch
Inclosure

09

Beaulieu River

Golf Course

CH

Dunces
Arch

Longwater Lawn

THE
CUSTARDS

3   Custards

1 QUEEN'S PAR
2 EMPRESS RD

Fox
Hill

Row
Hill

QUEENS RD

PRINCES CRES

SOUTHAMPTON RD

WELLANDS
RD

PEMBERTON RD

PO

PRINCES
CT

PRINCES
CT

Cemy

Meml

HIGH ST   A35

B3056

RUFUS
CT

P
i

Hotel
Mus

SHAG'S
MEADOW

Bolton's
Bench

White
Moor

08

GOSPORT LA

THE MEADOWS

The
Bench

P

The Ridge

A35

Goose
Green

BROOKLANDS

A337

2

Irons Hill
Walk

BEAULIEU RD

B30

Clayhill

Matley Ridge

CLAY HILL

PARK CL

BEECHEN LA

HILARY CL

The Crown
& Stirrup
(PH)

Pondhead
Inclosure

Pondhead

Parkhill
(Hotel)

Holmhill
Passage

07

Beechen La

Parkhill
Lawn

Little Holmhill
Inclosure

1

Park Ground
Inclosure

Denny Inclosure

Litt
Holm

Park
Hill

P

A337

06

30   **A**   **31**   **B**   **32**   **C**

121
146

D
E
F

Camp and Caravan Site

Churchplace Inclosure

Langley Cottage
P

Nature Quest

Langley Wood

DEERLEAP LA

4

Ashurst Wood

Church Place

P

The Homestead

NEW COTTS

Deerleap Inclosure

09

Home Farm

Ashurst Lodge

Longdown Inclosure

3

Ashurst Walk

Fulliford Bog

Beaulieu River

Peel Hill

08

Matley Heath

Matley Holms

Matley Wood

Fulliford Passage

Caravan and Camping Site
P

King's Passage

Withycombe Shade

2

Decoy Pond Farm

Matley Bog

Matley Passage

07

Church Place

Black Down

Caravan and Camping Site

P

P

1

P

Stag Park

Shatterford Bottom

STATION COTTS

Hotel

Beaulieu Road Sta

Denny Wood

B3056

06

123
101

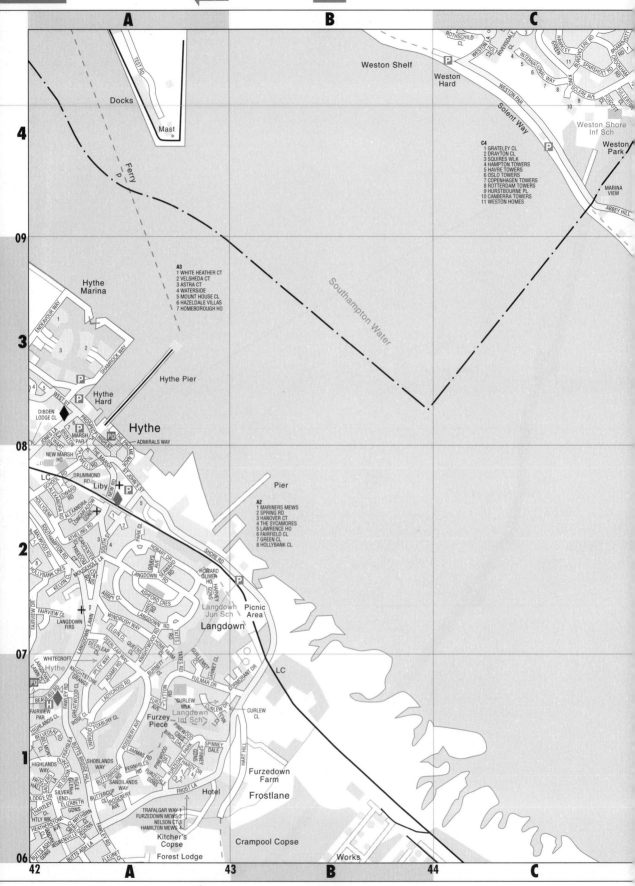

Weston Shelf

Docks

Mast

4

Ferry

09

Hythe Marina

A3
1 WHITE HEATHER CT
2 VELSHEDA CT
3 ASTRA CT
4 WATERSIDE
5 MOUNT HOUSE CL
6 HAZELDALE VILLAS
7 HOMEBOROUGH HO

Weston Hard

Solent Way

Weston Shore Inf Sch

Weston Park

Weston Homes

C4
1 GRATELEY CL
2 DRAYTON CL
3 SQUIRES WLK
4 HAMPTON TOWERS
5 HAVRE TOWERS
6 OSLO TOWERS
7 COPENHAGEN TOWERS
8 ROTTERDAM TOWERS
9 HURSTBOURNE PL
10 CANBERRA TOWERS
11 WESTON HOMES

MARINA VIEW

ABBEY HILL

3

Hythe Pier

Southampton Water

Hythe Hard

DIBDEN LODGE CL

Hythe

ADMIRALS WAY

NEW MARSH HO

08

LC

Liby

Pier

A2
1 MARINERS MEWS
2 SPRING RD
3 HANOVER CT
4 THE SYCAMORES
5 LAWRENCE HO
6 FAIRFIELD CL
7 GREEN CL
8 HOLLYBANK CL

SHORE RD

2

HOWARD OLIVER HO

HARVEY GDNS

Langdown Jun Sch

Picnic Area

Langdown

LC

07

WHITECROFT

Hythe

FAIRVIEW PAR

Langdown Firs

Langdown Inf Sch

CURLEW WLK

CURLEW CL

Furzey Piece

1

HIGHLANDS WAY

Furzedown Farm

Frostlane

Hotel

TRAFALGAR WAY 1
FURZEDOWN MEWS 2
NELSON CT 3
HAMILTON MEWS 4

Kitcher's Copse

Crampool Copse

Works

Forest Lodge

06

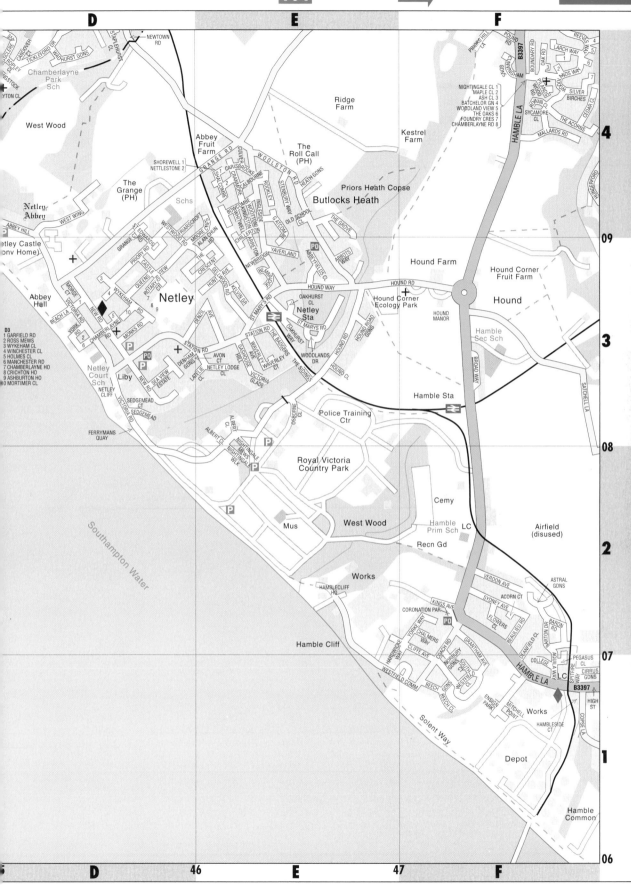

A
B
C

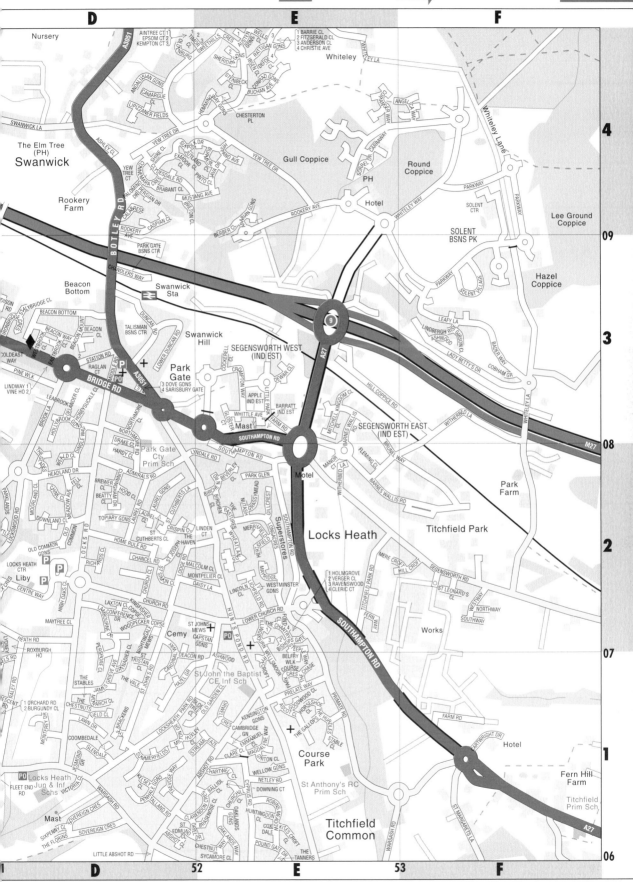

D E F

4

09

Heytesbury Farm

Crockerhill
The Old Vine (PH)
CHALK PIT COTTS

Carpenters Copse

Homerhill Copse

Pigeonhouse Coppice

Bere Farm

Albany Farm

Charity Farm

Moor Coppice

3

Dean Farm

Roche Court (Boundary Oak Prep Sch)

Whitedell Farm

Wallington River

08

Hellyers Farm

North Fareham

POOK LA

NINE ELMS LA

Spurlings Farm

North Fareham Farm

Down Barn Farm
BOARHUNT RD

2

FURZE HALL

Cemy

Greenwood

FAREHAM

St Christophers

Fareham Ind Pk

Pennant Pk

North Wallington

Supermarket

RIVERDALE COTTS

STANDARD WAY

Fareham Hts

Fort Wallington Ind Est

07

North Wallington

Harrison Prim Sch

Riverside Terr

Wallington

Kings Way

M27

1

L Ctr

Liby

C Ctr

WALLINGTON WAY A32

Ellerslie House

Downend

Mus

WESTERN WAY

EASTERN WAY

CAMS HILL

Golf Course

PORTCHESTER RD

A27

06

D 58 E 59 F

131 109

A B C

4

B2177

Carmans Copse

STAPLE CROSS

Staplecross Copse

Walton Heath

Mitchellar

BLACKHOUSE LA

Prior's Hold Farm

Carmans Farm

Lodge Farm

Vernons Farm

COMMON LA

Lodge Coppice

Friar's Coppice

NORTON

09

Wallington River

Boarhunt Mill
Grub Coppice

Mill Coppice

Ham Coppice

Bridge St

Newman's Bridge

Castle Farm

BACK LA

NORTON CL

CASTLE RD

Kings Way

Dirtystile Copse

Ham Farm

FAREHAM RD

WEST ST

Royal Naval Cotts

PO

HIGH ST

3

Manor Farm

Ashleydown Coppice

Boarhunt

Ashley Down Farm

Stroud Coppice

Southwick

Southw Park

The Wildern

Perrige's Coppice

Marls Rows

B2

08

BOARHUNT RD

Damson Row

MONUMENT LA

Offwell Farm

PORTCHESTER LA

CROOKED WALK LA

2

SWIVELTON LA

Monument Farm

Mountemoor's Coppice

Mus

P

Nelson's Monument

07

Fort Nelson

PORTSDOWN HILL RD

Mast

Mast

JAMES CALLAGHAN DR

Fort Southw

CORNAWAY RD

P

Ports Down

SKEW RD

High Tor

WINTERBO

M27

The Mount

NELSON LA

1 2 3 4 5 6 7 8 9

1

Chalk Pit

Upper Cornaway La

LECKFORD CL

EXTON

WALTHAM CL

NYEWOOD AVE

ANSON GR

BENEDICT WAY

KINGSCOTE RD

ALMOND

HILLSLEY RD

RIDGEWA

BROWNING AVE

KILMISTON DR

WETLN CL

ROGATE GDNS

CARLTON RD

KEATS AVE

WORDSWORTH AVE

COLERIDGE RD

FALMOUTH AVE

TUDOR

SAXON CL

DORE AVE

STEEP

HILL D

PENTI RD RISE

CHAUCER AVE

MACAULAY AVE

MASERFIELD

BRIDGES AVE

BUDE CL

HELSTON

Winnham Farm

Lancaster CL

DANES RD

MERLIN GDNS

HARTING GDNS

FROXFIELD GDNS

BURITON CL

GRAMONTROSE AVE

SOUTHWICK AVE

EDWARD GR

SHELLEY AVE

NEWBOLT RD

TRURO RD

MOUSEHOLE RD

PEDEN CL

Cams Bridge

JUTE CL

SOLENT AVE

ISLAND VIEW WLK

GRINDLE CL

RED BARN AVE

LAVEROCK LEA

LEITH AVE

SEAVIEW AVE

DRYDEN AVE

SAUNDERS HO

HILLSIDE CRES

CONNIGAR

THE PINES

Crem

BOXWOOD CL

NORTHFIELD PARK

HAWTHORN CL

ROBINSON CT

CANNON'S BARN CL

LINDEN LEA

Northern Schs

HILL VIEW RD

RICHMOND RISE

MORNINGSIDE AVE

PO

RAYMOND RD

06

60 A 61 B 62 C

D   E   F

Wynn's Copse

Little Belney Copse

Belney Farm

Jays Copse

Great Belney Copse

Place Wood

Sheepwash Farm

4

Assells Copice

Hazelhook Coppice

Graysland Hummock

sells ow

Wanstead Farm

Short's Coppice

Dunsland Coppice

Hobern Coppice

Lyeheath Farm

Ward's Coppice

09

POULTER LA

NORTH RD W

WOOD LA

NORTH RD E

WEST RD

MAIN DR

SOUTH RD

EAST RD

PRIORY RD

HMS Dryad

Lye Heath

Littlehunts Coppice

Wayfarer's Walk

Newlandsmoor Coppice

Southwick House

CH

Comphouse Moor Coppice

Portland Coppice

Cooper Hill

3

Southwick Park Naval Recreation Centre

Golf Course

PINSLEY DR

Comphouse Farm

Sawyer's Wood

Greathunts Coppice

PURBROOK HEATH RD

Southwick Park Lake

Hookheath Farm

Broomground Coppice

Potwell Coppice

08

DROVE RD

PITYMOOR LA

PIGEON HOUSE LA

Potwell Farm

Broomfield House

Pitymoor Coppice

Miller's Coppice

Pinsley Coppice

Potwell House

New Barns

Pinsley Plantation

Ford

MILL LA

Mill Farm

2

Bushy Coppice

WIDLEY WLK

Pigeon House Farm

07

PORTSDOWN HILL RD

SOUTHWICK RD

Paulsgrove Chalk Pit

BUTTERFLY DR

CHALK PIT RD

LIME GR

Fort Widley

Mast

1

BURY HO

NDSBURY RD

LEOMINSTER HO

Ports Down

Mus

PORTSDOWN HILL RD

B2177

FERN 2 3

SLEY RD

UTH CL

M27

BEVERSTON CRES

Paulsgrove

LEOMINSTER RD

DORSTONE RD

MEADOWSWEET WAY

HOLBEACH CL

DERSINGHAM CL

SOUTHWICK HILL RD

FORT WIDLEY MARRIED QUARTERS

BEECHURST CRES

NORTH CRES

HATHERLEY RD

WOOFFERTON RD

ELKSTONE RD

WINCHCOMBE RD

SEVERN CL

CLEEVE

BLAKEMERE CRES

HARLESTON RD

SHERINGHAM RD

MABLETHORPE RD

LOWESTOFT RD

NORWICH RD

PETERBOROUGH RD

ARGAN CL

KINTYRE RD

SHETLAND CL

BRESLER HO

WINCHCOMBE RD

DORMINGTON RD

LEDBURY RD

WILLERSLEY CL

WALSINGHAM CL

Wymering

Queen Alexandra

B2177

ISLAY GDNS

ORKNEY RD

BIRDLIP RD

COLESBOURNE RD

MORTIMER RD

LUDLOW CRES

KINGSLAND CL

RAPSON CL

CREDENHILL CL

WASHBROOK RD

HARWICH RD

COLCHESTER RD

CAVELL DR

A3

Liby

HEMPSTED RD

ARTILLERY CL

ABBEYDORE RD

BROMLEY RD

FITZPATRICK CT

BRAINTREE RD

MAIDSTONE CRES

HYTHE RD

SEVENOAKS RD

DEAL CL

WYMERING LA

BOSTON RD

H

D   64   E   65   F   **06**

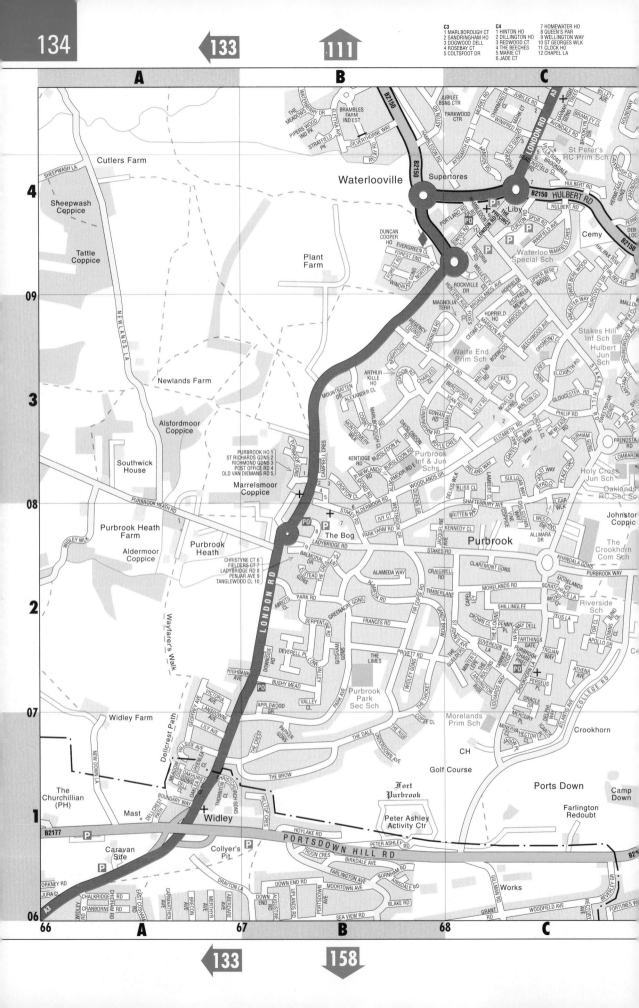

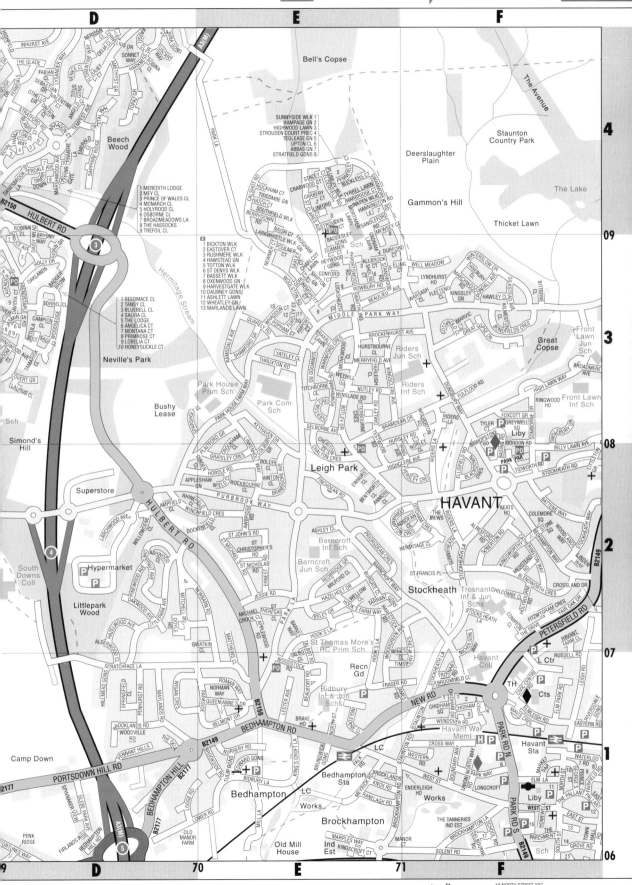

D · E · F

Holme Farm

Sussex Border Path

The Groves

Stubbermere

Racton Common

Pond Cottage

Pond Copse

Brickkiln Ponds

WOODBERRY LA

EMSWORTH COMMON RD

Westbourne Common

Valley Farm

Longcopse Hill

Cricket Gd

Monk's Farm

MONK'S HILL

SYDENHAM TERR
COVINGTON RD

1 SILVERLOCK PL
2 LANSDOWN TERR

Hollybank Farm

LONG COPSE LA

SCHOOL LA

BYERLEY CL
ELLESMERE
ORCH
WHITLEY
WILLOW GDNS
RIVER ST

2
COMMONSIDE

Commonside

Westbourne Cty Prim Sch

BECKENHAM TERR

MILL RD

PARADISE LA

Westbourne

MANCHESTER TERR

NORTH ST

CROCKFORD
TAYLORS
HAROLD
EDGE RD
HOMEFIELD
CHURCHER
RD

Hampshire Farm

KING ST
CHURCH RD
THE GROVE

OLD RECTORY
RIVERMEAD CT
1
2
3
PO
NEW RD

WESTBOURNE RD

New Brighton

ELDERFIELD

WICKOR WAY
WICKOR CL

WRD CRES

WESTBOURNE AVE
COMSON

DANBURY CT

Sussex Border Path

WESTBOURNE CL

MILL LA

EW BRIGHTON RD
LEWIS RD
RACTON RD
DANNEATON CL

Lumley Croft

Lumley Mill Farm

Lumley

1 VICTORIA TERR
2 RAGLAN TERR
3 LUMLEY TERR

LUMLEY RD
1
2
3

THE ROOKERY

WOODFIELD PARK RD

PARK LA

Sindle's Farm

Aldsworth

Aldsworth Manor

Aldsworth Common

Didmans Copse

River Ems

FOXBURY LA

Deepsprings

Chantry Farm

Cemy

CEMETERY LA

WHITECHIMNEY ROW

CHURCH VIEW 1
VICTORIA TERR 2
JUBILEE TERR 3

Lumley Farm

BROOK COTTS

OLD FARM LA

SOUTH LA

The Bourne Com Coll

PARK RD

HASLEMERE RD

BOURNE VIEW

CLOVELLY RD

ST JOHN'S RD

MANOR GDNS

ROMAN RD

MANOR RD

MANOR WAY

New Barn Cottage

NEWBARN LA

Walderton

MONUMENT LA

Racton Mon

B2147

Ell Bridge

Ellbridge Buildings

Ractonpark Wood

COMMON RD

Woodmancote

Woodmancote Farm

Bishop Barn Farm

Manor House

WOODMANCOTE LA

Woodmancote (PH)

DUFFIELD LA

WALNUT TREE DR

South Lane Farm

A27

WEST VIEW COTTS

SOUTH LA

CHESHIRE WAY

LAUDER CL

FRASER GDNS

BREACH AVE

STEIN RD

BANNELL CL

MOUNTWOOD RD

MERRIVALE CT

SMALLCUTS AVE

GLENWOOD CT

OVERTON RD

HARTLAND CT

PRIORS CL

KELSEY AVE

EAST FIELD CL

FURLSTON GR

Breach

Loveders Farm

PRIORS LEAZE LA

COOKS LA

HURSTWOOD AVE

GUILDFORD CL

INLANDS RD

Inlands Farm

Inlands

5 · 76 · E · 77 · F

09
4
3
08
2
07
1
06

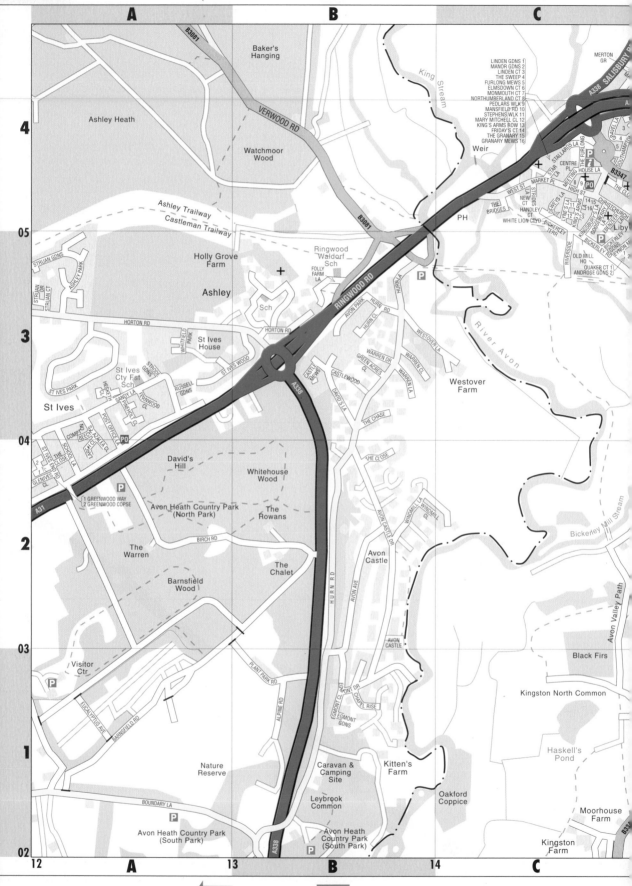

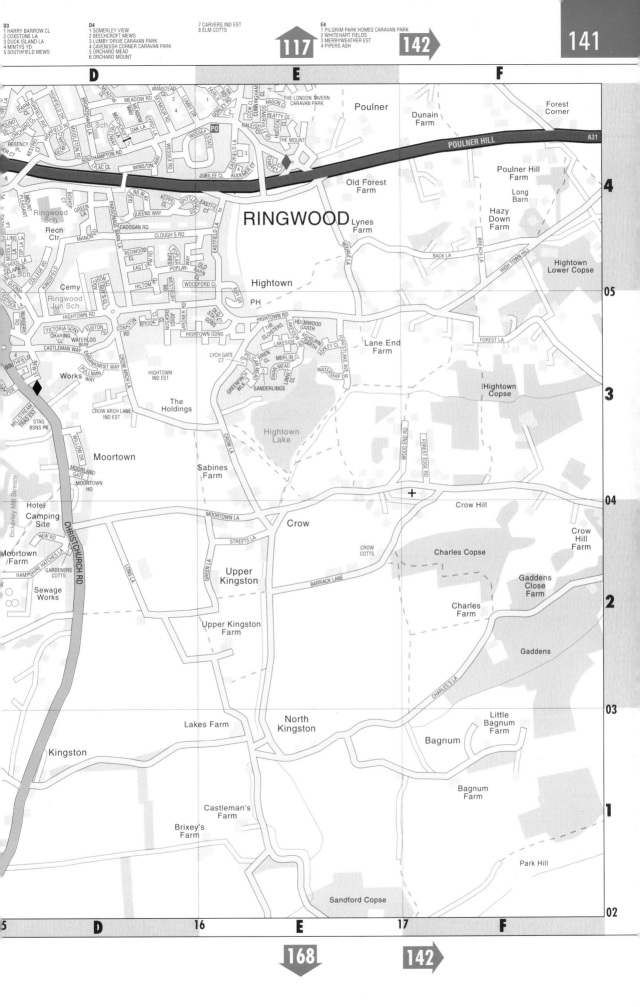

A31

Picket Plain

Ridley Wood

Ridley Green

Picket Hill

4

Foulford

Foulford Bottom

Mill Lawn Brook

Vereley Wood

Turf Croft Farm

Vereley Farm

Foulford Farm

05

Mast

Vereley

Smugglers Road

Vereley Hill

Box Berry Hill

Burley Croft

Whitemoor

Hurn Farm

3

Common Moor

COACH HILL LA

Broad Bottom

Forest Farm

FOREST LA

Vales Moor

RINGWOOD RD

Little Castle Common

RANDALL S LA

PO

FOREST RD

Knaves Ash

04

Burley Street

CHARLES S LA

Stocks Farm

TYRELLS LA

CROW HILL TOP

Castle Hill

Sandys

LONGMEAD RD

Gritenbury Farm

Black Bush

2

Sandy Shoot

Strodgemoor Bottom

Burley Hill House

ESGHAILE LA

CLO

GARDEN RD

Coffins Holms

Campden House

COPSE RD

CASTLE HILL LA

HONEY LA

03

Church Moor

Bagnum Rough

WARNES LA

POUND LA

Cranes Moor

Burley Beacon

MEADOW CL

Kingston Great Common

Burnt Axon

Shappe

1

SHAPPEN HILL LA

Pound Farm

Bagnum Bog

Brown Loaf

Chubb's Farm

Slap

02

18   A   19   B   20   C

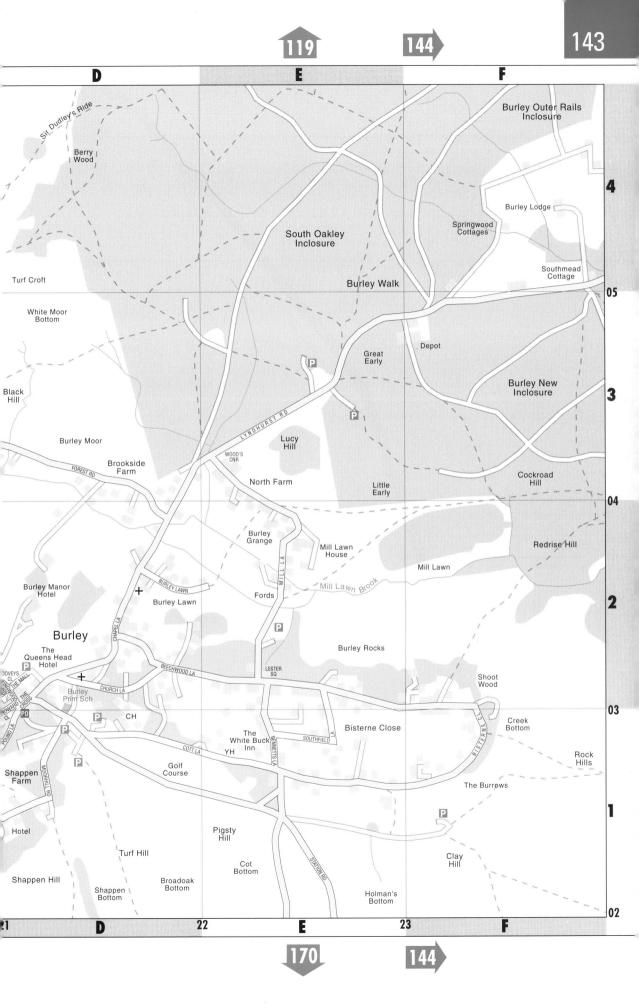

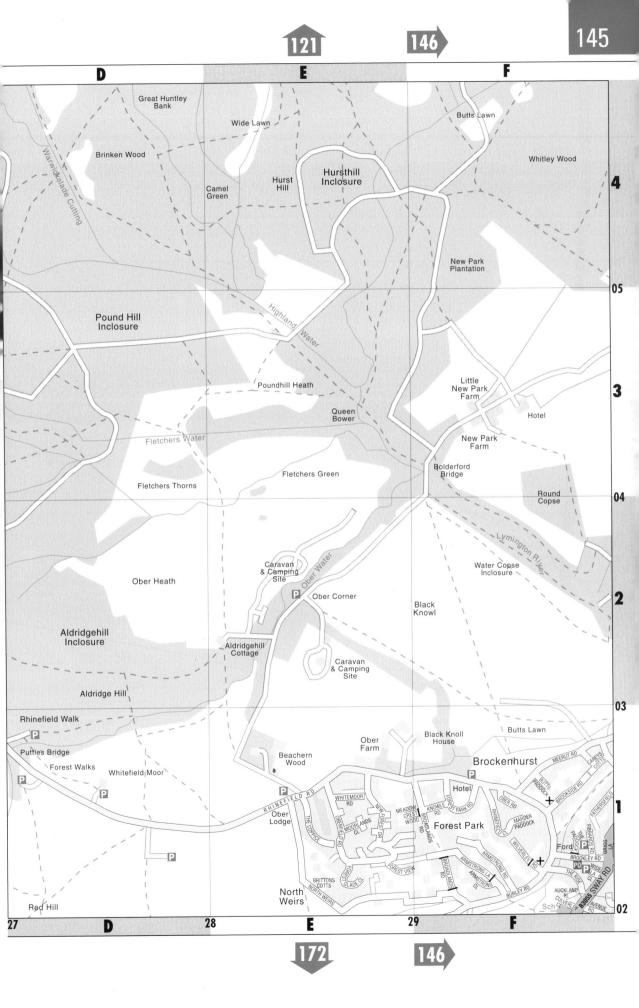

D
E
F

4

05

3

04

2

03

1

02

Great Huntley Bank
Wide Lawn
Butts Lawn
Brinken Wood
Whitley Wood
Camel Green
Hurst Hill
Hursthill Inclosure
New Park Plantation

Warwickslade Cutting

Highland Water

Pound Hill Inclosure

Poundhill Heath

Little New Park Farm

Hotel

Queen Bower

Fletchers Water

New Park Farm

Fletchers Green
Bolderford Bridge

Fletchers Thorns

Round Copse

Lymington River

Ober Water

Ober Heath

Caravan & Camping Site

Water Copse Inclosure

Ober Corner

Black Knowl

Aldridgehill Inclosure

Aldridgehill Cottage

Caravan & Camping Site

Aldridge Hill

Rhinefield Walk

Black Knoll House

Butts Lawn

Puttles Bridge

Ober Farm

Brockenhurst

MEERUT RD

CARRYS COTTS

Forest Walks

Beachern Wood

Whitefield Moor

Hotel

BUTTS PADDOCK

BROOKSIDE RD

FATHERSFIELD

RHINEFIELD RD

WHITEMOOR RD

OBER RD

Ford

FIBBARDS RD

HIGHS

Ober Lodge

THE COPPICE

OBERFIELDS RD

MOORLANDS CL

NEW FOREST DR

MEADOW CREST RD

KNOWLE WOOD

BROOKLANDS RD

Forest Park

RHINEFIELD CL

MARDEN PADDOCK

WILVERLEY RD

PO

P

WIDE LA

THE RISE

B3055 SWAY RD

BRITTONS COTTS

FOREST GLADE CL

FOREST VIEW

NORTH WEIRS

BROADLANDS RD

ARMSTRONG LA

ARMSTRONG CL

BROOKLEY RD

AUCKLAND PL

CULVERLEY RD

AVENUE RD

North Weirs

BURLEY RD

Red Hill

Sch

145
122

A B C

4

05

3

04

2

03

1

02

30 31 32

A337

Spaniards
Hole

King's
Hat

Parkhill
Inclosure

Hollands
Wood

Ramnor
Inclosure

Stubby Copse
Inclosure

Pignal
Inclosure

Camp
Site

Balmer
Lawn

Standing
Hat

Pound

Perrywood
Haseley
Inclosure

Victoria
Tilery
Cottage

Pignalhill
Inclosure

Ford

Hotel

B3055

BALMER LAWN RD

Jacks
Wood

Balmerlawn

Bridge
Farm

Warren
Farm

Whitley Ridge

Hotel

New Copse
Inclosure

MARTINS RD

WATERS GREEN

PARK

MEERUT RD

RINGWOOD
TERR

Hotel

Brockenhurst

LYNDHURST RD

B3055

1 WATERS GREEN
2 WATERS GREEN CT

BURFORD
LA

HORLOCK
RD

FATHERSFIELD

GREGG LA

CHESTNUT
RD

FOREST
RD

SUTTON PL

2

Brockenhurst
Coll

Warren
Farm

Old Mill
House

Lymington River

Longbow

Perrywood
Ivy
Inclosure

B3055

HOMEFORDE
HO

BROOKLEY RD

AUCKLAND
AVE

HALL NO 1

GREENWAYS RD

NORTH RD

NO 2 CL

MILL LA

Ivy
Wood

Irons
Hill

Perrywood
Ironshill
Inclosure

LC

A337

B3055

LYMINGTON
RD

AUCKLAND
RD

A B C

145
173

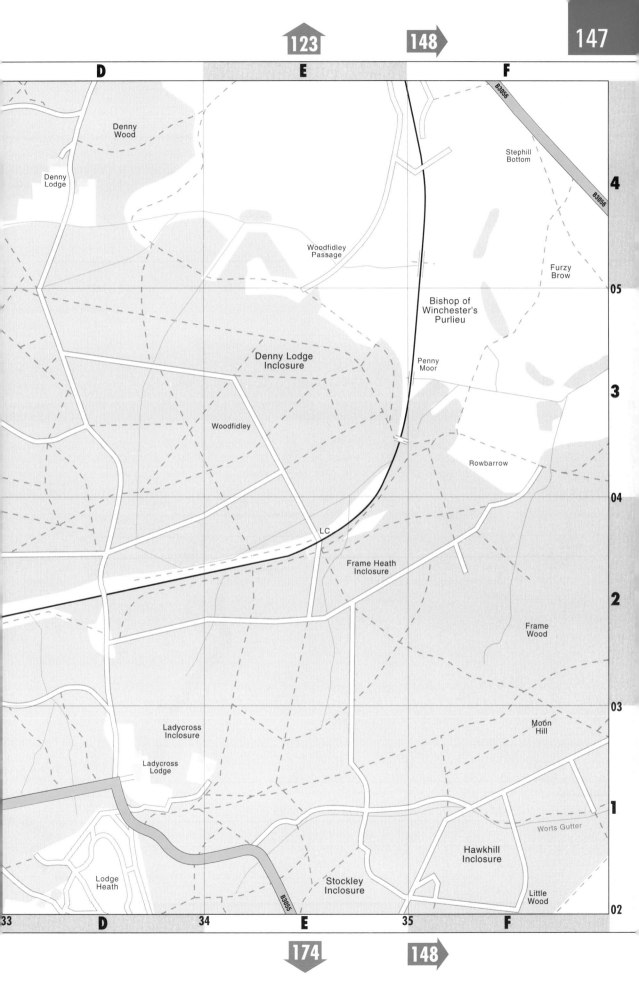

A B C

King's Hat
Cottage

Buck Hill

Ferny Crofts
(Scout Ctr)

4

King's Hat
Inclosure

B3056

Gurnetfields
Furzebrake

P

Ford

Culverley
Old Farm

Starpole
Pond

05

Pig
Bush

NORTH LA

Foxhunting
Inclosure

Culverley
Farm

P

Gurnet
Fields

North
Gate

3

Honey
Hill

Shepton
Bridge

Shepton Water

The House
in the Wood

Halfpenny
Green

P

Penerley Water

Penerley
Wood

Beaulieu River

Little Goswell
Copse

04

Little Honeyhill
Wood

Penerley
Gate

Penerley
Farm

Hides Hill La

Penerley
Lodge

Hartford
Bridge

Tantany
Wood

Leygreen
Farm

Hides
Close

2

Stubbs Wood

Black
Bridge

Hartford
Copse

P

Abbotstanding
Wood

P

03

Wood La

P

The National
Motor Mus

Beaulieu Abbey
(remains of)

Works Gutter

Palace
House

1

P

FURZEY LA

PALACE LA B3054

Furzey
Lodge

Pit
Copse

Hotel

Mill

PONDSIDE FLATS 1
DITTON COTTS 2
CLITHEROE COTTS 3

B3054

P

HIGH ST

PO

2
3

B3056

B3054

Beaulieu
Prim Sch

Beaulieu

36 **A** 37 **B** 38 **C**

D E F

Dibden
Inclosure

The
Noads

A326

B3054

PRU
BEAULIEU RD
LUMEDALE RD
WHINGFIELD RD
CRETE COTTS
CRETE RD
VILLIERS RD
ARNWOOD AVE
BARCLAY MEWS
CLARKLEY CR
HAWLEY RD

SOLENT RD
MONKS WLK
HEATHERSTONE AVE
CORBOULD RD
BUTTS ASH LA
FOREST FRONT

ROMAN RD
BEVERLEY RD
FOREST MEADOW

Nature
Reserve

4

HYTHE BY PASS

A326

Fawley
Inclosure

Crabhat
Inclosure

Flash Pond

05

BEAULIEU RD

Harford
House

3

Solent Way

Beaulieu Heath

Stonyford
Pond

Holbury
Purlieu

Hartford Heath

04

Great Goswell
Copse

Hilltop
Farm

2

Hill Top

Hilltop
Wood

Hilltop
House

Royal Oak
(PH)

03

Boarman
Pond

Stock Water

Moonhills
Gate

Moonhills LA

Moonhills
Copse

P

1

PALACE LA

Home
Farm

Otterwood
Gate

Cowleys La

Carpenters
Cottage

SUMMER LA

Otterwood
Farm House

Cowleys
Copse

DOCK LA

Otterwood

02

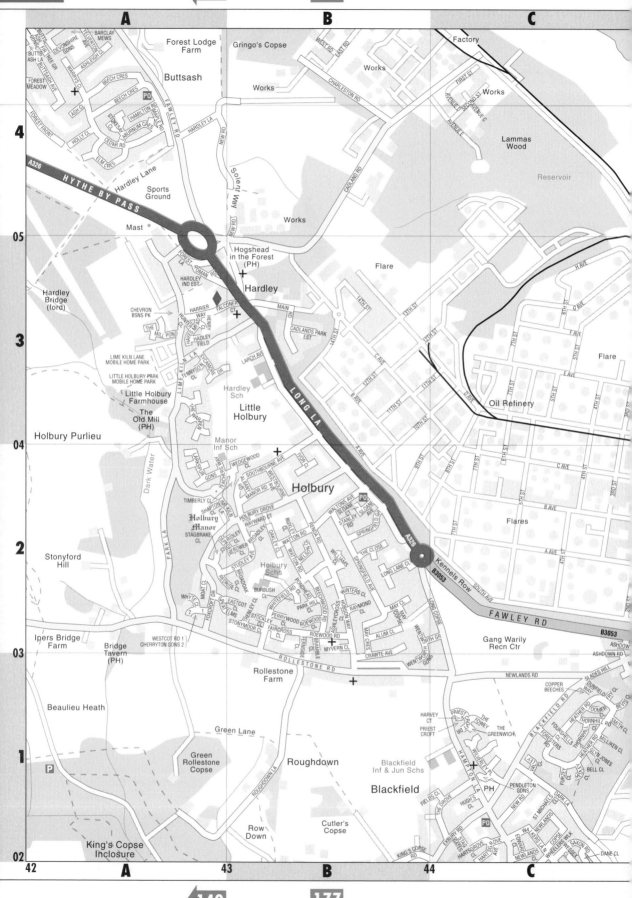

127
152

D   E   F

Jetty

4

Southampton Water

Cadland Creek

05

Pier

Marine Terminal

Foreshore N

3

North Trestle Rd

Foreshore S

Pier

Burma Rd

PL P.H. RD

Burma Rd S

Pier

Jetty Rd

South Trestle Rd

Cadland Rd

Old Agwi Rd

04

Bitumen Rd

Agitator Rd

Seps 4 Rd

2ND ST

C. Ave

Flume End Rd

Ashlett Creek

2

1ST ST

Rye Paddock La

Fawley

Churchfields

Copthorne Cotts

Hamlet Ct

Marsh La

Copthorne Cl

The Jolly Sailor (PH)

A Ave

Church Cl

Sherring Rd

Thorne La

Fawley Inf Sch

Orchard Cl

India Rd

PO

Admirals Cl

Church La

Woodville Ave

Ashlett Rd

Stonehills

Southview

The Paddocks

The Square

Ashlett Cl

Ashlett

School Rd

School Rd

Denny Cl

Falcon Fields

The Lane

Chestnut Rd

Whites La

2

Fawley Bsns Ctr

Liby

FAWLEY RD

FAWLEY BY PASS

03

The Pentagon

Blackfield Rd

Meadow Way

Charles Ley Ct

Ashlett Mews1

Rhyme Hall Mews 2

Chapel La

P

Stone Hill Farm

Stonehills

Fields Farm

Northern Access Rd

Northern Rd

Eastern Rd

Fawley Power Station

1

Fields Heath

Badminston Farm

Switch House Rd

Central Way N

Haleway Rd

Western Rd

Boiler Rd

Wright Way

Channel Mouth Rd

Swing Bridge

Tom's Down

Badminston Common

Badminston La

Badminston Drove

B3053

Chy

Inner La

Southern Rd

Quayside Rd

02

45   D   46   E   47   F

178
152

151
128

A   **B**   **C**

Hamble
Point
Marina

River Hamble

DIBLES RD

FLEET END BOTTOM

SANDY
CROFT

BEVIS CL

SHELLCROFT

ASPEN AVE

ELMDALE CL

SPRUCE

Sch

CHURCH RD

BIRCHDALE
CL

QUEEN'S RD

MEADCROFT CL

CHEVIOT GN

SPENCER
CL

OAKWOOD

NEW RD

HEWETTS RISE

ROMFORD RD

OSBORNE RD

HORNBY CL

BEECHWOOD

LARCHDALE
CL

NEWTOWN RD

PITCHPONDS RD

GLEN RD

HOWERTS CL

UPPER SPINNEY

JUMAR CL

SUSAN AVE

LOWER SPINNEY

FLEET END RD

4

Newtown

Warsash Maritime
Ctr
(Southampton Inst)

Hook Lake

Solent Court
Farm

05

Hamble Spit

Nature
Reserve

HOOK PARK RD

Solent
Court

Solent Way

Hook
Park

SOLENT DR

COMES LA

Workman's Lane

CHILLING LA

3

04

Southampton Water

Solent Breezes
Caravan Site

2

02

Calshot

P

Stanswood Bay

P

B3053

03

Hillhead

01   **48**   **49**

Lifeboat
Sta

Pier

1

Calshot Castle

Nature
Reserve

Calshot
Activities
Ctr

02

48   **A**   **49**   **B**   **50**   **C**

151

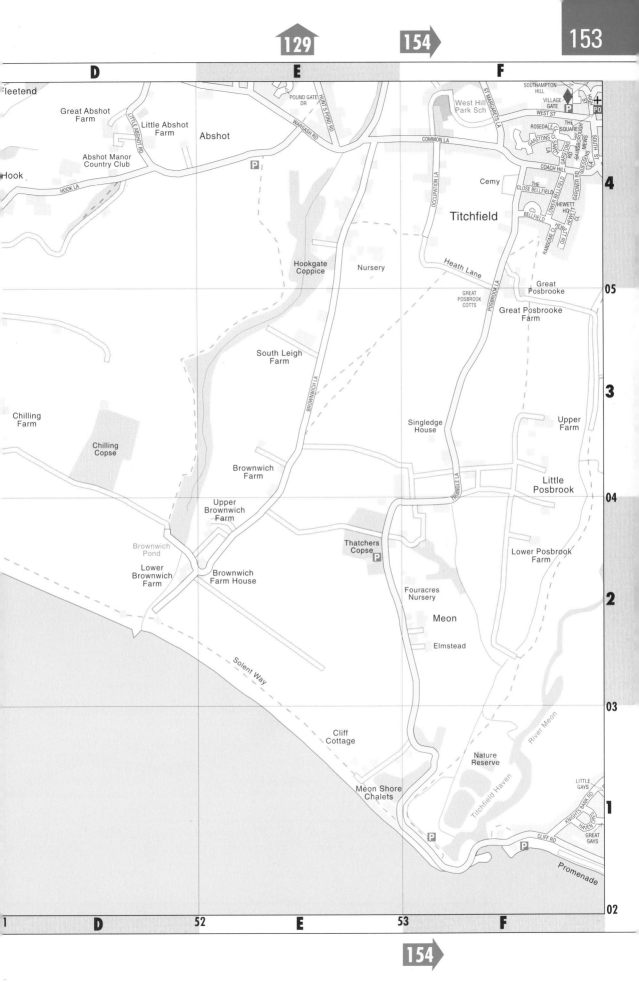

Fleetend

Great Abshot
Farm

Little Abshot
Farm

Abshot

Abshot Manor
Country Club

Hook

HOOK LA

LITTLE ABSHOT RD

WARSASH RD

POUND GATE DR

HUNT'S POND RD

COMMON LA

West Hill
Park Sch

SOUTHAMPTON
HILL

WEST ST

ST MARGARET'S LA

WEST HILL
GATE

VILLAGE
GATE

THE
SQUARE

ROSEDALE CL

GARSTONS CL

GARSTONS
RD

GAINSBOROUGH
MEWS

GARDNER RD

GEESENS
LA

SOUTH ST

HIGH ST

PO

Cemy

THE
CLOSE BELLFIELD

Hookgate
Coppice

Nursery

COACH HILL

Titchfield

Heath Lane

LOWER BELLFIELD

RANSOME RD

HEWETT
RD

HEWETT
CL

BELLFIELD

HEWETT
HO

4

Great
Posbrooke

GREAT
POSBROOK
COTTS

Great Posbrooke
Farm

05

South Leigh
Farm

BROWNWICH LA

POSBROOK LA

Singledge
House

Upper
Farm

3

Chilling
Farm

Chilling
Copse

Brownwich
Farm

Upper
Brownwich
Farm

TRIANGLE LA

Little
Posbrook

04

Brownwich
Pond

Lower
Brownwich
Farm

Brownwich
Farm House

Thatchers
Copse

Fouracres
Nursery

Lower Posbrook
Farm

Meon

2

Solent Way

Elmstead

03

Cliff
Cottage

Nature
Reserve

River Meon

Meon Shore
Chalets

Titchfield Haven

LITTLE
GAYS

1

KNIGHTS BANK RD

HAVEN

GREAT
GAYS

CLIFF RD

Promenade

02

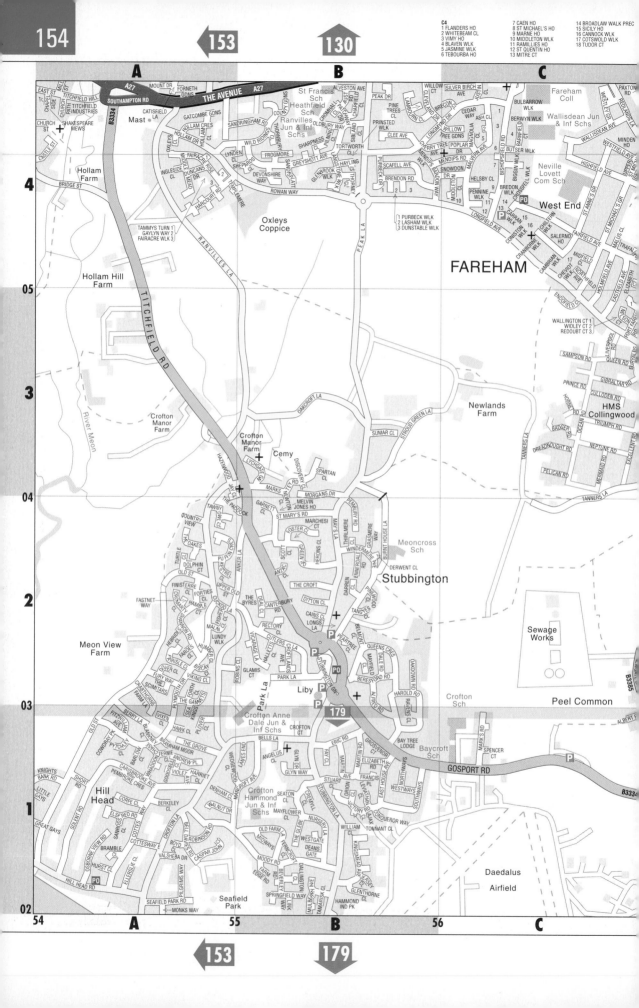

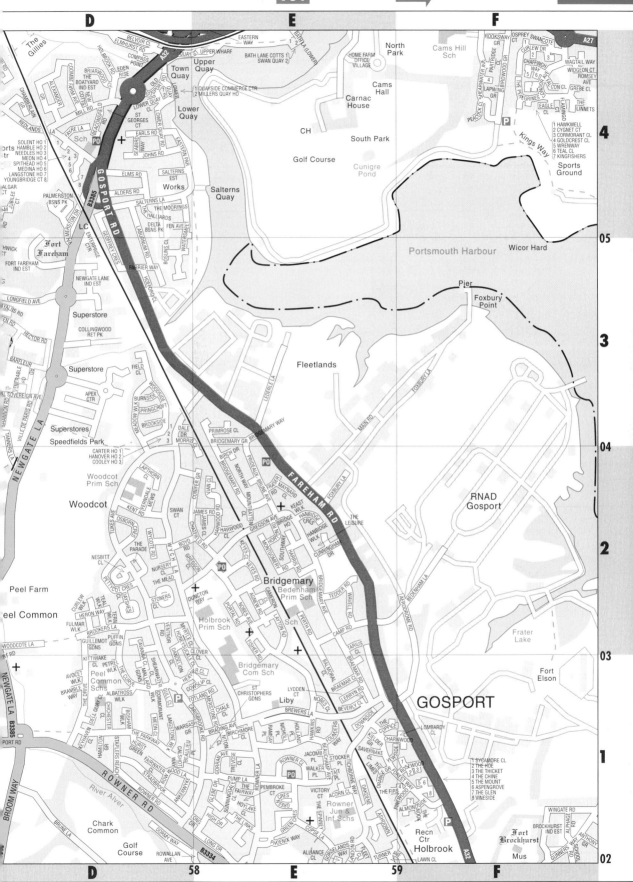

155
132

A **B** **C**

Crem

SIMPSON CL

WINNHAM DR

SEVERN CL

THE MARKET

ROCKINGHAM WAY

BOXWOOD CL

BOXWOOD DR

DORE AVE

DOORE AVE

THE HILLWAY

HILL RD

KELVIN GR

JUBILEE AVE

ALLAWAY AVE

CONNAUGHT LA

Westfield Jun Sch

King Richard Sch

A27

PORTCHESTER RD

Cornaway Bridge

Red Barn Cty Prim Sch

THE CROSSWAY

Portchester Sta

PORTSDOWN

Saxon Shore Inf Sch

CONNAUGHT LA

SHOREHAVEN

FARMLA

ROMSEY AVE

BEAULIEU

ASHTEAD CL

THE QUEENSWAY

THE CLOSE

THE KINGSWAY

THE FAIRWAY

THE DOWNSWAY

ST HELENA WAY

ST JAMES RD

STATION RD

NEW TOWN

GARDEN CT

MURRILLS EST

NEELANDS GR

EDGEFIELD GR

COLTSMEAD

HATHERLEY CRES

WINNHAM DR 1
TRENT WLK 2
AVON WLK 3
MERROW CL 4
RUDGEWICK CL 5
STONELEIGH CL 6

QUINTRELL AVE

Wicor Prim Sch

HATHERLEY DR

WEST ST

EAST ST

SOUTHAMPTON RD

4

CORNAWAY LA

NELSON AVE

SINODS

WHITEHAVEN

WESTLAND GR

Liby

WEST ST

NEW PAR

THE LEAWAY

ST HELENA WAY

THE KEEP

CASTLE TRAD EST

HAMILTON RD

1 PRIORY CT
2 PARRY CL
3 HOPKINS CL
4 ELGAR CL
5 SULLIVAN CL

Portchester

BRENCHLEY CL

CENTRAL RD

KENYA RD

JOHN AVE

ALLENBY GR

VINCENT GR

FROBISHER GR

KING GEORGE RD

PRIORY

RUSSELL BLDGS

QUEEN MARY RD

SUNNINGDALE RD

ASSHETON CT

CRANLEIGH RD

ORCHARD GR

SAMPORT

SEAFIELD RD

WELLINGTON GR

CLIVE GR

SHRUBBERY LA

Portchester Com Sch

CASTLE GR

MYRTLE AVE

CASTLE ST

COW LA

Castle Prim Sch

05

Wicor Farm

SESSIONS

SSHG

TATTERSHALL CRES

GATE HOUSE RD

TATTERSHALL CRES

WICOR MILL LA

FOXBURY GR

NORGETT WAY

CORAL CL

SEAWAY GR

MARINA GR

COPPINS GR

KENT GR

GROVE AVE

WHITE HART LA

1 MARLBOROUGH GR
2 GLADSTONE GDNS

OLIVE GR

NEVILLE CRES

EDGAR CRES

COOPER GR

WINDSOR RD

YORK GDNS

Castle St E GR

Wicor Path

WATERSIDE LA

Wicor Path

MORAUNT DR

ALBION CL

AUDRET CL

Works

KILWICH WAY

WINDMILL GR

HARBOUR VIEW

Kings Way

KILWICH WAY

COPPINS GR

MERTON CRES

MERTON GR

ROMAN GR

WESTBROOK

BAYLY AVE

BENHAM GR

WOTHAM

DENVILLE AVE

CASTLE GR

WICOR PATH

Cemy

HOSPITAL LA

CHURCH RD

Portchester Castl
and remains of
ROMAN FORT

3

ALTON GR

LANSDOWN AVE

LONSDALE AVE

KENWOOD RD

WEBB RD

BEACHWAY

04

Pewit Island

2

Portsmouth Harbour

03

RNAD Gosport

1

GUNNERS

HACKETT WAY

BLACKTHORN DR

WANDESFORD PL

FRATER LA

QUAY LA

ANTHONY GR

RICHARD GR

PARKER CL

STANLEY CL

NAISH

ORCHARD CL

CHESTNUT WLK

02

60 | A | 61 | B | 62 | C

D4
1 PADDOCK WLK
2 WATERSEDGE RD
3 DELLFIELD CL
4 BELNEY HO
5 WINDERMERE HO
6 PAULSGROVE ENT CTR

E4
1 ARTILLERY CL
2 DOWNTON HO
3 COTSWOLD HO
4 MELLOR CL
5 MALDON RD
6 HADLEIGH RD

7 HOCKLEY CL
8 PEBMARSH RD
9 WYMERING MANOR CL
10 BLACKWATER CL

F4
1 GLEBEFIELD GDNS
2 TANKERTON CT

F4
3 DYMCHURCH HO
4 NEPTUNE HO
5 MALLOW CL
6 ELIZABETH CT
7 STUART CT
8 TUDOR CT

F4
9 WINDSOR CT
10 ODEON BLDGS
11 CHIPSTEAD RD
12 CHIPSTEAD HO
13 NORTHERN BLDGS
14 ALDROKE ST

15 BEATRICE MEWS
16 ORFORD CT
17 GLENLEIGH CT
18 GLENLEIGH AVE
19 MEGAN CT
20 SELWYN CT
21 VINE CT

133   158   157

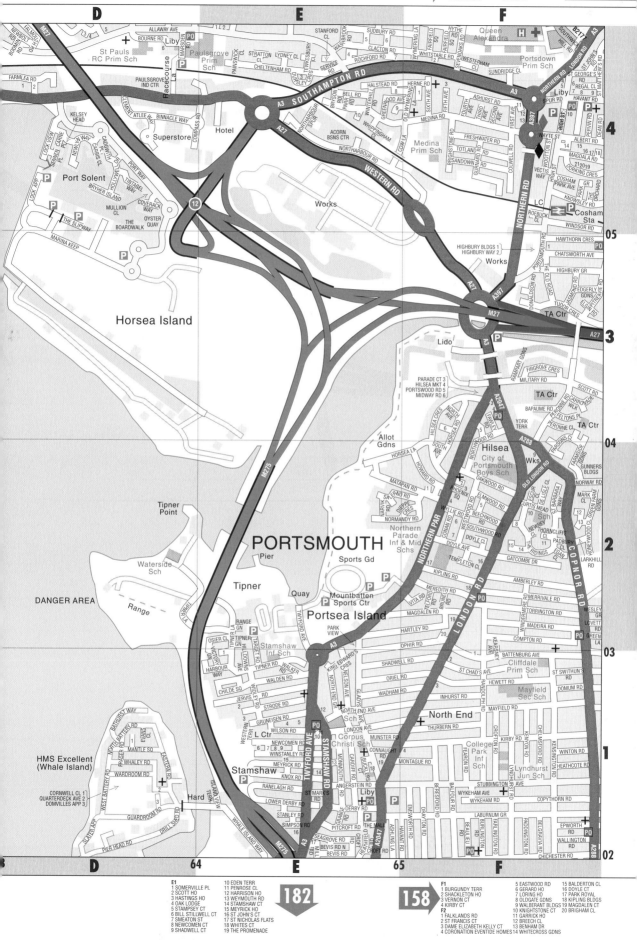

182   158

E1
1 SOMERVILLE PL
2 SCOTT HO
3 HASTINGS HO
4 OAK LODGE
5 STAMPSEY CT
6 BILL STILLWELL CT
7 SMEATON ST
8 NEWCOMEN CT
9 SHADWELL CT
10 EDEN TERR
11 PENROSE CL
12 HARRISON HO
13 VERNON CT
14 STAMSHAW RD
15 MEYRICK HO
16 ST JOHN'S CT
17 ST NICHOLAS FLATS
18 WHITES CT
19 THE PROMENADE

F1
1 BURGUNDY TERR
2 SHACKLETON HO
3 VERNON CT
4 KIRBY CT
F2
1 FALKLANDS RD
2 ST FRANCIS CT
3 DAME ELIZABETH KELLY CT
4 CORONATION EVENTIDE HOMES

5 EASTWOOD RD
6 GERARD HO
7 LORING HO
8 OLDGATE GDNS
9 BERWERANT BLDGS
10 KNIGHTSTONE CT
11 GARRICK HO
12 BREECH CL
13 BENHAM DR
14 WHITECROSS GDNS

15 BALDERTON CL
16 DOYLE CT
17 PARK ROYAL
18 KIPLING BLDGS
19 MAGDALEN CT
20 BRIGHAM CL

158

A4
1 WALBERTON CT
2 DOMEY CT
3 PARK MANSIONS
4 WIDLEY CT

157 134

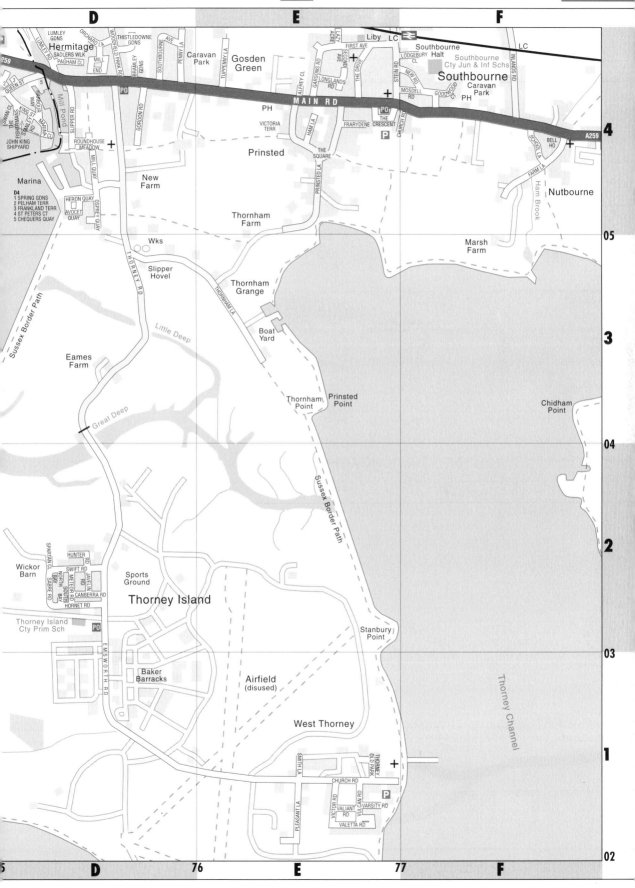

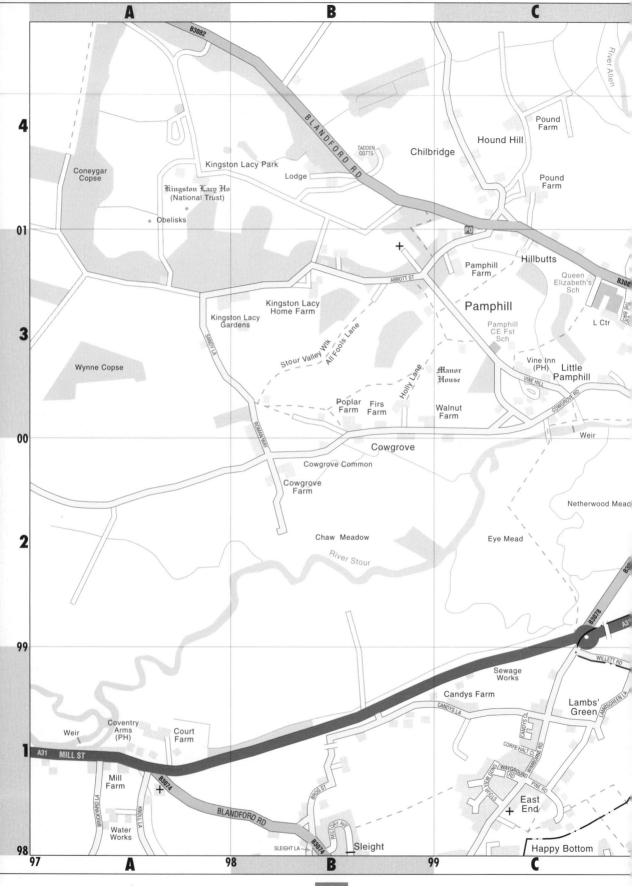

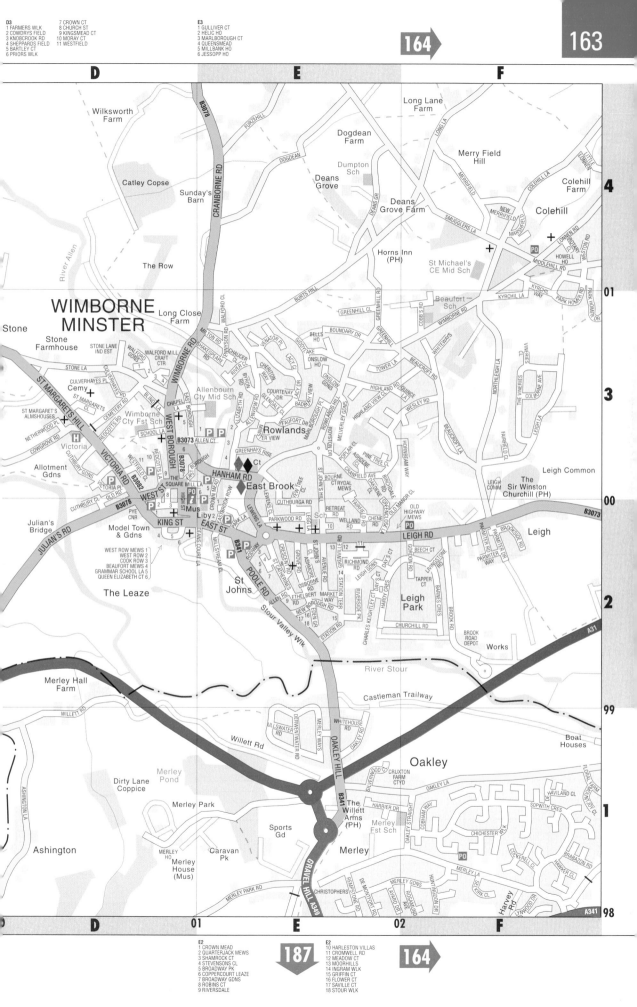

163

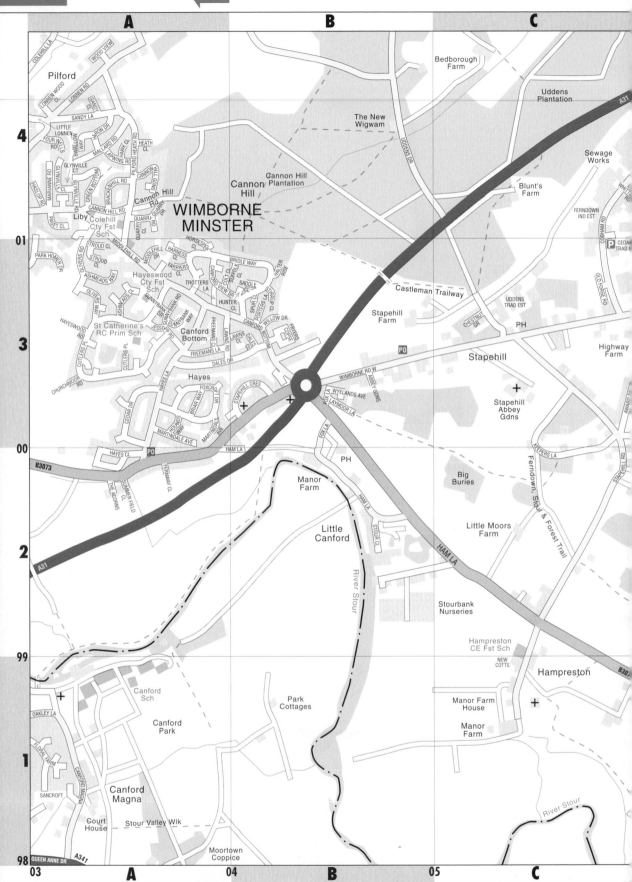

163

188

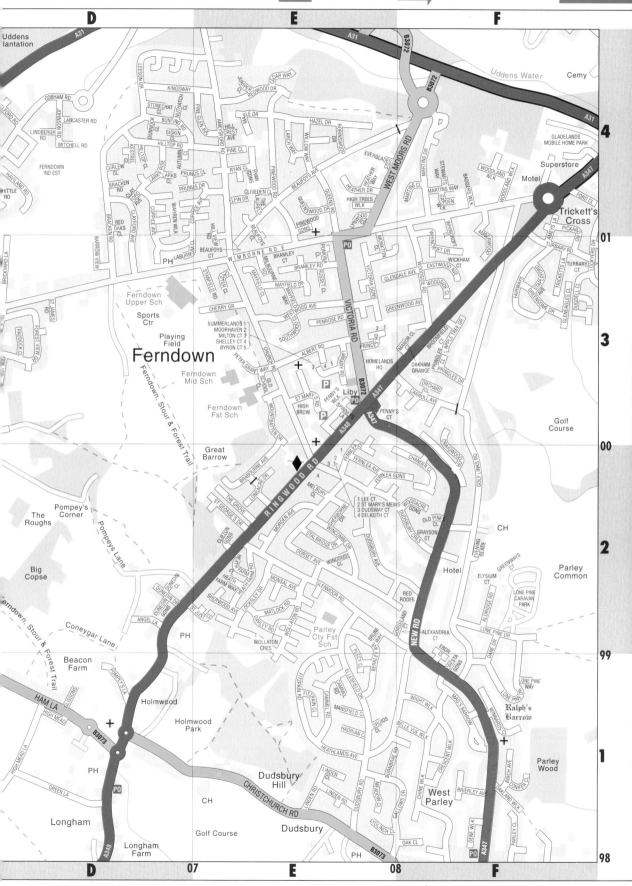

165
139

A   B   C

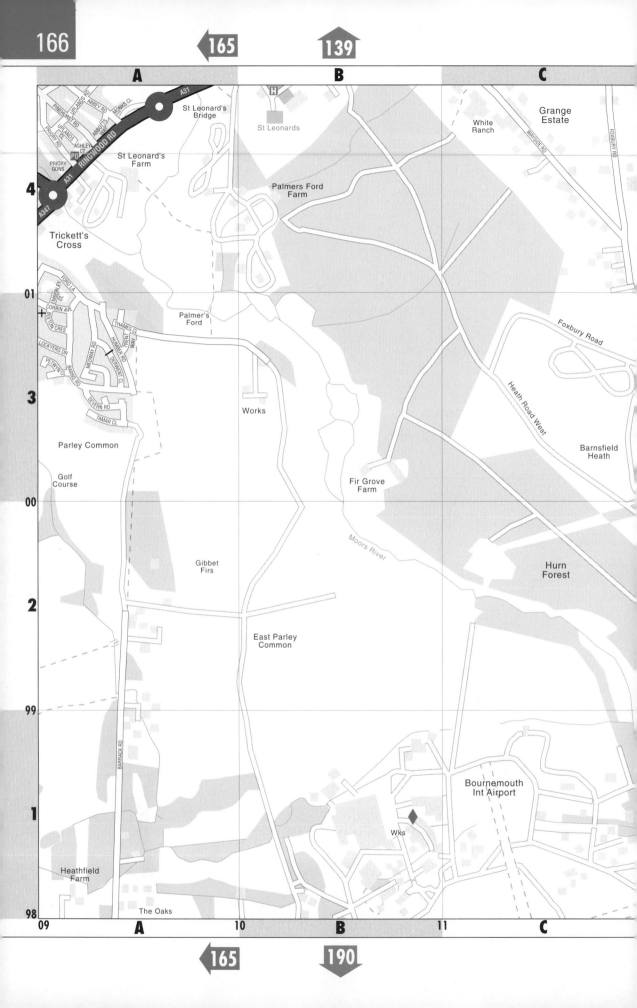

A31

St Leonard's Bridge

St Leonards

H

Grange Estate

White Ranch

FOXBURY RD

WAYSIDE RD

UPLANDS RD
ABBEY RD
MONKS CL
PINEHURST RD
UPLANDS
PRIORY RD
ASHLEY CT
ABBOTS
RINGWOOD RD
PO
St Leonard's Farm
Palmers Ford Farm
A347
PRIORY GDNS
A31

4

Trickett's Cross

01

+
AMBERLEY
FORD LA
CORBIN AVE
BOLTON CRES
LOCKYERS DR
PELWYN CL
BARNS RD
MEDWAY RD
HUMBER RD
THAMES CL
TRENT WAY
DERWENT CL
Palmer's Ford

Foxbury Road

3

SEVERN RD
TAMAR CL

Works

Heath Road West

Barnsfield Heath

Parley Common

Golf Course

Fir Grove Farm

00

Gibbet Firs

Moors River

Hurn Forest

2

East Parley Common

99

BARRACK RD

1

Bournemouth Int Airport

Wks

Heathfield Farm

98

The Oaks

09   A   10   B   11   C

165
190

167
141

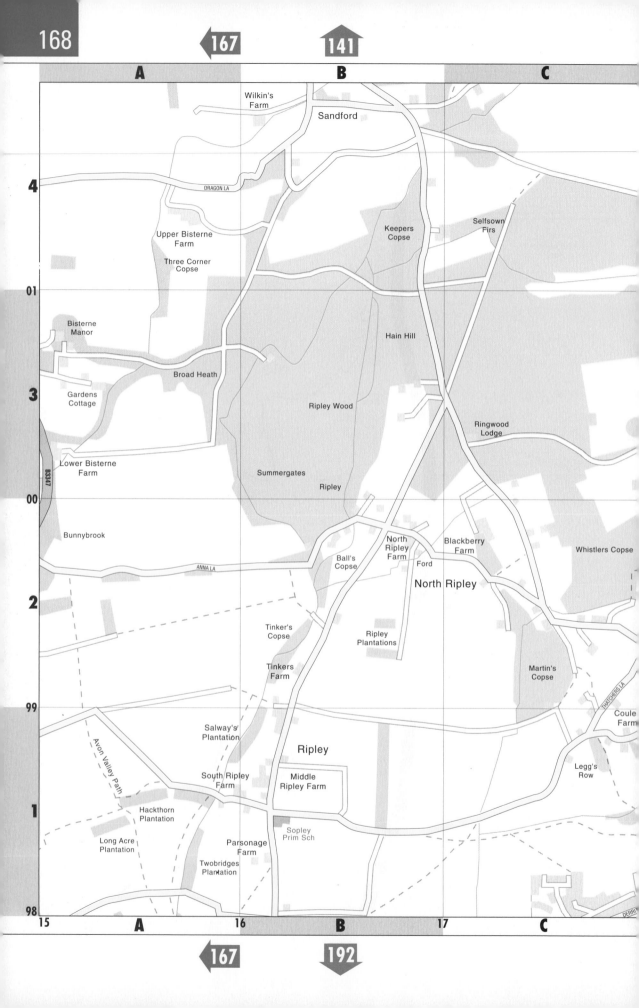

A B C

Wilkin's Farm

Sandford

4

DRAGON LA

Keepers Copse

Selfsown Firs

Upper Bisterne Farm

Three Corner Copse

01

Bisterne Manor

Hain Hill

Broad Heath

3

Gardens Cottage

Ripley Wood

Ringwood Lodge

B3347

Lower Bisterne Farm

Summergates

Ripley

00

Bunnybrook

North Ripley Farm

Blackberry Farm

Whistlers Copse

ANNA LA

Ball's Copse

Ford

North Ripley

2

Tinker's Copse

Ripley Plantations

Martin's Copse

Tinkers Farm

THATCHERS LA

99

Coule Farm

Salway's Plantation

Avon Valley Path

Ripley

Legg's Row

South Ripley Farm

Middle Ripley Farm

1

Hackthorn Plantation

Sopley Prim Sch

Long Acre Plantation

Parsonage Farm

Twobridges Plantation

DERRI

98

15 A 16 B 17 C

D
E
F

4

01

Slap Bottom

Burbush Hill

Whitten
Pond

Dur Hill Inclosure
Dur Hill Down

Bisterne Common

Lugden Bottom

Whitten Bottom

Avon
Clump
Whitefield
Hill

3

Avon
Tyrell

Hillside
Farm

White
Lodge

Thorney Hill
Holms

Home
Farm

CROSS
WAYS

Magpie Green

00

Black Firs

Devils Den

Shirley Common

Pigsty Hill

Thorneywood
Farm

2

North
Braggers

Lane End
Farm
Thorneywood

King
Braggers

Thorney
Hill

Purlieu

Shirley
House

Hill Farm

99

Shirley Farm

Prink's
Wood

Howen
Copse

Nature
Reserve

Hill Farm

Shirley

Stibb's Copse

Tothill

Jopps
Plantation

1

Burnt House
Farm

Poors Common

Poors Copse

Heathfield
Farm

New
Merryfield
Farm

MT
PLEASANT
DR

WEDGWOOD
GDNS

HEATHFIELD
HO

98

D
19
E
20
F

169
143

A

B

C

Holmsley Bog

Goatspen Plain

Clayhill Bottom

Scrape Bottom

4

Anthony's Bee Bottom

P

HOLMSLEY PASS

STATION RD

Scrape Rd

Wilverley Cottage

Holmsley Walk

Gravel Pit

P

01

Holmsley Ridge

Holmsley Lodge

Lodge Hill

The Old Station

3

Little Holmsley

Cardinal Hat

Holmsley Inclosure

Avon Water

Mill

P

Magpie Bottom

Great Hat

Hanging Shoot

Holmsley Toll House

00

Brownhill Inclosure

Pigsty Hat

Stony Moors

Wootton Copse Inclosure

2

Bell's Hat

Holmsley Caravan & Camp Site

B3058

P

Wootton Old Farm

BROWNHILL RD

WOOTTON FARM RD

WILVERLEY RD

Mast

P

RHINEFIELD RD

99

Little Wootton Inclosure

HOLMSLEY RD

Wattons Farm

Wootton Heath Farm

Plain Heath

FOREST RD

1

Manor Farm

NORTH DR

B30

Valesmoo Farm

LYNDHURST RD

Forest Lodge

A35

Willie's Holms

Portnall's Farm

98

Hole Copse

21

A

22

B

23

C

194

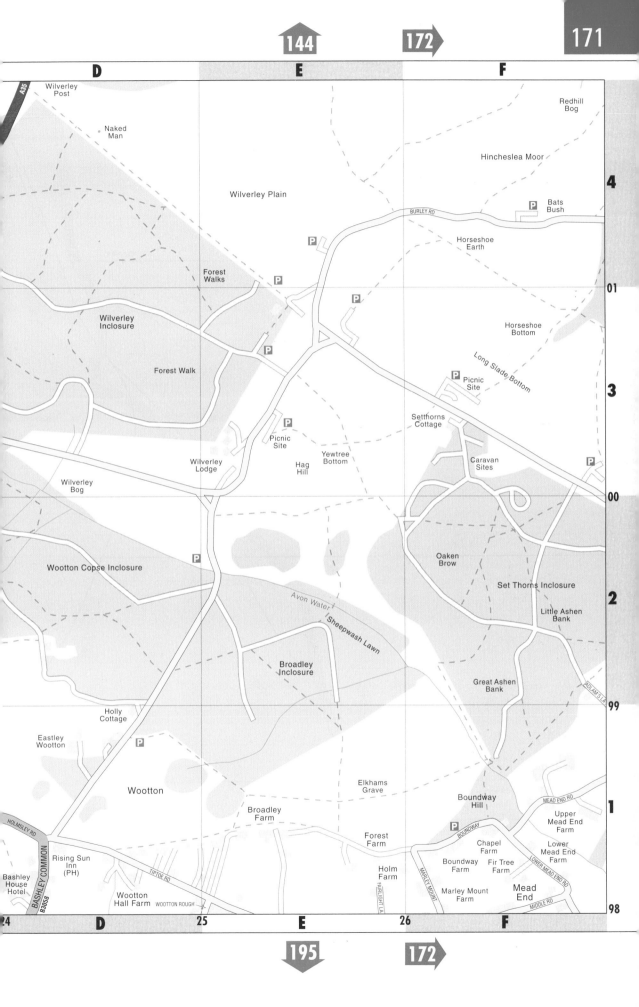

A35

Wilverley
Post

Naked
Man

Redhill
Bog

Hincheslea Moor

Wilverley Plain

4

BURLEY RD

P   Bats
Bush

Horseshoe
Earth

Forest
Walks

P

P

01

Wilverley
Inclosure

P

Horseshoe
Bottom

Long Slade Bottom

Forest Walk

P   Picnic
Site

3

Setthorns
Cottage

P

Picnic
Site

Caravan
Sites

P

Wilverley
Lodge

Hag
Hill

Yewtree
Bottom

Wilverley
Bog

00

P

Oaken
Brow

Wootton Copse Inclosure

Set Thorns Inclosure

Avon Water

Little Ashen
Bank

2

Sheepwash Lawn

Broadley
Inclosure

Great Ashen
Bank

ADLAM'S LA

99

Holly
Cottage

Eastley
Wootton

P

Wootton

Elkhams
Grave

Boundway
Hill

MEAD END RD

1

HOLMSLEY RD

Broadley
Farm

Upper
Mead End
Farm

P

Boundway

Chapel
Farm

Lower
Mead End
Farm

Rising Sun
Inn
(PH)

Forest
Farm

Boundway
Farm

Fir Tree
Farm

LOWER MEAD END RD

Bashley
House
Hotel

Holm
Farm

MARLEY MOUNT

Mead
End

BASHLEY COMMON

B3058

TIPTOE RD

Wootton
Hall Farm

WOOTTON ROUGH

Marley Mount
Farm

FAIRLIGHT LA

MIDDLE RD

98

A   **B**   **C**

4

01

3

00

2

99

1

98

White Moor

Furzey
Cottage

Pound
Farm

Brockenhurst
CE Prim Sch
Brookley Farm

RAILWAY TERR 1
AVENUE RD 2

PARTRIDGE RD

HIGHWOOD RD

Highwood
PRU

TATTENHAM RD
THE
LAURELS

ADDISON
RD

B3055

Five Thorns Hill

BURLEY RD

Furzy
Hill

South
Weirs

SOUTH WEIRS

Worthys
Farm

Westbeams
Stables

COLLYERS
RD

WOODLANDS
RD

SWAY RD

Brokenhurst
Copse

Trenley Lawn

Farm
Cottage

CH

Brokenhurst Manor
Golf Club

TILLEBARN LA

Hincheslea Wood

Blackhamsley
House

Golf Course

Lymington
Junction

Latchmoor
House

Hincheslea Bog

Blackhamsley
Hill

Cater's Cottage

B3055

Three
Beech
Bottom

Setley Plain

Marlpit
Oak

Milking Pound Bottom

Cemy

QUARR
HO

BUILDOWNE WLK

MANCHESTER RD

ISLAND
VIEW

BOND
RD

KITCHENS RD

OXFORD
TERR

JORDANS LA

LITTLE
BURN

Widden Bottom

BRIGHTON RD

HAWTHORN
DR

RHINERS
CL

GILPIN HILL

LD CL

CURRANT WAY

OAKENBROW

THE
CLOSE

STAG
FORD
RISE

MIDDLE
RD

HIGHFIELD RD

ANDERWOOD DR

WIDDEN CL

HIGHFIELD
GDNS

NORMANDY
CL

MEAD END RD

CRUSE CL

HYDE CL

SET THORNS RD

CRITTAL

CENTENARY CL

BADGERS
CL

CHURCH LA

ST JAMES

DURNSTOWN

PH

Durns Town

PITMORE LA

SHIRLEY HOLMS

HERON

Sway
St Luke's
CE Prim Sch

WESTBEAMS RD

BACK LA

1

Rushcroft
Farm

Sway Sta

PO
STATION RD

ROWAN CL

HOLLIES
CL

Sway

SWAY PARK
IND EST

TEBOURBA
COTTS

BIRCHY HILL

B3055

OLD VICARAGE LA

COOMBE LA

CHAPEL LA

Little
Purley
Farm

Manor Farm

Hilltop

Eastwoods

P

27   **A**   28   **B**   29   **C**

D
E
F

4

01

3

00

2

99

1

A337

←LYMINGTON RD

Brockenhurst Sta

AVENUE RD
EAST BANK RD
WOODSIDE

Brockenhurst Park

Brockenhurst Park Stables

Perrywood Ironshill Inclosure

Furze Hill

Bakers Copse

Dilton

Tile Barn Farm

Dilton Copse

TILE BARN LA

CHURCH LA

Newlands Copse

Holly Bush Farm

Setley

Dawkins Bottom

Roydon Manor

Dilton Gardens

The Filly Inn

Setley Farm

Calveslease Copse

Setley Common

Lymington River

Howe Copse

Blazemore Farm

SANDY DOWN

Sandy Down

Heywood Farm

HURSTLY LA

COBBLERS CNR

LOWER SANDY DOWN LA

The Old Mill House

Race Plain

Heywood Manor

Rodlease Rough

The Hobler (PH)

CHURCH LA

Battramsley Lodge

ROYDEN LA

RODLEASE LA

Boldre Grange

Great Oaks Farm

Dunsford Farm

Rodlease House

Slade Farm

JEALOUS LA

Battramsley

Boldre

Pilley

William Gilpin CE Prim Sch

GILPIN CL

Shirley Holms

SHIRLEY HOLMS

Battramsley Farm

BATTRAMSLEY CROSS

A331

The Red Lion (PH)

Hill House Sch

BOLDRE LA

SWAY LOW LA

Pilley Hill

PILLEY HILL

SCHOOL LA

Fleur-de-lys Inn

BURNT HOUSE LA

HUDSON DAVIES CL

Passford Water

Battramsley House

ROPE HILL

TWEED LA

0

D

31

E

32

F

98

A **B** **C**

Stockley
Inclosure

Stockley
Cottage

B3055

Hawkhill
Inclosure

B305

Lodge Heath

P

P

4

Dilton Common

01

Dilton
Farm

Hatchet Moor

Beaulieu Heath

P

3

Little Dilton
Farm

Two Bridges
Bottom

B305

00

Sheffield
Copse

Greenmoor

Deep Moor

2

Whitemoor
Rough

Crockford Stream

P

Crockford Bridge

99

Allot
Gdns

Lower Crockford Bottom

P

Pilley
Bailey

Fords

WOOD HOUSE LA

P

Bull
Hill

Norley Inclosure

Wormstall
Wood

1

PILLEY BAILEY

MAY LA

PILLEY GN

PILLEY ST

PD

LUCKY LA

JORDANS LA

HOLLY LA

BURNT HOUSE LA

Pilley

BULL HILL

P

Norley
Farm

98

WARBORNE LA

B3054

NORLEYWOOD RD

33 **A** **34** **B** **35** **C**

B3054

The Lodge

B3055

Hatchet Gate

Hazelcopse Farm

HATCHET LA

Bunkers Hill

Jarvis's Copse

4

Hatchet Pond

P

Hatchet Mill

MASSEYS LA

Swinesleys Farm

Beufre Farm

P

HEATH LA

WITHEBS LA

PAGES LA

GAZA AVE

MATTHEWS LA

EAST BOLDRE RD

SNEVHS LEASE

CHAPEL LA

WALLACE LA

WARTON PL

PO

Grindingstone Cottages

Cemy

01

Sewage Works

Knights Copse

STRANBERRY FIELDS

CHURCH LA

NEW INN LA

NEW INN COTTS

CRIPPLE GATE LA

High Wood

3

Bagshot Moor

The Turfcutters Arms (PH)

Newhouse Farm

East Boldre

00

Peaked Bottom

Gravelly Copse

Lodge Farm

2

Peaked Hill

Newhouse Copse

Harepath

Newlands Cottage

99

Wormstall Hill

Newlands Plantation

Longmead Copse

Horsebush Bottom

Newlands

Ford

Broomhill Farm

Broom Hill

Bergerie Rough

1

Upper Beckheath Plantation

Horsemoor Copse

98

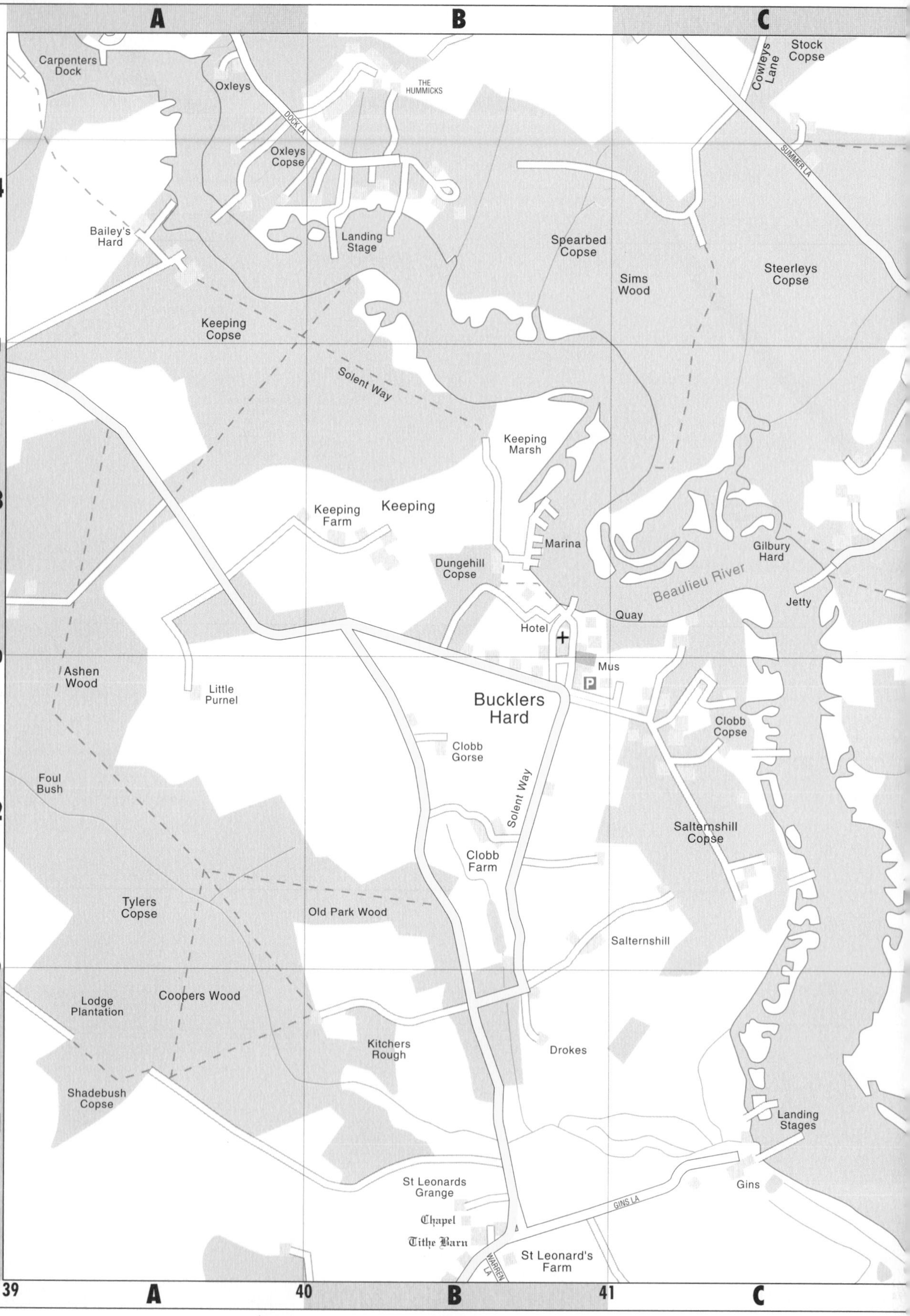

175
149

A **B** **C**

Carpenters Dock

Oxleys

THE HUMMICKS

Stock Copse

Cowleys Lane

Oxleys Copse

DOCK LA

SUMMER LA

4

Bailey's Hard

Landing Stage

Spearbed Copse

Sims Wood

Steerleys Copse

Keeping Copse

01

Solent Way

Keeping Marsh

3

Keeping Farm

Keeping

Marina

Gilbury Hard

Dungehill Copse

Beaulieu River

Jetty

Quay

Hotel

Mus

00

Ashen Wood

Little Purnel

P

Bucklers Hard

Clobb Copse

Clobb Gorse

Foul Bush

Solent Way

Salternshill Copse

2

Clobb Farm

Tylers Copse

Old Park Wood

Salternshill

99

Coopers Wood

Lodge Plantation

Kitchers Rough

Drokes

Shadebush Copse

Landing Stages

1

Gins

St Leonards Grange

GINS LA

Chapel

Tithe Barn

WARREN LA

St Leonard's Farm

98

39 **A** 40 **B** 41 **C**

D

Row Down

KING'S COPSE RD

East Stock
Copse

Kings Copse
Inclosure

Meadow Close
Copse

Gatewood
Bridge

P

Cemy

Ford

Blackwell
Common

E

WHEELERS
WLK

JANES CL

HAMPTON
GDNS

HAMPTON CL

NORTHAMPTON LA

WHITEHAVEN
HOME PK

HOLLY RD

CHAPEL LA

HAMPTON LA

WALKER'S LANE N

WESSEX CL
VIKING

CEDRIC CL
SAXON RD

DANE CL

NORMAN RD

WALKER'S

Blackfield
Recn
Gd

THORNBURY AVE

WALKER'S LANE S

GREEN LA

4

Gatewood Farm
House

Gatewood Hill

THE G LADE

STROUD
WAY CL

KING'S PCE

LEA RD

CHALEWOOD RD

NICHOLAS RD

ST FRANCIS RD

MOPLEY CL

MOPLEY

CLARE GDNS

Langley

FOREST GATE

01

Nursery

CHARNWOOD

FORESTERS
GATE

ROWLAND
WAY

BERNWOOD

SLEY
GR

WYCHWOOD DR

LANGLEY
LODGE
GDNS

HOME FARM LA

FORGE RD

1 THE MEWS
2 FOXY PADDOCK
3 FOXLANDS
4 FOX'S WLK
5 FOXGLADE

PH

Yard Wood

SUMMER LA

Main Drive

Exbury
Bridge

Nursery

Exbury
Gdns

CRESCENT
COTTS

NEW
COTTS

WEST COMMON

WEST COMMON

HOMER
MOBILE HOME PARK

West Common

Dark Water

LEPE RD

Whitefield
Farm

3

Witchers
Copse

Exbury
House

PO

Recn Grd

Exbury

Chale
Wood

East
Wood

Whitefield
Rough

St Mary's
Spring

Upper
Exbury

00

East Hill
Farm

Salterns
Copse

The
Green

2

Aldermoor

Haxland
Pits

Lepe
Farm

Pophams
Wood

Grassy
Copse

The
Moor

Lower Exbury
House

Three
Stones

Little Haxland
Copse

99

Inchmery
House

Lower Exbury

Quay

Lepe
House

Groynes

1

98

42   D   43   E   44   F

A B C

Tom's Down

Mopley Pond

Badminston Common

B3053

Ower La

Ower Farm

Ower

Solent View

PO

Calshot Cl

Calshot

The Flying Boat (PH)

Bus Dro

Elmfield La

Cristan Cl

Castle La

B3053

B3053

Hillhead

4

Mopley

Dean's Bridge

North Solent Nature Reserve

Sprat's Down

Spratsdown Plantation

Eaglehurst

01

King's Rew Copse

Stanswood Common

Stanswood Rd

Stanswood Farm

Stanswood

Nelson's Place

3

Bourne Gap

Stanswood Bay

00

Stone Farm Cottages

Cadland House

Stanswood Copse

Allwoods Copse

2

Stone

Dark Water

Lepe Rd

Stone Farm

Pits Copse

99

Lepe

COASTGUARD COTTS

P

IRB Sta (Summer only)

P

Stansore Point

Stanswood Bay

1

P

Lepe Country Park

Stone Point

98

45

A

46

B

47

C

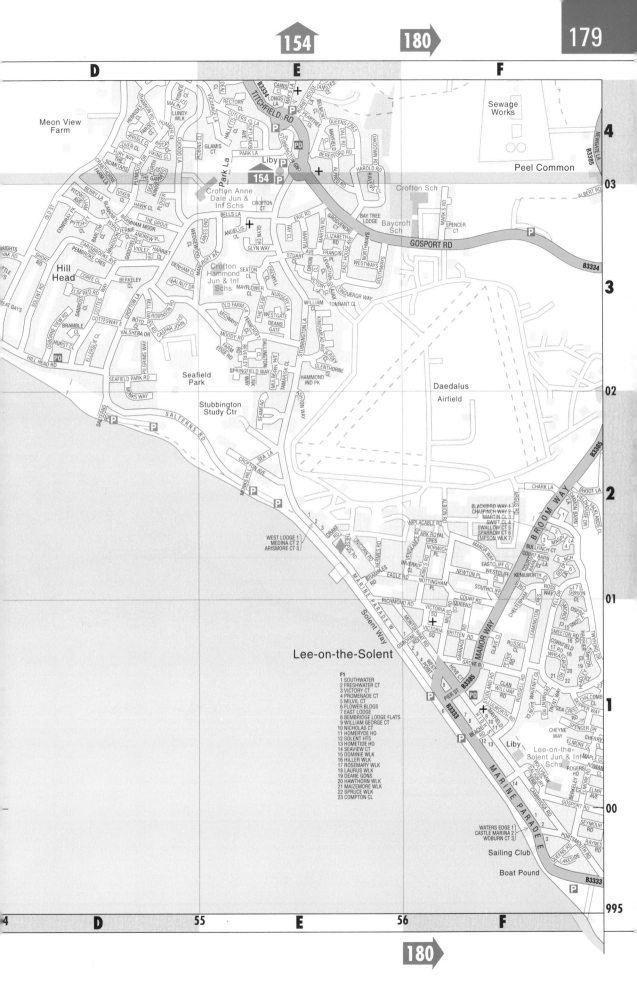

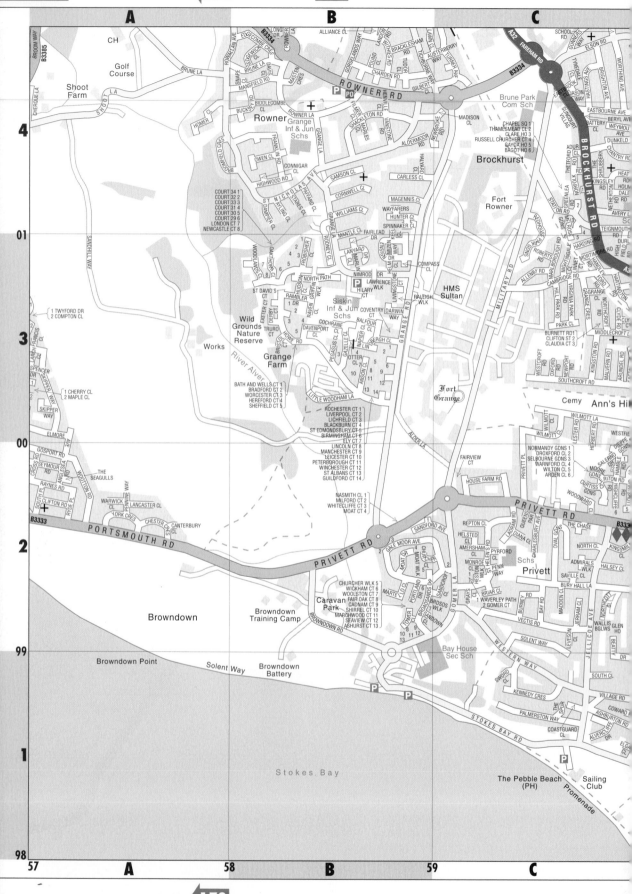

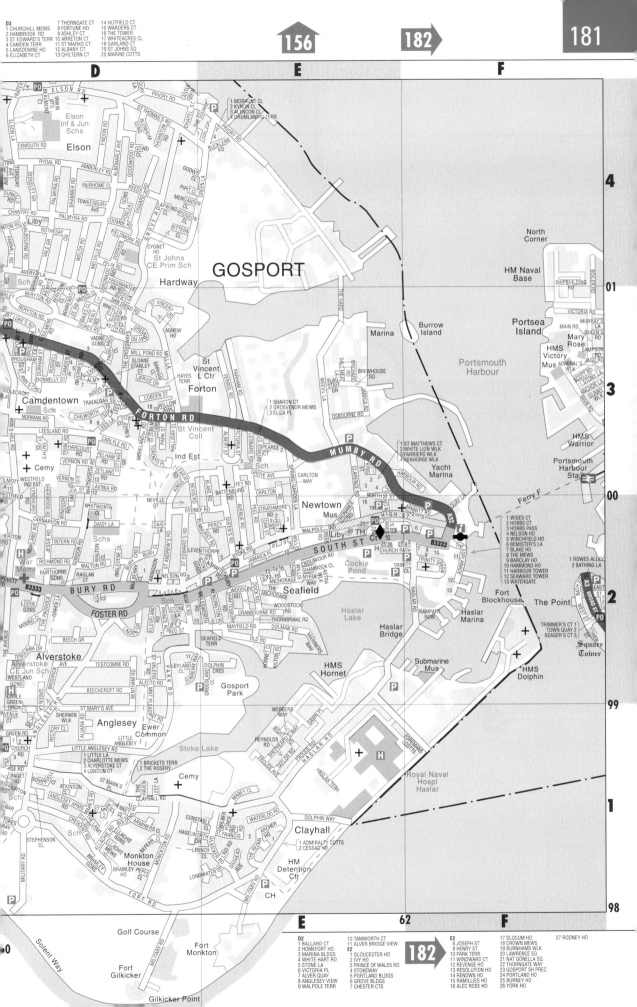

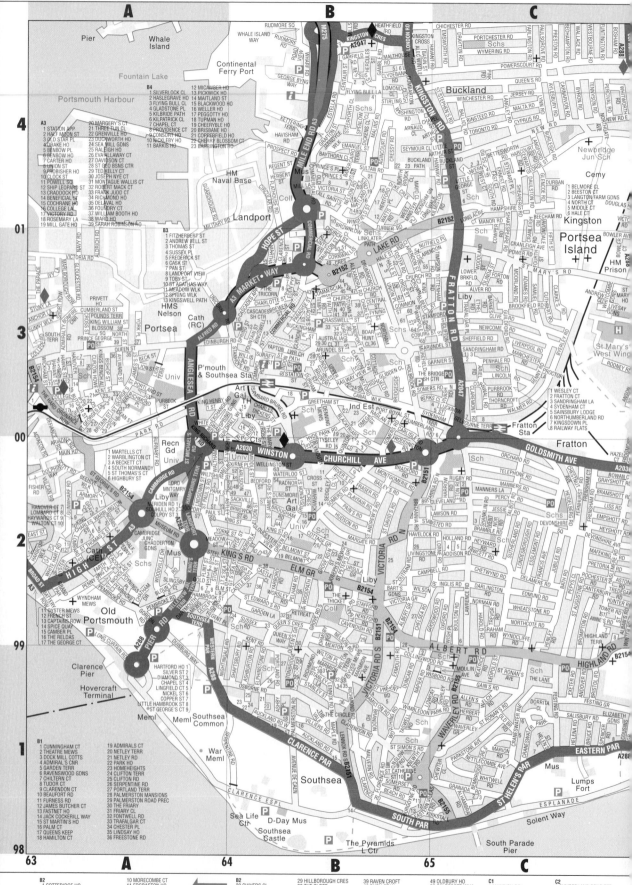

B3
14 ARUNDELWAY SH ARC
15 GUILDHALL SQ
16 DOROTHY DYMOND ST
17 HARRY LAW HALL
18 DUGALD DRUMMOND ST
19 WILMCOTE HO

20 WILMCOTE GDNS
21 OMEGA HO
22 MAXSTOKE CL
23 RELWAL HO
24 TADHURST ST
25 WINDSOR HO
26 DALE PARK HO

27 EAST SURREY ST
28 ANGMERING HO
29 CANBERRA HO
30 MELBOURNE HO
31 PERTH HO
32 DARWIN HO
33 SYDNEY HO

34 SETTLERS CL
35 DURBAN HO
36 NICHOLSON GDNS
37 CANFIELD HO
38 FAREHAM HO
39 HORNDEAN HO
40 BURSLEDON HO

157

B3
41 PETERSFIELD HO
42 CHALTON HO
43 SPICER ST
44 CATISFIELD HO
45 TITCHFIELD HO
46 BLENDWORTH HO

47 DROXFORD HO
48 ROGATE HO
49 CORNWALLIS HO
50 LOWER WINGFIELD ST
51 FAWCETT RD
52 CHEKELIA HO
53 SELHURST HO

54 REIGATE HO
55 REDHILL HO
56 BOXGROVE HO
57 MIDHURST HO
58 CROWN CT
59 KING ALBERT ST
60 FITZROY WLK

61 LORDS CT
62 HARLEY WLK
63 WIMPOLE CT
64 WIGMORE CT
65 LITTLE COBURG ST

B2
1 COTTERIDGE HO
2 FORBURY RD
3 BLACKFRIARS CL
4 ARTHUR POPE HO
5 HANDSWORTH HO
6 LADYWOOD HO
7 HYDE PARK RD
8 ALDWELL ST
9 LOWER FORBURY RD

10 MORECOMBE CT
11 EDGBASTON HO
12 TIPTON HO
13 GROSVENOR HO
14 CANNOCK LWR
15 LOUIS FLAGG HO
16 FRANK MILES HO
17 HOMERISE HO
18 HOMESEA HO
19 ROSLYN HO

B2
20 CHIVERS CL
21 MILVERTON HO
22 HOMEGROVE HO
23 WINDSOR LA
24 EASTFIELDS
25 HEATHERLEY CT
26 BAYSWATER HO
27 KEYES CT

29 HILLBOROUGH CRES
30 THE CLOSE
31 GREYFRIARS CT
32 QUEEN'S PL
33 SUSSEX TERR
34 SUSSEX PL
35 WOODPATH HO
36 WILBERFORCE RD
37 PARK CT
38 BUSH HO

181

39 RAVEN CROFT
40 BUSH ST W
41 SOUTH ST
42 GLOUCESTER TERR
43 GLOUCESTER PL
44 OCKENDON CL
45 PRICE REGENT CT
46 ELDON CT
47 STRATFORD HO
48 ATHERSTONE WLK

49 OLDBURY HO
50 CALDECOTE HO
51 LONGBRIDGE HO
52 LEAMINGTON HO
53 PICTON HO
54 PONSONBY HO

C1
1 MANSION HO
2 MANSION CT
3 ROSTREVOR LA
4 CRANESWATER GATE
5 CRANESWATER MEWS
6 NORMAN CT
7 DOLPHIN CT
8 CRESTA CT

C2
1 CUMBERLAND BSNS CTR
2 PRIORY CT
3 EMBASSY CT
4 GRENVILLE RD
5 NORLAND RD
6 BRANDON CT
7 WHITE CLOUD PK
8 WHITE CLOUD PL

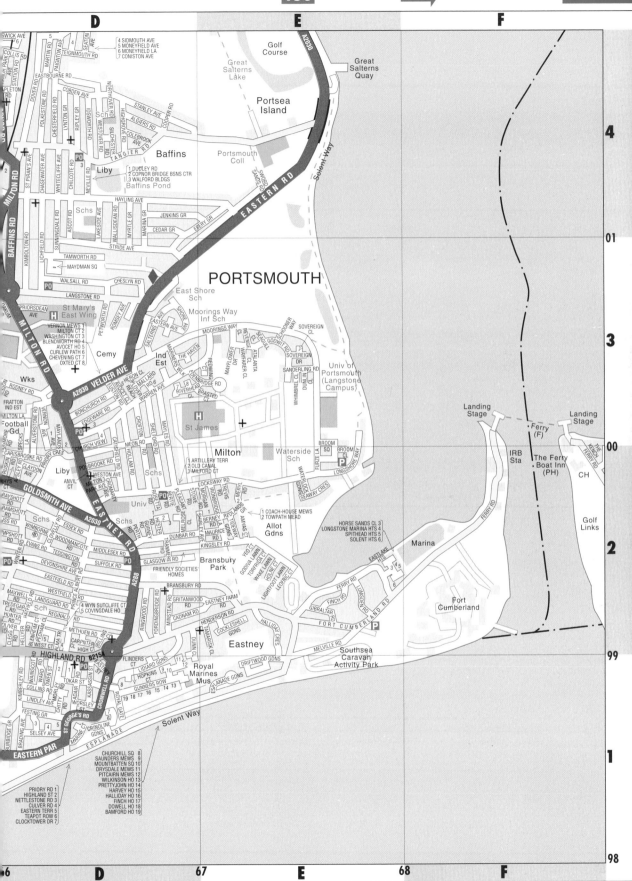

D E F

4

01

3

00

2

99

1

98

PORTSMOUTH

Golf Course

Great Salterns Lake

Great Salterns Quay

Portsea Island

Portsmouth Coll

Baffins

Liby

1 DUDLEY RD
2 COPNOR BRIDGE BSNS CTR
3 WALFORD BLDGS

Baffins Pond

4 SIDMOUTH AVE
5 MONEYFIELD AVE
6 MONEYFIELD LA
7 CONISTON AVE

HAYLING AVE

JENKINS GR

CEDAR GR

TAMWORTH RD

MAYDMAN SQ

WALSALL RD

LANGSTONE RD

PO

East Shore Sch

Moorings Way Inf Sch

St Mary's East Wing

H

VERNON MEWS 1
MILTON CT 2
WASHINGTON CT 3
BLENDWORTH RD 4
AVOCET HO 5
CURLEW PATH 6
CHEVENING CT 7
OXTED CT 8

Cemy

Ind Est

Sovereign CL

Sovereign DR

Moorings Way

The Haven

Wks

A2030 VELDER AVE

Football Gd

FRATTON IND EST

PO

H
St James

Liby

Univ

1 ARTILLERY TERR
2 OLD CANAL
3 MILFORD CT

Milton

Waterside Sch

P

Univ of Portsmouth (Langstone Campus)

Landing Stage

Landing Stage

Ferry (F)

IRB Sta

The Ferry Boat Inn (PH)

CH

GOLDSMITH AVE

Schs

Schs

PO

1 COACH-HOUSE MEWS
2 TOWPATH MEAD

Allot Gdns

HORSE SANDS CL 3
LONGSTONE MARINA HTS 4
SPITHEAD HTS 5
SOLENT HTS 6

Marina

Golf Links

Bransbury Park

Friendly Societies Homes

BRANSBURY RD

EASTNEY RD

Fort Cumberland

FORT CUMBERLAND RD

Eastney

EASTNEY FARM RD

P

HIGHLAND RD
B2154

PO

FLINDERS CT

Royal Marines Mus

GUNNERS ROW

Southsea Caravan Activity Park

ST GEORGE'S RD

Solent Way

ESPLANADE

EASTERN PAR

CHURCHILL SQ 8
SAUNDERS MEWS 9
MOUNTBATTEN SQ 10
DRYSDALE MEWS 11
PITCAIRN MEWS 12
WILKINSON HO 13
PRETTYJOHN HO 14
HARVEY HO 15
HALLIDAY HO 16
FINCH HO 17
DOWELL HO 18
BAMFORD HO 19

PRIORY RD 1
HIGHLAND ST 2
NETTLESTONE RD 3
CULVER RD 4
EASTERN TERR 5
TEAPOT ROW 6
CLOCKTOWER DR 7

A   B   C

DAW LA

WEST LA

A3022

Cam
Site

WOODLANDS LA

BRIGHTS LA

DENHILL CL

SALTMARSH LA

GARDENS
LA

HOWORTH LA

Higworth
Caravan Site

GLEBE CL

DOVER
CT

ATHERLEY

MANOR RD

Newtown

NORTH SHORE RD

CHARL
TON CL

GILBERT
MEAD

NEWTOWN
LA

SYCAMORE
DR

FAXHOMS REACH

Rook
Farm

THE
KENCH

Pier

FLINDERS WAY

STATION RD

PAGES WAY

SOUTHLEIGH
GR

The Kench

Sinah
Farm

Hotel

WARREN
CL

SINAH LA

PARK RD

PO

RICHMOND DR

RICHMOND CL

GRAYLAND
CL

JAMES
CL

SPINNAKER

LENSTER
GDNS

OLD HURDS

ST MARY'S RD

HILDEN CT

WALNUT
TREE C

BRIARWO

GREEN

OAKWON

Ferry Rd

HARBOUR RD

LIME GR

ST CATHERINE'S RD

ST AUBYN'S PATH

ST THOMAS AVE

STAUNTON AVE

West
Town

BENWELL CT

GARDEN CL

OAKWON

ELM CLOSE
ESTATE

Sinah Common

LINKS LA

ST
CATHERINES
CT

ST HELEN'S RD

FERNHURST CL

BACON LA

WINSTON
CL

HOLLOW LA

Golf Links

ST
GEORGES
CL

THE
GORSEWAY

Gorseway

WEST
MEAD

STAMFORD AVE

MAGPIE

GREEN LA

OLD
TIMBERS

13

WESTFIELD CT

VICTORIA AVE

Club
House

SEA FRONT

12

3

4

Hotel

A3023

ST JOHNS
CL

OLD
CENTURY

ORCHARD
CL

ALEXANDRA AVE

TUDOR CL

Gunner
Point

BAY VIEW
CT

5

NORFOLK CRES

10

11

8 9

BEACH RD

Westfield

PH

The Beach

CHICHESTER
AVE

South Hayling

BAY VIEW MEWS 1
WARD CT 2
STAMFORD LODGE 3
ROPLEY CT 4
NORFOLK MEWS 5
FAIRMEAD CT 6
OCEAN CT 7
NICHOLAS CT 8
PADWICK CT 9
ANNES CT 10
VICTORIA CT 11
MARK ANTHONY CT 12
WESTFIELD OAKS 13

Hayling Bay

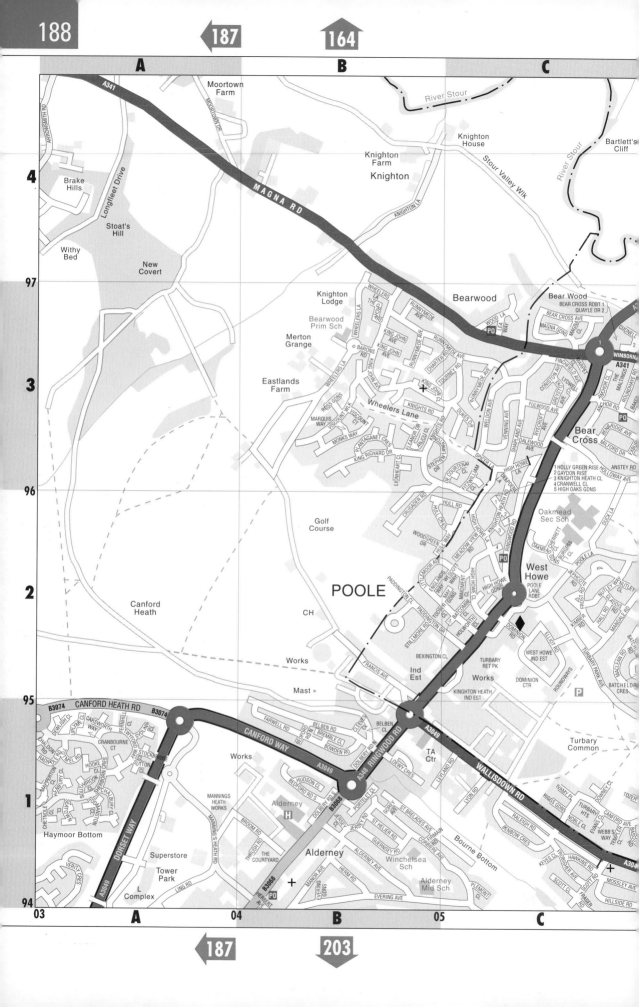

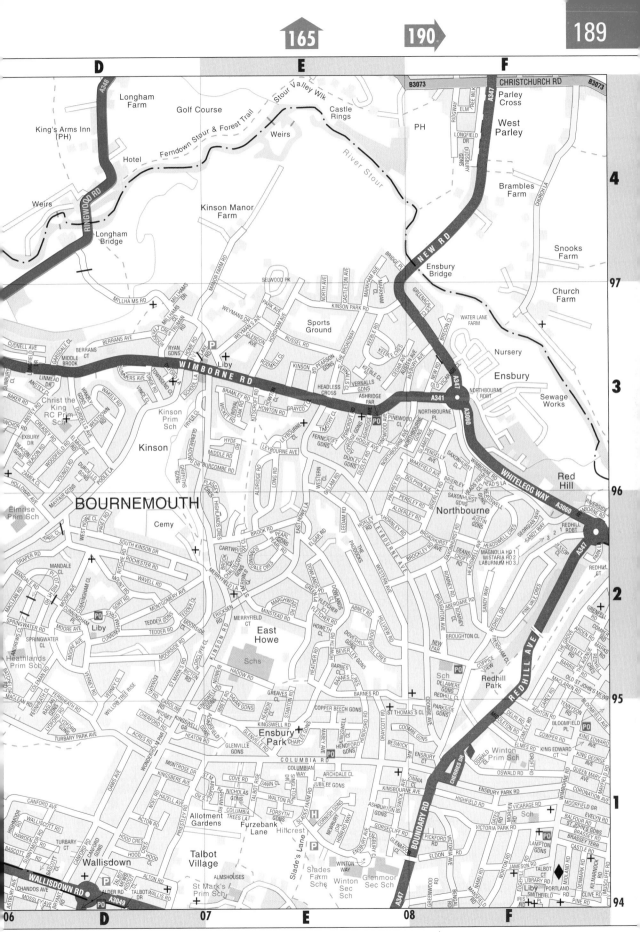

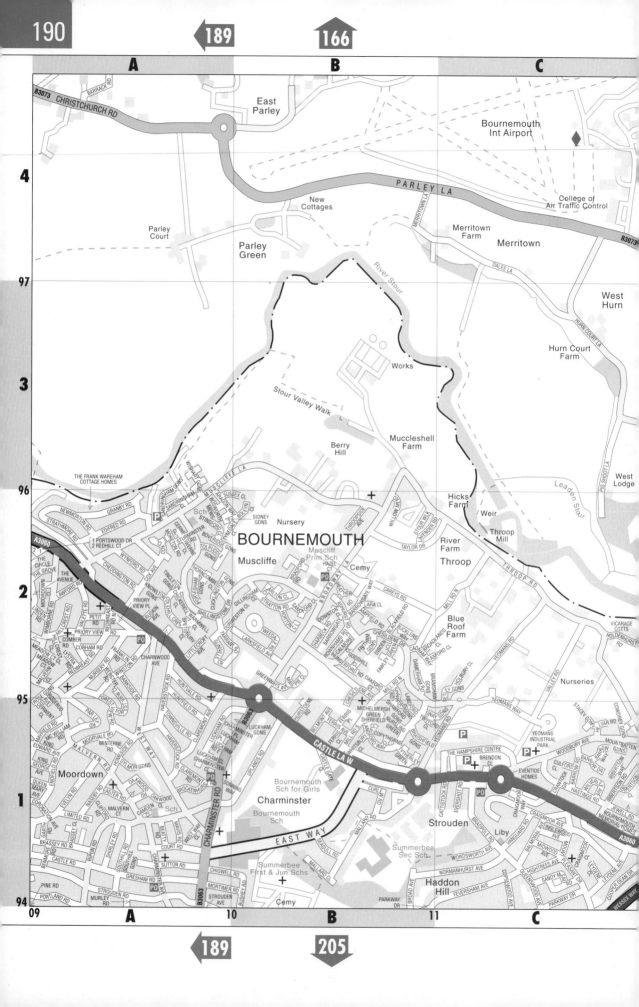

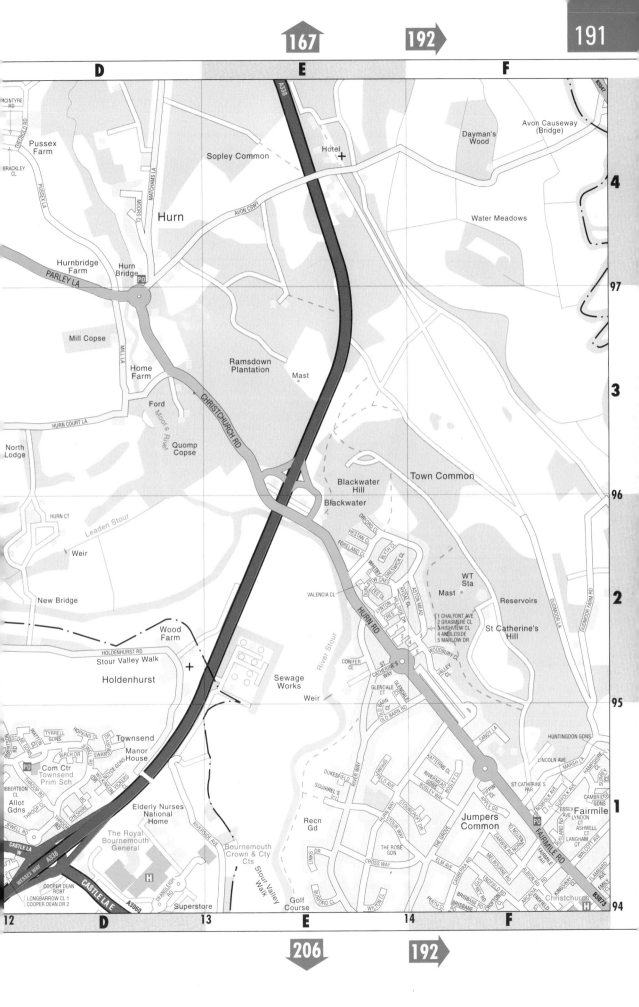

D   E   F

4
97
3
96
2
95
1
94

Pussex Farm
Brackley Cl
Mcintyre Rd
Freebold Rd
Matchams La
Moors Cl
Pussex La
Hurn
Avon Cswy
Sopley Common
Hotel
Dayman's Wood
Avon Causeway (Bridge)
B3347
Water Meadows
Hurnbridge Farm
Hurn Bridge
PO
PARLEY LA
A338
Mill La
Mill Copse
Home Farm
Ford
Moor's River
Quomp Copse
Hurn Court La
CHRISTCHURCH RD
Ramsdown Plantation
Mast
Town Common
North Lodge
Hurn Ct
Leaden Stour
Weir
Blackwater Hill
Blackwater
Orford Cl
Hestan Cl
Foreland Cl
Whitby Cres
Creswick Cl
Blyth Cl
New Bridge
Valencia Cl
Quartes Cl
Lynton Cl
Hillside Dr
Aston Mead
WT Sta
Mast
Reservoirs
Duodmoor La
Duodmoor Farm Rd
St Catherine's Hill
1 Chalfont Ave
2 Grasmere Cl
3 Highview Cl
4 Ambleside
5 Marlow Dr
Wood Farm
Holdenhurst Rd
Stour Valley Walk
Holdenhurst
Sewage Works
Weir
River Stour
HURN RD
Conifer Cl
ST Catherine's Way
Glendale Cl
Glendale Ct
Old Barn Rd
Old Barn Rd
Woodbury Cl
Valley Cl
Huntingdon Gdns
Townsend
Manor House
Tyrrell Gdns
Watton Gdns
Hopkins Cl
Birch Dr
Jewell Rd
Swans Cl
Motor Gdns
Vickers Cl
Wilkinson Rd
Throop Rd
Cheshire Cl
Allot Gdns
Throop Cl
Jewell Rd
Castle La W
A338
WESSEX WAY
Com Ctr
Townsend Prim Sch
PO
Ibbertson Cl
Elderly Nurses National Home
The Royal Bournemouth General
Riverside Ave
Bournemouth Crown & Cty Cts
Stour Valley Walk
Golf Course
Dukesfield
Squirrel's Cl
Recn Gd
Links Dr
Burrord Rd
Wilton Cl
Cross Way
River Way
Snibs Cl
Field Ave
High Way
Stourcroft Dr
Katterns Cl
Rivermead Gdns
Bosley Way
Bossley Cl
Sandy La
St Catherine's Par
Pippin Cl
Apple Gr
The Grove
Elm Ave
The Rose Gdn
Perth Cl
Canberra Rd
Brisbane Rd
Brisbane
Enfield Rd
Melbourne Rd
Darwin Ave
Albion Rd
Fairmile Rd
Drofton Cl
Arcadia Rd
Enfield Rd
Kingsway
B3073
Jumpers Common
Lincoln Ave
Marsh La
Hampshire Gdns
Norfolk Ave
Suffolk Ave
Surrey Cl
St Catherine's Par
Cambridge Gdns
Essex Ave
Fairmile
Lyndon Ct
Ashwell Ct
Langham Ct
Flambard Rd
Emily Cl
PO
Christchurch
H
Cooper Dean Rdbt
Longbarrow Cl 1
Cooper Dean Dr 2
Deansleigh Rd
CASTLE LA E
A3060
Superstore
H

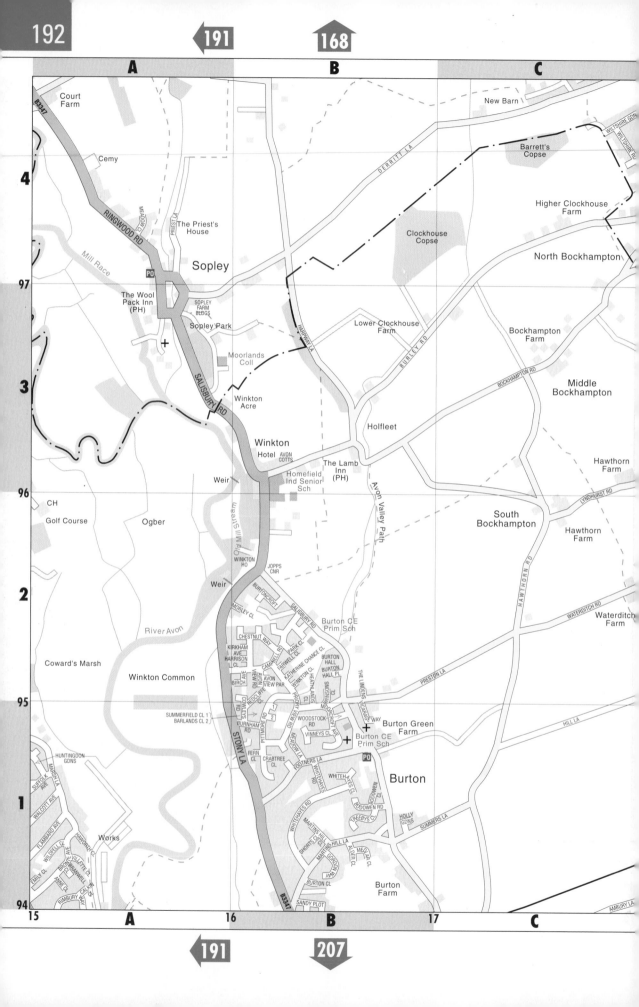

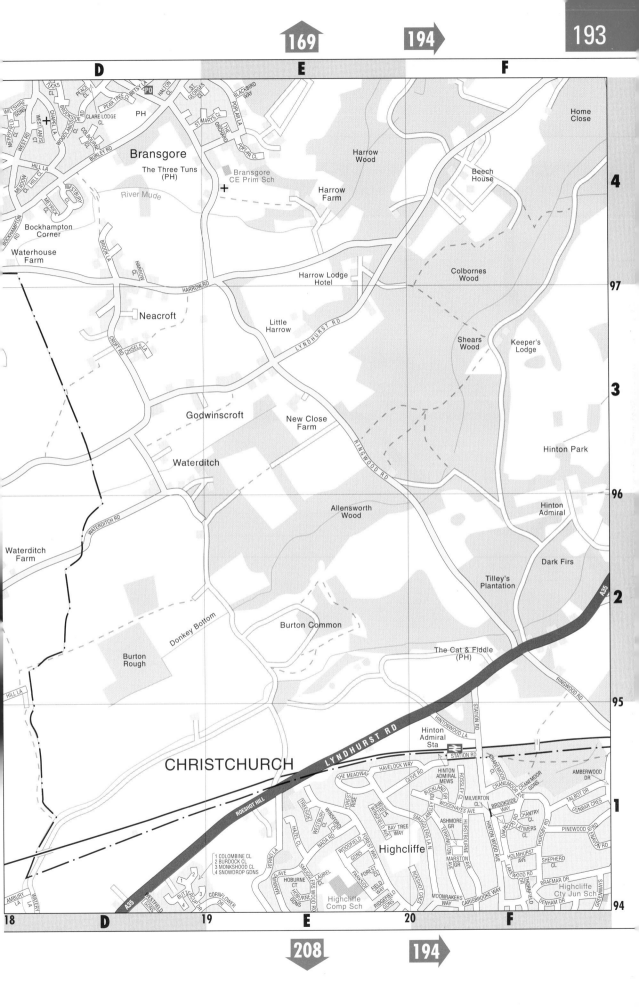

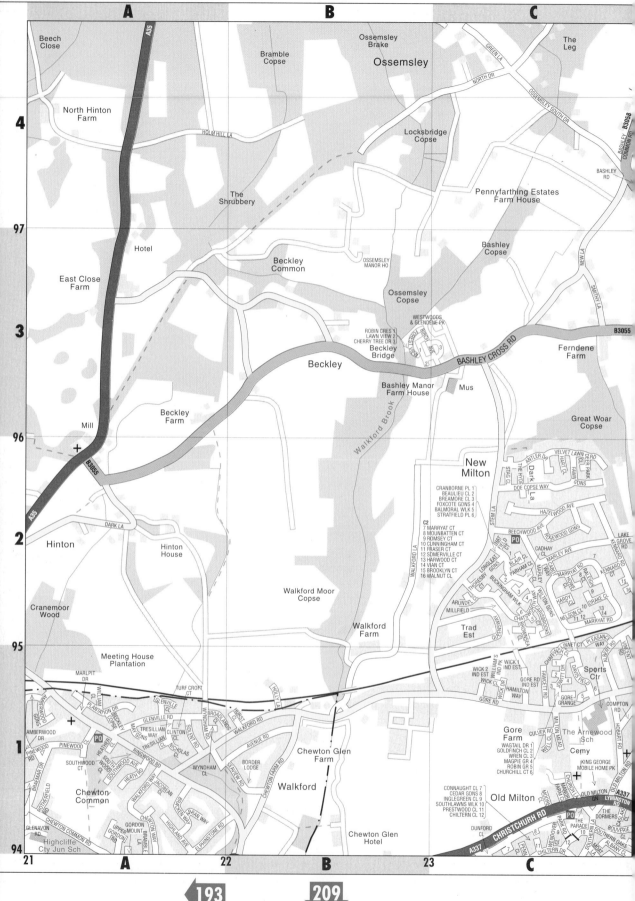

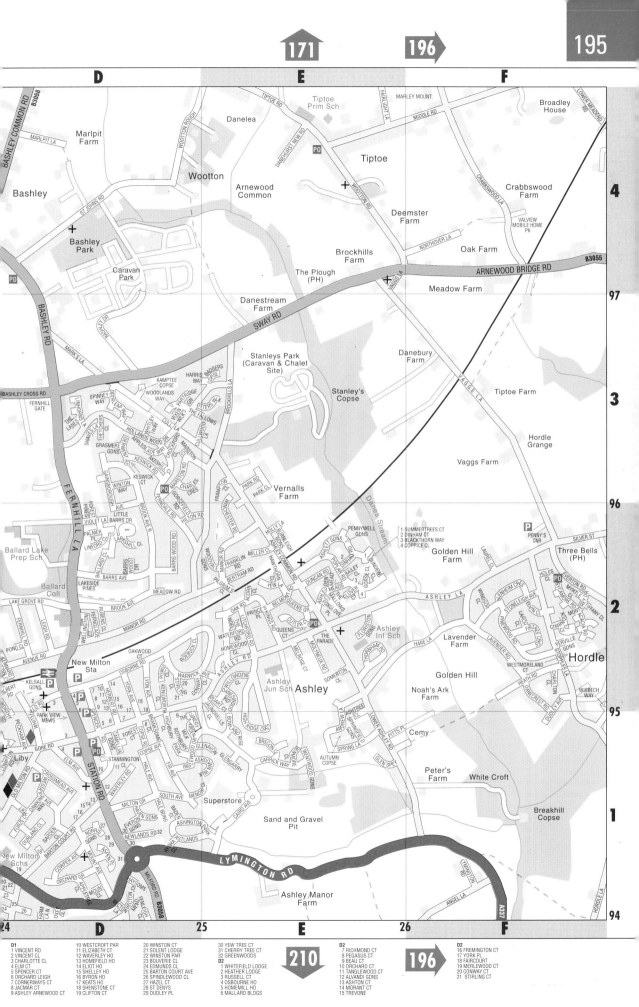

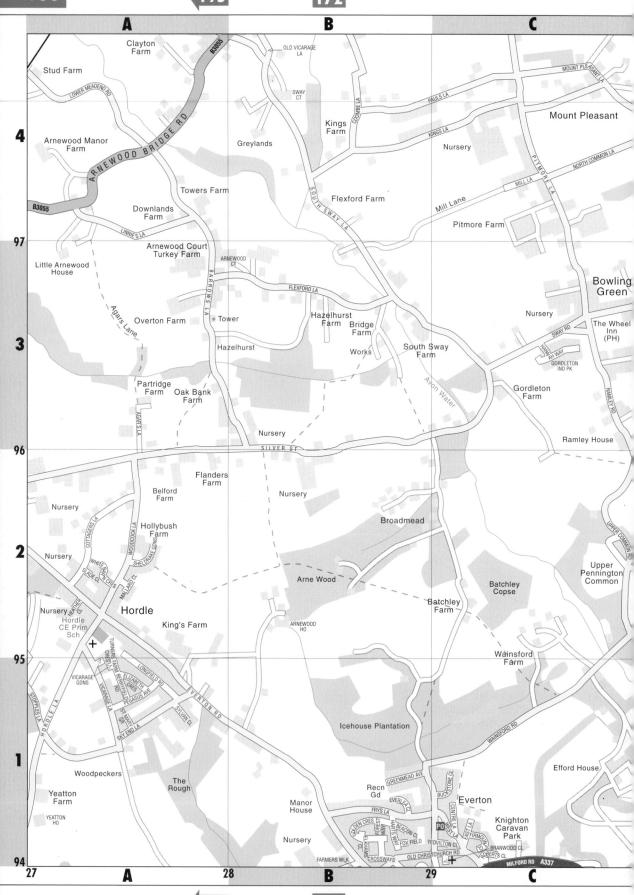

A   **B**   **C**

Stud Farm

Clayton Farm

B3055

Old Vicarage La

Sway Ct

Kings Farm

Mount Pleasant La

Pauls La

Kings La

Nursery

Mount Pleasant

4

Arnewood Manor Farm

Greylands

Towers Farm

Arnewood Bridge Rd

B3055

Downlands Farm

Linnies La

South Sway La

Flexford Farm

Mill Lane

Mill Lane

Mill La

Pitmore La

North Common La

Pitmore Farm

97

Little Arnewood House

Arnewood Court Turkey Farm

Arnewood Ct

Barrows La

Flexford La

Bowling Green

Nursery

The Wheel Inn (PH)

Agars Lane

Overton Farm

Tower

Hazelhurst

Hazelhurst Farm

Bridge Farm

Works

South Sway Farm

Avon Water

Nursery

Sway Rd

Haw La

Ah Way

Gordleton Ind Pk

Gordleton Farm

Ramley Rd

Ramley House

3

Partridge Farm

Oak Bank Farm

Agars La

Nursery

Silver St

96

Flanders Farm

Nursery

Broadmead

Upper Common Rd

Nursery

Belford Farm

Cottagers La

Woodcock La

Hollybush Farm

Sheldrake Gdns

Mallard Cl

White Barn Cres

Slade Cl

Nursery

Arne Wood

Arnewood Ho

Batchley Farm

Batchley Copse

Upper Pennington Common

2

Nursery

Weather Cl

Hordle

King's Farm

Wainsford Farm

Nursery

Hordle CE Prim Sch

Turners Farm Cres

Bewfield Rd

Elizabeth Cres

Pegasus Ave

Longfield Rd

Sylvan Cl

Everton Rd

Wainsford Rd

95

Stopples La

Hordle La

Vicarage Gdns

Vicarage La

St Mary Gr

Sky End La

Icehouse Plantation

Efford House

1

Woodpeckers

The Rough

Greenmead Ave

Everlea Ct

Buckland Rd

Branwood Cl

Efford House

Yeatton Farm

Yeatton Ho

Manor House

Nursery

Recn Gd

Frys La

Golden Cres

Beacon Cl

Fox Field

Forest St

Harts Way

Blackhams

Crossways

Farmers Wlk

Yeovilton Cl

Centre La

West La

East Firmount

Po

Everton

Old Christchurch Rd

Roberts Cl

Milford Rd A337

Knighton Caravan Park

94

27   **A**   **28**   **B**   **29**   **C**

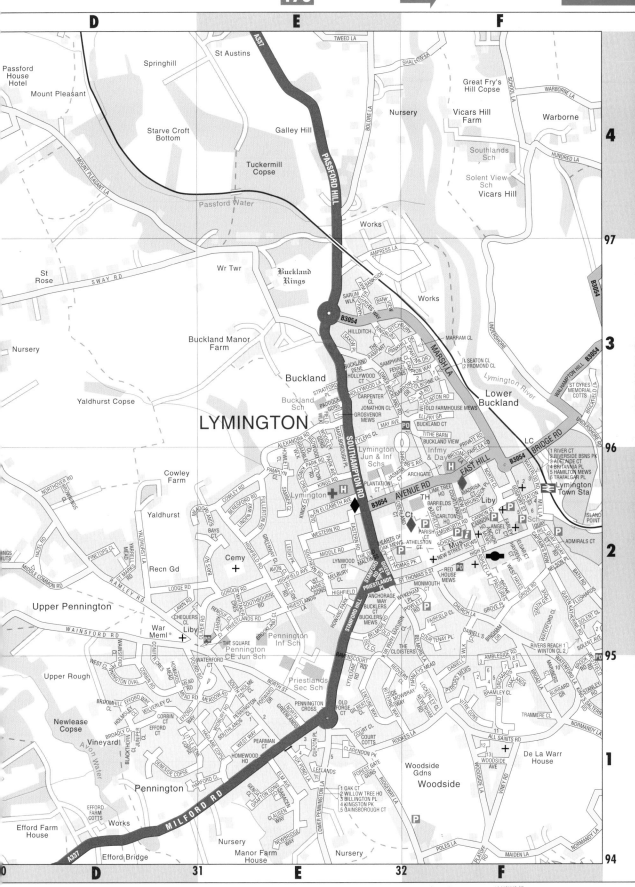

F1
1 PYRFORD GDNS
2 VICTORIA PL
3 GOLD MEAD CL
4 PEARMAIN DR
5 PEARTREE CT
6 PIPPIN CL
7 WORCESTER PL
8 BROADMEAD CL
9 RUSSET CL
10 MONKS CT
11 CONFERENCE PL
12 CHURCH MEAD
13 WOODSIDE CL

D · E · F

4

97

3

96

2

95

1

94

Norley
Copse

NORLEYWOOD RD

Forestside
Farm

East End
Bridge

Bridge
Farm

East End
Arms
(PH)

NEW
COTTS

Otters
Hill
Copse

MILL LA

TANNERS LA

BROOM HILL

ROWES LA

East End

Coombes Gate
Farm Kennels

Ravensbeck
Farm

Sowley
Brooms

Solent Way

Boscoppa

PITTS DEEP LA

Pitts
Deep

Quay

Upper Beckheath
Plantation

Beck
Farm

Beck Farm
Cottages

Thorns
Cottages

Hardings
Wood

Thorns
Cottages

Thorns
Farm

Sowley Pond

SOWLEY LA

Sowley
House

Sowley
Farm

BROWNS LA

Solent Way

SANDPIT LA

Whitehouse
Copse

Colgrims

THORNS LA

D · 37 · E · 38 · F

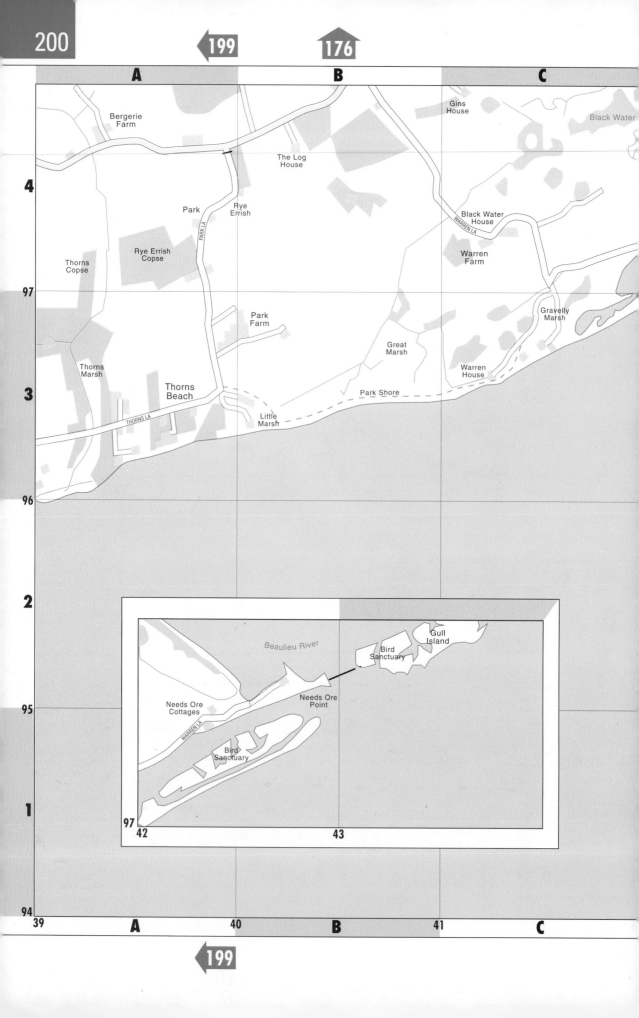

A   B   C

4

97

3

96

Bergerie
Farm

The Log
House

Gins
House

Black Water

Park   Rye
Errish

Thorns
Copse

Rye Errish
Copse

PARK LA

Black Water
House

WARREN LA

Warren
Farm

Gravelly
Marsh

Park
Farm

Great
Marsh

Warren
House

Thorns
Marsh

Thorns
Beach

THORNS LA

Park Shore

Little
Marsh

2

95

1

94

Beaulieu River

Gull
Island

Bird
Sanctuary

Needs Ore
Cottages

WARREN LA

Needs Ore
Point

Bird
Sanctuary

97

42   43

39   40   41

A   B   C

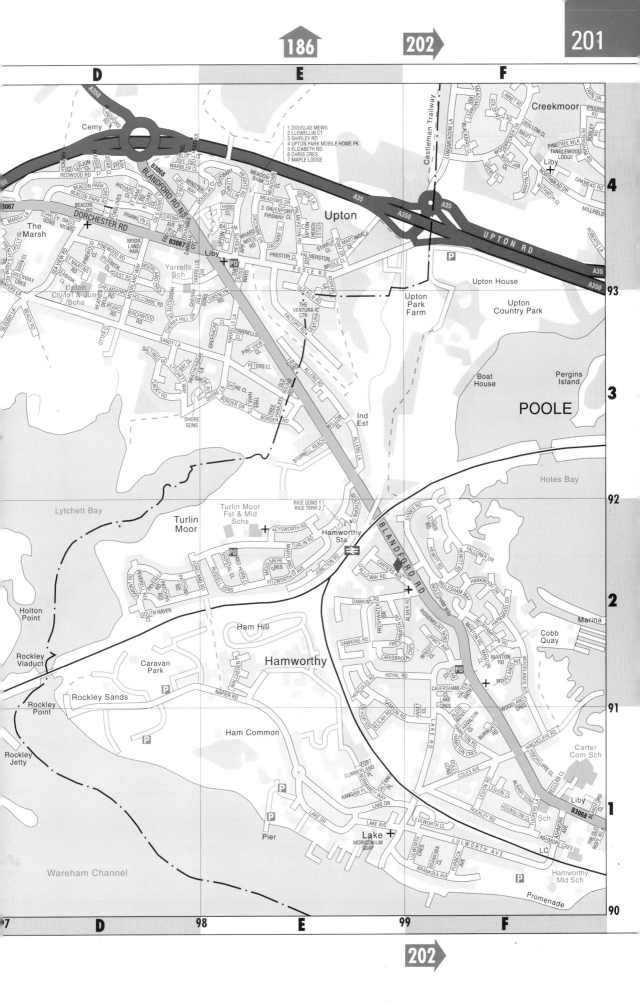

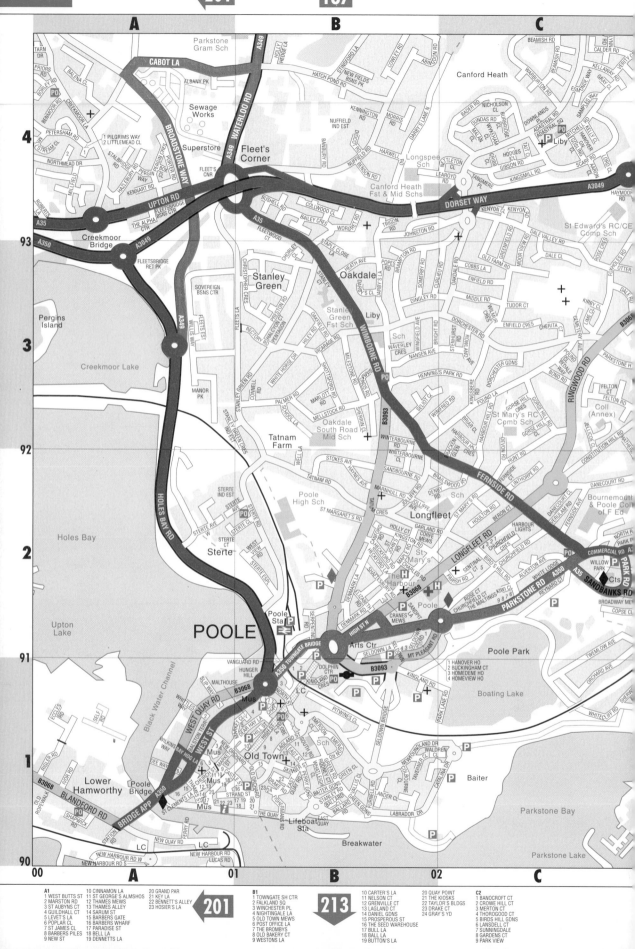

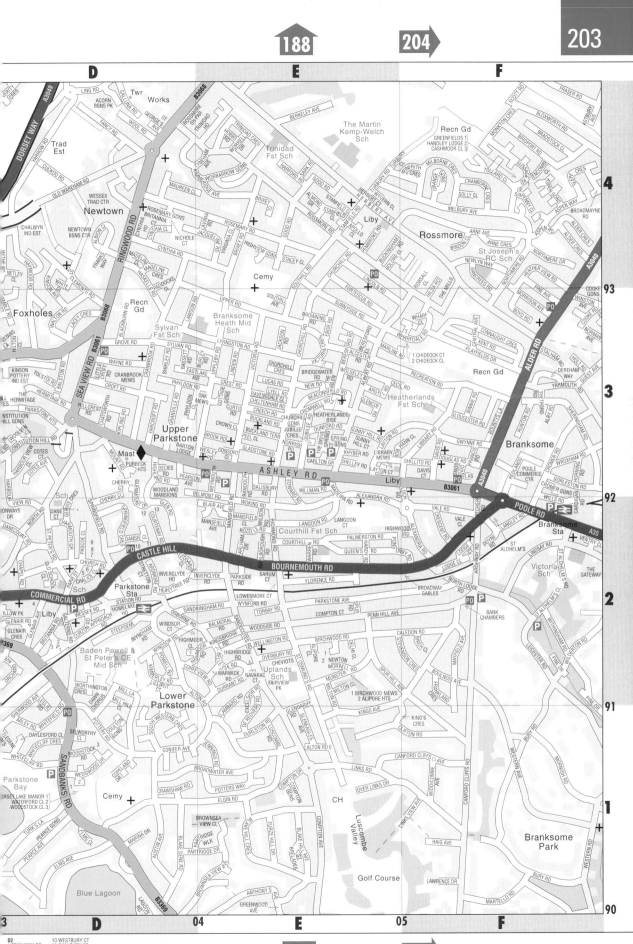

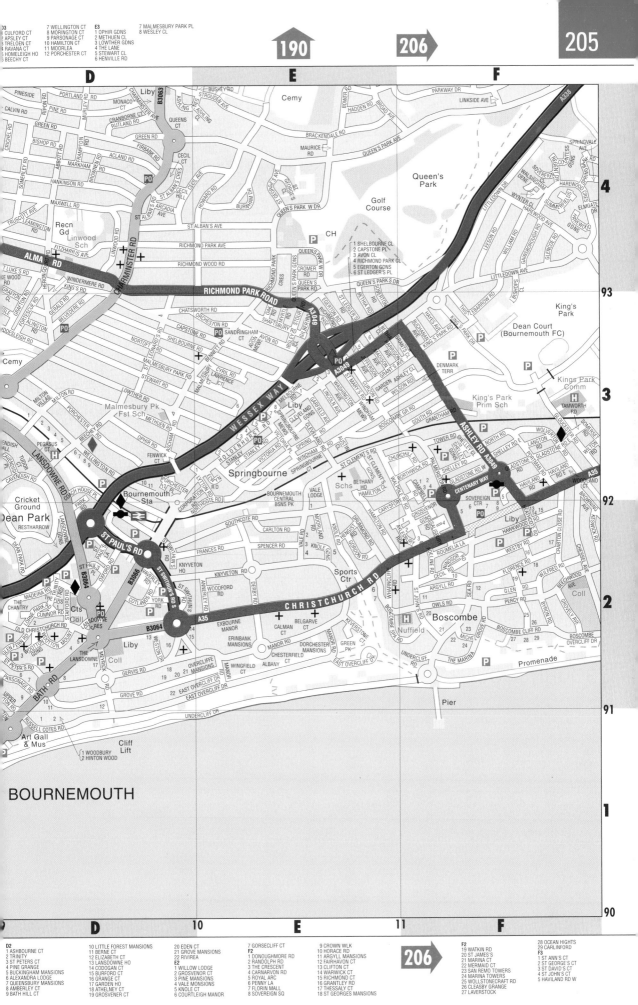

BOURNEMOUTH

BOURNEMOUTH

Littledown House
Littledown
Superstore
Golf Course
New Iford Bridge
Iford
Christchurch
Cemy
Dorset Grange
River Stour
Stour Valley Wlk
Iford Bridge Home Pk
Juniper Flats
Stourfield Schs
Tuckton
Homefield Sch
River Pk
The Moorings
Pokesdown Sta
Cemy
Pokesdown
West Southbourne
Southbourne
St Peter's RC Sec Sch
Boscombe Promenade
Cliff Lift
Southbourne Promenade
Southbourne Sands
Promenade
Poole Bay

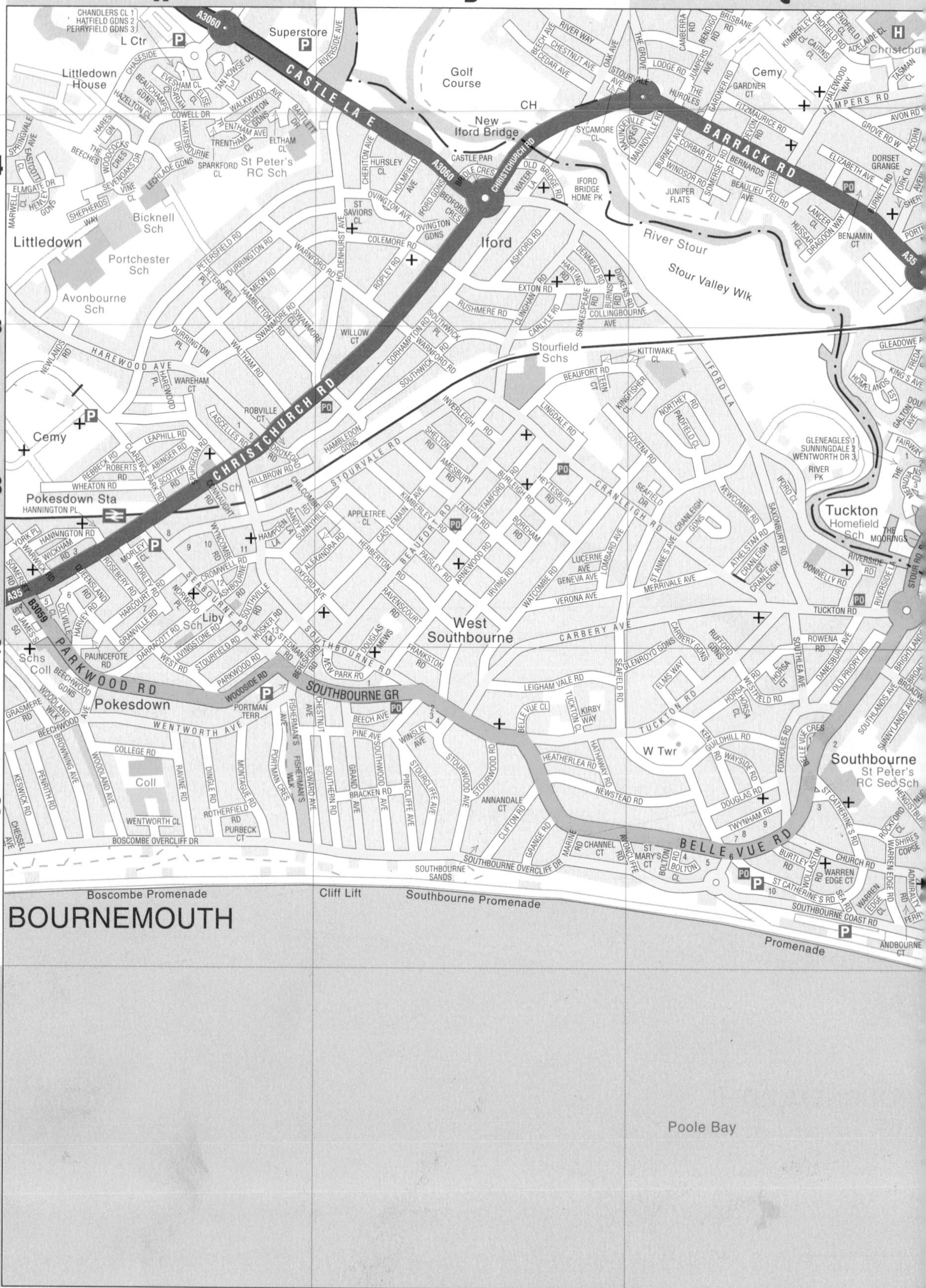

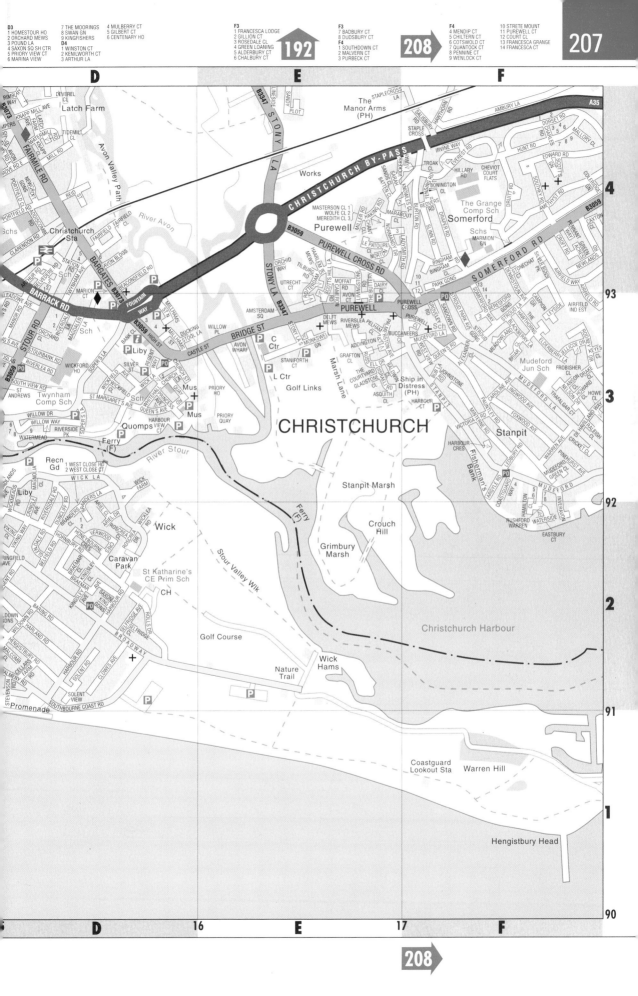

209
195

A **B** **C**

ALBANY MOAT CL
BARTON COURT AVE
FRIARS WLK
FARM LA TN
CHESTNUT AVE
ASHMORE AVE
UPLANDS AVE
WESTBURY CL
LANGTON LA
HEDGERLEY
FENLEIGH CL
GREEN LA
NEWTON RD
B3058
MILFORD RD

Ashley
Bridge

A337 LYMINGTON RD

HORDLE LA

HIGHLANDS RD

GREENACRE
THE CLOSE
SPINACRE
ROYSTON PL
ARLINGTON CT
SEAWAY
BARTON COMMON LA

Home
Farm

Ashley
Clinton

CHRISTCHURCH RD

Downton

PH

Durlston Court
Sch

BARTON CROFT
BECTON LA
SILVERDALE
THE WILLOWS
THE MARTELLS
Angels
Cottage

Danes Stream

SUNNYFIELD CL
FARM LA S
DILLY LA
MITCHELL CL
DANES CL
SOLENT DR
THE FAIRWAY
MAPLE CL
BARTON COMMON RD

4

5
MEADOW WAY
1 ALDBURY CT
2 DOLPHIN PL
3 HIGH MARRYATS
4 LYNRIC CL
5 WHITE KNIGHTS
CH

Hordle
Bridge

DOWNTON LA

93

BARTON CT
GROVE RD
SECOND MARINE AVE
BARTON LN
GREENSIDE CT
MARINE DR E
Sewage
Works
Barton
Common

Golf Course

Taddiford
Farm

Hordle Ho
Sch

P

Barton Cliff

Becton Bunny

P

Hordle Manor
Farm

CLIFF RD

B3

3

Barton on Sea

92

Christchurch Bay

2

91

1

90

24 **A** 25 **B** 26 **C**

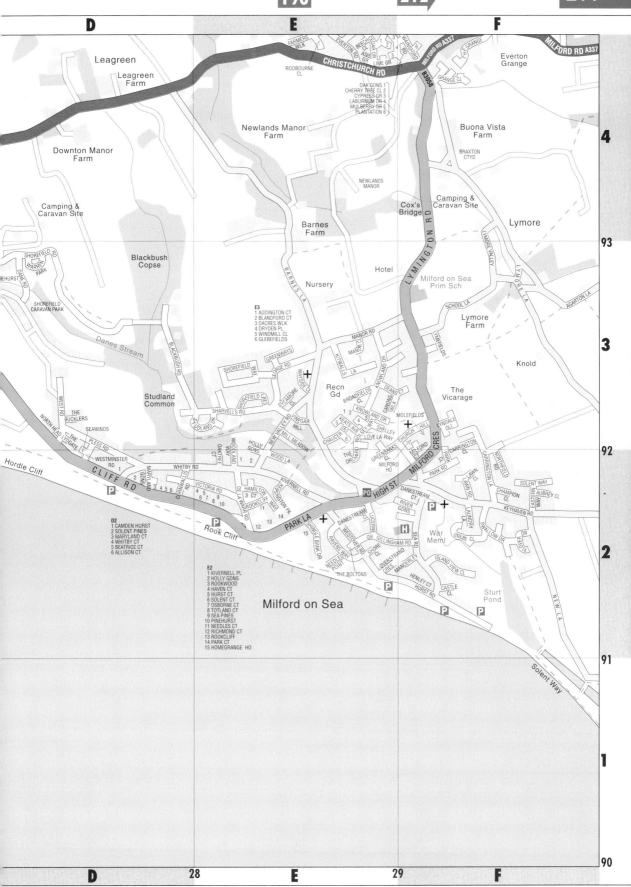

211
197

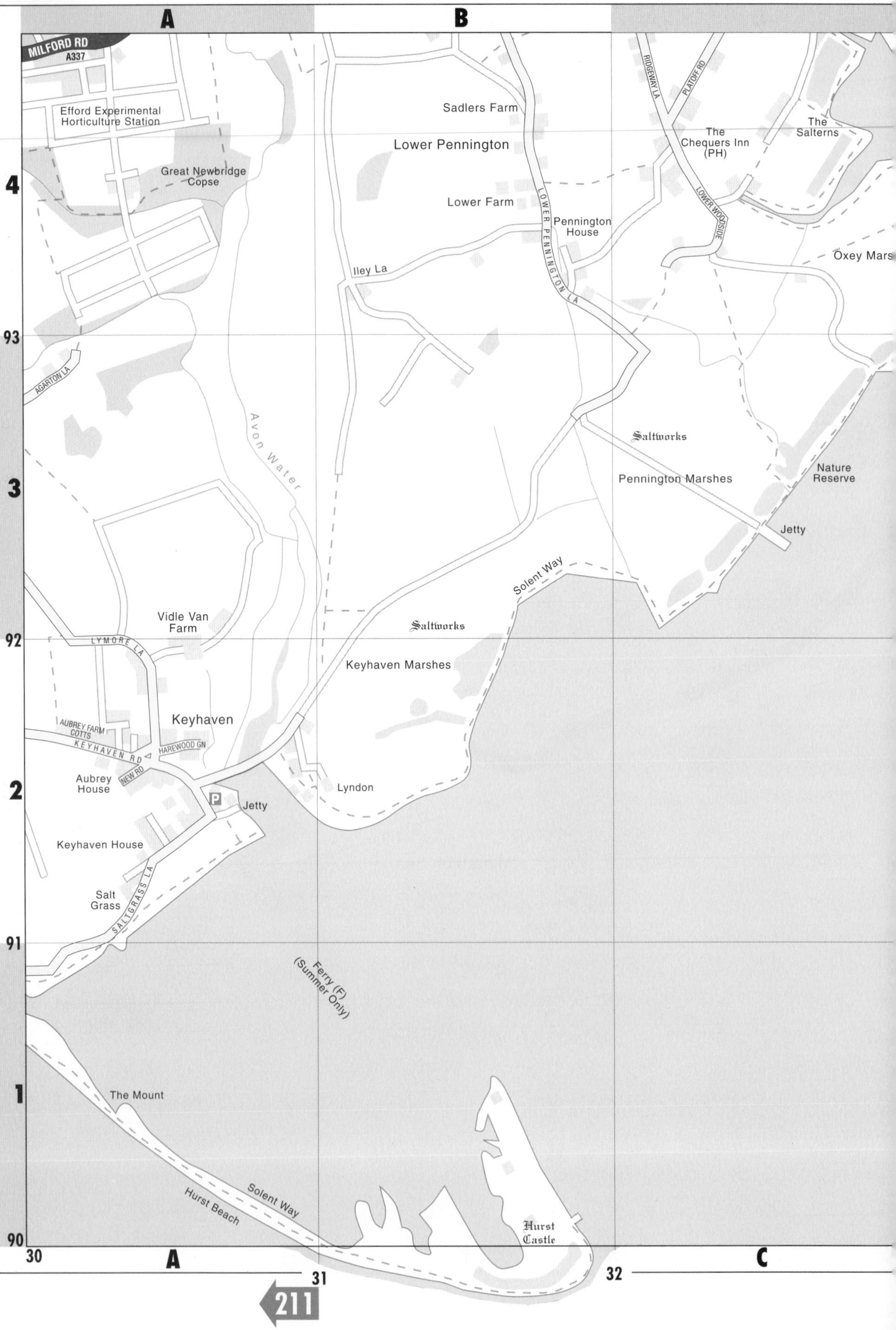

A
B
MILFORD RD
A337
Efford Experimental Horticulture Station
Great Newbridge Copse
Sadlers Farm
Lower Pennington
Lower Farm
LOWER PENNINGTON LA
Pennington House
Iley La
RIDGEWAY LA
PLATOFF RD
The Chequers Inn (PH)
The Salterns
LOWER WOODSIDE
Oxey Mars
4
93
AGARTON LA
Avon Water
Saltworks
Pennington Marshes
Nature Reserve
Jetty
3
Solent Way
Vidle Van Farm
Saltworks
92
LYMORE LA
Keyhaven Marshes
AUBREY FARM COTTS
Keyhaven
KEYHAVEN RD
HAREWOOD GN
NEW RD
Aubrey House
2
P
Jetty
Lyndon
Keyhaven House
Salt Grass
SALTGRASS LA
91
Ferry (F) (Summer Only)
1
The Mount
Solent Way
Hurst Beach
Hurst Castle
90
30
A
31
32
C

211

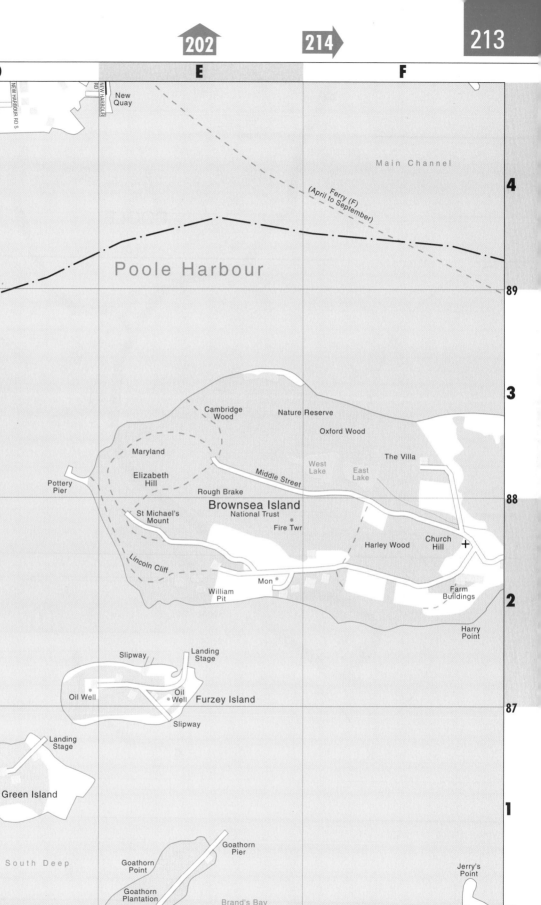
D

E

F

Marina

NEW HARBOUR RD S

NEW HARBOUR RD

New
Quay

Main Channel

4

Ferry (F)
(April to September)

Poole Harbour

89

3

Cambridge
Wood

Nature Reserve

Oxford Wood

Maryland

The Villa

Elizabeth
Hill

West
Lake

East
Lake

Middle Street

Pottery
Pier

Rough Brake

88

Brownsea Island

St Michael's
Mount

National Trust

Fire Twr

Harley Wood

Church
Hill

Lincoln Cliff

Mon

William
Pit

Farm
Buildings

2

Harry
Point

Slipway

Landing
Stage

Oil Well

Oil
Well

Furzey Island

87

Slipway

Landing
Stage

Green Island

1

Goathorn
Pier

South Deep

Goathorn
Point

Jerry's
Point

Goathorn
Plantation

Brand's Bay

86

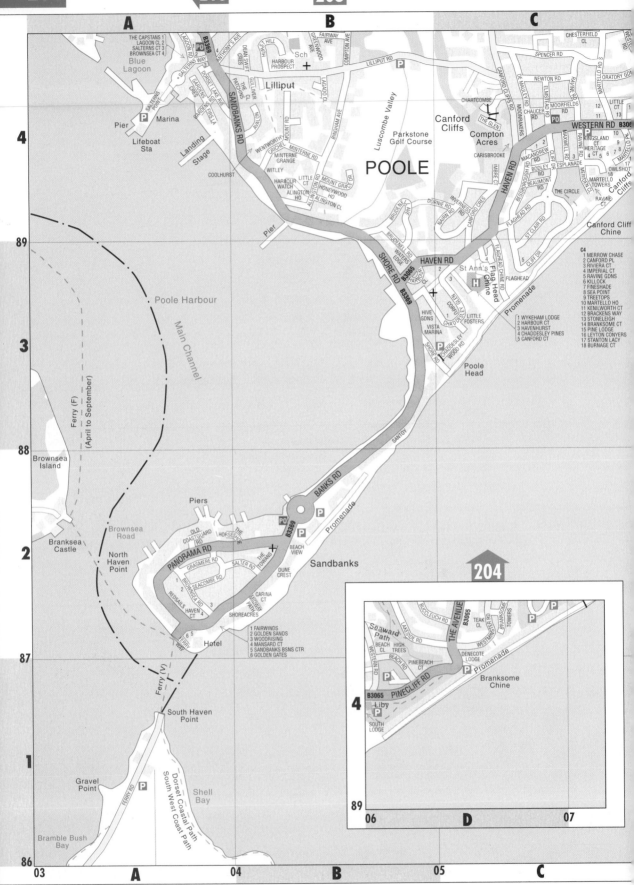

A | B | C

4

Blue Lagoon

THE CAPSTANS 1
LAGOON CL 2
SALTERNS CT 3
BROWNSEA CT 4

B3369

PO

Pier
Marina

Lifeboat Sta

Landing Stage

Coolhurst

SANDBANKS RD

SALTERNS WAY

ANTHONY'S AVE

DORSET LAKE AVE

GARDENS CL

GULLIVER RD

DEAN SWIFT CRES

SPA HILL

THE CL

HARBOUR PROSPECT

Sch

LILLIPUT RD

Lilliput

FAIRWAY AVE

GREENWOOD AVE

COMPTON AVE

LAGADO RD

BINGHAM AVE

PO

Luscombe Valley

Parkstone Golf Course

POOLE

CHARTCOMBE

THE GLEN

Canford Cliffs

Compton Acres

CHESTERFIELD CL

SPENCER RD

NEWTON RD

MARTELLO RD

ORATORY GDNS

MOORFIELDS

LITTLE CT

WESTERN RD B306

KINGSLAND CT

HERITAGE

CHAUCER RD

MOONRAKERS

CARISBROOKE

IMBRE CT

HAVEN RD

MACANDREW RD

CLIFF DR

BODLEY RD

ESPLANADE

BEAUMONT RD

THE CIRCLE

MARTELLO TOWERS

OWLSHOT

RAVINE CT

Canford Cliffs

89

Poole Harbour

Main Channel

Pier

SHORE RD

B3065

B3069

St Ann's

H

Flag Head Chine

FLAGHEAD CHINE RD

Promenade

Canford Cliff Chine

C4
1 MERROW CHASE
2 CANFORD PL
3 RIVIERA CT
4 IMPERIAL CT
5 RAVINE GDNS
6 KILLOCK
7 FINESHADE
8 SEA POINT
9 TREETOPS
10 MARTELLO HO
11 KENILWORTH CT
12 BRACKENS WAY
13 STONELEIGH
14 BRANKSOME CT
15 PINE LODGE
16 LEYTON CONYERS
17 STANTON LACY
18 BURNAGE CT

3

Ferry (F) (April to September)

HIVE GDNS

Vista Marina

Little Fosters

1 WYKEHAM LODGE
2 HARBOUR CT
3 HAVENHURST
4 CHADDESLEY PINES
5 CANFORD CT

P

88

Brownsea Island

Branksea Castle

Brownsea Road

North Haven Point

Piers

OLD COASTGUARD

THE HORSESHOE

PANORAMA RD

Grasmere Rd

SALTER RD

THE TOWANS

BEACH VIEW

DUNE CREST

Sandbanks

BANKS RD

PO

B3369

P

Promenade

SANTOY

204 ↑

2

SEACOMBE RD

BROWNSEA

HAVEN RD

REDSAILS

CARINA CT

SHOREACRES

1 FAIRWINDS
2 GOLDEN SANDS
3 WOODRISING
4 MANSARD CT
5 SANDBANKS BSNS CTR
6 GOLDEN GATES

THE AVENUE

BUCCLEUCH RD

LAKESIDE RD

TEAK CL

BRANKSOME TOWERS

B3065

P

P

Seaward Path

BEACH CL

HIGH TREES

WESTMINSTER RD

WESTERN RD

BEACH RD

PINEBEACH CT

DENECOTE LODGE

P

Promenade

Branksome Chine

87

Ferry (V)

South Haven Point

Hotel

PINECLIFF RD

B3065

4

Liby

P

SOUTH LODGE

1

Gravel Point

FERRY RD

P

Shell Bay

Dorset Coastal Path
South West Coast Path

89

06 | **D** | 07

86

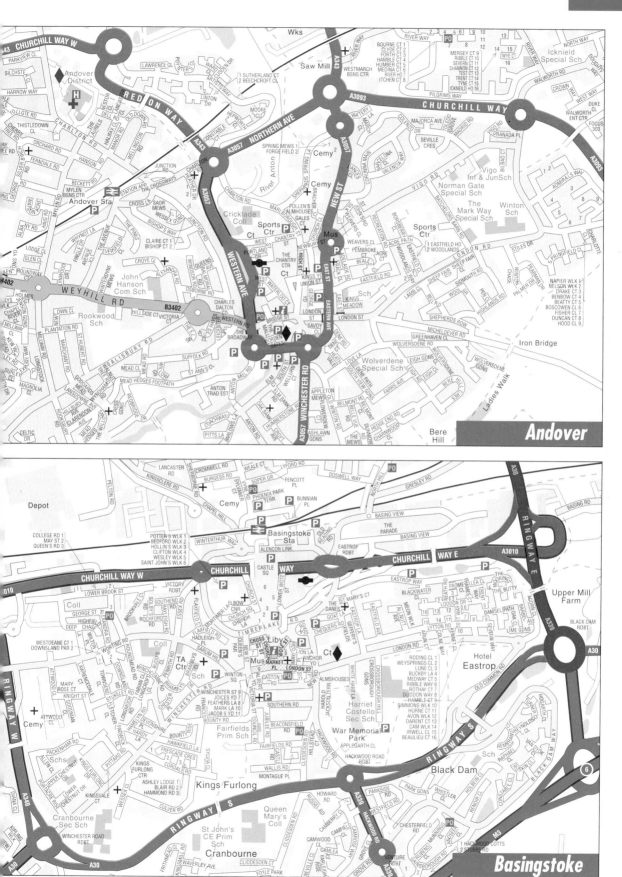

Andover

Basingstoke

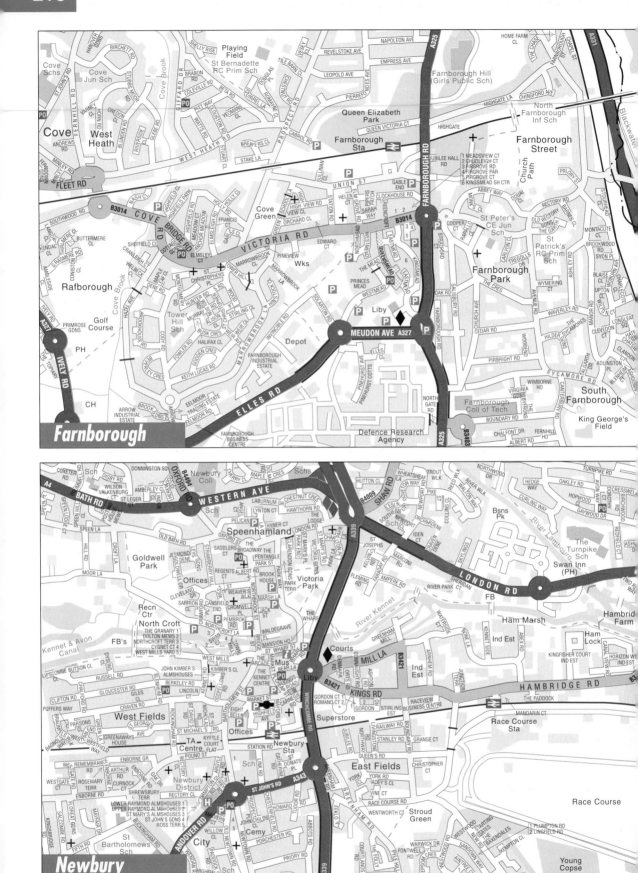

Farnborough

Newbury

Street names are listed alphabetically and show the locality, the Postcode District, the page number and a reference to the square in which the name falls on the map page

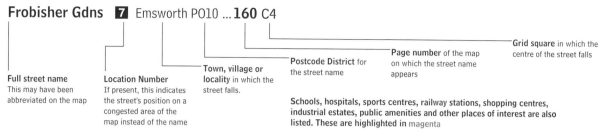

Frobisher Gdns **7** Emsworth PO10 ... **160** C4

Full street name
This may have been abbreviated on the map

Location Number
If present, this indicates the street's position on a congested area of the map instead of the name

Town, village or locality in which the street falls.

Postcode District for the street name

Page number of the map on which the street name appears

Grid square in which the centre of the street falls

Schools, hospitals, sports centres, railway stations, shopping centres, industrial estates, public amenities and other places of interest are also listed. These are highlighted in magenta

Abbreviations used in the index

App **Approach**	Cl **Close**	Ent **Enterprise**	La **Lane**	Rdbt **Roundabout**
Arc **Arcade**	Comm **Common**	Espl **Esplanade**	N **North**	S **South**
Ave **Avenue**	Cnr **Corner**	Est **Estate**	Orch **Orchard**	Sq **Square**
Bvd **Boulevard**	Cotts **Cottages**	Gdns **Gardens**	Par **Parade**	Strs **Stairs**
Bldgs **Buildings**	Ct **Court**	Gn **Green**	Pk **Park**	Stps **Steps**
Bsns Pk **Business Park**	Ctyd **Courtyard**	Gr **Grove**	Pas **Passage**	St **Street, Saint**
Bsns Ctr **Business Centre**	Cres **Crescent**	Hts **Heights**	Pl **Place**	Terr **Terrace**
Bglws **Bungalows**	Dr **Drive**	Ho **House**	Prec **Precinct**	Trad Est **Trading Estate**
Cswy **Causeway**	Dro **Drove**	Ind Est **Industrial Estate**	Prom **Promenade**	Wlk **Walk**
Ctr **Centre**	E **East**	Intc **Interchange**	Ret Pk **Retail Park**	W **West**
Cir **Circus**	Emb **Embankment**	Junc **Junction**	Rd **Road**	Yd **Yard**

Town and village index

Abbotswood 28 A2	Compton 90 C1	Havant 135 F2	Netley Marsh 100 A3	Southbourne 161 F4
Alderholt 92 C3	Compton (Winchester) .. 31 E4	Hawkley 19 F4	New Milton 194 C2	Southsea 182 B1
Ampfield 29 E2	Coombe Bisset 23 F4	Hayling Island 185 D4	Newbridge 74 C2	Southwick 132 C3
Ashurst 100 A2	Corfe Mullen 186 B3	Hedge End 105 E3	Nomansland 73 E4	St Leonards 139 E2
Awbridge 26 C2	Cosham 158 A3	High Cross 18 C1	North Baddesley 53 F3	Standon 9 D1
Bartley 99 D3	Cowplain 111 F2	Highcliffe 208 C4	North Boarhunt 109 D1	Steep 40 B4
Barton on Sea 209 F3	Cranbourne 91 D4	Hill Brow 21 D1	North Hayling 160 B2	Stubbington 154 B2
Beaulieu 148 C1	Croucheston 22 A4	Hoe Gate 109 F4	Nursling 77 E3	Swanmore 84 B3
Beauworth 35 D4	Curdridge 106 C4	Holbury 150 B2	Oakley 163 F1	Swanwick 129 D4
Bishop's Waltham 83 E4	Damerham 68 B3	Holt Heath 138 A3	Otterbourne 31 E2	Sway 172 A1
Bishopstoke 56 C2	Dean 59 F2	Hordle 195 F2	Ower 75 F3	Thorney Island 161 D2
Bisterne Close 143 E1	Denmead 111 D3	Horndean 112 B4	Owslebury 33 D2	Three Legged Cross ... 138 C4
Blackfield 177 F4	Dibden Purlieu 125 F1	Horton Heath 81 E4	Pamphill 162 C3	Timsbury 27 E3
Blashford 117 D2	Downton 47 D4	Hurn 191 D4	Pentridge 42 A1	Titchfield 153 F4
Boldre 173 E1	Droxford 61 D1	Hursley 30 A4	Petersfield 40 B2	Totton 100 C4
Botley 106 A4	Durley 82 A3	Hythe 126 A3	Plaitford 50 A2	Twyford 32 A3
Bournemouth 206 A2	East Boldre 175 E3	Ibsley 117 D4	Poole 202 A2	Upham 58 C3
Braishfield 28 B4	East Dean 4 A1	Keyhaven 212 A2	Portchester 156 B4	Upton 201 E4
Bramdean 15 E2	East End 199 D4	Kilmeston 14 B1	Portmore 198 A4	Verwood 114 C2
Bramshaw 73 F2	East Meon 38 B1	Kings Worthy 2 B3	Portsea Island 182 C3	Walderton 137 F4
Bransgore 193 D4	East Tytherley 4 C4	Kingston 167 F4	Portsmouth 157 F2	Warnford 36 C2
Breamore 70 A4	East Wellow 51 D3	Landford 49 E2	Privett 17 E1	Warsash 128 B1
Broadstone 187 D2	Eastleigh 55 F2	Langrish 39 E2	Purbrook 134 C2	Waterlooville 134 B4
Brockenhurst 145 F1	Edmondsham 91 D2	Langstone 159 F4	Rake 21 F2	West Dean 3 E2
Brook 74 A1	Emery Down 121 E3	Lee-on-the-Solent 179 E1	Ramsdean 39 E1	West End 80 C1
Brown Sea Island 213 E2	Emsworth 136 C1	Lepe 178 A1	Redlynch 47 F3	West Meon 37 D2
Bucklers Hard 176 B2	Exbury 177 D3	Linwood 118 A4	Ringwood 141 E4	West Moors 138 C2
Buriton 65 E3	Fair Oak 57 E1	Liss 21 D2	Ripley 168 B1	West Parley 189 F4
Burley 143 D2	Fareham 131 D2	Littleton 1 A3	Rockbourne 44 C1	West Tisted 16 B4
Bursledon 128 A4	Fawley 151 D2	Lockerley 4 C1	Rogate 41 F3	West Wellow 50 C2
Burton 192 B1	Ferndown 165 D3	Locks Heath 129 E2	Romsey 52 C3	Westbourne 137 D2
Cadnam 98 C4	Finchdean 113 E3	Lover 48 A3	Rowland's Castle 113 E1	Whiteparish 24 A2
Calshot 178 C4	Fordingbridge 69 F1	Lymington 197 D2	Rownhams 77 F4	Whitsbury 45 D2
Chalton 89 E3	Fratton 182 C2	Lyndhurst 121 F3	Sandbanks 214 B2	Wick 46 B4
Chandler's Ford 55 E4	Fritham 72 C1	Marchwood 101 F1	Shawford 31 F4	Wickham 108 A2
Cheriton 14 B3	Frogham 94 C4	Martin 43 D2	Shedfield 107 E4	Wimborne Minster 163 D3
Chidden 86 C4	Froxfield Green 39 E4	Meonstoke 61 E3	Sherfield English 25 E1	Winchester 10 B3
Chilcomb 12 A3	Godshill 70 C1	Michelmersh 6 B1	Soberton 85 E3	Woodgreen 70 C4
Chilworth 54 B1	Gosport 181 E4	Milford on Sea 211 E2	Sopley 192 A4	Woodlands 114 A3
Christchurch 207 E3	Hamble-le-Rice 128 A1	Minstead 98 A2	South Harting 66 C2	Wootton 171 D1
Clanfield 88 A3	Hambledon 86 B1	Mottisfont 5 F1	South Hayling 184 C1	
Colden Common 32 A1	Hamworthy 201 E2	Netley 127 D3	Southampton 102 B2	

1st St SO45 151 D2
2nd St SO45 151 D2
3rd St SO45 150 C2
4th St SO45 150 C2
5th St SO45 150 C2
6th St Fawley SO45 150 C2
Fawley SO45 150 C2
7th St SO45 150 C2
8th St SO45 150 C2
9th St SO45 150 B2
10th St SO45 150 B3
11th St SO45 150 B3
12th St SO45 150 B3
13th St SO45 150 B3
14th St SO45 150 B3
A Ave SO45 150 B2
A'beckett Ct PO1 182 A2
Aaron Cl BH17 202 C4
Aaron Ct SO40 101 F1
Abbas Gr PO9 135 E4
Abbey Cl SO45 126 A2
Abbey Ct 15 SO15 102 C4
Abbey Ent Ctr SO51 53 E3
Abbey Gdns BH21 164 B3
Abbey Hill SO31 127 D4
Abbey Hill Cl SO23 2 A1
Abbey Hill Rd SO23 1 C1
Abbey Pas SO23 11 D4
Abbey Rd Fareham PO15 130 B1
West Moors BH22 166 A4
Abbey The SO51 52 C4
Abbey Water 9 SO51 52 C4
Abbeyfield Dr PO15 130 B1
Abbeyfield House 7 SO18 103 F4
Abbeyfields Cl SO31 127 E3
Abbots Cl Christchurch BH23 208 C4
Waterlooville PO7 134 B2
Abbots Way Fareham PO15 130 B1
Netley SO31 127 E3
Abbots Well Rd SP6 94 C4
Abbotsbury Rd
Bishopstoke SO50 56 C1
Corfe Mullen BH18 186 C3
Abbotsfield SO40 100 C4
Abbotsfield Cl SO16 78 B3
Abbotsford SO40 99 D3
Abbotstone Ave PO9 136 A2
Abbotswood Cl SO51 28 B1
Abbotswood GM Jun Sch
SO40 100 C4
Abbott Rd BH9 205 D4
Abbott St BH21 162 B3
Abbotts Ann Rd SO22 1 B2
Abbotts Cl SO23 2 A1
Abbotts Ct
15 Southampton SO17 79 D1
Winchester SO22 1 C1
Abbotts Dro SO51 50 C1
Abbotts Rd Eastleigh SO50 55 F1
Winchester SO23 2 A1
Abbotts Way Southampton SO17 79 D1
West Moors BH22 166 A4
Abercrombie Gdns SO16 78 A2
Aberdare Ave PO6 158 A4
Aberdare Rd BH10 189 F2
Aberdeen Cl PO15 130 C2
Aberdeen Rd SO17 79 E1
Aberdour Cl SO18 104 A4
Abingdon Cl PO12 181 D2
Abingdon Dr BH23 209 E4
Abingdon Gdns SO16 78 C2
Abingdon Rd BH17 202 B4
Abinger Rd BH7 206 A3
Abney Rd BH10 189 E2
Above Bar St SO14 102 C3
Abraham Cl SO30 105 E3
Abshot Cl PO14 129 D1
Abshot Rd PO14 129 E1
Acacia Ave BH31 115 E3
Acacia Gdns PO8 112 A3
Acacia Rd Hordle SO41 195 F2
Southampton SO19 103 F3
Ackworth Rd PO3 158 A3
Acland Rd BH9 205 D4
Acorn Bsns Ctr PO6 157 E4
Acorn Bsns Pk BH12 203 D4
Acorn Cl Christchurch BH23 206 C4
Cosham PO6 158 C4
Gosport PO13 155 E1
Marchwood SO40 102 A1
New Milton BH25 195 E2
St Leonards BH24 139 F2
Acorn Cotts BH31 114 C4
Acorn Ct SO31 127 F2
Acorn Dr SO16 77 F4
Acorn Gdns PO8 112 A3
Acorn Gr SO52 54 C2
Acorn Workshops SO14 103 D4
Acorns The Bursledon SO31 127 F4
Wimborne Minster BH21 164 A2
Acre La PO7 112 B1
Acres Rd BH11 189 D1
Actaeon Rd PO1 182 A2
Acton Rd BH10 189 D1
Ad Astro Fst Sch BH17 187 F1
Adair Rd PO4 183 D1
Adames Rd PO1 182 C3
Adams Cl SO30 81 D2
Adams Rd SO45 126 A1
Adams Terr PO6 158 B3
Adams Wood Dr SO40 101 F1
Adamsfield Gdns BH10 189 E1
Adamson Cl SO53 55 E4
Adastral Rd BH17 202 C4
Adastral Sq BH17 202 C4
Adcock Ct SO16 77 F4
Adderbury Ave PO10 136 C2
Addington Ct 1 SO41 211 E3
Addington Pl BH23 207 E3
Addis Sq 35 SO17 79 D1
Addiscombe Rd BH23 207 D4
Addison Cl Romsey SO51 28 A1
Winchester SO22 10 B3
Addison Rd Brockenhurst SO42 172 C4
Eastleigh SO50 56 A3
Locks Heath SO31 128 C3
Portsmouth PO5 182 C2
Addison Sq BH24 141 D4
Adelaide Cl BH23 206 C4
Adelaide Ct SO41 197 F2
Adelaide La 40 BH1 204 C2
Adelaide Pl 9 PO16 131 E1
Adelaide Rd SO17 103 E4
Adeline Rd BH5 205 F2
Adey Cl SO19 104 A1
Adhurst Rd PO9 136 A2
Adlam's La SO41 172 A1
Admiral Park The PO3 158 A2
Admiral's Cnr 4 PO5 182 B1
Admiral's Wlk PO1 181 F3
Admirals Cl SO45 151 D2
Admirals Ct
Hamble-le-Rice SO31 128 A1
Lymington SO41 197 F2
19 Portsmouth PO5 182 B1
Admirals Rd SO31 129 D2
Admirals Way SO45 126 A3
Admirals Wlk
Bournemouth BH2 204 B1
Gosport PO12 180 C2
Admiralty Cotts PO12 181 E1
Admiralty Rd
Bournemouth BH6 206 C2
Portsmouth PO1 182 A3
Admiralty Way SO40 101 F2
Adsdean Cl PO9 135 F2
Adstone La PO3 158 B2
Adur Cl PO12 180 C4
Aerodrome Rd PO13 155 F2
Africa Dr SO40 124 C4
Agar's La SO41 196 A3
Agarton La SO41 211 F3
Aggis Farm Rd BH31 114 C3
Agincourt Rd PO2 182 B4
Agitator Rd SO45 151 E2
Agnew House PO12 181 D3
Agnew Rd PO13 155 E2
Aikman La SO40 100 A4
Ailsa La SO19 103 E2
Ainsdale Rd PO6 134 B1
Ainsley Gdns SO50 56 A3
Aintree Cl SO50 81 E4
Aintree Ct SO31 129 D4
Aintree Dr PO7 112 A1
Aintree Rd SO40 76 B1
Airetons Cl BH18 187 E2
Airfield Ind Est BH23 207 F3
Airfield Rd BH23 207 F3
Airfield Way BH23 207 F4
Airlie Cnr SO22 10 C3
Airlie Rd SO22 10 C3
Airport Service Rd PO3 158 A2
Airspeed Rd
Christchurch BH23 208 A4
Portsmouth PO3 158 B1
Ajax Cl PO14 179 E3
Akeshill Cl BH25 195 D3
Alameda Rd PO7 134 B2
Alameda Way PO7 134 B2
Alan Chun House SO31 127 E4
Alan Ct 16 BH23 209 D4
Alan Drayton Way SO50 56 C1
Alan Gr PO15 130 C1
Alandale Rd SO19 104 B2
Albacore Ave SO31 128 C1
Albany BH1 205 E2
Albany Cl BH25 194 C1
Albany Ct
Bishop's Waltham SO32 83 D4
12 Gosport PO12 181 D3
Albany Dr
Bishop's Waltham SO32 83 D4
Three Legged Cross BH21 114 C1
Albany Gdns BH15 201 F1
Albany Park Ct SO17 102 C4
Albany Pk BH17 202 A4
Albany Rd
Bishop's Waltham SO32 83 D4
Holbury SO45 150 B2
Portsmouth PO5 182 B2
Romsey SO51 52 C4
Southampton SO15 102 B3
Albatross Wlk PO13 155 D1
Albemarle Ave PO12 181 D4
Albemarle Rd BH3 204 C4
Albermarle Ct SO17 79 E2
Albert Cl SO31 127 E3
Albert Gr PO5 182 B2
Albert Rd
Bishop's Waltham SO32 83 D4
Bournemouth BH1 204 C2
Corfe Mullen BH21 186 B3
Cosham PO6 157 F4
6 Eastleigh SO50 56 A3
Ferndown BH22 165 E3
Hedge End SO30 105 D3
New Milton BH25 194 C1
Poole BH12 203 E3
Portsmouth PO4, PO5 182 C1
Stubbington PO14 179 F3
Albert Rd N SO14 103 D2
Albert Rd S SO14 103 D2
Albert St PO12 181 E3
Albion Cl Poole BH12 203 D4
Portchester PO16 156 A3
Albion Pl 3 SO14 102 C2
Albion Rd Christchurch BH23 191 F1
Fordingbridge SP6 69 F1
Lee-on-the-Solent PO13 179 F2
Albion Towers 1 SO14 103 D2
Albion Way BH31 114 B4
Albretia Ave PO8 111 F2
Albury Pl SO53 30 A1
Alby Rd BH12 203 F3
Alcantara Cres SO14 103 D2
Alcester Rd BH12 203 E3
Alchorne Pl PO3 158 A2
Aldbury Ct 1 BH25 210 A4
Alder Cl Burton BH23 192 B1
Colden Common SO21 57 D4
Hythe SO45 125 E2
Marchwood SO40 101 F1
Romsey SO51 53 E3
Alder Cres BH12 203 F4
Alder Dr SP6 92 C3
Alder Hill Dr SO40 100 A4
Alder Hills BH12 204 A4
Alder Hills Ind Est BH12 204 A4
Alder La PO13 180 B3
Alder Rd Poole BH12 203 F3
Southampton SO16 78 A2
Alderbury Ct 5 BH23 207 F3
Alderfield GU32 40 C2
Alderholt Rd SP6 69 D1
Alderley Rd BH10 189 F2
Alderman Quilley Sch SO50 55 F1
Alderman Quilley Sch The
SO50 56 A1
Aldermoor Ave SO16 78 A2
Aldermoor Cl SO16 78 B2
Aldermoor Rd Gosport PO13 180 B4
Southampton SO16 78 A2
Waterlooville PO7 134 B2
Aldermoor Rd E PO7 134 B3
Alderney Ave BH12 188 B1
Alderney Cl SO16 77 F2
Alderney Hospl BH12 188 B1
Alderney Mid Sch BH12 188 B1
Alders Rd PO16 155 D4
Aldershot House 37 PO9 136 A3
Alderwood Ave SO53 55 D3
Alderwood Cl PO9 135 D2
Aldis Gdns BH15 201 F1
Aldrich Rd PO1 182 A3
Aldridge Cl PO8 88 B3
Aldridge Rd Bournemouth BH10 189 E3
Ferndown BH22 165 F2
Aldroke St 14 PO6 157 F4
Aldsworth Cl PO6 158 B4
Aldsworth Gdns PO6 158 B4
Aldwell St 8 PO5 182 B2
Alec Rose House 16 PO12 181 E2
Alec Rose La PO1 182 B3
Alec Wintle House PO2 182 B4
Alecto Rd PO12 181 D2
Alencon Cl PO12 181 E4
Alexander Cl
Christchurch BH23 207 F3
Totton SO40 100 B4
Waterlooville PO7 134 B3
Alexander Ct SO19 103 F1
Alexander Gr PO16 155 D4
Alexander House PO11 185 F1
Alexandra Ave PO11 184 C1
Alexandra Cl SO45 126 A2
Alexandra Lodge 6 BH1 205 D2
Alexandra Rd
Bournemouth BH6 206 B3
Chandler's Ford SO53 55 F4
Fordingbridge SP6 69 F1
Hedge End SO30 105 D3
Hythe SO45 126 A2
Lymington SO41 197 E3
Poole BH14 203 F2
Portsmouth PO1 182 B3
Southampton SO15 102 C3
Alexandra St PO12 181 D3
Alexandra Terr SO23 10 C4
Alexandra Way SO30 106 A4
Alexandria Ct BH22 165 F2
Alford Rd BH3 204 B4
Alfred Cl SO40 100 B4
Alfred Rd Portsmouth PO1 182 A3
Stubbington PO14 154 B2
Alfred Rose Ct SO18 79 F2
Alfred St SO14 103 D3
Alfrey Cl PO10 161 E4
Alfriston Ct SO19 104 B2
Alfriston Gdns SO19 104 A2
Algiers Rd PO3 183 D4
Alhambra Rd PO4 182 C1
Alington 18 BH4 204 B2
Alington Cl BH14 214 B4
Alington House BH14 214 B4
Alington Rd BH3 205 D3
Alipore Cl BH14 203 E2
Alipore Hts BH14 203 E2
All Saints CE Com Prim Sch
SO23 11 D3
All Saints House 19 SO14 103 D2
All Saints Rd SO41 197 F1
All Saints' Rd PO1 182 B4
All Saints' St PO1 182 B3
Allan Gr SO51 53 D4
Allaway Ave Cosham PO6 157 D4
Portchester PO6 157 D4
Allbrook Ct PO9 135 E3
Allbrook Hill Eastleigh SO50 56 A4
Otterbourne SO50 56 A4
Allbrook Knoll SO50 56 A4
Allbrook Way SO50 56 A4
Allcot Rd PO3 158 A1
Allen Ct BH21 163 E3
Allen Rd Hedge End SO30 105 E4
Wimborne Minster BH21 163 E2
Allen Water Dr SP6 69 F1
Allen's Rd PO4 182 C1
Allenbourn Cty Mid Sch BH21 163 E3
Allenby Cl BH17 187 D1
Allenby Gr PO16 156 B4
Allenby Rd Broadstone BH17 187 D1
Gosport PO12 180 C3
Allendale Ave PO10 136 C2
Allens La Hamworthy BH16 201 E3
Meonstoke SO32 61 E3
Allens Rd Hamworthy BH16 201 E3
Upton BH16 201 E3
Allenview Rd BH21 163 E3
Allerton Cl SO40 76 B1
Alliance Cl PO13 180 B4
Allington La SO30 80 C3
Allington Manor Farm
Bsns Ctr SO50 80 C4
Allington Manor Sch SO50 80 C4
Allington Rd Poole BH14 214 B4
Southampton SO15 101 E4
Allison Ct 6 SO41 211 D2
Allison House SO30 105 E4
Allmara Dr PO7 134 C2
Allotment Rd Hedge End SO30 105 D3
Locks Heath SO31 128 C3
Alma House SO14 103 D4
Alma La SO32 58 A1
Alma Rd Bournemouth BH9 205 D4
Romsey SO51 52 C4
Southampton SO14 103 D4
Alma St PO12 181 D3
Alma Terr PO4 183 D2
Almatade Rd SO18 104 A4
Almer Rd BH15 201 F2
Almond Cl Cosham PO6 158 C4
Waterlooville PO8 112 B2
Almond Ct 11 SO15 102 B3
Almond Gr BH12 203 E4
Almond Rd SO15 102 B3
Almondsbury House 8 PO6 132 C1
Almondsbury Rd PO6 132 C1
Almondside PO13 155 F1
Almshouses BH10 189 E1
Alpha Ctr The BH17 202 A4
Alphage Rd PO12 155 F1
Alpine Cl SO18 104 A4
Alpine Rd Ashurst SO40 99 F2
St Leonards BH24 140 B1
Alresford Rd
Chilcomb SO21, SO23 12 B4
Havant PO9 135 F2
Winchester SO21, SO23 11 E4
Alsford Rd PO7 134 B3
Alswitha Terr 27 SO23 2 A1
Alten Rd PO7 111 E1
Althorpe Dr PO3 158 B2
Alton Cl SO50 57 D1
Alton Ct 12 SO23 2 A1
Alton Gr PO16 156 B3
Alton House SO18 103 F4
Alton Rd Bournemouth BH10 189 D1
Poole BH14 203 E2
Alton Rd E BH14 203 E1
Alum Chine Rd BH4 204 A2
Alum Cl SO45 150 B2
Alum Way Portchester PO16 131 F1
Southampton SO18 104 A4
Alumdale Rd BH4 204 A1
Alumhurst Rd BH4 204 A1
Alvandi Gdns 12 BH25 195 D2
Alvara Rd PO12 181 D1
Alver Bridge View 11 PO12 181 D2
Alver Quay 7 PO12 181 D2
Alver Rd Gosport PO12 181 D2
Portsmouth PO1 182 C3
Alvercliffe Dr PO12 180 C1
Alverstoke CE Jun Sch PO12 181 D1
Alverstoke Ct PO12 181 D1
Alverstoke Inf Sch PO12 181 D1
Alverstone Rd PO4 183 D3
Alverton Ave BH15 202 C2
Alverton Hall BH4 204 B1
Alveston Ave PO14 154 B4
Alyne House SO15 102 C4
Alyth Rd BH3 204 B3
Ambassador Cl BH23 208 A3
Ambassador Ind Est BH23 208 A3
Amber Rd BH21 186 B2
Amberley Cl Botley SO30 106 A4
Christchurch BH23 208 C4
North Baddesley SO52 53 F3
Amberley Ct
8 Bournemouth BH1 205 D2
Totton SO40 100 C3
Amberley Rd Clanfield PO8 88 B3
Gosport PO12 181 D4
Portsmouth PO2 157 F2
Amberslade Wlk SO45 125 F1
Amberwood BH22 165 F3
Amberwood Cl SO40 76 B1
Amberwood Dr BH23 193 F1
Amberwood Gdns BH23 194 A1
Ambledale SO31 128 C2
Ambleside
Bishop's Waltham SO32 83 D4
Christchurch BH23 191 F2
Hedge End SO30 105 E3
Ambleside Gdns SO19 104 A2
Ambleside Rd SO41 197 F2
Ambury La BH23 207 F4
Amersham Cl PO12 180 C2
Amesbury Rd BH6 206 B3
Amethyst Gr PO7 135 D4
Amethyst Rd BH23 207 F4
Amey Ind Est GU32 40 C2
Ameys La BH22 165 F4
Ameysford Rd BH22 165 E4
Amira Ct 9 BH2 204 C2
Amoy St SO15 102 C3
Ampfield CE Prim Sch SO51 29 E2
Ampfield Cl PO9 135 D2
Ampfield Rd BH8 190 B2
Amport Cl SO22 1 B2
Amport Ct PO9 135 E3
Ampress La SO41 197 E3
Ampthill Rd SO15 102 A4
Amsterdam Sq BH23 207 E3
Amyas Ct PO4 183 E2
Ancasta Rd SO14 103 D4
Anchor Cl Bournemouth BH11 188 C3
Christchurch BH23 208 A3
Anchor Ct SO14 103 D1
Anchor La PO1 182 A3
Anchor Mews SO41 197 F2
Anchor Rd BH11 188 C3
Anchorage Rd PO3 158 A2
Anchorage The PO12 181 E2
Anchorage Way SO41 197 E2
Ancrum Lodge BH4 204 A2
Andalusian Gdns SO31 129 D4
Andbourne Ct BH6 206 C2
Anderby Rd SO16 77 E1
Anderson Cl Havant PO9 136 A2
Romsey SO51 28 B1
Swanwick PO15 129 E4
Anderson's Rd SO14 103 D2
Anderwood Dr SO41 172 A1
Andes Cl SO14 103 E2
Andes Rd SO16 77 D2
Andlers Ash Rd GU33 20 C2
Andover Cl BH23 208 A4
Andover House 27 PO9 136 A3
Andover Rd Portsmouth PO4 182 C1
Southampton SO15 102 B3
Winchester SO21, SO22, SO23 1 C1
Andover Rd N SO22 1 C2
Andover Road Ret Pk SO23 1 C1
Andree Ct BH23 209 D4
Andrew Bell St 2 PO1 182 B3
Andrew Cl Hythe SO45 126 A1
Portsmouth PO1 182 C3
Totton SO40 100 B4
Andrew Cres PO7 111 E1
Andrew La BH25 195 E1
Andrew Pl PO14 179 D3
Andrewes Cl SO32 83 E4
Andrews Cl BH11 189 D2
Andromeda Rd SO16 77 F2
Androse Gdns BH24 140 C3
Anfield Cl SO50 57 E1
Anfield Ct SO50 57 D1
Angel Cres SO19 104 A3
Angel Ct SO41 197 F2
Angel La Barton on Sea BH25 210 B4
Ferndown BH22 165 D2
Angelica Ct PO7 135 D3
Angelica Gdns SO50 81 E4
Angelica Way PO15 129 F4
Angeline Cl BH23 208 C4
Angelo Cl PO7 135 D4
Angelus Cl PO14 179 E3
Angerstein Rd PO2 157 E1
Anglers Way SO31 128 B4
Anglesea Ct SO15 78 A1
Anglesea Rd
Lee-on-the-Solent PO13 180 A2
Portsmouth PO1 182 A3
Southampton SO15 78 A1
Anglesea Terr SO14 103 D2
Anglesey Arms Rd PO12 181 D1
Anglesey Rd PO12 181 D1
Anglesey View 8 PO12 181 D2
Anglewood Mnsns 9 BH4 204 B2
Anglo-European Coll of
Chiropractic BH5 206 A2
Angmering House 28 PO1 182 B3
Angus Cl PO15 130 C2
Anjou Cl BH11 188 B3
Anjou Cres PO15 130 B1
Anker La PO14 154 B2
Ankerwyke PO13 155 D1
Anmore Cl PO9 135 E2
Anmore Cnr PO7 111 D2
Anmore Dr PO7 111 E1
Anmore La PO7 111 E3
Anmore Rd PO7 111 D2
Ann's Hill Rd PO12 181 D3
Anna La BH23 168 A2
Annandale Ct BH6 206 B2
Anne Cl BH23 192 A1
Anne Cres PO7 134 C3
Annerley Rd BH1 205 E2
Annes Ct PO11 184 C1
Annet Cl BH15 201 F1
Anson Cl Christchurch BH23 207 F3
Gosport PO13 180 B3
Ringwood BH24 141 E4
Anson Dr SO19 104 B3
Anson Gr PO16 132 C1
Anson Rd PO4 183 D3
Anstey Cl BH11 189 D3
Anstey Rd Bournemouth BH11 189 D3
Romsey SO51 28 A1
Antell's Way SP6 93 D3
Anthill Cl PO7 110 B3
Anthony Gr PO12 156 A1
Anthony Way PO10 136 C2
Anthony's Ave BH14 203 E1
Antigua House 5 PO6 132 C1
Antler Dr BH25 194 C2
Anton Cl SO51 53 E4

Anvil Cl PO7 — 112 B1
Anvil Cres BH18 — 186 C3
Anvil Ct PO4 — 183 D2
Anzac Cl PO14 — 154 B2
Apex Ctr PO14 — 155 D3
Apless La PO7 — 110 A2
Apollo Cl BH12 — 203 E4
Apollo Dr PO7 — 134 C2
Apollo Rd SO53 — 55 F4
Apple Cl BH12 — 204 A2
Apple Gr BH23 — 191 F1
Apple Ind Est PO15 — 129 E3
Apple Tree Cl SP5 — 47 E4
Apple Tree Gr BH22 — 165 F3
Apple Tree Rd SP6 — 92 C3
Applemore Coll SO45 — 125 E2
Applemore Recn Ctr SO45 — 125 E2
Appleshaw SO22 — 1 B2
Appleshaw Gn PO9 — 135 E2
Appleslade Way BH25 — 195 D3
Appleton Rd Fareham PO15 — 130 B1
   Southampton SO18 — 79 F1
Appletree Cl SO30 — 106 A4
Appletree Rd SP5 — 47 E4
Applewood Gdns SO19 — 104 A2
Applewood Gr PO7 — 134 B2
Applewood Pl SO40 — 100 B3
Applewood Rd PO9 — 135 E2
Appollo Pl SO18 — 104 A4
Approach Rd BH14 — 203 D2
Approach The PO3 — 158 A1
April Cl Bournemouth BH11 — 189 D2
   Southampton SO18 — 104 A4
April Gr SO31 — 128 C2
Apsley Cres BH17 — 187 E1
Apsley Ct 2 BH8 — 205 D3
Apsley Rd SO53 — 30 A1
Apsley Rd PO4 — 183 D2
Aquila Way SO31 — 127 F1
Aquitanis House 6 SO14 — 103 E3
Arabian Gdns PO15 — 129 E4
Aragon Way BH9 — 190 A2
Arbour Ct 15 SO22 — 10 C4
Arcade BH4 — 204 A2
Arcade The
   37 Bournemouth BH1 — 204 C2
   Liss GU33 — 20 C3
Arcadia Ave BH8 — 205 D4
Arcadia Cl SO16 — 78 B2
Arcadia Rd BH23 — 191 E1
Arch Farm Ind Est SP6 — 69 F2
Archdale Cl BH10 — 189 E1
Archer House PO12 — 181 E1
Archers SO15 — 102 C3
Archers Cl SO40 — 76 B1
Archers Rd Eastleigh SO50 — 56 A2
   Southampton SO15 — 102 C4
Archery Gdns SO19 — 103 F1
Archery Gr SO19 — 103 F1
Archery La Fareham PO16 — 131 E1
   Winchester SO22 — 10 C4
Archery Rd SO19 — 103 F1
Archgate SO41 — 197 F2
Archway Rd BH14 — 203 F2
Arden Cl Gosport PO12 — 180 C2
   Southampton SO18 — 80 A1
Arden Rd BH9 — 189 F2
Arden Wlk BH25 — 195 D1
Ardingly Cres SO30 — 81 E1
Ardington Rise PO7 — 134 C2
Ardmore BH14 — 203 D2
Ardnave Cres SO16 — 78 C3
Argosy Cl SO31 — 128 C1
Argus Rd PO13 — 179 F2
Argyle Cres PO15 — 130 C1
Argyle Rd Christchurch BH23 — 207 F3
   Southampton SO15 — 103 D3
Argyll Mansions 11 BH5 — 205 F2
Argyll Rd Bournemouth BH5 — 205 F2
   Poole BH12 — 203 E3
Ariadne Rd PO1 — 182 A2
Ariel Cl BH6 — 207 D2
Ariel Dr BH6 — 207 D2
Ariel Rd PO1 — 182 C3
Arismore Ct PO13 — 179 E2
Ark Royal Cres PO13 — 179 F2
Arle Cl PO8 — 88 B2
Arley Rd BH14 — 203 D1
Arlington Ct BH25 — 210 A4
Arlington Pl
   30 Winchester SO23 — 2 A1
   2 Winchester SO23 — 11 D4
Arliss Rd SO16 — 78 A1
Arlott Ct SO15 — 102 C4
Armada Cl SO16 — 77 F4
Armada Dr SO45 — 125 F1
Armadale House 20 SO14 — 103 E3
Arminers Cl PO12 — 181 D1
Armitage Ave SO45 — 125 F1
Armory La PO1 — 182 A2
Armstrong Cl
   Brockenhurst SO42 — 145 F1
   Waterlooville PO7 — 111 E1
Armstrong Ct SO16 — 77 F3
Armstrong La SO42 — 145 F1
Armstrong Rd SO42 — 145 F1
Armsworth La SO32 — 85 F1
Arnaud Cl PO2 — 182 B4
Arne Ave BH12 — 203 F4
Arne Cres BH12 — 203 F4
Arnewood Bridge Rd SO41 — 196 A4
Arnewood Ct
   Bournemouth BH2 — 204 C1
   Sway SO41 — 196 B3
Arnewood House SO41 — 196 B2

Arnewood Rd BH6 — 206 B3
Arnewood Sch The BH25 — 194 C1
Arnheim Cl SO16 — 78 B2
Arnheim Rd SO16 — 78 B2
Arnold Cl BH22 — 138 C2
Arnold Rd Eastleigh SO50 — 80 A4
   Southampton SO17 — 79 E1
   West Moors BH22 — 138 C2
Arnolds Cl BH25 — 209 F4
Arnside Rd PO7 — 134 C4
Arnwood Ave SO45 — 149 F4
Arragon Ct PO7 — 135 D4
Arran Cl PO6 — 133 F1
Arran Way BH23 — 194 A1
Arras House PO15 — 130 B2
Arreton SO31 — 127 E3
Arreton Ct 10 PO12 — 181 D3
Arrow Cl Eastleigh SO50 — 56 A2
   Southampton SO19 — 103 E1
Arrowsmith Ct BH18 — 187 D3
Arrowsmith La PO21 — 187 F4
Arrowsmith Rd PO21 — 187 F4
Arters Lawn SO40 — 124 B3
Arthur Cl PO4 — 204 C3
Arthur Kille House PO7 — 134 B3
Arthur Pope House 4 PO5 — 182 B2
Arthur Rd Christchurch BH23 — 207 D4
   Eastleigh SO50 — 56 A2
   Southampton SO15 — 102 B3
   Winchester SO23 — 2 A1
Arthur St PO2 — 182 C4
Arthurs Gdns SO30 — 81 D2
Artillery Cl 1 PO6 — 157 E4
Artillery Terr PO4 — 183 D2
Arun Cl BH24 — 80 A1
Arun Way SO51 — 50 B2
Arundel Cl BH25 — 194 C2
Arundel Ct Inf Sch PO1 — 182 B3
Arundel Ct Jun Sch PO1 — 182 B3
Arundel Dr PO16 — 131 D1
Arundel House 19 SO14 — 103 E3
Arundel Rd Eastleigh SO50 — 56 A3
   Gosport PO12 — 180 C3
   Totton SO40 — 101 D4
Arundel St PO1 — 182 B3
Arundel Way BH24 — 208 C4
Arundel Way Sh Arc 14 PO1 — 182 B3
Ascham Rd BH8 — 205 D3
Ascot Cl PO14 — 129 E1
Ascot Rd Broadstone BH18 — 187 D2
   Fair Oak SO50 — 81 E4
   Portsmouth PO3 — 183 D4
Ascupart House 22 SO17 — 103 D4
Ascupart St SO14 — 103 D2
Asford Gr SO50 — 56 B2
Ash Cl Alderholt SP6 — 93 D3
   Bursledon SO31 — 127 F4
   Colden Common SO21 — 32 A1
   Fareham PO14 — 154 C4
   Gosport PO12 — 181 D2
   Hythe SO45 — 150 A4
   North Baddesley SO52 — 53 F3
   Romsey SO51 — 53 E3
   Southampton SO19 — 104 B3
   Upton BH16 — 201 D4
   Waterlooville PO8 — 111 F1
Ash Gr Ashurst SO40 — 100 B2
   Hordle SO41 — 211 E4
   Ringwood BH24 — 141 E4
Ash Rd SO40 — 100 A1
Ash Tree Rd SO18 — 79 F1
Ashbarn Cres SO22 — 10 C3
Ashbourne Ct 1 BH1 — 205 D2
Ashbourne Rd BH5 — 206 A3
Ashbridge Rise SO53 — 30 A1
Ashburn Garth PO14 — 141 E3
Ashburnham Cl SO19 — 103 E3
Ashburton Gdns BH10 — 189 E1
Ashburton House 9 SO41 — 127 D3
Ashburton Rd Gosport PO12 — 180 C1
   Portsmouth PO5 — 182 B1
Ashby Cres SO40 — 100 B4
Ashby Pl PO5 — 182 B1
Ashby Rd Southampton SO19 — 104 A2
   Totton SO40 — 100 B4
Ashcroft Ct 9 GU32 — 40 C2
Ashcroft La PO8 — 113 D3
Ashdene 16 SO15 — 102 A4
Ashdene BH21 — 163 E3
Ashdene Rd SO40 — 100 B2
Ashdown Bournemouth BH2 — 204 B1
   Fawley SO45 — 150 C2
   Gosport PO12 — 155 E1
Ashdown Cl
   Chandler's Ford SO53 — 30 B1
   Poole BH17 — 187 F1
Ashdown Dr SO53 — 30 B1
Ashdown Rd Blackfield SO45 — 150 C1
   Chandler's Ford SO53 — 30 B1
Ashdown Sch SO17 — 187 F1
Ashdown Way SO51 — 53 D4
Ashdown Wlk BH25 — 195 E1
Ashe Rd 45 PO9 — 136 A3
Ashen Cl SO53 — 55 E4
Ashford Chace GU32 — 19 F1
Ashford Cl SP6 — 69 E1
Ashford Cres SO45 — 126 A3
Ashford Rd Bournemouth BH6 — 206 B4
   Fordingbridge SP6 — 93 E4
Ashington Cl PO8 — 112 A2
Ashington Gdns BH21 — 186 C4
Ashington La BH21 — 163 D1
Ashington Park SO41 — 195 D1
Ashlea SO50 — 57 E1
Ashleigh Cl SO45 — 150 A4
Ashlett Cl SO45 — 151 E2
Ashlett Gdns BH25 — 195 E2

Ashlett Lawn 11 PO9 — 135 E3
Ashlett Mews SO45 — 151 D2
Ashlett Rd SO45 — 151 E2
Ashley Arnewood Ct 9 BH25 — 195 D1
Ashley Cl Bournemouth BH1 — 205 F3
   Havant PO9 — 135 E2
   Horndean PO8 — 111 F3
   Ringwood BH24 — 141 E4
   Swanwick SO31 — 129 D4
   Winchester SO23 — 1 B2
Ashley Common Rd BH25 — 195 E2
Ashley Cres SO19 — 104 B1
Ashley Cross SP 6 — 71 F1
Ashley Ct Bursledon SO31 — 105 D1
   9 Gosport PO12 — 181 D3
   West Moors BH22 — 166 A4
Ashley Dr N BH24 — 139 F3
Ashley Dr S BH24 — 139 F3
Ashley Dr W BH24 — 139 F3
Ashley Gdns
   Chandler's Ford SO53 — 55 F3
   Shedfield SO32 — 83 F2
Ashley Heath Ind Est BH21 — 139 D4
Ashley House SO51 — 52 C3
Ashley Inf Sch BH25 — 195 E2
Ashley Jun Sch BH25 — 195 E2
Ashley La Hordle SO41 — 195 F2
   Lymington SO41 — 197 F2
   New Milton BH25 — 195 F2
Ashley Meadows SO51 — 53 D4
Ashley Meads BH25 — 195 E2
Ashley Park BH24 — 140 A3
Ashley Rd
   Bournemouth BH1, BH7 — 205 F3
   New Milton BH25 — 195 E2
   Poole BH14 — 203 E3
Ashley Wlk PO6 — 158 A3
Ashleycross Cl SO45 — 150 B2
Ashling Cl Bournemouth BH8 — 205 E4
   Denmead PO7 — 110 C2
Ashling Cres BH8 — 205 D4
Ashling Gdns PO7 — 110 C2
Ashling La PO7 — 157 E1
Ashling Park Rd PO7 — 110 C2
Ashlyn Cl PO15 — 130 B1
Ashmead Rd SO16 — 77 F2
Ashmeads Cl BH21 — 164 A3
Ashmeads Way BH21 — 164 A3
Ashmede BH4 — 204 B1
Ashmore BH21 — 163 E2
Ashmore Ave
   Barton on Sea BH25 — 210 A4
   Hamworthy BH15 — 201 F1
Ashmore Cl BH25 — 24 A2
Ashmore Cres BH15 — 201 F1
Ashmore Gr BH23 — 193 F1
Ashmore La West Dean SP5 — 24 A3
   Whiteparish SP5 — 24 A3
Ashmore Rd SO22 — 1 B1
Ashridge Ave BH10 — 189 E3
Ashridge Cl SO15 — 102 C4
Ashridge Gdns BH10 — 189 E3
Ashridge Par BH10 — 189 E3
Ashstead Cl PO16 — 156 A4
Ashton Cl SO32 — 59 D1
Ashton Cross SO51 — 51 D1
Ashton Ct 13 BH25 — 195 D2
Ashton House SO19 — 103 F1
Ashton La SO32 — 59 D1
Ashton Pl SO53 — 30 A1
Ashton Rd BH9 — 189 F1
Ashton Way PO14 — 179 E2
Ashtree Cl BH25 — 195 E1
Ashtree Ct SO53 — 55 E2
Ashurst Bridge Rd
   Netley Marsh SO40 — 100 B3
   Totton SO40 — 100 B3
Ashurst Cl Ashurst SO40 — 100 A1
   Southampton SO19 — 104 A1
   Winchester SO22 — 1 B2
Ashurst Ct PO12 — 180 B2
Ashurst Hospl (Geriatric)
   SO40 — 100 A1
Ashurst (New Forest) Sta
   SO40 — 100 A1
Ashurst Rd Bournemouth BH8 — 190 B2
   Cosham PO6 — 157 F4
   West Moors BH22 — 138 C2
Ashwell Ct BH23 — 191 F1
Ashwood
   Swanwick, Whiteley PO15 — 129 F3
   Titchfield SO31 — 129 E3
Ashwood Cl Havant PO9 — 135 D2
   South Hayling PO11 — 185 D2
Ashwood Dr BH18 — 187 E2
Ashwood Gdns
   Southampton SO16 — 78 C2
   Totton SO40 — 100 B4
Ashwood Lodge 1 PO16 — 131 D1
Aspen Ave SO31 — 152 B4
Aspen Cl Colden Common SO21 — 57 D4
   Hedge End SO30 — 105 D4
Aspen Dr BH31 — 115 D3
Aspen Gdns BH12 — 203 F4
Aspen Holt SO16 — 79 D3
Aspen Pl BH25 — 195 D1
Aspen Rd BH12 — 203 F4
Aspen Way Poole BH12 — 203 F4
   Waterlooville PO8 — 112 A3
Aspen Wlk SO40 — 100 A4
Aspengrove PO13 — 155 F1
Asquith Cl BH21 — 207 E3
Assheton Ct PO16 — 156 B4
Astbury Ave BH12 — 189 D1
Aster Rd SO16 — 79 E2
Astley St PO5 — 182 B2

Aston Mead BH23 — 191 F2
Aston Rd Portsmouth PO4 — 182 C2
   Waterlooville PO7 — 134 B4
Astra Ct 3 SO45 — 126 A3
Astra Wlk PO12 — 181 E2
Astral Gdns SO31 — 127 F2
Astrid Cl PO11 — 185 E2
Asturias Way SO14 — 103 E2
Asylum Rd SO15 — 103 D3
Atalanta Cl PO4 — 183 E3
Atheling Rd SO45 — 126 A2
Athelney Ct 18 BH1 — 205 D2
Athelstan Rd
   Bournemouth BH1 — 206 C3
   Southampton SO19 — 103 F3
Athelston Ct SO41 — 197 E2
Athena Ave PO7 — 134 C2
Athena Cl SO31 — 57 D2
Athena Ct BH24 — 140 B3
Atherfield Rd SO16 — 77 F2
Atherley Rd
   South Hayling PO11 — 184 C3
   Southampton SO15 — 102 B3
Atherley Sch SO16 — 77 D3
Atherstone Wlk 48 PO5 — 182 B2
Atkins Pl PO15 — 130 B2
Atkinson Cl PO12 — 181 D1
Atlantic Cl SO14 — 103 D1
Atlantic Park View SO18 — 80 A1
Atlantis Ave PO7 — 134 C1
Attwood Cl SP6 — 92 C3
Attwoods Dro SO21 — 10 B1
Aubrey Cl SO41 — 211 F2
Aubrey Farm Cotts SO41 — 212 A2
Auckland Ave SO42 — 146 A1
Auckland Pl SO42 — 146 A1
Auckland Rd
   Christchurch BH23 — 208 B4
   Southampton SO15 — 101 F4
Auckland Rd E PO5 — 182 B1
Auckland Rd W PO5 — 182 B1
Audemer Ct PO14 — 141 E4
Audrayton Ct 9 BH6 — 206 C2
   Southampton SO18 — 103 D3
Audret Cl PO16 — 156 A3
Augustine Rd Cosham PO6 — 158 B4
   Southampton SO14 — 103 D3
Augustus Cl SO53 — 55 F4
Augustus Way SO53 — 55 F4
Auriol Dr PO9 — 159 D1
Aust Rd PO14 — 154 B4
Austen Ave
   Bournemouth BH10 — 189 F3
   Winchester SO22 — 10 B2
Austen Cl Totton SO40 — 100 B3
   Winchester SO22 — 2 A1
Austen Gdns PO15 — 129 E4
Auster Cl BH23 — 208 A4
Austerberry Way PO13 — 180 C4
Austin Ave BH14 — 203 D1
Austin Cl BH1 — 205 E3
Austin Ct PO7 — 133 D1
Australia Cl PO1 — 182 B3
Autumn Cl BH22 — 165 D4
Autumn Copse BH25 — 195 E1
Autumn Pl 18 SO17 — 79 D1
Autumn Rd SO40 — 102 A1
Avalan Ct SO22 — 10 C3
Avalon BH24 — 214 B4
Avalon Ct PO10 — 136 C1
Avebury Ave BH10 — 189 F3
Avebury Gdns SO53 — 30 A1
Avenger Cl SO53 — 55 D3
Avens Cl SO30 — 81 E3
Avenue C SO45 — 150 C4
Avenue Campus (Univ of
   Southampton) SO17 — 79 D1
Avenue Ct Gosport PO12 — 181 D1
   Poole BH13 — 204 A2
   1 Southampton SO17 — 102 C4
Avenue D SO45 — 150 C4
Avenue De Caen PO5 — 182 B1
Avenue E SO45 — 150 C4
Avenue La 20 BH2 — 204 C2
Avenue Rd
   Bournemouth BH2 — 204 C2
   Brockenhurst SO42 — 172 C4
   Christchurch BH23 — 206 C4
   Christchurch, Walkford BH23 — 194 B1
   Fareham PO14 — 130 C1
   Gosport PO12 — 181 D2
   Lymington SO41 — 197 F2
   New Milton BH25 — 195 D2
   North Hayling PO11 — 160 A2
   Southampton SO14 — 103 D4
   Wimborne Minster BH21 — 163 E2
   Winchester SO22 — 10 C4
Avenue Sh Ctr The 21 BH2 — 204 C2
Avenue The
   Bishop's Waltham SO32 — 83 D4
   Bournemouth BH9 — 189 F2
   Fareham PO14 — 130 B1
   Gosport PO12 — 181 D2
   Petersfield GU31 — 40 C2
   Poole BH13 — 204 A1
   Southampton SO17 — 102 C4
   Twyford SO21 — 32 A3
   West Moors BH22 — 138 C2
Avery La PO12 — 181 D4
Avington Cl SO50 — 56 B3
Avington Ct SO16 — 78 C2
Avington Gn PO9 — 136 A3
Avocet Cl PO4 — 183 D3
Avocet House PO13 — 183 D3
Avocet Quay PO10 — 161 D4
Avocet Wlk PO13 — 155 D1
Avon Ave BH24 — 140 B2
Avon Bldgs BH23 — 207 D4
Avon Castle BH24 — 140 B2
Avon Castle Dr BH24 — 140 B2

Avon Cl Bournemouth BH8 — 205 E3
   Lee-on-the-Solent PO13 — 179 F1
   Lymington SO41 — 197 E2
   Petersfield GU32 — 40 C1
Avon Cotts BH23 — 192 B3
Avon Cres SO51 — 53 E4
Avon Cswy BH23 — 191 E4
Avon Ct Christchurch BH23 — 207 E3
   Fordingbridge SP6 — 69 F1
   Netley SO31 — 127 E3
   2 Waterlooville PO8 — 111 F2
Avon Dyke SP5 — 46 C3
Avon Farm Cotts BH23 — 167 F2
Avon Gdns BH23 — 169 D1
Avon Gr SO53 — 55 E3
Avon Heath Ctry Pk
   (North Pk) BH24 — 140 A2
Avon Heath Ctry Pk
   (South Pk) BH24 — 167 E4
Avon House Bournemouth BH2 — 204 C1
   8 Southampton SO14 — 103 E3
Avon Meade SP6 — 69 F1
Avon Meadow SP5 — 46 C4
Avon Mews BH8 — 205 E3
Avon Park BH24 — 140 B3
Avon Rd Bournemouth BH8 — 205 E3
   Southampton SO18 — 79 F1
   West Moors BH22 — 138 C1
Avon Rd E BH23 — 207 D4
Avon Rd W BH23 — 206 C4
Avon Run Cl BH23 — 208 A3
Avon Run Rd BH23 — 208 A3
Avon View SP6 — 70 B1
Avon View Par BH23 — 192 B2
Avon View Rd BH23 — 192 B2
Avon Way SO30 — 80 C1
Avon Wharf BH23 — 207 E3
Avon Wlk PO16 — 156 A4
Avonborne Way SO53 — 55 D4
Avonbourne Sch BH7 — 206 A4
Avoncliffe Rd BH6 — 206 C2
Avondale Ct SO17 — 79 D1
Avondale Rd Portsmouth PO1 — 182 C4
   Waterlooville PO7 — 134 C4
Avonlea Sch BH24 — 141 D4
Award Rd BH21 — 164 C3
Awbridge Prim Sch SO51 — 26 B3
Awbridge Rd PO9 — 135 E2
Axford Cl BH8 — 190 B2
Aylen Rd PO3 — 158 A1
Aylesbury Rd
   Bournemouth BH1 — 205 F2
   Portsmouth PO2 — 182 C4
Ayling Cl PO13 — 180 B4
Aylward St PO1 — 182 A3
Aynsley Ct SO15 — 102 B4
Aysgarth Rd PO7 — 134 C4
Aysha Cl PO13 — 195 D1
Azalea Cl BH24 — 140 A3
Azura Cl BH31 — 139 D3

B Ave Fawley SO45 — 150 B3
   Fawley SO45 — 150 C2
Back La Mottisfont SO51 — 5 F3
   Ringwood BH24 — 141 F4
   Southwick PO17 — 132 C3
   Sway SO41 — 172 B1
Back of the Walls
   Southampton SO14 — 103 D1
   Southampton SO14 — 103 D2
Back St SO23 — 10 C2
Bacon Cl SO19 — 103 F1
Bacon La PO11 — 184 C2
Badbury Cl BH18 — 187 E2
Badbury Ct 7 BH23 — 207 F3
Badbury View BH21 — 163 E3
Badbury View Rd BH21 — 186 B4
Baddesley Cl SO52 — 53 F3
Baddesley Gdns PO9 — 135 E4
Baddesley Rd SO53 — 30 A1
Baden Cl BH14 — 195 D1
Baden Powell & St Peter's
   CE Mid Sch BH14 — 203 D2
Baden Powell Way 13 SO51 — 52 C4
Bader Cl SO30 — 105 E4
Bader Rd BH17 — 202 C4
Bader Way PO15 — 129 F3
Badger Brow PO7 — 175 D3
Badger Cl Bishopstoke SO50 — 56 C1
   Fareham PO15 — 130 B1
Badger Ct SO50 — 56 C1
Badger Farm Rd SO22 — 10 B2
Badger Rd PO14 — 154 C3
Badger Way BH31 — 114 C3
Badger Wood Pl SO18 — 79 F1
Badgers Cl St Leonards BH24 — 139 F3
   Sway SO41 — 172 B1
Badgers Copse BH25 — 195 E3
Badgers The SO31 — 127 E3
Badgers Wlk Ferndown BH22 — 165 F4
   Hythe SO45 — 125 F1
Badminston Dro SO45 — 178 B4
Badminston La SO45 — 151 E2
Badshear La SO24 — 14 C4
Baffins Rd PO3 — 183 D4
Bagber Rd SO40 — 100 C4
Bagot House PO12 — 180 C3
Bagshot Mews SO19 — 103 F2
Baigent Cl SO23 — 11 E4
Bailey Cl Botley SO30 — 106 A3
   New Milton BH25 — 195 E2
   Winchester SO22 — 10 B3
Bailey Cres BH15 — 202 B4
Bailey Gn SO18 — 80 A1
Bailey's Rd PO5 — 182 B2

Baiter Gdns BH15 .... 202 B1
Baker Rd BH11 .... 189 D3
Baker St PO1 .... 182 B4
Bakers Dro SO16 .... 77 F3
Bakers Farm Rd BH31 .... 114 C4
Balaclava Rd SO18 .... 104 A4
Balcombe Rd BH13 .... 204 A2
Balderton Cl 15 PO2 .... 157 F2
Baldwin Ct BH23 .... 207 E3
Balena Cl BH17 .... 202 A4
Balfour Cl Christchurch BH23 .. 208 B4
Gosport PO13 .... 180 B3
Balfour Dr GU33 .... 20 C2
Balfour Rd Bournemouth BH9 .. 189 F1
Portsmouth PO2 .... 157 F1
Southampton SO19 .... 104 B3
Ball La 18 BH15 .... 202 B1
Ballam Cl BH16 .... 201 E4
Ballard Cl New Milton BH25 .. 195 D2
Poole BH15 .... 202 B1
Southampton SO16 .... 77 E1
Ballard Coll BH25 .... 195 D2
Ballard Ct 1 BH12 .... 181 D2
Ballard Lake Prep Sch BH25 . 195 D2
Ballard Rd BH15 .... 202 B1
Balliol Cl PO14 .... 129 E1
Balliol Rd PO2 .... 182 C4
Balmer Lawn Rd SO42 .... 146 A2
Balmoral Ave BH8 .... 190 C1
Balmoral Cl
Chandler's Ford SO53 .... 55 D4
Gosport PO13 .... 155 E1
Southampton SO16 .... 78 B3
Balmoral Ct
7 Christchurch BH23 .... 209 D4
6 Southampton SO17 .... 103 D4
Southampton, Millbrook SO15 .. 102 A3
Balmoral Dr BH2 .... 134 B2
Balmoral House BH2 .... 204 B2
Balmoral Rd Fareham PO15 .. 130 C2
Poole BH14 .... 203 E2
Balmoral Way
Petersfield GU32 .... 40 C2
Rownhams SO16 .... 77 F3
Balmoral Wlk BH25 .... 194 C2
Balston Rd BH23 .... 203 D3
Balston Terr BH15 .... 202 A1
Baltic St SO30 .... 80 C1
Bamford House PO4 .... 183 D1
Banbury Ave SO17 .... 104 B2
Banbury Rd BH17 .... 202 B4
Banfurly Gdns SO45 .... 125 F1
Bangor Rd SO15 .... 102 A3
Banister Cl 13 SO15 .... 102 C4
Banister Gdns SO15 .... 102 C4
Banister Grange 16 SO15 .... 102 C4
Banister Inf Sch SO15 .... 102 C4
Banister Mews SO15 .... 102 C4
Banister Rd SO15 .... 102 C4
Bank Chambers BH14 .... 203 F2
Bank Cl BH23 .... 207 D3
Bank Side SO18 .... 79 E2
Bank St SO32 .... 83 E4
Bankhill Dr SO41 .... 197 E3
Banks Rd BH13 .... 214 B2
Banks The SO51 .... 26 A3
Bankside SO41 .... 197 E3
Bankside Rd BH9 .... 190 A2
Bankview SO41 .... 197 E3
Bannerman Rd GU32 .... 40 C2
Banning St SO51 .... 52 C3
Bannister Ct SO40 .... 101 D4
Banocroft Ct 1 BH15 .... 202 C4
Banstead Rd BH18 .... 187 D3
Bapaume Rd PO3 .... 157 F3
Bar End Ind Est SO23 .... 11 D3
Bar End Rd SO23 .... 11 D3
Bar Gate & Guildhall(Mus)
SO14 .... 102 C2
Barbe Baker Ave SO30 .... 80 B1
Barberry Way BH31 .... 115 E3
Barbers Gate 15 BH15 .... 202 A1
Barbers Piles 8 BH15 .... 202 A1
Barbers Wharf 16 BH15 ...... 202 A1
Barclay House PO12 .... 181 D2
Barclay Mansions BH2 .... 204 C3
Barclay Mews Hythe SO45 .. 149 F4
Hythe SO45 .... 150 A4
Bardon Way PO14 .... 154 B4
Barfield Cl SO23 .... 11 D3
Barfields SO41 .... 197 F2
Barfields Cl SO41 .... 197 F2
Barfleur Cl PO15 .... 130 B1
Barfleur Rd PO14 .... 155 D3
Barford Cl SO53 .... 55 D4
Barford La SP5 .... 47 D4
Bargate Ctr 8 SO14 .... 103 D2
Bargate St SO14 .... 102 C2
Bargates BH23 .... 207 D4
Barham Cl PO12 .... 181 D3
Barham Rd GU32 .... 40 C2
Baring Rd Bournemouth BH6 .. 207 D2
Winchester SO23 .... 11 D4
Barker Mill Cl SO16 .... 77 F3
Barkis House 11 PO1 .... 182 B4
Barkshire Ct 7 SO15 .... 102 C4
Barlands SO18 .... 192 B1
Barle Cl SO18 .... 80 A1
Barley Down Dr SO22 .... 10 B2
Barleycorn Wlk SO40 .... 98 C4
Barlow Cl PO14 .... 179 D3
Barn Cl Emsworth PO10 ...... 160 B4
Upton BH16 .... 201 D4
Barn Fold PO7 .... 112 B1
Barn Rd BH18 .... 187 D2

Barnaby Cl SP5 .... 46 B4
Barnbrook Rd SO31 .... 128 C2
Barncroft Inf Sch PO9 .... 135 E2
Barncroft Jun Sch PO9 .... 135 E2
Barncroft Way PO9 .... 135 D2
Barnes Cl Bournemouth BH10 .. 189 E2
Locks Heath SO31 .... 128 B2
Southampton SO19 .... 104 B3
West Wellow SO51 .... 50 C2
Winchester SO23 .... 10 C3
Barnes Cres
Bournemouth BH10 .... 189 E2
Wimborne Minster BH21 ..... 163 F2
Barnes La Locks Heath SO31 . 128 C2
Milford on Sea SO41 .... 211 E3
Barnes Rd Bournemouth BH10 .. 189 E2
Portsmouth PO1 .... 182 C3
Southampton SO19 .... 104 B3
Barnes Wallis Rd PO15 ...... 129 E2
Barnes Way PO9 .... 135 E3
Barnet Side La GU32 .... 18 B3
Barney Evans Cres PO8 ...... 111 E2
Barney Hayes La SO40 .... 99 D4
Barnfield BH23 .... 208 B4
Barnfield Cl Southampton SO19 . 103 F1
Southbourne PO10 .... 137 F1
Barnfield Ct Fareham PO14 .. 154 C4
Southampton SO19 .... 103 F1
Barnfield Flats SO19 .... 103 F1
Barnfield Rd Petersfield GU31 .. 41 E2
Southampton SO19 .... 103 F1
Barnfield Way SO19 .... 103 F1
Barns Rd SO32 .... 166 A3
Barnsfield Cres SO40 .... 100 B4
Barnside Way GU33 .... 20 C2
Barnsland SO30 .... 80 B2
Barnwood Rd PO15 .... 130 B1
Baron Cl SO18 .... 104 A4
Barons Ct 8 BH12 .... 204 A2
Barons Mead SO16 .... 77 F2
Barons Rd BH11 .... 188 B3
Barrack Lane PO14 .... 141 E2
Barrack Rd Christchurch BH23 . 206 C4
Ferndown BH22 .... 166 A1
Barratt Ind Est PO15 .... 129 E3
Barrie Cl PO15 .... 129 E4
Barrie Rd BH9 .... 189 F2
Barrington Cl SO50 .... 55 F3
Barrington Ct 31 SO17 .... 79 D1
Barrington House 23 PO1 ... 182 B4
Barrow Down Gdns SO19 .... 104 C3
Barrow Dr BH8 .... 190 C1
Barrow Hill Rd SO40 .... 75 E2
Barrow Rd BH8 .... 190 C1
Barrow View BH22 .... 165 D3
Barrow Way BH8 .... 190 C1
Barrowgate Rd BH8 .... 190 B2
Barrowgate Way BH8 .... 190 B2
Barrows La Landford SP5 .... 49 E3
Sway SO41 .... 196 A3
Barrs Ave BH25 .... 195 D2
Barrs Wood Dr BH25 .... 195 D2
Barrs Wood Rd BH25 .... 195 D2
Barry Gdns BH18 .... 186 C3
Barry Rd SO19 .... 104 A3
Barters Cl SO16 .... 77 F1
Barters La BH18 .... 186 C2
Bartholomew La 25 SO23 .... 2 A1
Bartlett Cl PO15 .... 130 C2
Bartlett Dr BH7 .... 206 A4
Bartlett House 18 SO17 ...... 103 D4
Bartletts Comm SP6 .... 94 C4
Bartletts The SO31 .... 128 A1
Bartley Ave SO40 .... 100 C3
Bartley CE Sch SO40 .... 99 D4
Bartley Ct 5 BH21 .... 163 D3
Bartley Rd SO40 .... 99 E2
Barton Cl SO51 .... 53 D4
Barton Common La BH25 .... 210 A4
Barton Common Rd BH25 .... 210 A4
Barton Court Ave BH25 ...... 210 A4
Barton Court Rd BH25 .... 195 D1
Barton Cres SO18 .... 79 F1
Barton Croft BH25 .... 210 A4
Barton Ct BH25 .... 210 A3
Barton Ctr The BH25 .... 78 A1
Barton Dr Barton on Sea BH25 . 209 F4
Hamble-le-Rice SO31 .... 127 F2
Hedge End SO30 .... 105 E4
Barton Gn BH25 .... 210 A3
Barton Gr PO3 .... 158 A2
Barton House BH25 .... 209 F4
Barton La BH25 .... 209 F4
Barton Lodge BH12 .... 203 D3
Barton Park Ind Est SO50 .... 56 B1
Barton Peveril Coll SO50 .... 55 F1
Barton Rd SO50 .... 56 B2
Barton Way PO15 .... 209 F4
Barton Wood Rd BH25 .... 209 F4
Bartons Rd
Fordingbridge SP6 .... 69 E1
Havant PO9 .... 136 A2
Bartons The
Fordingbridge SP6 .... 69 E1
Hedge End SO30 .... 105 D3
Bartonside Rd BH25 .... 209 F4
Bartram Rd SO40 .... 101 D3
Barwell Gr PO10 .... 136 C2
Barwell Terr SO30 .... 105 E3
Bascott Cl BH11 .... 189 D1
Bascott Rd BH11 .... 189 D1
Bashley Common Rd BH25 .. 195 D4
Bashley Cross Rd BH25 ...... 194 C3
Bashley Dr BH25 .... 195 D3
Bashley Rd BH25 .... 195 D3
Basin St PO2 .... 182 B4
Basing Dean GU34 .... 17 F2
Basing House SO15 .... 102 B4

Basing Mews SO32 .... 83 E4
Basing Rd PO9 .... 135 F3
Basing Way SO53 .... 55 C2
Basingstoke Rd SO23 .... 2 B4
Basingwell St SO32 .... 83 E4
Bassett Ave SO16 .... 78 A3
Bassett Cl SO16 .... 78 C2
Bassett Cres E SO16 .... 78 C2
Bassett Cres W SO16 .... 78 C2
Bassett Ct SO16 .... 78 C2
Bassett Dale SO16 .... 78 C3
Bassett Gdns SO16 .... 78 C2
Bassett Gn SO16 .... 79 D3
Bassett Green Cl SO16 ...... 79 D3
Bassett Green Ct SO16 ...... 79 D3
Bassett Green Dr SO16 ...... 79 D3
Bassett Green Inf Sch SO16 . 79 D2
Bassett Green Jun Sch SO16 . 79 D2
Bassett Green Rd SO16 ...... 79 D3
Bassett Heath Ave SO16 .... 78 C3
Bassett Meadow SO16 ...... 78 C3
Bassett Mews SO16 .... 78 C3
Bassett Rd BH12 .... 203 D3
Bassett Row SO16 .... 78 C3
Bassett Wlk 7 PO9 .... 135 E3
Bassett Wood Dr SO16 ...... 79 D3
Bassett Wood Mews SO16 .. 78 C3
Bassett Wood Rd SO16 ...... 79 D3
Batchelor Cres BH11 .... 188 C4
Batchelor Gn SO31 .... 127 F4
Batchelor Rd BH11 .... 188 C2
Batcombe Cl BH11 .... 188 C2
Bath & Wells Ct PO13 .... 180 B3
Bath Cl SO18 .... 104 A3
Bath Hill Ct 9 BH1 .... 205 D2
Bath La 11 PO16 .... 131 E1
Bath La (lower) 13 PO16 .... 131 E1
Bath Lane Cotts PO16 .... 155 E4
Bath Rd Bournemouth BH1 .. 205 D2
Emsworth PO10 .... 160 C4
Lymington SO41 .... 197 F2
Portsmouth PO4 .... 182 C2
Southampton SO18 .... 104 A3
Bath Sq PO1 .... 181 F2
Bath St SO14 .... 103 D4
Bathing La PO1 .... 181 F2
Bathurst Way PO2 .... 157 D1
Batten Cl BH23 .... 207 E4
Batten Rd SP5 .... 46 C4
Battenburg Ave PO2 .... 157 F1
Battenburg Rd PO12 .... 181 E3
Battens Way PO9 .... 135 F2
Batterley Dro PO9 .... 91 F2
Battery Cl PO12 .... 180 C4
Battery Hill
Bishop's Waltham SO32 ..... 83 D4
Winchester SO22 .... 10 B3
Battery Row PO1 .... 182 A2
Battle Cl SO31 .... 129 D2
Battramsley Cross SO41 .... 173 E1
Baverstock Rd BH12 .... 204 A4
Baxter Rd SO19 .... 104 C3
Bay Cl Southampton SO19 ... 104 A2
Three Legged Cross BH21 ... 138 C3
Upton BH16 .... 201 D3
Bay Hog La BH15 .... 202 A1
Bay Rd Gosport PO12 .... 180 C2
Southampton SO19 .... 104 A2
Bay Tree Lodge PO14 .... 179 E3
Bay Tree Way BH23 .... 193 E1
Bay Trees SO19 .... 104 C3
Bay View Ct PO11 .... 184 B1
Bay View Mews PO11 .... 184 B1
Baybridge La SO21 .... 33 E2
Baybridge PO9 .... 136 A3
Baycroft Sch PO14 .... 179 F3
Bayly Ave PO16 .... 156 B3
Bays Cl SO41 .... 197 E2
Bays Rd SO41 .... 197 E2
Bayswater House 27 PO5 ... 182 B2
Baythorn Cl PO2 .... 182 B4
Beach Ave BH25 .... 209 F4
Beach Cl BH13 .... 214 B2
Beach La SO31 .... 127 D3
Beach Rd Emsworth PO10 ... 160 C4
Lee-on-the-Solent PO13 .... 179 F1
Poole BH13 .... 214 C4
Portsmouth PO5 .... 182 B1
South Hayling PO11 .... 184 C2
Upton BH16 .... 201 D3
Beach View BH13 .... 214 B2
Beachcroft BH13 .... 204 A2
Beachway PO16 .... 156 B3
Beacon Bottom SO31 .... 129 D3
Beacon Cl Hordle SO41 ...... 196 B1
Locks Heath SO31 .... 129 D3
Rownhams SO16 .... 77 E3
Beacon Ct Christchurch BH23 . 208 C4
Fordingbridge SP6 .... 69 E2
Beacon Dr BH23 .... 208 C4
Beacon Gdns BH18 .... 186 C2
Beacon Hill La
Droxford SO32 .... 60 C3
Meonstoke SO32 .... 61 E3
Beacon Mews SO30 .... 104 B4
Beacon Mount SO31 .... 129 D3
Beacon Park Cres BH16 ..... 201 D4
Beacon Park Rd BH16 .... 201 D4
Beacon Rd
Bournemouth BH2 .... 204 C1
Broadstone BH18 .... 186 C2
Upton BH16 .... 201 D4
West End SO30 .... 104 B4
Beacon Sq PO10 .... 160 C4
Beacon Way Broadstone BH18 . 186 C2
Locks Heath SO31 .... 129 D3
Beaconsfield Ave PO6 .... 158 A4

Beaconsfield Rd
Christchurch BH23 .... 207 D4
Fareham PO16 .... 155 D4
Poole BH12 .... 203 E3
Waterlooville PO7 .... 134 C4
Bealing Cl SO16 .... 79 D2
Beamish Rd BH17 .... 202 C4
Bear Cross Ave BH11 .... 188 C3
Bear Cross Rdbt BH11 .... 188 C3
Bearslane Cl SO40 .... 76 B1
Bearwood Prim Sch BH11 ... 188 B3
Beatrice Ct 5 SO41 .... 211 D2
Beatrice Mews 15 PO6 ...... 157 F4
Beatrice Rd Portsmouth PO4 .. 182 C1
Southampton SO15 .... 102 B4
Beatrice Royal Art Gal SO50 . 55 F1
Beattie Rise SO30 .... 81 E1
Beatty Cl Locks Heath SO31 .. 129 D2
Ringwood BH24 .... 141 E4
Beatty Dr PO12 .... 180 C2
Beatty Rd BH9 .... 190 A1
Beaty Ct SO19 .... 104 B3
Beau Ct 31 Bournemouth BH4 .. 204 B2
9 New Milton BH25 .... 195 D2
Beauchamp Ave PO13 .... 155 E1
Beauchamps Gdns BH7 ..... 206 A4
Beaucroft La BH21 .... 163 F3
Beaucroft Rd Shedfield SO32 . 83 F2
Wimborne Minster BH21 .... 163 F3
Beaufort Ave PO16 .... 130 C1
Beaufort Ct BH23 .... 208 A4
Beaufort Dr
Bishop's Waltham SO32 ..... 83 E4
Wimborne Minster BH21 .... 163 D2
Beaufort Mews BH21 .... 163 D2
Beaufort Rd Bournemouth BH6 . 206 B3
Havant PO9 .... 135 D1
10 Portsmouth PO5 .... 182 B1
Winchester SO23 .... 10 C3
Beaufoys Ave BH22 .... 165 E4
Beaufoys Cl BH22 .... 165 E4
Beaufoys Cl BH22 .... 165 E3
Beaulieu Abbey SO42 .... 148 C1
Beaulieu Ave
Christchurch BH23 .... 206 C4
Havant PO9 .... 135 E3
Portchester PO16 .... 156 A4
Beaulieu Cl New Milton BH25 . 194 C2
Southampton SO16 .... 78 A3
Winchester SO22 .... 1 B2
Beaulieu House 12 SO15 .... 102 C4
Beaulieu Pl PO13 .... 155 D1
Beaulieu Prim Sch SO42 .... 148 C1
Beaulieu Rd Beaulieu SO42 . 149 E3
Bournemouth BH4 .... 204 A1
Christchurch BH23 .... 206 C4
Eastleigh SO50 .... 56 A2
Hamble-le-Rice SO31 .... 127 F2
Hythe SO45 .... 125 F1
Lyndhurst SO42 .... 122 B2
Lyndhurst SO43 .... 122 B2
Marchwood SO40 .... 124 C3
Portsmouth PO2 .... 157 F1
Beaulieu Road Sta SO42 .... 123 E1
Beaumaris Cl SO53 .... 55 D2
Beaumond Gn SO22 .... 10 C4
Beaumont Cl Fareham PO15 . 130 B2
Southampton SO16 .... 78 C2
Beaumont Ct PO12 .... 181 D4
Beaumont Pl SO40 .... 101 D4
Beaumont Rd Poole BH13 ... 214 C4
Totton SO40 .... 101 D4
Beaumont Rise PO15 .... 130 B2
Beauworth Ave SO18 .... 104 B4
Beaver Dr SO50 .... 57 D1
Beaver Ind Est BH23 .... 208 A3
Beccles Cl BH15 .... 201 F1
Becher Rd BH14 .... 203 F2
Beck Cl SO31 .... 128 C2
Beck St PO1 .... 182 A3
Beckenham Terr PO10 .... 137 D2
Beckford La PO17 .... 109 F1
Beckham La GU32 .... 40 B2
Beckhampton Rd BH15 ...... 201 F2
Beckley Copse BH23 .... 194 A1
Becton Cl BH25 .... 210 A4
Becton Mead BH25 .... 195 D1
Bedale Way BH15 .... 202 C3
Bedales Sch GU32 .... 40 C4
Bedenham La PO13 .... 155 F2
Bedenham Prim Sch PO13 .. 155 E2
Bedfield House SO23 .... 2 A3
Bedfield La SO23 .... 2 A3
Bedford Ave SO19 .... 103 F1
Bedford Cl Fordingbridge SP6 . 69 F2
Havant PO9 .... 160 A4
Hedge End SO30 .... 105 E3
Bedford Cres BH7 .... 206 B4
Bedford Pl SO15 .... 102 C3
Bedford Rd N BH12 .... 188 B1
Bedford Rd S BH12 .... 188 B1
Bedford St Gosport PO12 ... 181 D2
Portsmouth PO5 .... 182 B2
Bedhampton Hill PO9 .... 135 D1
Bedhampton Rd Havant PO9 . 135 D1
Portsmouth PO2 .... 182 C4
Bedhampton Sta PO9 .... 135 E1
Bedhampton Way PO9 ...... 135 F2
Bedwell Cl SO16 .... 77 F3
Beech Ave Bournemouth BH6 . 206 B2
Christchurch BH23 .... 206 B4
Southampton SO18 .... 103 F4
Beech Cl Hordle SO41 .... 196 B1
Broadstone BH18 .... 186 C2
Chandler's Ford SO53 .... 30 B1
Hamble-le-Rice SO31 .... 127 F1

Beech Cl Continued
Hordle SO41 .... 211 D4
Romsey SO51 .... 53 E2
Verwood BH31 .... 114 C2
Waterlooville PO8 .... 111 F2
Winchester SO22 .... 10 A2
Beech Cnr SO32 .... 81 F2
Beech Copse SO22 .... 1 A1
Beech Cres SO45 .... 150 A4
Beech Ct Southampton SO19 . 103 F2
Wimborne Minster SO21 ... 163 F2
Beech Gdns SO31 .... 127 D3
Beech Gr Gosport PO12 ..... 181 D2
Owslebury SO21 .... 33 D2
South Hayling PO11 .... 185 D2
Beech Grange SP5 .... 49 E1
Beech House SO16 .... 78 C4
Beech La GU34 .... 139 F1
Beech Rd Ashurst SO40 ..... 100 A1
Chandler's Ford SO53 .... 55 E4
Clanfield PO8 .... 88 B3
Fareham PO15 .... 130 C1
Hedge End SO30 .... 105 E4
Southampton SO15 .... 102 A3
Beech Way PO8 .... 112 A1
Beech Wood Cl PO18 .... 187 D2
Beecham Rd PO1 .... 182 C4
Beechbank Ave BH17 .... 186 C1
Beechcroft BH1 .... 205 D3
Beechcroft Cl
Chandler's Ford SO53 .... 55 E3
Fareham PO16 .... 130 B1
Beechcroft La BH24 .... 141 D4
Beechcroft Mews 2 BH24 .. 141 D4
Beechcroft Rd PO12 .... 181 D3
Beechcroft Way SO53 .... 55 E4
Beechdale Cl SO40 .... 76 B1
Beechdale Wlk SO40 .... 76 B1
Beechen La SO43 .... 122 A2
Beeches Hill SO32 .... 59 E1
Beeches The Awbridge SO51 . 26 C3
Bournemouth BH7 .... 206 A4
Fair Oak SO50 .... 57 E1
4 Waterlooville PO7 .... 134 C4
West Wellow SO51 .... 50 B2
Beechey Ct 6 BH8 .... 205 D3
Beechey Rd BH8 .... 205 D3
Beechfield 30 BH4 .... 204 B2
Beechfield Ct SO15 .... 102 A4
Beechmount SO16 .... 78 C3
Beechmount Rd SO16 .... 78 C3
Beechwood SP6 .... 69 E1
Beechwood Ave
Bournemouth BH5 .... 205 F2
New Milton BH25 .... 194 C2
Waterlooville PO7 .... 134 C3
Beechwood Cl
Chandler's Ford SO53 .... 30 A1
Locks Heath SO31 .... 152 B4
Beechwood Cres SO53 ...... 30 A1
Beechwood Ct
Bournemouth BH2 .... 204 C1
Liss GU33 .... 21 D3
Beechwood Gdns
Bournemouth BH5 .... 206 A2
Southampton SO18 .... 103 F4
Beechwood Jun Sch SO18 .. 103 F4
Beechwood La BH24 .... 143 D2
Beechwood Lodge 3 PO16 . 131 D1
Beechwood Rd Cadnam SO40 . 99 D3
Holbury SO45 .... 150 B2
Portsmouth PO2 .... 157 F2
West Moors BH22 .... 138 C1
Beechwood Rise SO18 ...... 80 B1
Beechwood Way SO45 ...... 125 E1
Beechworth Rd PO9 .... 136 A1
Beehive Cotts PO11 .... 131 D1
Beehive Wlk PO1 .... 182 A2
Beeston Ct PO1 .... 182 C4
Beggar's La SO23 .... 11 D4
Begonia Rd SO16 .... 79 D2
Behrendt Cl PO12 .... 181 D3
Belben Cl BH12 .... 188 B1
Belben Rd BH12 .... 188 B1
Belbins SO51 .... 27 F2
Belfield Rd BH6 .... 207 D2
Belfry Wlk PO14 .... 129 E1
Belgarve Ct BH1 .... 205 E2
Belgrave Ind Est
Southampton, Millbrook SO14 . 103 E3
Southampton, Portswood SO17 . 79 E1
Belgrave Rd Poole BH13 .... 204 A4
Southampton SO17 .... 79 E1
Belgravia Rd PO2 .... 157 F1
Bell Cl SO45 .... 150 C1
Bell Cres PO7 .... 134 C3
Bell Davies Rd PO14 .... 179 D3
Bell Heather Cl BH16 .... 201 D4
Bell Hill GU32 .... 40 C3
Bell Hill Ridge GU32 .... 40 C3
Bell House PO18 .... 161 F4
Bell La 18 BH15 .... 202 A1
Bell Rd PO6 .... 157 E4
Bell St Romsey SO51 .... 52 C4
Southampton SO14 .... 103 D2
Bellair House PO9 .... 136 A1
Bellair Rd PO9 .... 136 A1
Bellamy Ct SO17 .... 103 E4
Belle Vue Cres BH6 .... 206 C2
Belle Vue Gdns 2 BH6 ..... 206 C2
Belle Vue Gr BH6 .... 138 C1
Belle Vue Mansions 7 BH6 . 206 C2
Belle Vue Rd
Bournemouth BH6 .... 206 C2
Poole BH14 .... 203 E2
Belle Vue Wlk BH22 .... 165 F1

Bellemoor Rd SO15 ... 78 B1
Bellemoor Sec Sch (Boys) SO15 ... 78 B1
Belleview Terr PO5 ... 182 A2
Bellevue La PO10 ... 136 C1
Bellevue Rd Eastleigh SO50 ... 56 A2
Southampton SO15 ... 103 D3
Bellevue Terr 7 SO14 ... 103 D3
Bellfield PO14 ... 153 F4
Bellflower Cl BH23 ... 208 A4
Bells House BH21 ... 163 E3
Bells La PO14 ... 179 E3
Belmont Ave BH8 ... 190 B1
Belmont Cl Horndean PO8 ... 88 B2
Hythe SO45 ... 126 A1
Stubbington PO14 ... 154 B2
Verwood BH31 ... 115 D3
Belmont Gr PO9 ... 135 E1
Belmont Pl PO5 ... 182 B2
Belmont Rd
Chandler's Ford SO53 ... 55 E2
New Milton BH25 ... 195 E2
Poole BH14 ... 203 E3
Southampton SO17 ... 103 D4
Belmont St PO5 ... 182 B2
Belmore Cl PO1 ... 182 C4
Belmore La
Lymington SO41 ... 197 F2
Owslebury SO21 ... 33 F2
Upham SO32 ... 34 A2
Belmore Rd SO41 ... 197 E2
Belmour Lodge 26 BH4 ... 204 B2
Belney House 4 PO6 ... 157 D4
Belstone Rd SO40 ... 100 C4
Belton Rd SO19 ... 104 A2
Belvedere Cl GU32 ... 40 C2
Belvedere Rd
Bournemouth BH3 ... 205 D3
Christchurch BH23 ... 207 D4
Hythe SO45 ... 126 A1
Belvidere House 12 SO14 ... 103 E3
Belvidere Rd SO14 ... 103 E3
Belvidere Terr SO14 ... 103 E3
Belvoir Cl PO16 ... 155 D4
Bembridge SO31 ... 127 E3
Bembridge Cl SO16 ... 79 E3
Bembridge Cres PO4 ... 182 C1
Bembridge Ct PO11 ... 185 E1
Bembridge Dr PO11 ... 185 E1
Bembridge House PO11 ... 185 D1
Bembridge Lodge Flats
8 PO13 ... 179 F1
Bemister Rd BH9 ... 205 D4
Bemister's La PO12 ... 181 F2
Benbow Cl PO8 ... 112 B4
Benbow Cres BH12 ... 188 C1
Benbow Gdns SO40 ... 76 B1
Benbow House 6 PO1 ... 182 A3
Benbow Pl 5 PO1 ... 182 A3
Benbridge Ave BH11 ... 188 C3
Bencraft Ct SO16 ... 79 D3
Bendigo Rd BH23 ... 206 C4
Benedict Cl SO51 ... 53 E4
Benedict Way PO16 ... 132 C1
Beneficial St 14 PO1 ... 182 A3
Benellen Ave BH4 ... 204 B2
Benellen Gdns BH4 ... 204 B2
Benellen Rd BH4 ... 204 B3
Benellen Towers BH4 ... 204 B2
Bengal Rd BH9 ... 204 C4
Benger's La SO51 ... 5 E1
Benham Dr 13 PO3 ... 157 F2
Benham Gr PO16 ... 156 B3
Benhams Farm Cl 8 SO18 ... 80 A1
Benhams Rd SO18 ... 80 A1
Benjamin Ct BH23 ... 206 C4
Benmoor Rd BH17 ... 202 A4
Benmore Cl BH25 ... 195 E1
Benmore Gdns SO53 ... 55 D4
Benmore Rd BH9 ... 190 A1
Bennett House 11 BH4 ... 204 B2
Bennett Rd BH8 ... 205 E3
Bennett's Alley 22 BH15 ... 202 A1
Bennetts La BH24 ... 143 E1
Bennion Rd BH10 ... 189 E2
Benridge Cl BH18 ... 187 D2
Bensgreen La GU32 ... 18 C2
Benson Cl BH23 ... 169 D1
Benson Rd Poole BH17 ... 202 B4
Southampton SO15 ... 102 A4
Bentham Rd PO12 ... 181 D2
Bentham Way SO31 ... 128 B4
Benthem Ct SO16 ... 79 D2
Bentley Cl Horndean PO8 ... 112 B4
Kings Worthy SO23 ... 2 A3
Bentley Cres PO16 ... 130 C1
Bentley Ct Havant PO9 ... 136 A3
16 Southampton SO17 ... 79 D1
Bentley Gr SO18 ... 104 B4
Bentley Rd BH9 ... 189 F2
Bentworth Cl PO9 ... 135 E2
Benwell Ct PO11 ... 184 C2
Bepton Down GU31 ... 41 D2
Berber Cl PO15 ... 129 E4
Bercote Cl SO22 ... 1 A3
Bere Cl
Broadstone BH17 ... 187 E1
North Baddesley SO53 ... 55 D4
Winchester SO22 ... 1 B1
Bere Farm La PO17 ... 131 F4
Bere Rd PO7 ... 110 C2
Beresford Cl
Chandler's Ford SO53 ... 55 F3
Poole BH12 ... 203 E3
Waterlooville PO7 ... 134 C3
Beresford Gdns
Chandler's Ford SO53 ... 55 F3
Christchurch BH23 ... 207 F3
Beresford Rd
Bournemouth BH6 ... 206 A2
Chandler's Ford SO53 ... 55 F3
Lymington SO41 ... 197 E2
Poole BH12 ... 203 E3
Portsmouth PO2 ... 157 F1
Stubbington PO14 ... 154 B2
Bereweeke Ave SO22 ... 1 C1
Bereweeke Cl SO22 ... 1 C1
Bereweeke Rd SO22 ... 1 C1
Bereweeke Way SO22 ... 1 C1
Bergen Cres SO30 ... 105 E3
Berkeley Ave BH12 ... 203 E4
Berkeley Cl Southampton SO15 ... 102 C4
Stubbington PO14 ... 179 D3
Verwood BH31 ... 114 C4
Berkeley Ct PO13 ... 179 F1
Berkeley Gdns SO30 ... 105 E3
Berkeley Rd
Bournemouth BH3 ... 204 C4
Southampton SO15 ... 102 C3
Berkeley Sq PO9 ... 136 A1
Berkley Ave BH22 ... 165 E1
Berkshire Cl PO1 ... 182 C3
Bermuda Ct
9 Christchurch BH23 ... 209 D4
22 Southampton SO17 ... 79 D1
Bermuda House 3 PO6 ... 132 C1
Bernard Ave PO6 ... 158 A4
Bernard Powell House PO9 ... 136 A1
Bernard St SO14 ... 103 D2
Bernard Cl BH23 ... 206 C4
Berne Ct 11 BH1 ... 205 D2
Berney Rd PO4 ... 183 E2
Bernina Ave PO7 ... 111 E1
Bernina Cl PO7 ... 111 E1
Bernwood Gr SO45 ... 177 F4
Beron Ct BH15 ... 202 C2
Berrans Ave BH11 ... 189 D3
Berrans Ct BH11 ... 189 D3
Berry Cl SO30 ... 105 E3
Berry La Stubbington PO14 ... 179 D3
Twyford SO21 ... 32 A4
Berrydown Rd PO9 ... 135 E4
Berryfield Rd SO41 ... 196 A1
Berrylands GU33 ... 21 D4
Bernards Cl BH23 ... 206 C4
Berrywood Gdns SO30 ... 105 D4
Berrywood Prim Sch SO30 ... 81 E1
Berthon House SO51 ... 52 C3
Bertie Rd PO4 ... 183 D2
Bertram Rd BH25 ... 195 E2
Berwick Rd BH3 ... 204 C3
Berwyn Ct BH18 ... 187 D2
Berwyn Wlk PO14 ... 154 C4
Beryl Ave PO12 ... 180 C4
Beryton Cl PO12 ... 181 D3
Beryton Rd PO12 ... 181 D3
Besomer Dro SP5 ... 47 F3
Bessborough Rd BH13 ... 214 C4
Bessemer Cl BH31 ... 115 E2
Beswick Ave BH10 ... 189 E1
Bethany House BH1 ... 205 E3
Bethany Jun CE Sch BH1 ... 205 E3
Bethia Cl BH8 ... 205 E3
Bethia Rd BH8 ... 205 E3
Betsy Cl BH23 ... 169 D1
Betsy La BH23 ... 169 D1
Betteridge Dr SO16 ... 77 E3
Bettesworth Rd PO1 ... 182 C4
Bettiscombe Cl BH17 ... 187 F1
Betula Cl PO7 ... 135 D3
Beulah Rd SO16 ... 78 A1
Bevan Cl SO19 ... 103 F1
Bevan Rd PO8 ... 112 A3
Beverley Cl PO14 ... 129 E2
Beverley Gdns
Bournemouth BH10 ... 189 E2
Bursledon SO31 ... 104 C1
Romsey SO51 ... 28 B1
Swanmore SO32 ... 84 A3
Beverley Gr PO6 ... 134 C1
Beverley Grange 29 BH4 ... 204 B2
Beverley Hts SO18 ... 79 F2
Beverley Rd Hythe SO45 ... 149 F4
Stubbington PO14 ... 179 E3
Beverly Cl PO13 ... 155 E1
Beverston House 4 PO6 ... 133 D1
Beverston Rd PO6 ... 133 D1
Bevis Cl Blackfield SO45 ... 150 C1
Locks Heath SO31 ... 152 B4
Bevis Rd Gosport PO12 ... 181 D3
Portsmouth PO2 ... 157 E1
Bevis Rd N PO2 ... 157 E1
Bevois Gdns SO14 ... 103 D4
Bevois Hill SO14 ... 103 D4
Bevois Mansions 23 SO14 ... 103 D4
Bevois Mews 24 SO14 ... 103 D4
Bevois Town Prim Sch SO14 ... 103 D4
Bevois Valley Rd SO14 ... 103 D4
Bexington Cl BH11 ... 188 C2
Beyne Rd SO22 ... 10 A2
Bickerley Gdns BH24 ... 140 C3
Bickerley Rd BH24 ... 140 C3
Bickerley Terr BH24 ... 140 C4
Bicknell Ct 10 BH4 ... 204 B2
Bicknell Sch BH7 ... 206 A4
Bickton Wlk 1 PO9 ... 135 E3
Bicton Rd BH11 ... 189 D2
Bidbury Inf Sch PO9 ... 135 E1
Bidbury Jun Sch PO9 ... 135 E1
Bidbury La PO9 ... 135 E1
Biddenfield La Shedfield SO32 ... 107 E3
Wickham PO17 ... 107 E3
Biddlecombe Cl PO13 ... 180 B4
Biddlesgate Ct 10 SO14 ... 102 C2
Bideford Cl SO16 ... 77 F1
Big Tree Cotts SO32 ... 85 E3
Biggin Wlk PO14 ... 154 C4
Bilberry Cl SO31 ... 128 C1
Bilberry Ct 8 SO22 ... 10 C4
Bilberry Dr SO40 ... 101 F1
Bill Stillwell Ct 6 PO2 ... 157 E1
Billett Ave PO7 ... 134 C4
Billing Cl PO4 ... 183 D2
Billington Gdns SO30 ... 81 E1
Billington Pl SO41 ... 197 E1
Billy Lawn Ave PO9 ... 135 F3
Bilton Bsns Pk PO3 ... 158 B1
Bindon Cl Poole BH12 ... 203 F4
Southampton SO16 ... 78 A1
Bindon Ct 5 SO18 ... 103 F4
Bindon Rd SO16 ... 78 A1
Bingham Ave BH14 ... 214 B4
Bingham Cl
Christchurch BH23 ... 207 F4
Verwood BH31 ... 115 D2
Bingham Dr Lymington SO41 ... 197 F2
Verwood BH31 ... 115 D2
Bingham Rd
Bournemouth BH9 ... 205 D4
Christchurch BH23 ... 207 F4
Verwood BH31 ... 115 D2
Binnacle Way PO6 ... 157 D4
Binness Way PO6 ... 158 C4
Binnie Rd BH12 ... 203 F3
Binstead Cl SO16 ... 79 E3
Binsteed Rd PO2 ... 182 C4
Birch Ave Burton BH23 ... 192 B2
Ferndown BH22 ... 165 F1
New Milton BH25 ... 194 B3
Birch Cl Colden Common SO21 ... 56 C4
Corfe Mullen BH21 ... 186 B3
Liss GU33 ... 21 D2
Poole BH14 ... 203 F2
Romsey SO51 ... 53 E3
Southampton SO16 ... 78 A1
St Leonards BH24 ... 139 E2
Waterlooville PO8 ... 111 F2
Birch Ct Southampton SO18 ... 104 A4
3 Winchester SO22 ... 10 B3
Birch Dale SO45 ... 126 A1
Birch Dr Bournemouth BH8 ... 191 D1
Gosport PO13 ... 155 E2
Birch Gr Eastleigh SO50 ... 56 A3
West Moors BH22 ... 138 B1
Birch Hill PO17 ... 109 D2
Birch House SO16 ... 78 C4
Birch Rd Chilworth SO16 ... 79 D4
Hedge End SO30 ... 105 E4
Southampton SO16 ... 78 A2
St Leonards BH24 ... 140 A2
Birch Tree Cl PO10 ... 136 C2
Birch Tree Dr PO10 ... 136 C2
Birch Wood SO19 ... 104 C3
Birchdale Cl SO31 ... 152 B4
Birchdale Rd BH21 ... 163 E3
Birchen Cl SO31 ... 129 E2
Birchen Rd SO31 ... 129 E2
Birches Cl The SO52 ... 53 F3
Birches The SO18 ... 104 A4
Birchglade SO40 ... 76 B1
Birchlands SO40 ... 100 B3
Birchmore Cl PO13 ... 155 E1
Birchwood Cl BH23 ... 208 C4
Birchwood Ct 8 SO18 ... 103 F4
Birchwood Dr SP6 ... 93 D3
Birchwood Gdns SO30 ... 105 E4
Birchwood Lodge 7 PO16 ... 131 D1
Birchwood Mews BH14 ... 203 E2
Birchwood Rd Poole BH14 ... 203 E2
Upton BH16 ... 201 D3
Birchy Hill SO41 ... 172 B1
Bird's Hill Rd BH15 ... 202 C2
Birdham Rd PO11 ... 185 F1
Birdlip Cl PO8 ... 112 A3
Birdlip Rd PO6 ... 133 D1
Birds Hill Gdns 5 BH15 ... 202 C2
Birdwood Gr PO16 ... 155 F4
Birinus Rd SO23 ... 2 A1
Birkdale Ave PO6 ... 134 B1
Birkdale Ct BH18 ... 187 D3
Birkdale Rd BH18 ... 187 D3
Birmingham Ct PO13 ... 180 B3
Biscay Cl PO14 ... 154 A2
Bishearne Gdns GU33 ... 20 C3
Bishop Ct BH24 ... 141 D4
Bishop Rd BH9 ... 205 D4
Bishop St PO1 ... 182 A3
Bishop's La SO32 ... 83 E4
Bishop's Palace SO32 ... 83 E4
Bishop's Waltham Inf Sch SO32 ... 83 E4
Bishop's Wood Rd PO17 ... 84 B1
Bishops Cl Bournemouth BH7 ... 205 F4
Poole BH12 ... 204 B4
Totton SO40 ... 100 C4
Bishops Cres SO19 ... 103 F2
Bishops Ct SO50 ... 56 B3
Bishops Gate PO14 ... 129 E2
Bishops La SO32 ... 84 A1
Bishops Rd SO19 ... 103 F2
Bishopsfield Rd PO14 ... 154 C4
Bishopstoke La SO50 ... 56 C4
Bishopstoke Manor SO50 ... 56 B2
Bishopstoke Rd Eastleigh SO50 ... 56 B2
Havant PO9 ... 135 F3
Bisley Ct SO19 ... 104 A2
Bisterne Cl BH24 ... 143 F1
Bittern Cl PO12 ... 181 D4
Bitterne CE Inf & Jun Sch SO19 ... 103 F3
Bitterne Cl PO9 ... 135 F3
Bitterne Cres SO19 ... 104 A3
Bitterne Manor House SO18 ... 103 E4
Bitterne Manor Prim Sch SO18 ... 103 E4
Bitterne Park Inf Sch SO17 ... 79 E1
Bitterne Park Jun Sch SO17 ... 79 E1
Bitterne Park Sec Sch SO18 ... 79 F1
Bitterne Park Triangle SO18 ... 79 E1
Bitterne Rd SO19 ... 104 A3
Bitterne Rd E SO18 ... 104 B4
Bitterne Rd W SO18 ... 103 F4
Bitterne Sta SO18 ... 103 E4
Bitterne Way Lymington SO41 ... 197 E1
Southampton SO19 ... 103 F3
Verwood BH31 ... 115 D3
Bitumen Rd SO45 ... 151 D2
Black Hill BH31 ... 115 D3
Black La SP5 ... 48 A2
Black Moor Rd BH31 ... 115 E2
Black Swan Bldgs 12 SO22 ... 10 C4
Blackberry Cl PO8 ... 88 B2
Blackberry La BH23 ... 207 F3
Blackberry Terr SO14 ... 103 D4
Blackbird Cl Broadstone BH17 ... 201 F4
Waterlooville PO8 ... 111 F2
Blackbird Rd SO50 ... 55 E1
Blackbird Way
Bransgore BH23 ... 193 E4
Lee-on-the-Solent PO13 ... 179 F2
Blackbrook Bsns Pk PO15 ... 130 C1
Blackbrook House Dr PO15 ... 130 C1
Blackbrook Park Ave PO15 ... 130 C1
Blackbrook Rd PO15 ... 130 B1
Blackburn Ct PO13 ... 180 B3
Blackburn Rd BH12 ... 203 D3
Blackbush Rd SO41 ... 211 D3
Blackbushe Cl SO16 ... 77 F3
Blackcap Cl PO9 ... 113 D1
Blackdown Cl SO45 ... 125 E1
Blackdown Cres PO9 ... 135 F2
Blackfield Inf & Jun Schs SO45 ... 150 C1
Blackfield La BH22 ... 138 C2
Blackfield Rd Blackfield SO45 ... 150 C1
Bournemouth BH8 ... 190 B2
Blackfriars Cl 3 PO1 ... 182 B2
Blackfriars Rd PO1 ... 182 B3
Blackhill Rd SO51 ... 74 C4
Blackhorse La SO32 ... 83 F1
Blackhouse La PO17 ... 109 D1
Blackmoor Wlk 26 PO9 ... 136 A3
Blackmore La GU32 ... 18 C2
Blacksmith Cl BH21 ... 186 B3
Blackthorn Cl Lymington SO41 ... 197 D1
Southampton SO19 ... 103 F3
Blackthorn Dr Gosport PO12 ... 156 A1
South Hayling PO11 ... 185 E2
Blackthorn Gn SO21 ... 57 D4
Blackthorn Rd
South Hayling PO11 ... 185 E1
Southampton SO19 ... 103 F3
Blackthorn Way
New Milton BH25 ... 195 E2
Verwood BH31 ... 115 D3
Blackthorn Wlk PO7 ... 112 B1
Blackwater Cl 10 PO6 ... 157 E4
Blackwater Dr Oakley BH21 ... 187 E4
Totton SO40 ... 76 B1
Blackwater Gr SP6 ... 92 C3
Blackwater Mews SO40 ... 76 B1
Blackwood House 15 PO1 ... 182 B4
Bladon Cl PO9 ... 136 B2
Bladon Rd SO16 ... 78 B1
Blair Ave BH14 ... 203 E2
Blair Cl BH25 ... 194 C2
Blake Cl SO16 ... 77 E3
Blake Dene Rd BH14 ... 203 D1
Blake Hill Ave BH14 ... 203 E1
Blake Hill Cres BH14 ... 203 E1
Blake House PO12 ... 181 F2
Blake Rd Cosham PO6 ... 134 B1
Gosport PO12 ... 181 E3
Blakemere Cres PO6 ... 133 E1
Blakeney Rd SO16 ... 77 E1
Blakesley La PO3 ... 158 B2
Blanchard Rd SO32 ... 83 D4
Blandford Cl BH15 ... 201 F1
Blandford Ct 2 SO41 ... 211 E3
Blandford House SO16 ... 77 F1
Blandford Rd
Coombe Bissett SP5 ... 23 E4
Corfe Mullen BH21 ... 186 B4
Hamworthy BH15 ... 201 E2
Pamphill BH21 ... 162 B4
Upton BH16 ... 201 E2
Blandford Rd N BH16 ... 201 D4
Blaney Way BH21 ... 186 B3
Blankney Cl PO14 ... 179 D3
Blann Cl SO16 ... 77 E3
Blashford Lakes Study Ctr BH24 ... 117 D2
Blaven Wlk 4 PO14 ... 154 C4
Bleaklow Cl SO16 ... 101 F4
Blechynden Terr SO15 ... 102 C3
Blencowe Dr SO52 ... 54 C3
Blendworth Cres PO9 ... 135 F2
Blendworth Fst Sch PO8 ... 112 C4
Blendworth House 46 PO1 ... 182 B3
Blendworth La Horndean PO8 ... 112 C4
Southampton SO18 ... 104 B4
Blendworth Rd PO4 ... 183 D3
Blenheim Ave SO17 ... 79 D1
Blenheim Cl
North Baddesley SO52 ... 54 C2
Totton SO40 ... 100 C3
Blenheim Cres SO41 ... 195 F2
Blenheim Ct
25 Bournemouth BH4 ... 204 B2
Portsmouth PO4 ... 183 D2
Southampton SO17 ... 79 D1
Blenheim Dr BH23 ... 208 A3
Blenheim Gdns Gosport PO12 ... 181 D4
Havant PO9 ... 136 B1
Hythe SO45 ... 125 E1
Southampton SO17 ... 79 D1
Blenheim House
4 Eastleigh SO50 ... 56 A1
Romsey SO51 ... 53 D4
Blenheim Rd Eastleigh SO50 ... 56 A1
Waterlooville PO8 ... 112 A3
Blighmont Ave SO15 ... 102 A3
Blighmont Cres SO15 ... 102 A3
Blind La Fair Oak SO30 ... 81 E3
West End SO30 ... 81 E3
Wickham PO17 ... 107 F3
Wimborne Minster BH21 ... 163 D3
Bliss Cl PO7 ... 134 C3
Blissford Cl PO9 ... 136 A3
Blissford Cross SP6 ... 94 C4
Blissford Hill SP6 ... 94 C4
Blissford Rd SP6 ... 94 C4
Bloomfield Pl BH9 ... 189 F1
Bloomsbury Wlk SO19 ... 103 F1
Blossom Cl SO30 ... 105 F3
Blount Rd PO1 ... 182 A2
Bloxworth Rd BH12 ... 203 F4
Blue Anchor La 15 SO14 ... 102 C2
Blue Ball Hill SO23 ... 11 D4
Bluebell Cl Christchurch BH23 ... 208 A4
Waterlooville PO7 ... 135 D3
Bluebell Copse SO31 ... 128 C1
Bluebell La BH17 ... 186 C1
Bluebell Rd SO16 ... 79 E2
Blueprint Portfield Rd PO3 ... 158 A1
Blundell La SO31 ... 105 E1
Blyth Cl Christchurch BH23 ... 191 E2
Southampton SO16 ... 77 E1
Blythe Rd BH21 ... 186 B3
Blythswood Ct BH25 ... 209 F4
Boakes Pl SO40 ... 100 B1
Boardwalk The PO6 ... 157 D4
Boarhunt Cl PO1 ... 182 B3
Boarhunt Rd PO17 ... 131 F2
Boatyard Ind Est The PO16 ... 155 D4
Bob Hann Cl BH12 ... 203 E3
Bockhampton Rd
Bransgore BH23 ... 192 C3
Burton BH23 ... 192 C3
Bodley Rd BH13 ... 214 C4
Bodmin Rd Bishopstoke SO50 ... 56 C1
Portchester PO6 ... 157 D4
Bodorgan Rd BH2 ... 204 C2
Bodowen Cl BH23 ... 192 B1
Bodowen Rd BH23 ... 192 B1
Bodycoats Rd SO53 ... 55 E3
Bognor Rd BH18 ... 186 C2
Bohemia La SP5 ... 47 F2
Boiler Rd Fawley SO45 ... 151 F1
Portsmouth PO1 ... 181 F4
Bolde Cl PO3 ... 158 A2
Boldens Rd PO12 ... 181 D1
Bolderwood Cl SO50 ... 56 C1
Bolderwood Ornamental Dr SO43 ... 120 B1
Boldre Cl Barton on Sea BH25 ... 209 E4
Havant PO9 ... 135 E2
Poole BH12 ... 203 E4
Boldre La SO41 ... 197 E4
Boldrewood Con Ctr (Univ of Southampton) SO16 ... 78 C2
Boldrewood Rd SO16 ... 78 C2
Boleyn CL BH9 ... 190 A2
Bolhinton Ave SO40 ... 101 E1
Bolton Cl BH6 ... 206 C2
Bolton Cres BH22 ... 166 A3
Bolton Ct 4 BH6 ... 206 C2
Bolton Rd BH6 ... 206 C2
Boltons The
Milford on Sea SO41 ... 211 E2
Waterlooville PO7 ... 134 C2
Bonchurch Cl SO16 ... 79 E3
Bonchurch Rd PO4 ... 183 D3
Bond Ave BH22 ... 138 B2
Bond Cl SO41 ... 172 A2
Bond Rd Poole BH15 ... 202 C3
Southampton SO18 ... 79 F1
Bond St SO14 ... 103 E3
Bondfields Cres PO9 ... 135 F3
Bones La GU31 ... 65 E3
Bonfire Cnr PO1 ... 182 A3
Bonham Rd BH3 ... 204 C4
Boniface Cl SO40 ... 100 B4
Boniface Cres SO16 ... 77 F2
Bonington Cl BH23 ... 207 F4
Bonner Cotts SP5 ... 4 C4
Boothby Cl SO40 ... 101 D3
Border Dr BH16 ... 201 E3
Border Lodge BH23 ... 194 B1
Border Rd Hamworthy BH16 ... 201 E3
Upton BH16 ... 201 E3
Bordon Rd PO9 ... 135 F3
Boredean La Froxfield GU32 ... 39 E3
Langrish GU32 ... 39 E3
Boreham Rd BH6 ... 206 B3
Borley Rd BH17 ... 202 A4
Borough Gr GU32 ... 40 C1
Borough Hill GU32 ... 40 C2
Borough Rd Petersfield GU32 ... 40 B1
Petersfield GU32 ... 40 C2
Borough The SP5 ... 46 C4
Borrowdale Rd SO16 ... 77 F1
Borthwick Rd BH1 ... 205 F3
Boscobel Rd SO22 ... 1 C1
Boscombe Cliff Rd BH5 ... 205 F2
Boscombe Gr Rd BH1 ... 205 E3

Boscombe Overcliff Dr BH5 .. 206 A2
Boscombe Spa Rd BH5 .... 205 E2
Bosham Rd PO2 .... 182 C4
Bosham Wlk PO13 .... 155 D1
Bosley Cl BH23 .... 191 F1
Bosley Way BH23 .... 191 F1
Bosmere Gdns PO10 .... 136 C1
Bosmere Jun Sch PO9 .... 159 F4
Bosmere Rd PO11 .... 185 F1
Bossington Cl SO16 .... 77 F3
Boston Cl SO53 .... 55 E4
Boston Lodge 22 BH4 .... 204 B2
Boston Rd PO6 .... 133 F1
Bosuns Cl PO16 .... 155 D3
Bosville SO50 .... 56 A3
Boswell Cl Botley SO30 .... 106 A3
Southampton SO19 .... 104 B3
Bosworth Mews BH9 .... 190 A2
Botany Bay Rd SO19 .... 104 A2
Botley CE Prim Sch SO30 .... 106 A4
Botley Dr PO9 .... 135 E3
Botley Gdns SO19 .... 104 C2
Botley Hill SO30 .... 106 A3
Botley Rd
Bishop's Waltham SO32 .... 82 C1
Curdridge SO32 .... 82 C1
Fair Oak SO50 .... 57 E1
Fair Oak, Wildern SO50 .... 81 E4
Hedge End SO30 .... 81 D1
North Baddesley SO52 .... 53 E3
Romsey SO51 .... 53 E3
Southampton SO19 .... 104 B2
Swanwick SO31 .... 129 D4
West End SO30 .... 81 D1
Botley Sta SO30 .... 106 B4
Bottings Est SO30 .... 106 A4
Bottom La SO51 .... 50 C2
Boulnois Ave BH14 .... 203 F2
Boultbee Cotts SO43 .... 121 E3
Boulter La SO17 .... 133 D4
Boulton Rd PO5 .... 182 C2
Bound La PO11 .... 185 D1
Boundary Cl SO15 .... 101 F4
Boundary Dr PO9 .... 163 E3
Boundary La BH24 .... 139 F1
Boundary Rd
Bournemouth BH10 .... 189 F1
Burslelon SO31 .... 127 F4
Boundary Way Havant PO9 .. 135 F1
Waterlooville PO7 .... 134 A1
Boundstone SO45 .... 125 F2
Boundway SO41 .... 171 F1
Bountys La BH12 .... 203 F3
Bourne Ave Bournemouth BH4 .. 204 C2
Southampton SO15 .... 78 B1
Bourne Cl Bournemouth BH4 .. 204 B2
Horndean PO8 .... 112 A4
Otterbourne SO21 .... 31 D2
West Wellow SO51 .... 50 B2
Bourne Com Coll The PO10 .. 137 E1
Bourne Cotts SP6 .... 44 C1
Bourne Ct
24 Bournemouth BH2 .... 204 C2
Wimborne Minster BH21 ..... 163 F3
Bourne La Netley Marsh SO40 .. 99 E3
Twyford SO21 .... 32 A3
Bourne Pines 3 BH4 .... 204 C2
Bourne Rd Cosham PO6 ...... 157 D4
Netley Marsh SO40 .... 99 E3
Southampton SO15 .... 102 B3
Bourne Valley Rd BH12 ...... 204 A3
Bourne View PO10 .... 137 E1
Bournefields SO21 .... 32 A4
Bournemouth Ave PO12 ..... 181 D4
Bournemouth Central
Bsns Pk BH1 .... 205 E3
Bournemouth Coll
of Art & Design BH12 ...... 204 B4
Bournemouth Crown & Cty
Cts BH7 .... 191 E1
Bournemouth House 20 PO9 .. 136 A3
Bournemouth Int Airport
BH23 .... 190 C4
Bournemouth Int Ctr BH2 .. 204 C1
Bournemouth Memorial
Homes BH8 .... 190 C1
Bournemouth Nuffield
Hospl BH8 .... 205 D3
Bournemouth & Poole Coll
Annexe The BH1 .... 205 D2
Bournemouth & Poole Coll
of F Ed BH14 .... 202 C2
Bournemouth & Poole Coll
of F Ed (Annex) BH14 ...... 202 C3
Bournemouth & Poole
Coll The BH1 .... 205 D2
Bournemouth Rd
Chandler's Ford SO53 .... 55 E2
Chilworth SO53 .... 55 E2
Lyndhurst SO43 .... 121 F3
Poole BH14 .... 203 E2
Bournemouth Sch BH8 .... 190 B1
Bournemouth Sch for Girls
BH8 .... 190 B1
Bournemouth Sta BH1 .... 205 D2
Bournemouth Univ BH12 .... 204 B4
Bournewood Dr BH4 .... 204 B2
Bourton Gdns BH7 .... 206 A4
Bouverie Cl 23 SO45 .... 195 D1
Boveridge Gdns BH9 .... 190 A2
Bovington Cl BH17 .... 187 F1
Bowater Cl SO40 .... 76 B1
Bowater Way SO40 .... 76 B1
Bowcombe SO31 .... 127 E4
Bowden La SO17 .... 79 E1

Bowden Rd BH12 .... 188 B1
Bower Cl Holbury SO45 ...... 150 B2
Southampton SO19 .... 103 F1
Bower Rd BH8 .... 205 E4
Bowers Cl PO8 .... 112 A2
Bowers Hill SP5 .... 47 F4
Bowerwood Cotts SP6 .... 93 E4
Bowerwood Rd SP6 .... 93 E4
Bowes Hill PO9 .... 113 E2
Bowes-Lyon Ct PO8 .... 112 A4
Bowland Rise New Milton BH25 .. 195 E4
North Baddesley SO52 .... 55 D4
Bowland Way SO45 .... 177 F4
Bowler Ave PO1 .... 182 C3
Bowler Ct PO1 .... 182 C3
Bowman Ct SO19 .... 104 A2
Box Cl BH17 .... 202 A4
Boxgrove House 56 PO1 .... 182 B3
Boxwood Cl Portchester PO16 .. 132 A1
Waterlooville PO7 .... 134 C3
Boyatt Cres SO50 .... 56 A4
Boyatt La Eastleigh SO50 .... 56 A4
Otterbourne SO21 .... 56 A4
Boyatt Wood Sh Ctr 7 SO50 .. 56 A3
Boyd Cl PO14 .... 179 D3
Boyd Rd Gosport PO13 .... 155 D2
Poole BH12 .... 203 F3
Boyes La SO21 .... 32 A1
Boyle Cres PO7 .... 134 B3
Boyne Mead Rd SO23 .... 2 B4
Boyne Rise SO23 .... 2 A4
Boynton Cl SO53 .... 55 D4
Brabant Cl PO15 .... 129 D4
Brabazon Dr BH23 .... 208 A4
Brabazon Rd PO15 .... 163 F1
Brabourne Ave BH22 .... 165 E2
Bracken Cl
North Baddesley SO52 .... 54 A4
St Leonards BH24 .... 139 E2
Bracken Cres SO50 .... 56 A3
Bracken Glen BH15 .... 202 C3
Bracken La SO16 .... 78 A1
Bracken Lodge 3 BH6 .... 206 C2
Bracken Pl SO16 .... 79 D4
Bracken Rd Bournemouth BH6 .. 206 B2
Ferndown BH22 .... 165 D4
North Baddesley SO52 .... 54 A2
Petersfield GU31 .... 41 E1
Bracken Way BH21 .... 194 A1
Brackendale Ct BH21 .... 138 C4
Brackendale Rd BH8 .... 205 E4
Brackenhill BH13 .... 204 A1
Brackenhill Rd BH21 .... 164 A4
Brackens The Hythe SO45 .. 125 E2
Locks Heath SO31 .... 129 D1
Brackens Way 12 BH13 ..... 214 C4
Brackenway Rd SO53 .... 55 E4
Bracklesham Cl SO19 .... 103 F2
Bracklesham Rd Gosport PO13 .. 180 B4
South Hayling PO11 .... 185 D1
Brackley Cl SO50 .... 57 D2
Brackley Cl BH23 .... 191 E4
Brackley Way SO40 .... 100 B4
Bradburne Rd BH2 .... 204 C2
Bradford Cl PO13 .... 180 B3
Bradford Rd Bournemouth BH9 .. 190 B2
Portsmouth PO5 .... 182 B2
Brading Ave Gosport PO13 .. 155 E1
Portsmouth PO4 .... 183 D1
Brading Cl SO16 .... 79 E3
Bradley Ct 24 PO9 .... 136 A3
Bradley Gn SO16 .... 78 A2
Bradley Peak SO22 .... 1 B1
Bradley Rd SO22 .... 1 B2
Bradly Rd PO15 .... 130 B1
Bradpole Rd BH8 .... 190 C1
Bradshaw Cl SO50 .... 57 F1
Bradstock Cl BH12 .... 203 F4
Braehead SO45 .... 125 F1
Braemar Ave Bournemouth BH6 .. 207 D2
Cosham PO6 .... 158 A4
Braemar Cl Bournemouth BH6 .. 207 D2
Fareham PO15 .... 130 C2
Gosport PO13 .... 155 E1
Braemar Dr BH23 .... 193 F1
Braemar Rd PO13 .... 155 E1
Braeside Cl Southampton SO19 .. 103 F3
Winchester SO22 .... 10 A2
Braeside Cres SO19 .... 103 F3
Braeside Rd Southampton SO19 .. 103 F3
St Leonards BH24 .... 139 F2
West Moors BH22 .... 138 C2
Braidley Rd BH2 .... 204 C2
Brailswood Rd BH15 .... 202 C2
Braintree Rd PO6 .... 133 E1
Braishfield Cl SO16 .... 77 F1
Braishfield Gdns BH8 .... 190 B1
Braishfield Prim Sch SO51 .. 28 B3
Braishfield Rd
Abbotswood SO51 .... 28 B2
Braishfield SO51 .... 28 B2
Havant PO9 .... 136 A2
Romsey SO51 .... 28 B2
Brake House PO9 .... 135 E1
Bramar Ct BH4 .... 204 B1
Bramber Rd PO12 .... 181 D4
Bramble Cl Alderholt SP6 .... 93 D3
5 Eastleigh SO50 .... 56 A3
Havant PO9 .... 136 B2
Holbury SO45 .... 150 B2
Stubbington PO14 .... 179 D3
Bramble Ct 2 GU31 .... 41 E2
Bramble Dr SO51 .... 28 B1
Bramble Hill SO53 .... 55 D2
Bramble La Christchurch BH23 .. 194 A1
Clanfield PO8 .... 88 A4
Locks Heath SO31 .... 128 C3
Bramble Mews SO18 .... 104 A4

Bramble Rd Petersfield GU31 .. 41 E2
Portsmouth PO4 .... 182 C2
Bramble Way Bransgore BH23 .. 169 D1
Gosport PO13 .... 155 D1
Bramble Wlk SO41 .... 197 E3
Brambles Cl SO21 .... 57 D4
Brambles Farm Ind Est PO7 .. 134 B4
Brambles Rd PO13 .... 179 E2
Brambling Cl SO16 .... 78 A3
Brambling Rd PO9 .... 113 D1
Bramblings The SO40 .... 100 B4
Brambridge SO50 .... 56 C4
Brambridge House SO21 ..... 31 E1
Brambridge Rd SO21, SO50 .. 56 C4
Bramdean Dr PO9 .... 135 F3
Bramdean Mews SO19 ...... 103 F2
Bramdean Rd SO18 .... 104 B4
Bramham Moor PO14 .... 179 D3
Bramley Cl Lymington SO41 .. 197 F1
Waterlooville PO7 .... 134 C4
Bramley Cres SO19 .... 104 A1
Bramley Ct BH22 .... 165 E3
Bramley Gdns Fair Oak SO50 .. 81 E3
Gosport PO12 .... 181 D1
Hermitage PO10 .... 161 D4
Bramley House Gosport PO12 .. 181 D1
Hedge End SO30 .... 105 D3
Bramley Rd
Bournemouth BH10 .... 189 E3
Ferndown BH22 .... 165 E3
Bramleys The SP5 .... 24 A2
Brampton La PO3 .... 158 B2
Brampton Manor SO16 .... 78 C3
Brampton Rd BH15 .... 202 B3
Brampton Tower SO16 .... 78 C3
Bramshaw SO22 .... 1 B2
Bramshaw Ct 41 PO9 .... 136 A3
Bramshaw Gdns BH8 .... 190 B2
Bramshaw Way BH25 .... 209 E4
Bramshott Rd Portsmouth PO4 .. 182 C2
Southampton SO19 .... 126 C4
Bramston Rd SO15 .... 102 B4
Bramwell Ct SO18 .... 104 A3
Branches La SO51 .... 25 F2
Branders Cl BH6 .... 207 D3
Branders La BH6 .... 207 D3
Brandon Ct 6 PO5 .... 182 C2
Brandon Rd PO5 .... 182 B1
Brandwood Ct 4 BH14 ...... 203 D2
Branksea Ave SO15 .... 201 F1
Branksea Cl BH15 .... 201 F1
Branksome Ave SO15 .... 78 B1
Branksome Cl
New Milton BH25 .... 195 D1
Winchester SO22 .... 10 A3
Branksome Ct 14 BH13 ...... 214 C4
Branksome Dene Rd BH4 ... 204 A1
Branksome Heath Mid Sch
BH12 .... 203 E3
Branksome Hill Rd
Bournemouth BH4 .... 204 A3
Poole BH13 .... 204 A3
Branksome Sta BH12 .... 203 F2
Branksome Towers BH13 ... 214 F2
Branksome Wood Gdns BH2 .. 204 B2
Branksome Wood Rd
Bournemouth BH2, BH4 ..... 204 B2
Poole BH12 .... 204 B2
Bransbury Cl SO16 .... 78 B2
Bransbury Rd PO4 .... 183 D2
Bransgore Ave PO9 .... 135 E2
Bransgore CE Prim Sch BH23 .. 193 E4
Bransgore Gdns BH23 .... 169 E3
Bransley Cl SO51 .... 28 A1
Branwell Cl BH23 .... 192 A1
Branwood Cl SO41 .... 196 C1
Brasenose Cl PO14 .... 129 E1
Brasher Cl SO50 .... 57 D1
Brassey Cl BH9 .... 190 A1
Brassey Rd Bournemouth BH9 .. 190 A1
Winchester SO22 .... 1 C1
Brassey Terr BH9 .... 189 F1
Brasted Ct PO4 .... 183 E3
Braunston Cl PO6 .... 133 D1
Braxall Lawn PO9 .... 135 E3
Braxton Ctyd SO41 .... 211 F4
Braxton House 1 SO23 .... 11 E4
Breach Ave PO10 .... 137 F1
Breach La BH24 .... 141 F4
Breamore CE Prim Sch SP6 .. 70 A4
Breamore Cl Eastleigh SO50 .. 56 A3
New Milton BH25 .... 194 C2
Breamore Countryside Mus
SP6 .... 46 A1
Breamore House SP6 .... 46 A2
Breamore Rd SO18 .... 104 B4
Brean Cl SO16 .... 77 F1
Brearley Cl BH23 .... 209 D4
Brecon Ave PO6 .... 158 A4
Brecon Cl Bournemouth BH10 .. 189 F2
Chandler's Ford SO53 .... 55 D2
Fareham PO14 .... 154 C4
Hythe SO45 .... 125 F2
New Milton BH25 .... 195 E1
Brecon Rd SO19 .... 104 B3
Bredenbury Cres PO6 .... 133 E1
Bredon Wlk PO14 .... 154 C4
Bredy Cl BH17 .... 187 E1
Breech Cl 12 PO3 .... 157 F2
Bremble Cl BH17 .... 188 B1
Brenchley Cl PO16 .... 156 A4
Brendon Cl Bournemouth BH8 .. 190 C1
Hythe SO45 .... 125 E1
Brendon Gr SO16 .... 101 F4
Brendon Rd PO14 .... 154 B4
Brent Ct PO10 .... 160 C4
Brentwood Cres SO18 .... 80 A1
Breton Cl PO15 .... 129 D4

Brewells La GU33 .... 21 F2
Brewer Cl SO31 .... 129 D2
Brewer St PO1 .... 182 B3
Brewers La Gosport PO13 .. 155 E1
West Tisted SO24 .... 17 E4
Brewhouse Sq PO12 .... 181 E3
Brewster Ct PO8 .... 112 A2
Briar Cl Christchurch BH23 .. 207 F3
Gosport PO12 .... 180 C2
Poole BH15 .... 202 C3
Waterlooville PO8 .... 112 A3
Briar Way Romsey SO51 ...... 28 B1
Wimborne Minster BH21 .... 164 A3
Briar Wood GU33 .... 21 D4
Briar's The PO7 .... 111 E1
Briardene Ct SO40 .... 100 C4
Briarfield 28 BH4 .... 204 B2
Briarfield Gdns PO8 .... 112 A3
Briarswood Cl SO16 .... 78 A1
Briarswood Rd BH16 .... 201 E4
Briarswood Rise SO45 .... 125 E1
Briarwood PO16 .... 155 D4
Briarwood Gdns PO11 .... 184 C2
Briarwood Rd SO40 .... 100 B3
Brick Kiln La SO24 .... 17 C4
Brick La BH23 .... 169 F2
Brickets Terr PO12 .... 181 D1
Brickfield La Boldre SO41 ... 197 F3
Chandler's Ford SO53 .... 55 E3
Brickfield Rd SO17 .... 79 E1
Brickmakers Rd SO21 .... 56 C4
Brickwoods Cl SO51 .... 53 D4
Brickworth Rd SP5 .... 24 A2
Brickyard La Broadstone BH21 .. 162 A1
Ferndown BH21 .... 165 D3
Brickyard Rd SO32 .... 84 A2
Bridefield Cl PO8 .... 111 E2
Bridefield Cres PO8 .... 111 E2
Bridge App BH15 .... 202 A1
Bridge Cl SO31 .... 105 D1
Bridge Cotts SO51 .... 50 C2
Bridge Ct SO51 .... 52 C3
Bridge House PO13 .... 155 E2
Bridge Industries PO16 ...... 131 E2
Bridge Mead SO32 .... 61 E3
Bridge Meadows GU33 .... 20 C2
Bridge Pl BH10 .... 189 E4
Bridge Rd Bursledon SO31 .. 128 B3
Emsworth PO10 .... 136 C1
Locks Heath SO31 .... 128 B3
Lymington SO41 .... 197 F3
Romsey SO51 .... 53 D4
Southampton SO19 .... 103 E2
Swanwick SO31 .... 128 B3
Bridge Sh Ctr The PO1 ..... 182 C3
Bridge St Christchurch BH23 .. 207 E3
Fordingbridge SP6 .... 69 F1
Southwick PO17 .... 132 C3
Titchfield PO14 .... 154 A4
Wickham PO17 .... 108 A2
34 Winchester SO23 .... 11 D4
Bridge Terr
Compton(Hants) SO21 .... 31 F3
33 Southampton SO14 ...... 103 D2
Bridgefoot Dr PO16 .... 131 E1
Bridgefoot Hill PO16 .... 131 E1
Bridgefoot Path PO10 .... 160 C4
Bridgemary Ave PO13 .... 155 E3
Bridgemary Com Sch PO13 .. 155 E1
Bridgemary Gr PO13 .... 155 E2
Bridgemary Rd PO13 .... 155 E2
Bridgemary Way PO13 .... 155 E3
Bridgers Cl SO16 .... 77 F3
Bridges Ave PO6 .... 132 C1
Bridges Cl SO50 .... 55 F2
Bridges The BH24 .... 140 C4
Bridgeside Cl PO8 .... 182 B3
Bridget Cl PO8 .... 112 B4
Bridgewater Rd BH12 .... 203 E3
Bridgeway Ct SO40 .... 101 D4
Bridgwater Ct SO15 .... 102 B3
Bridle Cl BH16 .... 201 E4
Bridle Cres BH7 .... 206 B4
Bridle Way BH21 .... 164 B3
Bridleways BH31 .... 114 C3
Bridlington Ave SO15 .... 102 B4
Bridport Ct SO15 .... 102 B3
Bridport Rd Poole BH12 ..... 203 F4
Verwood BH31 .... 114 C3
Bridport St PO1 .... 182 B3
Brierley Ave BH22 .... 165 F1
Brierley Cl BH10 .... 189 F3
Brierley Rd BH10 .... 189 F2
Brigantine Rd SO31 .... 128 C1
Brigham Cl 20 PO2 .... 157 F2
Brighstone Cl SO16 .... 79 E3
Bright Rd BH15 .... 202 B3
Brightlands Ave BH6 .... 206 C3
Brighton Ave PO12 .... 180 C4
Brighton Rd
Southampton SO15 .... 102 C4
Sway SO41 .... 172 A1
Brights La PO11 .... 184 C3
Brightside PO7 .... 134 B3
Brightside Rd SO16 .... 77 F1
Brightstone Rd PO6 .... 157 F4
Brindle Cl SO16 .... 79 D3
Brinsons Cl BH23 .... 192 B2
Brinton La SO45 .... 126 A3
Brinton's Rd SO14 .... 103 D3
Brinton's Terr SO14 .... 103 D3
Brisbane House 20 PO1 ..... 182 A4
Brisbane Rd BH23 .... 191 F1
Bristol Ct PO13 .... 180 B3
Bristol Rd PO4 .... 182 C1
Britain St PO1 .... 182 A3
Britannia Ct BH12 .... 203 D4

Britannia Gdns SO30 .... 81 D2
Britannia Pl SO41 .... 197 E2
Britannia Rd Poole BH14 .... 203 D2
Portsmouth PO5 .... 182 B2
Southampton SO14 .... 103 D3
Britannia Rd N PO5 .... 182 B2
Britannia Way BH23 .... 208 A4
Britannic House 22 SO14 .. 103 E3
Britnell House 6 GU31 .... 40 C2
Briton St SO14 .... 103 D2
Britten Rd PO13 .... 179 F1
Britten Way PO7 .... 134 C2
Brittons Cotts SO42 .... 145 E1
Brixey Cl BH12 .... 203 E4
Brixey Rd BH12 .... 203 E4
Brixworth Cl 11 PO6 .... 133 D1
Broad Ave BH8 .... 205 E4
Broad Chalke Down SO22 .. 10 B2
Broad Croft PO9 .... 113 E2
Broad Gdns PO6 .... 158 C4
Broad Gn 5 SO14 .... 103 D2
Broad Way Denmead PO7 .. 110 A3
Lymington SO41 .... 197 F1
North Baddesley SO52 .... 53 F3
Southampton SO14 .... 102 C2
Swanmore SO32 .... 84 A3
Broad Mead Rd GU23 .... 114 C1
Broad Oak SO30 .... 105 F4
Broad St PO1 .... 181 F2
Broad View La SO22 .... 10 A2
Broad Way Froxfield GU32 .. 39 F4
Hamble-le-Rice SO31 .... 127 F3
Broad Woods La SO51 .... 51 D3
Broadbent Cl SO16 .... 77 F3
Broadcut PO16 .... 131 E1
Broadfields Cl SO41 .... 211 E3
Broadhill La SP6 .... 94 B4
Broadhurst Ave BH10 .... 189 F2
Broadland Cotts GU32 .... 41 D3
Broadlands Ave
Bournemouth BH6 .... 206 C2
Eastleigh SO50 .... 56 A3
Waterlooville PO7 .... 134 C4
Broadlands Cl
Bournemouth BH8 .... 190 B2
Christchurch BH23 .... 194 A1
Broadlands Rd
Brockenhurst SO42 .... 145 F1
Southampton SO17 .... 79 D2
Broadlaw Walk Prec 14 PO14 .. 154 C4
Broadley Cl SO45 .... 150 B2
Broadly Cl SO41 .... 197 D1
Broadmayne Rd BH12 .... 204 A4
Broadmead 6 SO41 .... 197 F1
Broadmead Flats SO16 .... 77 E3
Broadmead Rd SO16 .... 77 E3
Broadmeadow Cl SO40 ..... 100 C4
Broadmeadows La PO7 ..... 135 D4
Broadmere Ave PO9 .... 135 F3
Broadmoor Rd BH21 .... 186 B4
Broadoak Cl SO45 .... 150 B2
Broads The BH21 .... 162 C3
Broadsands Dr PO12 .... 180 B2
Broadsands Wlk PO12 .... 180 C2
Broadshard La BH24 .... 141 D4
Broadstone Cty Fst Sch
BH18 .... 187 D2
Broadstone Cty Mid Sch
BH18 .... 187 E3
Broadstone Way
Broadstone BH17 .... 202 A4
Broadstone, Fleet's Cnr BH18 .. 186 C1
Broadwater Ave BH14 .... 203 E1
Broadwater Rd Romsey SO51 .. 52 C3
Southampton SO18 .... 79 F2
Broadway BH6 .... 207 D2
Broadway Cl BH12 .... 204 A3
Broadway Gables BH14 ..... 203 F2
Broadway Gdns 7 BH21 .... 163 E2
Broadway La
Bournemouth BH8 .... 190 B2
Horndean PO8 .... 111 E4
Broadway Mews BH14 ...... 202 C2
Broadway Pk 5 BH21 .... 163 E2
Broadway The
Bournemouth BH10 .... 189 E3
5 Southampton, Bitterne Pk
SO18 .... 79 F1
Southampton, Portswood SO17 .. 79 D1
Southampton, Thornhill Pk SO18 .. 104 B4
Winchester SO23 .... 11 D4
Brockenhurst Ave PO9 ...... 135 E3
Brockenhurst CE Prim Sch
SO42 .... 172 C4
Brockenhurst Coll SO42 ..... 146 A1
Brockenhurst Rd BH9 .... 190 A1
Brockenhurst Sta SO42 ..... 173 D4
Brockhampton La PO9 ...... 135 F1
Brockhampton Rd PO9 ...... 135 E1
Brockhills La BH25 .... 195 E3
Brockhurst Ind Est PO12 ... 155 F1
Brockhurst Inf Sch PO12 ... 180 C2
Brockhurst Jun Sch PO12 .. 181 D4
Brockhurst Rd PO12 .... 180 C4
Brocklands SO40 .... 135 E1
Brockley Rd BH10 .... 189 F2
Brocks Cl SO45 .... 125 E1
Brocks Pine BH24 .... 139 F2
Brockwood Bottom SO32 ... 36 C4
Brodrick Ave PO12 .... 181 D2
Brog St BH21 .... 162 B1
Brokenford Ave SO40 .... 100 C4
Brokenford Bsns Ctr SO40 .. 100 C4
Brokenford La SO40 .... 100 C4
Brombys The 7 BH15 .... 202 B1
Bromley House BH12 .... 204 A3

Bromley Rd SO18 .... 79 F1
Brompton Rd PO4 .... 182 C2
Bromyard Cres PO6 .... 133 E1
Bronte Ave BH23 .... 192 A1
Bronte Cl SO40 .... 100 B3
Bronte Way SO19 .... 103 F3
Bronwen Ct SO19 .... 104 A1
Brook Ave Locks Heath SO31 .. 128 B2
  New Milton BH25 .... 195 D2
Brook Ave N BH25 .... 195 D2
Brook Cl Bournemouth BH10 .. 189 E2
  North Baddesley SO52 .... 54 A2
Brook Cnr SO43 .... 74 A1
Brook Cotts
  King's Somborne SO51 .... 6 B3
  Westbourne PO10 .... 137 D2
Brook Ct Romsey SO51 .... 52 C3
  13 Southampton SO15 .... 102 B3
Brook Dr BH31 .... 115 D2
Brook Farm Ave PO15 .... 130 C1
Brook Gdns PO10 .... 160 B4
Brook Hill SO41 .... 198 C4
Brook La Botley SO30 .... 105 F3
  Bransgore BH23 .... 193 D4
  Corfe Mullen BH21 .... 186 B3
  Hambledon PO7 .... 86 B3
  Locks Heath SO31 .... 128 C2
  Woodgreen SP6 .... 70 C4
Brook Meadow PO15 .... 130 C1
Brook Rd Bournemouth BH10 .. 189 E2
  Fair Oak SO50 .... 57 E1
  Lymington SO41 .... 197 F1
  Poole BH12 .... 203 E3
  Southampton SO18 .... 104 A4
  Wimborne Minster BH21 ...... 163 F2
Brook Road Depot BH21 ...... 163 F2
Brook St SO32 .... 83 E4
Brook Terr SP6 .... 93 F4
Brook Valley SO16 .... 78 A1
Brook Way
  Christchurch BH23 .... 208 B4
  Romsey SO51 .... 28 A1
Brook Wlk SO40 .... 76 B1
Brookdale Cl
  Broadstone BH18 .... 187 D2
  Waterlooville PO7 .... 134 C4
Brooke Cl SO23 .... 2 A4
Brookers La PO13 .... 155 D2
Brookfield Cl PO9 .... 135 F1
Brookfield Com Sch SO31 .. 128 C2
Brookfield Gdns SO31 .... 128 C2
Brookfield Pl SO17 .... 79 D1
Brookfield Rd Fair Oak SO50 .. 57 E1
  Portsmouth PO1 .... 182 C3
Brookfields SO51 .... 50 B2
Brookland Cl SO41 .... 197 E2
Brooklands Bournemouth BH4 .. 204 A2
  Lyndhurst SO43 .... 122 A2
Brooklands Rd
  Bishop's Waltham SO32 .... 83 E4
  Havant PO9 .... 135 D1
Brookley Rd SO42 .... 146 A1
Brooklyn Cl SO21 .... 31 E2
Brooklyn P PO7 .... 134 C4
Brooklynn Cl SO32 .... 83 F1
Brookman Ct SO18 .... 104 A4
Brookmead Way PO9 .... 159 F4
Brooks Cl BH24 .... 141 D3
Brooks Cl SO51 .... 1 C1
Brookside Gosport PO13 ...... 155 D2
  Ibsley SP6 .... 94 B1
  Landford SP5 .... 49 E2
  Totton SO40 .... 100 C3
Brookside Ave SO15 .... 101 F4
Brookside Cl Bransgore BH23 .. 169 D1
  Denmead PO7 .... 110 C2
Brookside Cvn Pk BH21 ...... 186 A2
Brookside House SO18 .... 79 F2
Brookside Rd
  Bransgore BH23 .... 193 D4
  Brockenhurst SO42 .... 145 F1
  Havant, Bedhampton PO9 .... 135 E1
  Wimborne Minster BH21 ...... 163 F2
Brookside Way
  Christchurch BH23 .... 193 F1
  Southampton SO18 .... 79 F1
  West End SO30 .... 80 C2
Brookvale Ct 14 SO17 .... 79 D1
Brookvale Rd SO17 .... 79 D1
Brookwood Ave SO50 .... 55 F2
Brookwood Ind Est SO50 .... 56 A2
Brookwood Rd SO16 .... 101 E4
Broom Cl Portsmouth PO4 .... 183 E2
  Waterlooville PO7 .... 135 D3
Broom Hill SO41 .... 199 D4
Broom Hill Way SO50 .... 56 A4
Broom Rd
  Petersfield GU31 .... 41 E1
  Poole BH11 .... 188 B1
Broom Sq PO4 .... 183 E3
Broom Way
  Lee-on-the-Solent PO13 ...... 179 F2
  Stubbington PO13 .... 179 F2
Broomfield Ave PO9 .... 189 F1
Broomfield Cres PO13 .... 180 A4
Broomfield Ct BH23 .... 165 F3
Broomfield Dr SP6 .... 93 D3
Broomfield La SO41 .... 197 F2
Broomhill SP5 .... 49 E1
Broomhill Cl SO41 .... 197 D1
Brooms Gr SO19 .... 104 B2
Broomy Cl SO45 .... 125 E2
Brougham La PO12 .... 181 D3
Brougham Rd PO5 .... 182 B2
Broughton St PO12 .... 181 D3
Broughton Cl BH10 .... 189 F2

Broughton Cl
  Bournemouth BH10 .... 189 F2
  4 Southampton SO16 .... 78 A1
Broughton Ct PO3 .... 158 B2
Broughton Rd SO43 .... 121 F3
Brow The PO7 .... 134 B1
Browndown Rd PO13 .... 180 B2
Brownen Rd BH9 .... 205 D4
Brownhill Cl SO53 .... 55 E4
Brownhill Ct SO16 .... 77 F2
Brownhill Gdns SO53 .... 55 E4
Brownhill Rd
  Brockenhurst BH25 .... 170 C2
  Chandler's Ford SO53 .... 55 E4
  North Baddesley SO52 .... 54 A2
Brownhill Way Nursling SO16 .. 77 E2
  Southampton SO16 .... 77 E2
Browning Ave
  Bournemouth BH5 .... 206 A2
  Portchester PO6 .... 132 C1
  Southampton SO19 .... 104 B3
Browning Cl Eastleigh SO50 .... 55 F2
  Totton SO40 .... 100 B4
Browning Dr SO22 .... 10 B4
Browning Rd BH12 .... 203 E3
Brownings Cl SO41 .... 197 D2
Brownlow Ave SO19 .... 104 A3
Brownlow Cl PO1 .... 182 B4
Brownlow Ct 23 BH4 .... 204 B2
Brownlow Gdns SO19 .... 104 A3
Browns La Beaulieu SO41 ...... 199 E3
  Damerham SP6 .... 68 A3
Brownsea Ave BH21 .... 186 B3
Brownsea Cl BH25 .... 194 C2
Brownsea Ct SO18 .... 103 F4
Brownsea Island (NT) BH15 .. 213 E2
Brownsea View Ave SO18 .. 203 E1
Brownsea View Cl BH14 .... 203 E1
Brownwich La PO14 .... 153 E3
Browsholme Cl 2 SO50 ...... 56 A3
Broxburn Cl SO53 .... 30 C1
Broxhead Rd PO9 .... 136 A3
Bruce Cl PO16 .... 131 D2
Bruce Rd PO4 .... 182 C1
Brudenell Ave BH13 .... 214 B4
Brudenell Rd BH13 .... 214 B3
Brue Cl SO53 .... 55 D4
Brune La Gosport PO13 ...... 180 A4
  Stubbington PO13 .... 155 D1
Brune Park Com Sch PO13 .. 180 C4
Brune Way BH22 .... 165 E2
Brunei House SO16 .... 79 D3
Brunel Cl Hedge End SO30 .... 81 F1
  Verwood BH31 .... 115 E2
Brunel Rd Portsmouth PO2 .. 157 F2
  Southampton SO15 .... 101 E4
  Totton SO40 .... 76 C2
Brunel Way PO15 .... 129 E2
Brunstead Pl BH12 .... 204 A3
Brunstead Rd BH12 .... 204 A2
Brunswick Cl SO50 .... 57 D2
Brunswick Gdns PO9 .... 135 E1
Brunswick Pl
  Lymington SO41 .... 197 F2
  Southampton SO15 .... 103 D3
Brunswick Rd SO50 .... 57 D2
Brunswick Sq SO14 .... 103 D2
Brunswick St PO5 .... 182 B2
Brushers BH23 .... 169 F2
Bruyn Ct 5 PO4 .... 70 A1
Bruyn Rd SP6 .... 70 A1
Bryanston Rd SO19 .... 103 F3
Bryanstone Rd BH3 .... 204 C4
Bryant Rd BH12 .... 204 A4
Bryher Island PO6 .... 157 D4
Brympton Cl SP6 .... 69 E1
Bryony Cl Broadstone BH18 .. 186 C2
  Locks Heath SO31 .... 128 C1
Bryony Gdns SO50 .... 81 E3
Bryony Way PO7 .... 135 D4
Bryson Rd PO6 .... 157 E4
Bub La BH23 .... 207 F3
Bubb La SO32 .... 81 E2
Buccaneers Cl BH23 .... 207 F3
Buccleuch Rd BH13 .... 204 A1
Buchan Ave PO15 .... 129 E4
Buchan Ct SO45 .... 125 E1
Buchanan Ave BH7 .... 205 F3
Buchanan Rd SO16 .... 77 F3
Buckby La PO3 .... 158 B2
Bucketts Farm Cl SO32 ...... 84 A3

Bucklers Ct Havant PO9 ...... 135 E4
  Lymington SO41 .... 197 E2
  Portsmouth PO2 .... 157 E1
Bucklers Hard Maritime
  Mus SO42 .... 176 B3
Bucklers Mews SO41 .... 197 E2
Bucklers Rd PO12 .... 181 E4
Bucklers The SO41 .... 211 D3
Bucklers Way BH8 .... 190 B2
Bucklershard Rd SO42 ...... 176 B3
Buckley Ct SO16 .... 78 A1
Buckmore Ave GU32 .... 40 B2
Bucks Head Hill SO32 .... 61 E3
Bucksey Rd PO13 .... 180 B4
Buckstone Cl SO41 .... 195 D2
Buckthorn Cl Broadstone BH17 .. 186 C1
  Totton SO40 .... 100 A4
Budden's La PO17 .... 108 C4
Buddens Rd PO17 .... 108 A2
Buddle Hill SP6 .... 94 B2
Budds La SO51 .... 27 F1
Budds Lane Trad Est SO51 .... 27 F1
Bude PO6 .... 132 C1
Bugdens La BH31 .... 115 D3
Bugle St SO14 .... 102 C2
Bulbarrow Wlk PO14 .... 154 C4
Bulbeck Rd 16 PO9 .... 135 F1
Buldowne Wlk SO41 .... 172 A2
Bull Hill Boldre SO41 .... 174 A1
  Rake GU33 .... 21 F2
Bull La Minstead SO43 .... 98 B2
  Poole BH15 .... 202 B1
  Shedfield SO32 .... 83 E2
Bullar Rd SO18 .... 103 F4
Bullar St SO14 .... 103 D3
Bullfinch Cl Broadstone BH17 .. 186 C1
  Totton SO40 .... 100 B4
Bullfinch Ct PO13 .... 179 F2
Bullrush Cl SO45 .... 125 F1
Bulls Copse La PO8 .... 112 A3
Bulls Dro SP5 .... 4 A3
Bunkers Hill PO7 .... 110 B2
Bunns La PO7 .... 109 F3
Bunny La Michelmersh SO51 .. 27 F3
  Sherfield English SO51 .... 25 D2
Bunstead La SO21 .... 30 B4
Bunting Gdns PO8 .... 111 F2
Bunting Rd BH22 .... 165 D4
BUPA Hospl PO9 .... 136 B3
Burbidge Gr PO4 .... 183 D1
Burbush Cl SO45 .... 150 B2
Burcombe La SO41 .... 117 F1
Burcombe Rd BH10 .... 189 E3
Burcote Dr PO3 .... 158 A2
Burdale Dr PO11 .... 185 E2
Burdock Cl BH23 .... 193 D1
Bure Cl BH23 .... 208 A3
Bure Haven Dr BH23 .... 208 A3
Bure Homage Gdns BH23 .. 208 A3
Bure Homage La BH23 ...... 208 A3
Bure La BH23 .... 208 A3
Bure Pk BH23 .... 208 A3
Bure Rd BH23 .... 208 A3
Burford Cl BH23 .... 191 E1
Burford Ct 15 BH1 .... 205 D2
Burford La SO42 .... 146 A1
Burgate Cl PO9 .... 135 E2
Burgate Cross SP6 .... 70 A3
Burgate Fields SP6 .... 70 A2
Burgate Sch The SP6 .... 70 A2
Burgesmede House 13 GU32 .. 40 C2
Burgess Cl Bournemouth BH11 .. 188 C2
  South Hayling PO11 .... 185 E1
Burgess Ct SO16 .... 79 D2
Burgess Gdns SO16 .... 78 C2
Burgess Rd SO16, SO17 .... 79 D2
Burghclere Rd Havant PO9 .. 136 A3
  Southampton SO19 .... 126 C4
Burgoyne Rd Portsmouth PO5 .. 182 B1
Burgundy Cl SO31 .... 128 C1
Burgundy Terr 1 PO2 .... 157 F1
Buriton Cl PO16 .... 132 B1
Buriton Ct SO19 .... 103 F2
Buriton Prim Sch GU31 ...... 65 E3
Buriton Rd SO22 .... 1 B2
Buriton St PO1 .... 182 B3
Burke Dr SO19 .... 104 B3
Burleigh Rd Bournemouth BH6 .. 206 B3
  Portsmouth PO1 .... 182 C4
Burley Cl Barton on Sea BH25 .. 209 E4
  Chandler's Ford SO53 .... 55 D2
  15 Havant PO9 .... 136 A3
  Verwood BH31 .... 114 C3
Burley Ct 4 SO17 .... 79 D1
Burley Down SO53 .... 55 D2
Burley House 5 SO16 .... 102 A4
Burley Lawn BH24 .... 143 D2
Burley Prim Sch BH24 ...... 143 D2
Burley Rd Bransgore BH23 .. 193 D4
  Brockenhurst SO42 .... 172 C4
  Burton BH23 .... 192 B3
  Poole BH12 .... 203 E3
  Winchester SO22 .... 1 B2
Burling Terr 1 BH12 .... 204 A2
Burlington Arc 34 BH1 ...... 204 C2
Burlington Ct SO19 .... 104 A3
Burlington Mans 1 SO15 .. 102 B4
Burlington Rd
  Portsmouth PO2 .... 157 F1
  Southampton SO15 .... 102 C3
Burma House SO18 .... 79 F2
Burma Rd SO51 .... 52 C3
Burma Rd N SO45 .... 151 D3
Burmese Cl PO15 .... 129 E4
Burn Cl BH31 .... 115 D2
Burnaby Ct BH4 .... 204 B1

Burnaby Rd Bournemouth BH4 .. 204 B1
  Portsmouth PO1 .... 182 A4
Burnage Ct 18 BH13 .... 214 C4
Burnbake Rd BH31 .... 115 D3
Burnbank Gdns SO40 .... 100 C4
Burnbrae Rd BH22 .... 165 E1
Burnett Ave BH23 .... 206 C4
Burnett Cl Hythe SO45 ...... 126 A1
  Southampton SO18 .... 79 F1
  Winchester SO22 .... 1 B1
Burnett Rd Christchurch BH23 .. 206 C4
  Gosport PO12 .... 180 C3
Burnetts Fields SO50 .... 81 E4
Burnetts Gdns SO50 .... 81 E4
Burnetts La Fair Oak SO50 .... 81 E3
  West End SO30,SO32 .... 81 E3
Burney House 25 PO12 ...... 181 E2
Burney Rd PO12 .... 180 C2
Burngate Rd BH15 .... 201 F1
Burnham Beeches SO53 ...... 55 D3
Burnham Chase SO18 .... 104 B3
Burnham Dr BH8 .... 205 E4
Burnham Rd Burton BH23 .. 192 B1
  Cosham PO6 .... 134 B1
  Fordingbridge SP6 .... 69 F2
Burnham Wood PO16 .... 131 D2
Burnhams Wlk 19 PO12 .... 181 E2
Burnleigh Gdns BH25 ...... 195 E2
Burns Cl SO50 .... 55 F1
Burns Pl SO16 .... 78 A1
Burns Rd Bournemouth BH6 .. 206 B4
  Eastleigh SO50 .... 55 F1
  Southampton SO19 .... 104 B3
Burnside Christchurch BH23 .. 208 B4
  Gosport PO13 .... 155 D3
  Waterlooville PO7 .... 112 A1
Burnt House La Boldre SO41 .. 174 A1
  Bransgore BH23 .... 169 D1
  Stubbington PO14 .... 154 B2
Burr Cl SO21 .... 56 C4
Burrard Gr SO41 .... 197 F1
Burridge Rd SO31 .... 106 A1
Burrill Ave PO6 .... 158 A4
Burrows Cl PO9 .... 136 A2
Burrows La BH31 .... 114 C4
Bursledon House 40 PO1 .... 182 B3
Bursledon Pl PO7 .... 134 B3
Bursledon Rd Hedge End SO30 .. 105 D3
  Southampton SO19, SO31 ...... 104 B3
  Waterlooville PO7 .... 134 B3
Bursledon Sta SO31 .... 128 A4
Bursledon Jun & Inf Sch
  SO31 .... 128 A4
Burt's La Holt Heath BH21 .... 138 A4
  Verwood BH31 .... 138 A4
Burtley Rd BH6 .... 206 C2
Burton CE Prim Sch BH23 .. 192 B2
  St Leonards BH24 .... 139 F3
Burton Hall BH23 .... 192 B1
Burton Hall Pl BH23 .... 192 B2
Burton Rd Christchurch BH23 .. 207 F4
  Poole BH13 .... 204 A2
  Southampton SO15 .... 102 C3
Burtoncroft BH23 .... 192 B2
Burts Hill BH21 .... 163 E3
Burwood Gr PO11 .... 185 D2
Bury Cl PO12 .... 181 D2
Bury Cres PO12 .... 181 D2
Bury Farm SO30 .... 106 B2
Bury Hall La PO12 .... 180 C2
Bury House 18 PO16 .... 131 D1
Bury La SO40 .... 101 D3
Bury La Gosport PO12 ...... 181 D2
  Marchwood SO40 .... 101 F2
  Poole BH13 .... 203 F1
Bus Dro SO45 .... 178 C4
Bush House 38 PO5 .... 182 B2
Bush St E PO5 .... 182 B2
Bush St W 40 PO5 .... 182 B2
Bushell Rd BH15 .... 202 B4
Bushells Farm SP6 .... 93 F4
Bushey Rd BH8 .... 190 B1
Bushmead Dr BH24 .... 139 F3
Bushy Mead PO7 .... 134 B2
Busket La SO23 .... 11 D4
Busketts Way SO40 .... 100 A1
Butcher St PO1 .... 182 A3
Butcher's Cnr SO43 .... 73 F2
Bute Dr BH23 .... 209 D4
Butlers Cl SO51 .... 4 C1
Butlers La BH24 .... 117 E1
Butser Ct PO8 .... 88 B2
Butser Wlk Fareham PO14 .... 154 C4
  Petersfield GU31 .... 41 D2
Butt La SP5 .... 22 A4
Butt's Cl SO19 .... 104 B3
Butt's Cres SO19 .... 104 B3
Butt's Rd SO19 .... 104 B2
Butt's Sq SO19 .... 104 B2
Buttercup Cl Hedge End SO30 .. 105 D3
  Hythe SO45 .... 126 A1
Buttercup Dr BH23 .... 193 D1
Buttercup Way SO31 .... 128 C2
Butterfield Rd SO16 .... 78 C2
Butterfly Dr PO6 .... 133 D1
Buttermere Cl SO16 .... 77 F1
Buttermere House 24 PO6 .... 133 E1
Buttery The BH23 .... 207 E4
Button's La 19 Poole BH15 .... 202 B1
  West Wellow SO51 .... 50 C2
Butts Ash Gdns SO45 ...... 126 A3
Butts Ash La SO45 .... 149 F4
Butts Bridge Hill SO45 ...... 126 A1
Butts Farm La SO32 .... 83 E4
Butts Paddock SO42 .... 145 E2

Butts The SO32 .... 61 E3
Buttsash Ave SO45 .... 150 A4
Buttsbridge Rd SO45 .... 126 A1
By Pass Rd SO51 .... 52 C3
By the Wood SO40 .... 76 B1
Byams La SO40 .... 102 A1
Bye Rd SO31 .... 128 B4
Byerley Cl PO10 .... 137 D3
Byerley Rd PO1 .... 182 C3
Byeways SO45 .... 125 F1
Byrd Cl PO7 .... 134 C3
Byres The PO14 .... 154 B2
Byron Ave SO22 .... 10 B4
Byron Cl
  Bishop's Waltham SO32 .... 83 F4
  Fareham PO16 .... 131 D1
Byron Ct Ferndown BH22 .. 165 E3
  Southampton SO15 .... 102 C3
Byron House 16 BH25 .... 195 D1
Byron Rd Barton on Sea BH25 .. 209 E4
  Bournemouth BH5 .... 205 F2
  Eastleigh SO50 .... 56 A2
  Portsmouth PO2 .... 182 C4
  Southampton SO19 .... 104 B3
  Wimborne Minster BH21 ...... 163 E3

C Ave SO45 .... 150 C2
Cable St 22 SO14 .... 103 E3
Cabot Dr PO14 .... 125 E2
Cabot La BH17 .... 202 A4
Cabot Way BH25 .... 194 C2
Cadgwith Pl PO6 .... 157 D4
Cadhay Cl PO15 .... 194 C2
Cadland Ct SO14 .... 103 E1
Cadland Rd Fawley, SO45 ...... 151 D3
  Fawley, Hardley SO45 .... 150 A4
Cadlands Park Est SO45 .... 150 B3
Cadnam Ct PO12 .... 180 B2
Cadnam La SO40 .... 74 C1
Cadnam Lawn PO9 .... 135 E4
Cadnam Rd PO4 .... 183 D2
Cadnam Way BH8 .... 190 B2
Cadogan Rd BH24 .... 141 D4
Cador Dr PO16 .... 156 A3
Caen House 7 PO14 .... 154 C4
Caerleon Ave SO19 .... 104 B3
Caerleon Dr SO19 .... 104 B3
Caernarvon Gdns SO53 ...... 55 D2
Caesar's Way BH18 .... 186 C3
Cains Cl PO14 .... 154 B2
Caird Ave BH25 .... 195 E1
Cairns Cl BH23 .... 206 C4
Cairo Terr PO2 .... 182 B4
Caister Cl SO16 .... 78 A2
Calabrese SO31 .... 129 D4
Calbourne SO31 .... 127 E4
Calcott La SO32 .... 82 C2
Caldecote Wlk 50 PO5 ...... 182 B2
Calder Cl SO16 .... 101 F4
Calder Rd BH17 .... 202 C4
Calderwood Dr SO19 .... 104 A2
Caledon Rd BH14 .... 203 F2
Caledonia Dr SO45 .... 125 E2
Caledonian Cl BH23 .... 208 A4
Calkin Cl SO16 .... 192 A1
Calluna Rd BH12 .... 203 D4
Calman Ct BH1 .... 205 E2
Calmore Cl BH8 .... 190 B2
Calmore Cres SO40 .... 76 A1
Calmore Dr SO40 .... 76 A1
Calmore Gdns SO40 .... 100 B4
Calmore Ind Est SO40 ...... 76 C1
Calmore Inf Sch SO40 ...... 76 B1
Calmore Jun Sch SO40 ...... 76 B1
Calmore Rd SO40 .... 100 B4
Calpe Ave SO43 .... 121 F3
Calshot Activities Ctr SO45 .. 152 A1
Calshot Castle SO45 .... 152 A1
Calshot Cl SO45 .... 178 C4
Calshot Ct SO14 .... 103 E1
Calshot Dr SO53 .... 55 D2
Calshot Rd Fawley SO45 .... 151 D1
  Havant PO9 .... 135 E4
Calshot Way PO13 .... 155 D1
Calvin Rd BH9 .... 204 C4
Camargue Cl SO31 .... 129 D4
Camber Pl PO1 .... 182 A2
Cambria Dr SO45 .... 125 E2
Cambrian Cl SO31 .... 105 D1
Cambrian Wlk PO14 .... 154 C4
Cambridge Ct 15 SO14 ...... 103 D4
Cambridge Dr SO53 .... 55 E2
Cambridge Gdns BH23 ...... 191 F1
Cambridge Gn
  Chandler's Ford SO53 .... 55 E1
  Titchfield PO14 .... 129 E1
Cambridge Junc PO1 .... 182 A2
Cambridge Rd
  Bournemouth BH2 .... 204 B2
  Gosport PO12 .... 180 C3
  Lee-on-the-Solent PO13 ...... 179 F1
  Portsmouth PO1 .... 182 A2
  Southampton SO14 .... 103 D4
Camcross Cl 7 PO6 .... 133 D1
Camden Cl BH9 .... 190 A1
Camden Hurst 1 SO41 ...... 211 D2
Camden St SO19 .... 181 D3
Camden Terr 4 PO12 .... 181 D3
Camel Green Rd SP6 .... 93 D3
Camelia Cl SO52 .... 54 A3
Camelia Gdns SO18 .... 80 A1
Camelia Gr SO50 .... 57 F1
Camellia Cl BH21 .... 114 C1
Camellia Ct 2 SO18 .... 79 F1

Camellia Gdns BH25 .... 195 D1
Camelot Cres PO16 .... 132 A1
Cameron PO13 .... 155 E2
Cameron Ct SO16 .... 77 F3
Cameron Rd BH23 .... 207 E4
Camley Cl SO19 .... 103 F1
Cammel Rd BH22 .... 165 E1
Camp Rd PO13 .... 155 E2
Campbell Cres PO7 .... 134 B3
Campbell Ct SO50 .... 57 E1
Campbell Mews SO18 .... 104 B4
Campbell Rd Bournemouth BH1 .. 205 F3
  Burton BH23 .... 192 B2
  Eastleigh SO50 .... 56 A1
  Portsmouth PO5 .... 182 C2
Campbell St SO14 .... 103 E3
Campbell Way SO50 .... 57 E1
Campion Cl Fair Oak SO50 .... 81 E3
  Locks Heath SO31 .... 128 C1
  Waterlooville PO7 .... 135 D3
Campion Dr SO51 .... 28 B1
Campion Gr BH23 .... 207 F3
Campion Rd SO19 .... 104 B3
Campion Way
  Kings Worthy SO23 .... 2 B4
  Lymington SO41 .... 197 F3
Cams Bay PO16 .... 131 F1
Cams Hill Hambledon PO7 .... 86 A1
  Portchester PO16 .... 131 F1
Cams Hill Sch PO16 .... 155 F4
Canada Cnr GU31 .... 66 C3
Canada Pl SO16 .... 78 C2
Canada Rd Southampton SO19 .. 103 F1
  West Wellow SO51 .... 50 B1
Canal Cl SO31 .... 28 A1
Canal Wlk Portsmouth PO1 .... 182 B3
  Romsey SO51 .... 52 C4
  Southampton SO14 .... 103 D2
Canberra House 29 PO1 .... 182 B3
Canberra Rd
  Christchurch BH23 .... 191 F1
  Nursling SO16 .... 77 D2
  Thorney Island PO10 .... 161 D2
Canberra Towers 10 SO19 .... 126 C4
Candlemas Pl 12 SO17 .... 103 D4
Candover Ct SO19 .... 127 D4
Candy La SO19 .... 104 C3
Candys Cl BH21 .... 162 C1
Candys La BH21 .... 162 C1
Canford Ave BH11 .... 189 D1
Canford Bottom BH21 .... 164 B3
Canford Cl Shedfield SO32 .... 107 F4
  Southampton SO16 .... 77 E1
Canford Cliffs Ave BH14 .... 203 F1
Canford Cliffs Rd BH13 .... 203 F1
Canford Cres BH13 .... 214 C4
Canford Ct BH13 .... 214 C4
Canford Gdns BH21 .... 189 D1
Canford Heath Fst
  & Mid Schs BH17 .... 202 B4
Canford Heath Rd
  Broadstone BH17 .... 187 F1
  Poole BH17 .... 187 F1
Canford Magna BH21 .... 164 A1
Canford Pl 2 BH13 .... 214 C4
Canford Rd Bournemouth BH11 .. 189 D1
  Poole BH15 .... 202 B2
Canford Sch BH21 .... 164 A1
Canford View Dr BH21 .... 164 A3
Canford Way BH12 .... 188 B1
Canhouse La GU33 .... 21 F2
Cannock Terr 14 PO5 .... 182 B2
Cannock Wlk 16 PO14 .... 154 C4
Cannon Cl BH18 .... 187 D1
Cannon Hill Gdns BH21 .... 164 A4
Cannon Hill Rd BH21 .... 164 A4
Cannon House SO41 .... 197 F2
Cannon St Lymington SO41 .... 197 F2
  Southampton SO15 .... 102 B4
Cannon's Barn Cl PO16 .... 132 B1
Canoe Cl SO31 .... 128 C1
Canon Ct 5 SO50 .... 57 E1
Canon St SO23 .... 10 C4
Canons Wlk SO41 .... 211 E3
Cantell Sec Sch SO16 .... 79 D2
Canterbury Ave SO19 .... 104 B2
Canterbury Cl
  Lee-on-the-Solent PO13 .... 180 A2
  West Moors BH22 .... 138 C1
Canterbury Dr SO45 .... 125 E2
Canterbury Rd
  Portsmouth PO4 .... 182 C2
  Stubbington PO14 .... 154 B2
Canterton La SO43 .... 98 A4
Canton St SO15 .... 102 C3
Canute Dr BH23 .... 169 D1
Canute House 25 SO14 .... 103 D2
Canute Rd Southampton SO14 .. 103 D2
  6 Winchester SO23 .... 11 D3
Canvey St SO16 .... 77 F1
Capel Ley PO7 .... 134 C2
Capella Ct BH2 .... 204 C1
Capella Gdns SO45 .... 125 E2
Capers End La SO32 .... 82 C1
Capesthorne BH23 .... 208 A3
Capital House 5 SO22 .... 10 C4
Capon Cl SO18 .... 79 F2
Capstan Ct SO14 .... 103 D1
Capstan Gdns SO31 .... 129 E2
Capstans The BH14 .... 214 A4
Capstone Pl BH8 .... 205 E1
Capstone Rd BH8 .... 205 E1
Captain's Pl SO14 .... 103 D2
Captain's Row SO41 .... 197 F2
Captains Row PO1 .... 182 B3

Caradon Pl BH31 .... 114 B4
Carberry Dr PO16 .... 156 B4
Carbery Ave BH6 .... 206 B3
Carbery Ct PO9 .... 135 E4
Carbery Gdns BH6 .... 206 C3
Carbery La 3 BH6 .... 206 B2
Carbery Row 2 BH6 .... 206 B2
Carbis Cl PO13 .... 157 D4
Cardew Rd GU33 .... 21 D2
Cardiff Rd PO13 .... 157 E1
Cardigan Rd
  Bournemouth BH9 .... 204 C4
  Poole BH12 .... 203 F2
Cardinal Dr PO7 .... 112 A1
Cardinal Way SO31 .... 129 D1
Cardington Ct SO16 .... 77 F2
Carey Rd Bournemouth BH9 .. 189 F2
  Southampton SO19 .... 104 B3
Careys Cotts SO42 .... 145 F1
Careys Rd BH8 .... 190 B2
Carina Ct BH13 .... 214 B2
Carisbrook Cres BH15 .... 201 E2
Carisbrooke Netley SO31 .... 127 E4
  Poole BH13 .... 214 C4
Carisbrooke Ave PO14 .... 179 D3
Carisbrooke Cl PO9 .... 136 A1
Carisbrooke Cres SO53 .... 55 F3
Carisbrooke Ct
  4 Christchurch BH23 .... 209 D4
  New Milton BH25 .... 194 C2
  Romsey SO51 .... 28 A1
Carisbrooke Dr SO19 .... 103 F3
Carisbrooke Rd Gosport PO13 . 155 E1
  Portsmouth PO4 .... 183 D2
Carisbrooke Way BH23 .... 193 F1
Carless PO13 .... 180 B4
Carlinford 29 BH5 .... 205 F2
Carlisle Ct 2 SO16 .... 102 A4
Carlisle Rd Portsmouth PO1 .. 182 B3
  Southampton SO16 .... 102 A4
Carlton Ave BH25 .... 209 F4
Carlton Cres SO15 .... 102 C3
Carlton Ct 5 SO15 .... 102 C4
Carlton Gr BH12 .... 203 E3
Carlton House 197 F2
Carlton Pl SO15 .... 102 C3
Carlton Rd Bournemouth BH1 .. 205 E2
  Gosport PO12 .... 181 D3
  Portchester PO16 .... 132 C1
  Southampton SO15 .... 102 B4
Carlton Way PO12 .... 181 D3
Carlyle Rd Bournemouth BH6 .. 206 B3
  Gosport PO12 .... 181 D3
Carlyn Dr SO53 .... 55 E4
Carmans La SO21 .... 31 E4
Carmarthen Ave PO6 .... 158 A4
Carnarvon Rd
  4 Bournemouth BH1 .... 205 F2
  Gosport PO12 .... 181 D2
  Portsmouth PO2 .... 182 C4
Carnation Rd SO16 .... 79 E2
Carne Cl SO53 .... 55 E4
Carne Pl PO6 .... 157 D4
Caroline Ave BH23 .... 207 F3
Caroline Gdns PO15 .... 130 B1
Caroline Rd BH11 .... 189 D2
Carolyn Cl SO19 .... 103 F1
Carpathia Cl SO18 .... 80 A1
Carpenter Cl Hythe SO45 .... 126 A2
  Lymington SO41 .... 197 E3
  Portsmouth PO4 .... 183 D2
Carradale BH23 .... 208 A4
Carran Wlk PO14 .... 154 C4
Carraway PO15 .... 129 E4
Carrbridge Cl BH3 .... 204 B4
Carrbridge Gdns BH3 .... 204 B4
Carrbridge Rd BH3 .... 204 B4
Carrick Way BH25 .... 195 E1
Carrington Cl SO41 .... 211 F3
Carrington House
  6 Eastleigh SO50 .... 56 A1
  33 Southampton SO17 .... 79 D1
Carrington La SO41 .... 211 F2
Carrol Cl SO50 .... 57 E1
Carroll Ave BH22 .... 165 F3
Carroll Cl BH12 .... 204 A3
Carronade Wlk PO3 .... 157 F3
Carronades The 19 SO14 .... 103 D3
Carshalton Ave PO6 .... 158 A4
Carsworth Way BH17 .... 188 A1
Carter Com Sch SO41 .... 201 F1
Carter House Gosport PO13 .. 155 D3
  7 Portsmouth PO1 .... 182 A3
Carter's Clay Rd SO51 .... 26 A3
Carter's La 10 BH15 .... 202 B1
Carters Ave BH15 .... 201 E2
Carters Cl SP6 .... 47 E2
Carthage Cl SO53 .... 55 D4
Cartref BH31 .... 114 C3
Cartwright Cl BH10 .... 189 E2
Cartwright Dr PO15 .... 129 F1
Carvers Ind Est 7 BH24 .... 141 D4
Carvers La BH24 .... 141 D4
Carysfort Rd BH1 .... 205 E2
Cascades App PO1 .... 182 B3
Cascades Sh Ctr PO1 .... 182 B3
Cashmoor Cl BH12 .... 203 F4
Cask St 6 PO1 .... 182 B3
Caslake Cl BH25 .... 194 C1
Caspar John Cl PO14 .... 179 D3
Caspian Cl SO31 .... 129 D4
Cassel Ave BH13 .... 204 A1
Castle Ave Christchurch BH23 .. 208 C4
  Havant PO9 .... 136 A1
  Winchester SO23 .... 10 C4
Castle Cl Milford on Sea SO41 .. 211 F2
  Portsmouth PO5 .... 182 B2
Castle Court Sch BH21 .... 186 A4

Castle Ct
  3 Christchurch BH23 .... 209 D4
  4 Southampton, Bitterne Pk
   SO18 .... 79 F1
  Southampton, Millbrook SO15 .. 102 A3
Castle Farm Ct PO17 .... 108 A1
Castle Gate Cl BH8 .... 190 B1
Castle Gdns GU32 .... 40 C2
Castle Gr PO16 .... 156 B4
Castle Hill La BH24 .... 142 C2
  Winchester SO22 .... 10 C4
Castle Hts 3 SO18 .... 79 F1
Castle La Chandler's Ford SO53 .. 55 D2
  Fawley SO45 .... 178 C4
  North Baddesley SO52 .... 54 C2
  6 Southampton SO14 .... 102 C2
Castle La E BH7 .... 206 B4
Castle La W BH8, BH9 .... 190 B1
Castle Marina PO13 .... 179 F1
Castle Meadow SP5 .... 46 C4
Castle Mews BH23 .... 140 B3
Castle Par BH7 .... 206 B4
Castle Prim Sch PO16 .... 156 B4
Castle Rd Bournemouth BH9 .. 190 A1
  Netley SO31 .... 127 D3
  Portsmouth PO5 .... 182 B2
  Rowland's Castle PO9 .... 113 D1
  Southampton SO18 .... 79 F1
  Southwick PO17 .... 132 C3
Castle Sq 8 SO14 .... 102 C2
Castle St Christchurch BH23 .. 207 E3
  Poole BH15 .... 202 B1
  Portchester PO16 .... 156 B4
  Southampton SO14 .... 103 D4
  Titchfield PO15 .... 154 A4
Castle Trad Est PO16 .... 156 C4
Castle View PO12 .... 181 D4
Castle View Rd PO16 .... 156 C3
Castle Way SO14 .... 102 C2
Castle Woods SP5 .... 47 E3
Castledene Cres BH14 .... 203 D1
Castlemain Ave BH6 .... 206 B3
Castleman Ct BH22 .... 138 B2
Castleman Way BH24 .... 141 D3
Castlemans La PO11 .... 160 A1
Castleshaw Cl SO16 .... 101 F4
Castleton Ave BH10 .... 189 E4
Castleway PO9 .... 136 A1
Castlewood Ave BH24 .... 140 B3
Catalina Cl BH23 .... 208 A3
Catalina Dr BH15 .... 202 C1
Catamaran Cl SO31 .... 128 C1
Cateran Cl SO16 .... 101 F4
Cathay Gdns SO45 .... 125 E2
Cathedral View 5 SO23 .... 11 D3
Catherine Cl SO30 .... 80 C1
Catherine Cres SP5 .... 46 B4
Catherine Gdns SO30 .... 80 C1
Catherington CE Inf Sch PO8 .. 88 A1
Catherington Hill PO8 .... 88 A2
Catherington La
  Horndean PO8 .... 112 A4
  Waterlooville PO8 .... 112 A4
Catherington Way PO9 .... 135 F2
Catisfield House 44 PO1 .... 182 B3
Catisfield La PO15 .... 130 A1
Catisfield Rd Fareham PO15 .. 130 A1
  Portsmouth PO4 .... 183 D2
Caton Cl BH12 .... 204 A4
Cattistock Rd BH8 .... 190 C1
Catways SO21 .... 30 A1
Causeway SO31 .... 52 B3
Causeway Cres SO40 .... 101 D4
Causeway Ct 6 SO18 .... 103 F4
Causeway Farm PO8 .... 112 A3
Causeway The
  Petersfield GU31 .... 40 C1
  Portchester PO16 .... 131 F1
Cavalier Cl SO45 .... 125 E2
Cavalier Ct PO6 .... 158 B4
Cavan Cres BH17 .... 187 D1
Cavanna Cl SO31 .... 155 D1
Cavell Dr PO6 .... 133 F1
Cavendish Cl Romsey SO51 .. 28 A1
  Waterlooville PO7 .... 134 C4
Cavendish Corner Cvn Pk
  4 BH24 .... 141 D4
Cavendish Dr PO7 .... 134 C4
Cavendish Gr
  Southampton SO17 .... 102 C4
  Winchester SO23 .... 2 A2
Cavendish Hall BH1 .... 205 D3
Cavendish Mews 2 SO15 .. 102 C4
Cavendish Pl BH1 .... 205 D3
Cavendish Rd
  Bournemouth BH1 .... 205 D3
  Portsmouth PO5 .... 182 B2
Caversham Cl
  Hamworthy BH15 .... 201 F2
  Southampton SO19 .... 104 A2
  West End SO30 .... 80 B1
Cawdor Rd BH3 .... 204 B4
Cawte Rd SO15 .... 102 B3
Cawte's Pl PO16 .... 131 E1
Caxton Ave SO19 .... 104 A3
Caxton Cl BH23 .... 208 A4
Cecil Ave Ashurst SO40 .... 100 B1
  Bournemouth BH8 .... 205 E4
  Southampton SO15, SO16 .... 78 A1
Cecil Cl BH21 .... 186 C3
Cecil Ct BH8 .... 205 D4
Cecil Gr PO5 .... 182 B2
Cecil Hill BH8 .... 205 D4
Cecil Pl PO5 .... 182 A2
Cecil Rd Bournemouth BH5 .. 205 D1
  Poole BH12 .... 203 E3
  Southampton SO19 .... 103 F2

Cecil Villas SO17 .... 79 E1
Cedar Ave Bournemouth BH10 .. 189 E3
  Christchurch BH23 .... 206 B4
  Southampton SO15 .... 102 B4
  St Leonards BH24 .... 139 F2
Cedar Cl Bursledon SO31 .... 127 F4
  Gosport PO12 .... 156 A1
  Hedge End SO30 .... 105 E4
  Kings Worthy SO23 .... 2 A1
  Upton BH16 .... 201 D4
  Waterlooville PO7 .... 134 C3
Cedar Cres
  North Baddesley SO52 .... 53 F3
  Waterlooville PO8 .... 112 B3
Cedar Ct Bournemouth BH4 .. 204 A1
  12 Fareham PO16 .... 131 E1
Cedar Dr Hordle SO41 .... 211 E4
  Wimborne Minster BH21 .. 164 A3
Cedar Gdns
  Barton on Sea BH25 .... 194 C1
  Southampton SO14 .... 103 D4
Cedar Gr PO3 .... 183 D4
Cedar Lawn SO51 .... 28 B1
Cedar Mount BH4 .... 204 B2
Cedar Pl BH23 .... 169 D1
Cedar Rd Eastleigh SO50 .... 55 F1
  Hythe SO45 .... 150 A4
  Southampton SO14 .... 103 D4
Cedar Specl Sch The SO16 .... 77 F2
Cedar Trad Pk BH21 .... 164 C3
Cedar Way Fareham PO14 .. 154 C4
  Ferndown BH22 .... 165 E4
Cedar Wlk 18 SO50 .... 10 C4
Cedar Wood Cl Fair Oak SO50 .. 57 F1
  Totton SO40 .... 100 B4
Cedarmount SO43 .... 121 F2
Cedars The BH4 .... 204 B2
Cedarwood SO23 .... 2 B4
Cedarwood Lodge 6 PO16 .. 131 D1
Cedric Cl SO45 .... 177 F4
Celandine Ave
  Locks Heath SO31 .... 128 C1
  Waterlooville PO8 .... 112 A2
Celandine Cl
  Christchurch BH23 .... 208 A4
  North Baddesley SO52 .... 54 C3
Celia Ct PO7 .... 135 D4
Cellars Farm Rd BH6 .... 207 D2
Cement Terr 7 SO14 .... 102 C2
Cemetery Ave BH15 .... 202 C3
Cemetery La Denmead PO7 .. 110 C3
  Westbourne PO10 .... 137 E2
Cemetery Rd
  Southampton SO15 .... 102 C4
  Wimborne Minster BH21 .. 163 D3
Centaur St PO2 .... 182 B4
Centenary Cl SO41 .... 172 B1
Centenary House 6 BH23 .. 207 D4
Centenary Way BH1, ... 205 F3
Central Ave Corfe Mullen BH21 .. 186 B4
  Poole BH12 .... 203 F3
Central Bridge SO14 .... 103 D2
Central Dr BH2 .... 204 C3
Central Prec The SO53 .... 55 E3
Central Rd Cosham PO6 .... 158 B4
  Portchester PO16 .... 156 A4
  Southampton SO14 .... 103 D1
Central St SO14 .... 182 B3
Central Station Bridge SO15 .. 102 C3
Central Way N SO45 .... 151 F1
Centre La SO41 .... 196 C1
Centre Pl BH24 .... 140 C4
Centre Way SO31 .... 129 D2
Centurion Ind Pk SO18 .... 103 E4
Cerdic Mews SO31 .... 128 A2
Cerne Abbas BH13 .... 204 A1
Cerne Cl Bournemouth BH9 .. 190 A2
  North Baddesley SO52 .... 53 F2
  West End SO18 .... 80 A1
Cessac House PO12 .... 181 E1
Chadderton Gdns PO1 .... 182 A2
Chaddesley Glen BH13 .... 214 C3
Chaddesley Pines BH13 .... 214 C3
Chaddesley Wood Rd BH13 .. 214 C3
Chadwell Ave SO19 .... 104 A2
Chadwick Rd SO50 .... 55 F1
Chafen Rd SO18 .... 103 E4
Chaffey Cl BH24 .... 141 E4
Chaffinch Cl Broadstone BH18 .. 186 C1
  New Milton BH25 .... 194 C1
  Totton SO40 .... 100 B4
Chaffinch Gn PO8 .... 111 F2
Chaffinch Way
  Lee-on-the-Solent PO13 .... 179 F2
  Portchester PO16 .... 155 F4
Chalbury Cl BH17 .... 188 A1
Chalbury Ct
  6 Christchurch BH23 .... 207 F3
  11 Poole BH14 .... 203 D2
Chaldecott Gdns BH10 .... 189 E2
Chaldon Rd BH17 .... 187 F1
Chale Cl PO13 .... 155 E1
Chalewood Rd SO45 .... 177 F4
Chalfont Ave SO19 .... 191 E2
Chalfont Ct 6 SO16 .... 78 A1
Chalice Cl BH14 .... 203 D2
Chalice Ct SO30 .... 105 D3
Chalk Cl SP5 .... 47 E4
Chalk Hill Soberton SO32 .... 85 E3
  West End SO18 .... 80 B1
Chalk Hill Rd PO8 .... 112 B4
Chalk La PO17 .... 131 D4
Chalk Pit Cotts PO17 .... 131 D4
Chalk Ridge PO8 .... 88 B2
Chalkpit Rd PO6 .... 133 D1
Challenger Way SO45 .... 125 D1
Challis Ct 18 SO14 .... 103 D2

Chalmers Way SO31 .... 127 F2
Chaloner Cres SO45 .... 126 A1
Chalton Cres PO9 .... 135 E2
Chalton House 42 PO1 .... 182 B3
Chalton La PO8 .... 88 B3
Chalvington Ct SO53 .... 55 E3
Chalvington Rd SO53 .... 55 E2
Chalwyn Ind Est BH12 .... 203 D4
Chalybeate Cl SO16 .... 78 A1
Chalybeate Hospl SO16 .... 78 A1
Chamberlain Gr PO14 .... 155 D4
Chamberlain Hall SO16 .... 79 D2
Chamberlain Rd SO17 .... 79 D2
Chamberlayne Ct SO52 .... 54 A2
Chamberlayne House
  7 SO31 .... 127 D3
Chamberlayne Park Sch
   .... 104 A1
Chamberlayne Park Sch
  SO19 .... 127 D3
Chamberlayne Rd
  Bursledon SO31 .... 127 F4
  Eastleigh SO50 .... 56 A1
  Netley SO31 .... 127 D3
Chambers Ave SO51 .... 53 D4
Chambers Cl SO16 .... 77 E3
Champion Cl SO41 .... 211 F2
Chancel Rd SO31 .... 129 D2
Chancellors La SO32 .... 81 F2
Chanctonbury House 22 PO5 . 182 B2
Chander Cl BH22 .... 165 F2
Chandler's Ford Ind Est SO53 .. 55 D3
Chandler's Ford Inf SO53 . 55 E3
Chandler's Ford Inf
  Sch (Annexe SO53 .... 55 E4
Chandlers Cl
  Bournemouth BH7 .... 206 A4
  South Hayling PO11 .... 185 E1
Chandlers Way SO31 .... 129 D3
Chandos Ave BH12 .... 204 A4
Chandos House 14 SO14 .... 103 D2
Chandos St 26 SO14 .... 103 D2
Channel Ct
  Barton on Sea BH25 .... 209 F4
  Bournemouth BH6 .... 206 B2
Channel Mouth Rd SO45 .... 151 F1
Channel Way SO14 .... 103 E2
Channels Farm Rd SO16 .... 79 E3
Chant Cl BH23 .... 207 E4
Chantrell Wlk PO15 .... 130 B2
Chantry BH23 .... 193 F1
Chantry Rd Gosport PO12 .. 181 D4
  Horndean PO8 .... 112 A4
  Southampton SO14 .... 103 D2
Chantry The
  Bournemouth BH1 .... 205 D2
  Locks Heath PO14 .... 129 E2
Chapel Cl Braishfield SO51 .... 28 B3
  Corfe Mullen BH21 .... 186 B3
Chapel Cres SO19 .... 104 A2
Chapel Ct 7 PO1 .... 182 B4
Chapel Dro Fair Oak SO50 .... 81 E4
  Hedge End SO30 .... 105 D3
Chapel La Blackfield SO45 .... 177 F4
  Bransgore BH23 .... 193 D4
  Burley BH24 .... 143 D2
  Chilcomb SO21, SO23 .... 12 A4
  Corfe Mullen BH21 .... 186 B3
  Curdridge SO32 .... 106 C4
  East Boldre SO42 .... 175 E3
  Fawley SO45 .... 151 D1
  Lockerley SO51 .... 26 A3
  Lyndhurst SO43 .... 121 F2
  Michelmersh SO51 .... 27 E4
  Nomansland SP5 .... 73 E4
  Otterbourne SO50 .... 31 D1
  Poole BH15 .... 202 B1
  Redlynch SP5 .... 47 F3
  Sherfield English SO51 .... 26 A3
  Sway SO41 .... 172 B1
  Totton SO40 .... 100 C3
  13 Waterlooville PO7 .... 134 C4
  Wimborne Minster BH21 .. 163 D3
Chapel Rd Locks Heath SO31 .. 128 C3
  Poole BH14 .... 203 D2
  Soberton SO32 .... 85 D1
  Southampton SO14 .... 103 D2
  Swanmore SO32 .... 84 A3
  West End SO30 .... 80 C1
Chapel Rise BH24 .... 140 B1
Chapel Sq PO12 .... 180 C4
Chapel St East Meon GU32 .... 38 B1
  Gosport PO12 .... 181 D4
  Petersfield GU32 .... 40 C2
  Portsmouth PO2 .... 182 A2
  Southampton SO14 .... 103 D2
Chapelside PO14 .... 154 A4
Chaplains Ave PO8 .... 111 E2
Chaplains Cl PO8 .... 111 E2
Charborough Rd BH18 .... 187 D2
Charden Ct SO18 .... 104 A4
Charden Rd Bishopstoke SO50 .. 57 D1
  Gosport PO13 .... 180 A4
Charfield Cl Fareham PO14 .. 154 B4
  Winchester SO22 .... 10 C3
Charing Cl BH24 .... 141 D3
Chark La PO13 .... 179 F2
Charlcot Lawn PO9 .... 135 E3
Charlecote Dr SO53 .... 55 D4
Charlecote Mews 10 SO22 .. 10 C4
Charlemont Dr 15 PO16 .... 131 E1
Charles Cl Waterlooville PO7 .. 134 B3
  Winchester SO23 .... 2 A1
Charles Cres BH25 .... 195 D3
Charles Dickens Jun Sch PO1 182 B4
Charles Dickens St PO1 .... 182 B3
Charles Gdns BH10 .... 189 E1

Charles Keightley Ct BH21 ...... 163 E2
Charles Knott Gdns SO15 .... 102 C4
Charles Ley Ct SO45 .... 151 D2
Charles Rd Christchurch BH23 .... 207 F4
Poole BH15 .... 202 B2
Charles St Petersfield GU32 ...... 40 C2
Portsmouth PO1 .... 182 B3
Southampton SO14 .... 103 D2
Charles Watts Way SO30 .... 105 D4
Charles Wyatt House 26 SO14 103 D4
Charles's La BH24 .... 141 F2
Charlesbury Ave PO12 .... 180 C2
Charleston Cl PO11 .... 184 C2
Charleston Rd SO45 .... 150 B4
Charlesworth Dr PO7 .... 111 E1
Charlesworth Gdns PO7 .... 111 E1
Charliejoy Gdns 18 SO14 .... 103 E3
Charlotte Cl Christchurch BH23 208 A3
3 New Milton BH25 .... 195 D1
Poole BH12 .... 204 B4
Charlotte Ct
Chandler's Ford SO53 .... 55 F4
Southampton SO19 .... 103 F1
Charlotte Mews PO12 .... 181 D1
Charlotte Pl SO14 .... 103 D3
Charlotte St PO1 .... 182 B3
Charlton Cl Bournemouth BH9 .. 190 B2
Hordle SO41 .... 195 F2
Charlton Rd SO15 .... 102 B4
Charltons The BH2 .... 204 C3
Charminster Ave BH9 .... 190 A1
Charminster Cl
Bournemouth BH8 .... 190 A1
Waterlooville PO7 .... 134 C4
Charminster Pl BH8 .... 190 B1
Charminster Rd BH8 .... 205 D4
Charmouth Gr BH14 .... 203 D2
Charmouth Terr 5 SO16 .... 78 A1
Charmus Rd SO40 .... 76 A1
Charmwen Cres SO30 .... 80 B1
Charnock Cl SO41 .... 195 F2
Charnwood Ave BH9 .... 190 A2
Charnwood Cl
Chandler's Ford SO53 .... 30 B1
Totton SO40 .... 76 B1
West Moors BH22 .... 138 C1
Charnwood Cres SO53 .... 30 B1
Charnwood Dr SP6 .... 69 F2
Charnwood Gdns SO53 .... 30 B1
Charnwood Way SO45 .... 177 F4
Chartcombe BH13 .... 214 C4
Charter Rd BH11 .... 188 B3
Chartergrove House 16 GU31 .. 40 C2
Charterhouse Way SO30 .... 81 E1
Chartfield SO14 .... 129 E1
Chartwell Cl Eastleigh SO50 ... 56 A3
Titchfield PO14 .... 129 E1
Chartwell Dr PO9 .... 136 B2
Chase Cl GU33 .... 21 D2
Chase Farm Cl SO32 .... 83 F2
Chase Gr SO32 .... 83 F2
Chase Rd GU33 .... 21 D2
Chase The Gosport PO12 .... 180 C2
St Leonards BH24 .... 140 B3
Titchfield PO14 .... 129 E1
Verwood BH31 .... 115 E3
Chaseside BH7 .... 206 A4
Chasewater Ave PO3 .... 183 D4
Chatburn Ave PO8 .... 111 F2
Chatfield Rd PO13 .... 155 F2
Chatham Dr PO4 .... 182 A2
Chatham Rd SO22 .... 10 B3
Chatsworth Ave PO6 .... 158 A3
Chatsworth Cl PO15 .... 130 B1
Chatsworth Rd
Bournemouth BH8 .... 205 E3
Eastleigh SO50 .... 56 A3
Poole BH14 .... 203 D3
Southampton SO19 .... 104 A3
Chatsworth Way BH25 .... 194 C2
Chaucer Ave PO6 .... 132 C1
Chaucer Cl Fareham PO16 ...... 130 C1
Waterlooville PO7 .... 111 F1
Wimborne Minster BH21 .... 163 E3
Chaucer Dr SO40 .... 211 E3
Chaucer Ind Est SO23 .... 2 B1
Chaucer Rd Poole BH13 .... 214 C4
Southampton SO19 .... 104 B3
Chaundler Rd SO23 .... 2 A1
Chaveney Cl SO45 .... 125 F1
Chawton Cl Southampton SO18 104 B4
Winchester SO22 .... 1 B2
Cheam Rd BH18 .... 186 C2
Cheam Way SO40 .... 76 B1
Cheater's La SP6 .... 92 B4
Cheddar Cl SO19 .... 103 F2
Cheddington Rd BH9 .... 190 A2
Chedington Cl BH17 .... 187 F1
Chedworth Cres PO6 .... 133 D1
Cheeryble House 19 PO1 .... 182 B4
Chelmsford Rd
Portsmouth PO2 .... 157 F1
Upton BH16 .... 201 D4
Chelsea Rd PO5 .... 182 B2
Cheltenham Cres PO13 .... 179 F2
Cheltenham Ct 26 SO17 .... 79 D1
Cheltenham Gdns SO30 .... 81 E2
Cheltenham Rd Cosham PO6 ... 157 E4
Poole BH12 .... 203 D3
Chelveston Cres SO16 .... 78 A2
Chelwood Gate SO16 .... 78 C3
Chene Rd BH21 .... 163 D2
Cheping Gdns SO30 .... 106 A3
Chepstow Cl
North Baddesley SO53 .... 55 D3
Totton SO40 .... 100 B4
Chepstow Court PO7 .... 112 A1
Chequers Cl SO41 .... 197 E2

Chequers Quay 5 PO10 .... 161 D4
Cherbourg Prim Sch SO50 ...... 56 A1
Cherbourg Rd SO50 .... 56 A1
Cherford Rd BH11 .... 189 D1
Cherita Ct BH15 .... 202 C3
Cheriton Ave
Bournemouth BH7 .... 206 B4
Southampton SO18 .... 104 B4
Cheriton Cl Havant PO9 .... 135 E2
Horndean PO8 .... 112 A4
Winchester SO22 .... 1 B1
Cheriton Ct 7 SO15 .... 102 B3
Cheriton La SO24 .... 15 D4
Cheriton Prim Sch SO24 .... 14 B3
Cheriton Rd Eastleigh SO50 .... 55 F1
Gosport PO12 .... 180 C2
Winchester SO22 .... 10 C4
Cheriton Way BH21 .... 163 E3
Cherque La PO13 .... 180 A4
Cherrett Cl BH11 .... 188 C2
Cherries Dr BH9 .... 189 F1
Cherry Blossom Ct 22 PO1 ..... 182 B4
Cherry Cl
Lee-on-the-Solent PO13 .... 180 A3
Poole BH14 .... 203 D2
Cherry Ct Poole BH14 .... 203 D3
14 Southampton SO17 .... 103 D4
Cherry Drove SO50 .... 81 E3
Cherry Gdns SO32 .... 83 E4
Cherry Gr BH22 .... 165 E3
Cherry Hill Gdns BH16 .... 201 D3
Cherry Hill Gr BH16 .... 201 D3
Cherry Tree Ave
Fareham PO14 .... 154 B4
Waterlooville PO8 .... 112 A4
Cherry Tree Cl Hordle SO41 .... 211 E4
St Leonards BH24 .... 139 E2
Cherry Tree 31 BH25 .... 195 D1
Cherry Tree Dr BH25 .... 194 C3
Cherry Wlk SO15 .... 102 B4
Cherrygarth Rd PO15 .... 130 B1
Cherryton Gdns SO45 .... 150 A2
Cherrywood Gdns
South Hayling PO11 .... 185 D2
Totton SO40 .... 100 B4
Chervil Cl PO8 .... 88 B1
Cherville Ct SO51 .... 52 C4
Cherville St SO51 .... 52 C4
Cherwell Cres SO16 .... 101 F4
Cherwell Gdns SO53 .... 55 E3
Cherwell House SO16 .... 101 F4
Cheshire Dr BH8 .... 191 D1
Cheshire Way PO10 .... 137 E1
Chesil St SO23 .... 11 D4
Chesil Terr 37 SO23 .... 11 D4
Chesildene Ave BH8 .... 190 B2
Chesildene Dr BH8 .... 190 B2
Cheslyn Rd PO3 .... 183 D4
Chessel Ave Bournemouth BH5 . 205 F2
Southampton SO19 .... 103 F3
Chessel Cres SO19 .... 103 F4
Chester Cres PO13 .... 180 A2
Chester Ct SO16 .... 78 B1
Chester Cts 7 PO12 .... 181 E2
Chester Pl 34 PO5 .... 182 B1
Chester Rd Poole BH13 .... 204 A1
Southampton SO18 .... 80 A1
Winchester SO23 .... 11 D4
Chesterfield Cl BH13 .... 214 C4
Chesterfield Rd BH1 .... 205 E2
Chesterfield Rd PO3 .... 183 D4
Chesterton Gdns PO8 .... 111 F2
Chesterton Pl SO31 .... 129 E4
Chestnut Ave Ashurst SO40 ... 100 B2
Barton on Sea BH25 .... 210 A4
Bournemouth BH6 .... 206 B2
Chandler's Ford SO53 .... 55 E1
Christchurch BH23 .... 206 B4
2 Colden Common SO21 ...... 31 F1
Eastleigh SO50, SO53 .... 55 E1
Havant PO9 .... 135 D2
Ibsley BH24 .... 116 A3
Littleton SO22 .... 1 A2
Portsmouth PO4 .... 182 C2
Waterlooville PO8 .... 112 B3
Chestnut Cl
Chandler's Ford SO53 .... 55 E2
Denmead PO7 .... 110 C2
Romsey SO51 .... 53 E3
West End SO30 .... 80 B2
Chestnut Ct
Rowland's Castle PO9 .... 136 A4
8 Southampton SO17 .... 79 D1
Chestnut Gr BH21 .... 164 C3
Chestnut Lodge SO16 .... 78 C2
Chestnut Rd
Brockenhurst SO42 .... 146 A1
Southampton SO16 .... 78 A4
Chestnut Rise Droxford SO32 .. 61 D1
Eastleigh SO50 .... 55 E1
Chestnut Way Burton BH23 .... 192 B2
Titchfield PO14 .... 129 E1
Chestnut Wlk Botley SO30 ..... 105 F4
Gosport PO12 .... 156 A1
Chestnuts The SO31 .... 129 D1
Chetnole Cl BH17 .... 188 A1
Chettle Rd SO19 .... 104 C3
Chetwode Way BH17 .... 187 D1
Chetwynd Dr SO16 .... 78 C2
Chetwynd Rd Portsmouth PO4 . 182 C2
Southampton SO16 .... 78 C3
Chevening Ct PO4 .... 183 D3
Cheviot Court Flats BH23 .... 207 F4
Cheviot Ct SO16 .... 101 F4
Cheviot Dr SO45 .... 125 E2
Cheviot Gn SO31 .... 152 B4
Cheviot Rd SO16 .... 101 F4
Cheviot Way BH31 .... 114 C3

Cheviot Wlk PO14 .... 154 C4
Cheviots BH14 .... 203 E2
Chevron Bsns Pk SO45 .... 150 A3
Chewter Cl PO4 .... 182 C1
Chewton Common Rd BH23 .... 209 D4
Chewton Farm Rd BH23 .... 194 B1
Chewton Lodge BH23 .... 209 D4
Chewton Way BH23 .... 194 A1
Cheyne Gdns BH4 .... 204 B1
Cheyne Way PO13 .... 179 F1
Chichester Ave PO11 .... 185 D2
Chichester Cl Gosport PO13 ... 155 D1
Hedge End SO30 .... 81 E1
Locks Heath SO31 .... 128 C2
West Wellow SO51 .... 51 D1
Chichester House PO9 .... 136 A2
Chichester Rd
North Hayling PO11 .... 160 B1
Portsmouth PO2 .... 182 C4
Ringwood BH24 .... 117 E1
Southampton SO18 .... 104 A4
Chichester Way BH23 .... 208 A3
Chichester Wlk BH21 .... 163 F1
Chickenhall La SO50 .... 56 B1
Chickerell Cl BH9 .... 190 A2
Chidden Cl GU32 .... 38 B1
Chidden Holt SO53 .... 55 D3
Chideock Cl BH12 .... 203 F3
Chideock Ct BH12 .... 203 F3
Chidham Cl PO9 .... 135 F1
Chidham Dr PO9 .... 135 F1
Chidham Rd PO6 .... 134 A1
Chidham Sq PO9 .... 135 F1
Chidham Wlk 1 PO9 .... 135 F1
Chigwell Rd BH8 .... 190 A1
Chilbolton Ave SO22 .... 10 B4
Chilbolton Cl 16 Havant PO9 .. 136 A3
Winchester SO22 .... 10 B4
Chilcomb Cl PO13 .... 179 F1
Chilcomb Rd SO18 .... 104 B4
Chilcombe Cl PO9 .... 135 F2
Chilcombe Hts 38 SO23 .... 11 D4
Chilcombe La Chilcomb SO23 .. 11 F3
Winchester SO23 .... 11 E3
Chilcombe Rd BH6 .... 206 A3
Chilcote Rd PO3 .... 183 D4
Childe Sq PO2 .... 157 E1
Chilfrome Cl BH17 .... 187 E1
Chilgrove Rd PO6 .... 158 B4
Chilham Cl SO50 .... 56 A4
Chillenden Ct SO40 .... 100 B3
Chillerton SO31 .... 127 E4
Chilling La SO31 .... 152 C3
Chillington Gdns SO53 .... 30 A1
Chilly Hill SP6 .... 94 C4
Chilmark Ct GU33 .... 20 C2
Chilsdown Way PO7 .... 134 C2
Chiltern Cl
Barton on Sea BH25 .... 194 C1
Poole BH12 .... 204 A3
Totton SO40 .... 100 B3
Chiltern Dr
5 Christchurch BH23 .... 207 F4
13 Eastleigh SO50 .... 181 D3
7 Portsmouth PO5 .... 182 B1
Verwood BH31 .... 114 C3
Chiltern Gr SO16 .... 101 F4
Chiltern Wlk PO14 .... 154 C4
Chilworth Cl SO16 .... 54 B1
Chilworth Gdns PO8 .... 88 B2
Chilworth Gr PO12 .... 181 D3
Chilworth Manor Hotel
& Con Ctr SO16 .... 54 B1
Chilworth Rd SO16 .... 54 C1
Chimes The BH4 .... 204 A2
Chine Ave SO19 .... 103 F3
Chine Cl SO31 .... 129 D2
Chine Cres BH2 .... 204 B1
Chine Crescent Rd BH2 .... 204 B1
Chine The PO13 .... 155 F1
Chine Wlk BH22 .... 165 F1
Chinham Rd SO40 .... 99 E3
Chipstead House 12 PO6 .... 157 F4
Chipstead Rd 11 PO6 .... 157 F4
Chisels La BH23 .... 193 D3
Chisholm Cl SO16 .... 77 F3
Chiswell Rd BH17 .... 187 E1
Chitty Rd PO4 .... 183 D1
Chivers Cl 20 PO5 .... 182 B2
Chorley Cl BH15 .... 202 B3
Chris Cres BH11 .... 201 E4
Christ the King RC
Prim Sch BH11 .... 189 D3
Christchurch Bay Rd BH25 ..... 209 F4
Christchurch By-Pass BH23 .... 207 E4
Christchurch Cty Jun Sch
BH23 .... 207 D4
Christchurch Cty Prim Sch
BH23 .... 207 D4
Christchurch Gdns
Waterlooville PO7 .... 134 A1
1 Winchester SO23 .... 10 C3
Christchurch Hospl BH23 .... 206 C4
Christchurch Rd
Barton on Sea BH25 .... 209 E4
Bournemouth BH1, BH7 .... 205 E2
Ferndown BH22 .... 165 E1
Hordle SO41 .... 211 E4
Hurn BH23 .... 191 E3
Ringwood BH24 .... 141 D4
Winchester SO23 .... 10 C3
Winchester SO23 .... 10 C4
Christchurch Sta BH23 .... 207 D4
Christie Ave PO15 .... 129 E4
Christine Ct 9 SO18 .... 103 F4
Christopher Cres BH15 .... 202 B3
Christopher Way PO10 .... 136 C1

Christophers BH21 .... 163 E1
Christyne Ct PO7 .... 134 B2
Church Cl Bishopstoke SO50 ... 56 B2
Clanfield PO8 .... 88 A3
Locks Heath SO31 .... 129 D2
Minstead SO43 .... 98 B1
North Baddesley SO52 .... 54 A2
Church End SO15 .... 102 B4
Church Farm SP6 .... 93 F4
Church Farm Cl SO45 .... 125 D3
Church Hatch SP5 .... 47 D4
Church Hill Milford on Sea SO41 211 F2
Redlynch SP5 .... 47 F3
Verwood BH31 .... 114 C3
West End SO30 .... 80 B1
Church La Awbridge SO51 ...... 26 C2
Boldre SO41 .... 173 F1
Botley SO30 .... 106 A3
Braishfield SO51 .... 28 B4
Bramdean SO24 .... 15 E2
Brockenhurst SO42 .... 173 D4
Burley BH24 .... 143 D2
Bursledon SO31 .... 128 A4
Christchurch BH23 .... 207 D3
Colden Common SO21 .... 56 C4
Curdridge SO32 .... 106 B4
Damerham SP6 .... 68 B2
Durley SO32 .... 81 F3
East Boldre SO42 .... 175 E3
Fawley SO45 .... 151 D2
Ferndown BH22 .... 189 F4
Froxfield GU34 .... 17 E2
Hambledon PO7 .... 86 B2
Havant PO9 .... 160 A4
Hedge End SO30 .... 105 D3
Itchen Abbas SO21 .... 2 C3
Kings Worthy SO23 .... 2 B3
Littleton SO22 .... 1 A3
Lymington SO41 .... 197 F2
Lyndhurst SO43 .... 121 F3
Mottisfont SO51 .... 5 F1
New Milton BH25 .... 194 C1
North Hayling PO11 .... 160 B2
Nursling SO16 .... 76 C3
Plaitford SO51 .... 50 A3
Romsey SO51 .... 52 C4
Sherfield English SO51 .... 25 E2
17 Southampton SO14 .... 102 C2
Southampton, Highfield SO17 .. 79 D1
Swanmore SO32 .... 84 B3
Sway SO41 .... 172 A1
Twyford SO21 .... 32 A4
West Meon GU32 .... 37 E3
Church Mead 12 SO41 .... 197 F1
Church Path
3 Emsworth PO10 .... 160 C4
Fareham PO14, PO16 .... 131 E1
Gosport PO12 .... 181 E2
Horndean PO8 .... 112 B3
Titchfield PO14 .... 154 A4
Church Path N PO1 .... 182 B3
Church Pl SO51 .... 52 C4
Church Rd Bishopstoke SO50 ... 56 B3
Bournemouth BH6 .... 206 C2
Ferndown BH22 .... 165 E3
Gosport PO12 .... 181 D1
Locks Heath SO31 .... 129 D2
Locks Heath, Warsash SO31 ... 152 B4
Michelmersh SO51 .... 6 B1
Poole BH14 .... 203 D2
Portchester PO16 .... 156 C3
Portsmouth PO1 .... 182 B3
Romsey SO51 .... 52 C4
Shedfield SO32 .... 107 F4
Soberton PO17 .... 109 E3
South Hayling PO11 .... 185 D3
Southampton SO19 .... 103 E1
Southbourne PO10 .... 161 F4
Steep GU32 .... 40 C4
Swanmore SO32 .... 84 A3
Thorney Island PO10 .... 161 E1
Three Legged Cross BH21 ...... 114 C1
Westbourne PO10 .... 137 D2
Church St Christchurch BH23 .. 207 D3
East Meon GU32 .... 38 C1
Fordingbridge SP6 .... 93 F4
Liss GU33 .... 20 C3
Poole BH15 .... 202 A1
Portsmouth PO1 .... 182 B3
Romsey SO51 .... 52 C4
Southampton SO15 .... 78 B1
Titchfield PO14 .... 154 A4
Upham SO32 .... 58 C3
8 Wimborne Minster BH21 ... 163 D3
Church View
Portsmouth PO4 .... 183 D3
Shedfield SO32 .... 107 F4
Westbourne PO10 .... 137 D2
Church View Cl SO19 .... 104 A2
Church Wlk SP5 .... 48 A3
Churcher Cl PO12 .... 180 B2
Churcher Rd PO10 .... 137 D2
Churcher's Coll GU31 .... 41 D2
Churchers Coll Jun Sch GU32 .. 40 C2
Churchfield BH31 .... 114 C3
Churchfield Cres BH15 .... 202 B2
Churchfield Ct BH15 .... 202 C2
Churchfield La BH24 .... 93 F1
Churchfield Rd
Petersfield GU31 .... 41 D1
Poole BH15 .... 202 C2
Churchfields SO45 .... 151 D2
Churchfields Rd SO21 .... 32 A3
Churchill Ave SO32 .... 59 D1
Churchill Cl Alderholt SP6 ...... 92 C3
Titchfield PO14 .... 129 E1
Churchill Cres BH12 .... 203 E3

Cha – Cla 225

Churchill Ct Cosham PO6 .... 158 C4
New Milton BH25 .... 194 C1
Waterlooville PO8 .... 112 A3
Churchill Dro BH21 .... 91 E4
Churchill Dr PO10 .... 136 C2
Churchill Gdns BH12 .... 203 E3
Churchill House SO18 .... 104 B4
Churchill Mews 1 PO12 .... 181 D3
Churchill Rd Bournemouth BH1 . 205 E3
Poole BH12 .... 203 E3
Wimborne Minster BH21 .... 163 F2
Churchmoor Rd BH21 .... 164 A3
Churchward Gdns SO30 .... 81 E1
Cinderford Cl 51 PO6 .... 133 D1
Cinnamon Ct SO15 .... 102 C3
Cinnamon La 10 BH15 .... 202 A1
Circle The Bournemouth BH9 .. 190 A2
Poole BH13 .... 214 C4
Portsmouth PO5 .... 182 B1
Circular Rd PO1 .... 182 B4
Cirrus Gdns SO31 .... 127 F1
City Bsns Ctr SO23 .... 11 D4
City Commerce Ctr 29 SO14 .. 103 D2
City Ind Pk SO15 .... 102 C2
City of Portsmouth Boys
Sch PO7 .... 157 F2
City of Portsmouth Girls'
Sch PO1 .... 182 C3
City of Toronto Homes SO16 . 101 F4
City Rd SO23 .... 10 C4
Civic Centre Rd Havant PO9 .... 135 F1
Southampton SO14 .... 102 C3
Civic Way PO16 .... 131 E1
Clacton Rd PO6 .... 157 E4
Claire Ct BH23 .... 209 D4
Claire Gdns PO8 .... 88 B1
Clamp Gr 4 SO21 .... 56 C4
Clandon Dr SO50 .... 55 F3
Clanfield Cl SO53 .... 55 E3
Clanfield Dr SO53 .... 55 E3
Clanfield House 37 PO1 .... 182 B3
Clanfield Jun Sch PO8 .... 88 A4
Clanfield Rd SO18 .... 104 B4
Clanfield Way SO53 .... 55 E3
Clanwilliam Rd PO13 .... 179 F1
Clare Cl PO14 .... 129 E1
Clare Gdns Blackfield SO45 .... 177 F4
Petersfield GU31 .... 41 E2
Clare House PO12 .... 180 C4
Clare Lodge Cl BH23 .... 169 D1
Claremont Ave BH9 .... 190 A1
Claremont Cl 1 SO50 .... 56 A3
Claremont Cres SO15 .... 102 A4
Claremont Gdns PO7 .... 134 C2
Claremont Rd
Bournemouth BH9 .... 190 A1
Portsmouth PO1 .... 182 C3
Southampton SO15 .... 102 A4
Clarence Espl PO5 .... 182 B1
Clarence House 5 SO14 .... 103 E3
Clarence Par PO5 .... 182 B1
Clarence Park Rd BH7 .... 206 B3
Clarence Rd Gosport PO12 .... 181 E3
Lyndhurst SO43 .... 121 F3
3 Poole BH14 .... 203 D2
Portsmouth PO5 .... 182 B1
Clarence St PO1 .... 182 B3
Clarendon Cl
Broadstone BH18 .... 187 D2
10 Romsey SO51 .... 28 A1
Clarendon Cres PO14 .... 129 E1
Clarendon Ct
Bournemouth BH2 .... 204 B1
9 Portsmouth PO5 .... 182 B1
Clarendon Pk SO41 .... 197 E1
Clarendon Pl PO1 .... 182 B3
Clarendon Rd
Bournemouth BH4 .... 204 B2
Broadstone BH18 .... 186 C2
Christchurch BH23 .... 207 D4
17 Havant PO9 .... 135 F1
Portsmouth PO5 .... 182 B1
Southampton SO16 .... 102 A4
Clarendon St PO1 .... 182 B3
Clark's Cl BH24 .... 141 D4
Clarke's Rd PO1 .... 182 C3
Claude Ashby Cl SO18 .... 79 F2
Claudeen Cl SO18 .... 79 F3
Claudeen Ct SO19 .... 104 C3
Claudia Ct PO12 .... 180 C3
Claudius Cl SO53 .... 55 F4
Claudius Gdns SO53 .... 55 F4
Clausen Way SO41 .... 197 E1
Clausentum Cl SO53 .... 55 F4
Clausentum Rd
Southampton SO14 .... 103 D4
Winchester SO23 .... 10 C3
Clave Cl PO13 .... 179 F1
Claxton St PO1 .... 182 B3
Clay Hill SO43 .... 122 A2
Clay St SP5 .... 24 A2
Claybank Rd PO3 .... 158 A1
Claybank Spur PO3 .... 158 A1
Claydon Ave PO4 .... 183 D2
Clayfields Sports Ctr SO45 .... 125 E2
Clayford Ave BH22 .... 165 D4
Clayford Cl BH17 .... 187 E1
Clayhall Rd PO12 .... 181 D1
Clayhill Cl SO32 .... 83 E2
Claylake Dr BH31 .... 115 D3
Claylands Ct SO32 .... 83 D4
Claylands Rd SO32 .... 83 D4
Claypit La GU32 .... 18 B3

Claypits La SO45 ...... 125 E2
Cleasby Cl SO16 ...... 101 F4
Cleasby Grange **28** BH5 ...... 205 F4
Clease Way SO21 ...... 31 E4
Clee Ave PO14 ...... 154 B4
Cleethorpes Rd SO19 ...... 104 A2
Cleeve Cl PO6 ...... 133 D1
Cleeves Cl BH12 ...... 188 B1
Cleeves The SO40 ...... 100 B3
Clegg Rd PO4 ...... 183 D2
Clem's Way SO51 ...... 5 D1
Clematis Cl BH23 ...... 208 B4
Clement Atlee Way PO6 ...... 157 D4
Clement Mews BH4 ...... 204 A2
Cleric Ct PO14 ...... 129 E2
Cleveland Cl BH25 ...... 209 E4
Cleveland Ct
 Bournemouth BH2 ...... 204 B1
 7 Southampton SO18 ...... 80 A1
Cleveland Dr Fareham PO14 ...... 154 B4
 Hythe SO45 ...... 125 E1
Cleveland Gdns BH1 ...... 205 E3
Cleveland Rd
 Bournemouth BH1 ...... 205 E3
 Gosport PO12 ...... 181 D2
 Portsmouth PO5 ...... 182 C2
 Southampton SO18 ...... 79 F1
Clevelands Cl SO53 ...... 30 A1
Clewers Hill SO32 ...... 83 E3
Clewers La SO32 ...... 83 F2
Cliff Cres BH25 ...... 209 F4
Cliff Dr Christchurch BH23 ...... 208 B3
 Poole BH13 ...... 214 C3
Cliff House **10** BH6 ...... 206 C2
Cliff Rd Milford on Sea SO41 ...... 211 D2
 Southampton SO15 ...... 102 B3
 Stubbington PO14 ...... 153 F1
Cliff Terr BH25 ...... 209 F3
Cliff Way SO21 ...... 103 E2
Cliff Way SO21 ...... 31 E4
Cliffdale Prim Sch PO2 ...... 157 F1
Cliffdale Sec Sch PO6 ...... 158 A3
Cliffe Ave SO21 ...... 127 E2
Cliffe Rd BH25 ...... 209 F4
Clifford Dibben Mews
 1 SO14 ...... 103 D4
Clifford Pl SO50 ...... 57 E1
Clifford Rd BH9 ...... 190 A1
Clifford St **11** SO14 ...... 103 D3
Clifton Cres PO7 ...... 111 D2
Clifton Ct
 13 Bournemouth BH5 ...... 205 F2
 19 New Milton BH25 ...... 195 D1
 15 Southampton SO15 ...... 102 A4
Clifton Gdns Ferndown BH22 ...... 165 E2
 14 Southampton SO15 ...... 102 A4
 West End SO18 ...... 80 B1
Clifton Hill SO21 ...... 10 C4
Clifton Lodge SO15 ...... 102 A4
Clifton Lodge No 1 **13** SO22 ...... 10 C4
Clifton Lodge No 2 **14** SO22 ...... 10 C4
Clifton Rd
 Bournemouth BH6 ...... 206 B2
 Lee-on-the-Solent PO13 ...... 180 A2
 Poole BH14 ...... 203 F1
 23 Portsmouth PO5 ...... 182 B1
 Southampton SO15 ...... 102 A4
 Winchester SO22 ...... 10 C4
Clifton St Gosport PO12 ...... 180 C3
 Portsmouth PO1 ...... 182 B3
Clifton Terr **24**
 Portsmouth PO5 ...... 182 B1
 Winchester SO22 ...... 10 C4
Clinghan Rd BH6 ...... 206 B4
Clinton Cl BH23 ...... 194 A1
Clinton Rd Lymington SO41 ...... 197 F3
 Waterlooville PO7 ...... 111 E1
Clipper Cl SO31 ...... 128 C1
Clitheroe Cotts SO42 ...... 148 C1
Clive Gr **19** BH4 ...... 204 B2
Clive Gr PO14 ...... 156 B4
Clive Rd Bournemouth BH9 ...... 189 F1
 Christchurch BH23 ...... 193 F1
 Portsmouth PO1 ...... 182 C3
Cliveden Cl BH22 ...... 165 E4
Clock House **12** PO7 ...... 134 C4
Clock St **10** PO1 ...... 182 A3
Clocktower Dr PO4 ...... 182 B2
Cloisters The Fareham PO15 ...... 130 B1
 Lymington SO41 ...... 197 F2
 Ringwood BH24 ...... 141 E3
 Southampton SO16 ...... 79 D2
Close Bellfield The PO14 ...... 153 F4
Close The
 Barton on Sea BH25 ...... 210 A4
 Broadstone BH18 ...... 186 C2
 Colden Common SO21 ...... 31 E1
 Cosham PO6 ...... 158 A4
 Fordingbridge SP6 ...... 94 B4
 Hamble-le-Rice SO31 ...... 128 A2
 Hedge End SO30 ...... 105 D3
 Holbury SO45 ...... 150 B2
 Langrish GU32 ...... 39 E2
 Portchester PO16 ...... 156 B4
 30 Portsmouth PO5 ...... 182 B2
 Redlynch SP5 ...... 47 E4
 Ringwood BH24 ...... 140 C4
 Southampton SO18 ...... 104 B4
 St Leonards, Avon Castle BH24 ...... 140 A3
 St Leonards, St Ives BH24 ...... 140 A2
 Sway SO41 ...... 172 A4
 Whitsbury SP6 ...... 45 D2
Closewood Rd PO7 ...... 111 D1
Clough La BH24 ...... 142 C2
Clough's Rd BH24 ...... 141 D4

Clovelly Rd Emsworth PO10 ...... 160 C4
 North Hayling PO11 ...... 160 B2
 Portsmouth PO4 ...... 183 D2
 Southampton SO14 ...... 103 D3
 Southampton PO10 ...... 137 E1
Clover Cl Christchurch BH23 ...... 208 A4
 Gosport PO13 ...... 155 E2
 Locks Heath SO31 ...... 128 C1
Clover Ct New Milton BH25 ...... 195 E2
 Waterlooville PO7 ...... 135 D3
Clover Dr BH17 ...... 186 C1
Clover Nooke SO15 ...... 101 E4
Clover Way Hedge End SO30 ...... 105 D3
 Romsey SO51 ...... 53 E4
Clovers The BH12 ...... 204 A4
Clowes Ave BH6 ...... 207 D2
Club House La SO32 ...... 83 F2
Clump Hill BH21 ...... 114 A1
Clyde Cl PO12 ...... 180 C3
Clyde House **24** SO14 ...... 103 E3
Clyde Rd Broadstone BH17 ...... 187 D1
 Gosport PO12 ...... 180 C3
Clydebank Rd PO2 ...... 182 B4
Clydesdale Rd PO15 ...... 129 D4
Clydesdale Way SO40 ...... 100 A4
Coach Hill PO14 ...... 153 F4
Coach Hill Cl SO53 ...... 55 D2
Coach Hill La BH24 ...... 142 C3
Coach House Pl BH1 ...... 205 D3
Coach Rd SO31 ...... 127 F2
Coach Rd The
 East Tytherley SP5 ...... 4 C4
 West Tytherley SP5 ...... 4 B4
Coach-House Mews PO4 ...... 183 E2
Coachmans Copse SO18 ...... 80 A1
Coachmans Halt PO7 ...... 86 B1
Coal Park La SO31 ...... 128 B4
Coalville Rd SO19 ...... 104 A2
Coastguard Cl PO12 ...... 180 C1
Coastguard Cotts Exbury SO45 ...... 178 A1
 Havant PO9 ...... 159 F3
 Lymington SO41 ...... 198 A1
Coastguard Way BH23 ...... 207 F3
Coat Gdns SO45 ...... 126 A2
Coates Rd SO19 ...... 104 B2
Coates Way PO7 ...... 134 C3
Cobb's Rd BH21 ...... 163 F3
Cobbett Cl SO22 ...... 10 B3
Cobbett Ct **15** SO18 ...... 103 F4
Cobbett Rd SO18 ...... 103 F4
Cobbett Way SO30 ...... 105 F4
Cobblers Cnr SO41 ...... 173 D2
Cobblewood PO10 ...... 136 C2
Cobbs La PO11 ...... 202 C3
Cobden Ave Portsmouth PO3 ...... 183 D4
 Southampton SO18 ...... 103 F4
Cobden Cres SO18 ...... 103 F4
Cobden Ct SO18 ...... 103 F4
Cobden Gdns SO18 ...... 79 F1
Cobden Hts SO18 ...... 79 F1
Cobden Marine Ct SO17 ...... 103 E4
Cobden Rise SO18 ...... 79 F1
Cobden St PO12 ...... 181 D3
Cobham Cl PO15 ...... 129 F3
Cobham Rd Bournemouth BH9 ...... 190 A2
 Ferndown BH21 ...... 165 D4
Cobham Way SO30 ...... 105 F4
Coblands SO40 ...... 100 B4
Coburg House **6** SO14 ...... 103 E3
Coburg St Portsmouth PO1 ...... 182 B3
 Southampton SO14 ...... 103 E3
Cochrane Cl PO13 ...... 180 B3
Cochrane House **15** PO1 ...... 182 A3
Cockerell Cl Locks Heath PO15 ...... 129 E3
 Oakley BH21 ...... 163 F1
Cockleshell Cl SO31 ...... 128 C1
Cockleshell Gdns PO4 ...... 183 E2
Cocklydown La SO40 ...... 100 B3
Cockshott La GU32 ...... 19 E1
Codogan Ct **14** BH1 ...... 205 D2
Cogdean Cl BH21 ...... 186 C4
Cogdean Way BH21 ...... 186 C4
Cogdean Wlk BH21 ...... 186 C4
Cogdeane Rd BH17 ...... 187 E1
Coghlan Cl PO16 ...... 131 D1
Coker Cl SO22 ...... 10 C4
Colborne Ave BH21 ...... 163 F3
Colborne Cl SO41 ...... 197 F3
Colbourne Cl Bransgore BH23 ...... 193 D4
 Poole BH15 ...... 202 B1
Colbourne Ct **6** SO23 ...... 2 A1
Colburn Cl PO13 ...... 77 E1
Colbury Gr PO9 ...... 135 E3
Colchester Ave SO50 ...... 56 C2
Colchester Rd PO6 ...... 133 F1
Cold East Cl SO31 ...... 128 C3
Cold Harbour Cl PO17 ...... 107 F2
Coldeast Hospl SO31 ...... 128 C3
Coldeast Way SO31 ...... 128 C3
Colden Common Cty
 Prim Sch PO18 ...... 56 C4
Coldharbour Farm Rd PO10 ...... 136 C1
Coldharbour La SO16 ...... 77 D4
Coldhill La PO8 ...... 111 F4
Cole Hill SO32 ...... 85 E3
Cole's La SP5 ...... 48 C3
Colebrook Ave
 Portsmouth PO3 ...... 183 D4
 Southampton SO15 ...... 78 B1
Colebrook Pl SO23 ...... 11 D4
Colebrook St SO23 ...... 11 D4
Colehill Cres BH9 ...... 190 A2
Colehill Cty Fst Sch BH21 ...... 164 A4
Colehill La BH21 ...... 163 F4
Coleman St SO14 ...... 103 D2
Colemore Rd BH7 ...... 206 B4
Colemore Sq PO9 ...... 135 F2

Colenso Rd PO16 ...... 131 D1
Coleridge Cl SO31 ...... 128 B1
Coleridge Ct SO19 ...... 104 B3
Coleridge Gdns PO8 ...... 111 F2
Coleridge Gn BH23 ...... 207 F4
Coleridge Rd PO6 ...... 132 C1
Coles Ave BH15 ...... 201 F1
Coles Cl SO21 ...... 32 A4
Coles Gdns BH15 ...... 201 F1
Coles Mede SO21 ...... 31 D2
Colesbourne Rd PO6 ...... 133 D1
Coleson Rd SO18 ...... 103 F4
Coleville Ave SO45 ...... 151 D2
Colin Cl BH21 ...... 186 B3
Colinton Ave PO16 ...... 132 B1
Collard Way **4** GU33 ...... 20 C2
College Cl
 Hamble-le-Rice SO31 ...... 127 F1
 Rowland's Castle PO9 ...... 113 E1
College La **16** PO1 ...... 182 A3
Coll of Air Traffic Control
 BH23 ...... 190 C4
College Park Inf Sch PO2 ...... 157 F1
College Pl **6** SO15 ...... 103 D3
College Rd
 Bournemouth BH5 ...... 206 A2
 Portsmouth PO1 ...... 182 A3
 Ringwood BH24 ...... 141 D4
 Southampton SO19 ...... 103 F1
 Waterlooville PO7 ...... 134 C2
College St
 Petersfield GU31, GU32 ...... 40 C2
 Portsmouth PO1 ...... 182 A3
 Southampton SO14 ...... 103 D2
 Winchester SO23 ...... 11 D4
College Wlk SO23 ...... 11 D3
Collett Cl SO30 ...... 81 D1
Colley Cl SO23 ...... 2 A2
Collier Cl SO17 ...... 103 E4
Collingbourne Ave BH6 ...... 206 B4
Collingbourne Dr SO53 ...... 55 D3
Collington Cres PO6 ...... 133 D1
Collingwood House PO15 ...... 130 B1
Collingwood Rd
 Portsmouth PO5 ...... 182 B1
 West Moors BH21 ...... 138 C3
Collingwood Ret Pk PO14 ...... 155 D3
Collins House SO53 ...... 55 E3
Collins' Ley SO21 ...... 30 B4
Collins La Ringwood BH24 ...... 141 D4
 South Harting GU31 ...... 66 C4
Collins Rd PO4 ...... 183 D1
Collis Rd PO3 ...... 183 D4
Collwood Cl BH15 ...... 202 B4
Collyers Rd SO42 ...... 172 C4
Colne Ave SO16 ...... 77 E1
Colne Ct SO16 ...... 77 F1
Colombine Cl BH23 ...... 193 D1
Colonnade Rd **5** BH5 ...... 206 A3
Colonnade Rd W **4** BH5 ...... 206 A3
Colonnade The SO19 ...... 103 E2
Colpoy St PO5 ...... 182 A2
Colson Cl **46** SO23 ...... 11 D4
Colson Rd SO23 ...... 11 D4
Colt Cl Rownhams SO16 ...... 77 F3
 Wimborne Minster BH21 ...... 164 B3
Colts Rd SO16 ...... 77 F4
Coltsfoot Cl SO30 ...... 105 D4
Coltsfoot Dr Locks Heath SO31 ...... 128 C1
 5 Waterlooville PO7 ...... 134 C3
Coltsfoot Wlk SO51 ...... 28 B1
Coltsmead PO6 ...... 156 C4
Columbia Rd BH10 ...... 189 E1
Columbia Trees La BH10 ...... 189 E1
Columbian Way BH10 ...... 189 E1
Colvedene Cl SO21 ...... 31 F1
Colville Cl BH5 ...... 206 A3
Colville Dr SO32 ...... 83 E4
Colville Rd
 6 Bournemouth BH5 ...... 206 A3
 Cosham PO6 ...... 158 A4
Colwell Cl SO16 ...... 101 E4
Colwell Rd PO6 ...... 157 F4
Combe Down SO21 ...... 31 E4
Combe Rd GU33 ...... 21 D1
Comber Rd BH9 ...... 190 A2
Comet Way BH23 ...... 208 A3
Comfrey Cl Horndean PO8 ...... 88 B1
 Romsey SO51 ...... 28 B1
Comines Way SO18 ...... 104 C4
Comley Hill PO9 ...... 136 B3
Comley Rd BH9 ...... 189 F1
Commercial Pl PO1 ...... 182 B3
Commercial Rd
 Bournemouth BH2 ...... 204 C2
 Poole BH14 ...... 203 D2
 Portsmouth PO1 ...... 182 B3
 Southampton SO15 ...... 102 C3
 Totton SO40 ...... 101 D4
Commercial St SO18 ...... 104 A4
Commodore Ct **30** SO14 ...... 103 D2
Common Barn La PO13 ...... 179 F2
Common Cl SO53 ...... 55 E4
Common Gdns SO53 ...... 55 E4
Common Hill Rd SO21 ...... 28 B3
Common La Southwick PO17 ...... 132 C4
 Titchfield PO14 ...... 153 F4
Common Rd
 Chandler's Ford SO53 ...... 55 E4
 Westbourne PO10 ...... 137 F3
 Whiteparish SP5 ...... 24 A1
Common St PO1 ...... 182 B3
Commonside PO10 ...... 137 D3
Compass Cl PO3 ...... 180 B3
Compass Point PO16 ...... 155 D4
Compass Rd PO6 ...... 157 D4
Compton Acres BH13 ...... 214 C4

Compton Ave BH14 ...... 203 E1
Compton Beeches BH24 ...... 140 A3
Compton CE Prim Sch SO21 ...... 31 E4
Compton Cl Eastleigh SO50 ...... 55 F3
 Havant PO9 ...... 135 F2
 23 Lee-on-the-Solent PO13 ...... 179 F1
 Winchester SO22 ...... 10 A2
Compton Cres SO53 ...... 139 D1
Compton Cl **3** Havant PO9 ...... 135 F1
 Poole BH14 ...... 203 E2
Compton Dr BH14 ...... 203 E1
Compton Gdns BH14 ...... 203 E1
Compton House **4** SO16 ...... 102 A4
Compton Rd New Milton BH25 ...... 195 D1
 Portsmouth PO2 ...... 157 F2
 Totton SO40 ...... 101 D4
 Winchester SO23 ...... 10 C4
Compton St SO21 ...... 31 E4
Compton & Up Marden
 CE Sch PO18 ...... 90 C1
Compton Way SO22 ...... 10 A2
Compton Wlk **21** SO14 ...... 103 D3
Compton's Dr SO51 ...... 50 A3
Conan Rd PO2 ...... 157 F2
Condor Ave PO16 ...... 155 F4
Condor Cl Southampton SO19 ...... 103 E2
 West Moors BH31 ...... 139 D3
Coney Gn **4** SO23 ...... 2 A1
Conference Dr SO31 ...... 129 D2
Conference Pl **11** SO41 ...... 197 F1
Conford Dr PO9 ...... 135 E3
Congleton Cl SO43 ...... 98 B2
Conifer Ave BH14 ...... 203 D1
Conifer Cl Christchurch BH23 ...... 191 E2
 Ferndown BH22 ...... 165 F1
 Hythe SO45 ...... 125 F2
 St Leonards BH24 ...... 139 E2
 Waterlooville PO8 ...... 112 A1
 Winchester SO22 ...... 1 C1
Conifer Cres SO41 ...... 197 D2
Conifer Gr PO13 ...... 155 E2
Conifer Mews PO16 ...... 132 B1
Conifer Rd SO16 ...... 78 A2
Conigar Rd PO10 ...... 136 C2
Coniston Ave
 Bournemouth BH11 ...... 188 C3
 Portsmouth PO3 ...... 183 D4
Coniston Cl BH31 ...... 114 C3
Coniston Gdns SO30 ...... 105 E3
Coniston House **19** PO6 ...... 133 D1
Coniston Rd Eastleigh SO50 ...... 55 F1
 Ringwood BH24 ...... 141 D3
 Southampton SO16 ...... 101 E4
Coniston Wlk PO14 ...... 154 C4
Connaught Cl BH25 ...... 194 C1
Connaught Cres BH12 ...... 203 F3
Connaught Hall SO18 ...... 79 E2
Connaught La PO6 ...... 156 C4
Connaught Pl PO9 ...... 136 A1
Connaught Rd
 Bournemouth BH4 ...... 206 A3
 Havant PO9 ...... 136 A1
 Portsmouth PO2 ...... 157 E1
Connell Rd BH15 ...... 202 B3
Connemara Cres PO15 ...... 129 D4
Connigar Cl PO13 ...... 180 B4
Conqueror Way PO14 ...... 179 E3
Conrad Gdns PO15 ...... 129 E4
Conservatory The **38** SO23 ...... 11 D4
Consort Cl Eastleigh SO50 ...... 56 A3
 Poole BH12 ...... 203 E3
Consort House **9** PO1 ...... 182 B4
Consort Rd SO50 ...... 56 A3
Constable Cl Gosport PO12 ...... 181 D1
 Southampton SO19 ...... 104 B1
Constables Gate SO22 ...... 10 C4
Constantine Ave SO53 ...... 55 F3
Constantine Cl SO53 ...... 55 F3
Constitution Hill Gdns BH14 ...... 203 D1
Constitution Hill Rd BH14 ...... 203 D1
Consulate House **32** SO14 ...... 103 D2
Convent Cl PO10 ...... 160 C4
Convent La PO10 ...... 160 C4
Conway Cl Chandler's Ford SO53 ...... 55 D2
 New Milton BH25 ...... 195 D2
Conway Ct **20** BH25 ...... 195 D1
Conways Dr BH14 ...... 203 D2
Cook Cl BH24 ...... 141 E4
Cook Row BH21 ...... 163 D2
Cook St SO14 ...... 103 D2
Cooke Gdns BH12 ...... 203 F3
Cooke Rd BH12 ...... 203 F3
Cooks La Awbridge SO51 ...... 27 D2
 Lockerley SO51 ...... 25 F4
 Southbourne PO10 ...... 137 D1
 Totton SO40 ...... 76 B1
Cooley House PO13 ...... 155 D3
Coolhurst BH14 ...... 214 B4
Coombe Ave BH10 ...... 189 F2
Coombe Farm Ave PO16 ...... 155 D4
Coombe Gdns BH10 ...... 189 F1
Coombe La SO41 ...... 196 B4
Coombe Rd East Meon GU32 ...... 63 E4
 Gosport PO12 ...... 181 D2
Coombe Road Terr GU32 ...... 63 E4
Coombedale SO31 ...... 129 D1
Coombs PO8 ...... 88 B1
Cooper Dean Dr BH8 ...... 190 C1
Cooper Dean Rdbt BH7, BH8 ...... 191 D1
Cooper Gr PO16 ...... 156 B3
Cooper Rd Ashurst SO40 ...... 100 B3
 Portsmouth PO3 ...... 183 D4
Cooper's Cl West End SO18 ...... 80 B1
 West Wellow SO51 ...... 51 D1
Cooper's La SO19 ...... 103 E2
Coopers La BH31 ...... 114 C1
Copeland Dr BH14 ...... 203 D1
Copeland Rd SO16 ...... 77 F1

Copenhagen Towers **7** SO19 ...... 126 C4
Copinger Cl SO40 ...... 100 B3
Copnor Bridge Bsns Ctr PO3 ...... 183 D4
Copnor Inf & Jun Sch PO3 ...... 158 A1
Copnor Rd PO2 ...... 157 F2
Copper Beech Cl BH12 ...... 204 A2
Copper Beech Dr PO6 ...... 158 A4
Copper Beech Gdns BH10 ...... 189 E1
Copper Beeches SO45 ...... 150 C1
Copper St PO5 ...... 182 A2
Coppercourt Leaze **6** BH21 ...... 163 E2
Copperfield House **21** PO1 ...... 182 B4
Copperfield Rd SO16 ...... 79 D3
Copperfields SO40 ...... 100 A4
Coppers Cl SP6 ...... 93 D3
Coppice Ave BH22 ...... 165 E4
Coppice Cl New Milton BH25 ...... 195 E2
 St Leonards BH24 ...... 139 F2
 Winchester SO22 ...... 1 B1
Coppice Hill SO32 ...... 83 E4
Coppice Rd SO40 ...... 76 B1
Coppice The
 Brockenhurst SO42 ...... 145 E1
 Christchurch BH23 ...... 208 A4
 Gosport PO13 ...... 155 E1
 Waterlooville PO8 ...... 112 A3
Coppice View BH10 ...... 189 F2
Coppice Way PO15 ...... 130 B2
Coppins Gr PO16 ...... 156 B3
Copse Ave BH25 ...... 195 D1
Copse Cl Liss GU33 ...... 21 D2
 North Baddesley SO52 ...... 53 F2
 Otterbourne SO21 ...... 31 E2
 Petersfield GU31 ...... 41 E2
 Poole BH14 ...... 202 C2
 Totton SO40 ...... 100 C3
 Waterlooville PO7 ...... 134 B1
Copse Cvn Pk The SO40 ...... 99 E3
Copse La Chilworth SO16 ...... 54 C1
 Gosport PO13 ...... 155 E1
 Hamble-le-Rice SO31 ...... 127 F1
 North Hayling PO11 ...... 160 A1
Copse Rd Burley BH24 ...... 142 C1
 New Milton BH25 ...... 195 D1
 Southampton SO18 ...... 80 A1
 Verwood BH31 ...... 114 C3
Copse The Chandler's Ford SO53 ...... 55 F3
 Fareham PO15 ...... 130 B2
 Romsey SO51 ...... 28 B1
Copse View SO19 ...... 104 C3
Copse Way BH23 ...... 208 C4
Copsewood Ave BH8 ...... 190 C1
Copsewood Rd Ashurst SO40 ...... 100 B2
 Hythe SO45 ...... 125 F2
 Southampton SO18 ...... 79 F1
Copsey Cl PO6 ...... 158 B4
Copsey Gr PO6 ...... 158 B4
Copthorne Cotts SO45 ...... 151 E2
Copthorne La SO45 ...... 151 E2
Copythorn Rd PO2 ...... 157 F1
Copythorne CE Fst Sch SO40 ...... 75 D1
Copythorne Cres SO40 ...... 75 E2
Coracle Cl SO31 ...... 128 C1
Coral Cl PO16 ...... 156 B3
Coral Ct **3** BH12 ...... 204 A2
Coralin Gr PO7 ...... 112 A1
Coram Cl **3** SO23 ...... 2 A1
Corbar Rd BH23 ...... 206 C4
Corbett Rd PO7 ...... 134 B3
Corbiere Ave BH12 ...... 188 C1
Corbiere Cl SO16 ...... 77 F2
Corbin Ave PO12 ...... 166 A3
Corbin Ct SO41 ...... 197 D1
Corbin Rd SO41 ...... 197 D1
Corbould Rd SO45 ...... 149 F4
Corby Cres PO3 ...... 158 A2
Cordelia Cl SO45 ...... 125 E2
Corfe Cl PO14 ...... 179 D3
Corfe Halt Cl BH21 ...... 162 C1
Corfe Hills Sch BH18 ...... 186 C3
Corfe Lodge Rd BH18 ...... 186 B2
Corfe Mews BH15 ...... 202 B2
Corfe View Rd
 Corfe Mullen BH21 ...... 186 B3
 Poole BH14 ...... 203 E2
Corfe Way BH18 ...... 186 C2
Corfu BH13 ...... 214 C3
Corhampton Cres PO9 ...... 135 E2
Corhampton La Droxford SO32 ...... 60 B3
 Meonstoke SO32 ...... 61 D3
Corhampton Rd BH6 ...... 206 B3
Coriander Dr SO40 ...... 100 B4
Coriander Way PO15 ...... 129 E4
Corinna Gdns SO45 ...... 125 E2
Corinthian Rd SO53 ...... 55 F4
Cork La SO40 ...... 101 F4
Cormorant Cl PO16 ...... 155 F4
Cormorant Dr SO45 ...... 126 B1
Cormorant Wlk PO13 ...... 155 D1
Corn Market SO51 ...... 52 C4
Cornaway La PO16 ...... 156 A4
Cornbrook Gr PO7 ...... 112 B1
Cornel Rd SO19 ...... 103 F3
Cornelia Cres BH12 ...... 204 A3
Cornelius Dr PO7 ...... 112 A1
Corner Mead PO7 ...... 110 C2
Cornerways Ct **7** BH25 ...... 195 D1
Cornes Cl SO22 ...... 10 B4
Cornfield Rd PO16 ...... 131 D2
Cornfield Rd PO13 ...... 179 F1
Cornflower Cl SO31 ...... 128 C2
Cornflower Dr BH23 ...... 208 B4
Cornforth Rd BH23 ...... 76 B1
Cornish Gdns BH10 ...... 189 E1
Cornpits La SP6 ...... 68 B2
Cornwall Cl **4** SO18 ...... 80 A1

Cornwall Cres SO18 .... 79 F1
Cornwall Rd
Chandler's Ford SO53 .... 55 E2
Portsmouth PO1 .... 182 C3
Southampton SO18 .... 79 F1
Cornwallis Cres PO1 .... 182 B3
Cornwallis House 40 PO1 ...... 182 B3
Cornwallis Rd SO41 .... 211 D2
Cornwell Cl Gosport PO13 ...... 180 B4
Portsmouth PO2 .... 157 D1
Coronado Rd PO13 .... 181 D4
Coronation Ave
Bournemouth BH9 .... 189 F1
Upton BH16 .... 201 D4
Coronation Cl BH31 .... 114 C4
Coronation Eventide
Homes 4 PO2 .... 157 F2
Coronation Homes SO18 ...... 104 B4
Coronation Par SO31 .... 127 F2
Coronation Rd
South Hayling PO11 .... 185 F1
Swanmore SO32 .... 84 A3
Verwood BH31 .... 114 C4
Coronation Terr SP6 .... 69 D1
Corporation Rd BH1 .... 205 E3
Corpus Christi RC Prim Sch
Bournemouth BH5 .... 206 A3
Portsmouth PO2 .... 157 F1
Corsair Dr SO45 .... 125 E2
Corscombe Cl BH17 .... 187 F1
Cort Way PO15 .... 130 B2
Cortina Way SO30 .... 105 E3
Corvette Ave SO31 .... 128 C1
Cosford Cl SO50 .... 57 D1
Cosham Park Ave PO6 .... 157 F4
Cosham Sta PO6 .... 157 F4
Cossack Gn 6 SO14 .... 103 D2
Cossack La 11 SO23 .... 11 D4
Cossack Lane House 13 SO23 .. 11 D4
Cosworth Dr SO45 .... 125 E2
Cotes Ave BH14 .... 203 D3
Cotes Ct BH14 .... 203 D3
Cotlands Rd BH1 .... 205 D2
Cotsalls SO50 .... 57 E1
Cotswold Cl Havant PO9 ...... 135 F3
Hythe SO45 .... 125 E2
Verwood BH31 .... 114 C3
Cotswold Ct
6 Christchurch BH23 .... 207 F4
12 Southampton SO17 .... 79 D1
Cotswold House 3 PO6 ...... 157 E4
Cotswold Rd SO16 .... 101 F4
Cotswold Wlk 17 PO14 ...... 154 C4
Cott La BH24 .... 143 D1
Cott St SO32 .... 84 B2
Cott Street La SO32 .... 84 C2
Cottage Cl PO7 .... 110 C2
Cottage Gdns BH12 .... 203 E3
Cottage Gr Gosport PO12 ...... 181 D3
Portsmouth PO5 .... 182 B3
Cottage Grove Prim Sch PO5 182 B2
Cottage La GU32 .... 19 F2
Cottage Mews SP6 .... 69 F1
Cottage View PO1 .... 182 B3
Cottagers La SO41 .... 196 A2
Cottages The SP6 .... 94 A2
Cotteridge House 1 PO1 ...... 182 B2
Cottes Way PO14 .... 179 D3
Cottesway E PO14 .... 179 D3
Cotton Cl Bishopstoke SO50 ... 56 C2
Corfe Mullen BH18 .... 186 C3
Cotton Dr PO10 .... 136 C2
Cotwell Ave PO8 .... 112 A2
Coulmere Rd PO12 .... 181 D3
Coulsdon Rd SO30 .... 105 E3
Coultas Rd SO53 .... 30 C1
Council Hos Lockerley SO51 ... 26 A3
Sopley BH23 .... 167 F1
Countess Cl BH21 .... 187 F4
Countess Gdns BH7 .... 205 F4
Country View Stubbington PO14 154 A2
West Wellow SO51 .... 50 C2
County Gdns PO14 .... 154 B4
Course Park Cres PO14 ...... 129 E1
Court 29 PO13 .... 180 B3
Court 30 PO13 .... 180 B3
Court 31 PO13 .... 180 B3
Court 32 PO13 .... 180 B3
Court 33 PO13 .... 180 B3
Court 34 PO13 .... 180 B3
Court Barn Cl PO13 .... 179 F2
Court Barn La PO13 .... 179 F2
Court Cl 12 Christchurch BH23 .. 207 F4
Cosham PO6 .... 158 A4
Lymington SO41 .... 197 E1
Southampton SO18 .... 104 A3
Totton SO40 .... 76 B1
Court Cotts SO41 .... 197 E1
Court Hill SP6 .... 68 C3
Court La PO6 .... 158 A4
Court Lane Inf Sch PO6 ...... 158 A4
Court Lane Jun Sch PO6 ...... 158 A4
Court Mead PO6 .... 158 A4
Court Rd Bournemouth BH9 ...... 190 A1
Kings Worthy SO23 .... 2 B3
Lee-on-the-Solent PO13 ...... 179 F2
Southampton SO15 .... 102 C4
Court Royal Mews SO15 ...... 102 C4
Courtenay Dr BH21 .... 163 E3
Courtenay Pl SO41 .... 197 F2
Courtenay Rd Poole BH14 ...... 203 D2
Winchester SO23 .... 2 A1
Courthill Fst Sch BH14 ...... 203 E2
Courthill Rd BH14 .... 203 E2
Courtier Cl SO45 .... 125 E2
Courtland Gdns SO16 .... 79 D3
Courtlands SO41 .... 197 F2
Courtlands Terr PO8 .... 112 A2

Courtleigh Manor 6 BH5 ...... 205 E2
Courtmount Gr PO6 .... 158 A4
Courtney Pl BH21 .... 186 B3
Courtyard The
Christchurch BH23 .... 207 E3
14 Petersfield GU31 .... 40 C2
Poole BH21 .... 188 B1
8 Romsey SO51 .... 52 C4
Cousins Gr PO4 .... 182 C1
Cove Rd BH10 .... 189 E1
Covena Rd BH6 .... 206 C3
Coventry Cl BH21 .... 186 B2
Coventry Cres BH17 .... 187 D1
Coventry Ct Gosport PO13 ...... 180 B3
7 Winchester SO23 .... 2 A1
Coventry Rd SO15 .... 102 C3
Coverack Way PO6 .... 157 D4
Covert Gr PO7 .... 135 D3
Covert The SO51 .... 53 D3
Covingdale House PO4 .... 183 D2
Covington Rd PO10 .... 137 D3
Cow La Cosham PO6 .... 157 E4
Portchester PO16 .... 156 B4
Cowan Rd PO7 .... 134 B3
Coward Rd PO12 .... 180 C1
Cowdray Cl Bishopstoke SO50 ... 56 C1
Southampton SO16 .... 78 A2
Cowdray Pk PO14 .... 179 D3
Cowdrey Gdns BH8 .... 190 C1
Cowdrys Field 2 BH21 ...... 163 D3
Cowell Dr BH21 .... 206 A4
Cowes La SO31 .... 152 B3
Cowgrove Rd BH21 .... 162 C3
Cowleas Cl SO51 .... 26 C3
Cowleas Cotts SO51 .... 26 C3
Cowley Cl SO16 .... 77 F1
Cowley Rd Lymington SO41 ...... 197 E2
Poole BH17 .... 202 B4
Cowleys Rd BH23 .... 192 B1
Cowper Ave BH25 .... 195 D1
Cowper Rd Bournemouth BH9 ... 189 F1
Portsmouth PO1 .... 182 C4
Southampton SO19 .... 104 B3
Cowpitts La SO23 .... 11 E1
Cowplain Sch PO8 .... 111 F1
Cowslip Cl Gosport PO13 ...... 155 E1
Locks Heath SO31 .... 128 C1
Cowslip Rd BH18 .... 186 C1
Cowslip Way SO51 .... 28 B1
Cox Ave BH9 .... 190 A2
Cox Cl BH9 .... 190 A2
Cox Dale PO14 .... 129 E1
Cox Row SO53 .... 55 E2
Cox's Dr SO19 .... 104 A1
Cox's La SO19 .... 103 E2
Coxes Meadow GU32 .... 40 C3
Coxford Cl SO16 .... 78 A1
Coxford Dro SO16 .... 78 A2
Coxford Rd SO16 .... 78 A2
Coxs Hill SO21 .... 32 A4
Coxstone La 2 BH24 .... 141 D3
Coy Pond Rd BH12 .... 204 A3
Crab Orchard Way BH21 ...... 114 C1
Crabapple Cl SO40 .... 100 B4
Crabbs Way SO40 .... 100 A4
Crabden La PO8 .... 88 C1
Crableck La SO31 .... 128 B3
Crabthorne Farm La PO14 ...... 154 A2
Crabton Close Rd BH5 ...... 205 F2
Crabtree SO16 .... 77 F1
Crabtree Cl BH23 .... 192 B1
Crabwood Cl SO16 .... 77 F1
Crabwood Ct PO9 .... 135 E4
Crabwood Dr SO30 .... 80 C1
Crabwood Rd SO16 .... 77 F1
Cracknore Hard SO40 .... 102 A1
Cracknore Hard La SO40 ...... 102 A1
Cracknore Rd SO15 .... 102 B3
Craddock House
13 Portsmouth PO1 .... 182 A3
2 Winchester SO23 .... 11 E4
Craigmoor Ave BH8 .... 190 C1
Craigmoor Cl BH8 .... 190 C1
Craigmoor Way BH8 .... 190 C1
Craigside Rd BH24 .... 139 E2
Craigwell Rd PO7 .... 134 B2
Craigwood Dr PO14 .... 165 F2
Crammpoor La SO51 .... 28 C1
Cranberry Cl SO40 .... 101 F1
Cranborne Cres BH12 ...... 203 F4
Cranborne Ct
Bournemouth BH9 .... 205 D4
14 Bournemouth, Westbourne
BH4 .... 204 B2
Cranborne Gdns SO53 ...... 30 A1
Cranborne Pl BH25 .... 194 C2
Cranborne Rd
Alderholt SP6, BH21 .... 92 A3
Bournemouth BH2 .... 204 C1
Cosham PO6 .... 134 A1
Wimborne Minster BH21 ...... 163 E4
Cranborne Wlk PO14 .... 154 C4
Cranbourne Ct SO15 .... 78 B1
Cranbourne Ct BH17 .... 188 A1
Cranbourne Dr SO21 .... 31 D2
Cranbourne Pk SO30 .... 105 E2
Cranbourne Rd PO12 .... 181 E2
Cranbrook Mews BH12 ...... 203 D3
Cranbrook Rd BH12 .... 203 D3
Cranbury Ave SO14 .... 103 D3
Cranbury Cl Downton SP5 ...... 46 C3
Otterbourne SO21 .... 31 D2
Cranbury Cres SO19 .... 103 F2
Cranbury Gdns SO31 .... 104 C1
Cranbury Pl SO14 .... 103 D3
Cranbury Rd Eastleigh SO50 ... 56 A1
Southampton SO19 .... 103 F2

Cranbury Terr 3 SO14 ...... 103 D3
Cranbury The 2 SO14 ...... 103 D3
Cranbury Towers 4 SO14 ...... 103 D3
Crane Cl BH31 .... 114 C3
Crane Dr BH31 .... 114 C4
Crane Way BH21 .... 139 D3
Cranemoor Ave BH23 .... 193 F1
Cranemoor Cl BH23 .... 193 F1
Cranemoor Gdns BH23 ...... 193 F1
Cranes Mews BH15 .... 202 B2
Craneswater Ave PO4 .... 182 C1
Craneswater Gate 4 PO4 ...... 182 C1
Craneswater Jun Sch PO4 ...... 182 C1
Craneswater Mews 5 PO4 ...... 182 C1
Craneswater Park PO4 .... 182 C1
Cranfield Rd BH23 .... 163 E3
Cranford Gdns SO53 .... 55 D4
Cranford House 5 SO17 ...... 79 D1
Cranford Rd GU32 .... 40 C1
Cranford Way SO17 .... 79 D1
Cranleigh Ave PO1 .... 182 C3
Cranleigh Cl BH6 .... 206 C3
Cranleigh Ct BH6 .... 206 C3
Cranleigh Gdns BH6 .... 206 C3
Cranleigh House
Hedge End SO30 .... 81 E2
Southampton SO17 .... 103 D4
Cranleigh Paddock SO43 ...... 121 F3
Cranleigh Rd
Bournemouth BH6 .... 206 C3
Hedge End SO30 .... 105 E3
Portchester PO16 .... 156 A4
Portsmouth PO1 .... 182 C3
Cranmer Cl SO16 .... 77 E3
Cranmer Rd BH9 .... 204 C4
Cranmore SO31 .... 127 E4
Cransley Gr BH4 .... 204 B1
Crantock Gr BH8 .... 190 C1
Cranwell Cl
Bournemouth BH11 .... 188 C2
Bransgore BH23 .... 169 D1
Cranwell Cl SO16 .... 77 F3
Cranworth Rd SO22 .... 1 C1
Crasswell St PO1 .... 182 B3
Craven Ct PO15 .... 130 C2
Craven Rd SO53 .... 55 E3
Craven St 18 SO14 .... 103 D3
Crawford Cl SO16 .... 77 E3
Crawford Dr PO16 .... 130 C2
Crawley Ave PO9 .... 136 A3
Crawley Hill SO51 .... 50 C1
Crawshaw Rd BH14 .... 203 D1
Crawte Ave SO45 .... 150 B1
Creasey Rd BH11 .... 189 D3
Credenhill Rd PO6 .... 133 E1
Creech Rd BH12 .... 203 E3
Creedy Gdns SO18 .... 80 A2
Creek End PO10 .... 160 C4
Creek Rd Gosport PO12 ...... 181 E2
South Hayling PO11 .... 185 E1
Creekmoor La BH17 .... 202 A4
Creighton Rd SO15 .... 101 F3
Cremorne Pl 10 GU32 ...... 40 C2
Cremyll Cl PO14 .... 179 E3
Crescent Cl SO22 .... 10 A2
Crescent Cotts SO45 .... 177 D3
Crescent Ct BH25 .... 209 F4
Crescent Dr BH25 .... 209 F4
Crescent House 3 SO14 ...... 56 A2
Crescent Prim Sch The SO50 ... 56 A2
Crescent Rd
Bournemouth BH2 .... 204 C2
Fareham PO16 .... 131 D1
Gosport PO12 .... 181 D1
Locks Heath SO31 .... 128 C1
North Baddesley SO52 ...... 53 F3
Poole BH14 .... 203 F2
Verwood BH31 .... 115 D3
Wimborne Minster BH21 ...... 163 E2
Crescent The
Barton on Sea BH25 .... 209 E4
3 Bournemouth BH7 .... 205 F2
Eastleigh SO50 .... 56 A2
Marchwood SO40 .... 101 F1
Netley SO31 .... 127 E3
Netley Marsh SO40 .... 99 F2
Romsey SO51 .... 53 D4
Southampton SO19 .... 104 A1
Southbourne PO10 .... 161 E4
Twyford SO21 .... 32 A3
Upham SO32 .... 58 B1
Waterlooville PO7 .... 134 B2
Crescent Wlk BH22 .... 165 F1
Cressey Rd SO51 .... 52 C4
Cressy Rd PO2 .... 182 B4
Crest Cl PO16 .... 131 E1
Crest Rd BH12 .... 203 E3
Crest The PO7 .... 134 B1
Crest Way SO19 .... 104 B2
Cresta Ct 8 PO4 .... 182 C1
Cresta Gdns BH22 .... 165 F1
Crestland Ct PO8 .... 112 A2
Crestwood Com Sch SO50 ... 55 F3
Crete Cotts SO45 .... 125 F1
Crete La SO45 .... 125 F1
Crete Rd SO45 .... 125 F1
Cribb Cl BH17 .... 202 A4
Crichel Mount Rd BH14 ...... 214 B4
Crichel Rd BH9 .... 205 D4
Crichton House 9 SO31 ...... 127 D3
Cricket Cl BH23 .... 207 F3
Cricket Dr PO8 .... 112 A3
Cricklemede SO32 .... 83 E4
Cricklewood Cl SO32 .... 83 E4
Crigdon Cl SO16 .... 101 F4
Crimea Rd BH9 .... 204 C4
Cringle Ave BH6 .... 207 D2
Crinoline Gdns PO4 .... 183 D1

Cripple Gate La Beaulieu SO42 175 E1
East Boldre SO42 .... 175 E3
Cripstead La SO23 .... 10 C3
Crispen Cl BH21 .... 208 C2
Crispin Cl Fair Oak SO50 ...... 81 E3
Locks Heath SO31 .... 129 D2
Crisspyn Cl PO8 .... 112 A3
Criterion Arc 39 BH1 .... 204 C2
Crittall Cl SO41 .... 172 B1
Crockford Cl BH25 .... 195 D3
Crockford Rd PO10 .... 137 D2
Croft Cl BH21 .... 186 B4
Croft Hts SP5 .... 24 A2
Croft La PO11 .... 159 F1
Croft Rd Bournemouth BH9 ...... 189 F1
Bransgore BH23 .... 193 D3
Christchurch BH23 .... 207 F4
Poole BH12 .... 203 D3
Portsmouth PO2 .... 157 C1
Ringwood BH24 .... 141 E4
Croft The Chandler's Ford SO53 ... 55 E2
Croucheston SP5 .... 22 B4
Stubbington BH22 .... 154 B2
Totton SO40 .... 76 B1
Croftlands Ave PO14 .... 154 B2
Crofton Anne Dale Jun
& Inf Schs PO14 .... 179 E3
Crofton Ave PO13 .... 179 E2
Crofton Cl Christchurch BH23 ... 191 F1
Southampton SO17 .... 79 D1
Waterlooville PO7 .... 134 B3
Crofton Ct PO14 .... 179 E3
Crofton Hammond Jun
& Inf Schs PO14 .... 179 E3
Crofton La PO14 .... 179 D3
Crofton Rd
Portsmouth, Milton PO4 ...... 183 D1
Portsmouth, North End PO2 ...... 157 F1
Crofton Sch PO14 .... 179 F3
Crofton Way Locks Heath SO31 ... 128 B1
Swanmore SO32 .... 84 A3
Cromalt Cl SO45 .... 125 E1
Cromarty Ave PO4 .... 183 D2
Cromarty Cl PO14 .... 154 A2
Cromarty Rd SO16 .... 77 F3
Crombie Cl PO8 .... 111 F2
Cromer Gdns BH12 .... 203 F3
Cromer Rd Bournemouth BH8 ...... 205 E4
Cosham PO6 .... 133 F1
Poole BH12 .... 203 F3
Southampton SO16 .... 77 F1
Cromhall Cl PO14 .... 154 B4
Crompton Way PO15 .... 129 E3
Cromwell Pl 9 BH5 .... 206 A3
Cromwell Rd
Bournemouth BH5 .... 206 A3
Poole BH12 .... 203 E3
Portsmouth PO4 .... 183 D1
Southampton SO15 .... 102 C4
11 Wimborne Minster BH21 ...... 163 E2
Winchester SO22 .... 10 C3
Crondall Ave PO9 .... 135 F3
Crood Ct 7 PO16 .... 131 E1
Crooked Hays Cl SO40 ...... 101 F1
Crooked Walk La PO17 ...... 132 C2
Crookham Cl PO9 .... 135 E2
Crookham Rd SO19 .... 126 C4
Crookhorn Com
Sch The PO7 .... 134 C2
Crookhorn La Soberton SO32 ... 85 E4
Waterlooville PO7 .... 134 C2
Crosby Rd BH4 .... 204 B1
Crosfield Cl SO51 .... 51 D1
Cross Keys Pas 22 SO23 ...... 11 D4
Cross La SO32 .... 59 D1
Cross Lanes BH24 .... 117 E4
Cross Rd
Lee-on-the-Solent PO13 ...... 180 A2
Southampton SO19 .... 103 F4
Cross St
Bishop's Waltham SO32 ...... 83 E4
Portsmouth PO5 .... 182 B2
Portsmouth, Portsea PO1 ...... 182 A3
Winchester SO23 .... 10 C4
Cross The Burley BH24 ...... 143 D2
East Meon GU32 .... 38 B1
Cross Trees SP6 .... 46 A1
Cross Way Christchurch BH23 ... 191 E1
Compton(Hants) SO21 ...... 31 E3
Havant PO9 .... 135 F1
Cross Ways BH23 .... 169 E3
Crossbill Cl PO8 .... 112 A4
Crossfell Wlk PO14 .... 154 C4
Crosshouse Rd SO14 .... 103 E2
Crossland Cl PO12 .... 181 E2
Crossland Dr PO9 .... 136 A2
Crossley Ct SO15 .... 102 B3
Crossmead Ave BH25 .... 195 D1
Crossway The PO16 .... 156 B4
Crossways SO41 .... 196 B1
Crossways Cl SP5 .... 46 C4
Crossways The Denmead PO7 ... 111 D4
Gosport PO12 .... 181 D2
Upton BH16 .... 201 E4
Crosswell Cl SO19 .... 104 B3
Crouch La BH24 .... 114 A4
Croucher's Croft SO22 ...... 1 B1
Crow Arch La BH24 .... 141 E4
Crow Arch Lane Ind Est
BH24 .... 141 D1
Crow Cotts BH24 .... 141 E2
Crow Hill Top BH24 .... 142 A3
Crow La BH24 .... 141 E3
Crowder Terr SO22 .... 10 C3
Crowders Gr 1 SO21 ...... 56 C4
Crowe Hill Ct 2 BH15 ...... 202 C2
Crown Cl Poole BH12 .... 203 E3
Waterlooville PO7 .... 134 C2

Crown Ct
58 Portsmouth PO1 .... 182 B3
7 Wimborne Minster BH21 ...... 163 E2
Crown Mead 1 BH21 ...... 163 E2
Crown Mews 18 PO12 ...... 181 E2
Crown St Portsmouth PO1 ...... 182 B3
Southampton SO15 .... 102 A4
Crown Wlk 9 BH7 .... 205 F2
Crows Nest La SO32 .... 81 F1
Crowsbury Cl PO10 .... 136 C2
Crowsport SO31 .... 128 A2
Crowther Cl SO19 .... 104 B2
Croydon Cl SO16 .... 78 A2
Crummock Rd SO53 .... 55 D4
Crusader Rd
Bournemouth BH11 .... 188 B2
Bournemouth BH8 .... 105 E3
Crusader Way SO52 .... 54 C3
Cruse Cl SO41 .... 172 A1
Cruxton Farm Ctyd BH21 ...... 163 E1
Crystal Way PO7 .... 135 D4
Cucklington Gdns BH9 ...... 190 A2
Cuckmere La SO16 .... 101 E4
Cuckoo Bushes La SO53 ...... 55 E4
Cuckoo Hill Way BH23 ...... 169 E1
Cuckoo La
22 Southampton SO14 ...... 102 C2
Stubbington PO14 .... 154 A2
Cuckoo Rd BH12 .... 203 D4
Cudnell Ave BH11 .... 189 D3
Cudworth Mead SO30 .... 81 E1
Cuffnells Cl BH24 .... 117 D4
Cul-de-sac PO4 .... 209 E4
Culford Ave SO40 .... 100 C3
Culford Cl BH8 .... 190 C1
Culford Ct 1 BH8 .... 205 D3
Culford Way SO40 .... 100 C3
Cull Cl BH12 .... 204 B4
Cull La BH25 .... 195 D3
Culliford Cres BH17 .... 187 F1
Culloden Cl PO15 .... 130 C1
Culloden Rd PO14 .... 154 C3
Cullwood La BH25 .... 195 E3
Culver SO31 .... 127 E4
Culver Cl SO16 .... 77 E1
Culver Dr PO11 .... 185 E1
Culver Mews 29 SO23 ...... 11 D4
Culver Rd New Milton BH25 ...... 194 C1
Portsmouth PO4 .... 183 D1
28 Southampton SO23 ...... 11 D4
Culverhayes Pl BH21 .... 163 D3
Culverhayes Rd BH21 .... 163 D3
Culverin Sq PO3 .... 158 A2
Culverlands Cl SO32 .... 107 F4
Culverley Cl SO42 .... 145 F1
Culverwell Gdns 21 SO23 ...... 10 C4
Culvery Gdns SO18 .... 80 A1
Cumber Rd SO31 .... 128 C2
Cumberland Ave
Chandler's Ford SO53 ...... 55 F3
Emsworth PO10 .... 136 C2
Cumberland Bsns Ctr 1 PO1 182 C1
Cumberland Cl SO53 .... 55 F3
Cumberland House(Mus &
Aquarium) PO5 .... 182 C1
Cumberland Inf Sch PO4 ...... 183 D1
Cumberland Pl SO15 .... 102 C3
Cumberland Rd PO1 .... 182 C2
Cumberland St
Portsmouth PO1 .... 182 A3
Southampton SO14 .... 103 D2
Cumberland Way SO45 ...... 125 E2
Cumbrian Way SO16 .... 101 F4
Cummins Gn SO31 .... 105 D1
Cumnor Rd BH1 .... 205 D2
Cunard Ave SO15 .... 102 B4
Cunard Rd SO14 .... 103 D1
Cundell Way SO23 .... 2 A4
Cunningham Ave SO32 ...... 83 D4
Cunningham Cl
Bournemouth BH11 .... 189 D2
Christchurch BH23 .... 208 A3
Ringwood BH24 .... 141 E4
Cunningham Cres
Bournemouth BH11 .... 189 D2
Southampton SO19 .... 104 A2
Cunningham Ct
10 New Milton BH25 .... 194 C2
1 Portsmouth PO5 .... 182 B1
Cunningham Dr Gosport PO13 ... 155 F2
Locks Heath SO31 .... 129 D2
Cunningham Gdns SO31 ...... 127 F4
Cunningham House SO32 ...... 83 D4
Cunningham Pl BH11 .... 189 D2
Cunningham Rd
Horndean PO8 .... 112 B4
Waterlooville PO7, PO8 ...... 134 B3
Cupernham Cl SO51 .... 28 A1
Cupernham Inf Sch SO51 ...... 28 A1
Cupernham Jun Sch SO51 ...... 28 A1
Cupernham La
Abbotswood SO51 .... 28 A1
Romsey SO51 .... 28 A1
Curdridge Cl 33 PO9 ...... 136 A3
Curdridge La Curdridge SO32 ... 83 E2
Shedfield SO32 .... 83 E2
Curdridge Prim Sch SO32 ...... 106 B4
Curlew Cl Emsworth PO10 ...... 160 C4
Ferndown BH22 .... 165 D4
Hythe SO45 .... 126 A3
Southampton SO16 .... 78 A3
Curlew Dr Waterside SO45 ...... 126 A1
Portchester PO16 .... 155 F4
Curlew Gdns PO8 .... 111 F2
Curlew Path PO4 .... 183 D3

Curlew Rd Bournemouth BH8 .... 190 B1
 Christchurch BH23 .... 208 A3
Curlew Sq SO50 .... 55 F1
Curlew Wlk Gosport PO13 ...... 155 D2
 Hythe SO45 .... 126 A1
Curlews The BH31 .... 115 D3
Curlieu Rd BH15 .... 202 B3
Curtis Mead PO12 .... 157 F2
Curtis Rd BH12 .... 203 E3
Curtiss Gdns PO12 .... 180 C2
Curve The Gosport PO13 .... 155 D1
 Horndean PO8 .... 111 F3
Curzon Ct
 32 Bournemouth BH4 .... 204 B2
 Southampton SO16 .... 78 B2
Curzon Howe Rd PO1 .... 182 A3
Curzon Pl SO41 .... 197 E1
Curzon Rd Bournemouth BH1 .... 205 E3
 Poole BH14 .... 203 D2
 Waterlooville PO7 .... 134 C4
Curzon Way BH23 .... 208 B4
Custards Rd SO43 .... 121 F3
Custards The SO43 .... 122 A3
Cut Throat La Droxford SO32 ... 61 D1
 Swanmore SO32 .... 84 B3
Cutbush La Southampton SO18 ... 80 A2
 Southampton SO18 .... 104 A4
 West End SO18 .... 80 A2
Cuthbert Rd PO1 .... 182 C3
Cuthburga Rd BH21 .... 163 E2
Cuthbury CI BH21 .... 163 D2
Cuthbury Gdns BH21 .... 163 D3
Cutler CI New Milton BH25 .... 195 E2
 Poole BH12 .... 204 B4
Cutlers La PO14 .... 154 B2
Cutlers Pl BH21 .... 164 A3
Cutter Ave SO31 .... 128 C1
Cutts Arch Droxford SO32 ..... 85 D3
 Soberton SO32 .... 85 D3
Cygnet Ct PO16 .... 155 F4
Cygnet House PO12 .... 181 D4
Cygnet Rd PO6 .... 158 C4
Cygnus Gdns SO45 .... 125 E2
Cynthia CI BH12 .... 203 D4
Cynthia House BH12 .... 203 D4
Cynthia Rd BH12 .... 203 D4
Cypress Ave SO19 .... 103 F3
Cypress Cres PO8 .... 112 A3
Cypress Gdns Botley SO30 ..... 106 A4
 Totton SO40 .... 100 B4
Cypress Gr SO41 .... 211 E4
Cyprus Rd Portsmouth PO2 ..... 182 C4
 Titchfield PO14 .... 129 E1
Cyril Rd BH8 .... 205 E3

D Ave SO45 .... 150 C3
D-Day Mus PO5 .... 182 B1
Dacombe CI BH16 .... 201 E4
Dacombe Dr BH16 .... 201 E4
Dacres Wlk 3 SO41 .... 211 E3
Daffodil Rd SO16 .... 79 E2
Daggons Rd SP6 .... 92 B3
Dahlia Rd SO17 .... 79 D2
Daintree CI SO19 .... 104 B2
Dairy CI Broadstone BH21 ..... 186 A2
 Christchurch BH23 .... 207 E4
Dairy La SO16 .... 77 D3
Dairymoor PO17 .... 108 A2
Daisy La Gosport PO12 .... 181 D2
 Locks Heath SO31 .... 129 E2
Daisy Mead PO7 .... 135 D4
Daisy Rd SO16 .... 79 D2
Dakota CI BH23 .... 208 A4
Dale CI Littleton SO22 .... 1 A3
 Poole BH15 .... 202 C3
Dale Dr PO13 .... 155 D3
Dale Park House 23 PO1 .... 182 B3
Dale Rd Hythe SO45 .... 125 F2
 Poole BH15 .... 202 C3
 Southampton SO16 .... 78 B1
 Stubbington SO14 .... 154 B2
Dale The PO7 .... 134 B1
Dale Valley CI SO16 .... 78 B1
Dale Valley Gdns SO16 .... 78 B1
Dale Valley Rd Poole BH15 .... 202 C4
 Southampton SO16 .... 78 B2
Dales CI BH21 .... 164 B3
Dales Dr BH21 .... 164 A3
Dales La BH23 .... 190 C4
Dales Way SO40 .... 100 A4
Dalewood Ave BH11 .... 188 C3
Dalewood Rd PO15 .... 130 B1
Dalkeith Rd Broadstone BH21 .. 186 B2
 Poole BH13 .... 204 A1
Dalling Rd BH12 .... 204 A3
Dallington CI PO14 .... 179 E3
Dalmally Gdns SO18 .... 103 F4
Dalmeny Rd BH6 .... 207 D2
Dalzell 31 SO23 .... 2 A1
Damask Gdns PO7 .... 112 A1
Dame Elizabeth
 Kelly Ct 3 PO2 .... 157 F2
Damen CI SO30 .... 105 D3
Damerham Rd BH8 .... 190 B2
Dampier CI PO13 .... 180 B4
Damson Hill SO32 .... 60 A1
Danbury Ct PO10 .... 137 D1
Dances Way PO11 .... 184 C2
Dandelion CI PO13 .... 155 D1
Dando Rd PO7 .... 111 D2
Dandy's Ford La SO51 .... 25 F1
Dane CI SO45 .... 150 C1
Dane Ct BH14 .... 203 D4
Dane Dr BH22 .... 165 F2
Dane Rd SO41 .... 211 D3

Danebury CI PO9 .... 135 F3
Danebury Gdns SO53 .... 55 D2
Danebury Way SO16 .... 77 E2
Danecourt CI PO14 .... 202 C2
Danecourt Rd BH14 .... 202 C2
Danecrest Rd SO41 .... 195 F2
Danehurst SO41 .... 211 D3
Danehurst New Rd SO41 .... 195 E4
Danemark CI 4 SO23 .... 11 D4
Danes CI BH25 .... 210 A4
Danes Rd Awbridge SO51 .... 26 B2
 Portchester PO16 .... 132 A1
 23 Winchester SO23 .... 2 A1
Danesbrook La PO7 .... 135 D4
Danesbury Ave BH6 .... 206 C2
Danestream CI SO41 .... 211 E2
Danestream Ct SO41 .... 211 F2
Daneswood Rd BH25 .... 195 E2
Daniel Gdns 14 BH15 .... 202 B1
Daniell's CI SO41 .... 197 F2
Daniell's Wlk SO41 .... 197 F2
Dannybrook BH23 .... 208 A3
Dansie CI BH14 .... 203 D2
Dapple Pl SO40 .... 102 A1
Darby's CI BH15 .... 202 B3
Darby's Cnr BH17 .... 187 E1
Darby's La BH15 .... 202 B3
Darby's La N BH17 .... 202 B4
Dark La Blackfield SO45 ...... 150 C1
 Bransgore BH23 .... 194 A2
Darley Rd BH22 .... 165 E2
Darlington Gdns SO15 .... 78 B1
Darlington Rd PO4 .... 182 C2
Darnan House 28 SO14 .... 103 D4
Darracott Rd BH5 .... 206 A3
Darren CI PO14 .... 154 B2
Darren Ct 9 PO16 .... 131 D1
Darrian Ct BH16 .... 201 D4
Dart House SO18 .... 103 F4
Dart Rd SO18 .... 80 A2
Dartington Rd SO50 .... 56 B3
Dartmouth Mews PO5 .... 182 A2
Dartmouth Rd PO4 .... 158 A1
Darwin Ave BH23 .... 191 F1
Darwin CI 4 SO41 .... 204 A2
Darwin House 32 PO1 .... 182 B3
Darwin Rd Eastleigh SO50 ..... 56 A2
 Southampton SO15 .... 102 C4
Darwin Way PO13 .... 180 B3
Daubney Gdns 10 PO9 .... 135 E3
Daulston Rd PO1 .... 182 C4
Davenport CI Gosport PO13 .... 180 B3
 Upton BH16 .... 201 E4
Daventry La PO3 .... 158 B2
David Ct SO51 .... 53 D3
David Hart Bsns Ctr SP5 ...... 46 C4
David's La BH24 .... 140 B3
Davidia Ct PO7 .... 135 D3
Davidson Ct 27 PO1 .... 182 A3
Davis CI PO13 .... 180 B4
Davis CI BH12 .... 203 F3
Davis Field BH25 .... 194 C1
Davis Rd BH12 .... 203 F3
Daw La PO11 .... 184 C4
Dawkins Rd BH15 .... 201 E2
Dawkins Way BH25 .... 195 D1
Dawlish Ave SO15 .... 102 B4
Dawn Chorus BH14 .... 203 D2
Dawn CI BH10 .... 189 E1
Dawn Gdns SO22 .... 10 B3
Dawnay CI SO16 .... 79 E3
Daws Ave BH11 .... 189 D1
Dawson Rd SO19 .... 104 B1
Day La PO8 .... 111 F4
Day's Ct BH21 .... 163 E2
Daylesford BH14 .... 203 D1
Dayrell CI SO40 .... 76 A1
Dayshes CI PO13 .... 155 D2
Dayslondon Rd PO7 .... 134 C2
De Courtenai CI BH11 .... 188 C3
De Grouchy La SO17 .... 79 D1
De Haviland Ct SO41 .... 163 F1
De Havilland House BH23 ...... 208 A3
De Havilland Way BH23 .... 208 A3
De La Warr Rd SO41 .... 211 E2
De Lisle CI PO2 .... 157 F2
De Lisle Rd BH3 .... 204 C4
De Lunn Bldgs 5 SO23 .... 11 D4
De Mauley Rd BH13 .... 214 C4
De Montfort Rd BH21 .... 163 E1
De Mowbray Way SO41 .... 197 E1
De Port Hts SO32 .... 61 E3
De Redvers Rd BH14 .... 203 E1
Deacon CI SO19 .... 104 A3
Deacon Cres SO19 .... 104 A3
Deacon Gdns BH11 .... 189 D3
Deacon Rd Bournemouth BH11 ... 189 D3
 Locks Heath SO31 .... 129 D1
 Southampton SO19 .... 104 A3
Deacon Trad Est SO50 .... 56 B1
Deadman Hill SP 6 .... 71 E3
Deal CI PO14 .... 154 B2
Deal Rd PO6 .... 133 F1
Dean CI Hamworthy BH15 .... 201 F2
 Winchester SO22 .... 1 B1
Dean Court
 (Bournemouth FC) BH7 .... 205 F3
Dean Ct Hedge End SO30 .... 105 E4
 Horndean PO8 .... 112 B4
 Southampton SO18 .... 104 A4
 4 Southampton, Bitterne
 Manor SO18 .... 103 F4
Dean La
 Bishop's Waltham SO32 ...... 59 F2
 Rowland's Castle PO8 .... 113 E3
 Sparsholt SO22 .... 1 A1
 Whiteparish SP5 .... 24 A2

Dean La Continued
 Winchester SO22 .... 1 A1
Dean Park Cres BH1 .... 204 C2
Dean Park Rd BH1 .... 204 C2
Dean Rd Cosham PO6 .... 157 F4
 Fair Oak SO50 .... 57 E1
 Southampton SO18 .... 104 A4
 West Dean SP5 .... 3 D1
 West Tytherley SP5 .... 3 A1
Dean St PO1 .... 182 A3
Dean Sta SP5 .... 3 E2
Dean Swift Cres BH14 .... 214 B4
Dean Villas PO17 .... 130 C4
Dean's Rd 13 BH5 .... 206 A3
Deane Ct 52 PO9 .... 136 A3
Deane Down Dro SO22 .... 1 A2
Deane Gdns 19 PO13 .... 179 F1
Deane's Park Rd PO16 .... 131 E1
Deanery The SO53 .... 55 D4
Deanfield CI SO31 .... 127 F1
Deans Court La SO41 .... 163 E2
Deans Ct SO41 .... 211 E3
Deans Gate PO14 .... 179 E3
Deans Gr SO41 .... 163 E4
Deans The BH1 .... 204 C2
Deanscroft Rd BH10 .... 189 F2
Deansfield CI SO51 .... 53 D4
Deansleigh Rd BH7 .... 191 D1
Deanswood Dr PO7 .... 111 F1
Dear Hay La BH15 .... 202 B1
Dearing CI SO43 .... 121 F2
Debney Lodge PO7 .... 134 C4
Decies Rd BH14 .... 203 D3
Dee CI SO53 .... 55 D3
Dee Way BH15 .... 202 A1
Deep Dell PO8 .... 112 A3
Deepdene SO18 .... 103 F4
Deepdene La BH11 .... 188 C3
Deeping CI SO19 .... 103 F1
Deeping Gate PO7 .... 135 D4
Deer Park BH25 .... 194 C2
Deer Sanctuary BH24 .... 119 F3
Deerhurst CI SO40 .... 100 B3
Deerhurst House 3 PO6 .... 133 D1
Deerleap CI SO45 .... 126 A2
Deerleap La SO40 .... 100 B1
Deerleap Way Hythe SO45 ...... 126 A2
 New Milton BH25 .... 195 D3
Defender Rd SO19 .... 103 E2
Defender Wlk SO19 .... 103 E2
Defiance Rd PO1 .... 182 A2
Defoe CI PO15 .... 129 E4
Delamere Gdns BH10 .... 189 F2
Delamere Rd PO4 .... 182 C2
Delaval House 35 PO1 .... 182 A3
Delft CI SO31 .... 128 C2
Delft Gdns PO8 .... 111 E1
Delft Mews BH23 .... 207 E3
Delhi CI BH14 .... 203 E2
Delhi Rd BH9 .... 189 F1
Delilah Rd BH15 .... 201 E1
Delius Ave SO19 .... 104 B2
Delius Wlk PO7 .... 134 C3
Delkeith Ct BH22 .... 165 E2
Dell CI Broadstone BH18 ...... 186 C2
 Fair Oak SO50 .... 57 E1
 Waterlooville PO7 .... 134 A1
Dell Cotts SO24 .... 15 F1
Dell Piece East PO8 .... 112 B3
Dell Piece West PO8 .... 112 B3
Dell Quay CI PO13 .... 155 D1
Dell Rd Southampton SO18 ..... 79 F1
 Winchester SO23 .... 11 D1
Dell The Barton on Sea BH25 .. 209 E4
 Havant PO9 .... 135 D1
 Portchester PO16 .... 131 E1
 Southampton FC SO15 .... 102 C3
Dellcrest Path PO7 .... 134 A1
Dellfield GU32 .... 18 C1
Dellfield CI
 14 Cosham PO6 .... 133 D1
 8 Cosham PO6 .... 157 D4
Delme CI 15 PO16 .... 131 D1
Delme Dr PO16 .... 131 D1
Delme Sq 21 PO16 .... 131 D1
Delph Rd BH21 .... 187 E4
Delphi Way PO7 .... 134 C1
Delta Bsns Pk PO16 .... 155 D4
Delta CI BH23 .... 208 A4
Dempsey CI SO19 .... 104 A2
Denbigh CI Eastleigh SO50 .... 55 F3
 Totton SO40 .... 100 B3
Denbigh Dr PO16 .... 130 C1
Denbigh Gdns SO16 .... 78 C2
Denby Rd BH15 .... 202 C2
Dene CI Chilworth SO16 .... 78 C4
 Locks Heath SO31 .... 128 C2
 Ringwood BH24 .... 117 E1
Dene Hollow PO6 .... 158 B4
Dene Rd SO40 .... 100 B1
Dene Way SO40 .... 100 B2
Dene Wlk BH22 .... 165 F1
Denecote Lodge BH13 .... 214 D4
Deneside Copse SO41 .... 197 D1
Deneve Ave BH17 .... 187 E1
Denewood Copse BH22 .... 138 B2
Denewood Rd BH22 .... 138 B2
Denewulf CI SO32 .... 83 E4
Denham CI Broadstone BH17 .... 187 F2
 Stubbington SO41 .... 179 D3
 Winchester SO23 .... 1 C1
Denham Ct SO23 .... 2 A1
Denham Dr BH21 .... 193 F1
Denham Gdns SO31 .... 127 D3
Denham's Cnr SO32 .... 81 E3
Denhill CI PO11 .... 184 C3
Denison Rd BH17 .... 187 E1

Denmark La BH15 .... 202 B2
Denmark Rd
 Bournemouth BH9 .... 189 F1
 Poole BH15 .... 202 B2
Denmark Terr BH1 .... 205 F3
Denmead BH25 .... 195 E2
Denmead Cvn Pk PO7 .... 111 D2
Denmead Inf Sch PO7 .... 111 D2
Denmead Jun Sch PO7 .... 111 D2
Denmead Rd
 Bournemouth BH6 .... 206 B4
 Southampton SO18 .... 104 B4
Dennet House SO23 .... 2 B1
Dennetts La 19 BH15 .... 202 A1
Denning Mews PO1 .... 182 B2
Dennis Rd BH21 .... 186 B3
Dennis Way GU33 .... 21 D2
Dennison CI 8 SO15 .... 102 A4
Dennistoun Ave PO7 .... 207 F4
Denny CI SO45 .... 151 D2
Densome Cnr SP 6 .... 71 D3
Denville Ave PO16 .... 156 B3
Denville CI PO6 .... 158 C4
Denvilles CI PO9 .... 136 A1
Denwood Rd BH4 .... 204 A2
Denzil Ave Netley SO31 .... 127 E3
 Southampton SO14 .... 103 D3
Depedene CI SO45 .... 150 B2
Derby Ct PO13 .... 180 B3
Derby House 5 SO50 .... 56 A1
Derby Rd Bournemouth BH1 ..... 205 E2
 Eastleigh SO50 .... 55 F1
 Portsmouth PO2 .... 157 F1
 Southampton SO14 .... 103 D3
Dereham Way BH12 .... 203 F3
Deridene Ct SO40 .... 100 B3
Derlyn Rd PO16 .... 131 D1
Derritt La Bransgore BH23 .... 192 B4
 Sopley BH23 .... 192 B4
Dersingham CI PO6 .... 133 F1
Derwent CI Bournemouth BH9 ... 190 A1
 Ferndown BH22 .... 166 A3
 Horndean PO8 .... 88 B1
 Stubbington PO14 .... 154 B2
 West End SO18 .... 80 A1
Derwent Rd
 Lee-on-the-Solent PO13 ..... 179 F1
 New Milton BH25 .... 195 D3
 Southampton SO16 .... 77 F1
Derwentwater Rd BH21 .... 163 E1
Desborough CI 9 PO6 .... 133 D1
Desborough Rd SO50 .... 56 A1
Devenish Rd SO22 .... 1 B2
Deverel CI BH22 .... 207 D4
Deverell Pl PO7 .... 134 B2
Devine Gdns SO50 .... 56 C1
Devon CI SO53 .... 55 E2
Devon Dr SO53 .... 55 E2
Devon Rd Christchurch BH23 ... 206 C4
 Poole BH15 .... 202 C3
 Portsmouth PO3 .... 158 A2
Devonshire Ave PO4 .... 183 D2
Devonshire Gdns
 Bursledon SO31 .... 105 D1
 Hythe SO45 .... 150 A4
Devonshire Inf Sch PO4 .... 182 C2
Devonshire Mansions
 10 SO15 .... 102 C3
Devonshire Rd SO15 .... 102 C3
Devonshire Sq PO4 .... 182 C2
Devonshire Way PO14 .... 154 B4
Dew La SO50 .... 55 F2
Dewar CI PO15 .... 129 E3
Deweys La BH24 .... 140 C4
Dewlands Pk BH31 .... 114 B3
Dewlands Rd BH31 .... 114 B3
Dewlands Way BH31 .... 114 C3
Dewlish CI BH17 .... 188 A1
Dewsbury Ct 3 SO18 .... 80 A1
Dhekelia CI 52 PO1 .... 182 B3
Dial CI BH23 .... 169 E1
Diamond CI SP6 .... 93 F4
Diamond Ct SP6 .... 93 F4
Diamond St PO5 .... 182 A2
Diana CI PO12 .... 180 C2
Diana Ct BH23 .... 209 D4
Diana Way BH21 .... 186 C4
Dibben Wlk SO51 .... 28 B1
Dibble Dr SO52 .... 53 F2
Dibden CI Bournemouth BH8 .... 190 B2
 Havant PO9 .... 135 E2
Dibden Lodge CI SO45 .... 125 F3
Dibles Rd SO31 .... 128 C1
Dickens CI PO2 .... 182 B4
Dickens Dell SO40 .... 100 A4
Dickens Mus PO1 .... 182 B4
Dickens Rd BH6 .... 206 B4
Dickson Pk PO17 .... 108 A2
Didcot Rd Poole BH17 .... 202 B4
 Southampton SO15 .... 78 B1
Dieppe Cres PO2 .... 157 F2
Dieppe Gdns PO12 .... 180 C2
Dight Rd PO12 .... 181 E1
Diligence CI SO31 .... 105 D1
Dillington House 2 PO7 ...... 134 C4
Dilly La BH25 .... 210 A4
Dimond CI SO18 .... 79 F1
Dimond Hill SO18 .... 79 F1
Dimond Rd SO18 .... 79 F1
Dingle Rd BH5 .... 206 A2
Dingle Way SO31 .... 129 D3
Dingley Rd BH15 .... 202 B3
Dinham Ct BH25 .... 195 E2
Dinham Rd BH25 .... 195 D2
Dinsey CI SO16 .... 101 F4
Diprose Rd BH12 .... 186 C4
Disa House SO15 .... 102 C3
Discovery CI PO14 .... 154 B3

Disraeli Rd BH23 .... 207 E3
Ditcham Cres PO9 .... 135 F2
Ditcham Park Sch GU31 .... 89 F4
Ditchbury SO41 .... 197 E3
Ditton CI PO14 .... 154 B2
Ditton Cotts SO42 .... 148 C1
Dock La SO42 .... 149 D1
Dock Mill Cotts 3 PO5 ...... 182 B1
Dock Rd PO12 .... 181 E2
Dockenfield CI PO9 .... 135 E2
Doctor's Hill SO51 .... 26 A2
Doctors La GU32 .... 37 E3
Dodds La SO32 .... 84 B3
Dodwell La SO31 .... 105 D2
Doe Copse Way BH25 .... 194 C2
Dogdean BH21 .... 163 E4
Dogkennel La PO7 .... 86 C2
Dogwood Dell 7 PO7 .... 134 C3
Dogwood Rd BH18 .... 186 C1
Dolbery Rd N BH12 .... 188 B1
Dolbery Rd S BH12 .... 188 B1
Dolman Rd PO12 .... 181 E2
Dolphin Ave BH10 .... 189 F3
Dolphin CI 11 SO50 .... 56 C1
Dolphin Cres PO12 .... 181 E2
Dolphin Ct
 7 Portsmouth PO5 .... 182 C1
 Stubbington PO14 .... 154 A2
Dolphin Ctr BH15 .... 202 B2
Dolphin Hill SO21 .... 32 A3
Dolphin Pl 2 BH25 .... 210 A4
Dolphin Way Gosport PO12 ..... 181 E1
 Portsmouth PO1 .... 182 A2
Dolton Rd SO16 .... 77 F2
Dome Al SO23 .... 11 D4
Domey Ct 2 PO6 .... 158 A4
Dominie Wlk 18 PO13 .... 179 F1
Dominion Ctr BH11 .... 188 C2
Dominion Rd BH11 .... 188 C2
Domum Rd Portsmouth PO2 ...... 157 F1
 Winchester SO23 .... 11 D3
Domvilles App PO2 .... 157 F3
Donaldson Rd PO6 .... 157 F3
Doncaster Rd SO50 .... 80 A4
Donigers CI SO32 .... 84 A3
Donigers Dell SO32 .... 84 A3
Donkey La SO30 .... 106 A4
Donnelly Rd BH6 .... 206 C3
Donnelly St PO12 .... 181 D3
Donnington Ct 19 SO23 ...... 2 A1
Donnington Dr
 Chandler's Ford SO53 .... 55 D2
 Christchurch BH23 .... 208 A4
Donnington Gr SO17 .... 79 E1
Donoughmore Rd 1 BH1 .... 205 F2
Dorcas CI PO7 .... 112 A1
Dorchester Ct SO15 .... 102 C4
Dorchester Gdns BH15 .... 202 C3
Dorchester Mansions BH1 ...... 205 E4
Dorchester Rd Poole BH15 ..... 202 C3
 Upton BH16 .... 201 D4
Dore Ave PO16 .... 132 B1
Dores CI Braishfield SO51 .... 29 D4
 Hursley SO51 .... 29 D4
Doric CI SO53 .... 55 F4
Dorking Cres PO6 .... 157 F4
Dorland Gdns SO40 .... 100 B3
Dorlands Rd PO8 .... 112 B4
Dormers The BH25 .... 194 C1
Dormington Rd PO6 .... 133 F1
Dormy CI SO31 .... 128 B2
Dormy Way PO13 .... 155 D1
Dornie Rd BH13 .... 214 C4
Dornmere La PO7 .... 135 D4
Dorothy Dymond St 16 PO1 ... 182 B3
Dorrick Ct 17 SO15 .... 102 C4
Dorrien Rd PO12 .... 181 E4
Dorrita Ave PO8 .... 112 A2
Dorrita CI PO4 .... 182 C1
Dorrits The SO40 .... 100 A4
Dorset Ave BH22 .... 165 E2
Dorset CI PO8 .... 112 A3
Dorset Grange BH23 .... 206 C4
Dorset Heavy Horse Ctr
 BH21 .... 91 E1
Dorset Lake Ave BH14 .... 214 A4
Dorset Lake Manor BH14 .... 203 D1
Dorset Rd Bournemouth BH4 .... 204 B3
 Chandler's Ford SO53 .... 55 E2
 Christchurch BH23 .... 207 F4
Dorset St SO14 .... 103 D3
Dorstone Rd PO6 .... 133 E1
Dorval House 23 SO15 .... 102 C4
Dorval Manor 24 SO15 .... 102 C4
Douglas Ave BH23 .... 207 D3
Douglas CI BH16 .... 201 E4
Douglas Cres SO19 .... 104 B3
Douglas Gdns Havant PO9 ...... 136 A2
 Poole BH12 .... 203 F3
Douglas Mews
 Bournemouth BH6 .... 206 B3
 Upton BH16 .... 201 E4
Douglas Rd Bournemouth BH6 ... 206 C2
 Poole BH12 .... 203 F3
Douglas Way SO45 .... 125 F2
Doulton Gdns BH14 .... 203 D1
Doussie CI BH16 .... 201 D4
Dove CI PO8 .... 111 F2
Dove Dale SO50 .... 56 C1
Dove Gdns SO31 .... 129 D3
Dove La SO51 .... 29 D4
Dover CI Poole BH13 .... 204 A2
 Stubbington SO16 .... 154 A2
Dover Ct PO11 .... 184 C3
Dover Rd Poole BH13 .... 204 A2
 Portsmouth PO3 .... 183 D4
Dover St SO14 .... 103 D4
Dovercourt Rd PO6 .... 158 A3

Doveshill Cres BH10 ..... 189 E2
Doveshill Gdns BH10 ..... 189 E2
Doveys Cl BH24 ..... 143 D2
Dowds Cl SO30 ..... 105 D4
Dowell House PO4 ..... 183 D1
Dowlands Cl BH10 ..... 189 E2
Dowlands La BH10 ..... 189 E2
Dowlands Rd BH10 ..... 189 E2
Down End PO6 ..... 134 B1
Down End Rd PO6 ..... 134 B1
Down Farm La SO23 ..... 1 C4
Down Farm Pl PO8 ..... 88 B1
Down Lodge Cl SP6 ..... 93 D3
Down Rd Horndean PO8 ..... 88 A1
Horndean PO8 ..... 112 B4
Down's Park Ave SO40 ..... 101 D3
Down's Park Cres SO40 ..... 101 D3
Down's Park Rd SO40 ..... 101 D3
Downend Rd PO16 ..... 131 F1
Downey Cl BH11 ..... 188 C1
Downham Cl PO8 ..... 111 F2
Downhouse Rd PO8 ..... 88 A2
Downing Ct PO14 ..... 129 E1
Downland Cl Botley SO30 ..... 105 F4
Locks Heath SO31 ..... 129 D2
Downland Pl SO30 ..... 105 D3
Downlands Cl SP5 ..... 46 C3
Downlands Pl BH17 ..... 202 C4
Downlands Rd SO22 ..... 10 A2
Downley Rd PO9 ..... 136 A2
Downs Cl PO7 ..... 134 C2
Downscroft Gdns SO30 ..... 105 D4
Downside PO13 ..... 155 E1
Downside Ave SO19 ..... 104 A3
Downside Rd
Waterlooville PO7 ..... 134 B2
Winchester SO22 ..... 1 A1
Downsway The PO16 ..... 156 B4
Downton Cl BH8 ..... 190 B2
Downton Cty Sec Sch SP5 ..... 46 C4
Downton Hill SP5 ..... 47 E4
Downton House ▣ PO6 ..... 157 E4
Downton La SO41 ..... 210 C4
Downton Rd SO18 ..... 79 F1
Downview Rd SP6 ..... 43 D2
Downwood Cl
Fordingbridge SP6 ..... 69 E1
Hythe SO45 ..... 125 E1
Downwood Way PO8 ..... 88 B1
Doyle Ave PO2 ..... 157 F2
Doyle Cl PO2 ..... 157 F2
Doyle Ct ▣ Portsmouth PO2 ..... 157 F2
Southampton SO19 ..... 103 F1
Doyle House PO9 ..... 135 D2
Doyne Rd BH14 ..... 203 F2
Dradfield La SO32 ..... 109 E4
Draffatts House SO15 ..... 102 B4
Dragon La BH23 ..... 168 A4
Dragon St GU31,GU32 ..... 40 C2
Dragoon Cl SO19 ..... 104 B2
Dragoon Way BH23 ..... 206 C4
Drake Cl Christchurch BH23 ..... 207 F3
Locks Heath SO31 ..... 129 D3
Marchwood SO40 ..... 102 A1
New Milton BH25 ..... 194 C2
Ringwood BH24 ..... 117 E1
Drake Ct ▣ BH15 ..... 202 B1
Drake House ▣ PO1 ..... 182 A3
Drake Rd Bishopstoke SO50 ..... 56 C2
Lee-on-the-Solent PO13 ..... 179 E2
Poole BH15 ..... 202 B1
Drakes Cl SO45 ..... 125 F1
Drakes Ct SO40 ..... 102 A2
Draper Rd Bournemouth BH11 .. 189 D2
Christchurch BH23 ..... 207 F4
Drapers Copse Cvn Site
SO45 ..... 125 E2
Draycote Rd PO8 ..... 88 B2
Draycott Rd BH10 ..... 189 E1
Drayton Cl ▣ SO19 ..... 126 C4
Drayton La PO6 ..... 134 A1
Drayton Pl SO40 ..... 100 B4
Drayton Rd PO2 ..... 157 F1
Drayton St SO22 ..... 10 B3
Dreadnought Rd PO14 ..... 154 C3
Dresden Dr PO8 ..... 111 F2
Dreswick BH23 ..... 191 E2
Drew Cl BH12 ..... 204 B4
Drift Rd Clanfield PO8 ..... 88 B2
Fareham PO16 ..... 131 E1
Drift The PO9 ..... 113 D1
Driftwood Gdns
Portsmouth PO4 ..... 183 E1
Totton SO40 ..... 100 B3
Drill Shed Rd PO12 ..... 157 D1
Drinkwater Cl SO50 ..... 55 F2
Drive The Fareham PO16 ..... 131 D1
Gosport PO13 ..... 155 D1
Havant PO9 ..... 135 F2
Plaitford SO51 ..... 25 D1
Poole BH12 ..... 203 E3
Sherfield English SO51 ..... 25 D1
Southbourne PO10 ..... 161 E4
Totton SO40 ..... 100 C3
West End SO30 ..... 80 A2
West Wellow SO51 ..... 51 D1
Drove Cl SO21 ..... 31 F3
Drove Rd Southampton SO19 .. 104 A2
Southwick PO17 ..... 133 D2
Drove The Blackfield SO45 ..... 150 C1
Durley SO32 ..... 82 B4
Fair Oak SO50 ..... 81 E3
Swanmore SO32 ..... 84 A3
Totton SO40 ..... 76 A1
Twyford SO21 ..... 31 F3
West End SO30 ..... 80 C2
West Wellow SO51 ..... 50 C2

Droxford Cl PO12 ..... 180 C2
Droxford House ▣ PO1 ..... 182 B3
Droxford Jun Sch SO32 ..... 61 D1
Droxford Rd
Bournemouth BH6 ..... 206 A3
Swanmore SO32 ..... 84 B3
Druids Cl BH22 ..... 165 E1
Druitt Rd BH23 ..... 207 F4
Drum Cl SO52 ..... 40 C2
Drum Mead GU32 ..... 40 C2
Drumlanrig Terr PO12 ..... 181 E4
Drummond Ct
▣ Eastleigh SO50 ..... 56 A3
Southampton SO19 ..... 103 F2
Drummond Rd
Bournemouth BH1 ..... 205 E2
Hedge End SO30 ..... 81 E1
Hythe SO45 ..... 126 A2
Portsmouth PO1 ..... 182 B3
Drummond Way SO53 ..... 55 D4
Drury Rd BH4 ..... 204 A1
Dryden Ave SO19 ..... 132 C1
Dryden Cl Fareham PO16 ..... 131 D1
St Leonards BH24 ..... 139 F3
Waterlooville PO7 ..... 111 F1
Dryden Pl ▣ SO41 ..... 211 E3
Dryden Rd SO19 ..... 104 C3
Drysdale Mews PO4 ..... 183 D1
Duart Ct BH25 ..... 195 E2
Duck Island La ▣ BH24 ..... 141 D3
Duck La BH11 ..... 188 C2
Ducking Stool La BH23 ..... 207 D3
Duckmead La GU33 ..... 21 D3
Duckworth House ▣ PO1 ..... 182 A3
Duddon Cl SO18 ..... 80 A1
Dudleston Heath Dr PO8 ..... 112 A1
Dudley Ave Fordingbridge SP6 ..... 69 F2
Hordle SO41 ..... 195 F2
Dudley Gdns BH10 ..... 189 E3
Dudley Pl ▣ BH25 ..... 195 D1
Dudley Rd Bournemouth BH10 .. 189 E3
Portsmouth PO3 ..... 183 D4
Dudley Terr GU33 ..... 21 D3
Dudmoor Farm Rd BH23 ..... 191 F2
Dudmoor La BH23 ..... 191 F2
Dudsbury Ave BH22 ..... 165 E2
Dudsbury Cres BH22 ..... 165 F2
Dudsbury Ct ▣ BH23 ..... 207 F3
Dudsbury Gdns BH22 ..... 189 F4
Dudsbury Rd BH22 ..... 165 E1
Dudsway Ct BH22 ..... 165 E2
Duffield La SO17 ..... 137 F2
Dugald Drummond St ▣ PO1 182 B3
Dugdell Cl BH22 ..... 165 F3
Duisburg Way PO5 ..... 182 A1
Duke Cres PO1 ..... 182 B4
Duke Rd SO30 ..... 105 E3
Duke St SO14 ..... 103 D2
Dukes Cl GU32 ..... 40 B2
Dukes Ct SO32 ..... 83 E4
Dukes Mead BH11 ..... 188 C3
Dukes Mill Ctr ▣ SO51 ..... 52 C4
Dukes Rd Gosport PO12 ..... 181 D3
Southampton SO14 ..... 103 E4
Dukes Wood Dr SO45 ..... 126 A1
Dukesfield BH23 ..... 191 E1
Dulsie Rd BH3 ..... 204 B4
Dumbarton Cl PO2 ..... 182 B4
Dumbleton Cl SO19 ..... 104 C2
Dumbleton's Towers SO19 ..... 104 C2
Dummer Ct PO9 ..... 135 E3
Dummer Rd SO51 ..... 28 B4
Dumpers Drove SO50 ..... 81 E3
Dumpton St BH21 ..... 163 E4
Dunbar Cl SO16 ..... 77 F3
Dunbar Cres BH23 ..... 193 F1
Dunbar Rd Bournemouth BH3 .. 204 C3
Portsmouth PO4 ..... 183 D2
Dunbridge La Awbridge SO51 .. 26 C4
Mottisfont SO51 ..... 26 C4
Dunbridge Sta SO51 ..... 5 E1
Duncan Cl SO19 ..... 103 F1
Duncan Cooper House PO7 .. 134 B4
Duncan Ct SO19 ..... 104 B3
Duncan Rd Locks Heath SO31 .. 129 D3
New Milton BH25 ..... 195 E2
Portsmouth PO5 ..... 182 B1
Duncans Dr PO14 ..... 154 A4
Duncliff Rd BH6 ..... 207 D2
Duncombe Dr BH24 ..... 116 B2
Duncombe Rd GU32 ..... 63 E4
Duncton Rd PO8 ..... 88 B3
Duncton Way PO13 ..... 155 E2
Dundas La PO3 ..... 158 A1
Dundas Rd PO3 ..... 158 A1
Dundas Rd BH17 ..... 202 C4
Dundas Spur PO3 ..... 158 A1
Dundee Cl PO15 ..... 130 C2
Dundee Rd SO17 ..... 79 E1
Dundonald Cl
South Hayling PO11 ..... 185 D3
Southampton SO19 ..... 103 E1
Dundridge La
Bishop's Waltham SO32 ..... 60 B1
Droxford SO32 ..... 60 B1
Dundry Way SO30 ..... 105 E4
Dune Crest BH13 ..... 214 B2
Dunedin Cl BH22 ..... 165 D2
Dunedin Dr BH22 ..... 165 D2
Dunedin Gdns BH22 ..... 165 D2
Dunedin Gr BH23 ..... 208 B4
Dunfield Way SO45 ..... 150 C1
Dunford Cl Barton on Sea BH25 209 F4
New Milton BH25 ..... 194 C1
Dunford Rd BH12 ..... 203 E3
Dunhurst (Bedales Jun Sch)
GU32 ..... 40 C3

Dunhurst Cl PO9 ..... 136 A2
Dunkeld Rd Bournemouth BH3 .. 204 C3
Gosport PO12 ..... 181 D4
Dunkirk Cl SO16 ..... 78 B2
Dunkirk Rd SO16 ..... 78 B2
Dunlin Cl Christchurch BH23 .. 208 A3
Portsmouth PO4 ..... 183 E3
Dunn Cl PO4 ..... 183 D2
Dunnings La SO52 ..... 53 F3
Dunnock Cl Ferndown BH22 .. 165 D4
Rowland's Castle PO9 ..... 113 D1
Dunsbury Way PO9 ..... 135 F3
Dunsmore Cl PO5 ..... 182 B2
Dunstable Wlk PO14 ..... 154 B4
Dunstans La BH15 ..... 203 D3
Dunster Cl SO16 ..... 78 B3
Durban Cl SO31 ..... 28 A1
Durban Ct ▣ SO15 ..... 102 C4
Durban House ▣ PO1 ..... 182 B3
Durban Rd PO1 ..... 182 C4
Durdells Ave BH11 ..... 189 D3
Durdells Gdns BH11 ..... 189 D3
Durford Ct PO9 ..... 135 E3
Durford Rd GU31 ..... 41 E2
Durham Gdns PO7 ..... 134 C3
Durham St Gosport PO12 ..... 181 D3
Portsmouth PO1 ..... 182 B3
Durland Cl BH25 ..... 195 D1
Durley Ave PO8 ..... 111 F2
Durley Brook Road SO32 ..... 81 F3
Durley CE Sch SO32 ..... 82 A3
Durley Chine Ct BH2 ..... 204 B1
Durley Chine Rd BH2 ..... 204 B1
Durley Chine Rd S BH2 ..... 204 B1
Durley Cres SO40 ..... 100 B3
Durley Gdns BH2 ..... 204 B1
Durley Hall Rd SO32 ..... 58 B1
Durley La SO32 ..... 82 B4
Durley Rd Bournemouth BH2 .. 204 C1
Durley SO32,SO50 ..... 81 F4
Fair Oak SO50 ..... 81 F4
Gosport PO12 ..... 181 D3
Durley Rd S BH2 ..... 204 B1
Durlston Court Sch BH25 ..... 210 A4
Durlston Cres BH23 ..... 191 E2
Durlston Rd Poole BH14 ..... 203 E1
Southampton SO16 ..... 77 E1
Durnford Rd SO14 ..... 103 D3
Durngate Pl SO23 ..... 11 D4
Durngate Terr SO23 ..... 11 D4
Durnstown SO41 ..... 172 B1
Durrant PRU PO9 ..... 136 A4
Durrant Rd
▣ Bournemouth BH2 ..... 204 C2
Poole BH15 ..... 203 E2
Durrant Way SO41 ..... 172 A1
Durrants Gdns PO9 ..... 136 A4
Durrants Rd PO9 ..... 136 A4
Durrington Pl BH7 ..... 206 A3
Durrington Rd BH7 ..... 206 A4
Dursley Cres PO6 ..... 157 E4
Durweston Cl BH9 ..... 190 A2
Dutton La SO50 ..... 56 A2
Dutton's Rd SO51 ..... 52 C4
Dyer Rd SO15 ..... 102 B4
Dymchurch House ▣ PO6 .. 157 F4
Dymewood Rd BH21 ..... 138 C2
Dymoke St PO10 ..... 136 C2
Dymott Cl SO15 ..... 102 B3
Dyneley Gn SO18 ..... 80 A1
Dyram Cl SO50 ..... 55 F3
Dysart Ave PO6 ..... 158 A4
Dyserth Cl SO19 ..... 104 A1
Dyson Dr SO23 ..... 2 A1

E Ave SO45 ..... 150 C3
Eadens La SO40 ..... 99 E4
Eagle Ave SO45 ..... 150 C3
Eagle Cl Chandler's Ford SO53 .. 55 D2
Portchester PO16 ..... 155 F4
Eagle House Sch BH14 ..... 203 D2
Eagle Rd
Lee-on-the-Solent PO13 ..... 179 E2
Poole BH12 ..... 204 A2
Eaglhurst ▣ BH12 ..... 204 A2
Eames La GU33 ..... 19 F4
Earle House ▣ SO23 ..... 11 E4
Earle Rd BH4 ..... 204 B1
Earley Ct SO41 ..... 197 F2
Earlham Dr BH14 ..... 203 E2
Earls Cl SO50 ..... 57 D1
Earls Rd Fareham PO16 ..... 155 D4
Southampton SO14 ..... 103 D4
Earlsdon St PO5 ..... 182 B2
Earlsdon Way BH23 ..... 208 C4
Earlsdon ▣ SO23 ..... 11 D4
Earlswood Dr SP6 ..... 92 C3
Earnley Rd PO11 ..... 185 F1
East Ave BH25 ..... 209 E4
East Avenue BH3 ..... 204 B3
East Bank Rd SO42 ..... 173 D4
East Bargate ▣ SO14 ..... 103 D2
East Boldre Rd SO42 ..... 175 E3
East Borough BH21 ..... 163 D4
East Cams Cl PO16 ..... 131 D1
East Cl PO5 ..... 209 E4
East Cliff Way BH23 ..... 208 B4
East Cosham Rd PO6 ..... 158 A4
East Ct Cosham PO6 ..... 158 A4
Portsmouth PO1 ..... 182 C4
East Dean Rd SO51 ..... 4 C1
East Dr SO50 ..... 56 C2
East Field Cl PO10 ..... 137 F1

East Hill SO41 ..... 197 F2
East Hill Cl PO16 ..... 131 E1
East Hill Dr GU33 ..... 21 D2
East Hoe Rd PO7 ..... 86 A2
East Horton Golf Ctr SO50 ..... 57 F1
East House Ave PO14 ..... 179 E3
East Howe La BH10 ..... 189 E2
East La SO41 ..... 196 C1
East Leigh Rd PO9 ..... 136 B2
East Links SO53 ..... 55 E1
East Lodge Fareham PO15 ..... 130 B1
▣ Lee-on-the-Solent PO13 ..... 179 F1
East Lodge Park PO6 ..... 158 C4
East Meon CE Prim Sch GU32 . 38 B3
East Overcliff Dr BH1 ..... 205 E2
East Pallant PO9 ..... 135 F1
East Park Terr SO14 ..... 103 D3
East Quay BH15 ..... 202 B1
East Quay Rd BH15 ..... 202 B1
East Rd Fawley SO45 ..... 150 B4
Southwick PO17 ..... 133 D3
East Shore Sch PO13 ..... 183 D3
East St Fareham PO14, PO16 ..... 131 E1
Hambledon PO7 ..... 86 B2
Havant PO9 ..... 135 F1
Poole BH15 ..... 202 B1
Portchester PO16 ..... 156 C4
Portsmouth PO1 ..... 182 A2
Southampton SO14 ..... 103 D2
Titchfield PO14 ..... 154 A4
Westbourne PO10 ..... 137 D2
Wimborne Minster BH21 ..... 163 E2
East Street Ctr ▣ SO14 ..... 103 D2
East Surrey St ▣ PO1 ..... 182 B3
East View Rd BH24 ..... 141 D4
East View Terr ▣ PO9 ..... 135 F1
East Way Bournemouth BH8 .. 190 B1
Corfe Mullen BH21 ..... 186 B3
East Woodhay Rd SO22 ..... 1 B2
Eastacre SO22 ..... 1 C1
Eastbourne Ave Gosport PO12 .. 180 C4
Southampton SO15 ..... 102 B4
Eastbourne Rd PO3 ..... 183 D4
Eastbrook Cl Gosport PO12 ..... 180 C4
Locks Heath SO31 ..... 129 D3
Eastbrook Row BH21 ..... 163 E2
Eastbury Ct BH23 ..... 207 F2
Eastchurch Cl SO16 ..... 77 F2
Eastcliff PO13 ..... 179 F2
Eastcot Cl SO45 ..... 150 B2
Eastcott Cl BH7 ..... 206 A4
Eastcroft Rd PO12 ..... 180 C3
Easter Rd BH9 ..... 190 A1
Eastern Ave PO4 ..... 183 D3
Eastern Ind Ctr PO6 ..... 158 B3
Eastern Par Fareham PO16 ..... 155 D4
Portsmouth PO4 ..... 182 C1
Eastern Rd Fawley SO45 ..... 151 F1
Havant PO9 ..... 136 A1
Lymington SO41 ..... 197 E2
Portsmouth PO3, PO6 ..... 158 B2
Portsmouth, Whale Is PO2 ..... 157 D1
Eastern Terr PO3 ..... 183 D1
Eastern Villas Rd PO4 ..... 182 B1
Eastern Way Fareham PO16 ..... 131 E1
Milford on Sea SO41 ..... 211 E2
Eastfield Ave PO14 ..... 154 C4
Eastfield Ct BH24 ..... 141 E4
Eastfield La BH24 ..... 141 E4
Eastfield Rd Portsmouth PO4 .. 183 D2
Southampton SO17 ..... 103 E4
Eastfields ▣ PO7 ..... 182 B2
Eastgate St
Southampton SO14 ..... 103 D2
Winchester SO23 ..... 11 D4
Eastlake Ave BH12 ..... 203 E3
Eastlake Cl GU31 ..... 41 E2
Eastlake Hts PO4 ..... 183 E2
Eastlands BH25 ..... 195 D1
Eastleigh Coll SO50 ..... 56 A1
Eastleigh Coll of F Ed SO50 ..... 56 A1
Eastleigh Rd SO50 ..... 57 E1
Eastleigh Sta SO50 ..... 56 A2
Eastleigh Town Mus SO50 ..... 56 A1
Eastman Cl SP5 ..... 47 D3
Eastmeare Ct SO40 ..... 100 B3
Eastney Farm Rd PO4 ..... 183 E2
Eastney Rd PO4 ..... 183 D2
Eastney St PO4 ..... 183 D1
Eastoke Ave PO11 ..... 185 E1
Easton La SO21 ..... 2 C2
Easton Lane Bsns Pk ▣ SO23 .. 11 D4
Eastover Ct ▣ PO9 ..... 135 E3
Eastville Rd SO50 ..... 57 E1
Eastways SO32 ..... 83 E4
Eastwood SO51 ..... 25 E1
Eastwood Ave BH25 ..... 165 F3
Eastwood Cl PO11 ..... 185 D3
Eastwood Rd ▣ PO2 ..... 157 F2
Eastworth Rd BH31 ..... 114 C4
Eaton Rd BH13 ..... 204 A1
Ebden Rd SO23 ..... 11 D4
Ebenezer La BH24 ..... 140 C4
Ebery Gr PO3 ..... 183 E4
Ebor Cl BH22 ..... 165 F1
Ebor Rd BH12 ..... 203 E3
Eccles Rd BH15 ..... 202 B1
Ecton La PO3 ..... 158 B2
Eddystone Rd SO40 ..... 76 B3
Edelvale Rd SO18 ..... 80 A1
Eden Ct ▣ BH1 ..... 205 D2
Eden Gr BH21 ..... 163 E2
Eden Rd SO18 ..... 80 A1
Eden Rise PO16 ..... 155 D2
Eden St ▣ PO1 ..... 182 B3
Eden Terr ▣ PO2 ..... 157 F2
Eden Wlk SO53 ..... 55 D2
Edenbridge Rd PO4 ..... 183 D2

Edgar Cres PO16 ..... 156 B3
Edgar Rd SO23 ..... 10 C3
Edgar Villas SO23 ..... 10 C3
Edgarton Rd BH17 ..... 187 E2
Edgbaston House ▣ PO5 ..... 182 B2
Edgecombe Cres PO13 ..... 180 B4
Edgehill Rd Bournemouth BH9 .. 189 F1
Southampton SO18 ..... 79 F1
Edgell Rd PO10 ..... 137 D2
Edgemoor Rd BH22 ..... 139 D1
Edgerly Gdns PO6 ..... 157 F3
Edgeware Rd PO4 ..... 183 D3
Edgewood Ct GU33 ..... 21 D1
Edifred Rd BH9 ..... 190 A2
Edinburgh Ct SO15 ..... 102 A3
Edinburgh Rd PO1 ..... 182 B3
Edington Cl SO32 ..... 83 D4
Edington Rd SO23 ..... 2 A1
Edmondsham House & Gdn
BH21 ..... 91 D2
Edmondsham Rd BH31 ..... 114 C4
Edmonsham Rd ▣ BH22 ..... 204 C2
Edmund Rd PO4 ..... 182 C2
Edmunds Cl
Barton on Sea BH25 ..... 195 D1
Hedge End SO30 ..... 105 E3
Edneys La PO7 ..... 111 D3
Edward Ave SO50 ..... 56 B2
Edward Cl SO45 ..... 150 C1
Edward Gdns PO9 ..... 135 E1
Edward Gr PO16 ..... 132 C1
Edward Rd
Bournemouth BH11 ..... 189 D2
Christchurch BH23 ..... 207 F4
Hythe SO45 ..... 126 A2
Poole BH14 ..... 203 E3
Southampton SO15 ..... 102 B4
Winchester SO23 ..... 10 C3
Edward's Cl ▣ PO6 ..... 133 D1
Edwards Cl PO8 ..... 111 F2
Edwin Jones Gn SO15 ..... 102 C4
Edwina Cl
North Baddesley SO52 ..... 54 A2
Ringwood BH24 ..... 117 E1
Southampton SO19 ..... 104 A3
Edwina Dr BH17 ..... 187 D1
Edwina House ▣ SO17 ..... 79 F2
Effingham Gdns SO19 ..... 104 B2
Efford Ct SO41 ..... 197 D1
Efford Farm Cotts SO41 ..... 197 D1
Efford Way SO41 ..... 197 D1
Egan Cl PO2 ..... 157 F2
Egbert Rd SO23 ..... 2 A1
Egdon Ct BH16 ..... 201 D4
Egdon Dr BH21 ..... 187 F4
Egerton Gdns BH8 ..... 205 E3
Egerton Rd BH8 ..... 205 E3
Eglantine Cl PO8 ..... 112 A2
Eglantine Wlk PO8 ..... 112 B2
Egmont Cl BH24 ..... 140 B1
Egmont Dr BH24 ..... 140 B1
Egmont Gdns BH24 ..... 140 B1
Egmont Rd BH16 ..... 201 D2
Eight Acres SO51 ..... 53 D4
Eileen Beard House PO9 ..... 136 A3
Elaine Gdns PO8 ..... 112 A3
Elan Cl SO18 ..... 80 A1
Elcombes Cl SO43 ..... 121 F3
Elder Cl Locks Heath SO31 ..... 128 C1
Marchwood SO40 ..... 102 A1
Winchester SO22 ..... 10 B2
Elder Gn SO21 ..... 57 D4
Elder Rd PO9 ..... 136 A2
Elderberry Cl PO8 ..... 88 B2
Elderberry La BH23 ..... 207 F3
Elderberry Way PO8 ..... 112 B2
Elderfield Cl PO10 ..... 137 D2
Elderfield Rd PO9 ..... 135 E4
Eldon Ave BH25 ..... 209 F4
Eldon Cl BH25 ..... 209 F4
Eldon Ct ▣ Poole BH14 ..... 203 D2
▣ Portsmouth PO5 ..... 182 B2
Eldon House ▣ SO14 ..... 103 D2
Eldon Pl BH4 ..... 204 A2
Eldon Rd Bournemouth BH9 .. 189 F1
Braishfield SO20, SO51 ..... 7 D3
King's Somborne SO20 ..... 7 D3
Eldon St PO5 ..... 182 B2
Eldridge Gdns SO51 ..... 52 C4
Eleanor Dr BH11 ..... 188 B3
Electron Way SO53 ..... 55 E3
Elettra Ave PO7 ..... 134 B4
Eleven Cross SP6 ..... 68 A3
Elfin Ct ▣ SO17 ..... 103 D4
Elfin Dr BH22 ..... 165 E4
Elgar Cl Gosport PO12 ..... 181 D1
Portchester PO6 ..... 156 C4
Southampton SO19 ..... 104 B2
Elgar Ct SO41 ..... 197 F2
Elgar Rd Bournemouth BH10 .. 189 E2
Southampton SO19 ..... 104 B2
Elgar Wlk PO7 ..... 134 C3
Elgin Cl Fareham PO15 ..... 130 C1
Hythe SO45 ..... 126 A2
Elgin Rd
Bournemouth BH2, BH4 ..... 204 B3
Cosham PO6 ..... 157 F3
Poole BH14 ..... 203 E1
Southampton SO15 ..... 102 B3
Eling Cl SO22 ..... 1 B2
Eling Hill SO40 ..... 101 D3
Eling Inf Sch SO40 ..... 101 D3
Eling La SO40 ..... 101 D3
Eling Mus SO40 ..... 101 D3
Eling Tide Mill SO40 ..... 101 D3

Eling View SO15 ... 101 E4
Elingfield Ct SO40 ... 101 D4
Eliot House
　[14] New Milton BH25 ... 195 D1
　Southampton SO17 ... 79 E1
Elise Cl BH7 ... 206 A4
Eliza Pl PO12 ... 181 E3
Elizabeth Ave BH23 ... 206 C4
Elizabeth Cl Downton SP5 ... 46 B4
　West End SO30 ... 80 B1
　Wickham PO17 ... 107 F2
Elizabeth Cres SO41 ... 196 A1
Elizabeth Ct
　[12] Bournemouth BH1 ... 205 D2
　[6] Cosham PO6 ... 157 F4
　Eastleigh SO50 ... 56 A2
　Fareham PO14 ... 154 C4
　[6] Gosport PO12 ... 181 D3
　[11] New Milton BH25 ... 195 D1
　Southampton, Aldermoor SO16 ... 78 A2
　Southampton, Portswood SO17 ... 79 E1
　West End SO30 ... 80 B1
Elizabeth Gdns
　Christchurch BH23 ... 208 B4
　Hythe SO45 ... 126 A1
　Portsmouth PO4 ... 182 C1
Elizabeth House SO40 ... 76 B1
Elizabeth Rd Poole BH15 ... 202 B2
　Stubbington PO14 ... 179 E3
　Upton BH16 ... 201 E4
　Waterlooville PO7 ... 134 C3
　Wickham PO17 ... 108 A2
　Wimborne Minster BH21 ... 163 E3
Elizabeth Way
　Bishop's Waltham SO32 ... 83 D4
　Eastleigh SO50 ... 56 A3
Elkhams Cl SO41 ... 196 B1
Elkstone Rd PO6 ... 133 D1
Ellachie Gdns PO12 ... 181 D1
Ellachie Mews PO12 ... 181 D1
Ellachie Rd PO12 ... 181 D1
Elland Cl SO50 ... 57 E1
Elldene Ct SO40 ... 100 C3
Ellen Gdns SO53 ... 55 D3
Ellen Wren House SO18 ... 79 F2
Ellerslie Cl PO14 ... 179 D3
Ellery Gr SO41 ... 197 F3
Ellesfield Dr BH22 ... 165 E1
Ellesmere Orch PO10 ... 137 D3
Ellingham Cross BH24 ... 116 C3
Ellingham Dr BH24 ... 116 B3
Ellingham Dro BH24 ... 117 D3
Ellingham Rd BH25 ... 209 E4
Elliot Cl SO40 ... 100 B4
Elliot Rd BH11 ... 188 C2
Elliot Rise SO30 ... 81 E1
Ellis Rd SO19 ... 104 C3
Ellisfield Rd PO9 ... 135 F2
Ellwood Ave SO19 ... 104 C3
Ellwood Cl SO19 ... 104 C3
Elm Ave Christchurch BH23 ... 191 F1
　Lymington SO41 ... 197 E3
　New Milton BH25 ... 195 D1
Elm Cl SO16 ... 78 C2
Elm Close Est PO11 ... 184 C2
Elm Cotts [8] BH24 ... 141 D4
Elm Cres Hythe SO45 ... 150 A4
　Uphham SO32 ... 58 C3
Elm Ct Chandler's Ford SO53 ... 30 B1
　[4] New Milton BH25 ... 195 D1
　Southampton, Sholing SO19 ... 103 F2
　[29] Southampton, Westwood Pk SO17 ... 79 D1
　Winchester SO22 ... 10 C4
Elm Gdns Bournemouth BH4 ... 204 B3
　West End SO30 ... 80 B2
Elm Gr Eastleigh SO50 ... 55 F1
　Gosport PO12 ... 181 D3
　Portsmouth PO5 ... 182 B2
　South Hayling PO11 ... 185 D2
Elm La PO9 ... 135 F1
Elm Park Rd PO9 ... 135 F1
Elm Rd Bishop's Waltham SO32 ... 83 F4
　Havant PO9 ... 160 A4
　Winchester SO22 ... 10 C4
Elm St Portsmouth PO1 ... 182 A1
　Southampton SO14 ... 103 D2
Elm Terr Liss GU33 ... 20 C3
　Southampton SO14 ... 103 D2
Elm Tree Wlk BH22 ... 189 F4
Elmdale GU31 ... 41 D2
Elmdale Cl SO31 ... 152 B4
Elmdale Gr SO51 ... 51 D1
Elmers Way BH23 ... 169 D1
Elmes Dr SO15 ... 101 F4
Elmes Rd BH9 ... 189 F1
Elmeswelle Rd PO8 ... 112 A3
Elmfield Cl SP5 ... 47 E3
Elmfield La SO45 ... 178 C4
Elmgate Dr BH7 ... 206 A4
Elmhurst Rd
　Bournemouth BH11 ... 189 D3
　Fareham PO16 ... 155 D4
　Gosport PO12 ... 181 E2
　West Moors BH22 ... 138 C1
Elmhurst Way BH22 ... 138 C1
Elmleigh Rd PO9 ... 135 F1
Elmore Ave PO13 ... 180 A3
Elmore Cl PO13 ... 179 F1
Elmore Dr BH24 ... 139 F3
Elmore Rd PO13 ... 179 F1
Elmrise Prim Sch BH11 ... 189 D2
Elms Ave BH14 ... 204 C3
Elms Cl Fordingbridge SP6 ... 69 D1
　Poole BH14 ... 203 D1

Elms Rd PO16 ... 155 D4
Elms Way BH6 ... 206 C2
Elmsdown Ct BH24 ... 140 C4
Elmsleigh Ct SO17 ... 79 D2
Elmsleigh Gdns SO16 ... 79 D2
Elmslie Gdns SO31 ... 104 C1
Elmstead Rd BH13 ... 214 C4
Elmtree Cl SO40 ... 100 A1
Elmtree Gdns [2] Eastleigh SO50 ... 56 A1
　Romsey SO51 ... 53 E3
Elmtree Rd PO6 ... 158 C4
Elmwood Ave Fordingbridge SP6 ... 69 E1
　Waterlooville PO7 ... 134 C3
Elmwood Cl SO19 ... 78 A1
Elmwood Lodge [2] PO16 ... 131 D1
Elmwood Rd PO12 ... 157 F2
Elmwood Way BH23 ... 209 D4
Elphinstone Rd
　Christchurch BH23 ... 194 A1
　Portsmouth PO5 ... 182 B1
Elsfred Rd PO14 ... 179 D3
Elson Inf Sch PO12 ... 181 D4
Elson Jun Sch PO12 ... 181 D4
Elson La PO12 ... 181 D4
Elson Rd PO12 ... 181 D4
Elstead Gdns PO7 ... 134 B2
Elstree Rd SO19 ... 103 F3
Eltham Cl BH7 ... 206 A4
Elvin Cl SO41 ... 195 F2
Elwell Gn PO11 ... 184 C2
Elwyn Rd BH1 ... 205 E3
Ely Ct PO13 ... 180 B3
Elysium Ct BH22 ... 165 F2
Emanuel St PO2 ... 182 B4
Embankment Way BH24 ... 141 D3
Embassy Ct [3] PO4 ... 182 C2
Emberley Cl BH22 ... 166 A3
Embley Cl SO40 ... 76 B1
Embley La SO51 ... 51 F4
Embley Park Ind Est SO51 ... 51 F4
Embley Park Jun Sch SO51 ... 52 C4
Embley Park Sch SO51 ... 51 F3
Embsay Rd SO31 ... 128 B4
Emer Cl SO52 ... 54 A3
Emerald Ct Southampton SO19 ... 104 A3
　Waterlooville PO7 ... 135 D4
Emerson Cl BH15 ... 202 B1
Emerson Rd BH15 ... 202 B1
Emily Cl BH23 ... 192 A1
Emmanuel Cl PO14 ... 129 E1
Emmanuel Mid Sch BH31 ... 114 C3
Emmett Rd SO16 ... 77 F3
Emmons Cl SO31 ... 128 A1
Empire Ct [12] PO9 ... 135 F1
Empress Pk SO14 ... 103 D4
Empress Rd
　Lyndhurst SO43 ... 121 F3
　Southampton, Bevois Valley SO14 ... 103 D4
　Southampton, Old Docks SO14 ... 103 D1
Empshott Rd PO4 ... 182 C2
Empson Wlk PO13 ... 179 F2
Emsbrook Dr PO10 ... 136 C1
Emsworth Common Rd PO10 ... 136 C3
Emsworth House Cl PO10 ... 136 C1
Emsworth Prim Sch PO10 ... 136 C1
Emsworth Rd Havant PO9 ... 136 A1
　Lymington SO41 ... 197 F2
　Portsmouth PO2 ... 157 F1
　Southampton SO15 ... 102 A4
　Thorney Island PO10 ... 161 D1
Emsworth Sta PO10 ... 136 C1
Encombe Cl BH12 ... 203 F4
Endeavour Cl [17] SO15 ... 102 A4
Endeavour Rd PO12 ... 181 E2
Endeavour Way SO45 ... 126 A3
Enderleigh House PO9 ... 135 F1
Enderwood Cl SO40 ... 100 A4
Endfield Cl BH23 ... 191 F1
Endfield Rd Bournemouth BH9 ... 190 A1
　Christchurch BH23 ... 191 F1
Endle St SO14 ... 103 D2
Endofield Cl PO14 ... 154 C3
Enfield Cres BH15 ... 202 C3
Enfield Gr SO19 ... 103 F2
Enfield Rd BH15 ... 202 C3
Englands Way BH11 ... 188 B2
Englefield Rd SO18 ... 103 E4
English Cl [18] SO51 ... 52 C4
English Rd SO15 ... 102 A4
Enmill La SO22 ... 9 F3
Ennel Copse SO52 ... 54 A2
Ennerdale Cl PO8 ... 88 B1
Ennerdale Gdns SO18 ... 80 A1
Ennerdale Rd
　Southampton SO16 ... 77 F1
　Stubbington SO14 ... 154 B2
Ensbury Ave BH10 ... 189 E1
Ensbury Cl BH10 ... 189 E1
Ensbury Cl BH10 ... 189 E1
Ensbury Park Rd BH9 ... 189 F1
Ensign Dr PO13 ... 180 B3
Ensign Park SO31 ... 127 F1
Enterprise Cl SO31 ... 128 C1
Enterprise Ctr Fareham PO14 ... 155 D3
　Portsmouth PO3 ... 158 A2
Enterprise Ind Est PO8 ... 112 B4
Enterprise Rd Chilworth SO16 ... 54 B1
　Horndean PO8 ... 112 B4
Enterprise Way SO14 ... 103 D1
Eperston Rd PO8 ... 112 A3
Epiphany CE Prim Sch BH9 ... 190 A2
Epping Cl SO18 ... 80 A1
Epsom Cl SO50 ... 81 E4
Epsom Ct PO15 ... 129 E4
Epworth Rd PO2 ... 157 F1
Erasmus Pk SO23 ... 2 B1
Eric Rd PO14 ... 179 E3

Erica Cl Locks Heath SO31 ... 128 C2
　Waterlooville PO8 ... 112 A2
Erica Dr PO21 ... 186 B3
Erica Way PO8 ... 112 A2
Ericksen Rd BH11 ... 189 E2
Erinbank Mansions BH1 ... 205 E2
Ernest Cl PO10 ... 136 C1
Ernest Rd Havant PO9 ... 135 E2
　Portsmouth PO1 ... 182 C4
Erpingham Rd BH12 ... 204 A3
Erskine Ct SO16 ... 77 F3
Erskine Rd SO22 ... 10 C4
Escombe Rd SO50 ... 56 B2
Escur Cl PO2 ... 157 F2
Esdaile Ct BH24 ... 142 C2
Esher Gr PO7 ... 111 E1
Eskdale Cl PO8 ... 88 B1
Eskdale House [16] PO6 ... 133 D1
Esmond Cl PO13 ... 179 F1
Esmonde Cl PO13 ... 179 F1
Esmonde Way BH17 ... 202 C4
Esplanade Poole BH13 ... 214 C4
　Portsmouth PO4 ... 183 D1
Esplanade Gdns PO4 ... 183 E1
Esplanade The PO12 ... 181 F2
Essex Ave BH23 ... 191 F1
Essex Gr SO53 ... 55 E1
Essex Rd PO4 ... 183 D2
Esslemont Rd PO4 ... 182 C2
Estella Rd PO2 ... 182 B4
Estridge Cl SO31 ... 105 D1
Ethel Rd PO1 ... 182 C3
Ethelbert Rd BH21 ... 163 E2
Ethelburt Ave SO16 ... 79 E3
Ethelred Gdns SO40 ... 100 B3
Eton Gdns BH4 ... 204 B2
Eton Rd PO5 ... 182 C2
Ettrick Rd BH13 ... 204 A1
Eucalyptus Ave BH24 ... 140 A1
European Way SO14 ... 103 D1
Euryalus Rd PO14 ... 155 D3
Euston Gr PO14 ... 141 D3
Euston Rd PO4 ... 183 D3
Eva Allaway Ct [26] PO1 ... 182 A3
Evans Cl Bournemouth BH11 ... 188 C1
　Portsmouth PO2 ... 157 D1
　St Leonards BH24 ... 139 F3
Evans Rd PO4 ... 183 D2
Evans St SO14 ... 103 D2
Evelegh Rd PO6 ... 158 B4
Evelyn Cl SO32 ... 83 F2
Evelyn Cres SO15 ... 102 B4
Evelyn Rd BH9 ... 190 A1
Evening Glade BH22 ... 165 F2
Evenlode Rd SO16 ... 77 F1
Eventide Homes BH8 ... 190 C1
Everdon La PO3 ... 158 B2
Everest Rd BH23 ... 207 F4
Everglades Ave PO8 ... 111 F2
Everglades Cl BH22 ... 165 E4
Evergreen Cl Marchwood SO40 ... 101 F1
　Three Legged Cross BH21 ... 114 B4
　Waterlooville PO7 ... 134 B4
Evergreens St Leonards BH24 ... 139 F3
　Totton SO40 ... 101 D3
Evering Ave BH12 ... 188 B1
Evering Gdns BH12 ... 188 B1
Everlea Cl SO41 ... 196 B1
Eversfield Gdns BH25 ... 195 D1
Evershot Rd BH8 ... 190 C1
Eversleigh BH2 ... 204 B1
Eversley Cres PO9 ... 135 F2
Eversley Pl SO22 ... 10 B3
Everton Rd SO41 ... 196 A1
Evesham Cl Bournemouth BH7 ... 206 A4
　Southampton SO16 ... 79 D3
Evesham Ct BH13 ... 204 A1
Ewart Cl SO45 ... 126 A3
Ewart Rd PO1 ... 182 C4
Ewell Way SO40 ... 76 B1
Ewhurst Cl PO9 ... 135 E2
Exbourne Manor BH1 ... 205 E2
Exbury Cl SO50 ... 56 C1
Exbury Dr BH11 ... 188 C3
Exbury Gdns SO45 ... 177 D3
Exbury Rd Blackfield SO45 ... 150 C1
　Havant PO9 ... 136 A3
Excellent Rd PO14 ... 154 C3
Excelsior Rd BH14 ... 203 E2
Exchange Rd PO1 ... 182 A3
Exeter Cl Eastleigh SO50 ... 55 F3
　Emsworth PO10 ... 136 C1
　Locks Heath SO31 ... 128 C2
　Southampton SO18 ... 80 A1
Exeter Cres BH2 ... 204 C1
Exeter Ct
　[10] Christchurch BH23 ... 209 D4
　Gosport PO13 ... 180 B3
Exeter La BH2 ... 204 C1
Exeter Park Mansions BH2 ... 204 C1
Exeter Park Rd BH2 ... 204 C1
Exeter Rd Bournemouth BH2 ... 204 C2
　Portsmouth PO4 ... 182 C1
　Southampton SO18 ... 104 A4
Exford Ave SO18 ... 104 B4
Exford Dr SO18 ... 104 B4
Exleigh Cl SO18 ... 104 A3
Exmoor Cl Swanwick PO15 ... 129 D4
　Totton SO40 ... 100 A4
Exmoor Rd SO14 ... 103 D3
Exmouth Gdns SO50 ... 81 E4
Exmouth Rd Gosport PO12 ... 181 D4
　Portsmouth PO5 ... 182 B1
Exmouth St SO14 ... 103 D3
Exton Gdns PO16 ... 132 B1
Exton Rd Bournemouth BH6 ... 206 B3
　Havant PO9 ... 136 A3
Eyebright Cl SO50 ... 81 E4

Eyeworth Wlk SO45 ... 125 E2
Eynham Ave SO19 ... 104 B3
Eynham Cl SO19 ... 104 B3
Eynon Mews BH24 ... 140 C3
Eyre Cl SO40 ... 100 B3

F Ave SO45 ... 150 C3
Faber Cl PO9 ... 136 A2
Faber Mews SO50 ... 53 D4
Fabers Yd [9] SO22 ... 10 C4
Fabian Cl PO7 ... 135 D4
Factory Rd Eastleigh SO50 ... 56 A1
　Hamworthy BH16 ... 201 E3
　Upton BH16 ... 201 E3
Fair Field SO51 ... 28 A1
Fair Gr PO7 ... 104 A3
Fair Isle PO14 ... 154 A2
Fair Lea BH2 ... 204 C1
Fair Oak Cl [4] Fair Oak SO50 ... 57 E1
　Gosport PO12 ... 180 B2
Fair Oak Cty Jun Sch SO50 ... 57 E1
Fair Oak Dr PO7 ... 135 F2
Fair Oak Inf Sch SO50 ... 57 E1
Faircre Rise PO14 ... 154 A4
Faircre Wlk PO14 ... 154 A4
Fairbourne Cl PO8 ... 111 F1
Fairclose Dr SO22 ... 1 A3
Faircourt [18] PO14 ... 154 C4
Faircross Cl SO45 ... 150 B2
Fairdown Ct SO23 ... 11 E4
Fairfax Cl SO22 ... 10 A3
Fairfax Ct SO19 ... 104 C3
Fairfax Mews SO19 ... 104 C3
Fairfield BH23 ... 207 D4
Fairfield Ave PO14 ... 154 C4
Fairfield Cl Christchurch BH23 ... 207 D4
　Hythe SO45 ... 125 F2
　Lymington SO41 ... 197 F2
　Wimborne Minster BH21 ... 163 F3
Fairfield Inf Sch PO9 ... 136 A1
Fairfield Rd
　Barton on Sea BH25 ... 209 F4
　Compton(Hants) SO21 ... 31 E3
　Havant PO9 ... 135 F1
　Wimborne Minster BH21 ... 163 E2
　Winchester SO21, SO22 ... 1 C1
Fairfield Sq PO6 ... 157 F4
Fairgate Ctr The SP6 ... 70 A2
Fairhavon Ct [12] BH5 ... 205 F2
Fairhome Cl PO12 ... 181 D4
Fairisle Inf Sch SO16 ... 77 F2
Fairisle Jun Sch SO16 ... 77 F2
Fairisle Rd SO16 ... 77 F2
Fairlands Montessori Sch SO32 ... 107 F4
Fairlawn Cl SO16 ... 77 F3
Fairlawn House [19] SO22 ... 10 C4
Fairlea Grange SO16 ... 78 C2
Fairlea Rd Emsworth PO10 ... 136 C2
　Lymington SO41 ... 197 F3
Fairlead Dr PO13 ... 180 B3
Fairlie BH2 ... 117 E1
Fairlie Cl SO30 ... 81 E2
Fairlie Pk BH24 ... 117 D1
Fairlight La SO41 ... 195 E4
Fairlight Lodge SO22 ... 10 B4
Fairmead Ct PO11 ... 184 C2
Fairmead Way SO40 ... 100 C3
Fairmead Wlk PO8 ... 112 A2
Fairmile Par BH23 ... 191 F1
Fairmile Rd BH23 ... 191 F1
Fairoak Rd Bishopstoke SO50 ... 57 D1
　Fair Oak SO50 ... 57 D1
Fairthorn Ct [2] BH2 ... 204 C2
Fairthorne Gdns PO12 ... 181 D2
Fairview Cl Hythe SO45 ... 126 A2
　Romsey SO51 ... 28 A1
Fairview Cres BH18 ... 187 D3
Fairview Ct PO12 ... 180 C2
Fairview Dr Broadstone BH18 ... 187 D3
　Hythe SO45 ... 126 A2
　Romsey SO51 ... 28 A1
Fairview Par SO45 ... 126 A1
Fairview Pk BH14 ... 203 E2
Fairview Rd BH18 ... 187 D3
Fairwater Cl PO13 ... 155 D4
Fairway Ave BH14 ... 214 B4
Fairway Bsns Ctr PO3 ... 158 B1
Fairway Dr BH23 ... 206 C3
Fairway Gdns SO16 ... 77 F3
Fairway Rd SO45 ... 125 F2
Fairway The
　Barton on Sea BH25 ... 210 A4
　Gosport PO13 ... 155 E1
　Portchester PO16 ... 156 B4
　Rowland's Castle PO9 ... 113 E1
Fairways ... 165 F3
Fairwinds BH13 ... 214 A2
Fairwood Rd BH31 ... 115 E3
Fairy Cross Way PO8 ... 112 A1
Falaise Rd SO16 ... 78 B2
Falcon Cl PO16 ... 155 F4
Falcon Dr BH23 ... 208 A3
Falcon Fields SO45 ... 151 D2
Falcon Gr PO3 ... 158 C4
Falcon Sq SO50 ... 55 F1
Falcon View SO22 ... 10 B2
Falcon Way SO32 ... 81 F1
Falconer Ct SO45 ... 150 B3
Falconer Dr BH15 ... 201 F2
Falkland Ct SO53 ... 55 E2
Falkland Rd
　Chandler's Ford SO53 ... 55 E2
　Southampton SO15 ... 102 A4
Falkland Sq [2] BH15 ... 202 B1
Falklands Cl PO13 ... 179 F2
Falklands Rd [1] PO2 ... 157 F2
Fallow Field SO22 ... 10 B2
Fallow Rd PO15

Fallows The BH25 ... 195 D3
Falstaff Way SO40 ... 100 C3
Fancy Rd BH12 ... 203 D4
Fanshawe St SO14 ... 103 D3
Far Ends [13] BH14 ... 203 D2
Far Meadow Way PO10 ... 160 A4
Farcroft BH12 ... 203 D3
Fareham Coll PO14 ... 130 C1
Fareham House [38] PO1 ... 182 B3
Fareham Hts PO16 ... 131 E2
Fareham Ind Pk PO16 ... 131 E2
Fareham Park CE Jun Sch PO15 ... 130 B2
Fareham Park Inf Sch PO15 ... 130 B2
Fareham Park Rd PO15 ... 130 B2
Fareham Rd Gosport PO13 ... 155 E2
　Southwick PO17 ... 132 C3
　Wickham PO17 ... 108 A2
Fareham Sta PO15 ... 130 C1
Faringdon Ct [16] SO23 ... 2 C1
Faringdon Rd SO18 ... 104 B4
Farleigh Cl PO9 ... 135 F2
Farley Cl Fair Oak SO50 ... 57 E1
　Winchester SO22 ... 10 A2
Farley Ct SO15 ... 78 B1
Farley La SO51 ... 7 F1
Farley Mount Ctry Pk SO21 ... 8 A4
Farley Mount Rd SO21 ... 9 D2
Farlington Ave PO6 ... 134 B1
Farlington Marshes (Nature Reserve) ... 158 C3
Farlington Rd PO2 ... 157 F1
Farm Cl Hamble-le-Rice SO31 ... 128 A4
　Ringwood BH24 ... 141 D4
Farm Edge Rd PO14 ... 179 E3
Farm La Christchurch BH23 ... 208 A3
　Southbourne PO18 ... 161 F4
Farm La (N) BH25 ... 210 A3
Farm La S BH25 ... 210 A4
Farm Rd Titchfield PO15 ... 129 F1
　West Moors BH22 ... 138 B1
Farm View PO10 ... 136 C2
Farm View Ave PO8 ... 88 A3
Farmdene Cl BH23 ... 208 B4
Farmers Wlk Hordle SO41 ... 211 E4
　[1] Wimborne Minster BH21 ... 163 D3
Farmery Ct SO18 ... 79 E2
Farmhouse Way PO8 ... 112 A3
Farmlea Rd PO6 ... 157 D4
Farmside Gdns PO3 ... 157 F2
Farnham Rd Liss GU33 ... 20 C2
　Poole BH12 ... 204 A4
　Steep GU32 ... 41 D4
Farnleys Mead SO41 ... 197 F1
Faroes Ct PO14 ... 154 A2
Farrier Way PO16 ... 155 D3
Farriers Cl BH21 ... 164 A3
Farriers Way PO7 ... 112 B1
Farriers Wlk PO12 ... 181 E3
Farringdon Rd PO9 ... 136 A2
Farringford Rd SO19 ... 104 B3
Farrington BH4 ... 204 B1
Farthing La PO1 ... 182 A2
Farthings Gate PO7 ... 134 C2
Farwell Cl BH23 ... 192 B2
Farwell Rd BH12 ... 188 B1
Fastnet Cl SO16 ... 77 F3
Fastnet House [13] PO5 ... 182 B1
Fastnet Way PO14 ... 154 A2
Fathersfield SO42 ... 145 F1
Fathoms Reach PO11 ... 184 C2
Faulston Cotts SP5 ... 22 B4
Faversham BH2 ... 204 B1
Fawcett Rd
　Barton on Sea BH25 ... 194 C1
　Portsmouth PO4 ... 182 C2
Fawley Bsns Ctr SO45 ... 151 D2
Fawley By Pass SO45 ... 151 D2
Fawley Ct [48] PO9 ... 136 A3
Fawley Gr BH8 ... 190 B2
Fawley Inf Sch SO45 ... 151 D2
Fawley La Froxfield GU34 ... 17 D2
　Owslebury SO21 ... 33 D4
Fawley Rd Fawley SO45 ... 150 C2
　Hythe SO45 ... 150 A4
　Portsmouth PO2 ... 157 F2
　Southampton SO15 ... 102 A3
Fawn Gdns BH25 ... 194 C2
Fay Cl PO14 ... 179 E3
Fayre La PO16 ... 155 D4
Fayrewood Ct BH31 ... 114 C4
Fearon Rd PO2 ... 157 F1
Felix Rd PO12 ... 181 D4
Fell Cl SO31 ... 129 D2
Fell Dr PO13 ... 179 F2
Felmer Dr SO23 ... 2 B4
Feltham Cl SO51 ... 53 E4
Felton Cres BH23 ... 208 C4
Felton Ct BH14 ... 202 C3
Felton Rd BH14 ... 202 C3
Feltons Pl PO3 ... 157 F3
Fen Ave PO16 ... 155 D4
Fenleigh Cl BH25 ... 195 D1
Fennel Gdns SO41 ... 197 F3
Fennell Cl PO7 ... 111 E1
Fenton Rd BH6 ... 206 B3
Fenwick Ct BH4 ... 205 D3
Fern Cl Alderholt SP6 ... 93 D3
　Burton BH23 ... 192 B1
　Petersfield GU31 ... 41 E2
Fern Cotts [2] PO16 ... 131 E1
Fern Ct SO18 ... 103 F4
Fern Hill Hythe SO45 ... 125 F2
　Southampton SO19 ... 103 F1
Fern Way PO15 ... 129 E2

Ferncroft Cl PO14 ...... 179 E3
Ferncroft Gdns BH10 ...... 189 E3
Ferncroft Rd BH10 ...... 189 E3
Ferndale Hedge End SO30 ...... 105 E3
  Waterlooville PO7 ...... 135 D4
Ferndale Mews PO13 ...... 155 D2
Ferndale Rd Marchwood SO40 .. 101 F1
  New Milton BH25 ...... 195 D3
Ferndene Way SO18 ...... 103 F4
Ferndown Ct SP6 ...... 69 E1
Ferndown Fst Sch BH22 ...... 165 E3
Ferndown Ind Est BH21 ...... 164 C4
Ferndown Mid Sch BH22 ...... 165 E3
Ferndown Upper Sch BH22 .. 165 D3
Ferneham Rd PO15 ...... 130 B1
Fernglade BH25 ...... 195 D2
Fernheath Cl BH9 ...... 189 D2
Fernheath Rd BH11 ...... 189 D2
Fernhill SO53 ...... 55 F3
Fernhill Cl BH17 ...... 188 A1
Fernhill Flats BH2 ...... 204 C2
Fernhill Gate BH25 ...... 195 D3
Fernhill La BH25 ...... 195 D2
Fernhill Rd BH25 ...... 195 D2
Fernhills Rd SO45 ...... 126 A1
Fernhurst Cl PO11 ...... 184 B2
Fernhurst Jun Sch PO4 ...... 182 C2
Fernhurst Rd PO4 ...... 182 C2
Fernie Cl PO14 ...... 179 D3
Fernlea Ave BH22 ...... 165 E2
Fernlea Cl Ferndown BH22 .. 165 E2
  St Leonards BH24 ...... 139 F2
Fernlea Gdns Ferndown BH22 .. 165 E2
  Southampton SO16 ...... 78 C2
Fernlea Way SO45 ...... 125 E2
Fernside Ave BH14 ...... 202 C2
Fernside Cl Holbury SO45 ...... 150 B2
  Southampton SO16 ...... 101 F4
Fernside Ct BH15 ...... 202 C2
Fernside Rd Bournemouth BH9 .. 204 C4
  Poole BH15 ...... 202 C2
  West Moors BH22 ...... 138 C1
Fernside Way SO50 ...... 57 F1
Fernside Wlk SO50 ...... 57 F1
Fernway Cl BH21 ...... 164 A2
Fernwood Cl BH24 ...... 140 A3
Fernwood Cres SO18 ...... 103 F4
Ferny Crofts (Scout Ctr) SO42 ...... 148 A4
Fernyhurst Ave SO16 ...... 77 F3
Ferris Ave BH8 ...... 190 B1
Ferris Cl BH8 ...... 190 B1
Ferris Pl BH8 ...... 190 B1
Ferrol Rd PO12 ...... 181 E3
Ferry Rd Bournemouth BH6 .. 206 C2
  Hamworthy BH15 ...... 202 A1
  Hythe SO45 ...... 125 F2
  Poole BH19 ...... 214 A1
  Portsmouth PO4 ...... 183 E2
  Portsmouth PO4 ...... 183 E2
  South Hayling PO11 ...... 184 A2
Ferry Way BH13 ...... 214 A2
Ferrybridge Gr SO30 ...... 105 E3
Ferrymans Quay SO31 ...... 127 D3
Festing Gr PO4 ...... 183 D1
Festing Rd PO4 ...... 182 C1
Feversham Ave BH8 ...... 190 C1
Fey Rd PO12 ...... 181 E3
Fibbards Rd SO42 ...... 145 F1
Field Cl Compton(Hants) SO21 .. 31 E3
  Gosport PO13 ...... 155 D3
  Locks Heath SO31 ...... 129 D1
  Romsey SO51 ...... 53 D4
  Southampton SO16 ...... 79 E3
Field End SO23 ...... 2 B4
Field Pl BH25 ...... 209 E4
Field View SO52 ...... 54 C3
Field Way Christchurch BH23 .. 193 E1
  Compton(Hants) SO21 ...... 31 E3
  Corfe Mullen BH21 ...... 186 C4
  Denmead PO7 ...... 110 C2
  Fordingbridge SP6 ...... 70 B1
Field Wlk SO41 ...... 197 E3
Fielden Cl SO52 ...... 53 F2
Fielders Ct PO7 ...... 134 B2
Fielders' Way SO51 ...... 51 D1
Fieldfare Cl PO8 ...... 88 B2
Fieldfare Ct SO40 ...... 100 B4
Fieldhouse Dr PO13 ...... 179 F2
Fieldmore Rd PO12 ...... 181 D4
Fields Cl SO45 ...... 150 C1
Fields The BH31 ...... 114 C4
Fieldway BH24 ...... 141 D4
Fifth Ave Cosham PO6 ...... 157 F4
  Havant PO9 ...... 136 A1
Fifth St PO1 ...... 182 C3
Filmer Cl PO13 ...... 180 B4
Filmorehill La GU34 ...... 17 D2
Filton Cl SO40 ...... 76 B1
Filton Rd SO41 ...... 197 E2
Finch House PO4 ...... 183 D1
Finch Rd PO4 ...... 183 E2
Finch's La SO21 ...... 31 F3
Finchdean Rd Havant PO9 ...... 135 E2
  Rowland's Castle PO9 ...... 113 E2
Finches The SO17 ...... 79 D1
Finchfield Ave BH11 ...... 188 C3
Finchmead La GU32 ...... 40 A2
Finchwood Farm Ind Units PO11 ...... 160 A1
Findon Rd PO12 ...... 181 D4
Fineshade BH13 ...... 214 C4
Finisterre Cl PO14 ...... 154 A2
Finlay Cl SO19 ...... 104 B2
Fiona Cl SO23 ...... 11 E4
Fir Ave BH25 ...... 195 D1
Fir Cl Lyndhurst SO43 ...... 121 F2
  West Moors BH22 ...... 138 C2

Fir Copse Rd PO7 ...... 134 B2
Fir Croft Dr SO53 ...... 55 E3
Fir Rd SO40 ...... 100 A1
Fir Tree Cl Fair Oak SO50 ...... 81 E4
  St Leonards BH24 ...... 139 E1
Fir Tree Ct SO18 ...... 104 A4
Fir Tree Gdns PO8 ...... 112 B3
Fir Tree Gr SO45 ...... 150 A4
Fir Tree Hill SP6 ...... 93 D3
Fir Tree La BH23 ...... 193 E1
Fir Tree Rd Cadnam SO40 ...... 99 D4
  South Hayling PO11 ...... 185 D2
Fir Vale Rd BH1 ...... 204 C2
Firbank Rd BH9 ...... 205 D4
Firecrest Cl SO16 ...... 78 A3
Firgrove Cl SO52 ...... 53 F2
Firgrove Cres PO3 ...... 157 F3
Firgrove Ct SO15 ...... 102 B4
Firgrove La PO17 ...... 108 C1
Firgrove Rd
  North Baddesley SO52 ...... 54 A3
  Southampton SO15 ...... 102 B4
Firlands Rise PO9 ...... 135 D1
Firmain Rd BH12 ...... 188 B1
Firmount Cl SO41 ...... 196 C1
Firs Ave PO8 ...... 111 F1
Firs Cres SO23 ...... 2 A4
Firs Dr SO30 ...... 105 D3
Firs Glen Rd
  Bournemouth BH9 ...... 204 C4
  Verwood BH31 ...... 115 D2
  West Moors BH22 ...... 138 C1
Firs La BH14 ...... 214 A4
Firs The Bournemouth BH1, ... 205 D2
  Chandler's Ford SO53 ...... 55 E2
  Gosport PO13 ...... 155 E1
  Southampton SO16 ...... 78 C2
Firshill BH23 ...... 208 C4
Firside Rd BH21 ...... 186 B2
First Ave Cosham PO6 ...... 157 F4
  Cosham, Farlington PO6 ...... 158 C4
  Havant PO9 ...... 136 A1
  Horndean PO8 ...... 88 B2
  Southampton SO15 ...... 101 E4
  Southbourne PO10 ...... 161 E4
First Marine Ave BH25 ...... 209 F4
First St SO45 ...... 150 C4
Firsway BH16 ...... 201 E4
Firtree Cres SO41 ...... 195 F2
Firtree La SO50 ...... 81 D4
Firtree Way SO19 ...... 104 A3
Firwood Pk (Cvn Pk) SO53 .. 55 E4
Fisgard Rd PO12 ...... 181 D4
Fisher Cl PO14 ...... 154 A2
Fisher Rd Gosport PO13 ...... 155 E2
  Portsmouth PO1 ...... 182 A2
Fisher's Rd SO40 ...... 101 D3
Fisherman's Ave BH5,BH6 ...... 206 A2
Fishermans Rd BH15 ...... 202 B1
Fishermans The PO10 ...... 161 E4
Fishermans Wlk PO11 ...... 185 F1
Fishers Gr PO6 ...... 158 C4
Fishers Hill PO15 ...... 130 A1
Fishery La PO11 ...... 185 E1
Fishlake Meadows SO51 ...... 28 A1
Fitzgerald Cl PO15 ...... 129 E4
Fitzharris Ave BH9 ...... 205 D4
Fitzherbert Rd PO6 ...... 158 B4
Fitzherbert Spur PO6 ...... 158 C4
Fitzherbert St PO1 ...... 182 B3
Fitzhugh House SO15 ...... 102 C3
Fitzhugh Pl SO15 ...... 102 C3
Fitzhugh St SO15 ...... 102 C3
Fitzmaurice Rd BH23 ...... 206 C4
Fitzpain Cl BH22 ...... 165 E1
Fitzpain Rd BH22 ...... 165 E1
Fitzpatrick Ct PO6 ...... 133 E1
Fitzroy Cl SO16 ...... 78 C4
Fitzroy Wlk PO1 ...... 182 B3
Fitzwilliam Ave PO14 ...... 179 D3
Fitzwilliam Cl BH11 ...... 188 C3
Fitzworth Ave BH16 ...... 201 E2
Fitzwygram Cres PO9 ...... 135 F2
Five Bridges Rd SO22 ...... 10 C2
Five Elms Dr SO51 ...... 53 E3
Five Heads Rd PO8 ...... 112 B4
Five Post La PO12 ...... 181 D3
Fivefields Cl SO23 ...... 11 E4
Fivefields Rd SO23 ...... 11 E4
Flag Staff Gn PO12 ...... 181 E3
Flag Wlk PO8 ...... 111 F2
Flaghead BH13 ...... 214 B4
Flaghead Chine Rd BH13 ...... 214 C3
Flaghead Rd BH13 ...... 214 C4
Flambard Ave BH23 ...... 192 A1
Flambard Rd BH14 ...... 203 E2
Flamborough Cl SO16 ...... 77 E2
Flamingo Ct PO16 ...... 155 F4
Flamston St SP5 ...... 22 A4
Flanders House PO14 ...... 154 C4
Flanders Ind Pk SO30 ...... 105 D4
Flanders Rd SO30 ...... 105 D4
Flathouse Rd PO1 ...... 182 B4
Flaxfields End SP6 ...... 69 F1
Fleet Cl PO13 ...... 155 E1
Fleet End Bottom SO31 ...... 152 C4
Fleet End Rd SO31 ...... 152 C4
Fleet Terr SO50 ...... 31 D1
Fleet's Cnr BH17 ...... 202 A4
Fleetend Cl PO9 ...... 135 F3
Fleets Est BH15 ...... 202 A3
Fleets La BH15 ...... 202 B3
Fleetsbridge Bsns Ctr BH17 .. 202 A4
Fleetsbridge Ret Pk BH17 .. 202 A3
Fleetwood Cl BH15 ...... 202 B4
Fleming Ave SO52 ...... 54 A4
Fleming Cl PO14 ...... 129 E2

Fleming Ct
  North Baddesley SO52 ...... 54 A2
  Southampton SO19 ...... 103 E1
Fleming Pl
  Colden Common SO21 ...... 31 F1
  Romsey SO51 ...... 52 C4
Fleming Rd SO17 ...... 79 E2
Fletcher Cl BH10 ...... 189 E2
Fletcher Rd BH10 ...... 189 E2
Fletchwood La SO40 ...... 99 F1
Fletchwood Rd SO40 ...... 100 A3
Fleuret Cl SO45 ...... 126 A1
Flexford Cl BH23 ...... 30 A1
Flexford Gdns PO9 ...... 136 A2
Flexford La SO41 ...... 196 B3
Flinders Ct PO4 ...... 183 D1
Flint Cl SO19 ...... 104 C2
Flint St PO5 ...... 182 A2
Floating Bridge Rd SO14 .. 103 E2
Floral Farm BH21 ...... 164 A1
Florence Cl SO51 ...... 51 D1
Florence Ct SO18 ...... 103 F4
Florence Rd Bournemouth BH5 . 205 F2
  Poole BH14 ...... 203 E2
  Portsmouth PO5 ...... 182 B1
  Southampton SO19 ...... 103 E1
Florentine Way PO7 ...... 135 D4
Florin Mall BH7 ...... 205 F2
Florins The Locks Heath PO14 . 129 D1
  Waterlooville PO7 ...... 134 C2
Floriston Gdns BH25 ...... 195 E2
Flower Bldgs PO13 ...... 179 F1
Flower La PO17 ...... 163 E2
Flowerdown Cl SO40 ...... 100 B4
Flowerdown House SO22 ...... 1 B2
Flowers Cl SO31 ...... 127 F2
Flowers La SO51 ...... 50 B3
Flum' E Rd SO45 ...... 151 E2
Flushards SO41 ...... 197 F2
Flying Bull Cl PO2 ...... 182 B4
Flying Bull Inf Sch PO2 ...... 182 B4
Flying Bull Jun Sch PO2 ...... 182 B4
Foldsgate Cl SO43 ...... 121 F3
Folkestone Rd PO3 ...... 183 D4
Folly Farm La BH24 ...... 140 B3
Folly Field SO32 ...... 83 E4
Folly La GU32 ...... 40 C2
Font Cl PO14 ...... 129 E2
Fontley Rd PO15 ...... 130 A3
Fontmell Rd BH18 ...... 187 E2
Fontwell Cl SO40 ...... 76 B1
Fontwell Gdns SO50 ...... 81 E4
Fontwell Mews PO7 ...... 112 A1
Fontwell Rd PO5 ...... 182 B1
Foord Rd SO30 ...... 105 D2
Football Gr SO43 ...... 98 B2
Footner Cl SO51 ...... 28 B1
Footners La BH23 ...... 192 B1
Forbes Cl SO16 ...... 77 F3
Forbes Rd SO23 ...... 2 A4
Forbury Rd PO1 ...... 182 B2
Ford Ave SO53 ...... 55 E2
Ford Cl BH22 ...... 165 F4
Ford La BH22 ...... 166 A4
Ford Rd PO2 ...... 180 C3
Fordingbridge Hospl SP6 ...... 69 F1
Fordingbridge Inf Sch SP6 ...... 69 F2
Fordingbridge Jun Sch SP6 ...... 69 F2
Fordingbridge Rd
  Alderholt SP6 ...... 93 D4
  Fordingbridge SP6 ...... 93 D4
  Portsmouth PO4 ...... 183 D2
Fordington Ave SO22 ...... 10 C4
Fordington Rd SO22 ...... 10 C4
Foreland Ct PO11 ...... 185 E1
Foreland Rd BH16 ...... 201 E2
Forelle Ctr The BH31 ...... 115 E2
Foremans Cotts PO12 ...... 181 F1
Foreshore N SO45 ...... 151 D3
Foreshore S SO45 ...... 151 D3
Forest Ave PO8 ...... 112 A2
Forest Cl Chandler's Ford SO53 . 55 E4
  Christchurch BH23 ...... 193 E1
  North Baddesley SO52 ...... 53 F3
  Shedfield SO32 ...... 83 F2
  Verwood BH31 ...... 115 E2
  Waterlooville PO8 ...... 111 F2
Forest Cnr GU33 ...... 21 D4
Forest Ct BH25 ...... 195 D1
Forest Edge SO45 ...... 151 D2
Forest Edge Cl BH24 ...... 139 E3
Forest Edge Dr BH24 ...... 139 E3
Forest Edge Rd BH24 ...... 141 F3
Forest Edge Sch SO40 ...... 100 C4
Forest End PO7 ...... 134 B4
Forest Front SO45 ...... 150 A4
Forest Gate SO45 ...... 177 E4
Forest Gate Gdns SO41 ...... 197 E1
Forest Gdns Lyndhurst SO43 .. 121 F3
  Shedfield SO32 ...... 83 F2
Forest Glade Cl SO42 ...... 145 E1
Forest Hall SO42 ...... 146 A1
Forest Hill Way SO45 ...... 125 F1
Forest Hills Dr SO18 ...... 79 F2
Forest La Fareham PO17 ...... 131 D4
  Holbury SO45 ...... 150 A4
  Ringwood BH24 ...... 141 F3
Forest Mead PO7 ...... 110 C2
Forest Meadow SO45 ...... 150 A4
Forest Park Rd SO42 ...... 145 E1
Forest Pines BH25 ...... 195 D2
Forest Rd Bransgore BH23 ...... 169 F2
  Burley BH24 ...... 142 C3
  Chandler's Ford SO53 ...... 55 E4
  Denmead PO7 ...... 110 B2

Forest Rd Continued
  Greatham GU33 ...... 20 C3
  Liss GU33 ...... 21 D3
  Nomansland SP5 ...... 73 E4
  Poole BH13 ...... 204 A1
  Redlynch SP5 ...... 47 F2
  Shedfield SO32 ...... 83 F2
  Swanmore SO32 ...... 83 F2
  Waterlooville PO7 ...... 134 B4
  West Moors BH22 ...... 138 C2
  Woodgreen SP6 ...... 47 F2
Forest Rise
  Christchurch BH23 ...... 193 E1
  Liss GU33 ...... 21 D3
Forest View
  Brockenhurst SO42 ...... 145 E1
  New Milton BH25 ...... 194 B3
  Southampton SO14 ...... 102 C2
Forest View Cl BH9 ...... 190 A1
Forest View Dr BH21 ...... 165 D3
Forest View Rd BH9 ...... 190 A1
Forest Way Christchurch BH23 . 193 E1
  Ferndown BH21 ...... 165 D3
  Gosport PO13 ...... 155 F1
  Hordle SO41 ...... 196 B1
  Netley Marsh SO40 ...... 76 A1
Forester Rd SO32 ...... 85 D1
Foresters Gate SO45 ...... 177 E4
Foresters Rd SO45 ...... 150 C1
Forestlake Ave BH24 ...... 141 E3
Forestside Ave PO9 ...... 136 A3
Forestside Gdns BH24 ...... 117 E1
Forestside The BH31 ...... 115 E3
Forge Cl SO31 ...... 105 D1
Forge Rd SO45 ...... 177 E4
Forneth Gdns PO15 ...... 154 A4
Forres Sandle Manor SP6 ...... 69 E1
Forster Rd SO14 ...... 103 D4
Forsyth Rd BH10 ...... 189 E1
Forsythia Cl SO30 ...... 105 D4
Forsythia Pl SO19 ...... 103 F3
Fort Brockhurst PO12 ...... 155 F1
Fort Cumberland Cl BH15 ...... 201 E1
Fort Cumberland Rd PO4 ...... 183 E2
Fort Fareham Ind Est PO14 .. 155 D3
Fort Fareham Rd PO14 ...... 154 C3
Fort Nelson PO16 ...... 132 A2
Fort Nelson Mus PO17 ...... 132 A2
Fort Rd Gosport PO12 ...... 181 D1
  Southampton SO19 ...... 103 F2
Fort Wallington Ind Est PO16 . 131 E1
Fort Widley Married Quarters PO6 ...... 133 F1
Fortescue Rd
  Bournemouth BH3 ...... 205 D3
  Poole BH12 ...... 203 E3
Forth Cl North Baddesley SO53 . 54 A3
  Stubbington BH24 ...... 154 A3
Forth House SO14 ...... 103 D4
Forties Cl PO14 ...... 154 A2
Forton Rd Gosport PO12 ...... 181 D3
  Portsmouth PO2 ...... 182 C3
Fortune Ct SO53 ...... 55 E3
Fortune House PO12 ...... 181 D3
Fortunes Way PO9 ...... 134 C1
Forum The PO9 ...... 135 F1
Forward Dr SO41 ...... 197 E1
Foster Ct PO14 ...... 154 B2
Foster Rd Gosport PO12 ...... 181 D2
  Portsmouth PO1 ...... 182 B3
Founders Way PO13 ...... 155 E1
Foundry Cres SO31 ...... 127 F4
Foundry Ct PO1 ...... 182 A3
Foundry Lane Prim Sch SO15 . 102 A4
Foundry Rd SP5 ...... 47 E4
Fountain Ct
  Colden Common SO21 ...... 31 F1
  Hedge End SO30 ...... 105 D3
Fountain St PO1 ...... 182 B3
Fountain Way BH23 ...... 207 D3
Four Acre SO30 ...... 106 A3
Four Cnrs SP6 ...... 68 A2
Four Marks Gn PO9 ...... 136 A3
Four Wells Rd BH21 ...... 164 A4
Fourposts Hill SO15 ...... 102 C3
Fourshells Cl SO45 ...... 150 C1
Fourth Ave Cosham PO6 ...... 157 F4
  Havant PO9 ...... 136 A1
Fourth St PO1 ...... 182 C3
Fowey Cl SO53 ...... 55 D3
Fowey The SO45 ...... 150 C1
Fowlers Rd SO30 ...... 105 D4
Fowlers Wlk SO16 ...... 54 B1
Fox Cl SO50 ...... 56 C1
Fox Field SO41 ...... 196 B1
Fox La Ferndown BH21 ...... 164 B3
  Winchester SO22 ...... 10 B3
Fox Pond La SO41 ...... 197 E1
Fox's Wlk SO45 ...... 177 E4
Foxbury Cl SO45 ...... 126 A1
Foxbury Gr PO16 ...... 156 A4
Foxbury La Gosport PO13 ...... 155 E3
  Westbourne PO10 ...... 137 E2
Foxbury Rd BH24 ...... 166 C4
Foxbury Special Sch The PO13 ...... 155 E2
Foxcombe Cl SO32 ...... 84 A3
Foxcote Gdns BH25 ...... 194 C4
Foxcote House PO6 ...... 132 C1
Foxcott Cl SO19 ...... 126 C4
Foxcott Gr PO9 ...... 135 F3
Foxcroft Dr Holbury SO45 ...... 150 A2
  Wimborne Minster BH21 ...... 164 A4
Foxes Cl Verwood BH31 ...... 114 C3
  Waterlooville PO7 ...... 134 C3
Foxes La SO51 ...... 50 C3

Foxglade SO45 ...... 177 F4
Foxglove Cl BH23 ...... 208 B4
Foxglove Pl BH25 ...... 195 E2
Foxgloves Fareham PO16 ...... 131 E2
  Upton BH16 ...... 201 D4
Foxgloves The SO30 ...... 105 E3
Foxhayes La SO45 ...... 177 E4
Foxhills Ashurst SO40 ...... 100 B2
  Verwood BH31 ...... 115 D3
Foxhills Cl SO40 ...... 100 B2
Foxhills Inf Sch SO40 ...... 100 B2
Foxhills Jun Sch SO40 ...... 100 B2
Foxholes BH6 ...... 206 C2
Foxholes Rd
  Bournemouth BH6 ...... 206 C2
  Poole BH15 ...... 202 C3
Foxlands SO45 ...... 177 F4
Foxlea SO15 ...... 102 C4
Foxlea Gdns PO12 ...... 181 D4
Foxlease Terr SO43 ...... 121 F2
Foxley Dr PO3 ...... 158 A2
Foxtail Gr PO12 ...... 125 F1
Foxwood Ave BH23 ...... 207 F3
Foxy Paddock SO45 ...... 177 F4
Foy Gdns SO31 ...... 128 B1
Foyes Ct SO15 ...... 102 B3
Fuyle Rd SO53 ...... 55 D3
Frampton Cl
  Colden Common SO21 ...... 31 F1
  New Milton BH25 ...... 195 E4
Frampton Pl BH24 ...... 141 D4
Frampton Rd BH9 ...... 205 D4
Frampton Way
  Kings Worthy SO23 ...... 2 B4
  Totton SO40 ...... 100 C3
Frances Ct BH23 ...... 209 D4
Frances Rd Bournemouth BH1 . 205 E2
  Waterlooville PO7 ...... 134 B2
Francesca Ct BH23 ...... 207 F3
Francesca Grange BH23 ...... 207 F4
Francesca Lodge BH23 ...... 207 F3
Francis Ave Bournemouth BH11 . 188 B2
  Portsmouth PO4 ...... 182 C2
Francis Cl PO13 ...... 180 A3
Francis Gdns SO23 ...... 2 A2
Francis Pl PO14 ...... 179 E3
Francis Rd Horndean PO8 ...... 88 B2
  Poole BH12 ...... 203 F3
Franconia Dr SO16 ...... 77 D2
Frank Judd Ct PO1 ...... 182 A3
Frank Miles House PO5 ...... 182 B2
Frank Wareham Cottage Homes The BH9 . 190 A2
Frankland Cres BH14 ...... 203 F2
Frankland Terr PO10 ...... 161 D4
Franklin Rd Bournemouth BH9 . 190 A2
  Gosport PO13 ...... 180 B4
  New Milton BH25 ...... 195 E2
  Twyford SO21 ...... 32 A4
Franklyn Ave SO19 ...... 104 A2
Franklyn Cl BH16 ...... 201 D4
Franks Way BH12 ...... 203 D4
Frankston Rd BH6 ...... 206 B2
Frarydene PO10 ...... 161 E4
Fraser Cl SO16 ...... 77 F3
Fraser Ct BH25 ...... 194 C2
Fraser Gdns PO10 ...... 137 F1
Fraser Rd Gosport PO13 ...... 155 E2
  Havant PO9 ...... 135 E1
  Kings Worthy SO23 ...... 2 B4
  Poole BH12 ...... 203 F4
  Portsmouth PO5 ...... 182 B2
  Portsmouth,Whale Is PO2 ...... 157 D1
Frater La PO14 ...... 156 A1
Fratton Ct PO1 ...... 182 C3
Fratton Ind Est PO4 ...... 183 D3
Fratton Park Portsmouth FC PO4 ...... 183 D3
Fratton Rd PO1 ...... 182 C3
Fratton Sta PO1 ...... 182 C3
Fratton Way SO50 ...... 57 E1
Frayslea SO45 ...... 126 A1
Freda Rd BH23 ...... 206 C3
Freda Routh Gdns SO50 ...... 57 E1
Frederica Rd BH9 ...... 204 C4
Frederick St
  Portsmouth PO1 ...... 182 B3
  Southampton SO14 ...... 103 D3
Free St SO32 ...... 83 E4
Freedom Ct SO45 ...... 126 A4
Freefolk Gn PO9 ...... 136 A3
Freegrounds Ave SO30 ...... 105 E3
Freegrounds Cl SO30 ...... 105 E3
Freegrounds Inf Sch SO30 .. 105 E3
Freegrounds Jun Sch SO30 .. 105 E3
Freegrounds Rd SO30 ...... 105 E3
Freemans Cl BH21 ...... 164 A4
Freemans La BH21 ...... 164 A4
Freemantle Bsns Ctr SO15 . 102 C3
Freemantle CE Inf Sch SO15 . 102 B3
Freemantle Cl SO19 ...... 103 F3
Freemantle Common Rd SO19 ...... 103 F3
Freemantle Rd PO12 ...... 181 D4
Freestone Rd BH25 ...... 182 B1
Fremington Ct BH25 ...... 195 D2
French Rd BH1 ...... 187 D1
French St Portsmouth PO1 ...... 182 A2
  Southampton SO14 ...... 102 C2
French's Farm Rd BH16 ...... 201 D4
Frenches La SO51 ...... 51 E4
Frenchmans Rd GU32 ...... 40 C2
Frenchmoor La East Dean SP5 . 3 F1
  West Tytherley SP5 ...... 3 F2
Frendstaple Rd PO7 ...... 135 D3

Frensham Cl
Bournemouth BH10 .... 189 F2
Hedge End SO30 .... 105 E3
Frensham Ct Hedge End SO30 .. 105 E3
Portsmouth PO4 .... 182 C2
Frensham Rd PO4 .... 182 C2
Freshfield Gdns PO7 .... 134 C4
Freshfield Rd SO15 .... 102 A4
Freshfield Sq SO15 .... 102 A4
Freshwater Ct
Chandler's Ford SO53 .... 30 C1
2 Lee-on-the-Solent PO13 .... 179 F1
Freshwater Dr BH15 .... 201 E2
Freshwater Rd
Christchurch BH23 .... 208 B3
Cosham PO6 .... 157 F4
Frewen Liby PO1 .... 182 A2
Friars Croft SO40 .... 76 B1
Friars Gate BH23 .... 208 B3
Friars Pond Rd PO15 .... 130 B1
Friars Rd Christchurch BH23 .. 208 A3
Eastleigh SO50 .... 55 F1
Friars Way SO18 .... 79 E2
Friars Wlk BH23 .... 210 A4
Friarscroft SO31 .... 127 D4
Friarsgate SO23 .... 11 D4
Friary Cl **51** PO5 .... 182 B1
Friary The **30** PO5 .... 182 B1
Friday's Ct BH24 .... 140 C4
Friendly Societies' Homes
PO4 .... 183 D2
Frinton Ct **6** BH14 .... 203 C2
Frith La PO17 .... 108 A4
Frith Lane End PO17 .... 108 A4
Fritham Cl SO40 .... 100 B4
Fritham Gdns BH8 .... 190 B2
Fritham Rd SO18 .... 104 B4
Frobisher Ave BH12 .... 188 C1
Frobisher Cl
Christchurch BH23 .... 207 F3
Gosport PO13 .... 180 B3
Ringwood BH24 .... 117 E1
Frobisher Ct SO40 .... 102 A2
Frobisher Gdns
7 Emsworth PO10 .... 160 C4
Southampton SO19 .... 104 B2
Frobisher Gr PO16 .... 156 B4
Frobisher House **9** PO1 ... 182 A3
Froddington Rd PO1 .... 182 B2
Frog La SP6 .... 93 F4
Froghall SO45 .... 126 A1
Frogham Gn PO9 .... 135 E3
Frogham Hill SP6 .... 94 B3
Frogmore PO14 .... 154 B4
Frogmore La Horndean PO8 .. 112 A3
Nursling SO16 .... 77 E2
Waterlooville PO8 .... 112 A3
Frogmore Rd PO4 .... 183 D3
Frome Cl SO40 .... 102 A1
Fromond Cl SO41 .... 197 F3
Fromond Rd SO22 .... 1 B2
Front Lawn Inf Sch PO9 ..... 135 F3
Front Lawn Jun Sch PO9 .... 135 F3
Frost La SO45 .... 126 A1
Frost Rd BH11 .... 188 C2
Frosthole Cl PO15 .... 130 C2
Frosthole Cres PO15 .... 130 C2
Froud Way BH21 .... 186 B2
Froude Ave PO12 .... 181 E1
Froude Rd PO12 .... 181 E1
Froxfield CE Inf Sch GU32 .... 18 C1
Froxfield Cl SO22 .... 1 B2
Froxfield Gdns PO16 .... 132 B1
Froxfield Rd PO9 .... 136 A3
Froyle Ct **54** PO9 .... 136 A3
Fry Cl Blackfield SO45 .... 150 C1
Hamble-le-Rice SO31 .... 128 A2
Fry's La SO32 .... 61 E2
Fryer Cl BH11 .... 189 D3
Fryern Arc SO53 .... 55 F4
Fryern Cl SO53 .... 55 F3
Fryern Court Rd SP6 .... 69 F3
Fryern Inf Sch SO53 .... 55 F3
Fryern Jun Sch SO53 .... 55 F3
Fryers Copse BH21 .... 164 B3
Fryers Rd BH21 .... 138 B4
Frys La SO41 .... 196 B1
Fuchsia Gdns SO16 .... 78 B1
Fulford Ct **2** SO22 .... 10 C4
Fulford Rd PO9 .... 135 F3
Fullerton Cl Havant PO9 ...... 136 A3
Southampton SO19 .... 126 C4
Fullerton Rd SO41 .... 197 E2
Fulmar Cl SO16 .... 78 A3
Fulmar Dr SO45 .... 126 A1
Fulmar Rd BH23 .... 208 A3
Fulmar Wlk PO13 .... 155 D2
Fulmer Wlk PO8 .... 111 F2
Fulwood Ave BH11 .... 188 C3
Funtington Rd PO2 .... 182 C4
Funtley Ct PO16 .... 130 C2
Funtley Hill PO16 .... 130 C2
Funtley La PO17 .... 130 C3
Funtley Rd PO15, PO17 ...... 130 C3
Furdies PO7 .... 110 C2
Furley Cl SO23 .... 11 D4
Furlong Mews BH24 .... 140 C4
Furlong The BH24 .... 140 C4
Furlonge House PO10 .... 136 C1
Furneaux Gdns PO16 .... 131 D2
Furnell Rd BH15 .... 202 B1
Furness Rd **11** PO5 .... 182 B1
Furniss Way PO11 .... 184 B2
Furnston Gr PO10 .... 137 F1
Fury Way PO14 .... 154 A2

Furze Cl SO19 .... 104 A3
Furze Croft BH25 .... 195 D1
Furze Hall PO16 .... 131 D2
Furze Hill Dr BH14 .... 203 E1
Furze La PO4 .... 183 E2
Furze Rd SO19 .... 104 A3
Furze Way PO8 .... 112 A2
Furzebrook Cl BH17 .... 187 F2
Furzedale Gdns SO45 .... 126 A1
Furzedale Park SO45 .... 126 A1
Furzedown Cotts SO20 .... 7 D4
Furzedown Cres **51** PO9 .. 136 A3
Furzedown House SO20 .... 7 D3
Furzedown Mews SO45 .... 126 A1
Furzedown Rd
King's Somborne SO20 .... 7 D4
Southampton SO17 .... 79 D1
Furzehall Ave PO16 .... 131 D2
Furzehill BH21 .... 163 E4
Furzelands Rd BH21 .... 138 C4
Furzeley Rd PO7 .... 110 C1
Furzey Ave SO45 .... 126 A1
Furzey Cl SO45 .... 150 C1
Furzey La SO42 .... 148 A1
Furzey Rd BH16 .... 201 D3
Furzley Ct PO9 .... 135 E3
Furzley La SO51 .... 74 B3
Furzley Rd SO51, SO40 .... 74 C2
Furzy Whistlers Cl BH23 ..... 169 C1
Futcher Sch PO6 .... 158 B4
Fyeford Cl SO16 .... 77 F3
Fyning St PO1 .... 182 B3

G Ave SO45 .... 150 C3
Gables Ct SO16 .... 78 C3
Gage Cl SO40 .... 102 A1
Gain's Rd PO4 .... 182 C1
Gainsborough Ave BH25 ...... 195 D3
Gainsborough Cl SO19 .... 104 B1
Gainsborough Ct
11 Bournemouth BH5 .... 206 A3
Lymington SO41 .... 197 E1
North Baddesley SO52 .... 54 A2
Gainsborough Mews PO14 ... 153 F4
Gainsborough Rd
Bournemouth BH7 .... 205 F4
St Leonards BH24 .... 139 F3
Gainsford Rd SO19 .... 103 F3
Galaxie Rd PO8 .... 112 A2
Gale Moor Ave PO12 .... 180 B2
Galleon Cl SO31 .... 128 C1
Gallia Ct SO15 .... 78 C1
Gallop Way BH12 .... 204 B4
Gallops The PO14 .... 129 E1
Galloway Rd BH15 .... 201 E2
Gallows Dr BH22 .... 165 F1
Galsworthy Rd SO40 .... 100 B4
Galt Rd PO6 .... 158 B4
Galton Ave BH23 .... 206 C3
Gamble Cl SO19 .... 103 F2
Gamble Rd PO2 .... 182 B4
Gamblins La SO32 .... 107 F4
Gang Warily Recn Ctr SO45 .. 150 C2
Ganger Farm La SO51 .... 28 B1
Ganger Rd SO51 .... 28 B1
Gannet Cl Hythe SO45 .... 126 A1
Southampton SO16 .... 78 A3
Gannets The PO14 .... 154 A2
Gar St SO22 .... 10 C4
Garage Cotts **2** GU32 .... 40 C2
Garbett Rd SO23 .... 11 E4
Garden City SO45 .... 125 D3
Garden Cl Lyndhurst SO43 .... 121 F3
New Milton BH25 .... 195 D1
South Hayling PO11 .... 184 C2
Garden Court Cotts BH22 .... 138 B2
Garden Ct Bournemouth BH1 ... 205 E3
Portchester PO16 .... 156 B4
Garden House **7** PO5 .... 205 D2
Garden La Portsmouth PO5 ... 182 B2
St Leonards BH24 .... 139 F2
16 Winchester SO23 .... 11 D4
Garden Mews SO31 .... 128 B1
Garden Rd BH24 .... 142 C2
Garden Terr **5** PO5 .... 182 B1
Garden Wlk BH22 .... 165 F4
Gardeners Cotts BH24 .... 141 D2
Gardeners La Awbridge SO51 .. 52 A2
Romsey SO51 .... 52 A2
Gardens Cres BH14 .... 214 A4
Gardens Ct **8** BH15 .... 202 C2
Gardens Rd BH14 .... 214 A4
Gardens The Hambledon PO7 .. 86 B2
Havant PO9 .... 136 A1
Gardiner Cl SO40 .... 102 A1
Gardiner Cl SO23 .... 206 C4
Gardner Rd Christchurch BH23 .. 206 C4
Ringwood BH24 .... 141 D3
Titchfield PO14 .... 153 F4
Garendon Ct SP6 .... 69 F1
Garfield Ave BH1 .... 205 E3
Garfield Cl SO32 .... 83 E4
Garfield Rd
Bishop's Waltham SO32 .... 83 E4
1 Netley SO31 .... 127 D3
Portsmouth PO2 .... 182 B4
Southampton SO19 .... 103 F4
Garland Ave PO10 .... 136 C2
Garland Ct **16** PO12 .... 181 D3
Garland Rd BH15 .... 202 B2
Garnett Cl PO14 .... 154 B2
Garnier Pk PO17 .... 108 A2
Garnier Rd SO23 .... 11 D1
Garnier St PO1 .... 182 C3
Garnock Rd SO19 .... 103 E1
Garratt Cl SO30 .... 81 E1
Garrett Cl SO19 .... 104 A1

Garrick Gdns SO19 .... 104 A1
Garrick House **11** PO2 .... 157 F2
Garrison Hill SO32 .... 61 D1
Garrow Dr SO41 .... 197 F3
Garsdale Cl BH11 .... 189 D3
Garsons Rd PO10 .... 161 E4
Garston Cl GU32 .... 63 E4
Garstons Cl PO14 .... 153 F4
Garstons Rd PO14 .... 153 F4
Garth Cl BH24 .... 139 E2
Garth Rd BH9 .... 190 A1
Garton Rd SO19 .... 103 E2
Gashouse Hill SO31 .... 127 E3
Gatcombe SO31 .... 127 E4
Gatcombe Ave PO3 .... 158 A1
Gatcombe Dr PO2 .... 157 F2
Gatcombe Gdns
Fareham PO14 .... 154 A4
West End SO18 .... 80 A1
Gatcombe Park Inf Sch PO2 .. 157 F2
Gate House Rd PO16 .... 156 A4
Gatehouse The **12** SO18 .... 103 F4
Gatekeeper Cl **10** SO23 ..... 11 E4
Gateway The BH13 .... 203 F2
Gatwick Cl SO16 .... 78 A2
Gaulter Cl PO9 .... 136 A2
Gavan St SO19 .... 104 B3
Gawn Pl PO12 .... 181 E1
Gayda House PO12 .... 180 C3
Gaydon Rise BH11 .... 188 C2
Gaylyn Way PO14 .... 154 A4
Gaza Ave SO42 .... 175 E3
Gaza House PO15 .... 130 B2
Gazelle Cl PO13 .... 180 B3
Gazing La SO51 .... 50 C2
Gazings The SO51 .... 50 C2
Geddes Way GU31 .... 41 E2
Gemini Cl SO16 .... 77 F2
General Johnson Ct **6** SO22 .. 10 B3
Geneva Ave BH6 .... 206 B3
Genoa Cl SO41 .... 197 E1
Gento Cl SO30 .... 105 F3
Geoffrey Ave PO7 .... 134 A1
Geoffrey Cres PO16 .... 155 D3
George Byng Way PO2 .... 182 B4
George Ct The PO1 .... 182 A2
George Eyston Dr SO22 .... 10 B3
George Rd SO41 .... 211 E3
George St Eastleigh SO50 ...... 56 A2
Gosport PO12 .... 181 E3
Portsmouth PO1, PO2 .... 182 C4
Georges Mews BH21 .... 186 B4
Georgian Cl BH24 .... 141 D4
Georgian Way BH10 .... 189 F2
Georgina Cl PO12 .... 204 B4
Gerald Rd BH3 .... 205 D3
Gerard Cres SO19 .... 104 B3
Gerard House **6** PO2 .... 157 F2
Germaine Cl BH23 .... 208 C4
Gervis Cres BH14 .... 203 D2
Gervis Pl BH2 .... 204 C2
Gervis Rd BH1 .... 205 D2
Gibbs Rd SO14 .... 102 C3
Gibraltar Cl PO15 .... 130 B1
Gibraltar Rd Gosport PO14 ... 154 C3
Portsmouth PO4 .... 183 E2
Gibson Cl
Lee-on-the-Solent PO13 .... 179 F2
Swanwick BH25 .... 129 F3
Gibson Rd BH17 .... 202 C4
Giddylake BH21 .... 163 E3
Gifford Cl PO15 .... 130 C2
Gilbert Cl Alderholt SP6 .... 93 D3
Gosport PO13 .... 180 B4
Lymington SO41 .... 197 E1
Gilbert Ct **5** BH23 .... 207 D4
Gilbert Mead PO11 .... 184 C2
Gilbert Rd BH1 .... 205 E3
Gilbert Way PO7 .... 134 C3
Gilbury Cl SO18 .... 79 F2
Giles Cl Fareham PO16 .... 131 D2
Gosport PO12 .... 181 D3
Hedge End SO30 .... 81 E1
Giles Hill SO23 .... 11 D4
Giles La SP5 .... 50 A2
Gilkicker Rd PO12 .... 181 E1
Gillam Rd BH10 .... 189 E3
Gillcrest PO14 .... 129 E2
Gillett Rd BH12 .... 204 B4
Gillies The **17** PO16 .... 131 D1
Gillingham Cl
Bournemouth BH9 .... 190 B2
Kings Worthy SO23 .... 2 B4
Gillingham Rd SO41 .... 211 E2
Gillion Ct **2** BH23 .... 207 F3
Gillman Rd PO6 .... 134 C1
Gilpin Cl Boldre SO41 .... 173 F1
Southampton SO19 .... 104 C3
Gilpin Hill SO41 .... 172 A1
Gins La SO42 .... 176 C1
Girton Cl PO14 .... 129 E1
Gitsham Gdns PO7 .... 134 B2
Gladdis Rd BH11 .... 188 C2
Glade The Blackfield SO45 .... 177 F4
Chandler's Ford SO53 .... 30 C1
Fareham PO16 .... 130 B2
South Hayling PO11 .... 185 E1
St Leonards BH24 .... 139 F3
Waterlooville PO7 .... 135 D4
Gladelands Cl BH18 .... 186 C2
Gladelands Mobile Home Pk
BH22 .... 165 F4
Gladelands Way BH18 .... 186 C2
Glades The SO31 .... 129 D2
Gladstone Cl BH23 .... 207 E3
Gladstone Gdns PO16 .... 156 B4
Gladstone Hill SO22 .... 10 C4
Gladstone Pl **4** PO2 .... 182 B4

Gladstone Rd
Bournemouth BH7 .... 205 F3
Gosport PO12 .... 181 D4
Poole BH12 .... 203 E3
Southampton SO19 .... 104 A3
Gladstone Rd E BH7 .... 205 F3
Gladstone Rd W BH1 .... 205 F3
Gladys Ave Portsmouth PO2 ... 157 E1
Waterlooville PO8 .... 112 A2
Glamis Ave BH10 .... 189 F3
Glamis Cl PO7 .... 135 D4
Glamis Ct PO14 .... 154 B2
Glamorgan Rd PO8 .... 88 A2
Glasgow Rd PO4 .... 183 D2
Glasslaw Rd SO18 .... 104 A4
Glasspool PO7 .... 110 C3
Gleadowe Ave BH23 .... 206 C3
Glebe Cl PO11 .... 184 C3
Glebe Cnr PO17 .... 108 A2
Glebe Ct Botley SO30 .... 106 A4
Fair Oak SO50 .... 57 E1
Southampton SO17 .... 79 D1
Glebe Dr PO13 .... 155 E1
Glebe La SP5 .... 49 E2
Glebe Meadow SP5 .... 4 A1
Glebe Park Ave PO9 .... 135 D1
Glebe Rd GU31 .... 65 E3
Glebe The PO14 .... 179 E3
Glebefield Gdns **1** PO6 ..... 157 F4
Glebefields **6** SO41 .... 211 E3
Glen Cl BH25 .... 209 E4
Glen Dale PO9 .... 113 E1
Glen Eyre Cl SO16 .... 79 D2
Glen Eyre Dr SO16 .... 79 D3
Glen Eyre Hall SO16 .... 79 D3
Glen Eyre Rd SO16 .... 78 C3
Glen Eyre Way SO16 .... 79 D2
Glen Fern Rd BH1 .... 205 D2
Glen House PO12 .... 180 C2
Glen Rd Bournemouth BH5 .... 205 F2
Locks Heath SO31 .... 128 C3
Southampton SO19 .... 103 E1
Swanwick SO31 .... 128 C4
Glen Spey BH25 .... 195 E1
Glen The Gosport PO13 .... 155 F1
Poole BH14 .... 203 E3
Poole, Canford Cliffs BH13 .... 214 C4
Glenair Ave BH14 .... 203 D2
Glenair Cres BH14 .... 203 D2
Glenair Rd BH14 .... 203 D2
Glenavon BH25 .... 195 E1
Glenavon Rd BH23 .... 193 F1
Glenbrook Wlk PO14 .... 154 B4
Glencarron Way SO16 .... 78 C2
Glencoe Rd Bournemouth BH7 .. 205 F4
Poole BH12 .... 203 E3
Portsmouth PO1 .... 182 C4
Glencoyne Gdns SO16 .... 77 F1
Glenda Cl SO31 .... 152 B4
Glendale Locks Heath SO31 .... 129 D1
Swanmore SO32 .... 84 A2
Glendale Ave BH22 .... 165 F3
Glendale Cl Christchurch BH23 .. 191 E2
Wimborne Minster BH21 .... 163 E3
Glendale Ct BH23 .... 191 E2
Glendale Rd BH6 .... 207 D2
Glendon Ave BH10 .... 189 E3
Glendowan Rd SO53 .... 55 D4
Glendrive BH25 .... 209 E4
Gleneagles BH23 .... 206 C3
Gleneagles Av BH14 .... 203 E1
Gleneagles Cl BH22 .... 165 F3
Gleneagles Dr PO7 .... 112 A1
Glenelg PO15 .... 130 C1
Glenesha Gdns PO15 .... 130 B1
Glenfern Hall BH4 .... 204 B3
Glenferness Ave BH3, BH4 ... 204 B3
Glenfield Ave SO18 .... 103 F4
Glenfield Cres SO18 .... 103 F4
Glenfield Inf Sch SO18 .... 103 F4
Glenfield Way SO18 .... 103 F4
Glengariff Rd BH14 .... 203 E2
Glengarry BH25 .... 195 E1
Glengarry Way BH23 .... 208 B3
Glenhurst Sch PO9 .... 136 A1
Glenives Cl BH24 .... 140 A2
Glenlea Cl SO30 .... 80 B1
Glenlea Dr SO30 .... 80 B1
Glenleigh Ave **18** PO6 ...... 157 F4
Glenleigh Ct **17** PO6 .... 157 F4
Glenleigh Pk PO9 .... 136 A1
Glenmeadows Dr BH10 .... 189 D3
Glenmoor Cl BH10 .... 189 E1
Glenmoor Rd
Bournemouth BH9 .... 204 C4
Ferndown BH22 .... 165 E2
Glenmoor Sec Sch BH10 ..... 189 E1
Glenmore Ct SO17 .... 103 D4
Glenmount Dr BH14 .... 203 D2
Glenn Rd SO30 .... 80 B1
Glenroyd Gdns BH6 .... 206 C2
Glenside Barton on Sea BH25 .. 209 D4
Hythe SO45 .... 125 F2
Glenside Ave SO19 .... 104 B3
Glenthorne Cl PO14 .... 179 E3
Glenthorne Meadow GU32 .... 38 C1
Glenthorne Rd PO3 .... 158 A1
Glenville Cl BH23 .... 194 A1
Glenville Gdns BH10 .... 189 E1
Glenville Rd
Bournemouth BH10 .... 189 E1
Christchurch BH23 .... 194 A1
Glenwood Ave SO16 .... 79 D3
Glenwood Cl BH22 .... 138 C1
Glenwood Gdns PO8 .... 111 F2
Glenwood La BH22 .... 138 C2

Glenwood Rd
Southbourne PO10 .... 137 F1
Verwood BH31 .... 114 C3
West Moors BH22 .... 138 C1
Glenwood Sch PO8 .... 111 F1
Glenwood Way BH22 .... 138 C1
Glidden Cl PO1 .... 182 B3
Glidden La PO7 .... 86 C2
Glissons BH22 .... 165 D1
Globe La BH15 .... 202 B1
Gloster Ct PO14 .... 129 E3
Gloucester Cl GU32 .... 40 B2
Gloucester Ct **8** GU32 .... 40 C2
Gloucester House **1** PO12 .. 181 E2
Gloucester Pl **43** PO5 .... 182 B2
Gloucester Rd
Bournemouth BH7 .... 205 F3
Poole BH12 .... 203 F3
Portsmouth PO1 .... 182 A3
Waterlooville PO7 .... 134 C3
Gloucester Terr **42** PO5 ..... 182 B2
Gloucester View PO5 .... 182 B2
Glyn Dr PO14 .... 179 E3
Glyn Jones Cl SO45 .... 150 C1
Glyn Way PO14 .... 179 E3
Glynville Cl BH21 .... 164 A4
Glynville Ct BH21 .... 164 A4
Glynville Rd BH21 .... 164 A4
Goathorn Cl BH16 .... 201 E2
God's House Tower (Mus)
SO14 .... 103 D1
Goddard Cl SO51 .... 79 D2
Godfrey Olson House **4** SO50 .. 56 A2
Godfrey Pink Way SO32 .... 83 E4
Godiva Lawn PO4 .... 183 E2
Godmanston Cl BH17 .... 188 A1
Godshill BH8 .... 190 B2
Godson House **14** SO23 .... 11 D4
Godwin Cl Emsworth PO10 ... 136 C2
Winchester SO22 .... 1 B1
Godwin Cres PO8 .... 88 B2
Godwins Field SO21 .... 31 E4
Godwit Cl PO12 .... 181 D4
Godwit Rd PO4 .... 183 E3
Gofton Ave PO6 .... 158 A4
Goggs La SP5 .... 47 F3
Gold Mead Cl **3** SO41 .... 197 F1
Gold Oak BH21 .... 91 F4
Gold St PO5 .... 182 A2
Goldcrest Cl Horndean PO8 ... 112 A4
Portchester PO16 .... 155 F4
Goldcrest Gdns SO16 .... 78 A3
Goldcrest La SO40 .... 100 B4
Golden Cres SO41 .... 196 B1
Golden Ct SO30 .... 80 C2
Golden Gates BH13 .... 214 A2
Golden Gr SO14 .... 103 D3
Golden Hind Park SO45 .... 125 F1
Golden Sands BH13 .... 214 A2
Goldfinch Cl BH25 .... 194 C1
Goldfinch La PO13 .... 179 F2
Goldfinch Rd BH17 .... 201 F4
Goldring Cl PO11 .... 185 D2
Goldsmith Ave PO4 .... 182 C2
Goldsmith Cl SO40 .... 100 B4
Goldsmith Inf Sch PO4 .... 182 C2
Goldsmith Rd SO50 .... 55 F1
Goldwire Dr SO52 .... 54 C3
Golf Course Rd SO16 .... 78 C3
Golf Links Rd Broadstone BH18 .. 187 D3
Ferndown BH22 .... 165 F2
Goliath Rd BH15 .... 201 E1
Gomer Ct PO12 .... 180 C2
Gomer Inf Sch PO12 .... 180 C2
Gomer Jun Sch PO12 .... 180 C2
Gomer La PO12 .... 180 C2
Good Acre Dr SO52 .... 54 C3
Good Rd BH12 .... 203 E4
Goodens The SO24 .... 14 B3
Goodison Cl SO50 .... 57 D1
Goodlands Vale SO30 .... 105 D4
Goodsell Cl PO14 .... 179 D3
Goodwin Cl SO16 .... 77 E1
Goodwood Cl Gosport PO12 ... 181 D4
Titchfield PO14 .... 129 E1
Waterlooville PO8 .... 112 A1
Goodwood Ct PO10 .... 161 F4
Goodwood Gdns SO40 .... 100 B4
Goodwood Rd Eastleigh SO50 ... 55 F2
Gosport PO12 .... 181 D4
Portsmouth PO5 .... 182 C2
Gooseberry La BH24 .... 140 C4
Gordleton Ind Pk SO41 .... 196 C3
Gordon Ave Southampton SO14 .. 103 D4
Winchester SO23 .... 11 E3
Gordon Bldgs SO15 .... 102 B4
Gordon Ct BH4 .... 204 B2
Gordon Mount BH23 .... 209 D4
Gordon Rd Bournemouth BH1 .. 205 E2
Chandler's Ford SO53 .... 30 B1
Christchurch BH23 .... 209 D4
Curdridge SO32 .... 83 D1
Fareham PO16 .... 131 D1
Gosport PO12 .... 181 D2
Hermitage PO10 .... 161 D4
Lymington SO41 .... 197 E2
Poole BH12 .... 204 A3
Portsmouth PO5 .... 182 A2
Waterlooville PO7 .... 134 B3
Wimborne Minster BH21 .... 163 F2
Winchester SO23 .... 11 D4
Gordon Rd S BH12 .... 204 A3
Gordon Terr SO19 .... 104 A1
Gordon Way BH23 .... 192 B1
Gore Grange BH25 .... 194 C1
Gore Rd BH25 .... 194 C1
Gore Rd Ind Est BH25 .... 194 C1
Gorey Ave BH12 .... 188 B1

ring Ave P08 .... 88 B2
ring Field SO22 .... 1 B1
rleston Rd BH12 .... 203 F3
rley Cross SP6 .... 94 A2
rley Cl P09 .... 135 E3
rley Lynch SP6 .... 94 B2
rley Rd BH24 .... 117 E1
rran Ave P013 .... 155 E1
race Cl Locks Heath SO31 .... 128 C1
New Milton BH25 .... 195 E2
St Leonards BH24 .... 139 E2
rse Down SO21 .... 33 D2
rse Hill BH15 .... 202 C3
rse Hill Cres BH15 .... 202 C3
rse Hill Rd BH15 .... 202 C3
rse La BH16 .... 201 E4
Petersfield GU31 .... 41 E2
rsecliff Ct 7 BH5 .... 205 E2
rsecliff Rd BH15 .... 189 E1
rsefield Rd BH25 .... 195 D2
rseland Ct BH22 .... 165 F2
rselands Rd SO18 .... 80 A1
rselands Way P013 .... 180 B4
rseway P011 .... 184 B2
rseway The P011 .... 184 B2
ort Cres SO19 .... 104 A2
ort Rd Bournemouth BH11 .. 189 D2
Broadstone BH17 .... 187 D1
osling Cl BH17 .... 202 C4
osport House 39 P09 .... 136 A3
osport La SO43 .... 122 A2
osport Rd
Fareham P014, P016 .... 155 D4
Lee-on-the-Solent P013 ...... 179 F1
Stubbington P014 .... 179 F3
osport Sh Prec 28 P012 .... 181 E2
osport St SO17 .... 197 F2
ough Cres BH17 .... 187 D1
over Rd SO16 .... 101 E4
race Dieu Gdns SO31 .... 104 C1
race La SP6 .... 70 C4
raddidge Way SO40 .... 100 B3
raemar La SO41 .... 25 E1
rafton Cl Bournemouth BH3 .. 205 D4
Christchurch BH23 .... 207 E3
rafton Gdns Lymington SO41 .. 197 E1
Southampton SO16 .... 78 B3
rafton Rd Bournemouth BH3 .. 205 D4
Winchester SO23 .... 10 C3
rafton St P02 .... 182 B4
raham Ct SO19 .... 104 A3
raham House 4 SO14 ...... 103 E3
raham Rd Gosport P012 .... 181 D4
Portsmouth P04 .... 182 C2
Southampton SO14 .... 103 E3
raham St SO14 .... 103 E3
rainger Gdns SO19 .... 104 B2
ranada Cl P08 .... 112 A2
ranada Rd Hedge End SO30 .. 105 D3
Portsmouth P04 .... 182 C1
ranary Mews BH24 .... 140 C4
ranary The BH24 .... 140 C4
ranby Gr SO17 .... 79 D2
ranby Rd BH9 .... 190 A2
rand Ave BH6 .... 206 B2
rand Par 20 Poole BH15 .... 202 A1
Portsmouth P04 .... 182 A2
South Hayling P011 .... 185 D1
range Cl Gosport P012 ...... 180 C3
Havant P09 .... 136 A1
Hordle SO41 .... 211 F4
Southampton SO18 .... 79 F2
Winchester SO23 .... 10 C2
range Cres P012 .... 180 C3
range Ct
16 Bournemouth BH1 .... 205 D2
Netley SO31 .... 127 D4
range Dr SO30 .... 105 E4
range Gdns BH12 .... 203 F4
range Inf Sch P013 .... 180 B4
range Jun Sch P013 .... 180 B4
range La P013 .... 180 B4
range Mews SO31 .... 28 B1
Grange Park Mobile Homes
SO30 .... 81 E1
Grange Rd Bournemouth BH6 .. 206 B2
Broadstone BH18 .... 187 D2
Christchurch BH23 .... 208 A4
Gosport P013 .... 180 B3
Hedge End SO30 .... 105 E4
Netley SO31 .... 127 D4
Petersfield GU32 .... 40 C1
Portsmouth P02 .... 157 E1
Southampton SO15 .... 78 A1
St Leonards BH24 .... 139 F1
Winchester SO23 .... 10 C2
range Road Bsns Ctr BH23 .. 208 A4
range Sch The BH23 .... 207 F4
range The Hordle SO41 .... 211 F4
8 Southampton SO15 .... 78 A1
Grangewood Ct SO50 .... 57 D1
Grangewood Gdns SO50 .... 57 D1
Grant Rd P06 .... 158 B4
Grant's Ave BH1 .... 205 E3
Grantham Ave SO31 .... 127 F2
Grantham Ct 3 SO50 .... 56 A1
Grantham Rd
Bournemouth BH1 .... 205 F3
Eastleigh SO50 .... 56 A1
Southampton SO19 .... 103 F3
Grantley Rd 16 BH5 .... 205 F2
Grants Cl BH1 .... 205 F3
Granville Cl P09 .... 136 A1
Granville Pl
32 Bournemouth BH1 .... 204 C2
Winchester SO23 .... 11 D3
Granville Rd Bournemouth BH5 . 206 A3
Poole SO22 .... 203 D2
Granville St SO14 .... 103 D2
Grasdean Cl 5 SO18 .... 80 A1
Grasmere SO50 .... 55 F1
Grasmere Cl Christchurch BH23 191 E2
West End SO18 .... 80 A1
Grasmere Ct SO16 .... 77 F1
Grasmere Gdns BH25 .... 195 D3
Grasmere House 18 P06 .... 133 D1
Grasmere Rd
Bournemouth BH5 .... 206 A2
Poole BH13 .... 214 A2
Grasmere Way P014 .... 154 B2
Grassmere Way P07 .... 112 B1
Grassymead P014 .... 129 E2
Grateley Cl 1 SO19 .... 126 C4
Grateley Cres P09 .... 135 E2
Gravel Cl SP5 .... 46 C4
Gravel Hill Broadstone BH18 .. 187 E3
Oakley BH21 .... 187 E3
Shedfield SO32 .... 84 A2
Swanmore SO32 .... 84 A2
Gravel La BH24 .... 140 C4
Gray Cl Locks Heath SO31 .. 128 C1
Poole BH17 .... 202 C4
Gray's Yd 24 BH1 .... 205 B1
Graycot Cl BH10 .... 189 D3
Grayland Cl P011 .... 184 C2
Grays Ave SO45 .... 126 A2
Grays Cl Colden Common SO21 .. 56 C4
Gosport P012 .... 180 C2
Romsey SO51 .... 53 D4
Grays Ct P01 .... 182 A2
Grayshott Cl SO22 .... 1 B2
Grayshott Rd Gosport P012 .. 180 C2
Portsmouth P04 .... 182 C2
Grayson Ct BH22 .... 165 F2
Great Copse Dr P09 .... 135 F3
Great Elms SO45 .... 150 A2
Great Field Rd SO22 .... 1 B2
Great Gays P014 .... 179 D3
Great Hanger GU31 .... 41 D2
Great Mead Denmead P07 .. 111 D2
Lyndhurst SO43 .... 121 F2
Great Minster St SO23 .... 11 D4
Great Posbrook Cotts P014 .. 153 F3
Great Southsea St P05 ...... 182 B2
Great Well Dr SO51 .... 53 D4
Greatbridge Rd
Awbridge SO51 .... 27 F1
Romsey SO51 .... 27 F1
Greatfield Way P09 .... 113 D2
Greatwood Cl SO45 .... 126 A1
Greaves Cl BH10 .... 189 E2
Grebe Cl Broadstone BH17 .. 201 F4
Christchurch BH23 .... 208 A3
Milford on Sea SO41 .... 211 F2
Portchester P016 .... 155 F4
Waterlooville P08 .... 111 F2
Green Acres BH23 .... 207 F4
Green Acres Cl BH24 .... 140 B3
Green Bottom BH21 .... 164 A4
Green Cl 7 Hythe SO45 .... 126 A2
Kings Worthy SO23 .... 2 A3
Netley Marsh SO40 .... 99 F2
Poole BH15 .... 202 B1
Whiteparish SP5 .... 24 A2
Green Cres P013 .... 155 E1
Green Dr SP6 .... 93 D3
Green Farm Gdns P03 ...... 157 F2
Green Gdns BH15 .... 202 B1
Green Hollow Cl P016 ...... 130 C2
Green Jacket Cl SO22 .... 10 C3
Green La Ampfield SO51 ...... 29 D1
Barton on Sea BH25 .... 210 A4
Bishop's Waltham SO32 ...... 83 E4
Blackfield SO45 .... 177 F4
Bournemouth BH10 .... 189 E2
Bursledon SO31 .... 104 C1
Chilworth SO16 .... 54 C1
Clanfield P08 .... 88 B3
Denmead P07 .... 110 C2
Downton SP5 .... 46 C4
Ferndown BH22 .... 165 D1
Fordingbridge SP6 .... 69 F1
Froxfield GU32 .... 18 C3
Gosport P012 .... 181 E4
Hamble-le-Rice SO31 .... 128 A1
Hambledon P7 .... 86 A2
Locks Heath SO31 .... 128 C1
New Milton BH25 .... 194 C4
Ower SO40 .... 76 A2
Portsmouth P03 .... 158 A2
Ringwood BH24 .... 141 D4
Ringwood, Upper Kingston
BH24 .... 141 E2
Rockbourne SP6 .... 69 E4
Soberton P07 .... 86 A3
South Hayling P011 .... 184 C2
Southampton SO16 .... 77 F1
Swanmore SO32 .... 84 B4
Swanwick SO31 .... 106 A1
Swanwick, Lwr Swanwick SO31 . 128 B4
Whitsbury SP6 .... 69 E4
Green Loaning 4 BH23 ...... 207 F3
Green Park Cl SO23 .... 2 A1
Green Park Rd SO16 .... 101 F4
Green Pk BH1 .... 205 D2
Green Pond Cnr P09 .... 136 A1
Green Pond La SO51 .... 29 E2
Green Rd
Bournemouth BH9 .... 205 D4
Gosport P012 .... 181 D1
Poole BH15 .... 202 B1
Portsmouth P05 .... 182 B2
Stubbington P014 .... 154 B2

Green The Liss GU33 .... 20 C3
Locks Heath SO31 .... 128 C3
Romsey SO51 .... 28 B1
Rowland's Castle P09 .... 113 E1
Whiteparish SP5 .... 24 A2
Green Wlk P015 .... 130 C2
Green's Cl SO50 .... 57 D1
Greenacre BH25 .... 210 A4
Greenacre Cl BH26 .... 201 E3
Greenacre Gdns P07 .... 134 B2
Greenbank BH13 .... 204 A2
Greenacres Cl BH10 .... 189 F3
Greenacres Dr SO21 .... 31 E2
Greenacres Special Sch SO22 . 1 C1
Greenaway La SO31 .... 128 B1
Greenbank Cres SO16 .... 78 C3
Greenbanks Cl SO41 .... 211 E2
Greenbanks Gdns P016 .... 131 E1
Greenclose La BH21 .... 163 E2
Greendale Cl
Chandler's Ford SO53 .... 55 F3
Fareham P015 .... 130 B2
Greendale The P015 .... 130 B2
Greenfield Gdns BH25 ...... 210 A4
Greenfield Rd BH15 .... 202 C4
Greenfield Rise P08 .... 112 A2
Greenfields Liss GU33 .... 21 D2
Poole BH12 .... 203 F4
Greenfields Ave SO40 .... 76 C1
Greenfields Cl SO40 .... 76 C1
Greenfinch Cl Broadstone BH17 186 C1
Eastleigh SO50 .... 55 E1
Greenfinch Wlk BH24 .... 141 E3
Greenhayes BH18 .... 187 E1
Greenhays Rise BH21 .... 163 E3
Greenhill Ave SO22 .... 10 C4
Greenhill Cl
Wimborne Minster BH21 .... 163 E3
Winchester SO22 .... 10 C4
Greenhill La Rownhams SO16 .. 77 F4
Wimborne Minster BH21 .... 163 E3
Greenhill Rd
Wimborne Minster BH21 .... 163 E3
Winchester SO22 .... 10 B4
Greenhill Terr SO22 .... 10 C4
Greenlea Cl P07 .... 134 A1
Greenlea Cres SO16 .... 79 E3
Greenlea Rd P012 .... 180 C4
Greenmead Ave SO41 ...... 196 B1
Greens Cl SO32 .... 83 D4
Greens Meade SP5 .... 47 E3
Greenside BH25 .... 210 A3
Greensleeves Ave BH18 .... 187 D3
Greensome Dr BH22 .... 165 F3
Greenway GU32 .... 38 C1
Greenway Cl SO41 .... 197 E2
Greenway Cres BH16 .... 201 D4
Greenway La GU31 .... 65 E3
Greenway Rd P012 .... 181 D3
Greenway The P010 .... 136 C2
Greenways
Chandler's Ford SO53 .... 55 F3
Christchurch BH23 .... 208 C4
Milford on Sea SO41 .... 211 E3
Southampton SO16 .... 79 E3
Swanmore SO32 .... 84 A3
Greenways Ave BH8 .... 190 B2
Greenways Ct BH22 .... 165 F2
Greenways Rd SO42 .... 146 A1
Greenwich The SO45 .... 150 C1
Greenwood Ave Cosham P06 .. 157 E4
Ferndown BH22 .... 165 F3
Poole BH14 .... 214 B4
Rownhams SO16 .... 77 E3
Greenwood Cl Eastleigh SO50 .. 55 F1
Fareham P016 .... 131 D2
Romsey SO51 .... 53 D4
Greenwood Copse BH24 .... 140 A2
Greenwood La SO32 .... 82 A4
Greenwood Rd BH9 .... 204 C4
Greenwood Way BH24 ...... 140 A2
Greenwoods 32 BH25 .... 195 D1
Greetham St P01 .... 182 B3
Gregory Gdns SO40 .... 76 B1
Gregory La SO32 .... 82 B3
Gregson Ave P013 .... 155 E2
Gregson Cl P013 .... 155 E2
Grenadier Cl SO31 .... 129 D1
Grendon Cl SO16 .... 79 D3
Grenehurst Way GU31 .... 40 C2
Grenfell Rd BH9 .... 189 F2
Grenfield Ct P010 .... 136 C2
Grenville Cl 1 BH24 .... 117 E1
Grenville Ct
6 Bournemouth BH4 .... 204 B2
12 Poole BH15 .... 202 B1
Southampton, SO15 .... 102 C4
Southampton, Bitterne Pk SO18 . 79 F2
Grenville Gdns SO45 .... 126 A1
Grenville House 22 P01 .... 182 A3
Grenville Rd
4 Portsmouth P05 .... 182 C2
Wimborne Minster BH21 .... 163 E2
Gresham Rd BH9 .... 190 A1
Gresley Gdns SO30 .... 81 E1
Greville Gn P010 .... 136 C2
Greville Rd SO15 .... 102 B4
Greycot Cl BH21 .... 138 C4
Greyfriars 19 SO23 .... 11 D4
Greyfriars Ct 31 P05 .... 182 B2
Greyfriars Rd P015 .... 130 B1
Greyhound Cl SO30 .... 81 D2
Greyladyes SO45 .... 128 A4
Greys Farm Cl BH24 .... 14 B2
Greyshott Ave P014 .... 154 B4
Greystoke Ave BH11 .... 188 C3
Greywell Ave SO16 .... 78 B2

Greywell Ct SO16 .... 78 B2
Greywell Sq P09 .... 135 F3
Griffen Cl SO50 .... 56 C1
Griffin Cl Southampton SO17 .. 103 E4
15 Wimborne Minster BH21 .. 163 E2
Griffin Ind Pk SO40 .... 76 C1
Griffin Wlk P013 .... 180 B3
Griffiths Gdns BH10 .... 189 D3
Griffon Cl SO31 .... 105 D1
Grigg La SO42 .... 146 A1
Grindle Cl P016 .... 132 B1
Gritanwood Rd P04 .... 183 D1
Grosvenor Cl BH10 .... 189 F3
Grosvenor Ct 19 BH1 .... 205 D2
Grosvenor Rd Southampton SO17 79 E1
St Leonards BH24 .... 139 E3
Grosvenor Ct
2 Bournemouth BH1 .... 205 E2
Christchurch BH23 .... 209 D4
Cosham P06 .... 158 C4
Romsey SO51 .... 53 E4
7 Southampton SO17 .... 79 E1
Stubbington P014 .... 179 E3
Grosvenor Dr SO23 .... 2 A1
Grosvenor Gdns
Bournemouth BH1 .... 205 F2
Southampton SO17 .... 79 E1
West End SO18 .... 104 B4
Grosvenor House 13 P05 .. 182 B2
Grosvenor Lodge 5 SO17 .. 79 E1
Grosvenor Mews
Gosport P012 .... 181 E3
Lymington SO41 .... 197 E3
8 Southampton SO17 .... 79 E1
Grosvenor Rd
Bournemouth BH4 .... 204 B2
Chandler's Ford SO53 .... 30 C1
Southampton SO17 .... 79 E1
Grosvenor Sq SO15 .... 102 C3
Grosvenor St P05 .... 182 B2
Grove Ave Gosport P012 .... 181 E3
Portchester P016 .... 156 B3
Grove Bldgs 6 P012 .... 181 E2
Grove Ct 14 P09 .... 135 F1
Grove Gdns SO19 .... 104 A1
Grove La SP5 .... 47 F4
Grove Mansions 21 BH1 .... 205 D2
Grove Mews SO19 .... 104 A1
Grove Pastures SO41 .... 197 F2
Grove Pl Lymington SO41 .. 197 F2
Southampton SO19 .... 104 A1
Grove Rd Barton on Sea BH25 .. 210 A4
Bournemouth BH1 .... 205 D2
Compton(Hants) SO21 .... 31 E3
Cosham P06 .... 158 B4
Fareham P016 .... 131 D1
Gosport P012 .... 181 D1
Lee-on-the-Solent P013 ...... 179 F1
Lymington SO41 .... 197 F2
Southampton SO15 .... 102 B4
Wimborne Minster BH21 .... 163 E2
Grove Rd E BH23 .... 207 D4
Grove Rd N BH23 .... 206 C4
Grove Rd S BH23 .... 206 C4
Grove Rd W BH23 .... 206 C4
Grove St SO14 .... 103 E3
Grove The Bournemouth BH9 .. 189 F2
Bursledon SO31 .... 105 D1
Christchurch BH23 .... 191 F1
Ferndown BH22 .... 165 E2
Netley SO31 .... 127 E4
Southampton SO19 .... 104 A1
Stubbington P014 .... 179 D3
Verwood BH31 .... 115 D3
Westbourne P010 .... 137 D2
Grovelands Rd SO22 .... 1 A1
Groveley Rd Bournemouth BH4 .. 204 A1
Christchurch BH23 .... 207 D4
Groveley Way SO51 .... 28 C1
Grovely Ave BH5 .... 205 F2
Groves Down SO51 .... 50 C2
Grundles SO31 .... 41 D2
Gruneisen Rd P02 .... 157 E2
Guardhouse Rd P01 .... 182 A4
Guardian Rd 30 SO17 .... 79 D1
Guardroom Rd P02 .... 157 D1
Gudge Heath La P015 ...... 130 C1
Guelders The P07 .... 134 C2
Guernsey Cl SO16 .... 77 F2
Guernsey Rd BH12 .... 188 B1
Guessens La P014 .... 153 F4
Guest Ave BH12 .... 204 A3
Guest Cl BH12 .... 204 A3
Guest Rd Bishopstoke SO50 .. 56 B2
Upton BH16 .... 201 D4
Guildford Ct P010 .... 137 F1
Guildford Rd Bournemouth BH4 .. 204 B2
Gosport P013 .... 180 B3
Guildford Dr SO53 .... 55 D2
Guildford Rd P01 .... 182 C3
Guildford St 30 SO14 ...... 103 E3
Guildhall Ct 4 BH15 .... 202 A1
Guildhall Sq 15 P01 .... 182 B3
Guildhall Wlk P01 .... 182 B3
Guildhill Rd BH6 .... 206 C2
Guillemot Cl SO45 .... 126 A1
Guillemot Gdns P013 .... 155 D2
Gull Cl P013 .... 155 D1
Gulliver Cl BH14 .... 214 B4
Gulliver Ct 3 BH21 .... 163 E3
Gulls The SO40 .... 101 F4
Gullycroft Mead SO30 ...... 105 D4
Gunners Bldgs P07 .... 157 F2
Gunners Pk SO32 .... 83 F4
Gunners Row P04 .... 183 D1
Gunners Way P012 .... 155 F1
Gunstore Rd P03 .... 158 A2

Gunville Cres BH9 .... 190 A2
Gunwharf Rd P01 .... 182 A2
Gurjun Cl P08 .... 201 D4
Gurkha Mus The SO22 .... 10 C3
Gurnard Rd P06 .... 157 F4
Gurnays Mead SO51 .... 50 C2
Gurney Rd Corfe Mullen BH21 .. 186 C3
Portsmouth P04 .... 183 D2
Southampton SO15 .... 102 B4
Gussage Rd BH12 .... 203 F4
Gutner La P011 .... 160 B1
Guy's Cl BH24 .... 141 D3
Gwatkin Cl P09 .... 135 E2
Gwen-Rhian Ct 10 SO15 .. 102 C4
Gwenlyn Rd BH16 .... 201 E3
Gwynne Rd BH12 .... 203 F3
Gypsy La BH24 .... 141 D4

H Ave SO45 .... 150 C3
Ha'penny Dell P07 .... 134 C2
Haarlem Mews BH23 .... 207 E4
Hack Dr SO21 .... 56 C4
Hacketts La SO32 .... 60 C1
Hackleys La SO51 .... 51 D3
Hackupps La SO51 .... 6 B1
Hackworth Gdns SO30 ...... 81 E2
Hadden Rd BH8 .... 205 E4
Hadden Cl P015 .... 130 C1
Haddon Dr SO50 .... 56 A3
Haddons Dr BH21 .... 138 B4
Hadleigh Gdns SO50 .... 56 A3
Hadleigh Rd 6 P06 .... 157 E4
Hadley Field SO45 .... 150 A3
Hadley Way BH18 .... 186 C2
Hadow Rd BH10 .... 189 E2
Hadrian Cl BH22 .... 165 E1
Hadrian Way Chilworth SO16 .. 78 C4
Corfe Mullen BH21 .... 186 C4
Hadrians Cl SO53 .... 55 F4
Haglane Copse SO41 .... 197 E1
Hahnemann Rd BH2 .... 204 C1
Haig Ave BH13 .... 203 F1
Haig Rd SO50 .... 57 D1
Haileybury Gdns SO30 ...... 81 E1
Haking Rd BH23 .... 207 E4
Halcyon Ct BH15 .... 202 B3
Halden Cl 2 SO51 .... 28 A1
Hale Ave BH25 .... 195 D1
Hale Ct P01 .... 182 C4
Hale Gdns BH25 .... 195 D1
Hale La SP6 .... 47 D2
Hale Prim Sch SP6 .... 47 E2
Hale St N P01 .... 182 B3
Hale St S P01 .... 182 B3
Hales Dr SO30 .... 105 D3
Halewood Way BH23 .... 206 C4
Half Moon St 2 P01 .... 182 A3
Halfpenny La P01 .... 182 A2
Halfway Rd SO45 .... 151 F1
Halifax Ct SO30 .... 80 B1
Halifax Rise P07 .... 134 C4
Halifax Way BH23 .... 208 A4
Hall Cl SO32 .... 83 E4
Hall Ct SO32 .... 107 D4
Hall Lands La SO50 .... 57 F1
Hall Rd BH11 .... 188 C2
Hall Way The SO22 .... 1 A3
Hallet Cl SO18 .... 80 A1
Hallett Rd P09 .... 136 A1
Halletts Cl P014 .... 154 B2
Halliards The P014 .... 155 D4
Halliday Cl P012 .... 181 D3
Halliday Cres P04 .... 183 E2
Halliday House P04 .... 183 D1
Halsey Cl P012 .... 180 C2
Halstead Rd Cosham P06 .. 157 E4
Southampton SO18 .... 79 F1
Halstock Cres BH17 .... 187 E1
Halter Path BH15 .... 201 F4
Halter Rise P04 .... 164 B3
Halterworth Cl SO51 .... 53 D4
Halterworth La SO51 .... 53 E4
Halterworth Prim Sch SO51 .. 53 E4
Halton Cl BH23 .... 193 D4
Haltons Cl SO40 .... 76 B1
Halyard Cl P013 .... 180 B4
Halyards SO31 .... 128 A2
Ham La Ferndown BH21 .... 164 C2
Gosport P012 .... 156 A1
Horndean P08 .... 112 A4
Southbourne P010 .... 161 E4
Wimborne Minster BH21 .... 164 B2
Hambert Way SO40 .... 100 C3
Hamble Cl SO31 .... 128 B1
Hamble Ct
Chandler's Ford SO53 .... 55 E3
Stubbington P014 .... 154 A2
3 Waterlooville P08 .... 111 F2
Hamble House P014 .... 155 D4
Hamble House Gdns SO31 ...... 128 A1
Hamble La Bursledon SO31 .. 127 F4
Hamble-le-Rice SO31 .... 127 F4
Waterlooville P08 .... 134 C3
Hamble Manor SO31 .... 128 A1
Hamble Prim Sch SO31 ...... 127 F2
Hamble Rd Gosport P012 .... 180 C2
Poole BH15 .... 203 D3
Hamble Sec Sch SO31 .... 127 F3
Hamble Springs SO32 .... 83 E4
Hamble Sta SO31 .... 127 F2
Hamblecliff House SO31 .... 127 E4
Hambledon Cl 2 SO22 ...... 1 B4
Hambledon Gdns BH6 ...... 206 B3
Hambledon Inf Sch P07 ...... 86 B2
Hambledon La SO32 .... 85 F2

Hambledon Par PO7 .... 111 E1
Hambledon Rd Clanfield PO8 .... 88 A3
Denmead PO7 .... 111 D2
Hambledon PO7 .... 110 B4
Waterlooville PO7, PO8 .... 111 D2
Hambleside Ct SO31 .... 127 F1
Hambleton Rd BH7 .... 206 A4
Hamblewood Botley SO30 .... 106 A3
Swanwick SO31 .... 128 B4
Hamblewood Ct SO30 .... 106 A3
Hambrook Rd 2 PO12 .... 181 D3
Hambrook St PO5 .... 182 A2
Hamdown Cres SO51 .... 51 D1
Hameldon Cl SO16 .... 101 F4
Hamilton Cl Bournemouth BH1 . 205 E3
Christchurch BH23 .... 207 F4
Hamworthy BH15 .... 201 F1
Havant PO9 .... 159 F4
Hamilton Cres BH15 .... 201 F1
Hamilton Ct
10 Bournemouth BH8 .... 205 D3
Milford on Sea SO41 .... 211 E2
18 Portsmouth PO5 .... 182 B1
22 Southampton SO17 .... 79 D1
Hamilton Gr PO13 .... 155 F3
Hamilton Mews Hythe SO45 ... 126 A1
Lymington SO41 .... 197 F2
Hamilton Pk SP5 .... 47 D4
Hamilton Rd Bishopstoke SO50 . 56 B2
Bournemouth BH1 .... 205 E2
Corfe Mullen BH21 .... 186 C3
Hamworthy BH15 .... 201 F1
Hythe SO45 .... 150 A4
Portchester PO6 .... 156 C4
Portsmouth PO5 .... 182 B1
Hamilton Way BH25 .... 194 C1
Hamlet Ct SO45 .... 151 D2
Hamlet Way PO12 .... 156 A1
Hammond House PO12 .... 181 F2
Hammond Ind Pk PO14 .... 179 E3
Hammond Rd PO15 .... 130 C1
Hammonds Cl SO40 .... 100 C4
Hammonds Gn SO40 .... 100 C4
Hammonds La SO40 .... 100 C4
Hammonds Way SO40 .... 100 C4
Hampage Gn PO9 .... 135 E4
Hampden La BH6 .... 227 F3
Hampden Ind Pk PO14 .... 179 E3
Hampreston CE Fst Sch BH21 .. 164 C2
Hampshire Ct
26 Bournemouth BH2 .... 204 C2
Chandler's Ford SO53 .... 55 E2
Hampshire Ctr The BH8 .... 190 C1
Hampshire Hatches La BH24 ... 141 D2
Hampshire Health &
Tennis Club The SO30 .... 80 C1
Hampshire House 28 BH2 ..... 204 C2
Hampshire St PO1 .... 182 C4
Hampshire Terr PO1 .... 182 A2
Hampton Cl Blackfield SO45 .... 177 F4
Waterlooville PO7 .... 135 D4
Hampton Dr BH24 .... 117 D1
Hampton Gdns SO45 .... 177 F4
Hampton Gr PO15 .... 130 A1
Hampton La Blackfield SO45 ... 150 C1
Winchester SO22 .... 1 B1
Hampton Towers 4 SO19 ...... 126 C4
Hamptworth Rd SP5 .... 48 B2
Hamtun Cres SO40 .... 76 C1
Hamtun Gdns SO40 .... 76 C1
Hamtun Rd SO19 .... 104 B2
Hamtun St 11 SO14 .... 102 C2
Hamworthy Fst Sch BH15 ...... 201 F1
Hamworthy Mid Sch BH15 ..... 201 F1
Hamworthy Sta BH16 .... 201 E2
Hanbidge Cres PO13 .... 155 E2
Hanbidge Wlk PO13 .... 155 E2
Handel Rd SO15 .... 102 C3
Handel Terr SO15 .... 102 C3
Handford Pl 2 SO15 .... 102 C3
Handley Ct BH24 .... 140 C4
Handley Lodge BH12 .... 203 F4
Handley Rd PO12 .... 180 C3
Handsworth House 5 PO5 ..... 182 B2
Hanger Way GU31 .... 41 D2
Hangers The SO32 .... 59 F1
Hanham Rd Corfe Mullen BH21 186 B3
Wimborne Minster BH21 .... 163 E3
Hankinson Rd BH9 .... 205 D4
Hanley Rd SO15 .... 102 B4
Hann Rd SO16 .... 77 F3
Hannah Gdns PO7 .... 134 C4
Hannah Way SO41 .... 196 C3
Hannay Rise SO19 .... 104 B3
Hannington Pl BH7 .... 206 A3
Hannington Rd
Bournemouth BH7 .... 206 A3
Havant PO9 .... 135 E4
Hanns Way SO50 .... 56 A1
Hanover Bldgs SO14 .... 103 D2
Hanover Cotts SO32 .... 36 C3
Hanover Ct 3 Hythe SO45 ..... 126 A2
Portsmouth SO16 .... 182 A2
Hanover Gdns PO16 .... 131 D2
Hanover Gn BH17 .... 202 C4
Hanover House Gosport PO13 . 155 D3
Poole BH15 .... 202 B2
Totton SO40 .... 101 D4
Hanover Lodge SO22 .... 10 C3
Hanover St PO1 .... 182 A3
Hants Corporate Pk SO53 ...... 55 D1
Hanway Rd PO1, PO2 .... 182 C4
Harbeck Rd BH8 .... 190 B2
Harborough Rd SO15 .... 102 C3

Harbour Cl BH13 .... 214 B3
Harbour Cres BH13 .... 207 F3
Harbour Ct
Barton on Sea BH25 .... 209 F4
Christchurch BH23 .... 207 F3
Poole BH13 .... 214 C3
Harbour Hill Cres BH15 .... 202 C3
Harbour Hill Rd BH15 .... 202 C3
Harbour Hospl The BH15 .... 202 B2
Harbour Lights 202 C2
Harbour Par SO15 .... 102 C2
Harbour Prospect BH14 .... 214 B4
Harbour Rd Bournemouth BH6 . 207 D2
Gosport PO12 .... 181 F3
South Hayling PO11 .... 184 B2
Harbour Tower PO12 .... 181 F2
Harbour View PO16 .... 156 B3
Harbour View Cl BH14 .... 203 D3
Harbour View Ct BH23 .... 207 D3
Harbour View Rd BH14 .... 203 D2
Harbour Watch BH14 .... 214 B4
Harbour Way Emsworth PO10 . 161 D4
Portsmouth PO2 .... 157 E1
Harbour Wlk PO1 .... 182 A2
Harbourne Gdns SO18 .... 80 A1
Harbourside PO9 .... 159 F3
Harbridge Ct PO9 .... 135 E4
Harbridge Dro BH24 .... 93 E2
Harcombe Cl BH17 .... 187 F2
Harcourt Cl PO8 .... 112 A2
Harcourt Mews 7 BH5 .... 206 A3
Harcourt Rd
Bournemouth BH5 .... 206 A3
Fareham PO14 .... 154 A4
Gosport PO12 .... 181 D3
Portsmouth PO1 .... 182 C4
Southampton SO18 .... 103 F4
Hard The Gosport PO12 .... 181 E3
Portsmouth PO1 .... 182 A3
Harding La SO50 .... 57 D2
Harding Rd PO12 .... 180 C3
Hardley Ind Est SO45 .... 150 A3
Hardley La SO45 .... 150 A4
Hardley Sch SO45 .... 150 B3
Hardman Ct PO3 .... 158 A2
Hardwick Rd SO53 .... 55 E3
Hardwicke Cl SO16 .... 77 F1
Hardwicke Way SO31 .... 127 F2
Hardy Cl Locks Heath SO31 .... 129 D2
New Milton BH25 .... 194 C2
Southampton SO15 .... 102 A3
West Moors BH22 .... 138 C1
Hardy Cres BH23 .... 163 E2
Hardy Dr SO45 .... 126 A1
Hardy Rd Corfe Mullen PO6 .... 158 C4
Eastleigh SO50 .... 56 A1
Poole BH14 .... 203 E2
West Moors BH22 .... 138 C1
Hare La Alderholt BH21 .... 91 F3
Hordle SO41 .... 195 F2
New Milton BH25 .... 195 F2
Harebell Cl PO16 .... 131 E2
Harefield Cl SO51 .... 53 D4
Harefield Inf Sch SO18 .... 104 A4
Harefield Jun Sch SO18 .... 104 A4
Harefield Rd SO17 .... 79 E2
Hares Gn BH7 .... 206 A4
Harestock Cl SO22 .... 1 B3
Harestock Cnr SO22 .... 1 B2
Harestock Prim Sch SO22 ...... 1 B2
Harestock Rd Havant PO9 .... 135 E2
Winchester SO22 .... 1 B2
Harewood Ave BH7 .... 206 A3
Harewood Cl SO40 .... 56 A4
Harewood Cres BH7 .... 205 F4
Harewood Gdns BH7 .... 205 F4
Harewood Gn SO41 .... 212 A2
Harewood Pl BH7 .... 206 A3
Harford Cl SO41 .... 197 E1
Harford Rd BH12 .... 203 E4
Harkness Dr PO7 .... 135 D4
Harkwood Dr BH15 .... 201 F2
Harland Cres SO15 .... 78 B1
Harland Rd BH6 .... 207 D2
Harlaxton Cl SO50 .... 55 F3
Harlech Dr SO53 .... 55 D2
Harlequin Gr PO15 .... 130 C1
Harleston Rd PO6 .... 133 E1
Harleston Villas 10 BH21 ...... 163 E2
Harley Ct SO31 .... 128 B1
Harley Wlk 62 PO1 .... 182 B3
Harlyn Rd SO16 .... 77 F1
Harness Cl BH21 .... 164 A3
Harold Cl SO40 .... 100 B3
Harold Rd Portsmouth PO4 ..... 182 C2
South Hayling PO11 .... 185 D1
Southampton SO15 .... 102 A4
Stubbington SO14 .... 154 B2
Westbourne PO10 .... 137 D2
Harold Terr PO10 .... 136 C1
Harpway La Burton BH23 .... 192 B3
Sopley BH23 .... 192 B3
Harrage The SO51 .... 52 C4
Harrier Cl Horndean PO8 .... 112 A4
Lee-on-the-Solent PO13 .... 179 F1
Southampton SO16 .... 78 A3
Harrier Dr BH21 .... 163 E1
Harrier Way Fawley SO45 .... 150 A3
Petersfield GU31 .... 41 E1
Harriers Cl BH23 .... 208 B4
Harriet Cl PO14 .... 179 D3
Harrington Ct BH23 .... 208 C4
Harris Ave SO30 .... 105 E4
Harris Rd PO13 .... 155 E2
Harris Way BH31 .... 195 D3
Harrison Ave BH1 .... 205 E4
Harrison Cl BH23 .... 192 B1
Harrison House 12 PO2 .... 157 E1

Harrison Prim Sch PO16 .... 131 D1
Harrison Rd Fareham PO16 ..... 131 D1
Southampton SO17 .... 79 E2
Harrison Way BH22 .... 138 C2
Harrison's Cut SO14 .... 103 D2
Harrow Cl BH23 .... 193 D4
Harrow Down SO22 .... 10 B2
Harrow La GU32 .... 40 C3
Harrow Rd Bransgore BH23 .... 193 D3
Portsmouth PO5 .... 182 C2
Harrowgate La PO7, PO8 .... 87 D1
Harry Barrow Cl 1 BH24 .... 141 D3
Harry Law Hall 17 PO1 .... 182 B3
Hart Ct BH25 .... 194 C2
Hart Ct SO19 .... 103 F2
Hart Hill SO45 .... 126 B1
Hart Plain Ave PO8 .... 111 F2
Hart Plain Jun & Inf Sch
PO7, PO8 .... 111 F1
Hartford House PO1 .... 182 A2
Harthill Dro SP5 .... 47 F3
Harting Cl PO8 .... 88 B2
Harting Down SO22 .... 41 D2
Harting Gdns PO16 .... 132 B1
Harting Rd BH6 .... 206 B4
Hartington Rd Gosport PO12 .. 180 C3
Southampton SO14 .... 103 D3
Hartland Ct PO10 .... 137 E1
Hartland's Rd PO16 .... 131 D1
Hartley Ave SO17 .... 79 D2
Hartley Cl Bishopstoke SO50 .. 57 D1
Hythe SO45 .... 126 A1
Hartley Rd Bishopstoke SO50 . 57 D1
Portsmouth PO2 .... 157 F2
Hartley Wlk SO45 .... 126 A1
Hartnell Ct BH21 .... 186 B3
Harts Farm Way PO9 .... 159 E4
Harts Way SO41 .... 196 B1
Hartsbourne Dr BH7 .... 206 A4
Hartsgrove Ave SO45 .... 150 C1
Hartsgrove Cl SO45 .... 150 C1
Hartwell Rd PO3 .... 158 A2
Hartwood Gdns PO8 .... 111 F1
Harvest Cl SO22 .... 10 B2
Harvest Rd PO7 .... 110 C2
Harvester Dr PO15 .... 130 A1
Harvester Way SO41 .... 197 E3
Harvestgate Wlk 9 PO9 .... 135 E3
Harvesting La GU32 .... 64 B3
Harvey Brown House PO11 ..... 185 D3
Harvey Cres SO31 .... 128 C1
Harvey Cl SO45 .... 150 C1
Harvey Gdns SO45 .... 126 A2
Harvey House PO4 .... 183 D1
Harvey Rd Bishopstoke SO50 .. 56 C1
Bournemouth BH5 .... 206 A3
Oakley BH21 .... 187 F4
Harwell Rd BH17 .... 202 B4
Harwich Rd PO6 .... 133 E1
Harwood Rd Gosport PO13 ..... 155 E2
Totton SO40 .... 100 B4
Harwood Ct 13 BH25 .... 194 C2
Harwood Pl SO23 .... 2 B4
Harwood Rd PO13 .... 155 E2
Haselbury Rd SO40 .... 100 C4
Haselworth Dr PO12 .... 181 D1
Haselworth Prim Sch PO12 .... 181 D2
Haskells Cl SO43 .... 121 F2
Haskells Rd BH12 .... 203 D4
Haslar Cres PO7 .... 111 E1
Haslar Rd PO12 .... 181 E1
Haslar Terr PO12 .... 181 E1
Haslegrave House 2 PO2 .... 182 B4
Haslemere Ave BH23 .... 209 D4
Haslemere Gdns PO11 .... 185 F1
Haslemere Pl BH23 .... 209 D4
Haslemere Rd Portsmouth PO4 182 C2
Southbourne PO10 .... 137 E1
Hasler Rd BH17 .... 187 E1
Haslop Rd BH21 .... 164 A4
Hassocks The PO7 .... 135 D4
Hastings Ave PO12 .... 180 C4
Hastings House 3 PO2 .... 157 E1
Hastings Rd Bournemouth BH8 190 C4
Broadstone BH17 .... 187 D1
Hatch Ct PO9 .... 135 E4
Hatch La GU33 .... 21 E2
Hatch Mead SO30 .... 80 B1
Hatch Pond Rd BH17 .... 202 B4
Hatchers Ls SO21 .... 33 D3
Hatchet Cl SP6 .... 47 E2
Hatchet La Beaulieu SO42 ...... 175 E4
East Boldre SO42 .... 175 E4
Hatchley La SO21 .... 58 A3
Hatfield Ct BH25 .... 194 C2
Hatfield Gdns BH7 .... 206 A4
Hatfield Rd PO4 .... 183 D2
Hathaway Cl SO50 .... 56 A2
Hathaway Gdns PO7 .... 112 A1
Hathaway Rd BH6 .... 206 B2
Hatherden Ave BH14 .... 202 C3
Hatherley Cres PO16 .... 156 A4
Hatherley Dr PO16 .... 156 A4
Hatherley Mans 4 SO15 .... 102 B4
Hatherley Rd Cosham PO6 ..... 133 D1
Winchester SO22 .... 1 C1
Hatley Rd SO18 .... 104 A4
Hatt La SO51 .... 5 F1
Havant Bsns Ctr PO9 .... 159 E4
Havant Coll 135 F1
Havant Farm Cl PO9 .... 135 F2
Havant Rd Cosham PO6 .... 158 B4
Emsworth PO10 .... 160 C4
Horndean PO8 .... 112 B4
North Hayling PO11 .... 159 F1
Portsmouth PO2 .... 182 C4
Havant St PO1 .... 182 A3
Havant Sta PO9 .... 135 F1

Havant War Meml Hospl PO9 .. 135 F1
Havant-By-Pass PO9 .... 160 A4
Havelock Cl SO31 .... 128 B1
Havelock Rd Locks Heath SO31 204 A3
Poole BH12 .... 204 A3
Portsmouth PO5 .... 182 B2
Southampton SO14 .... 102 C3
Havelock Way BH23 .... 193 E1
Haven Cres PO14 .... 153 F1
Haven Ct
4 Milford on Sea SO41 .... 211 E2
Poole BH13 .... 214 A2
Haven Gdns BH25 .... 195 D1
Haven Rd Corfe Mullen BH21 .. 186 B3
Poole BH13 .... 214 C4
South Hayling PO11 .... 185 F1
Haven The Eastleigh SO50 ..... 56 A3
Gosport PO12 .... 181 D1
Locks Heath SO31 .... 129 D2
Portsmouth PO4 .... 183 D3
Southampton SO19 .... 103 F2
Havendale SO30 .... 105 E3
Havenhurst BH13 .... 214 C3
Havenstone Way SO18 .... 79 E2
Haverstock Rd BH9 .... 190 A2
Haviland Rd
Bournemouth BH1, BH7 .... 205 F3
Ferndown BH21 .... 165 D4
Haviland Rd E BH7 .... 205 F3
Haviland Rd W 6 BH7 .... 205 F3
Havisham Rd PO2 .... 182 B4
Havre Towers 5 SO19 .... 126 C4
Hawden Rd BH11 .... 189 D1
Hawfinch Cl SO16 .... 78 A3
Hawk Cl Stubbington PO14 .... 179 D3
Wimborne Minster BH21 .... 164 A4
Hawkchurch Gdns BH17 .... 187 F1
Hawke St PO1 .... 182 A3
Hawker Cl BH21 .... 163 F1
Hawkeswood Rd SO18 .... 103 E4
Hawkewood Ave PO7 .... 111 E1
Hawkhill SO45 .... 125 F2
Hawkhurst Cl SO19 .... 104 A1
Hawkins Cl BH24 .... 117 E1
Hawkins Cl SO40 .... 101 F2
Hawkins Rd Gosport PO13 ..... 155 E1
Poole BH12 .... 188 C1
Hawkley Gr SO19 .... 126 C4
Hawkley Rd Hawkley GU33 .... 20 B3
Liss GU33 .... 20 B3
Hawks Mead GU33 .... 20 C3
Hawkwell PO16 .... 155 F4
Hawkwood Rd BH5 .... 205 F2
Hawley Cl PO9 .... 135 F3
Haworth Cl BH23 .... 192 A1
Hawstead Gn 4 PO9 .... 135 E3
Hawswater Cl SO16 .... 77 F1
Hawthorn Cl
Colden Common SO21 .... 57 D3
1 Fair Oak SO50 .... 57 E1
Hedge End SO30 .... 105 E3
New Milton BH25 .... 195 E2
Hawthorn Cres PO6 .... 158 A3
Hawthorn Ct 1 GU31 .... 41 E2
Hawthorn Dr Broadstone SO21 186 C1
Sway SO41 .... 172 A1
Hawthorn La SO31 .... 128 C3
Hawthorn Rd
Bournemouth BH9 .... 204 C4
Burton BH23 .... 192 C4
Denmead PO7 .... 110 C2
Horndean PO8 .... 88 B1
Hythe SO45 .... 125 F2
Southampton SO19 .... 79 D1
Hawthorn Wlk 20 PO13 .... 179 F1
Hawthorne Gr PO13 .... 185 D2
Hawthorne Rd SO40 .... 100 B4
Hawthorns The
Bishop's Waltham SO32 .... 83 D4
Christchurch BH23 .... 207 F3
Eastleigh SO50 .... 55 F1
Marchwood SO40 .... 102 A1
Southampton SO19 .... 104 A3
Hayburn Rd SO16 .... 77 F1
Haydens Ct SO41 .... 197 E2
Haydn Cl SO23 .... 2 A4
Haydock Cl SO40 .... 100 B4
Haydock Mews PO7 .... 112 A1
Haydon Br BH13 .... 204 A1
Hayes Ave BH7 .... 205 F3
Hayes Cl Fareham PO15 .... 130 B2
Wimborne Minster BH21 .... 164 A2
Hayes La BH24 .... 164 A1
Hayes Mead SO45 .... 150 A3
Hayes Terr PO12 .... 181 D3
Hayeswood Cty Fst Sch BH21 164 A3
Hayeswood Rd BH21 .... 164 A3
Hayle Rd SO18 .... 80 A1
Hayley Cl SO45 .... 149 F4
Hayling Ave PO3 .... 183 D4
Hayling Cl PO14 .... 154 A4
Hayling Sch The PO11 .... 185 D3
Haymoor Mid Sch PO17 .... 187 F1
Haymoor Rd BH15 .... 203 D4
Haynes Ave BH15 .... 202 B3
Haynes Way SO45 .... 125 F1
Hays Cotts GU32 .... 40 B3
Haysoms Cl BH25 .... 195 D1
Hayter Gdns SO51 .... 53 D4
Hayters Way SP6 .... 93 D3
Hayward Bsns Ctr PO9 .... 136 A2
Hayward Cl SO40 .... 100 B4
Hayward Cres BH31 .... 114 C3
Hayward La SO45 .... 150 B2
Hayward Way BH31 .... 114 C3
Haywards Cl PO16 .... 182 A2
Haywards Farm Cl BH31 .... 114 C3
Haywards La BH21 .... 186 B4

Hazel Cl Alderholt SP6 .... 93 E1
Chandler's Ford SO53 .... 30 E1
Christchurch BH23 .... 193 E3
Colden Common SO21 .... 32 A4
Hazel Ct Bournemouth BH9 .... 190 B4
27 New Milton BH25 .... 195 D1
Hazel Rd Locks Heath SO31 ... 182 C1
Hazel Dr SO41 .... 165 E1
Hazel Farm Rd SO40 .... 100 B1
Hazel Gr Ashurst SO40 .... 99 F1
Clanfield PO8 .... 88 B1
Locks Heath SO31 .... 129 D1
Winchester SO22 .... 10 B2
Hazel Rd Clanfield PO8 .... 88 B2
Lymington SO41 .... 197 D3
Southampton SO19 .... 103 E2
Hazel Wood Inf Sch SO40 ..... 100 B1
Hazelbank Cl PO13 .... 41 D2
Hazeldale Villas 6 SO45 .... 126 A1
Hazeldean Ct PO9 .... 113 D1
Hazeldean Dr PO9 .... 113 D1
Hazeldene BH18 .... 187 D1
Hazeldown Rd SO16 .... 77 F1
Hazeleigh Ave SO19 .... 103 F1
Hazeley Cotts SO21 .... 32 B2
Hazeley Gn 45 PO9 .... 136 A2
Hazeley Rd SO21 .... 32 B2
Hazelholt Dr PO9 .... 135 E1
Hazell Ave BH10 .... 189 D2
Hazelton Cl BH7 .... 206 A4
Hazelwood PO14 .... 154 A4
Hazelwood Ave Havant PO9 ... 135 D2
New Milton BH25 .... 194 C3
Hazelwood Dr BH31 .... 115 D3
Hazelwood Rd SO18 .... 80 A1
Hazlebury Rd BH17 .... 202 A4
Hazlemere Dr BH24 .... 141 D3
Hazleton Way PO8 .... 112 A1
Head Down GU31 .... 41 D2
Head's La BH10 .... 189 F3
Headbourne Worthy House
SO23 .... 2 A1
Headland Dr SO31 .... 129 D2
Headlands Adventure Ctr
BH24 .... 117 D2
Headlands Bsns Pk BH24 ...... 117 D3
Headlands The SP5 .... 46 C4
Headless Cross BH10 .... 189 E3
Headley Ct PO13 .... 179 F1
Headon View GU32 .... 37 E3
Heads Farm Cl BH10 .... 189 F3
Headswell Ave BH10 .... 189 F3
Headswell Cres BH10 .... 189 F3
Headswell Gdns BH10 .... 189 F3
Heanor Cl BH10 .... 189 E3
Hearne Gdns SO32 .... 84 A3
Hearts Of Oak Mews SO41 .... 197 E3
Heath Ave BH15 .... 202 B3
Heath Cl Fair Oak SO50 .... 57 E1
Horndean PO8 .... 112 A4
Wimborne Minster BH21 .... 164 A4
Heath Ct BH22 .... 40 C1
Heath Farm Cl BH22 .... 165 E4
Heath Farm Rd BH22 .... 165 E4
Heath Farm Way BH22 .... 165 E4
Heath Gdns SO31 .... 127 E4
Heath House Cl SO30 .... 105 D2
Heath House Gdns SO30 .... 105 D2
Heath House La SO30 .... 105 E2
Heath La SO42 .... 175 E4
Heath Lawns PO15 .... 130 B1
Heath Lodge GU31 .... 41 D1
Heath Rd Christchurch BH23 .. 194 A1
Hordle SO41 .... 195 F2
Locks Heath SO31 .... 129 D2
North Baddesley SO52 .... 54 A2
Petersfield GU31 .... 41 D2
Soberton SO32 .... 85 D1
Southampton SO19 .... 104 A3
St Leonards BH24 .... 139 E2
Heath Rd E GU31 .... 41 D1
Heath Rd N SO31 .... 128 C2
Heath Rd S GU31 .... 128 C2
Heath Rd W GU31 .... 41 D1
Heath The PO7 .... 111 D2
Heathcote Pl SO21 .... 30 A4
Heathcote Rd
Bournemouth BH5 .... 205 F2
Chandler's Ford SO53 .... 55 F3
Portsmouth PO2 .... 157 F1
Heathen St SO32 .... 82 A2
Heather Chase SO50 .... 57 D1
Heather Cl Bournemouth BH8 . 190 B2
Christchurch BH23 .... 194 A1
Corfe Mullen BH21 .... 186 C3
Gosport PO13 .... 155 D1
Hordle SO41 .... 196 A2
St Leonards BH24 .... 139 F2
Totton SO40 .... 100 C4
Waterlooville PO7 .... 134 C3
Heather Ct SO18 .... 104 B4
Heather Dell BH22 .... 165 E4
Heather Gdns PO15 .... 130 B2
Heather Lodge 2 BH25 .... 195 D2
Heather Rd Blackfield SO45 ... 150 C1
Bournemouth BH10 .... 189 E2
Petersfield GU31 .... 41 E2
Heather View Rd BH12 .... 203 F4
Heather Way BH22 .... 165 E4
Heatherbank Rd BH4 .... 204 B2
Heatherbrae Gdns SO52 .... 53 F2
Heatherbrae La BH16 .... 201 D3
Heatherdeane Rd SO17 .... 79 D3
Heatherdene Rd SO53 .... 30 C1
Heatherdown Way BH22 .... 139 D3
Heatherfield GU31 .... 65 E3

Heatherlands Fst Sch BH12 .... 203 F3
Heatherlands Rd SO16 .... 78 C4
Heatherlands Rise BH12 .... 203 B3
Heatherlea Rd BH6 .... 206 B2
Heatherley Ct 26 PO5 .... 182 B2
Heatherstone Rd SO45 .... 125 F1
Heatherton Mews PO10 .... 136 C1
Heatherview SO52 .... 53 F3
Heathfield SO45 .... 125 F1
Heathfield Ave Fareham PO15 . 130 B1
Poole BH12 .... 204 A4
Heathfield Cl
Chandler's Ford SO53 .... 30 B1
Southampton SO19 .... 104 A2
Heathfield House BH23 .... 169 F1
Heathfield Inf Sch SO19 .... 104 B1
Heathfield Jun Sch SO19 .... 104 B2
Heathfield Rd
Chandler's Ford SO53 .... 30 B1
Petersfield GU31 .... 41 E2
Portsmouth PO2 .... 157 E1
Southampton SO19 .... 104 B2
West Moors BH22 .... 139 D1
Heathfield Specl Sch PO14 ... 154 B4
Heathfield Way BH22 .... 138 C1
Heathlands Ave BH22 .... 165 E1
Heathlands Cl Burton BH23 ... 192 B2
Chandler's Ford SO53 .... 55 E4
Verwood BH31 .... 115 D3
Heathlands Prim Sch BH11 ... 189 D2
Heathlands Rd SO53 .... 55 E4
Heathwood Ave BH25 .... 209 F4
Heathwood Rd BH9 .... 204 C4
Heathy Cl BH25 .... 209 F4
Heaton Rd Bournemouth BH10 . 189 D1
Gosport PO12 .... 181 D4
Heavytree Rd BH14 .... 203 D2
Hebrides Cl PO14 .... 154 A2
Heckfield Cl PO9 .... 136 A3
Heckford La BH15 .... 202 B2
Heckford Rd
Corfe Mullen BH21 .... 186 B3
Poole BH15 .... 202 B2
Hector Cl PO7 .... 134 C1
Hector Rd PO14 .... 155 D3
Hedera Rd SO31 .... 128 C2
Hedge End Bsns Ctr SO30 ..... 81 D1
Hedge End Sta SO30 .... 81 E2
Hedge End Wlk 7 PO9 .... 136 A3
Hedgerley BH25 .... 210 A4
Hedgerow Cl SO16 .... 77 F4
Hedgerow Dr SO18 .... 80 A1
Hedgerow Gdns PO10 .... 136 C2
Hedley Cl SO45 .... 150 C1
Hedley Gdns SO30 .... 81 D2
Heidelberg Rd PO4 .... 182 C2
Heights App BH16 .... 201 E4
Heights Rd BH16 .... 201 E4
Heights The Fareham PO16 ..... 131 E1
Hedge End SO30 .... 105 D3
Helena Rd PO4 .... 182 C1
Helford Rd SO18 .... 80 A1
Helic House 2 BH21 .... 163 E3
Hellyer Rd PO4 .... 183 D2
Helm Cl PO13 .... 180 B3
Helsby Cl PO14 .... 154 C4
Helsted Cl PO12 .... 180 C2
Helston Dr PO10 .... 136 C2
Helston Rd PO6 .... 132 C1
Helvellyn Rd SO16 .... 101 F4
Helyar Rd BH8 .... 190 C1
Hemdean Gdns SO30 .... 80 B1
Hemlock Rd PO8 .... 111 F2
Hemlock Way SO52 .... 54 C3
Hemming Cl SO40 .... 100 C3
Hemmingway Gdns PO15 ..... 129 E4
Hempsted Rd PO6 .... 133 D1
Hemsley Wk PO8 .... 112 A2
Henbury Cl Corfe Mullen BH21 .. 186 B3
Poole BH17 .... 188 A1
Henbury Rise BH21 .... 186 B3
Henbury View Fst Sch BH21 .. 186 B3
Henbury View Rd BH21 .... 186 B3
Henderson Rd PO4 .... 183 D2
Hendford Gdns BH10 .... 189 D1
Hendford Rd BH10 .... 189 D1
Hengist Rd BH1 .... 205 E2
Hengistbury Rd
Barton on Sea BH25 .... 209 F4
Bournemouth BH6 .... 207 D2
Henley Ct SO41 .... 211 F2
Henley Gdns
Bournemouth BH7 .... 206 A4
Fareham PO15 .... 130 B2
Henley Rd PO4 .... 182 C2
Henning's Park Rd BH15 ...... 202 C3
Henry Beaufort Sec Sch SO22 ... 1 C2
Henry Cl SO45 .... 150 A3
Henry Cort Com Sch PO15 .... 130 A2
Henry Cort Dr PO15 .... 130 B2
Henry Rd Bishopstoke SO50 ... 56 B2
Southampton SO15 .... 102 B4
Henry St 9 Gosport PO12 ..... 181 E2
Southampton SO15 .... 102 C3
Henstead Ct 9 SO15 .... 102 C3
Henstead Rd SO15 .... 102 C3
Hensting La
Colden Common SO21 .... 32 C1
Owslebury SO21 .... 58 C1
Henty Rd SO16 .... 102 A4
Henville Cl PO3 .... 180 B4
Henville Rd 6 BH8 .... 205 E4
Henwood Down GU31 .... 41 D2
Hepworth Cl SO19 .... 104 B1
Herald Ind Est SO30 .... 81 D1
Herald Rd SO30 .... 81 D1
Herbert Ave BH12 .... 203 E4
Herbert Ct BH12 .... 203 E4

Herbert Hospl BH4 .... 204 A1
Herbert Rd Bournemouth BH4 .. 204 A1
Gosport PO12 .... 180 C3
New Milton BH25 .... 195 D2
Poole BH13 .... 204 A1
Portsmouth PO4 .... 182 C1
Redlynch SP5 .... 47 E3
Herbert St PO1 .... 182 B4
Herbert Walker Ave SO15 .... 102 B2
Herberton Rd BH6 .... 206 B3
Hercules Rd BH15 .... 201 E2
Hercules St PO2 .... 182 B4
Hereford Ct PO13 .... 180 B3
Hereford Rd PO5 .... 182 B2
Hereward Cl SO51 .... 53 D4
Heritage Ct BH13 .... 214 C4
Herm Rd BH12 .... 188 B1
Hermes Rd PO13 .... 179 E2
Hermitage Cl
Bishop's Waltham SO32 .... 83 D4
Havant PO9 .... 135 F2
Hermitage Gdns PO7 .... 134 C4
Hermitage Rd BH14 .... 203 D3
Hermitage The BH14 .... 203 D3
Hern La SP6 .... 94 A3
Herne Jun Sch GU31 .... 41 D2
Herne Rd Charlton PO6 .... 157 F4
Petersfield GU31 .... 41 D2
Heron Cl Portsmouth PO4 ..... 183 D3
Sway SO41 .... 172 A1
Heron Court Rd BH3, BH9 .... 205 A4
Heron Dr BH21 .... 164 A4
Heron La SO51 .... 27 E3
Heron Quay PO10 .... 161 D4
Heron Sq SO50 .... 55 F1
Heron Way PO13 .... 155 D2
Herons Cl PO14 .... 154 B2
Herons Ct PO11 .... 185 D3
Heronswood SO40 .... 76 B1
Herrick Cl SO19 .... 104 B2
Herriot Cl PO8 .... 112 A3
Herriot House PO8 .... 112 A1
Herstone Cl BH17 .... 187 F1
Hertford Cl SP6 .... 69 F2
Hertford Ct 12 BH23 .... 209 D4
Hertford Pl PO1 .... 182 B4
Hertsfield PO14 .... 129 E2
Hesketh Cl BH24 .... 140 A3
Hesketh House 8 SO15 .... 102 B3
Hestan Cl BH23 .... 191 E2
Hester Rd PO4 .... 183 D2
Hestia Cl SO51 .... 53 E4
Heston Way BH22 .... 138 B2
Heston Wlk PO12 .... 180 C2
Hewett Cl PO14 .... 153 F4
Hewett House PO14 .... 153 F4
Hewett Rd Portsmouth PO2 ... 157 F1
Titchfield PO14 .... 153 F4
Hewetts Rise SO31 .... 152 B4
Hewitt Cl PO14 .... 181 D4
Hewitt Rd BH15 .... 201 F2
Hewitt's Rd SO15 .... 102 B3
Heyes Dr SO19 .... 104 B2
Heysham Rd
Broadstone BH18 .... 187 D2
Southampton SO15 .... 102 A4
Heyshott Gdns PO8 .... 88 B2
Heyshott Rd PO4 .... 182 C2
Heytesbury Rd BH6 .... 206 B3
Heyward Rd PO4 .... 182 C2
Heywood Gdns PO9 .... 135 E3
Heywood Gr SO19 .... 104 C3
Hibberd Way BH10 .... 189 E1
Hibbs Cl BH16 .... 201 E4
Hickory Cl BH16 .... 201 D4
Hickory Dr SO22 .... 1 B2
Hickory Gdns SO30 .... 80 B2
High Barn Cotts SO32 .... 36 C2
High Brow SO21 .... 165 E3
High Cross SO32 .... 18 C1
High Cross La GU32 .... 18 B1
High Ct PO4 .... 183 D2
High Dr PO13 .... 155 E1
High Firs Gdns SO51 .... 53 E4
High Firs Rd Romsey SO51 .... 53 E4
Southampton SO19 .... 104 B3
High Howe Cl BH11 .... 188 C2
High Howe Gdns BH11 .... 188 C2
High Howe La BH11 .... 188 C2
High Lawn Way PO9 .... 135 F3
High Marryats 3 BH25 .... 210 A4
High Mead Fareham PO15 .... 130 C2
Ferndown BH22 .... 165 D1
High Mead La BH22 .... 165 D1
High Meadow SO19 .... 104 B3
High Oaks Cl SO31 .... 129 D2
High Oaks Gdns BH11 .... 188 C2
High Park Rd BH18 .... 186 C2
High Pines BH23 .... 208 B4
High Point SO18 .... 103 F4
High Rd SO16 .... 79 E2
High Ridge Cres BH25 .... 195 E1
High St Beaulieu SO42 .... 148 C1
Bishop's Waltham SO32 .... 83 E4
Botley SO30 .... 106 A4
Buriton GU31 .... 65 E3
Bursledon SO31 .... 128 A4
Christchurch BH23 .... 207 D3
Cosham PO6 .... 157 F4
Damerham SP6 .... 68 B3
Downton SP5 .... 47 D4
Droxford SO32 .... 61 D1
East Meon GU32 .... 38 C1
Eastleigh SO50 .... 56 A1
Emsworth PO10 .... 160 C4
Fareham PO14, PO16, PO17 . 131 E1
Fordingbridge SP6 .... 69 F1
Gosport PO12 .... 181 E2

High St continued
Hamble-le-Rice SO31 .... 128 A1
Hambledon PO7 .... 86 B2
Hythe SO45 .... 126 A3
Lee-on-the-Solent PO13 ..... 179 F1
Lymington SO41 .... 197 F2
Lyndhurst SO43 .... 121 F3
Meonstoke SO32 .... 61 E2
Milford on Sea SO41 .... 211 E3
Petersfield GU32 .... 40 C2
Poole BH15 .... 202 B1
Portsmouth PO1 .... 182 A4
Ringwood BH24 .... 140 C4
Shedfield SO32 .... 107 F4
Soberton SO32 .... 85 D2
9 Southampton SO14 .... 103 C2
Southwick PO17 .... 132 C3
St Leonards SO21 .... 139 F3
Titchfield PO14 .... 153 F4
Totton SO40 .... 101 D4
Twyford SO21 .... 32 A3
West End SO30 .... 80 B1
Wimborne Minster BH21 ...... 163 D2
Winchester SO21, SO23 ..... 10 C4
33 Southampton SO21, SO23 .. 11 D4
Woodgreen SP6 .... 70 C4
High St N PO5 .... 202 B2
High Town Hill BH24 .... 141 F4
High Trees Poole BH13 .... 214 D4
Waterlooville PO7 .... 134 C4
High Trees SO22 .... 1 C1
High Trees Wlk BH22 .... 165 E4
High View PO16 .... 132 B1
High View Way SO18 .... 103 F4
High Way BH18 .... 186 C2
High Wlk PO15 .... 130 C2
Highbank Ave PO7 .... 134 B2
Highbank Gdns SP6 .... 69 F1
Highbridge Rd
Colden Common, SO21 ...... 31 F1
Colden Common SO50, SO21 .. 56 B4
Poole BH14 .... 203 D2
Twyford SO21 .... 31 F1
Highbury Bldgs PO6 .... 157 F3
Highbury Cl Fair Oak SO50 .... 57 E1
New Milton BH25 .... 195 D1
Highbury Coll PO6 .... 158 A3
Highbury Gr PO6 .... 158 A3
Highbury Prim Sch PO6 ...... 158 A3
Highbury St PO1 .... 182 A2
Highbury Way PO6 .... 157 F3
Highclere Ave PO9 .... 135 F2
Highclere Rd SO16 .... 78 B2
Highclere Way SO53 .... 55 D2
Highcliff Ave SO14 .... 103 D4
Highcliffe Cnr BH23 .... 209 D4
Highcliffe Comp Sch BH23 .. 193 E1
Highcliffe Cty Jun Sch
Christchurch BH23 .... 193 F1
Christchurch BH23 .... 194 A1
Highcliffe Dr SO50 .... 56 A4
Highcliffe Rd
Christchurch BH23 .... 208 B4
Gosport PO12 .... 180 C2
Winchester SO23 .... 11 D3
Highcroft Ind Est PO8 .... 112 B4
Highcroft La PO8 .... 112 B4
Highcrown Mews SO17 .... 79 D1
Highcrown St SO17 .... 79 D1
Higher Blandford Rd BH18 ... 186 C3
Higher Merley La BH21 .... 186 C4
Highfield Lymington SO41 ..... 197 E2
Twyford SO21 .... 32 A3
Highfield Ave Fareham PO14 .. 154 C4
Lymington SO41 .... 197 E2
Ringwood BH24 .... 141 D4
Southampton SO15 .... 78 C2
Twyford SO21 .... 32 A3
Waterlooville PO7 .... 111 F1
Highfield Campus (Univ of
Southampton) SO17 .... 79 D2
Highfield CE Jun Sch SO17 ... 79 D1
Highfield CE Prim Sch SO17 .. 79 D1
Highfield Cl
Chandler's Ford SO53 .... 55 F3
Corfe Mullen BH21 .... 186 C3
Southampton SO17 .... 79 D1
Sway SO41 .... 172 A1
Waterlooville PO7 .... 111 F1
Highfield Cres SO17 .... 79 D1
Highfield Dr BH24 .... 141 D4
Highfield Gdns Liss GU33 .... 21 D2
Sway SO41 .... 172 A1
Highfield Hall SO17 .... 79 D1
Highfield House 12 BH14 .... 203 D3
Highfield La Redlynch SP5 .... 47 E3
Southampton SO17 .... 79 D1
Highfield Lodge 3 SO17 ...... 79 D1
Highfield Par PO8 .... 112 A1
Highfield Rd
Bournemouth BH9 .... 189 F1
Chandler's Ford SO53 .... 55 F3
Corfe Mullen BH21 .... 186 C3
Gosport PO12 .... 180 C2
Lymington SO41 .... 197 E2
Petersfield GU32 .... 40 C2
Portsmouth PO2 .... 182 B3
Ringwood BH24 .... 141 D4
Southampton SO17 .... 79 D1
West Moors BH22 .... 138 C2
Highfield Terr 17 SO22 .... 10 C4
Highfields SO31 .... 128 C1
Highgate Rd PO3 .... 158 A1
Highgrove Cl SO40 .... 100 B3
Highgrove Ind Pk PO3 .... 158 A2
Highgrove Rd PO3 .... 183 D4
Highland Ave BH23 .... 194 A1
Highland Cl PO10 .... 160 C4

Highland Rd Emsworth PO10 .... 136 C1
Poole BH14 .... 203 D3
Portsmouth PO4 .... 183 D1
Wimborne Minster BH21 ...... 163 E3
Highland St PO4 .... 183 D1
Highland Terr PO4 .... 182 C2
Highland View Cl BH21 .... 163 E3
Highlands Cl Hythe SO45 ..... 126 A1
North Baddesley SO52 .... 53 F3
Highlands Cres BH10 .... 189 E2
Highlands House SO19 .... 103 E2
Highlands Rd
Barton on Sea BH25 .... 210 A4
Cosham PO6 .... 158 B4
Fareham PO15, PO16 .... 130 B2
Highlands Way Hythe SO45 .. 125 F1
Whiteparish SP5 .... 24 A2
Highmoor Cl
Corfe Mullen BH21 .... 186 B3
Poole BH11 .... 203 D2
Highmoor Rd
Bournemouth BH11 .... 189 D1
Corfe Mullen BH21 .... 186 B3
Poole BH11 .... 203 E2
Highmount Cl SO23 .... 11 E3
Highnam Gdns SO31 .... 128 C2
Hightown Gdns BH24 .... 141 E3
Hightown Ind Est BH24 .... 141 D3
Hightown Prim Sch SO19 .... 104 C2
Hightown Rd BH24 .... 141 D3
Hightown Towers SO19 ...... 104 C2
Hightrees Ave BH8 .... 190 C1
Highview Cl BH23 .... 191 F2
Highview Gdns BH12 .... 203 E4
Highways Rd SO21 .... 31 E3
Highwood Cl SP6 .... 92 B3
Highwood La
North Baddesley SO51 .... 53 E4
Ringwood BH24 .... 117 F2
Highwood Lawn PO9 .... 135 E4
Highwood PRU SO42 .... 172 C4
Highwood Rd
Brockenhurst SO42 .... 172 C4
Gosport PO13 .... 180 B4
Poole BH14 .... 203 F2
Higworth La PO11 .... 184 C3
Hilary Ave PO6 .... 158 A4
Hilary Cl SO43 .... 122 A2
Hilary Ct PO13 .... 180 B3
Hilary Rd BH17 .... 187 E1
Hilda Ct 8 SO15 .... 102 C4
Hilda Gdns PO7 .... 111 D2
Hilda Pl 28 SO14 .... 103 E3
Hilda Rd BH12 .... 203 F4
Hilden Ct PO11 .... 184 C2
Hilden Way SO22 .... 1 A3
Hiley Rd BH15 .... 202 B3
Hill Brow Rd Hill Brow GU33 .. 21 D1
Liss GU33 .... 21 D1
Hill Cl Bransgore BH23 .... 193 D4
Fair Oak SO50 .... 57 E3
Hill Close SP6 .... 70 C4
Hill Coppice Rd PO15 .... 129 E3
Hill Croft PO15 .... 129 F2
Hill Dr PO15 .... 130 B2
Hill Farm Rd SO15 .... 102 C3
Hill Head Rd PO14 .... 179 D3
Hill House Sch SO41 .... 173 E1
Hill Houses La SO24 .... 14 A3
Hill La Bransgore BH23 .... 193 D4
Burton BH23 .... 192 C1
Colden Common SO21 .... 31 F1
Southampton SO15 .... 78 C1
Hill Park Rd Fareham PO15 ... 130 B2
Gosport PO12 .... 180 C3
Hill Pl SO31 .... 128 A4
Hill Rd PO16 .... 132 B1
Hill Rise SO21 .... 32 A3
Hill St Ower SO51, SO40 ..... 76 B3
Poole BH15 .... 202 B1
Hill Top SO22 .... 1 B3
Hill View GU32 .... 38 B1
Hill View Prim Sch BH10 .... 189 F2
Hill View Rd Braishfield SO51 .. 28 B3
Ferndown BH22 .... 165 E3
Michelmersh SO51 .... 27 E4
Portchester PO16 .... 132 B1
Hill Wlk PO15 .... 130 B2
Hillary Cl PO16 .... 130 C1
Hillary Rd BH23 .... 207 F4
Hillborough Cres 29 PO5 .... 182 B2
Hillbourne Fst & Mid Schs
BH17 .... 187 D1
Hillbourne Rd BH17 .... 187 D1
Hillbrow Cl Fareham PO15 ... 130 B2
Rowland's Castle PO9 .... 113 D1
Hillbrow Rd BH6 .... 206 A3
Hillbury Pk SP6 .... 93 D3
Hillbury Rd SP6 .... 93 D3
Hillcrest Ave
Chandler's Ford SO53 .... 55 F3
Ferndown BH22 .... 165 E4
Hillcrest Cl Bournemouth BH9 .. 190 A2
North Baddesley SO52 .... 53 F3
Hillcrest Dr SO53 .... 55 E3
Hillcrest Gdns SO32 .... 83 E2
Hillcrest Hospl BH10 .... 189 E1
Hillcrest Rd Bournemouth BH9 .. 190 A2
Corfe Mullen BH21 .... 186 B3
Hillcroft SP5 .... 47 E3
Hilldene Way SO30 .... 80 C1
Hillditch SO41 .... 197 E3
Hilldown Rd SO17 .... 79 D1
Hilldowns Ave PO2 .... 157 E1
Hiller Wlk 18 PO13 .... 179 F1
Hillgrove Rd SO18 .... 79 F2
Hillier Way SO23 .... 2 A1

Hillmead Gdns PO9 .... 135 D1
Hillrise SO32 .... 61 E3
Hillside Curdridge SO32 ...... 106 C4
Littleton SO22 .... 1 B3
Hillside Ave Romsey SO51 .... 53 D4
Southampton SO18 .... 79 F1
Waterlooville PO7 .... 134 A1
Hillside Cl Chandler's Ford SO53 . 55 E3
Horndean PO8 .... 88 B2
West Dean SP5 .... 3 E1
Winchester SO22 .... 1 B1
Hillside Cres PO6 .... 132 C1
Hillside Cty First Sch BH31 .. 114 C4
Hillside Dr BH23 .... 191 E2
Hillside Gdns BH21 .... 186 B2
Hillside Ind Est PO8 .... 112 B4
Hillside Mews BH21 .... 186 B2
Hillside Rd Corfe Mullen BH21 .. 186 B3
Lymington SO41 .... 197 E2
Poole BH12 .... 188 C1
Verwood BH31 .... 114 C4
Winchester SO22 .... 1 B1
Woodlands BH21 .... 114 A3
Hillside Wlk BH21 .... 114 A3
Hillsley Rd PO6 .... 132 C1
Hillson Dr PO15 .... 130 B2
Hillson House PO15 .... 130 B2
Hillsons Rd SO30 .... 106 B4
Hilltop Cl BH22 .... 165 D4
Hilltop Cres PO6 .... 134 B1
Hilltop Dr SO19 .... 104 B2
Hilltop Gdns PO8 .... 88 B2
Hilltop Rd Corfe Mullen BH21 .. 186 C3
Ferndown BH24 .... 165 D4
Hillview PO8 .... 112 B3
Hillview Rd Bournemouth BH10 . 189 E2
Hythe SO45 .... 125 F2
Hillway SO41 .... 197 F3
Hillway The
Chandler's Ford SO53 .... 55 E4
Portchester PO16 .... 156 B4
Hilly Cl SO21 .... 33 D2
Hillyfields SO16 .... 77 E2
Hilsea Cres PO2 .... 157 F3
Hilsea Mkt PO2 .... 157 F3
Hilsea Sta PO3 .... 158 A2
Hiltingbury Ave 32 PO9 ..... 136 A3
Hiltingbury Cl SO53 .... 30 A1
Hiltingbury Ct SO53 .... 30 A1
Hiltingbury Inf Sch SO53 ..... 30 B1
Hiltingbury Jun Sch SO53 .... 30 B1
Hiltingbury Rd SO53 .... 30 B1
Hiltom Rd BH24 .... 141 D4
Hilton Cl BH15 .... 203 D3
Hilton Rd Gosport PO12 ...... 181 D2
Hedge End SO30 .... 105 D4
New Milton BH25 .... 195 D2
Hinchcliffe Cl BH15 .... 201 F1
Hinchcliffe Rd BH15 .... 201 F1
Hinkler Rd SO19 .... 104 C3
Hinton Admiral Mews BH23 .. 193 F1
Hinton Admiral Sta BH23 .... 193 F1
Hinton Ampner House SO24 .. 14 C2
Hinton Cl SO50 .... 135 D2
Hinton Cres SO19 .... 104 C2
Hinton Hill SO24 .... 14 C2
Hinton House 1 PO7 .... 134 C4
Hinton Rd BH1 .... 204 C2
Hinton Wood BH1 .... 205 D1
Hinton Wood Ave BH23 ..... 193 F1
Hintonwood La BH23 .... 193 F1
Hipley Rd PO9 .... 136 A2
Hirst Rd SO45 .... 126 A2
Hispano Ave PO15 .... 129 E3
Hive Gdns BH13 .... 214 B3
Hives Way SO41 .... 197 E3
HMS Victory PO1 .... 181 F3
HMS Warrior PO1 .... 181 F3
Hoad's Hill PO17 .... 108 A1
Hoadlands GU31 .... 41 D2
Hobart Dr SO45 .... 126 A2
Hobart Rd BH25 .... 194 C1
Hobb La SO30 .... 105 E3
Hobbs Ct PO12 .... 181 F2
Hobbs Pass PO12 .... 181 F2
Hobbs Pk BH24 .... 139 F2
Hobbs Rd BH12 .... 203 E4
Hobby Cl PO3 .... 158 A2
Hobson Way SO45 .... 150 B2
Hoburne Ct BH23 .... 193 E1
Hoburne Gdns BH23 .... 193 E1
Hoburne La BH23 .... 208 B4
Hockham Ct PO9 .... 135 E4
Hockley Cl 7 PO6 .... 157 E4
Hockley Cotts Cheriton SO24 .. 13 F2
Twyford SO21 .... 32 A4
Hockley Golf Course SO23 ... 11 D1
Hocombe Dr SO53 .... 30 A1
Hocombe Park Cl SO53 ...... 30 B1
Hocombe Rd SO53 .... 30 B1
Hocombe Wood Rd SO53 .... 30 A1
Hodder Cl SO53 .... 55 D3
Hodges Cl Havant PO9 .... 136 A2
Poole BH17 .... 202 C4
Hoe La SO52 .... 53 E2
Hoe Rd SO32 .... 83 F4
Hoe St PO7 .... 109 F4
Hoe The PO13 .... 155 F1
Hoebrook Pl 6 SO51 .... 52 C4
Hoeford Ct PO16 .... 155 D3
Hogarth Cl Petersfield GU32 .. 41 D2
7 Romsey SO51 .... 28 A1
Southampton SO19 .... 104 B1
Hogs Lodge La PO8 .... 88 C4
Hogue Ave BH10 .... 189 E3

Hogwood La SO30 .... 80 C3
Holbeach Cl PO6 .... 133 F1
Holbein Lodge SO41 .... 198 A2
Holbrook Prim Sch PO13 .... 155 E2
Holbrook Rd Fareham PO16 .... 155 D4
Portsmouth PO1 .... 182 B3
Holbury Cl BH8 .... 190 C2
Holbury Ct 20 PO9 .... 136 A3
Holbury Dro SO45 .... 150 B2
Holbury Inf & Jun
Schs SO45 .... 150 B2
Holbury La
East Tytherley SO51 .... 4 B2
Lockerley SO51 .... 4 B2
Holcombe Rd BH16 .... 201 D3
Holcot La PO3 .... 158 B2
Holcroft Rd SO19 .... 104 C3
Holdaway Cl SO23 .... 2 B4
Holden La SO24 .... 34 C4
Holdenbury Ct PO3 .... 158 B2
Holdenhurst Ave BH7 .... 206 B4
Holdenhurst Cl PO8 .... 88 B1
Holdenhurst Rd
Bournemouth BH8 .... 205 E3
Bournemouth, Holdenhurst BH8 191 D2
Hole La Curdridge SO32 .... 83 D1
Soberton PO7 .... 110 A4
Holes Bay Rd BH15 .... 202 A2
Holes Cl SO41 .... 195 F2
Holkham Cl SO16 .... 77 F2
Hollam Cl PO14 .... 154 A4
Hollam Cres PO14 .... 154 A4
Hollam Dr PO14 .... 154 A4
Holland Cl SO53 .... 55 D2
Holland Pk SO31 .... 128 C2
Holland Pl Gosport PO13 .... 155 E1
Southampton SO16 .... 78 A1
Holland Rd
Portsmouth PO5 .... 182 C2
Southampton SO19 .... 103 E1
Totton SO40 .... 100 B4
Holland Way BH18 .... 186 C3
Hollands Cl SO22 .... 1 A3
Hollands Wood Dr BH25 .... 195 D3
Hollies Cl SO41 .... 172 A1
Hollies The SO51 .... 50 C2
Hollingbourne Cl SO18 .... 103 E4
Hollman Dr SO51 .... 52 B4
Hollow La PO11 .... 184 C2
Holloway Ave BH11 .... 188 C3
Holly Cl Hythe SO45 .... 150 A4
Locks Heath SO31 .... 128 C2
St Leonards BH24 .... 139 E2
Upton BH16 .... 201 D4
Holly Ct BH15 .... 202 B2
Holly Dell SO16 .... 78 C3
Holly Dr PO7 .... 135 D3
Holly Gdns Burton BH23 .... 192 B1
2 Milford on Sea SO41 ..... 211 E2
West End SO30 .... 80 B2
Holly Gr Fareham PO16 .... 130 C2
Verwood BH31 .... 114 C3
Holly Green Rise BH11 .... 188 C2
Holly Hatch Rd SO40 .... 100 C3
Holly Hedge La BH17 .... 202 B4
Holly Hill SO16 .... 78 C3
Holly Hill Cl SO16 .... 78 C3
Holly Hill La SO31 .... 128 B3
Holly Hill Mansions SO31 ..... 128 C2
Holly Hill Woodland Pk SO31 128 B2
Holly La Boldre SO41 .... 174 A1
Christchurch BH23 .... 194 B1
New Milton BH25 .... 195 E2
Holly Lodge
Chandler's Ford SO53 .... 55 E4
18 Poole BH12 .... 204 A2
Southampton SO17 .... 79 D1
Holly Oak Cl SO16 .... 78 A2
Holly Oak Rd SO16 .... 78 A2
Holly Rd Ashurst SO40 .... 100 A1
Blackfield SO45 .... 177 F4
Holly St PO12 .... 181 E2
Hollybank PO13 .... 179 F1
Hollybank Cl 8 Hythe SO45 ... 126 A2
Waterlooville PO8 .... 112 B3
Hollybank Cres SO45 .... 125 F2
Hollybank La PO10 .... 136 C2
Hollybank Rd SO45 .... 125 F2
Hollybrook Ave SO16 .... 78 B2
Hollybrook Cl SO16 .... 78 A1
Hollybrook Gdns SO31 .... 129 D3
Hollybrook Inf Sch SO16 .... 78 B2
Hollybrook Jun Sch SO16 .... 78 B2
Hollybrook Rd SO16 .... 78 B1
Hollydene SO45 .... 126 A1
Hollywell Dr PO6 .... 157 D4
Hollywood PO6 .... 157 D4
Hollywood Ct SO52 .... 53 F2
Hollywood Cl SO41 .... 197 E3
Hollywood La SO41 .... 197 E3
Holm Cl BH24 .... 117 E1
Holm Hill La BH23 .... 194 A4
Holman Cl PO8 .... 112 A1
Holmdale Rd PO12 .... 180 C4
Holme Cl SO41 .... 197 E1
Holme Rd BH23 .... 209 D4
Holmes Cl 5 SO31 .... 127 D3
Holmesland Dr SO30 .... 105 F4
Holmesland La SO30 .... 105 F4
Holmesland Wlk SO30 .... 105 F4
Holmfield Ave
Bournemouth BH7 .... 206 B4
Fareham PO14 .... 154 C4
Holmgrove PO14 .... 129 E2

Holmhurst Ave BH23 .... 193 F1
Holmsley Cl Lymington SO41 . 197 D1
Southampton SO18 .... 104 B4
Holmsley Ct SO40 .... 100 A4
Holmsley Pass BH24 .... 170 B4
Holmsley Rd
Brockenhurst BH25 .... 170 C1
New Milton BH25 .... 170 C1
Holmwood Garth BH24 .... 141 E3
Holne Ct PO4 .... 183 E2
Holnest Rd BH17 .... 187 E1
Holst Way PO7 .... 134 C3
Holt Cl PO17 .... 107 F2
Holt Ct SO19 .... 126 C4
Holt Down GU31 .... 41 D2
Holt Gdns PO9 .... 113 D2
Holt Rd Poole BH12 .... 203 F3
Southampton SO15 .... 102 C3
Verwood BH21 .... 138 B4
Holt View SO50 .... 56 C1
Holworth Rd BH11 .... 188 C2
Holy Cross Jun Sch PO14 ..... 134 C3
Holy Family RC Prim Sch
SO16 .... 77 E1
Holy Rood Est SO14 .... 103 D2
Holyborne Rd SO51 .... 53 D4
Holybourne Rd PO9 .... 135 F2
Holyrood Ave SO17 .... 79 D1
Holyrood Cl PO7 .... 135 D4
Holyrood House 12 SO14 ...... 103 D2
Holywell Cl BH17 .... 187 E2
Home Farm Bsns Ctr SP5 ..... 4 C3
Home Farm Cl SO45 .... 126 A2
Home Farm La SO45 .... 177 D3
Home Farm Office Village
PO16 .... 155 E4
Home Farm Rd BH31 .... 114 C3
Home Farm Way BH31 .... 114 C3
Home Field Dr SO16 .... 77 E3
Home Mead PO7 .... 110 C2
Home Rd BH11 .... 189 D3
Home Rule Rd SO31 .... 129 D2
Home Way GU31 .... 41 E2
Homeborough House
7 SO45 .... 126 A3
Homebridge House SP6 .... 69 F1
Homedale House BH15 .... 204 C3
Homedene House BH15 .... 202 B2
Homefayre House 19 PO16 ... 131 D1
Homefield SO51 .... 28 A1
Homefield Cotts GU33 .... 20 C3
Homefield House 13 BH25 .... 195 D1
Homefield Ind Prep Sch BH6 . 206 C3
Homefield Ind Senior Sch
BH23 .... 192 B3
Homefield Rd Cosham PO6 ... 158 B4
Westbourne BH10 .... 137 D2
Homefield Way PO8 .... 88 A3
Homeforde House SO42 .... 146 A1
Homefort House 2 PO12 .... 181 D2
Homegrange House 15 SO41 . 211 E2
Homegrove House 22 PO5 .... 182 B2
Homeheights 23 PO5 .... 182 B1
Homelake House BH14 .... 203 D2
Homelands Est BH23 .... 206 C3
Homelands House BH22 .... 165 E3
Homeleigh House 5 BH8 .... 205 D3
Homemead House SO51 .... 52 C3
Homemill House 5 BH25 .... 195 D2
Homeoaks House BH2 .... 204 C3
Homepoint House SO18 .... 104 A4
Homer Cl Gosport PO13 .... 180 A4
Waterlooville PO8 .... 111 F1
Homer Mobile Home Park
SO45 .... 177 D3
Homerise House 1 SO23 .... 11 D4
Homerose House 17 PO5 ...... 182 B4
Homeryde House 11 PO13 .... 179 F1
Homesea House 18 PO5 .... 182 B2
Homeside Rd BH9 .... 190 A1
Homespinney House SO18 .... 79 E1
Homestour House 1 BH23 .... 207 D3
Hometide House 13 PO13 ..... 179 F1
Homeview House BH15 .... 202 B2
Homewater House 7 PO7 ...... 134 C4
Homeway Cotts SO40 .... 101 D3
Homewell PO9 .... 135 F1
Homewood Cl BH25 .... 195 E2
Homewood House SO41 .... 197 E1
Honey La Burley BH24 .... 142 C1
Fareham PO15 .... 130 B3
Honeybourne Cres BH6 .... 207 D2
Honeycritch La GU32 .... 19 E2
Honeysuckle Cl Gosport PO13 155 D2
Locks Heath SO31 .... 129 D3
Winchester SO23 .... 10 C2
Honeysuckle Ct
Southampton SO18 .... 104 A4
Waterlooville PO8 .... 135 D3
Honeysuckle La BH17 .... 186 C1
Honeysuckle Rd SO16 .... 79 E2
Honeysuckle Way
Christchurch BH23 .... 208 A4
North Baddesley SO53 .... 55 D3
Honeywood Cl
Portsmouth PO3 .... 157 F2
Totton SO40 .... 76 B1
Honeywood House BH14 ...... 214 B4
Honister Cl SO16 .... 101 F4
Hood Cl
Bournemouth BH10 .... 189 D1
Locks Heath SO31 .... 129 D2
Hood Cres BH10 .... 189 D1
Hood Rd SO18 .... 104 A4
Hook Cl SO53 .... 30 C4
Hook Cotts SO31 .... 152 C4
Hook Cres SO53 .... 30 A1
Hook La PO14 .... 153 D4

Hook Park Rd SO31 .... 152 C3
Hook Rd Ampfield SO51 .... 29 F1
Chandler's Ford SO51 .... 29 F1
Hook Water Cl SO53 .... 30 A1
Hook Water Rd SO53 .... 30 A1
Hook with Warsash CE Prim
Sch SO31 .... 152 B4
Hook's Farm Way PO9 .... 135 E2
Hook's La PO9 .... 135 E2
Hooke Cl BH17 .... 188 A1
Hookpit Farm La SO23 .... 2 A4
Hookwood La SO51 .... 29 F1
Hop Cl BH16 .... 201 D4
Hope Lodge Sch
Southampton SO17 .... 79 D1
Southampton SO18 .... 103 F4
Hope Rd SO30 .... 80 C1
Hope St PO1 .... 182 B3
Hopfield Cl PO7 .... 134 C4
Hopfield House PO7 .... 134 C3
Hopfield Mews PO7 .... 134 C3
Hopkins Bsns Ctr BH23 .... 208 A4
Portchester PO6 .... 156 C4
Hopkins Ct PO4 .... 183 D1
Horace Rd 10 BH5 .... 205 F2
Hordle CE Prim Sch SO41 .... 196 A2
Hordle House Sch SO41 .... 210 C3
Hordle La SO41 .... 196 A1
Hordle Rd PO9 .... 135 E2
Horlock Rd SO42 .... 146 A1
Hornbeam Cl SO30 .... 105 D3
Hornbeam Gdns SO30 .... 80 B2
Hornbeam Rd PO9 .... 136 A2
Hornbeam Way BH21 .... 163 F3
Hornby Cl SO31 .... 152 B4
Hornchurch Rd SO16 .... 77 F2
Horndean CE Jun Sch PO8 ... 112 B4
Horndean Com Sch PO8 .... 112 A4
Horndean House 39 PO1 ...... 182 B3
Horndean Inf Sch PO8 .... 112 B4
Horndean Prec PO8 .... 112 B4
Horndean Rd PO10 .... 136 C2
Hornet Cl Fareham PO15 ...... 130 B1
Gosport PO12 .... 181 E2
Hornet Rd Gosport PO14 ...... 154 C3
Thorney Island PO10 .... 161 D2
Horning Rd BH12 .... 203 F3
Horns Drove SO16 .... 77 F3
Horns Hill Nursling SO16 ...... 77 E3
Soberton SO32 .... 85 D1
Horsa Cl BH6 .... 206 C2
Horsa Ct BH6 .... 206 C2
Horsa Rd BH6 .... 206 C2
Horse Sands Cl PO4 .... 183 E2
Horsea La PO2 .... 157 F2
Horsea Rd PO2 .... 157 F3
Horsebridge Rd PO9 .... 136 A2
Horsebridge Way SO16 .... 77 F3
Horsecroft 2 SO51 .... 52 C4
Horsefair Ct SO51 .... 52 C4
Horsefair Mews SO51 .... 52 C4
Horsefair The SO51 .... 52 C4
Horsepost La PO7 .... 87 D1
Horseshoe Cl Titchfield PO14 129 E1
Wimborne Minster BH21 ..... 164 A3
Horseshoe Ct
4 Bournemouth BH1 .... 204 C2
Downton SP5 .... 46 C4
Horseshoe Dr
Netley Marsh SO40 .... 76 A1
Romsey SO51 .... 28 A1
Horseshoe Lodge SO31 .... 128 C1
Horseshoe The BH13 .... 214 B2
Horsham Ave BH10 .... 189 E3
Horton Cl BH9 .... 190 B2
Horton Rd Gosport PO13 ..... 155 E2
St Leonards BH24 .... 139 F3
Verwood BH31 .... 114 A1
Horton Way Bishopstoke SO50 56 C1
Verwood BH31 .... 114 B3
Hosier's Gr 28 BH15 .... 202 A1
Hosker Rd BH5 .... 206 A3
Hospital La PO16 .... 156 C3
Hospital Rd SO32 .... 108 A4
Hotspur Cl SO45 .... 125 F3
Houchin St SO32 .... 83 E4
Houghton Cl 1 PO9 .... 136 A3
Houlton Rd BH15 .... 202 C2
Hound Cl SO31 .... 127 E3
Hound Manor SO31 .... 127 F3
Hound Rd SO31 .... 127 E3
Hound Road Gdns SO31 ...... 127 E3
Hound Way SO31 .... 127 E3
Hounds Way BH21 .... 164 A3
Houndwell Pl SO14 .... 103 D2
Hounsdown Ave SO40 .... 100 C3
Hounsdown Cl SO40 .... 100 C3
Hounsdown Sec Sch SO40 ... 100 C2
Hounslow Cl BH15 .... 201 F1
House Farm Rd PO12 .... 180 C2
Hove Ct PO13 .... 179 F1
Hoveton Gr SO53 .... 55 D4
Howard Cl Burley BH24 .... 143 D2
Chandler's Ford SO53 .... 55 E2
Christchurch BH23 .... 207 F3
Fair Oak SO50 .... 57 E1
Southampton SO18 .... 79 F2
Howard Oliver House SO45 ... 126 A2
Howard Rd Bournemouth BH8 205 E4
Portsmouth PO2 .... 157 F2
Southampton SO15 .... 102 B3
Verwood BH31 .... 114 C3
Howard's Gr SO15 .... 102 B4
Howards Mead SO41 .... 197 D1
Howe Cl Christchurch BH23 .. 207 F3
New Milton BH25 .... 194 C2
Howe La BH31 .... 114 C3
Howe Rd PO13 .... 180 B3

Howell House BH21 .... 163 F4
Howerts Cl SO31 .... 152 B4
Howeth Cl BH10 .... 189 E2
Howeth Rd BH10 .... 189 E2
Howlett Cl SO41 .... 197 E2
Howton Cl BH10 .... 189 E1
Howton Rd BH10 .... 189 E1
Hoxley Rd BH10 .... 189 E2
Hoyal Rd BH15 .... 201 E2
Hoylake Cl PO13 .... 155 E1
Hoylake Rd PO6 .... 134 B1
Hoyle Cl SO32 .... 58 B2
Hoylecroft Cl PO15 .... 130 C2
Hubert Rd SO23 .... 10 C2
Hudson Cl Gosport PO13 ...... 180 B3
Poole BH12 .... 188 B1
Ringwood BH24 .... 141 E4
Hudson Ct SO30 .... 100 B3
Hudson Davies Cl SO41 .... 173 F1
Hudson Rd PO5 .... 182 B2
Hugh's Cl SO45 .... 150 C1
Hughes Bsns Ctr BH23 .... 208 A4
Hulbert Jun Sch PO7 .... 134 C3
Hulbert Rd Havant PO9 .... 135 D2
Waterlooville PO7 .... 134 C4
Hull Cres BH11 .... 188 C2
Hull Rd BH11 .... 188 C2
Hull Way BH11 .... 188 C2
Hulles Way SO52 .... 53 F2
Hulse Lodge 4 SO15 .... 102 C4
Hulse Rd SO15 .... 102 C4
Hulton Cl SO19 .... 103 E1
Humber Cl PO14 .... 154 A2
Humber Gdns SO31 .... 105 D1
Humber Rd BH22 .... 166 A3
Hummicks The SO42 .... 176 B4
Hundred Acres PO17 .... 108 C2
Hundred Acres Rd
Soberton PO17 .... 108 C3
Wickham PO17 .... 108 C3
Hundred La SO41 .... 198 A4
Hundred The
Fordingbridge SP6 .... 69 F1
Romsey SO51 .... 52 C4
Waterlooville PO7 .... 111 E1
Hunger Hill PO1 .... 202 B1
Hungerfield Cl BH23 .... 169 D1
Hungerford SO31 .... 128 A4
Hungerford Hill SP6 .... 94 B3
Hungerford Rd BH8 .... 190 B2
Hunt Ave SO31 .... 127 E3
Hunt Cl Christchurch BH23 ... 207 F4
Poole BH15 .... 202 C2
Hunter Cl Christchurch BH23 . 208 A4
Gosport PO13 .... 180 B4
Holbury SO45 .... 150 A4
Wimborne Minster BH21 ..... 164 B3
Hunter Ct 10 SO15 .... 78 A1
Hunter Rd Portsmouth PO4 ... 183 D2
Thorney Island PO10 .... 161 D2
Hunters Chase SO32 .... 84 B2
Hunters Cl BH11 .... 115 E3
Hunters Cres Romsey SO51 .. 28 B1
Totton SO40 .... 100 A3
Hunters Hill SO40 .... 100 B2
Hunters Lodge PO15 .... 130 B1
Hunters Ride PO7 .... 134 C2
Hunters Way SO50 .... 57 D1
Huntfield Rd BH9 .... 190 A1
Huntingdon Cl
Titchfield PO14 .... 129 E1
Totton SO40 .... 76 C1
Huntingdon Dr PO7 .... 163 F1
Huntingdon Gdns BH23 ...... 192 A1
Huntley Cl 29 PO6 .... 133 D1
Huntly Rd BH3 .... 204 B4
Huntly Way SO18 .... 103 F4
Hunton Cl SO16 .... 78 B2
Hunts La SO21 .... 31 F4
Hunts Pond Rd PO14 .... 129 E2
Huntsbottom La
Hill Brow GU33 .... 21 D2
Liss GU33 .... 21 D2
Huntvale Rd BH9 .... 190 A2
Hurdle Way SO21 .... 31 E4
Hurdles The
Christchurch BH23 .... 206 C4
Titchfield PO14 .... 129 E1
Hurlingham Gdns SO16 ...... 79 D3
Hurn Cl BH24 .... 140 B3
Hurn Court La BH23 .... 190 C3
Hurn Ct 17 Havant PO9 ...... 136 A3
Hurn BH23 .... 191 D2
Hurn La BH24 .... 140 B3
Hurn Rd Christchurch BH23 . 191 D2
Hurn BH23 .... 191 D2
St Leonards BH24 .... 140 B2
Hurn Way BH23 .... 191 E1
Hurricane Dr SO16 .... 77 F3
Hursley Cl BH7 .... 206 B4
Hursley Ct SO53 .... 30 A1
Hursley Dr SO45 .... 177 F4
Hursley Rd
Chandler's Ford SO53 .... 55 E4
Havant PO9 .... 135 F2
Hurst Castle 212 B1
Hurst Cl Chandler's Ford SO53 55 D2
Christchurch BH23 .... 194 B1
Stubbington PO14 .... 179 D3
Totton SO40 .... 100 C4
Hurst Ct 6 Christchurch BH23 209 D4
5 Milford on Sea SO41 ..... 211 E2
Hurst Gr PO13 .... 155 D1
Hurst Green Cl PO8 .... 112 A4
Hurst Green Rd SO19 .... 104 A1
Hurst Hill BH14 .... 214 B4
Hurst La Colden Common SO21 58 A4
Froxfield GU34 .... 18 A2

Hurst Rd Milford on Sea SO41 211 E2
Ringwood BH24 .... 117 D2
Hurstbourne Ave BH23 .... 193 F1
Hurstbourne Cl PO9 .... 135 E2
Hurstbourne Pl 9 SO19 .... 126 C4
Hurstdene Rd BH8 .... 190 B3
Hurstly La SO41 .... 173 D2
Hurstville Dr PO7 .... 134 C4
Hurstwood Ave PO10 .... 137 F3
Hussar Cl BH23 .... 206 C4
Hussar Ct PO7 .... 111 E3
Hussey Pl 2 SO23 .... 2 A1
Hutfield Ct 16 PO12 .... 181 D3
Hutwood Rd SO16 .... 79 D4
Huxley Cl SO41 .... 129 D3
Huxley Ct SO45 .... 125 E3
Hyacinth Cl BH17 .... 186 C1
Hyde Abbey Rd SO23 .... 11 D4
Hyde Church La SO23 .... 2 A1
Hyde Church Path 24 SO23 2 A1
Hyde Cl Southampton SO15 . 78 B3
Sway SO41 .... 172 A3
Totton SO40 .... 100 A4
Winchester SO23 .... 1 C1
Hyde Gate SO23 .... 2 A1
Hyde House Gdns 22 SO23 . 2 A1
Hyde La Downton SP5 .... 46 B4
Fordingbridge SP6 .... 94 B3
Hyde Lodge Winchester SO22 1 C1
21 Winchester SO23 .... 2 A1
Hyde Park House 7 PO1 ..... 182 B3
Hyde Park Rd PO1 .... 182 B3
Hyde Prim Sch SP6 .... 94 B3
Hyde Rd BH10 .... 189 E3
Hyde St Portsmouth PO5 .... 182 B2
Winchester SO23 .... 2 A1
Hyde The BH25 .... 194 C2
Hyden Cross PO8 .... 63 F1
Hyden Farm La PO8 .... 87 E4
Hyden Wood PO8 .... 63 F1
Hylton Rd GU32 .... 40 C2
Hyman Way SO40 .... 100 C4
Hynes Ct 17 SO17 .... 103 D4
Hynesbury Rd BH23 .... 208 B3
Hythe-By-Pass SO45 .... 149 F4
Hythe-By-Pass SO45 .... 150 A4
Hythe Hospl SO45 .... 126 A1
Hythe Prim Sch SO45 .... 126 A2
Hythe Rd Cosham PO6 ...... 157 F4
Marchwood SO40 .... 124 C4
Poole BH15 .... 203 D4

I

Ibberton Cl BH8 .... 190 C1
Ibberton Rd BH8 .... 190 C1
Ibberton Way BH8 .... 190 C1
Ibbett Rd BH10 .... 189 E2
Ibbotson Way SO40 .... 100 B3
Ibsen Cl PO15 .... 129 E4
Ibsley Cl BH8 .... 205 E3
Ibsley Dro BH24 .... 94 A1
Ibsley Gr PO9 .... 135 E2
Icarus Pl PO7 .... 134 C1
Iddesleigh Rd BH3 .... 205 D3
Ideal Park Homes SO50 .... 56 C3
Idsworth Rd
Portsmouth PO3 .... 183 D4
Waterlooville PO8 .... 112 A1
Iford Bridge Home Pk BH6 . 206 B4
Iford Cl BH6 .... 206 C3
Iford Ct 14 PO9 .... 136 A3
Iford Gdns BH7 .... 206 B4
Iford La BH6 .... 206 C3
Ilex Cres SO31 .... 128 C2
Ilex Wlk PO11 .... 185 E1
Imber Dr BH23 .... 208 C4
Imber Rd SO23 .... 11 E4
Imber Way SO19 .... 104 B2
Imbre Ct BH13 .... 214 C4
Imperial Ave SO15 .... 102 A4
Imperial Ct 3 BH13 .... 214 C4
Imperial Pk SO14 .... 103 D4
Imperial Rd SO14 .... 103 D4
Imperial Way SO15 .... 102 B3
Implacable Rd PO13 .... 179 F2
Ingarth 8 BH21 .... 206 C2
Ingle Glen SO45 .... 126 A1
Ingle Gr SO40 .... 76 A1
Ingledene Cl Gosport PO12 . 181 D2
Havant PO9 .... 135 E1
Inglegreen Cl BH25 .... 194 C1
Inglesham Way BH15 .... 201 F2
Ingleside Cl PO14 .... 127 E4
Ingleside SO41 .... 154 A4
Ingleton Rd SO16 .... 77 E1
Inglewood Ave BH8 .... 190 C1
Inglewood Dr BH25 .... 195 D1
Inglewood Gdns SO50 ..... 57 E2
Inglis Rd PO5 .... 182 C2
Ingoldfield La SO32 .... 109 E4
Ingram Ct SO17 .... 103 E4
Ingram Wlk 14 BH21 .... 163 E2
Ingworth Rd BH12 .... 204 A3
Inhams La PO7 .... 110 B3
Inhurst Ave PO7 .... 135 D4
Inhurst Rd PO2 .... 157 F1
Inkerman Rd SO19 .... 103 E2
Inkpen Wlk PO9 .... 135 E4
Inlands Rd PO10 .... 161 F4
Inmans La GU32 .... 41 D3
Insley Cres BH18 .... 186 C3
International Way SO19 .... 126 C4
Inveravon BH23 .... 207 F2
Inverclyde House BH14 ..... 203 D2
Inverclyde Rd BH14 .... 203 E2
Invergordon Ave PO6 .... 158 A4
Inverkip Cl PO13 .... 179 F2
Inverleigh Rd BH6 .... 206 B3
Inverness Ave PO15 .... 130 C2

verness Rd Gosport PO12 ...... 181 D3
Poole BH13 .... 214 C4
Portsmouth PO1 .... 182 C4
onic Cl SO53 .... 55 F4
DW Ferry Terminal SO14 ...... 102 C1
ping Ave PO9 .... 135 F2
oley Way SO45 .... 126 A1
oswich Rd BH4 .... 204 A2
eland Way PO7 .... 134 C3
is Rd Bournemouth BH9 .... 189 F1
Southampton SO16 .... 79 D2
on Mill Cl PO15 .... 130 B2
onbridge Cres SO31 .... 129 D3
onbridge La PO4 .... 183 E2
onmill La PO15 .... 130 A3
onside Ct 12 SO14 .... 102 C2
vine Cl PO16 .... 131 D2
vine Way BH23 .... 207 F4
ving Rd Bournemouth BH6 ... 206 B3
Southampton SO16 .... 77 F1
well Cl SO53 .... 55 D3
win Hts PO12 .... 181 D4
saacs Cl BH12 .... 204 A4
sambard Brunel
Jun Sch PO2 .... 182 C4
sambard Brunel Rd PO1 ...... 182 B3
sis Cl SO16 .... 101 F4
sland Cl PO11 .... 160 A2
sland Point SO41 .... 197 F2
sland View BH9 .... 172 A4
sland View BH23 .... 208 A3
sland View Cl SO41 .... 211 E2
sland View Rd BH25 .... 209 E4
sland View Terr PO2 .... 157 F1
sland View Wlk PO16 .... 132 B1
slay Gdns PO6 .... 133 F1
tchen Ave SO50 .... 56 C1
tchen Cl Petersfield GU32 ..... 40 C1
West Wellow SO51 .... 50 B2
tchen Coll SO19 .... 104 A3
tchen Ct 4 Waterlooville PO8 ... 111 F2
43 Winchester SO23 .... 11 D4
tchen Ho 5 PO9 .... 136 A3
tchen Valley Ctry Pk SO30 ... 80 B3
tchen View SO18 .... 79 F2
tchenor Rd PO11 .... 185 F1
tchenside Cl SO18 .... 79 F2
tchin Cl SO40 .... 100 B3
thlca PO11 .... 185 D2
vamy PO11 BH11 .... 188 C1
vanhoe Rd SO15 .... 78 B1
vor Cl SO41 .... 150 B2
vor Rd Broadstone BH21 .... 186 B2
Poole BH15 .... 202 A1
vy Cl St Leonards BH24 .... 139 E2
Totton SO40 .... 76 C1
Winchester SO22 .... 10 C3
vy Cotts SO50 .... 31 D1
vy Ct PO7 .... 134 B2
vy Dene SO19 .... 104 B2
vy House 2 PO14 .... 181 E2
vy La Portsmouth PO1 .... 182 A3
Ringwood BH24 .... 117 D2
West End SO18 .... 80 B1
vy Orch PO8 .... 88 A3
vy Rd Oakley BH21 .... 187 E4
Southampton SO17 .... 103 E4
vyhouse La GU32 .... 18 C2
lwerne Cl BH9 .... 190 A2

Jack Cockerill Way 14 PO5 ... 182 B1
Jackdaw Cl PO8 .... 111 F2
Jackdaw Rise SO50 .... 55 E1
Jacklin Ct BH18 .... 187 D3
Jackman's Hill SO21 .... 33 D3
Jackmans Cl SO19 .... 103 E2
Jackson Cl PO6 .... 158 B3
Jackson Rd BH12 .... 203 E3
Jacmar Ct 8 BH25 .... 195 D1
Jacob's Gutter La SO40 .... 101 D2
Jacob's St PO1 .... 182 B3
Jacobean Cl BH23 .... 194 A1
Jacobs Cl Clanfield PO8 .... 88 B3
Romsey SO51 .... 53 D4
Jacobs Wlk SO40 .... 100 C3
Jacomb Pl SO13 .... 155 E1
Jacqueline Ave PO7 .... 134 B2
Jacqueline Rd BH12 .... 203 E4
Jade Ct 6 PO7 .... 134 C4
Jago Rd PO1 .... 181 F3
Jamaica Pl PO12 .... 181 E2
James Butcher Ct 12 PO5 ..... 182 B1
James Callaghan Dr PO17 .... 132 C1
James Cl Gosport PO13 .... 155 E2
South Hayling PO11 .... 184 C2
James Copse Rd PO8 .... 111 F3
James Ct SO51 .... 53 D3
James Grieve Ave SO31 .... 129 D3
James Howell Ct PO7 .... 110 C2
James Rd Gosport PO13 .... 155 E2
Havant PO9 .... 135 F1
Poole BH12 .... 204 A3
James St SO14 .... 103 D2
Jameson Rd Bournemouth BH9 ... 189 F1
Southampton SO19 .... 103 F2
Jamica Rd PO12 .... 181 E3
Janaway Gdns SO17 .... 103 E4
Janes Cl SO45 .... 177 F4
Janred Ct BH25 .... 209 F4
Janson Rd SO15 .... 102 B4
Jardnyce Wlk PO2 .... 182 B4
Jarvis Fields SO31 .... 128 A4
Jasmine Ct SO41 .... 197 F2
Jasmine Gr PO7 .... 135 D3
Jasmine Rd SO30 .... 105 D4
Jasmine Way PO8 .... 88 B3

Jasmine Wlk 6 PO14 .... 154 C4
Jasmond Rd PO6 .... 157 F3
Jason Pl PO7 .... 134 C1
Jason Way PO12 .... 180 C4
Jaundrells Cl BH25 .... 195 D3
Java Dr PO15 .... 129 E4
Javelin Rd PO10 .... 161 D2
Jay Cl Horndean PO8 .... 112 A4
Stubbington PO14 .... 154 A3
Jay's Ct BH23 .... 209 D4
Jealous La SO41 .... 173 D1
Jefferson Ave BH1 .... 205 E3
Jeffries Cl SO16 .... 77 F3
Jellicoe Ave PO12 .... 180 C2
Jellicoe Cl BH14 .... 202 C3
Jellicoe Dr BH23 .... 207 F3
Jenkins Cl SO30 .... 106 A4
Jenkins Gr PO3 .... 183 D4
Jenner Way SO51 .... 53 E4
Jennings Rd Poole BH14 .... 203 E1
Totton SO40 .... 101 D4
Jensen Ct SO15 .... 102 C4
Jephcote Rd BH11 .... 188 C2
Jermyns La Abbotswood SO51 .... 28 C2
Ampfield SO51 .... 28 C2
Jerome Ct SO19 .... 104 B3
Jerram Ct PO12 .... 180 C2
Jerrett's La SO16 .... 77 E2
Jersey Cl Poole BH12 .... 188 B3
Southampton SO16 .... 77 F2
Stubbington PO14 .... 179 E3
Jersey Rd Poole BH12 .... 188 B1
Portsmouth PO2 .... 182 C4
Jervis Court La
Bishop's Waltham SO32 .... 84 A4
Swanmore SO32 .... 84 A4
Jervis Dr PO12 .... 181 D3
Jervis Rd PO2 .... 157 E1
Jesmond Ave BH23 .... 208 C4
Jesmond Gr SO31 .... 129 D1
Jessamine Rd SO16 .... 78 A1
Jessica Ave BH31 .... 114 B4
Jessica Cl PO7 .... 112 A1
Jessie Rd Gosport PO12 .... 181 D2
Havant PO9 .... 135 E2
Portsmouth PO4 .... 182 C2
Jessop Cl Bournemouth BH10 ... 189 E3
Hythe SO45 .... 125 F3
Jessop Rd BH23 .... 164 A3
Jessop Wlk SO45 .... 125 F3
Jessopp House 6 BH21 .... 163 E4
Jetty Rd SO45 .... 151 D3
Jewell Rd BH8 .... 191 D1
Jewry St SO23 .... 11 D4
Jimmy Brown Ave BH22 .... 138 C3
Jinny La SO51 .... 27 F3
Joanna Cl SP5 .... 46 B4
Jockey La SO50 .... 56 C3
Jodrell Cl PO8 .... 112 B4
John Darling Mall SO50 .... 56 A2
John King Shipyard PO10 ..... 161 D4
John St SO14 .... 103 D2
John's Rd SO19 .... 103 E2
Johns Rd PO16 .... 155 D4
Johnson Rd BH21 .... 165 D4
Johnson St 2 SO14 .... 103 D2
Johnston Rd BH15 .... 202 B4
Johnstone Rd BH23 .... 207 F3
Jolliffe Ave BH15 .... 202 B2
Jolliffe Ct 16 GU32 .... 40 C2
Jolliffe Rd BH15 .... 202 B2
Jonas Nichols Sq SO14 .... 103 D2
Jonathan Rd PO15 .... 130 C1
Jonathon Cl SO41 .... 197 F3
Jones La SO45 .... 126 A3
Jopps Cnr BH23 .... 192 B2
Jordan House SO15 .... 102 B3
Jordans La Boldre SO41 .... 198 A4
Sway SO41 .... 172 B1
Joseph Nye Ct 30 PO1 .... 182 A3
Joseph St 8 PO12 .... 181 E2
Josian Wlk 10 SO14 .... 103 D3
Jowitt Dr BH25 .... 194 C1
Joyce Dickson Cl BH24 .... 141 D3
Joys Cl SO41 .... 198 C4
Joys Rd BH21 .... 138 C4
Jubilee Ave PO16 .... 156 C4
Jubilee Bsns Ctr PO7 .... 134 C4
Jubilee Cl Corfe Mullen BH21 ... 186 C4
Eastleigh SO50 .... 55 F1
Fordingbridge SP6 .... 69 E1
Ringwood BH24 .... 141 E4
Jubilee Cres BH12 .... 203 E3
Jubilee Ct PO14 .... 155 D4
Jubilee Gdns
Bournemouth BH10 .... 189 E1
Southampton SO18 .... 104 A4
Jubilee House PO10 .... 136 C1
Jubilee Rd Corfe Mullen BH21 ... 186 C4
Fordingbridge SP6 .... 69 E1
Gosport PO13 .... 181 D3
Poole BH12 .... 203 E3
Portchester PO16 .... 156 B4
Portsmouth PO4 .... 182 C4
Romsey SO51 .... 52 C4
Waterlooville PO7 .... 111 F1
Jubilee Terr Portsmouth PO5 ... 182 A2
Westbourne PO10 .... 137 D2
Julia Cl BH23 .... 208 C4
Julian Ct SO16 .... 78 C3
Julian Cl 1 SO18 .... 79 F1
Julian Rd SO19 .... 104 A2
Julian's Rd Pamphill BH21 .... 163 D2
Wimborne Minster BH21 .... 163 D2
Julie Ave PO15 .... 130 C1
Juliet Ct PO7 .... 135 D4
Julius Cl SO53 .... 55 F3

Julyan Ave BH12 .... 204 A4
Jumar Cl SO41 .... 152 B4
Jumpers Ave BH23 .... 206 C4
Jumpers Rd BH23 .... 206 C4
Junction Rd
Bournemouth BH9 .... 204 B4
Hamworthy BH16 .... 201 E2
Totton SO40 .... 101 D4
Juniper Cl Ferndown BH22 ... 165 E4
Lymington SO41 .... 197 D1
North Baddesley SO52 .... 53 F3
Three Legged Cross BH21 ..... 138 C4
Winchester SO22 .... 10 B3
Juniper Ct 12 SO18 .... 103 F4
Juniper Flats BH23 .... 206 C4
Juniper Rd Horndean PO8 ...... 88 B1
Southampton SO18 .... 103 F4
Juniper Sq PO9 .... 159 F4
Jupiter Cl SO16 .... 77 F2
Jupiter Way BH21 .... 186 C4
Jura Cl PO6 .... 133 F1
Jurd Way SO31 .... 104 C1
Jurds Lake Way SO19 .... 103 F1
Justin Cl PO14 .... 154 C4
Justin Gdns BH10 .... 189 F2
Justine Ct SO18 .... 104 A4
Justinian Cl SO53 .... 55 F4
Jute Cl PO16 .... 132 A1
Jutland Cl PO15 .... 129 D4

Kamptee Copse BH25 .... 195 D3
Kanes Hill SO19 .... 104 C3
Kanes Hill Prim Sch SO19 .... 104 C3
Kangaw Pl PO15 .... 201 E1
Karen Ave PO6 .... 158 B3
Kassassin St PO4 .... 183 D1
Kassel Ct PO7 .... 135 D4
Katherine Chance Cl BH23 ... 192 B2
Kathleen Rd SO19 .... 104 A2
Katrina Gdns PO11 .... 185 D3
Katrine Cres SO53 .... 55 D4
Katterns Cl BH23 .... 191 F1
Kayak Cl SO31 .... 128 C1
Kayleigh Cl SO40 .... 100 B3
Kealy Rd PO13 .... 181 D1
Kearsney Ave PO2 .... 157 F2
Keast Wlk PO13 .... 155 E2
Keats Ave Milford on Sea SO41 ... 211 E3
Portchester PO16 .... 132 C1
Keats Ct Waterlooville PO8 ... 111 F2
Winchester SO21, SO22 .... 10 C3
Keats House Havant PO9 ...... 135 F2
17 New Milton BH25 .... 195 D1
Keats Rd SO19 .... 104 B3
Keble Cl Chandler's Ford SO53 ... 55 E2
Hursley SO21 .... 30 A4
Keble Meml CE
Prim Sch SO53 .... 55 E2
Keble Rd SO53 .... 55 E2
Keble St SO18 .... 10 B3
Keeble Cl BH10 .... 189 E3
Keeble Cres BH10 .... 189 E3
Keeble Rd BH10 .... 189 E3
Keel Cl Gosport PO13 .... 180 B3
Portsmouth PO3 .... 158 B2
Keep The PO16 .... 156 B4
Keepers Cl SO53 .... 55 D3
Keepers La Ferndown BH21 .. 164 C3
Mottisfont SO51 .... 5 E1
Kefford Cl PO8 .... 112 A3
Keighley Ave BH18 .... 186 C1
Keith Cl PO12 .... 181 D3
Keith Rd BH3 .... 204 B4
Kelburn Cl SO53 .... 55 D4
Kellaway Rd BH17 .... 202 C4
Kellett Rd SO15 .... 102 C4
Kelly Cl BH17 .... 202 C4
Kelly Ct
10 Fareham PO16 .... 131 D1
2 Southampton, Bitterne SO18 ... 103 F4
Southampton, Lordswood SO16 ... 78 B3
Kelly House SO18 .... 79 F2
Kelly Rd PO7 .... 134 C3
Kelmscott Gdns SO53 .... 30 A1
Kelsall Gdns BH25 .... 195 D2
Kelsey Ave PO10 .... 137 F1
Kelsey Cl Liss GU33 .... 21 D3
Locks Heath PO14 .... 129 D1
Kelsey Head PO6 .... 157 D2
Kelston Cl SO15 .... 102 A4
Kelvin Cl SO45 .... 126 A3
Kelvin Gr Netley SO31 .... 127 E3
Portchester PO16 .... 156 B4
Kelvin Rd SO50 .... 55 F1
Kemp Rd BH9 .... 204 C4
Kempland La GU34 .... 17 C2
Kemps Quay Ind Pk SO18 ..... 103 E4
Kempton Cl PO15 .... 129 E4
Kempton Pk PO7 .... 112 A1
Kemshott Cl PO9 .... 135 E3
Ken Berry Ct PO9 .... 136 A3
Ken Rd BH6 .... 206 C2
Kench The PO11 .... 183 F2
Kendal Ave Portsmouth PO3 ... 158 A1
Southampton SO16 .... 101 E4
Kendal Cl Chandler's Ford SO53 ... 55 F4
Waterlooville PO8 .... 112 A2
Kendal Ct SO16 .... 77 F1

Kenilworth Rd
Portsmouth PO5 .... 182 B1
Southampton SO15 .... 102 C3
Kenmore Cl SO40 .... 100 C3
Kennard Ct BH25 .... 194 C3
Kennard Rd BH25 .... 194 C2
Kennart Rd BH17 .... 202 A4
Kennedy Ave PO15 .... 130 C2
Kennedy Cl PO7 .... 134 C2
Kennedy Cres PO12 .... 180 C1
Kennedy Rd SO16 .... 77 F2
Kennel La SO22 .... 1 B2
Kennet Cl Gosport PO12 .... 181 D1
Romsey SO51 .... 53 E4
West End SO18 .... 80 A2
Kennet Rd Petersfield GU32 ... 40 C1
Romsey SO51 .... 53 E4
Kenneth Ct 15 BH23 .... 209 D4
Kennington La SO40 .... 99 D4
Kennington Rd BH17 .... 202 B4
Kensington Cl SO50 .... 56 B3
Kensington Ct 3 SO17 .... 79 E1
Kensington Dr BH2 .... 204 B2
Kensington Fields SO45 .... 125 E1
Kensington Gdns PO14 .... 129 E1
Kensington Pk SO41 .... 211 E2
Kensington Rd Gosport PO12 ... 181 E2
Portsmouth PO2 .... 157 F1
Kenson Gdns SO19 .... 104 A2
Kent Gdns SO40 .... 100 B3
Kent Gr PO16 .... 156 B3
Kent House
20 Bournemouth BH4 .... 204 B2
27 Southampton SO14 .... 103 E3
Kent La BH24 .... 93 E1
Kent Rd Chandler's Ford SO53 ... 55 D2
Gosport PO13 .... 155 D2
Poole BH12 .... 203 F3
Portsmouth PO5 .... 182 B2
Southampton SO17 .... 79 E1
Kent St Portsmouth PO1 .... 182 A3
Southampton SO14 .... 103 E3
Kentidge Rd PO7 .... 134 B3
Kentish Rd SO15 .... 102 B4
Kenwood Rd PO16 .... 156 B3
Kenwyn Cl SO18 .... 80 A1
Kenya Rd PO16 .... 156 A4
Kenyon Cl BH15 .... 202 C4
Kenyon Rd Poole BH15 .... 202 C4
Portsmouth PO2 .... 157 F1
Keppel Cl BH24 .... 141 D4
Kerley Rd BH2 .... 204 C1
Kern Cl SO16 .... 77 F2
Kerrfield SO22 .... 10 B4
Kerrfield Mews SO22 .... 10 B4
Kerry Cl Chandler's Ford SO53 ... 55 E3
Lymington SO41 .... 197 E2
Kesteven Way SO18 .... 104 A4
Kestrel Cl
Bishop's Waltham SO32 .... 83 D4
Botley SO32 .... 81 F1
Clanfield PO8 .... 88 B2
Ferndown BH22 .... 165 E4
Marchwood SO40 .... 101 F1
Southampton SO16 .... 78 A3
Stubbington PO14 .... 154 A2
Upton BH16 .... 201 D4
Winchester SO22 .... 10 B2
Kestrel Ct BH24 .... 141 D4
Kestrel Dr BH23 .... 208 A3
Kestrel Pl PO6 .... 158 C4
Kestrel Rd SO50 .... 55 F1
Kestrel Way SP6 .... 93 D3
Keswick Ave PO3 .... 183 D4
Keswick Ct BH25 .... 195 D3
Keswick Rd
Bournemouth BH5 .... 206 A2
New Milton BH25 .... 195 D3
Southampton SO19 .... 103 E1
Keswick Way BH31 .... 114 C4
Kettering Terr PO2 .... 182 B4
Keverstone Ct BH1 .... 205 E2
Kevlyn Cres SO31 .... 104 C1
Kew La SO31 .... 128 A4
Kewlake La SO40 .... 74 B1
Key Cl 21 BH15 .... 202 A1
Keydell Ave PO8 .... 112 A3
Keydell Cl PO8 .... 112 A3
Keyes Cl Christchurch BH23 ... 207 F3
Gosport PO13 .... 155 E2
Poole BH12 .... 188 C1
Keyes Rd SO15 .... 155 E2
Keyhaven Cl PO13 .... 155 D1
Keyhaven Dr PO9 .... 135 E3
Keyhaven Rd SO41 .... 211 F2
Keynsham Rd SO19 .... 104 A3
Keysworth Ave BH25 .... 209 F4
Keysworth Rd BH16 .... 201 E2
Khandala Gdns PO7 .... 134 C2
Khartoum Rd SO17 .... 79 D1
Khyber Rd BH12 .... 203 E3
Kidmore La PO7 .... 110 C3
Kielder Cl SO53 .... 55 D4
Kielder Gr PO13 .... 155 E1
Kilbride 11 BH14 .... 204 A2
Kilbride Path 5 PO2 .... 182 B4
Kilham La SO22 .... 10 A3
Killarney Cl SO19 .... 104 C3
Killock 6 BH13 .... 214 C4
Kilmarnock Rd BH9 .... 189 F1
Kilmeston Cl PO9 .... 135 F3
Kilmeston Rd Cheriton SO24 ... 14 B2
Kilmeston SO24 .... 14 B1
Kilmington Way BH23 .... 208 C4
Kilmiston Cl PO16 .... 132 B1
Kilmiston Dr PO16 .... 132 B1
Kilmiston Rd PO1 .... 182 C4
Kiln Acre PO16 .... 131 D2

Kiln Cl Broadstone BH21 ...... 186 B2
Hythe SO45 .... 125 F2
Kiln Field GU33 .... 20 C3
Kiln Gn SO21 .... 57 D4
Kiln Hill SO32 .... 109 D4
Kiln La Braishfield SO51 .... 28 B3
Buriton GU31 .... 65 E3
Colden Common SO50 .... 31 E1
Otterbourne SO21 .... 31 E1
Redlynch SP5 .... 47 F4
Kiln Rd Fareham PO16, PO17 ... 131 D2
Portsmouth PO3 .... 158 A1
Kilnside PO7 .... 110 C2
Kilnyard Cl SO40 .... 76 B1
Kilpatrick Cl 6 PO12 .... 182 B4
Kilwich Way PO16 .... 156 A3
Kimber Rd BH11 .... 188 C2
Kimberley Cl
Christchurch BH23 .... 206 C4
Fair Oak SO50 .... 57 E1
Kimberley Ct SO19 .... 103 E1
Kimberley Rd
Bournemouth BH6 .... 206 B3
Poole BH14 .... 203 D2
Portsmouth PO4 .... 183 D1
Kimbers GU32 .... 40 C2
Kimbolton Rd PO3 .... 183 D3
Kimbridge Cnr SO51 .... 27 D4
Kimbridge Cres PO9 .... 136 A3
Kimbridge La SO51 .... 27 D4
Kimmeridge Ave BH12 .... 203 E4
Kimpton Cl PO13 .... 179 F1
Kimpton Ct 25 PO9 .... 136 A3
Kineton Rd SO15 .... 78 C3
King Albert Ct 59 PO1 .... 182 B3
King Albert St PO1 .... 182 B3
King Alfred Pl SO23 .... 2 A1
King Alfred Terr 28 SO23 .... 2 A1
King Alfred's Coll SO22 .... 10 C4
King Arthur's Ct PO6 .... 158 B4
King Charles St PO1 .... 182 A2
King Cl BH24 .... 139 F2
King Cup Ave SO18 .... 128 C2
King Edward Ave
Bournemouth BH9 .... 190 A1
Southampton SO16 .... 102 A4
King Edward St PO1 .... 182 B2
King Edward Pk(Cvn Pk) SO53 ... 55 D4
King Edward VI Sch SO15 ..... 102 C4
King Edward's Cres PO2 .... 157 E1
King Fisher Way BH23 .... 208 A3
King George Ave
Bournemouth BH9 .... 189 F1
Petersfield GU32 .... 40 C2
King George Mews 7 SO21 ... 40 C2
King George Mobile
Home Pk BH25 .... 194 C1
King George Rd PO16 .... 156 B4
King George's Ave SO15 .... 101 F4
King Harold St SO22 .... 10 C3
King Henry 1 St PO1 .... 182 A3
King John Ave
Bournemouth BH11 .... 188 B3
Portchester PO16 .... 156 A4
King John Cl BH11 .... 188 B3
King La GU32 .... 39 F4
King Richard 1 Rd PO1 .... 182 A2
King Richard Dr BH11 .... 188 B3
King Richard Sch PO6 .... 156 C4
King St Emsworth PO10 .... 161 D4
Gosport PO12 .... 181 E3
Portsmouth PO5 .... 182 B2
Southampton SO14 .... 103 D2
Westbourne PO10 .... 137 D2
Wimborne Minster BH21 .... 163 D2
King William St PO1 .... 182 A3
King's Arms La BH24 .... 140 C4
King's Arms Row BH24 .... 140 C4
King's Ave BH23 .... 206 C3
King's Cl SO53 .... 55 E4
King's Copse Rd SO45 .... 177 E4
King's Cres BH14 .... 203 F1
King's Croft La PO9 .... 135 E1
King's House 17 SO14 .... 103 D2
King's La GU32 .... 18 B2
King's Park Dr BH7 .... 205 E3
King's Park Prim Sch BH1 .... 205 F3
King's Park Rd
Bournemouth BH7 .... 205 E3
Southampton SO15 .... 103 D3
King's Rd Bournemouth BH3 ... 205 D4
Emsworth PO10 .... 160 C4
Fareham PO16 .... 131 D1
Lee-on-the-Solent PO13 .... 179 F2
Portsmouth PO5 .... 182 B2
Winchester SO22, SO23 .... 10 B3
King's Saltern Rd SO41 .... 198 A1
King's Sch (Prim) The SO30 ... 80 C2
King's Terr 1 PO10 .... 160 C4
Kingcup Cl BH18 .... 186 C1
Kingdom Cl PO15 .... 129 E3
Kingfisher Cl
Bournemouth BH6 .... 206 C3
Hamble-le-Rice SO31 .... 128 A2
Rowland's Castle PO9 .... 113 D1
South Hayling PO11 .... 185 D1
West Moors BH22 .... 138 C4
Kingfisher Copse SO31 .... 129 D2
Kingfisher Ct Havant PO9 ..... 136 A1
1 Southampton SO17 .... 79 D1
Kingfisher Rd SO50 .... 55 F1
Kingfisher Way
Marchwood SO40 .... 101 F1
Ringwood BH24 .... 117 D1
Romsey SO51 .... 52 C4

Kingfishers
 9 Christchurch BH23 .... 207 D3
 Portchester PO16 .... 155 F4
Kingfishers The BH31 .... 115 B4
Kinghton Heath
 Ind Est BH11 .... 188 C2
Kingland Cres BH15 .... 202 B1
Kingland Rd BH15 .... 202 B1
Kings Ave
 Hamble-le-Rice SO31 .... 127 F2
 Poole BH14 .... 203 E1
 Winchester SO22 .... 10 C3
Kings Bench Alley PO1 ...... 182 A3
Kings Cl Lymington SO41 .... 197 E2
 Lyndhurst SO43 .... 121 F3
 Rowland's Castle PO9 .... 113 D1
 Twyford SO21 .... 32 A4
 West Moors BH22 .... 138 C1
Kings Copse Ave SO30 .... 105 E3
Kings Copse Prim Sch SO30 .. 105 E3
Kings Copse Rd SO30 .... 105 E3
Kings Court Sch PO8 .... 88 A1
Kings Cres SO41 .... 197 E2
Kings Field SO31 .... 105 D1
Kings Field Gdns SO31 .... 105 D1
Kings Head Yd 25 SO23 ...... 11 C4
Kings Huts SO41 .... 197 D2
Kings La Chilcomb SO23 ...... 11 F3
 Sway SO41 .... 196 C4
Kings Mede PO8 .... 112 A3
Kings Park Com Hospl BH7 ... 205 F3
Kings Rd Chandler's Ford SO53 .. 55 E3
 Gosport PO12 .... 181 D3
 Lymington SO41 .... 197 E2
 New Milton BH25 .... 195 E2
 Petersfield GU32 .... 40 B2
 South Hayling PO11 .... 185 D3
Kings Ride SO45 .... 177 F4
Kings Sch The SO50 .... 57 D1
Kings Somborne Rd SO51 ..... 7 E1
Kings Way PO9 .... 113 D1
Kings Worthy Prim Sch SO23 .. 2 B3
Kingsbere Ave BH10 .... 189 D1
Kingsbere Gdns BH23 .... 209 D4
Kingsbere Rd BH15 .... 202 C3
Kingsbridge Rd BH14 .... 203 E2
Kingsbury Rd SO14 .... 103 D4
Kingsbury's La BH24 .... 140 C4
Kingsclere Ave Havant PO9 .. 135 E3
 Southampton SO19 .... 126 C4
Kingsclere Cl SO19 .... 103 F1
Kingscote House 7 PO6 ...... 132 C1
Kingscote Rd Cosham PO6 .... 132 C1
 Waterlooville PO8 .... 111 E2
Kingscroft PO9 .... 135 E1
Kingsdale Ct 7 SO22 .... 10 C4
Kingsdown Pl PO1 .... 182 C3
Kingsdown Rd PO7 .... 111 E1
Kingsdown Way SO18 .... 80 A1
Kingsey Ave PO10 .... 160 C4
Kingsfernsden La GU32 ...... 41 D3
Kingsfield Lymington SO41 ... 198 A1
 Ringwood BH24 .... 141 D4
Kingsfold Ave SO18 .... 79 F2
Kingsford Cl SP5 .... 47 E3
Kingsgate Rd SO14 .... 10 C3
Kingsgate St SO23 .... 11 D3
Kingsland Cl PO6 .... 133 E1
Kingsland Cl Poole BH13 .... 214 C4
 4 Southampton SO14 .... 103 D2
Kingsland House 18 SO14 .... 103 D3
Kingsland Mkt SO14 .... 103 D2
Kingsland Sq 3 SO14 .... 103 D2
Kingsleigh Fst Sch BH10 .... 189 E2
Kingsleigh Jun Sch BH10 .... 189 E2
Kingsleigh Sec Sch BH10 .... 189 E2
Kingsley Ave BH6 .... 207 D2
Kingsley Cl BH6 .... 207 D2
Kingsley Gdns SO40 .... 100 A4
Kingsley Gn PO9 .... 135 F3
Kingsley Pl SO22 .... 10 C3
Kingsley Rd Gosport PO12 ... 180 C4
 Portsmouth PO4 .... 183 E2
 Southampton SO15 .... 102 A4
Kingsmead PO17 .... 108 B4
Kingsmead Ave SO19 .... 179 E3
Kingsmead Ct
 12 Southampton SO15 ..... 78 A1
 9 Wimborne Minster BH21 .. 163 D3
Kingsmill Cl PO12 .... 180 C2
Kingsmill Rd BH17 .... 202 C4
Kingston SO31 .... 127 E4
Kingston Cres PO2 .... 182 B4
Kingston Cross PO2 .... 182 B4
Kingston Ct SO19 .... 77 F1
Kingston Gdns PO15 .... 130 B2
Kingston Lacy House (NT)
 BH21 .... 162 A4
Kingston Pk SO41 .... 197 E1
Kingston Rd Gosport PO12 ... 180 C3
 Poole BH15 .... 202 B2
 Portsmouth PO1, PO2 .... 182 C4
 Southampton SO15 .... 102 B3
Kingsway Chandler's Ford SO53 .. 55 F4
 Ferndown BH22 .... 165 D4
 North Hayling PO11 .... 160 A2
 Southampton SO14 .... 103 D3
Kingsway BH23 .... 191 F1
Kingsway Cl SO53 .... 55 F4
Kingsway Gdns SO53 .... 55 F4
Kingsway The PO16 .... 156 B4
Kingswell Cl BH10 .... 189 E1
Kingswell Gdns BH10 .... 189 D1
Kingswell Gr BH10 .... 189 D1

Kingswell Path 13 PO1 ...... 182 B3
Kingswell Rd BH10 .... 189 E1
Kingswell St PO1 .... 182 B3
Kingswood
 Bournemouth BH4 .... 204 B1
 Marchwood SO40 .... 102 A1
Kingsworthy Rd PO9 .... 135 F2
Kinloss Cl SO16 .... 78 A3
Kinnell Cl PO10 .... 160 C4
Kinross Cres PO6 .... 158 A4
Kinross Rd Bournemouth BH3 .. 204 C3
 Totton SO40 .... 100 C3
Kinsbourne Ave BH10 .... 189 E1
Kinsbourne Cl SO19 .... 104 C3
Kinsbourne Rise SO19 .... 104 C3
Kinsbourne Way SO19 .... 104 C3
Kinson Ave BH15 .... 203 D4
Kinson Gr BH10 .... 189 E3
Kinson Park Rd BH10 .... 189 E3
Kinson Pottery Ind Est BH14 .. 203 F4
Kinson Prim Sch BH11 ...... 189 D3
Kinson Rd BH10 .... 189 E2
Kinterbury Ct 9 SO17 ...... 103 D4
Kintyre Rd PO6 .... 133 F1
Kinver Cl SO51 .... 28 A1
Kiosks The 21 BH15 .... 202 B1
Kipling Bldgs 18 PO2 .... 157 F2
Kipling Ct SO19 .... 103 F1
Kipling Rd Eastleigh SO50 ... 55 F2
 Poole BH14 .... 203 D3
 Portsmouth PO2 .... 157 F2
Kirby Cl BH15 .... 202 C3
Kirby Ct 4 PO2 .... 157 F1
Kirby Rd PO2 .... 157 F1
Kirby Way BH6 .... 206 B2
Kirkham Ave BH23 .... 192 B2
Kirkstall Rd PO4 .... 182 C1
Kirkway BH18 .... 187 D2
Kirtley Cl PO6 .... 158 B3
Kirton Rd PO6 .... 158 B4
Kitchener Cres BH17 .... 187 D1
Kitchener Rd SO17 .... 79 E1
Kitchers Cl SO41 .... 172 A1
Kite Cl PO8 .... 111 F2
Kitnocks Hill SO32 .... 106 C4
Kitscroft Rd BH10 .... 189 E3
Kitt's La GU10 .... 16 B1
Kittiwake Cl
 Bournemouth BH6 .... 206 C3
 Gosport PO13 .... 155 D1
Kitwalls La SO41 .... 211 E3
Kitwood Gn 50 PO9 .... 136 A3
Kivernell Pl 1 SO41 .... 211 E2
Kivernell Rd SO41 .... 211 E2
Kiwi Cl BH15 .... 202 C2
Kleves Ct SO19 .... 104 A3
Knapp Cl BH23 .... 207 D4
Knapp La SO51 .... 29 E2
Knapp Mill Ave BH23 ...... 207 D4
Knapps Hard GU32 .... 37 D3
Knatchbull Cl SO51 .... 52 C4
Knellers La SO40 .... 100 B2
Knight Cl SO23 .... 2 A1
Knighton Heath Cl BH11 .... 188 C2
Knighton Heath Rd BH11 ... 188 C2
Knighton La BH21 .... 188 B4
Knighton Park BH25 .... 209 F4
Knighton Rd SO19 .... 103 F2
Knights Bank Rd PO14 ..... 153 F1
Knights Rd BH11 .... 188 B3
Knightsbridge Ct BH2 ...... 204 C1
Knightstone Ct 10 PO2 ..... 157 F2
Knightstone Gr BH22 ...... 138 B1
Knightstone Grange SO45 .. 126 A1
Knightwood Ave
 Havant PO9 .... 136 A3
 Lyndhurst SO43 .... 121 F3
Knightwood Cl Ashurst SO40 .. 100 A1
 Christchurch BH23 .... 208 B4
 Lyndhurst SO43 .... 121 F3
Knightwood Oak SO43 ..... 120 C1
Knightwood Rd
 Chandler's Ford SO52 ...... 55 D3
 Hythe SO45 .... 126 A2
 North Baddesley SO52 ...... 55 D3
Knobcrook Rd 3 BH21 ...... 163 D3
Knole Ct 5 BH1 .... 205 E2
Knole Gdns BH1 .... 205 E2
Knole Rd BH1 .... 205 E2
Knoll Gdns BH24 .... 139 F2
Knoll La BH21 .... 186 A4
Knoll Manor BH21 .... 204 C3
Knotgrass Rd SO31 .... 128 C1
Knowland Dr SO41 .... 211 E3
Knowle Hill SO50 .... 56 A4
Knowle Hospl PO17 .... 130 C4
Knowle La SO50 .... 57 F1
Knowle Rd SO42 .... 145 F1
Knowle Sidings SO17 ...... 130 B4
Knowles Cl BH23 .... 207 F4
Knowles Meadow GU33 .... 21 D1
Knowlton Gdns BH9 .... 190 A2
Knowlton Rd BH17 .... 187 F1
Knowsley Cres PO6 .... 158 A4
Knowsley Rd PO6 .... 157 F4
Knox Rd Havant PO9 ...... 135 E1
 Portsmouth PO2 .... 157 F1
Knyght Cl SO51 .... 53 D3
Knyveton Cl BH1 .... 205 D2
Knyveton Rd BH1 .... 205 E2
Kootenay Ave SO18 .... 104 C4
Kooyong SO52 .... 51 D1
Kynegils Rd SO22 .... 1 C1
Kynon Ct PO12 .... 181 E4
Kyrchil La BH21 .... 163 F3
Kyrchil Way BH21 .... 163 F4
Kytes La SO32 .... 82 B3

Labrador Dr BH15 .... 202 B1
Laburnum Ave PO6 .... 158 B4
Laburnum Cl Ferndown BH22 .. 165 D3
 North Baddesley SO52 ...... 54 A3
 Verwood BH31 .... 115 E3
Laburnum Cres SO45 .... 150 A4
Laburnum Ct SO19 .... 103 E2
Laburnum Dr SO41 .... 211 F4
Laburnum Gr Eastleigh SO50 .. 56 A2
 Portsmouth PO2 .... 157 F1
 South Hayling PO11 .... 185 D2
Laburnum House
 Bournemouth BH10 .... 189 F2
 Hedge End SO30 .... 105 E3
Laburnum Rd
 Fareham PO16 .... 155 D3
 Hedge End SO30 .... 105 E3
 Southampton SO16 .... 79 E2
 Waterlooville PO7 .... 134 B3
Lacey Cres BH15 .... 203 D3
Lackford Ave SO40 .... 100 C3
Lacon Cl SO18 .... 103 F4
Lacy Cl BH21 .... 163 E3
Lacy Dr BH21 .... 163 E3
Ladram Rd PO2 .... 180 C2
Lady Betty's Dr PO15 ...... 129 F3
Ladybridge Rd PO7 .... 134 B2
Ladycross Rd SO45 .... 126 A1
Ladysmith Rd BH23 .... 207 F4
Ladysmith Terr SO32 ...... 83 E4
Ladywood SO50 .... 55 F3
Ladywood House 6 PO1 .... 182 B2
Lagado Cl BH14 .... 214 B2
Lagland Ct 13 BH15 .... 202 B1
Lagland St BH15 .... 202 B1
Lagoon Cl BH14 .... 214 A4
Lagoon Rd BH14 .... 214 A4
Laidlaw Cl BH12 .... 204 A4
Lake Ave BH15 .... 201 E1
Lake Cres BH15 .... 201 F2
Lake Dr BH15 .... 201 E1
Lake Farm Cl SO30 .... 105 E4
Lake Grove Rd BH25 ...... 195 D2
Lake House SO15 .... 102 B3
Lake Rd
 Chandler's Ford SO53 ...... 55 F4
 Curdridge SO32 .... 106 C4
 Hamworthy BH15 .... 201 F1
 Portsmouth PO1 .... 182 B3
 Southampton SO19 .... 103 E1
 Verwood BH31 .... 115 D3
Lakeland Gdns SO40 ...... 101 F1
Lakelands Dr SO15 .... 102 B3
Lakes The SO32 .... 84 A2
Lakeside
 Fareham PO17 .... 130 C3
 Lee-on-the-Solent PO13 .... 179 F1
 Ower SO51 .... 75 E3
 Ringwood BH24 .... 141 E3
Lakeside Ave
 Portsmouth PO3 .... 183 D4
 Rownhams SO16 .... 77 F3
Lakeside Pines BH25 ...... 195 D2
Lakeside Rd BH13 .... 204 A1
Lakesmere Rd PO8 .... 112 B3
Lakeview Dr BH24 .... 141 E3
Lakewood Cl SO53 .... 55 E4
Lakewood Rd Ashurst SO40 .. 100 B2
 Chandler's Ford SO53 ...... 30 C1
 Christchurch BH23 .... 193 F1
Lambert Cl PO7 .... 134 C3
Lambourn Cl PO14 .... 154 B4
Lambourn Sq SO53 .... 55 D3
Lambourne Cl SO45 .... 125 F1
Lambourne Dr SO31 ...... 129 C2
Lambourne House SO30 ... 105 D3
Lambourne Rd SO18 ...... 80 A1
Lambs Cl BH17 .... 187 E1
Lambsgreen La BH21 ...... 162 C1
Lammas Rd SO45 .... 126 A1
Lampeter Ave PO6 .... 158 A4
Lampton Gdns BH9 .... 189 F1
Lamward Mansions 28 SO14 .. 103 D4
Lancaster Cl Bursledon SO31 .. 105 D1
 Christchurch BH23 .... 208 B4
 Corfe Mullen BH18 .... 186 C3
 Lee-on-the-Solent PO13 .... 180 A2
 Portchester PO16 .... 132 A1
Lancaster Ct SO30 .... 80 B1
Lancaster Dr
 Corfe Mullen BH18 .... 186 C3
 Verwood BH31 .... 114 C3
Lancaster Rd Ferndown BH21 .. 165 D4
 Southampton SO16 .... 77 F2
Lancaster Way PO7 .... 134 C3
Lancer Cl BH23 .... 206 C4
Lander Cl BH15 .... 202 B1
Landford CE Contr
 Prim Sch SP5 .... 49 E2
Landford Gdns BH8 .... 190 B1
Landford Way BH8 .... 190 B1
Landguard Rd
 Portsmouth PO4 .... 183 D2
 Southampton SO15 .... 102 B1
Landon Rd PO13 .... 180 A2
Landport St Portsmouth PO1 .. 182 A3
 Portsmouth PO1 .... 182 B3
Landport Terr PO1 .... 182 A2
Landport View 8 PO1 ..... 182 B3
Lands End Rd SO31 .... 128 B4
Landsdowne St PO5 .... 182 A2
Landseer Rd
 13 Bournemouth BH4 ..... 204 B2
 Southampton SO19 .... 104 B2
Lane End SO24 .... 17 E4
Lane End Cotts SP5 .... 49 E2
Lane End Rd PO10 .... 160 C4

Lane The
 4 Bournemouth BH8 ...... 205 E3
 Fawley SO45 .... 151 D2
 Portsmouth PO4 .... 181 D1
 Portsmouth PO4 .... 182 C1
Lanehays Rd SO45 .... 125 F2
Lanes End PO14 .... 179 E3
Lanes The BH25 .... 195 D3
Lanesbridge Cl SO40 ...... 99 F3
Langbar Cl SO19 .... 103 F3
Langbrook Cl PO9 .... 159 F4
Langdale Ave PO6 .... 158 A4
Langdale Cl SO16 .... 101 F4
Langdon Ct BH14 .... 203 E2
Langdon Rd BH14 .... 203 E2
Langdown Firs SO45 ...... 126 A2
Langdown Inf Sch SO45 ... 126 A1
Langdown Jun Sch SO45 ... 126 A1
Langdown Lawn SO45 ..... 126 A1
Langdown Lawn Cl SO45 ... 126 A1
Langdown Rd SO45 .... 126 A2
Langford La SP5 .... 47 F4
Langford Rd PO1 .... 182 C4
Langham Cl SO52 .... 53 F2
Langham Ct BH23 .... 191 F1
Langhorn Rd SO16 .... 79 E2
Langley Gdn SP6 .... 70 A2
Langley Lodge Gdns SO45 .. 177 F4
Langley Rd Christchurch BH23 .. 193 F1
 Poole BH14 .... 203 F2
 Portsmouth PO2 .... 182 C4
 Southampton SO15 .... 102 A3
Langrish Cl PO9 .... 136 A3
Langrish Hill GU32 .... 39 E2
Langrish Prim Sch GU32 .. 40 A2
Langrish Rd SO16 .... 78 A2
Langside Ave BH12 ...... 204 A4
Langside Sch BH12 ...... 204 A4
Langstone Ave PO9 ...... 159 F4
Langstone High St PO9 ... 159 F3
Langstone House BH12 ... 155 D4
Langstone Inf Sch PO3 ... 183 D4
Langstone Jun Sch PO3 ... 183 D4
Langstone Rd Havant PO9 .. 159 F4
 Portsmouth PO3 .... 183 D3
Langstone Wlk
 Fareham PO14 .... 154 B4
 Gosport PO13 .... 155 D1
Langton Cl
 Barton on Sea BH25 ...... 210 A4
 Winchester SO23 .... 1 C1
Langton Dene 27 BH4 .... 204 B2
Langton Farm Gdns PO1 .. 182 C4
Langton Rd
 Bishop's Waltham SO32 ... 83 E4
 Bournemouth BH7 .... 205 F3
Lanham La Sparsholt SO22 .. 10 A4
 Winchester SO22 .... 1 A1
Lankhills Rd SO22 .... 1 C1
Lankhills Sch SO22 .... 2 A1
Lansdell Rd 6 BH15 ...... 202 C2
Lansdown Ave PO16 ...... 156 B3
Lansdown Terr PO10 ..... 137 D3
Lansdowne Ave
 Waterlooville PO7 .... 134 C4
 Winchester SO23 .... 10 C3
Lansdowne Cl 3 SO53 .... 52 C4
Lansdowne Cres BH1 ..... 205 D2
Lansdowne Ct Romsey SO51 .. 52 C4
 3 Winchester SO23 ...... 10 C3
Lansdowne Gdns
 Bournemouth BH1 .... 205 D2
 Romsey SO51 .... 52 C4
Lansdowne Hill SO14 .... 102 C2
Lansdowne House
 13 Bournemouth BH1 .... 205 D2
 5 Gosport PO12 .... 181 D3
Lansdowne Rd
 Bournemouth BH1 .... 205 D3
 Southampton SO15 ...... 102 A4
Lansdowne The BH1 ..... 205 D2
Lantana Cl PO7 .... 134 C3
Lantern Ct SO22 .... 10 C3
Lanyard Dr PO13 .... 180 B3
Lapthorn Cl PO13 ...... 155 D2
Lapwing Cl Gosport PO12 .. 181 D4
 Horndean PO8 .... 112 A4
Lapwing Dr SO40 .... 100 B4
Lapwing Gr PO16 .... 155 F4
Lapwing Rd BH21 ...... 164 A4
Lara Cl BH8 .... 190 B2
Larch Ave SO45 .... 150 B3
Larch Cl Broadstone BH17 .. 186 C1
 Hordle SO41 .... 195 F2
 Kings Worthy SO23 ...... 2 A4
 Lee-on-the-Solent PO13 .. 180 A3
 St Leonards SO30 .... 80 B1
Larch Ct SO16 .... 78 A2
Larch Row SP6 .... 70 B1
Larch Way Bursledon SO31 .. 127 F4
 Ferndown BH22 .... 165 E4
Larchdale Cl SO31 ...... 152 B4
Larches Gdns PO15 ..... 130 B1
Larchfield Way PO8 ..... 112 B3
Larchwood Ave PO9 .... 135 D2
Larchwood Rd SO40 .... 100 B4
Larcombe Rd GU32 ..... 40 B1
Larg Dr SO22 .... 1 B2
Lark Hill Rise SO22 ..... 10 B2
Lark Rd Christchurch BH23 .. 208 A3
 Eastleigh SO50 .... 55 E1
Larkhill Rd PO3 .... 157 F2
Larks Cl BH22 .... 165 D4
Larks Rise BH22 .... 165 D4
Larksfield Ave BH9 ..... 190 B2
Larkshill CE BH25 ...... 195 D2
Larkspur Chase SO19 ... 104 C3

Larkspur Cl Locks Heath SO31 .. 128 C1
 Swanmore SO32 .... 84 A1
Larkspur Dr SO40 .... 124 C1
Larkspur Gdns Hedge End SO30 105 E1
 Holbury SO45 .... 150 A4
Larkwhistle Wlk PO9 .... 135 E1
Lascelles Ct 1 BH7 ...... 206 A4
Lascelles Rd BH7 .... 206 A4
Laser Cl SO31 .... 128 C1
Lasham Gn PO9 .... 136 A3
Lasham House 3 SO16 .. 102 A4
Lasham Wlk PO14 ...... 154 B4
Lashley Meadow PO7 ... 86 B4
Latch Farm Ave BH23 .. 207 D2
Latchmore Dr SO45 .... 125 E1
Latchmore Forest Gr PO8 .. 112 A4
Latchmore Gdns PO8 ... 111 F4
Latelie Cl SO31 .... 127 E3
Latham Cl SO50 .... 57 A
Latham Ct SO15 .... 102 A
Latham Rd Fair Oak SO50 .. 57 D
 Romsey SO51 .... 53 D
Latimer Ct Portsmouth PO3 .. 158 A
 11 Southampton SO17 .. 79 D
Latimer Gate 27 SO14 .. 103 D
Latimer Rd BH9 .... 204 C
Latimer St Romsey SO51 .. 52 C
 Southampton SO14 ..... 103 D
Latimers Cl BH23 ...... 193 F
Lauder Cl PO10 .... 137 F
Launcelyn Cl SO52 ..... 53 F
Launceston Dr SO50 ... 55 F
Laundry La SO41 ...... 211 F
Laundry Rd SO16 ...... 78 A
Laurel Cl Christchurch BH23 .. 193 E
 Corfe Mullen BH21 ..... 186 B
 Hordle SO41 .... 195 F
 Hythe SO45 .... 125 F
 Locks Heath SO31 ..... 129 D
 Southampton SO19 .... 103 E
 St Leonards BH24 ..... 139 F
Laurel Dr BH18 .... 187 E
Laurel Gdns Broadstone BH18 .. 187 E
 Locks Heath SO31 ..... 129 D
Laurel La BH24 .... 139 F
Laurel Rd Locks Heath SO31 .. 129 D
 Waterlooville PO8 ..... 112 B
Laurels The
 Brockenhurst SO42 .... 172 C
 Ferndown BH22 .... 165 D
Laurence Ct 2 SO50 ... 57 E
Laurence Gn PO10 .... 136 C
Lauriston Dr SO53 .... 30 A
Laurus PO7 .... 135 D
Laurus Wlk 18 PO13 .. 179 F
Lavant Ct 8 GU32 .... 40 C
Lavant Cl PO8 .... 112 A
Lavant Dr PO9 .... 136 A
Lavant St GU32 ...... 40 C
Lavender Cl
 Southampton SO19 ... 103 F
 Verwood BH31 .... 115 E
Lavender Rd
 Bournemouth BH8 .... 190 B
 Hordle SO41 .... 195 F
 Waterlooville PO7 .... 135 D
Lavender Villas 1 BH23 .. 209 D
Lavender Way BH18 .. 186 B
Laverock Lea PO16 ... 132 B
Laverstock 27 BH5 ... 205 F
Laverstoke Cl SO16 .. 77 F
Lavey's La PO15 ..... 130 A
Lavington Gdns SO52 .. 53 F
Lavinia Rd Gosport PO12 .. 181 D
 Poole BH12 .... 203 E
Lawford Rd BH9 ...... 190 A
Lawford Way SO40 ... 100 C
Lawn Cl Gosport PO13 .. 180 B
 Milford on Sea SO41 .. 211 F
Lawn Ct SO17 .... 103 D
Lawn Dr SO31 .... 129 D
Lawn House 17 SO23 .. 11 D
Lawn Rd Eastleigh SO50 .. 56 A
 Littleton SO22 .... 1 B
 Lymington SO41 ...... 197 D
 Milford on Sea SO41 .. 211 F
 Southampton SO17 ... 103 D
Lawn St 18 SO23 ..... 11 D
Lawn View BH25 ..... 194 B
Lawns Cl BH21 .... 164 B
Lawns Rd BH21 ...... 164 A
Lawns The BH23 ..... 209 D
Lawnside Rd SO15 ... 102 A
Lawnswood Cl PO8 .. 111 F
Lawrence Ave PO8 .. 111 F
Lawrence Ct
 Bournemouth BH8 ... 205 E
 Southampton SO19 .. 103 F
Lawrence Dr BH13 .. 203 F
Lawrence Gr SO19 .. 103 F
Lawrence House 5 SO45 .. 126 A
Lawrence La SP6 .... 94 A
Lawrence Rd Fareham PO15 .. 130 C
 Portsmouth PO5 ..... 182 C
 Ringwood BH24 ..... 117 F
Lawrence Sq 20 PO12 .. 181 E
Lawrence Wlk PO13 . 180 B
Lawson Cl SO31 .... 128 A
Lawson Ct 9 SO15 .. 78 A
Lawson Rd Poole BH12 .. 203 D
 Portsmouth PO5 ..... 182 C
Laxton Cl Locks Heath SO31 .. 129 D
 Southampton SO19 .. 104 A
Layard Dr BH21 .... 163 E
Laymoor La BH21 ... 164 B
Layton Cl SO31 .... 203 E
Layton Rd Gosport PO13 .. 155 E
 Poole BH12 .... 203 E

azy Acre PO10 .... 161 E4
e Patourel Cl BH23 .... 207 E4
ea Rd SO45 .... 177 F4
ea The BH31 .... 115 D3
ea Way BH11 .... 188 C3
eabrook SO31 .... 129 D3
eacock Cl SO32 .... 84 A3
eafy La PO15 .... 129 F3
ealand Gr PO6 .... 158 B4
ealand Rd PO6 .... 158 B4
eamington Cres PO13 ..... 179 F1
eamington House 52 PO5 .. 182 B2
eamington Rd BH9 .... 205 D4
eander Cl SO50 .... 56 A3
eaphill Rd BH7 .... 206 A3
ear Rd PO12 .... 181 D3
earoyd Rd BH17 .... 202 C4
easide Way SO16 .... 79 D3
eatherhead Gdns SO30 .... 81 E1
eaway The PO16 .... 156 B4
ebanon Rd SO15 .... 101 E4
echlade Gdns
  Bournemouth BH7 .... 206 A4
  Fareham PO15 .... 130 C2
eckford Cl
  Portchester PO16 .... 132 A1
  Southampton SO18 ...... 104 B4
eckford Rd PO9 .... 136 A3
edbury Rd
  Christchurch BH23 ...... 207 F3
  Cosham PO6 .... 133 E1
ederle La PO13 .... 155 E3
edgard LB BH14 .... 203 D2
ee Church La SO51 .... 76 C4
ee Ct BH22 .... 165 E2
ee Dro SO51 .... 53 D1
ee La SO16 .... 77 D4
ee Rd PO12 .... 181 D3
ee-on-the-Solent Inf Sch
  PO13 .... 179 F1
ee-on-the-Solent Jun Sch
  PO13 .... 179 F1
eedam Rd BH10 .... 189 E2
eelands SO41 .... 197 E1
eep La PO12 .... 181 D1
ees Cl BH23 .... 191 E2
ees La SO18 .... 181 D3
ees La N PO12 .... 181 D3
eesland CE Inf Sch PO12 .. 181 D2
eesland CE Jun Sch PO12 .. 181 D2
eesland Rd PO12 .... 181 D2
eeson Dr BH22 .... 165 D4
eeson Rd BH7 .... 205 F4
egg La BH21 .... 163 E2
egion Cl BH15 .... 201 F1
egion La SO23 .... 2 B4
egion Rd Hamworthy BH15 .. 201 F1
  South Hayling PO11 ..... 185 D2
eicester Ct SO13 .... 180 B3
eicester Rd Poole BH13 .. 203 F2
  Southampton SO15 ...... 78 B1
eicester Way SO23 .... 2 B1
eigh Comm BH21 .... 163 F2
eigh Ct SO50 .... 55 F2
eigh Gdns BH21 .... 163 E2
eigh House Hospl SO53 ... 55 E4
eigh La BH21 .... 163 F3
eigh Mansions 10 SO17 ... 79 D1
eigh Pk SO41 .... 197 E2
eigh Rd
  Chandler's Ford SO53 .. 55 F4
  Eastleigh SO50, SO53 .. 55 F2
  Fareham PO16 .... 131 D1
  Havant PO9 .... 135 F1
  New Milton BH25 .... 195 D2
  Southampton SO17 ..... 79 D1
  Wimborne Minster BH21 .. 163 F2
eigham Vale Rd BH6 ..... 206 B2
eighton Ave 7 SO15 ..... 102 A4
eighton Rd SO19 .... 103 F2
eisure The PO13 .... 155 E2
eith Ave PO16 .... 132 B1
emon Rd SO15 .... 102 A4
endorber Ave PO6 .... 158 A4
ennox Cl
  Chandler's Ford SO53 .. 55 F4
  Gosport PO12 .... 181 E1
  Southampton SO16 ..... 77 F3
ennox Rd N PO5 .... 182 B1
ennox Rd S PO5 .... 182 B1
ensyd Gdns PO8 .... 111 F3
ent Hill St 5 SO22 ...... 10 B3
entham Cl BH17 .... 187 E1
entune Way SO41 .... 197 E1
eofric Ct PO4 .... 183 E2
eominster Rd PO6 .... 133 D1
eonard Rd PO13 .... 181 E3
eonards Ct SO16 .... 101 E4
eopold Dr SO32 .... 83 D4
eopold St PO4 .... 182 C1
epe Ctry Pk SO45 .... 178 A1
epe Rd SO45 .... 178 A2
erryn Rd PO15 .... 155 E1
eslie Loader Ct SO50 .... 56 A2
eslie Loader House SO19 .. 103 F3
eslie Rd Bournemouth BH9 .. 204 C4
  Poole BH14 .... 203 D1
ester Ave PO9 .... 135 E1
ester Rd PO12 .... 180 C3
ester Sq BH4 .... 143 E2
even Cl BH4 .... 204 B3
even Cl Bournemouth BH4 .. 204 B2
  North Baddesley SO53 .. 55 D4
eventhorpe Ct PO12 ..... 181 E2
eveson Cl PO12 .... 180 C2
evet's La 5 BH15 .... 202 A1
eviathan Cl PO14 .... 179 E3

Lewens Cl BH21 .... 163 E2
Lewens La BH21 .... 163 E2
Lewes Cl SO50 .... 56 A3
Lewesdon Dr BH18 .... 186 C2
Lewin Cl SO21 .... 56 C4
Lewins Wlk SO31 .... 104 C1
Lewis Cl SO45 .... 125 E1
Lewis House 17 SO14 .... 103 D3
Lewis Rd PO10 .... 137 D2
Lewis Silkin Way SO16 ... 78 A2
Lewry Cl SO30 .... 105 E4
Lexby Rd SO40 .... 101 D3
Lexden Gdns PO11 .... 184 C2
Leybourne Ave
  Bournemouth BH10 .... 189 E2
  Southampton SO18 .... 104 A4
Leybourne Cl BH10 ..... 189 E3
Leydene Ave BH8 .... 190 C1
Leydene Cl BH8 .... 190 C1
Leyland Cl PO12 .... 181 D2
Leyland Rd PO12 .... 188 C1
Leyside BH23 .... 207 F3
Leyton Conyers 16 BH13 .. 214 C4
Leyton Rd SO14 .... 103 E3
Liam Cl PO9 .... 136 A2
Liberty Cl BH21 .... 139 D3
Liberty Rd PO17 .... 109 D4
Library Mews BH12 ..... 203 E3
Library Rd Bournemouth BH9 .. 189 F1
  Ferndown BH22 .... 165 E3
  Poole BH12 .... 203 F3
  Totton SO40 .... 101 D4
Lichen Way SO40 .... 101 F1
Lichfield Ct PO13 ...... 180 B3
Lichfield Rd
  Locks Heath PO14 .... 129 E2
  Portsmouth PO3 .... 183 D3
Liddel Way SO53 .... 55 D3
Liddiards Way PO7 ..... 134 C2
Lidiard Gdns PO4 ...... 183 D1
Lightfoot Lawn PO4 ... 183 E2
Lilac Cl BH31 .... 141 D4
Lilac Rd SO16 .... 79 D2
Lilley Cl SO40 .... 101 F1
Lilliput CE Fst Sch BH14 .. 214 B4
Lilliput Ct BH14 .... 203 D2
Lilliput Rd BH14 ...... 214 B4
Lily Ave PO7 .... 134 A1
Limberline Rd PO3 .... 158 A4
Limberline Spur PO3 .. 158 A3
Lime Ave SO19 .... 104 A3
Lime Cl Colden Common SO21 .. 57 D4
  Hythe SO45 .... 125 F1
  Poole BH15 .... 202 C3
  Southampton SO19 .. 104 A3
Lime Gdns SO30 ...... 80 B2
Lime Gr Cosham PO6 . 133 D1
  Hordle SO41 .... 211 E4
  South Hayling PO11 . 184 B2
Lime Kiln La SO45 .... 150 A3
Lime Kiln Lane
  Mobile Home Pk SO45 .. 150 A3
Lime St SO14 .... 103 D3
Lime Tree Cl SP6 .... 92 C3
Lime Tree House SO41 .. 197 F2
Lime Wlk Botley SO30 .. 105 F4
  Hythe SO45 .... 125 F1
Limekiln La
  Bishop's Waltham SO32 .. 59 F2
  East Meon GU32 ..... 64 B4
Limes Cl GU33 .... 20 C2
Limes The Gosport PO13 .. 155 E1
  Havant PO9 .... 159 F4
  Marchwood SO40 ... 102 A1
  Waterlooville PO7 .. 134 B2
Limetree Wlk 6 SO23 .. 11 E4
Limited Rd BH9 ...... 190 A1
Lin Brook Dr BH24 ... 117 E1
Linacre Rd SO19 .... 104 B3
Lincoln Ave Bournemouth BH1 .. 205 E3
  Christchurch BH23 .. 191 F1
Lincoln Cl Locks Heath PO14 .. 129 E2
  Romsey SO51 .... 28 A1
Lincoln Ct Gosport PO13 .. 180 B3
  Southampton SO15 .. 78 C1
  West End SO30 ..... 80 B1
Lincoln Rd Poole BH12 .. 203 E4
  Portsmouth PO1 .... 182 C3
Lincoln Rise PO8 .... 112 A3
Lincolns Rise SO50 .. 31 D1
Lind Cl PO7 .... 134 C2
Lind Rd PO12 .... 181 E1
Linda Gr PO8 .... 111 F2
Linda Rd SO45 .... 151 D1
Lindbergh Cl PO13 .. 180 B3
Lindbergh Rd BH21 .. 165 D4
Lindbergh Rise PO15 .. 129 F3
Linden Cl Ferndown BH22 .. 165 E1
  Shedfield SO32 ..... 83 F2
Linden Ct Locks Heath SO31 .. 129 E2
  Ringwood BH24 ..... 140 C4
  12 Romsey SO51 .... 52 C4
  West End SO18 ..... 80 A2
Linden Dr GU33 ..... 20 C2
Linden Gdns
  Hedge End SO30 ... 105 E3
  Ringwood BH24 .... 140 C4
Linden Gr
  Chandler's Ford SO53 .. 55 E4
  Gosport PO12 .... 181 D1
  South Hayling PO11 . 185 D2
Linden Lea PO16 .... 132 B1
Linden Rd
  Bournemouth BH9 .. 190 A2
  Ferndown BH22 .... 165 E1
  Poole BH12 .... 203 E3

Linden Rd Continued
  Romsey SO51 .... 52 C4
  Southampton SO16 . 78 A2
Linden Way Havant PO9 .. 135 F2
  Lymington SO41 .... 197 E2
  Waterlooville PO8 .. 112 B3
Linden Wlk SO52 ..... 53 F3
Lindens Cl PO10 ..... 136 C1
Lindens The BH23 ... 192 B2
Lindisfarne Cl PO6 .. 158 A4
Lindley Ave PO4 .... 183 D1
Lindsay House 35 PO5 .. 182 B1
Lindsay Manor 10 BH12 .. 204 A2
Lindsay Pk 15 BH13 .. 204 A2
Lindsay Rd Poole BH13 .. 204 A2
  Southampton SO19 . 104 C3
Lindum Cl 3 BH12 .. 204 A2
Lindway SO31 .... 129 D3
Lineside BH23 ...... 207 E4
Linford Cl SO45 .... 195 D2
Linford Cres SO16 .. 78 B2
Linford Ct PO9 ..... 135 E4
Linford House BH24 .. 117 F2
Linford Rd BH24 ... 117 E1
Ling Dale SO16 .... 78 C4
Ling Rd BH12 ...... 188 A1
Lingdale Pl 1 SO17 .. 103 D4
Lingdale Rd BH6 ... 206 B3
Lingfield Ct PO1 ... 182 A2
Lingfield Grange BH4 .. 204 A2
Lingwood Ave BH23 .. 207 F3
Lingwood Cl SO16 .. 78 C4
Lingwood Wlk SO16 . 78 C4
Linhorns La SO16 .. 195 D3
Link Rd Ringwood BH24 .. 141 E4
  Southampton SO16 . 77 F2
Link Rise BH21 .... 186 C3
Link The PO7 ..... 112 A1
Link Way PO14 ... 179 E3
Linkenholt Way PO9 .. 135 E2
Linklater Path PO1 .. 182 B4
Links Cl PO9 ...... 113 D1
Links Dr BH23 .... 191 E1
Links La
  Rowland's Castle PO9 .. 113 D1
  South Hayling PO11 . 184 B2
Links Rd Poole BH14 .. 203 E1
  Winchester SO22 ... 1 B1
Links The PO13 ... 155 E1
Links View Ave BH14 .. 203 F1
Links View Way SO16 . 78 C3
Linkside Ave BH8 .. 205 F4
Linmead Dr BH11 .. 189 D3
Linnet Cl Petersfield GU31 .. 41 E1
  Ringwood BH24 ... 141 E3
  Waterlooville PO8 . 111 F2
Linnet Ct Gosport PO12 .. 180 C3
  New Milton BH25 .. 194 C2
Linnet Rd BH17 ... 201 F4
Linnet Sq SO50 ... 55 E1
Linnets The
  Portchester PO16 .. 155 F4
  Totton SO40 ...... 100 A4
Linnies La SO41 .. 196 A4
Linthorpe Rd BH15 .. 202 C2
Linwood Cl SO45 .. 126 A1
Linwood Rd BH24 .. 205 D4
Linwood Sch BH9 . 205 D4
Lion Cl SO41 ..... 182 A3
Lion Terr PO1 .... 182 A3
Lionheart Cl BH11 .. 188 B3
Lionheart Way SO31 .. 105 D1
Lions Hall 23 SO22 .. 10 C4
Lions La BH24 ... 139 E3
Lions Wood BH24 .. 139 F2
Liphook House 33 PO9 .. 136 A3
Lipizzaner Fields SO31 .. 129 D4
Lippen La SO32 .. 36 C2
Lisbon Rd SO15 .. 102 B3
Lisle Cl Lymington SO41 .. 197 E1
  Winchester SO22 .. 10 A2
Lisle Court Rd SO41 .. 198 B2
Lisle Ct SO22 .... 10 C3
Lisle Way PO10 .. 136 C2
Liss Rd PO4 ..... 182 C2
Liss Schs GU33 .. 21 D1
Liss Sta GU33 ... 20 C2
Litchfield Cres SO18 .. 79 F1
Litchfield Rd
  Southampton SO18 .. 79 F1
  Winchester SO22 .. 1 B2
Litchford Rd BH25 .. 195 E2
Lith Ave PO8 .... 112 B4
Little Abshot Rd PO14 .. 153 D4
Little Anglesey PO12 .. 181 D1
Little Anglesey Rd PO12 .. 181 D1
Little Arthur St PO2 .. 182 C4
Little Ashton La SO32 .. 59 F2
Little Barn Pl GU33 .. 21 D2
Little Barrs Dr BH25 .. 195 D2
Little Bull La SO32 .. 83 E1
Little Burn SO41 .. 172 A1
Little Cnr PO7 ... 111 D2
Little Coburg St 65 PO1 .. 182 B3
Little Croft Rd BH12 .. 203 D3
Little Ct Poole BH14 .. 214 B4
  Poole, Canford Cliffs BH13 .. 214 C4
Little Dene Copse SO41 .. 197 D1
Little Dewlands BH31 .. 114 B3
Little Dro SP6 ... 70 C4
Little Forest
  Mansions 10 BH1 .. 205 D2
Little Forest Rd BH4 .. 204 C3
Little Fosters BH13 .. 214 C4
Little Gays PO14 .. 179 D3
Little George St PO1 .. 182 C4
Little Gr PO12 ... 181 D1
Little Green Orch PO12 .. 181 D1

Little Hambrook St PO5 .. 182 A2
Little Holbury Park
  Mobile Home Pk SO45 .. 150 A3
Little Hyden La PO8 .. 88 A4
Little Kimble Wlk SO30 .. 105 E3
Little La PO12 .... 181 D1
Little Lance's Hill SO19 .. 103 F3
Little Lonnen BH21 .. 163 F4
Little Mead PO7 .. 111 D2
Little Minster St 26 SO23 .. 11 D4
Little Oak Rd SO16 .. 78 C2
Little Park Cl SO30 .. 105 D3
Little Park Farm Rd PO15 .. 127 F2
Little Park Mansions PO17 .. 107 F2
Little Quob La SO30 .. 80 C1
Little Reynolds SO40 .. 100 B3
Little Shore La SO32 .. 83 E4
Little Southsea St PO5 .. 182 A2
Little Toller SO16 .. 78 C4
Little Woodfalls Dr SP5 .. 64 A2
Little Woodham La PO13 .. 180 B3
Littlecroft Ave BH9 .. 190 A2
Littledown Ave BH7 .. 205 F4
Littledown Dr BH7 .. 205 F4
Littlegreen Ave PO9 .. 136 A2
Littlegreen Sch PO18 .. 90 C2
Littlemead Cl BH17 .. 202 A4
Littlemeads SO51 .. 52 B4
Littlemill La SP6 .. 68 B3
Littlemoor Ave BH11 .. 188 B2
Littlepark Ave PO9 .. 135 D2
Littleton Gr PO9 .. 135 F2
Littleton La SO21 .. 1 A3
Littleton Rd SO22 .. 1 A1
Littlewood Gdns
  Locks Heath SO31 .. 128 C2
  West End SO30 ... 80 B1
Liverpool Ct PO13 .. 180 B3
Liverpool Rd Gosport PO14 .. 154 C3
  Portsmouth PO1 ... 182 C3
Liverpool St SO14 .. 103 D4
Livesay Gdns PO1 .. 182 C3
Livingston Rd BH12 .. 203 E3
Livingstone Ct PO13 .. 180 B3
Livingstone Rd
  Bournemouth BH5 .. 206 A3
  Christchurch BH23 .. 207 E4
  Portsmouth PO5 ... 182 B2
  Southampton SO14 .. 103 D4
  Wimborne Minster BH21 .. 163 F2
Llewellin Cl BH16 .. 201 E4
Llewellin Cl BH16 .. 201 E4
Lloyd Ave SO40 ... 101 F1
Loane Rd SO19 ... 103 F2
Lobelia Ct PO7 ... 135 D3
Lobelia Rd SO16 .. 79 E3
Locarno Rd PO3 .. 158 A1
Loch Rd BH14 .... 203 F3
Lock App PO6 .... 157 D4
Lock View PO6 ... 157 D4
Lock's Cotts SO45 .. 125 E3
Locke Rd SO30 ... 105 E4
Lockerley Cl SO41 .. 197 E1
Lockerley Cres SO16 .. 77 F1
Lockerley Endowed
  CE Prim Sch SO51 .. 5 D1
Lockerley Rd PO9 .. 136 A2
Lockhams Rd SO32 .. 106 C4
Locks Heath Ctr SO31 .. 129 D2
Locks Heath Jun & Inf Schs
  SO31 .... 129 D1
Locks Rd SO31 ... 129 D2
Locksheath Cl PO9 .. 135 E3
Locksheath Park Rd SO31 .. 129 D1
Locksley Dr BH22 .. 165 E2
Locksley Rd SO50 .. 55 F1
Locksway Rd PO4 .. 183 E2
Lockswood Rd SO31 .. 129 D2
Lockyer's Cty Mid Sch BH21 .. 186 B4
Lockyers Dr BH22 .. 165 F3
Lode Hill SP5 .... 47 D4
Loders Cl BH17 .. 187 E2
Lodge Ave PO6 .. 158 A4
Lodge Cl BH14 ... 203 F2
Lodge Dr SO45 .. 126 A1
Lodge Dro SP5 .. 47 E2
Lodge Hill PO17 .. 109 D3
Lodge Rd
  Christchurch BH23 .. 206 C4
  Havant PO9 .... 135 D1
  Locks Heath SO31 .. 129 D2
  Lymington SO41 .. 197 D2
  Southampton SO14 .. 103 D4
Lodge The
  Southampton SO15 .. 102 C4
  Waterlooville PO7 .. 135 D3
Lodge Vale SO51 .. 51 D1
Lodgebury Cl PO10 .. 161 F4
Lodowick Cl PO8 .. 88 B2
Loewy Cres BH12 .. 188 B1
Lofting Cl SO50 .. 56 C1
Logan Cl SO16 ... 77 F3
Lomax Cl SO30 ... 81 E1
Lombard Ave BH6 .. 206 B3
Lombard Ct PO1 .. 182 A2
Lombard St PO1 .. 182 A2
Lombardy Cl Gosport PO13 .. 155 F1
  Verwood BH31 .... 115 D3
Lombardy Rise PO7 .. 134 C3
Lomer La SP6 .... 93 E2
Lomond Cl PO12 .. 181 D2
Londesborough Rd PO4 .. 182 C2
London Ave PO2 .. 157 E1
London Ct SO30 .. 180 B3
  Gosport, Alverstoke PO12 .. 181 D1
London La BH23 .. 167 F1

London Rd Clanfield PO8 .. 88 B2
  Cosham PO7 .... 134 B2
  Hill Brow GU33 .... 21 D1
  Horndean PO8 ..... 88 B2
  Kings Worthy SO23 .. 2 A3
  Petersfield GU31 ... 41 D3
  Portsmouth PO2 .... 157 F2
  Southampton SO16 . 103 D3
  Steep GU31 .... 41 E3
  Waterlooville PO7, PO6 .. 134 B2
London Tavern
  Cvn Pk The BH24 .. 141 E4
Lone Barn La SO32 .. 60 C4
Lone Pine Cvn Pk BH22 .. 165 F2
Lone Pine Dr BH22 .. 165 F2
Lone Pine Way BH22 .. 165 F1
Lone Valley PO7 ... 134 B2
Long Acre Ct PO1 .. 182 C4
Long Beech Dr SO40 .. 100 B3
Long Cl Downton SP5 .. 46 C4
  Winchester SO22 .. 10 C3
Long Copse SO45 .. 150 C2
Long Copse Ct PO10 .. 136 C2
Long Copse La PO10 .. 137 D2
Long Curtain Rd PO5 .. 182 A1
Long Down GU31 .. 41 D2
Long Dr Gosport PO13 .. 155 E3
  West End SO30 ... 80 C1
Long La Bursledon SO31 .. 105 D1
  Holbury SO45 ..... 150 B3
  Marchwood SO40 .. 101 E4
  Ringwood BH24 ... 141 D2
  Wimborne Minster BH21 .. 163 F4
Long Lane Cl SO45 .. 150 B2
Long Priors GU32 .. 37 D3
Long Rd Bournemouth BH10 .. 189 E3
  Soberton SO32 .... 85 E3
Long Water Dr PO12 .. 181 E1
Long Wlk Itchen Abbas SO21 .. 2 C2
  Portsmouth PO1 ... 182 B4
Longacre GU33 ... 21 D2
Longacre Dr BH22 .. 165 E2
Longacres PO14 .. 129 E2
Longbarrow Cl BH8 .. 191 D1
Longbridge Cl SO40 .. 76 B1
Longbridge Cl SO40 .. 76 B1
Longbridge House 51 PO5 .. 182 B2
Longbridge Rd SO19 .. 103 E2
Longclose Rd SO30 .. 105 E4
Longcroft PO9 .... 135 F1
Longdean Cl 1 PO6 .. 133 D1
Longdown Dairy Farm SO40 .. 100 B1
Longespee Rd BH21 .. 187 F4
Longfield Rd PO14 .. 154 C4
Longfield Dr
  Bournemouth BH11 .. 189 D3
  Ferndown BH22 .... 189 F4
Longfield Rd Emsworth PO10 .. 136 C2
  Fair Oak SO50 ..... 57 E1
  Hordle SO41 ...... 196 A1
  Winchester SO23 .. 11 E4
Longfleet CE Comb Sch BH15 .. 202 B2
Longfleet Rd BH15 .. 202 C2
Longhouse Gn 9 SO23 .. 11 E4
Longlands Rd PO10 .. 161 E4
Longleat Gdns
  New Milton BH25 .. 194 C2
  Southampton SO16 .. 78 A2
Longmead GU33 .. 20 C2
Longmead Ave SO50 .. 56 B2
Longmead Cl PO9 .. 159 F4
Longmead Gdns PO9 .. 159 F4
Longmead Rd Burley BH24 .. 142 C2
  1 Southampton SO18 .. 80 A1
Longmeadow Gdns SO45 .. 126 A2
Longmeadow La BH17 .. 201 E4
Longmore Ave SO19 .. 103 E1
Longmore Cres SO19 .. 103 E1
Longmynd Dr PO14 .. 154 B4
Longridge Rd SO30 .. 105 E3
Longs La PO17 ... 154 B2
Longshore Way PO4 .. 183 E2
Longspee Sch BH17 .. 202 B4
Longstaff Gdns PO16 .. 130 C2
Longstock Cl SO19 .. 127 D4
Longstock Cres SO40 .. 100 C4
Longstock Rd PO9 .. 136 A3
Longstone House PO9 .. 136 A3
Longstone Marina Hts PO4 .. 183 E2
Longwood Ave PO8 .. 112 A4
Longwood Dean La
  SO32, SO23 .... 34 A3
Lonnen Rd BH21 .. 164 A4
Lonnen Wood Cl BH21 .. 164 A4
Lonsdale Ave Cosham PO6 .. 158 A4
  Portchester PO16 .. 156 B3
Lonsdale Rd BH3 .. 204 C3
Loose Hanger SP5 .. 47 F2
Loperwood SO40 .. 76 A1
Loperwood La
  Netley Marsh SO40 .. 76 A1
  Ower SO40 .... 76 A2
  Totton SO40 ...... 76 A1
Loraine Ave BH23 .. 209 E4
Lord Cl BH17 ..... 202 C4
Lord Montgomery Way PO1 .. 182 A2
Lord Mountbatten Cl SO18 .. 79 F2
Lord Wilson Sch SO31 .. 128 C2
Lord's Hill Ctr E SO16 .. 77 F2
Lord's Hill Ctr W SO16 .. 77 F2
Lord's Hill Way SO16 .. 78 A3
Lordington Cl PO6 .. 158 A4
Lords Ct 61 PO1 .. 182 B3
Lords St PO1 .... 182 B3

Lordswood SO50 ... 56 C4
Lordswood Cl SO16 ... 78 B2
Lordswood Ct SO16 ... 78 B2
Lordswood Gdns SO16 ... 78 B2
Lordswood Rd SO16 ... 78 B2
Loreille Cl SO16 ... 77 F4
Loring House 7 PO2 ... 157 F2
Lorne Park Rd BH1 ... 205 D2
Lorne Rd PO5 ... 182 C2
Lortemore Pl 7 SO51 ... 52 C4
Loughwood Cl SO50 ... 56 A3
Louis Flagg House 19 PO5 ... 182 B2
Lovage Gdns SO40 ... 100 B4
Lovage Way PO8 ... 88 B1
Lovatt Gr PO15 ... 130 B2
Love La Milford on Sea SO41 ... 211 E3
  Petersfield GU31 ... 41 D2
  Romsey SO51 ... 52 C4
  Twyford SO21 ... 32 A3
  Woodgreen SP6 ... 70 C4
Lovedean La Horndean PO8 ... 111 F3
  Waterlooville PO8 ... 111 F3
Lovedon La SO23 ... 2 B4
Lovett Rd PO3 ... 158 A2
Lovett Wlk SO22 ... 1 B2
Lowcay Rd PO5 ... 182 C1
Lowden Cl SO22 ... 10 B2
Lower Alfred St 8 SO14 ... 103 D3
Lower Ashley Rd BH25 ... 195 E1
Lower Banister St 7 SO15 ... 102 C3
Lower Bartons SP6 ... 69 F1
Lower Baybridge La SO21 ... 33 E1
Lower Bellfield PO14 ... 153 F4
Lower Bere Wood PO7 ... 134 C4
Lower Blandford Rd BH18 ... 187 D2
Lower Brook St 12 SO23 ... 11 D4
Lower Brookfield Rd PO1 ... 182 C3
Lower Brownhill Rd SO16 ... 77 E2
Lower Buckland Rd SO41 ... 197 E3
Lower Canal Wlk SO14 ... 103 D2
Lower Chase Rd Shedfield SO32 ... 83 F2
  Swanmore SO32 ... 83 F2
Lower Church Path PO1 ... 182 B3
Lower Church Rd PO14 ... 129 E2
Lower Common La BH21 ... 139 D4
Lower Common Rd SO51 ... 50 C2
Lower Crabbick La PO7 ... 110 A3
Lower Densome Wood SP6 ... 70 C4
Lower Derby Rd PO2 ... 157 E1
Lower Drayton La PO6 ... 158 A4
Lower Duncan Rd SO31 ... 129 D3
Lower Farlington Rd PO6 ... 158 C4
Lower Forbury Rd 9 PO5 ... 182 B2
Lower Golf Links Rd BH18 ... 187 D3
Lower Gr PO6 ... 45 D1
Lower Grove Rd PO9 ... 160 A4
Lower Heyshott GU31 ... 41 D2
Lower La SO32 ... 83 E4
Lower Lamborough La SO24 ... 14 B3
Lower Mead GU31 ... 41 D2
Lower Mead End Rd SO41 ... 171 F1
Lower Moors Rd SO21 ... 31 F1
Lower Mortimer Rd SO19 ... 103 E2
Lower Mullin's La SO45 ... 125 F2
Lower New Rd SO30 ... 80 B1
Lower Northam Rd SO30 ... 105 E4
Lower Pennington La SO41 ... 212 B4
Lower Quay PO16 ... 155 D4
Lower Quay Cl PO16 ... 155 D4
Lower Quay Rd PO16 ... 155 D4
Lower Rd PO9 ... 135 E1
Lower Sandy Down La SO41 ... 173 E2
Lower Spinney SO31 ... 152 B4
Lower St SO51 ... 28 A4
Lower St Helens Rd SO30 ... 105 E3
Lower Stanmore La SO23 ... 10 C3
Lower Swanwick Rd SO31 ... 128 B4
Lower Vicarage Rd SO19 ... 103 E2
Lower Wardown GU31 ... 41 D2
Lower William St SO14 ... 103 E3
Lower Wingfield St 50 PO1 ... 182 B3
Lower Woodside SO41 ... 212 C4
Lower York St SO14 ... 103 E3
Lowesmere Ct BH14 ... 203 E2
Lowestoft Rd PO6 ... 133 E1
Loweswater House 21 PO6 ... 133 D1
Lowford Hill SO31 ... 104 C1
Lowland Rd PO7 ... 110 C2
Lowry Gdns SO19 ... 104 B1
Lowther Gdns 3 BH8 ... 205 E3
Lowther Rd BH8 ... 205 D3
Loxwood Rd PO8 ... 111 F3
Luard Ct PO9 ... 136 A1
Lucas Cl SO16 ... 77 F3
Lucas Rd Poole BH15 ... 202 A1
  Poole, Upper Parkstone BH14 ... 203 E3
Luccombe Pl SO15 ... 78 B1
Luccombe Rd SO15 ... 78 B1
Lucerne Ave Bournemouth BH6 ... 206 B3
  Waterlooville PO7 ... 111 E1
Lucerne Gdns SO30 ... 105 D3
Lucerne Rd SO41 ... 211 E2
Luckham Cl BH9 ... 190 A1
Luckham Gdns BH9 ... 190 A1
Luckham Pl BH9 ... 190 A1
Luckham Rd BH9 ... 190 A1
Luckham Rd E BH9 ... 190 A1
Lucknow St PO1 ... 182 C3
Lucky La SO41 ... 174 A1
Ludcombe PO7 ... 110 C4
Ludlow Inf Sch SO19 ... 103 F2
Ludlow Jun Sch SO19 ... 103 F2
Ludlow Rd Cosham PO6 ... 133 E1
  Southampton SO19 ... 103 F2

Ludwell's La SO32 ... 83 F2
Lugano Cl PO7 ... 111 E1
Lukin Dr SO16 ... 77 E3
Lulworth Ave BH15 ... 201 F1
Lulworth Bsns Pk SO40 ... 76 C1
Lulworth Cl
  Chandler's Ford SO53 ... 55 D2
  Hamworthy BH15 ... 201 F1
  South Hayling PO11 ... 185 D1
  Southampton SO16 ... 77 F1
Lulworth Cres BH15 ... 201 F1
Lulworth Gn SO16 ... 77 F1
Lulworth Rd PO13 ... 179 F1
Lumby Dr BH24 ... 141 D4
Lumby Drive Cvn Pk 3 BH24 ... 141 D4
Lumley Gdns PO10 ... 161 D4
Lumley Rd PO10 ... 137 D1
Lumley Terr PO10 ... 137 D1
Lumsden Ave SO15 ... 102 B4
Lumsden Mans 3 SO15 ... 102 B4
Lumsden Rd SO40 ... 183 E2
Lundy Cl SO16 ... 77 F3
Lundy Wlk SO14 ... 154 A2
Lunedale Rd SO45 ... 149 F4
Lupin Rd SO16 ... 79 E3
Luscombe Rd BH14 ... 203 E1
Luther Rd BH9 ... 204 C4
Lutman St PO10 ... 136 C2
Luton Rd SO19 ... 104 A2
Luxton Cl SO30 ... 105 F4
Luzborough La SO51 ... 53 E3
Lyburn Ct SO16 ... 78 B2
Lyburn Cl SO16 ... 78 B2
Lyburn House SP5 ... 73 D4
Lyburn Rd SP5 ... 48 C1
Lych Gate BH24 ... 141 E3
Lychgate Dr PO8 ... 112 A4
Lychgate Gn PO14 ... 154 B3
Lydden Ct PO13 ... 155 E1
Lydford Gdns BH11 ... 189 D1
Lydford Rd BH11 ... 189 D1
Lydgate SO40 ... 100 B4
Lydgate Cl SO19 ... 104 B2
Lydgate Gn SO19 ... 104 B2
Lydgate Rd SO19 ... 104 B2
Lydgate The SO41 ... 211 D3
Lydiard Cl SO50 ... 56 A3
Lydlinch Cl BH22 ... 165 E1
Lydlynch Inf Sch SO40 ... 100 C4
Lydlynch Rd SO40 ... 100 C4
Lydney Cl PO6 ... 157 E4
Lydney Rd SO31 ... 128 C2
Lydwell Cl BH11 ... 188 C3
Lyell Rd BH12 ... 203 E4
Lymbourn Rd PO9 ... 136 A1
Lyme Cl SO50 ... 55 F3
Lyme Cres BH23 ... 208 C4
Lymefields SO41 ... 211 F3
Lymer La SO16 ... 77 E3
Lymer Villas SO16 ... 77 E3
Lymington Cath Sch SO41 ... 197 E2
Lymington CE Inf Sch SO41 ... 197 E2
Lymington Hospl SO41 ... 197 E2
Lymington Infmy & Day Hospl SO41 ... 197 E2
Lymington Jun Sch SO41 ... 197 E2
Lymington Pier Sta SO41 ... 198 A2
Lymington Rd
  Barton on Sea BH25 ... 195 E1
  Brockenhurst SO42 ... 146 A1
  Christchurch BH23 ... 208 C4
  Milford on Sea SO41 ... 211 E2
Lymington Town Sta SO41 ... 197 F2
Lymore La SO41 ... 211 F3
Lymore Valley SO41 ... 211 F3
Lynch Cl SO22 ... 1 C1
Lynch La GU32 ... 37 E2
Lyndale Cl SO41 ... 211 F3
Lyndale Rd SO31 ... 129 E2
Lynden Cl PO14 ... 154 A4
Lynden Gate SO19 ... 104 B2
Lyndhurst CE Inf Sch SO43 ... 121 F3
Lyndhurst Cl
  South Hayling PO11 ... 185 D2
  Winchester SO22 ... 1 B2
Lyndhurst Hill SO40 ... 98 C4
Lyndhurst House PO9 ... 135 F3
Lyndhurst Jun Sch PO2 ... 157 F1
Lyndhurst Rd Ashurst SO40 ... 100 A1
  Bransgore BH23 ... 193 E3
  Brockenhurst SO42 ... 146 A1
  Burley BH24 ... 143 E3
  Burton BH23 ... 193 E3
  Cadnam SO40 ... 98 C4
  Christchurch BH23 ... 193 E1
  Gosport PO12 ... 181 D2
  Landford SP5 ... 49 E2
  Portsmouth PO2 ... 157 F1
Lyndock Cl SO19 ... 103 F1
Lyndock Pl SO19 ... 103 F1
Lyndon Ct BH23 ... 191 F1
Lyndum Cl GU32 ... 40 C2
Lyne Pl PO8 ... 112 A3
Lyne's La SO41 ... 140 C4
Lynford Ave SO22 ... 1 C1
Lynford Way SO22 ... 1 C1
Lynn Cl SO18 ... 80 A2
Lynn Rd Poole BH17 ... 187 F1
  Portsmouth PO2 ... 182 C4
Lynric Cl 4 BH25 ... 210 A4
Lynton Cres BH23 ... 191 E2
Lynton Ct SO40 ... 100 C3
Lynton Gdns PO16 ... 130 C2
Lynton Gr PO3 ... 183 D4
Lynton Rd Hedge End SO30 ... 105 E4
  Petersfield GU32 ... 40 C2
Lynwood Ave PO8 ... 111 E2
Lynwood Cl BH22 ... 165 E4

Lynwood Ct
  Lymington SO41 ... 197 E2
  Winchester SO22 ... 1 C1
Lynwood Dr BH21 ... 187 F4
Lynx Cl SO50 ... 56 C1
Lyon Ave BH25 ... 195 D2
Lyon Rd BH12 ... 188 C1
Lyon St SO14 ... 103 D3
Lysander Cl BH23 ... 208 B4
Lysander Way PO7 ... 135 D2
Lyse Cl GU33 ... 20 C2
Lysses Ct PO16 ... 131 E1
Lyster Rd SP6 ... 70 A1
Lystra Rd BH9 ... 190 A2
Lytchett Dr BH18 ... 187 D2
Lytchett Way BH16 ... 201 D3
Lyteltane Rd SO41 ... 197 E1
Lytham Cl
  Broadstone BH18 ... 187 D2
  Southampton SO18 ... 80 A1
Lythe La GU32 ... 40 A3
Lytton Rd
  Bournemouth BH1 ... 205 E3
  Hythe SO45 ... 126 A1

M

Mabey Ave BH10 ... 189 E1
Mabey Cl PO12 ... 181 E1
Mablethorpe Rd PO6 ... 133 F1
Macandrew Rd BH13 ... 214 C4
Macarthur Cres SO18 ... 104 A4
Macaulay Ave PO6 ... 132 C1
Macaulay Rd BH18 ... 187 D2
Macklin House 16 SO22 ... 10 C4
Maclaren Rd BH9 ... 189 F2
Maclean Rd BH11 ... 188 C2
Macnaghten Rd SO18 ... 103 E4
Madden Cl PO12 ... 180 C2
Maddison St 5 SO14 ... 102 C2
Maddoxford La SO32 ... 82 A1
Maddoxford Way SO32 ... 81 F1
Madeira Rd
  Bournemouth BH1 ... 205 D2
  Poole BH14 ... 203 E3
  Portsmouth PO2 ... 157 F2
Madeline Cl BH12 ... 203 D4
Madeline Cres BH12 ... 203 D4
Madeline Rd GU31 ... 40 C2
Madison Ave BH1 ... 205 E3
Madison Cl PO13 ... 180 C4
Madison Ct 10 PO16 ... 131 E1
Madrisa Cl SO41 ... 197 F2
Mafeking Rd PO4 ... 182 C2
Maffey Ct SO30 ... 106 A4
Mag's Barrow BH22 ... 165 F1
Magazine La SO41 ... 102 A2
Magdala Rd Cosham PO6 ... 157 F4
  South Hayling PO11 ... 184 C2
Magdalen Ct 19 PO2 ... 157 F2
Magdalen Hill SO23 ... 11 D4
Magdalen Mews 41 SO23 ... 11 D4
Magdalen Rd PO2 ... 157 F2
Magdalene Way PO14 ... 129 E1
Magennis Cl PO13 ... 180 B4
Magna Cl BH11 ... 188 C3
Magna Gdns BH11 ... 188 C3
Magna Rd
  Bournemouth BH11 ... 188 B4
  Oakley BH11 ... 188 B4
Magnolia Cl
  Bournemouth BH6 ... 207 D3
  Fareham PO14 ... 154 C4
  Hythe SO45 ... 125 E2
  Verwood BH31 ... 115 C2
Magnolia Gr SO50 ... 57 F1
Magnolia House BH10 ... 189 F2
Magnolia Rd SO19 ... 103 F3
Magnolia Terr PO7 ... 134 C3
Magnolia Way PO8 ... 112 B2
Magpie Cl BH8 ... 190 B2
Magpie Dr SO40 ... 100 B4
Magpie Gdns SO19 ... 104 B2
Magpie Gr BH25 ... 194 C1
Magpie La
  Eastleigh SO50 ... 55 F1
  Lee-on-the-Solent PO13 ... 179 F2
Magpie Rd PO8 ... 113 E3
Magpie Wlk PO7 ... 111 E2
Maiden La SO41 ... 197 F1
Maidford Gr PO3 ... 158 B2
Maidment Cl BH11 ... 188 C2
Maidstone Cres PO6 ... 133 F1
Main Rd
  Colden Common SO21 ... 32 A1
  Compton(Hants) SO21 ... 31 D2
  Compton(Hants) SO21 ... 31 E3
  Fawley SO45 ... 150 B3
  Gosport PO13 ... 155 B3
  Hermitage PO10 ... 161 E4
  Hythe SO45 ... 125 E4
  Littleton SO22 ... 1 A3
  Marchwood SO40 ... 101 F1
  Otterbourne SO21 ... 31 D2
  Owslebury SO21 ... 33 D2
  Portsmouth PO1 ... 181 F3
  Portsmouth PO1 ... 182 A2
  Southbourne PO18 ... 161 E4
  Totton SO40 ... 100 C2
Mainstone SO51 ... 52 B3
Mainstream Ct SO50 ... 56 B2
Maisemore Gdns PO10 ... 160 B4
Maitland Cl SO21 ... 31 D2
Maitland St 14 PO1 ... 182 B4
Maitlands The BH2 ... 204 B1
Maizemore Wlk 21 PO13 ... 179 F1
Majestic Rd SO16 ... 77 D2
Majorca Mansions 11 BH2 ... 204 C2
Malan Cl BH17 ... 202 C4

Malcolm Cl
  Chandler's Ford SO53 ... 30 C1
  Locks Heath SO31 ... 129 D2
Malcolm Rd SO53 ... 30 C1
Malcomb Cl BH6 ... 207 D2
Malcroft Mews SO40 ... 102 A1
Maldon Cl SO50 ... 56 A2
Maldon Rd 5 Cosham PO6 ... 157 E4
  Southampton SO19 ... 103 F2
Malibres Rd SO53 ... 55 F4
Malin Cl Southampton SO16 ... 77 F2
  Stubbington PO14 ... 154 A2
Malins Rd PO2 ... 182 B4
Mall The Burley BH24 ... 143 E2
  Chandler's Ford SO53 ... 55 F4
Mallard Bldgs 8 BH25 ... 195 D2
Mallard Cl
  Bishop's Waltham SO32 ... 83 D4
  Bournemouth BH8 ... 190 B1
  Christchurch BH23 ... 208 A3
  Hordle SO41 ... 196 A2
  Romsey SO51 ... 52 C4
Mallard Gdns Gosport PO13 ... 155 D1
  Hedge End SO30 ... 81 E1
Mallard Rd
  Bournemouth BH8 ... 190 B1
  Portsmouth PO4 ... 183 D3
  Rowland's Castle PO9 ... 113 D1
  Wimborne Minster BH21 ... 164 A4
Mallards Rd SO31 ... 127 F4
Mallards The Fareham PO16 ... 131 D2
  Havant PO9 ... 159 F4
Mallory Cl BH23 ... 207 F4
Mallory Cres PO16 ... 131 D2
Mallow Cl Broadstone BH18 ... 186 C2
  5 Cosham PO6 ... 157 F4
  Locks Heath SO31 ... 128 C1
  Waterlooville PO7 ... 134 C3
Mallow Rd SO30 ... 105 D3
Mallows The BH25 ... 195 E2
Malmesbury Cl SO50 ... 57 E1
Malmesbury Ct BH8 ... 205 E3
Malmesbury Gdns SO22 ... 1 B1
Malmesbury Park Pl 7 BH8 ... 205 E3
Malmesbury Park Rd BH8 ... 205 E3
Malmesbury Pk Prim Sch BH8 ... 205 D3
Malmesbury Pl SO15 ... 102 B4
Malmesbury Rd Romsey SO51 ... 52 C4
  Southampton SO15 ... 102 B4
  St Leonards BH24 ... 139 F2
Maloney Mews PO11 ... 185 F1
Maloren Way BH22 ... 139 D1
Malory Cl SO19 ... 104 B3
Malt House 22 SO22 ... 10 C4
Malt La SO32 ... 83 E4
Malta Rd PO2 ... 182 C4
Malthouse
  Itchen Abbas SO21 ... 2 C1
  Romsey SO51 ... 52 C4
Malthouse Cotts SO16 ... 77 D4
Malthouse Gdns SO40 ... 101 F1
Malthouse La PO16 ... 131 D1
Malthouse Rd PO2 ... 182 B4
Maltings The
  Bournemouth BH11 ... 188 B4
  Fareham PO16 ... 131 E1
  Petersfield GU31 ... 40 C2
  Poole BH15 ... 202 C2
Malus Cl PO14 ... 154 C4
Malvern Ave PO14 ... 154 C4
Malvern Bsns Ctr SO16 ... 78 B1
Malvern Cl
  Bishop's Waltham SO32 ... 83 E4
  Bournemouth BH9 ... 190 A2
Malvern Ct Bournemouth BH9 ... 190 A1
  2 Christchurch BH23 ... 207 F4
Malvern Dr SO45 ... 125 E2
Malvern Gdns SO30 ... 81 E1
Malvern Mews PO10 ... 136 C1
Malvern Rd Bournemouth BH9 ... 190 A1
  Gosport PO12 ... 180 C2
  Hill Brow GU33 ... 21 D1
  Portsmouth PO5 ... 182 B1
  Southampton SO16 ... 78 B1
Malvern Terr PO10 ... 136 C1
Malwood Ave SO16 ... 78 B2
Malwood Cl PO9 ... 136 A3
Malwood Gdns SO40 ... 100 B4
Malwood Rd SO45 ... 126 A2
Malwood Rd W SO45 ... 125 F2
Manaton Way SO30 ... 81 D1
Manchester Rd
  6 Netley SO31 ... 127 D2
  Portsmouth PO1 ... 182 C3
  Sway SO41 ... 172 A2
Manchester Terr PO10 ... 137 D2
Mancroft Ave PO14 ... 179 E4
Mandale Cl BH11 ... 189 D2
Mandale Rd BH11 ... 188 C2
Mandela Way SO15 ... 102 C3
Manderley SO41 ... 211 F2
Manley Rd SO31 ... 104 C1
Manners La PO4 ... 182 C2
Manners Rd PO4 ... 182 C2
Manning Ave BH23 ... 193 E1
Manning's Heath Rd BH12 ... 188 A1
Manningford SO23 ... 2 A2
Mannings Heath Works BH12 ... 188 A1
Mannington Pl 19 BH2 ... 204 C2
Mannington Way BH22 ... 138 B1
Manns Cl SO18 ... 80 B1
Mannyngham Way SO51 ... 27 D2
Manor Ave BH12 ... 188 B1

Manor Cl Bursledon SO31 ... 104 C1
  Ferndown BH22 ... 165 F1
  Fordingbridge SP6 ... 69 F1
  9 Havant PO9 ... 135 F2
  Milford on Sea SO41 ... 211 E1
  Totton SO40 ... 100 C1
  Wickham PO17 ... 108 A2
  Winchester SO23 ... 11 D4
Manor Cres Bursledon SO31 ... 104 C1
  Cosham PO6 ... 158 A4
Manor Ct Havant PO9 ... 135 E3
  Locks Heath SO31 ... 129 E2
  Ringwood BH24 ... 140 C4
  Verwood BH31 ... 114 C3
Manor Farm Cl
  4 Bishopstoke SO50 ... 56 C4
  New Milton BH25 ... 194 C1
Manor Farm Ctry Pk SO31 ... 105 E2
Manor Farm Gr 3 SO50 ... 56 C4
Manor Farm La SO51 ... 6 C1
Manor Farm Rd
  Bournemouth BH10 ... 189 E4
  Fordingbridge SP6 ... 69 E1
  Southampton SO18 ... 79 F4
Manor Flats SO21 ... 31 F3
Manor Gdns Ringwood BH24 ... 140 C4
  Southbourne PO10 ... 137 E1
  1 Verwood BH31 ... 114 C3
Manor House Ave SO15 ... 101 F3
Manor Inf Sch Holbury SO45 ... 150 A2
  Portsmouth PO3 ... 182 C4
Manor La BH31 ... 114 C3
Manor Lodge Rd PO9 ... 113 D1
Manor Mews PO6 ... 158 B4
Manor Park Ave PO3 ... 183 D4
Manor Park House 14 SO18 ... 103 F4
Manor Pk BH15 ... 202 A3
Manor Rd Bishopstoke SO50 ... 56 C1
  Bournemouth BH1 ... 205 E2
  Chilworth SO16 ... 54 B1
  Christchurch BH23 ... 207 D3
  Durley SO32 ... 82 B4
  East Tytherley SP5 ... 4 C4
  Holbury SO45 ... 150 B2
  Hythe SO40 ... 125 D2
  Milford on Sea SO41 ... 211 E3
  New Milton BH25 ... 195 D2
  North Hayling PO11 ... 184 C3
  Portsmouth PO1 ... 182 C4
  Ringwood BH24 ... 141 D4
  South Hayling PO10 ... 137 E1
  Twyford SO21 ... 31 F3
  Verwood BH31 ... 114 C3
Manor Rd N SO19 ... 103 F2
Manor Rd S SO19 ... 103 F2
Manor Terr Bursledon SO31 ... 104 C1
  Durley SO32 ... 82 C4
Manor Villas PO17 ... 108 A2
Manor Way
  Lee-on-the-Solent PO13 ... 179 F1
  Lee-on-the-Solent PO13 ... 179 F2
  South Hayling PO11 ... 185 D1
  Southbourne PO10 ... 137 E1
  Verwood BH31 ... 114 C4
Manor Wks SO40 ... 101 D4
Mansard Ct BH13 ... 214 A2
Mansbridge Prim Sch SO18 ... 79 F2
Mansbridge Rd
  Eastleigh SO50 ... 56 A1
  Southampton SO18 ... 79 F2
Mansel Cl BH12 ... 204 B4
Mansel Ct SO16 ... 77 F1
Mansel Inf Sch SO16 ... 77 F1
Mansel Jun Sch SO16 ... 77 F1
Mansel Rd E SO16 ... 77 F1
Mansel Rd W SO16 ... 77 F1
Mansell Cl SO45 ... 125 F1
Mansfield Ave BH14 ... 203 E2
Mansfield Cl Ferndown BH22 ... 165 E1
  Poole BH14 ... 203 E2
Mansfield Rd
  Bournemouth BH9 ... 189 F1
  Gosport PO13 ... 180 B4
  Poole BH14 ... 203 E2
  Ringwood BH24 ... 140 C4
Mansion Ct 2 PO4 ... 182 C1
Mansion Rd
  1 Portsmouth PO4 ... 182 C1
  Southampton SO15 ... 102 B3
Manston Ct SO16 ... 77 F2
Mansvid Ave PO6 ... 158 A4
Mantle Cl PO13 ... 180 B4
Mantle Sq PO2 ... 157 D1
Manton Cl BH15 ... 201 F2
Manton Rd BH15 ... 201 F2
Maple Cl Barton on Sea BH25 ... 210 A4
  Bursledon SO31 ... 127 F4
  Christchurch BH23 ... 208 C4
  Emsworth PO10 ... 136 C1
  Fareham PO15 ... 130 B1
  Lee-on-the-Solent PO13 ... 179 F1
  Romsey SO51 ... 53 E3
Maple Cres PO8 ... 88 B3
Maple Ct SO19 ... 103 F1
Maple Dr Denmead PO7 ... 111 D2
  Ferndown BH22 ... 165 E4
  Kings Worthy SO23 ... 2 A4
Maple Gdns SO40 ... 100 B3
Maple House SO16 ... 78 C4
Maple Lodge BH16 ... 201 E4
Maple Rd Bournemouth BH9 ... 204 C4
  Hythe SO45 ... 150 A4
  Poole BH15 ... 202 B2
  Portsmouth PO5 ... 182 B1
  Southampton SO19 ... 103 F1
Maple Sq SO50 ... 55 F1
Mapleleaf Gdns 1 SO50 ... 56 A1

aples The SO53 .... 55 E4
apleton Rd SO30 .... 105 E3
apletree Ave PO8 .... 112 B2
aplewood Cl SO40 .... 100 B3
aplin Rd SO16 .... 77 E1
apperton Cl BH17 .... 188 A1
arabout Cl BH23 .... 207 E4
aralyn Ave PO7 .... 134 C3
arathon Pl SO50 .... 57 D1
arbream Cl SP6 .... 69 E1
archesi Ct PO14 .... 154 B2
archwood-By-Pass
  Hythe SO40 .... 124 C4
  Marchwood SO40 .... 124 C4
  Totton SO40 .... 101 D2
archwood CE Inf Sch SO40 .124 C4
archwood Ct PO12 .... 180 B2
archwood Ind Pk SO40 .... 101 F1
archwood Jun Sch SO40 .... 101 F1
archwood Rd
  Bournemouth BH10 .... 189 E2
  Havant PO9 .... 135 F3
  Southampton SO15 .... 102 A3
  Totton SO40 .... 101 E2
archwood Terr SO40 .... 101 F1
arcus Cl SO50 .... 57 D1
ardale Rd SO16 .... 101 E4
ardale Wlk SO16 .... 101 E4
arden Paddock SO42 .... 145 F1
arden Way GU31 .... 41 D2
ardon Cl SO18 .... 79 F1
are La SO21 .... 32 C3
argam Ave SO19 .... 103 F3
argards La BH31 .... 114 C3
argaret Cl PO7 .... 111 E1
argarita Rd PO15 .... 130 C1
argate Pl PO5 .... 182 B2
argery's Ct 20 PO1 .... 182 A3
arian Cl BH21 .... 186 B2
arianne Cl SO15 .... 101 E4
arianne Rd Poole BH12 .... 204 B4
  Wimborne Minster BH21 .... 164 A4
arie Ave SP5 .... 46 B4
arie Ct 5 PO7 .... 134 C4
arie Rd SO19 .... 104 B2
arigold Cl PO15 .... 130 C1
arina Bldgs 3 PO12 .... 181 D2
arina Cl PO10 .... 161 D4
arina Ct
  21 Bournemouth BH5 .... 205 F2
  Christchurch BH23 .... 209 D4
arina Dr BH14 .... 203 D1
arina Gr Portchester PO16 .. 156 B3
  Portsmouth PO3 .... 183 D4
arina Keep PO6 .... 157 D3
arina The BH5 .... 205 F2
arina Towers 24 BH5 .... 205 F2
arina View
  6 Christchurch BH23 .... 207 D3
  Netley SO31 .... 126 C4
arine Cotts 20 PO12 .... 181 D3
arine Ct Barton on Sea BH25 .. 209 E4
  Portsmouth PO4 .... 183 D1
arine Dr BH23 .... 209 F4
arine Dr E BH25 .... 210 A3
arine Drive W BH25 .... 209 F4
arine Par SO14 .... 103 D2
arine Parade E PO13 .... 179 E1
arine Parade W PO13 .... 179 E1
arine Rd BH6 .... 206 B2
arine Wlk PO11 .... 185 E2
ariner's Cl SO31 .... 128 A2
ariners Ct
  Christchurch BH23 .... 208 A3
  Lymington SO41 .... 197 F1
ariners Mews 1 SO45 .... 126 A2
ariners Way Gosport PO12 .. 181 E2
  Locks Heath SO31 .... 128 B1
arion Ct BH23 .... 207 D4
arion Rd PO4 .... 182 C1
aritime Ave SO40 .... 102 A2
aritime Mus SO14 .... 102 C2
aritime Way SO14 .... 103 D1
aritime Wlk SO14 .... 103 D1
arjoram Cres PO8 .... 112 A2
ark Anthony Ct PO11 .... 184 C2
ark Cl Portsmouth PO3 .... 157 F2
  Southampton SO15 .... 102 A4
ark Ct PO7 .... 134 C4
ark Way SO51 .... 4 B2
ark's La PO13 .... 195 D3
ark's Rd PO14 .... 179 E3
arkall Cl SO24 .... 14 B3
arken Cl SO31 .... 128 C2
arket Bldgs SO16 .... 79 E2
arket Cl BH15 .... 202 B1
arket La SO23 .... 11 D4
arket Par PO9 .... 135 F1
arket Pl Fordingbridge SP6 ... 69 F1
  Ringwood BH24 .... 140 C4
  Romsey SO51 .... 52 C4
  10 Southampton SO23 .... 103 D2
arket St Eastleigh SO50 .... 56 A1
  Poole BH15 .... 202 A1
  Winchester SO23 .... 11 D4
arket Way BH21 .... 163 E2
arketway PO1 .... 182 B3
arkham Ave BH10 .... 189 E3
arkham Cl BH10 .... 189 E3
arkham Rd BH9 .... 205 D4
arks Rd BH9 .... 189 F2
arks Terr SO32 .... 83 D4
arks Tey Rd PO14 .... 154 B3
arkway PO10 .... 136 B1
arlands Lawn 13 PO9 .... 135 F3
arlands Sh Ctr SO14 .... 102 C2

Marlands Sq 12 SO15 .... 102 C3
Marlborough Ct PO7 .... 134 B3
Marlborough Ct
  21 Bournemouth BH4 .... 204 B2
  Chandler's Ford SO53 .... 55 D2
  Hythe SO45 .... 125 F1
  7 Poole BH12 .... 204 A2
  1 Waterlooville PO7 .... 134 C1
  3 Wimborne Minster BH21 .. 163 F3
Marlborough Gdns SO30 .... 81 E2
Marlborough Gr SO16 .... 156 B4
Marlborough Mans 2 BH7 .. 206 A3
Marlborough Pk PO9 .... 136 B2
Marlborough Pl
  Lymington SO41 .... 197 E3
  Wimborne Minster BH21 .... 163 F3
Marlborough Rd
  Bournemouth BH4 .... 204 B2
  Chandler's Ford SO53 .... 30 C1
  Gosport PO13 .... 180 C3
  Poole BH14 .... 203 E2
  Southampton SO15 .... 102 A4
Marlborough Row PO1 .... 182 A3
Marldell Cl PO9 .... 136 A3
Marles Ct PO13 .... 180 B4
Marley Ave BH25 .... 194 C2
Marley Cl BH25 .... 194 C2
Marley Mount SO41 .... 171 F1
Marlhill Cl SO18 .... 79 F1
Marlin Cl PO13 .... 180 B3
Marline Rd BH12 .... 203 E4
Marlott Rd BH15 .... 202 B3
Marlow Cl PO15 .... 130 C2
Marlow Dr BH23 .... 191 F2
Marlow Rd SO32 .... 83 D4
Marlowe Ct
  Southampton SO19 .... 103 F1
  Waterlooville PO8 .... 111 E1
Marlpit Dr BH23 .... 194 A1
Marlpit La BH25 .... 195 D4
Marls Rd SO30 .... 105 F3
Marmion Ave PO5 .... 182 B1
Marmion Gn BH23 .... 207 F4
Marmion Rd PO5 .... 182 B1
Marne House 9 PO14 .... 154 C4
Marne Rd SO18 .... 104 A4
Marnhull Rd BH15 .... 202 B2
Marpet Cl BH11 .... 188 C3
Marples Way PO9 .... 135 E1
Marquis Way BH11 .... 188 B3
Marram Cl SO41 .... 197 F3
Marryat Christchurch BH23 .. 209 D4
  7 New Milton BH25 .... 194 C2
Marryat Rd BH25 .... 194 C2
Marsden Rd PO6 .... 157 D4
Marsh Cl PO6 .... 158 B3
Marsh Gdns SO30 .... 81 E1
Marsh House 20 SO14 .... 103 D2
Marsh La Breamore SP6 .... 70 A4
  Christchurch BH23 .... 191 F1
  Fawley SO45 .... 151 D2
  Lymington SO41 .... 197 F3
  Southampton SO14 .... 103 D2
  Upton BH16 .... 201 D4
Marsh Par PO14 .... 126 A2
Marsh The SO45 .... 126 A2
Marshal Rd BH17 .... 187 D1
Marshall Rd PO11 .... 185 E1
Marshfield BH21 .... 163 F4
Marshfield Cl SO40 .... 101 C1
Marshfield House PO6 .... 158 B4
Marshlands Rd PO6 .... 158 B4
Marshwood Ave
  Broadstone BH17 .... 187 F1
  Waterlooville PO7 .... 135 D4
Marston Cl BH23 .... 195 D3
Marston Gr BH23 .... 193 F1
Marston La PO13 .... 158 A2
Marston Rd New Milton BH25 .. 195 D3
  2 Poole BH15 .... 202 A1
  Southampton SO19 .... 104 C3
Martello Cl PO12 .... 180 B2
Martello House 10 BH13 .... 214 C4
Martello Pk BH13 .... 214 C4
Martello Rd BH13 .... 203 F1
Martello Rd S BH13 .... 214 C4
Martello Towers BH13 .... 214 C4
Martells Ct PO1 .... 182 A2
Martells The BH25 .... 210 A4
Martha St PO1 .... 182 B3
Martin Ave Denmead PO7 .... 111 D2
  Stubbington PO14 .... 179 E3
Martin Cl Broadstone BH17 .... 201 F4
  Lee-on-the-Solent PO13 .... 179 F2
  Swanmore SO32 .... 84 A2
Martin Kemp-Welch
  Sch The BH12 .... 203 E4
Martin Rd Havant PO9 .... 136 A2
  Portsmouth PO3 .... 183 D4
  Stubbington PO14 .... 179 E3
Martin St SO32 .... 83 D4
Martin's Rd SO42 .... 146 A1
Martindale Ave BH21 .... 164 A3
Martindale Terr SO16 .... 101 F4
Martingale Cl BH16 .... 201 E4
Martins Cl BH21 .... 165 E4
Martins Dr BH22 .... 165 E4
Martins Fields SO21 .... 10 B1
Martins Hill Cl BH23 .... 192 B1
Martins Hill La BH23 .... 192 B1
Martins The SO50 .... 57 E1
Martins Way BH22 .... 165 F4
Martley Gdns SO30 .... 81 E1
Marvic Ct PO9 .... 135 F3
Marvin Cl SO30 .... 105 E4
Marwell Cl BH7 .... 206 A4

Marwell Zoo SO21 .... 57 F4
Mary La PO8 .... 138 B1
Mary Mitchell Cl BH24 .... 140 C4
Mary Rose Cl PO1 .... 181 F3
Mary Rose Cl PO15 .... 130 C2
Mary Rose St The PO1 .... 182 B3
Marybridge Cl SO40 .... 100 C3
Marycourt Co-ed Sch PO12 .181 D1
Maryfield SO14 .... 103 D2
Maryland Cl SO18 .... 79 F2
Maryland Cl 3 SO41 .... 211 D2
Maryland Gdns SO41 .... 211 D2
Maryland Rd BH16 .... 201 E2
Masefield Ave PO6 .... 132 C1
Masefield Cl SO50 .... 55 F2
Masefield Cres PO8 .... 111 F2
Masefield Gr SO19 .... 104 B3
Mason Moor Prim Sch SO16 ... 101 F4
Masseys La SO42 .... 175 E4
Masten Cres PO13 .... 180 B4
Masters Ct BH4 .... 204 B2
Masterson Cl BH23 .... 207 E4
Matapan Rd PO2 .... 157 F2
Matchams La Hurn BH23 .... 167 D2
  St Leonards BH23 .... 167 D2
Matheson Rd SO16 .... 78 A3
Matilda Pl 3 SO23 .... 11 D4
Matley Gdns SO40 .... 100 A4
Matlock Rd PO12 .... 165 E2
Matthews Cl PO9 .... 135 E2
Matthews La SO42 .... 175 E3
Maturin Cl SO41 .... 197 E2
Maundeville Cres BH23 .... 206 B4
Maundville Rd BH23 .... 206 C4
Maunsell Way SO30 .... 81 E2
Maureen Cl BH11 .... 203 D4
Mauretania House 13 SO14 .. 103 E3
Mauretania Rd SO16 .... 77 D2
Maurice Rd Bournemouth BH8 .. 205 E4
  Portsmouth PO4 .... 183 D4
Maury's La SO51 .... 50 B2
Mavis Cres PO9 .... 135 F1
Mavis Rd PO2 .... 190 A1
Maxstoke Cl 22 PO1 .... 182 B3
Maxwell Rd Bournemouth BH9 .205 D4
  Broadstone BH18 .... 186 C2
  Poole BH13 .... 214 C4
  Portsmouth PO4 .... 183 D2
  Southampton SO19 .... 104 A2
May Cl SO41 .... 197 E3
May Bush La SO32 .... 85 D1
May Cl SO45 .... 150 B2
May Copse SO45 .... 150 B2
May Cres SO45 .... 150 B2
May Gdns
  Bournemouth BH11 .... 188 C2
  Christchurch BH23 .... 194 A1
May La SO41 .... 174 A1
May Rd SO15 .... 102 B4
May Tree Cl SO22 .... 10 B2
May's La PO14 .... 154 B2
Maybray King Way SO18 .... 104 A4
Maybush Cl 3 SO16 .... 78 A1
Maybush Rd SO16 .... 77 F1
Maycroft Cl 3 SO15 .... 102 A4
Maydman Sq PO3 .... 183 D3
Mayfair BH4 .... 204 B1
Mayfair Ct SO30 .... 106 A3
Mayfair Gdns
  Bournemouth BH11 .... 189 D2
  Southampton SO15 .... 102 C4
Mayfield PO13 .... 179 F1
Mayfield Ave Poole BH14 .... 203 F2
  Totton SO40 .... 100 C4
Mayfield Cl
  Ferndown BH22 .... 165 E3
  Stubbington PO14 .... 154 B2
Mayfield Dr BH22 .... 165 E3
Mayfield Rd
  Bournemouth BH9 .... 190 A1
  Fordingbridge SP6 .... 69 E1
  Gosport PO12 .... 181 E2
  Portsmouth PO2 .... 157 F1
  Southampton SO17 .... 79 E2
Mayfield Sch PO2 .... 157 F1
Mayfield Sec Sch PO2 .... 157 F1
Mayfield Way BH22 .... 165 E3
Mayflower Cl
  Chandler's Ford SO53 .... 55 D3
  Lymington SO41 .... 198 A1
  Stubbington PO14 .... 179 E3
Mayflower Ct 4 SO15 .... 102 C4
Mayflower Dr PO4 .... 183 E3
Mayflower Rd SO15 .... 102 A4
Mayflowers The SO17 .... 79 D2
Mayford Rd BH12 .... 204 A3
Mayhall Rd PO3 .... 158 A1
Mayhill La Droxford SO32 .... 84 C4
  Swanmore SO32 .... 84 C4
Maylands Ave PO4 .... 183 D3
Maylands Rd PO9 .... 135 D1
Mayles Cl PO17 .... 108 A2
Mayles La PO17 .... 107 F1
Mayles Rd PO4 .... 183 D3
Maylings Farm Rd PO16 .... 130 C2
Maylyn Rd SO40 .... 100 A4
Maynard Cl PO13 .... 155 E2
Maynard Pl PO8 .... 112 A4
Maynard Rd SO40 .... 100 C4
Mayo Cl PO1 .... 182 B4
Maypole Villas SO50 .... 56 A4
Mayridge PO14 .... 129 E2
Mays Firs SP6 .... 47 F1
Maytree Cl Fair Oak SO50 .... 57 E1
  Locks Heath SO31 .... 129 E2
Maytree Gdns PO8 .... 111 F2
Maytree Inf Sch SO14 .... 103 D3

Maytree Rd
  Chandler's Ford SO53 .... 30 B1
  16 Fareham PO16 .... 131 D1
  Southampton SO19 .... 104 A3
  Waterlooville PO8 .... 111 F2
Mayvale Cl SO40 .... 101 F1
Mayville High Sch PO5 .... 182 B1
McIntyre Rd BH23 .... 191 D4
McKinley Rd BH4 .... 204 B3
McWilliam Cl BH12 .... 204 B4
McWilliam Rd BH9 .... 190 A1
Meacher Cl SO40 .... 100 C4
Mead Cl Broadstone BH18 .... 187 D1
  Romsey SO51 .... 53 D4
Mead Cres SO18 .... 79 E2
Mead Ct
  Chandler's Ford SO53 .... 55 E3
  Southampton SO16 .... 79 E4
Mead End Rd Denmead PO7 ... 111 D2
  Sway SO41 .... 171 F1
Mead Rd
  Chandler's Ford SO53 .... 55 E3
  Lymington SO41 .... 197 D1
  Winchester SO23 .... 10 C2
Mead The Gosport PO13 .... 155 D2
  Hythe SO45 .... 125 F2
  Liss GU33 .... 20 C2
  Petersfield GU32 .... 40 B1
Mead Way PO16 .... 131 D2
Meadbrook Gdns SO53 .... 55 E3
Meadcroft Cl SO31 .... 152 B4
Meadend Rd PO9 .... 136 A3
Meadow Ave
  Fordingbridge SP6 .... 69 E1
  Locks Heath SO31 .... 129 D2
Meadow Cl Bransgore BH23 .. 193 D4
  Burley BH24 .... 142 C1
  Ferndown BH22 .... 165 E1
  Fordingbridge SP6 .... 69 E1
  North Baddesley SO52 .... 54 A2
  Ringwood BH24 .... 141 D4
  Shedfield SO32 .... 83 F2
  Sopley BH23 .... 192 A4
  Totton SO40 .... 100 C3
  West End SO30 .... 80 C1
Meadow Court Cl BH9 .... 190 A2
Meadow Croft Cl SO21 .... 31 E2
Meadow Ct
  Bournemouth BH9 .... 190 A2
  2 Emsworth PO10 .... 160 C4
  Fordingbridge SP6 .... 69 E1
  Whiteparish SP5 .... 24 B2
  12 Wimborne Minster BH21 ... 163 E2
Meadow Edge PO7 .... 134 A1
Meadow Farm La BH21 .... 186 B4
Meadow Gdns SO32 .... 83 F2
Meadow Gr
  Chandler's Ford SO53 .... 55 E2
  Verwood BH31 .... 115 D3
Meadow La Burton BH23 .... 192 B1
  Hamble-le-Rice SO31 .... 128 A1
Meadow Rd Lymington SO41 .. 197 E1
  New Milton BH25 .... 195 D3
  Ringwood BH24 .... 141 D4
Meadow Rise
  Corfe Mullen BH18 .... 186 C3
  Waterlooville PO8 .... 112 A2
Meadow St PO5 .... 182 A2
Meadow Terr 12 PO16 .... 131 D1
Meadow The Denmead PO7 .... 110 C2
  Romsey SO51 .... 28 A1
Meadow View Rd BH11 .... 188 C2
Meadow Way
  Barton on Sea BH25 .... 210 A4
  Fawley SO45 .... 151 D2
  Ringwood BH24 .... 141 D4
  Verwood BH31 .... 115 D3
  Winchester SO22 .... 10 B2
Meadow Wlk Gosport PO13 .... 155 D3
  1 Liss GU33 .... 20 C2
  11 Portsmouth PO1 .... 182 B3
Meadowbank BH16 .... 201 E4
Meadowbank Rd PO15 .... 130 B1
Meadowcrest Wood SO42 .... 145 E1
Meadowhead Rd SO16 .... 78 C2
Meadowland
  Christchurch BH23 .... 207 F3
  Kings Worthy SO23 .... 2 A4
Meadowlands Havant PO9 .... 136 A1
  Lymington SO41 .... 197 E2
  Rowland's Castle PO9 .... 113 E2
Meadowlands Jun &
  Inf Sch PO8 .... 111 F3
Meadowmead Ave SO15 .... 102 A4
Meadows Cl BH16 .... 201 E4
Meadows Dr BH16 .... 201 E4
Meadows The Fareham PO16 ... 131 E2
  Lyndhurst SO43 .... 122 A4
  Waterlooville PO8 .... 134 B4
Meadowside Cl SO18 .... 79 F2
Meadowsweet PO7 .... 112 A4
Meadowsweet Rd BH17 .... 201 F4
Meadowsweet Way
  Cosham PO6 .... 133 E1
  Fair Oak SO50 .... 81 E3
Meads The
  North Baddesley SO53 .... 55 D3
  Romsey SO51 .... 52 B4
Meadway The BH23 .... 193 E1
Mears Rd SO50 .... 57 E1
Meath Cl PO11 .... 185 E1
Medina Cl SO53 .... 55 F3
Medina Ct PO13 .... 180 C3
Medina House PO14 .... 155 D4
Medina Prim Sch PO6 .... 157 F4
Medina Rd Cosham PO6 .... 157 F4
  Southampton SO15 .... 78 A1
Medina Way BH23 .... 208 B3

Medlar Cl Burton BH23 .... 192 B1
  Hedge End SO30 .... 105 E3
Medley Pl 18 SO30 .... 105 E3
Medlicott Way SO32 .... 84 A2
Medstead Rd PO9 .... 135 F2
Medwall Gr SO19 .... 104 B3
Medway Dr SO53 .... 55 D4
Medway Rd BH22 .... 166 A3
Meerut Rd SO42 .... 145 F1
Meeting House La BH24 .... 140 C4
Megan Ct 19 PO6 .... 157 F4
Megan Rd SO30 .... 80 B1
Megana Way SO51 .... 28 B3
Meggeson Ave SO18 .... 80 A1
Melbourne Rd BH8 .... 191 F1
Melbourne Gdns SO30 .... 105 E3
Melbourne House 30 PO1 .... 182 B3
Melbourne Pl PO5 .... 182 B2
Melbourne Rd
  Bournemouth BH8 .... 205 E3
  Christchurch BH23 .... 191 F1
  Hedge End SO30 .... 105 E3
Melbourne St SO14 .... 103 D2
Melbury Ave BH12 .... 203 F4
Melbury Cl Ferndown BH22 .... 165 E2
  Lymington SO41 .... 197 E2
Melbury Ct 19 SO17 .... 79 D1
Melchet Cl SO51 .... 25 D1
Melchet Ct (St Edward's Sch)
  SO51 .... 25 D1
Melchet Rd SO18 .... 104 B4
Melick Cl SO40 .... 101 D1
Mellor Cl 4 PO6 .... 157 E4
Mellstock Rd BH15 .... 202 B3
Melrose Cl PO4 .... 183 D2
Melrose Ct New Milton SO40 .... 195 E1
  Totton SO40 .... 76 B1
Melrose Gdns PO12 .... 180 C4
Melrose Rd SO15 .... 78 B1
Melton Ct 1 BH21 .... 204 A2
Melverley Gdns BH21 .... 163 E3
Melville Cl SO16 .... 78 B3
Melville Rd
  Bournemouth BH9 .... 204 C4
  Gosport PO4 .... 181 D4
  Portsmouth PO4 .... 183 E2
Melvin Jones House PO14 .... 154 B2
Mendip Cl New Milton BH25 .... 195 E1
  Verwood BH31 .... 114 C3
Mendip Ct 4 BH23 .... 207 F4
Mendip Gdns SO45 .... 125 E1
Mendip Rd
  Southampton SO16 .... 101 F4
  Verwood BH31 .... 114 C3
Mendips Rd PO14 .... 154 C4
Mendips Wlk PO14 .... 154 B4
Mengham Ave PO11 .... 185 D1
Mengham Ct PO11 .... 185 D2
Mengham Inf Sch PO11 .... 185 D2
Mengham Jun Sch PO11 .... 185 D1
Mengham La PO11 .... 185 D2
Mengham Rd PO11 .... 185 D2
Menin House PO15 .... 130 B1
Menslands La Hambledon PO7 ... 86 A1
  Soberton PO7 .... 109 F4
Mentone Rd 2 BH14 .... 203 D2
Menzies Cl 2 SO16 .... 77 F3
Meon Cl Clanfield PO8 .... 88 B2
  Gosport PO13 .... 155 D1
  Petersfield GU32 .... 40 C2
  Romsey SO51 .... 53 E4
Meon Cres SO53 .... 55 E3
Meon Ct SO18 .... 104 B4
Meon Gdns SO32 .... 84 A3
Meon House SO14 .... 155 D4
Meon Jun & Inf Schs PO4 .... 183 D2
Meon Rd Bournemouth BH7 .... 206 A4
  Portsmouth PO4 .... 183 D2
  Romsey SO51 .... 53 E4
Meoncross Sch SO14 .... 154 B2
Meonstoke CE Inf &
  1st Year Jun Sch SO32 .... 61 E2
Meonwara Cres GU32 .... 37 E3
Mercer Way SO51 .... 53 D4
Merchants Pl 9 SO23 .... 11 D4
Merchants Wlk 21 SO14 .... 102 C2
Merchistoun Rd PO7 .... 112 B4
Mercury Cl SO16 .... 77 F2
Mercury Gdns SO31 .... 128 A2
Mercury Pl PO7 .... 134 C1
Merdon Ave SO53 .... 55 E4
Merdon Cl SO53 .... 55 E4
Merdon Ct SO53 .... 55 E4
Merdon Jun Sch SO53 .... 55 E4
Mere Croft PO15 .... 129 F2
Meredith Cl BH23 .... 207 E4
Meredith Gdns SO40 .... 100 B3
Meredith Inf Sch PO2 .... 182 C4
Meredith Lodge PO7 .... 135 D4
Meredith Rd PO2 .... 157 F2
Meredith Towers SO19 .... 104 C2
Meredun Cl SO21 .... 30 A4
Merepond La GU34 .... 17 F2
Merganser Cl PO12 .... 181 D4
Meriden Cl BH13 .... 214 C4
Meriden Ct 10 SO23 .... 2 A1
Meriden Rd PO5 .... 182 A2
Meridian Ctr 11 PO9 .... 135 F1
Meridians The BH23 .... 206 C3
Merino Way BH22 .... 138 C1
Merlewood Cl BH2 .... 204 C4
Merlewood Cl 19 BH25 .... 195 D2
Merley Dr BH23 .... 209 D4
Merley Fst Sch BH21 .... 163 E1
Merley Gdns BH21 .... 163 F1

Merley House BH21 .... 163 D1
Merley La BH21 .... 163 F1
Merley Park Rd
　Corfe Mullen BH21 .... 186 C4
　Oakley BH21 .... 163 E1
Merley Ways BH21 .... 163 E1
Merlin Cl
　Bishop's Waltham SO32 ...... 83 D4
　Ringwood BH24 .... 141 E3
Merlin Dr PO3 .... 158 A2
Merlin Gdns Hedge End SO30 .. 105 D4
　Portchester PO16 .... 132 A1
Merlin Lodge SO19 .... 103 E2
Merlin Way PO3 .... 208 A3
Mermaid Ct 22 BH5 .... 205 F2
Mermaid Rd PO14 .... 154 C3
Mermaid Way SO14 .... 103 D1
Merrick Way SO53 .... 55 D4
Merridale Rd SO19 .... 103 F3
Merriefield Ave BH18 .... 187 D3
Merriefield Cl BH18 .... 187 D3
Merriefield Dr BH18 .... 187 D3
Merrieleas Cl SO53 .... 55 E4
Merrieleas Dr SO53 .... 55 E4
Merriemeade Cl SO45 .... 125 F1
Merriemeade Par SO45 .... 125 F1
Merrifield BH21 .... 163 E4
Merritown La BH23 .... 190 B4
Merritt Ct SO53 .... 55 E2
Merrivale Ave BH6 .... 206 C3
Merrivale Cl SO45 .... 125 F2
Merrivale Ct PO10 .... 137 E1
Merrivale Rd PO2 .... 157 F2
Merrow Ave BH12 .... 204 A4
Merrow Chase 1 BH13 .... 214 C4
Merrow Cl PO16 .... 156 A4
Merry Gdns SO52 .... 54 A3
Merryfield PO14 .... 129 E2
Merryfield Ave PO9 .... 135 E3
Merryfield Cl BH23 .... 193 D4
Merryfield Ct BH10 .... 189 E2
Merryfield La BH10 .... 189 E2
Merryfield Rd GU31 .... 41 D2
Merryoak Gn SO19 .... 103 F3
Merryoak Rd SO19 .... 103 F3
Merrytree Cl SO51 .... 50 C2
Merryweather Est BH24 ...... 141 E4
Mersea Gdns SO19 .... 104 A2
Mersham Gdns SO18 .... 104 A4
Merstone Rd PO13 .... 155 E1
Merthyr Ave PO6 .... 158 A4
Merton Ave PO16 .... 156 B3
Merton Cl SP6 .... 69 F2
Merton Cres PO16 .... 156 A4
Merton Ct
　8 Christchurch BH23 .... 209 D4
　3 Poole BH15 .... 202 C2
Merton Gr BH24 .... 140 C4
Merton Rd Portsmouth PO5 .. 182 B1
　Southampton SO17 .... 79 D2
Meryl Rd PO4 .... 183 E2
Mesh Pond SP5 .... 46 B4
Mesh Rd SO51 .... 6 A1
Meteor Rd PO10 .... 161 D2
Methuen Cl 2 BH8 .... 205 E3
Methuen Rd Bournemouth BH8 .. 205 D3
　Broadstone BH17 .... 187 D1
　Portsmouth PO4 .... 183 D2
Methuen St SO14 .... 103 D4
Metuchen Way SO30 .... 105 E2
Mews Ct SO21 .... 31 D2
Mews La SO22 .... 10 C4
Mews The
　1 Blackfield SO45 .... 177 F4
　1 Bournemouth BH4 .... 204 B2
　Chandler's Ford SO53 .... 55 E2
　Gosport PO12 .... 181 F2
　Havant PO9 .... 135 F2
　Petersfield GU31 .... 41 D2
　Rownhams SO16 .... 77 F3
Mewsey Ct PO9 .... 135 E4
Mey Cl PO7 .... 135 D4
Meynell Cl SO50 .... 55 F2
Meyrick Cl BH23 .... 193 D4
Meyrick Park Cres BH3 .... 205 D2
Meyrick House 15 PO2 .... 157 E1
Meyrick Park Mans 5 BH2 .. 204 C3
Meyrick Rd Bournemouth BH1 .. 205 D2
　Havant PO9 .... 135 E1
　Portsmouth PO2 .... 157 E1
Micawber House 12 PO1 .... 182 B4
Michael Crook Cl PO9 .... 135 E2
Michael's Way SO45 .... 125 F2
Michaels Way SO50 .... 57 E1
Michelgrove Rd BH5 .... 205 F2
Michelmersh Cl SO16 .... 77 F3
Michelmersh Gr BH8 .... 190 B1
Michigan Way SO40 .... 100 A4
Mickleham Cl BH12 .... 204 A4
Midanbury Cres SO18 .... 79 F1
Midanbury Ct 10 SO18 .... 103 F4
Midanbury La SO18 .... 103 F4
Midanbury Wlk 1 SO18 ...... 103 F4
Midas Cl PO7 .... 134 C2
Middle Brook BH11 .... 189 D3
Middle Brook St SO23 .... 11 D4
Middle Common Rd SO41 ... 197 D2
Middle Ct PO1 .... 182 C4
Middle La BH24 .... 141 D4
Middle Mead PO14 .... 154 A4
Middle Meadow GU33 .... 21 D2
Middle Park Way PO9 .... 135 E2
Middle Rd
　Bournemouth BH10 .... 189 E3
　Locks Heath SO31 .... 129 D3

Middle Rd Continued
　Lymington SO41 .... 197 E2
　New Milton SO41 .... 195 F4
　North Baddesley SO52 .... 54 A2
　Poole BH15 .... 202 C3
　Southampton SO19 .... 104 A2
　Sway SO41 .... 172 A1
　Sway SO41 .... 195 F4
　Winchester SO22 .... 10 C4
Middle St Portsmouth PO5 ... 182 B2
　Southampton SO14 .... 103 D4
Middlebere Cres BH16 .... 201 E2
Middlebridge St SO51 .... 52 C3
Middlebrook SO32 .... 83 E4
Middlecroft La PO12 .... 180 C3
Middlehill Dr BH21 .... 164 A3
Middlehill Rd BH21 .... 164 A3
Middlesex Rd PO4 .... 183 D2
Middleton Cl Fareham PO14 .. 154 C4
　Southampton SO18 .... 80 A1
Middleton Rd
　Bournemouth BH9 .... 189 F1
　Ringwood BH24 .... 141 D4
Middleton Rise PO8 .... 88 B2
Middleton Wlk 10 PO14 ...... 154 C4
Midfield Cl PO14 .... 154 C4
Midhurst House 57 PO1 ...... 182 B3
Midland Rd BH9 .... 189 F1
Midlands Est SO30 .... 80 B1
Midlington Hill SO32 .... 85 D4
Midlington House SO32 .... 85 D4
Midlington Rd SO32 .... 85 D4
Midway SO45 .... 125 F2
Midway Path BH13 .... 214 B2
Midway Rd PO2 .... 157 F3
Midways PO14 .... 179 E3
Midwood Ave BH8 .... 190 C1
Milbeck Cl PO8 .... 112 A2
Milborne Cres BH12 .... 203 F4
Milbourne Rd BH22 .... 165 E3
Milburn Cl 12 BH4 .... 204 B2
Milburn Rd BH4 .... 204 A2
Milburns The SO51 .... 27 E4
Milbury Cres SO18 .... 104 A3
Milbury House PO6 .... 133 D1
Mildmay Ct 42 SO23 .... 11 D4
Mildmay St SO22 .... 10 B3
Mile End Rd PO2 .... 182 B4
Miles Cl PO11 .... 185 E1
Miles La SP5 .... 24 B3
Milestone Rd BH15 .... 202 B3
Milford Cl Havant PO9 .... 135 E2
　West Moors BH22 .... 138 C1
Milford Cres SO41 .... 211 E3
Milford Ct Gosport PO12 ..... 180 B2
　Milford on Sea SO41 .... 211 F2
　Portsmouth PO4 .... 183 D2
Milford Dr BH11 .... 188 C3
Milford Gdns SO53 .... 55 F3
Milford House SO41 .... 211 F3
Milford on Sea Prim Sch
　SO41 .... 211 F3
Milford Rd
　Barton on Sea BH25 .... 210 A4
　Lymington SO41 .... 197 D1
　Portsmouth PO1 .... 182 B3
Militair House BH31 .... 114 C4
Military Rd Fareham PO16 ... 131 E1
　Gosport PO12 .... 181 D1
　Gosport, Brockhurst PO13 .. 180 C3
　Gosport, Clayhall PO12 ...... 181 E1
　Portsmouth PO3 .... 157 F3
　Portsmouth PO1 .... 182 A4
Milkwood Ct SO40 .... 100 B4
Mill Cl Denmead PO7 .... 111 D2
　North Hayling PO11 .... 159 F1
　Nursling SO16 .... 77 E3
Mill Ct Fordingbridge SP6 ..... 69 F1
　4 Southampton SO17 .... 79 E1
Mill End Damerham SP6 .... 68 B2
　Hermitage PO9 .... 161 D4
Mill Gate House 19 PO1 ..... 182 A3
Mill Hill SO30 .... 106 A3
Mill Hill Cl BH14 .... 203 E2
Mill House Bsns Ctr SO19 ... 103 E2
Mill House Ctr SO40 .... 101 D4
Mill House Lodge SO50 .... 56 B2
Mill La Boldre SO41 .... 198 C3
　Brockenhurst SO42 .... 146 A1
　Burley BH24 .... 143 E2
　Christchurch BH23 .... 209 D4
　Croucheston SP5 .... 22 B4
　Droxford SO32 .... 61 D1
　Droxford SO32 .... 61 E1
　Durley SO32 .... 82 B2
　Gosport PO12 .... 181 D3
　Havant PO9 .... 159 F3
　Havant, Bedhampton PO9 ... 135 E1
　Hawkley GU33 .... 19 F4
　Hermitage PO10 .... 137 D1
　Hurn BH23 .... 191 D3
　Kings Worthy SO21 .... 2 B3
　Lymington SO41 .... 197 F2
　Minstead SO43 .... 98 C1
　Nursling SO16 .... 76 C2
　Petersfield GU31, GU32 .... 41 D3
　Poole BH14 .... 203 D2
　Portsmouth PO1 .... 182 B4
　Romsey SO51 .... 52 B4
　Sherfield English SO51 .... 25 F1
　Southwick PO17 .... 133 F2
　Steep GU32 .... 40 C4
　Steep Marsh GU32 .... 19 F1
　Sway SO41 .... 196 C4
　Titchfield PO15 .... 130 A1
　Westbourne PO10 .... 137 D1
　Wickham PO17 .... 108 A3
　Wimborne Minster BH21 .... 163 D3

Mill Meadow SO41 .... 211 E3
Mill Pond Rd PO12 .... 181 D3
Mill Pond The SO45 .... 150 A3
Mill Quay PO10 .... 161 D4
Mill Race View SP5 .... 46 C4
Mill Rd Christchurch BH23 ... 207 D4
　Denmead PO7 .... 111 D2
　Fareham PO16 .... 155 D4
　Gosport PO12 .... 181 D3
　Liss GU33 .... 21 D1
　Portsmouth PO2 .... 157 E1
　Southampton SO15 .... 102 A4
　Totton SO40 .... 101 D4
　Waterlooville PO7 .... 134 C3
　Westbourne PO10 .... 137 D2
Mill Rd N Bournemouth BH8 .. 190 B2
　Bournemouth BH8 .... 190 C2
Mill Rd S BH8 .... 190 B1
Mill Rise SO51 .... 5 E1
Mill Rythe Inf Sch PO11 ...... 185 D3
Mill Rythe Jun Sch PO11 ..... 185 D3
Mill Rythe La PO11 .... 185 D4
Mill St Broadstone BH21 ..... 162 A1
　Eastleigh SO50 .... 56 A2
　Titchfield PO15 .... 154 A4
Mill Way SO40 .... 100 C3
Millais Rd SO19 .... 103 F2
Milland Rd SO23 .... 11 D3
Millbank House
　14 Southampton SO14 .... 103 E3
　5 Wimborne Minster BH21 .. 163 E3
Millbank St SO14 .... 103 E3
Millbridge Gdns SO19 .... 104 A2
Millbrook Cl
　Chandler's Ford SO53 .... 55 D3
　Liss GU33 .... 21 D2
Millbrook Com Sch SO16 ...... 77 F2
Millbrook Dr PO9 .... 136 A3
Millbrook Flyover SO15 ...... 101 F4
Millbrook Point Rd SO15 ..... 102 A3
Millbrook Rd E SO15 .... 102 B3
Millbrook Rd W SO15 .... 102 A3
Millbrook Sta SO15 .... 102 A3
Millbrook Trad Est SO15 ..... 101 E4
Millcourt 6 SO50 .... 57 E1
Miller Cl BH5 .... 195 E2
Miller Dr PO16 .... 130 C1
Miller Rd BH23 .... 207 E4
Millers La SO22 .... 9 F2
Millers Quay House PO16 ... 155 D4
Millers Way SO45 .... 125 F1
Millfield Broadstone BH17 ... 201 F4
　Broadstone BH17 .... 202 A4
　New Milton BH25 .... 194 C4
Millhams Cl BH10 .... 189 D3
Millhams Dr BH10 .... 189 D3
Millhams Rd BH10 .... 189 D3
Millhams St BH23 .... 207 D3
Millhams St N BH23 .... 207 D3
Milliken Cl SO45 .... 150 C1
Mills The BH12 .... 203 F4
Millsom Cl Broadstone BH17 .. 202 A4
　Wimborne Minster BH21 .... 163 E2
Millstream Rise SO51 .... 52 B4
Millstream Trad Est BH24 .... 141 D3
Millverton Cl SO18 .... 104 A4
Millverton Cl SO40 .... 99 F2
Millyford Cl BH25 .... 209 E4
Milne Cl SO45 .... 125 E1
Milne Rd BH17 .... 187 D1
Milner Ct SO15 .... 102 B4
Milner Pl SO22 .... 10 C3
Milner Rd BH4 .... 204 B1
Milnthorpe La SO22 .... 10 C4
Milton Cl BH14 .... 203 E2
Milton Ct Ferndown BH22 ... 165 E3
　Portsmouth PO4 .... 183 D3
Milton Gr Locks Heath SO31 .. 129 D1
　New Milton BH25 .... 195 D1
Milton Mead BH25 .... 194 C1
Milton Par PO7 .... 111 F1
Milton Park Ave PO4 .... 183 D2
Milton Park Jun & Inf Schs
　PO4 .... 183 D2
Milton Rd
　Bournemouth BH8 .... 205 D3
　Eastleigh SO50 .... 56 A3
　Poole BH14 .... 203 E2
　Portsmouth PO3 .... 183 D3
　Southampton SO15 .... 102 C3
　Waterlooville PO7, PO8 ...... 111 F1
　Wimborne Minster BH21 .... 163 F1
Milton Villas BH8 .... 205 D3
Milverton Cl
　Christchurch BH23 .... 193 F1
　Totton SO40 .... 101 D3
Milverton House 21 PO5 ..... 182 B2
Milverton Rd Totton SO40 ... 101 D3
　Winchester SO22 .... 10 C4
Milvil Ct 5 PO13 .... 179 F1
Milvil Rd PO13 .... 179 F1
Mimosa Ave BH21 .... 187 F4
Mimosa Dr SO50 .... 57 F1
Mincingfield La SO32 .... 82 B3
Mincingfield Terr SO32 .... 82 B3
Minden House Fareham PO14 .. 154 C4
　Romsey SO51 .... 53 D4
Minden Way SO22 .... 10 B3
Minerva Cl PO7 .... 134 C1
Minley Ct PO9 .... 136 A3
Minnitt Rd PO12 .... 181 F2
Minstead Ave SO18 .... 104 B4
Minstead Cl SO22 .... 1 B2
Minstead Ct 4 SO17 .... 103 D4
Minstead Rd
　Bournemouth BH10 .... 189 E2
　Portsmouth PO4 .... 183 D2

Minstead Rural Studies Ctr
　SO43 .... 98 A1
Minster Cl PO15 .... 130 B1
Minster Ct 1 SO15 .... 102 B3
Minster La 27 SO23 .... 11 D4
Minster View BH21 .... 163 E3
Minster Way BH16 .... 201 D4
Mint Cl GU33 .... 21 D3
Mint The GU31,GU32 .... 40 C1
Minterne Cl SO30 .... 56 B3
Minterne Grange BH14 .... 214 B4
Minterne Rd
　Bournemouth BH9 .... 190 A1
　Christchurch BH23 .... 207 F3
　Poole BH14 .... 214 B4
Minton Mews BH2 .... 204 C3
Mintyns Hill SP6 .... 68 C4
Mintys Yd 4 BH21 .... 141 E3
Mirror Cl SO31 .... 128 C1
Mislingford Rd SO32 .... 84 B2
Missenden Acres SO30 .... 105 E4
Mission La PO8 .... 112 A2
Mission Rd BH18 .... 187 D1
Misslebrook La SO52 .... 54 B2
Mistletoe Gdns SO31 .... 128 C3
Mitchell Cl
　Barton on Sea BH25 .... 210 A4
　Locks Heath SO31 .... 129 E3
Mitchell Dr SO50 .... 57 E2
Mitchell Point SO31 .... 127 F1
Mitchell Rd Eastleigh SO50 ... 56 A1
　Ferndown BH21 .... 165 D4
　Havant PO9 .... 135 D2
　Poole BH17 .... 202 C4
Mitchell Way
　Eastleigh SO18 .... 79 F3
　Eastleigh SO50 .... 80 A4
　Portsmouth PO3 .... 158 A2
Mitchells Cl Redlynch SP5 ..... 47 E3
　Romsey SO51 .... 52 C4
Mitre Copse SO50 .... 56 C1
Mitre Ct 18 PO14 .... 154 C4
Mizen Way PO13 .... 180 B3
Mizzen Ct SO14 .... 103 D1
Moat Cl SO45 .... 150 A2
Moat Ct
　Bournemouth BH4 .... 204 B3
　Gosport PO12 .... 180 B2
Moat Dr PO12 .... 180 B2
Moat Hill SO18 .... 79 F2
Moat La BH25 .... 209 F4
Moat Wlk PO12 .... 180 B2
Mockbeggar La BH24 .... 117 D4
Moffat Rd BH23 .... 207 E4
Moggs Mead GU31 .... 41 D2
Mole Hill PO7 .... 134 C3
Molefields SO41 .... 211 F3
Molesworth Rd PO12 .... 181 E2
Molyneux Rd BH25 .... 195 E2
Momford Rd SO22 .... 10 A2
Mon Cres SO18 .... 104 B4
Monaco Cl BH9 .... 205 D4
Monarch Cl Locks Heath SO31 .. 129 D1
　Waterlooville PO7 .... 135 D4
Monarch Way SO30 .... 80 C1
Monastery Rd SO18 .... 103 F4
Monckton Rd Gosport PO12 .. 181 D1
　Portsmouth PO3 .... 158 A1
Moneyfield Ave PO3 .... 158 A1
Moneyfield La PO3 .... 183 D4
Moneyfly Rd BH31 .... 115 D3
Monk's Hill PO10 .... 137 D3
Monks Brook Cl SO50 .... 55 F1
Monks Brook Ind Pk SO53 .... 55 D3
Monks Cl BH22 .... 166 A4
Monks Ct 10 SO41 .... 197 F1
Monks Hill PO13 .... 179 E2
Monks Orch GU32 .... 40 C3
Monks Pl SO40 .... 100 B3
Monks Rd Netley SO31 .... 127 D3
　Winchester SO23 .... 2 A1
Monks Way
　Bournemouth BH11 .... 188 B3
　Eastleigh SO50 .... 55 F1
　Southampton SO18 .... 79 F2
　Stubbington PO14 .... 179 D2
Monks Wlk SO45 .... 149 F4
Monks Wood Cl SO16 .... 79 D3
Monkshood Cl BH23 .... 193 D1
Monkswell Gn BH23 .... 207 E3
Monkton Cl SO40 .... 100 B3
Monkton Cres BH12 .... 203 F4
Monkton House PO12 .... 181 D1
Monkton La SO40 .... 100 B3
Monkwood Cl PO9 .... 135 E3
Monkworthy Dr BH24 .... 139 F3
Monmouth Cl
　North Baddesley SO53 .... 55 D3
　Verwood BH31 .... 115 D2
Monmouth Ct
　Lymington SO41 .... 197 D2
　Ringwood BH24 .... 140 C4
Monmouth Dr BH31 .... 115 D2
Monmouth Gdns SO40 .... 100 B3
Monmouth Rd PO2 .... 157 E1
Monmouth Sq SO22 .... 10 A3
Monnow Gdns SO18 .... 80 A1
Monroe Cl PO12 .... 180 C2
Monsal Ave BH22 .... 165 E2
Montacute Sch BH17 .... 187 E1
Montacute Way BH23 .... 187 F4
Montagu Pk BH23 .... 209 D4
Montagu Rd BH23 .... 209 D4
Montague Ave SO19 .... 104 B2
Montague Cl SO19 .... 104 B2
Montague Gdns GU31 .... 41 E2

Montague Rd
　Bishopstoke SO50 .... 56 B1
　Bournemouth BH5 .... 206 A4
　Portsmouth PO2 .... 157 E1
Montague Wallis Ct 31 PO1 .. 182 A4
Montana Ct PO7 .... 135 D4
Montefiore House SO18 .... 79 E1
Monterey Dr Havant PO9 .... 136 A3
　Hordle SO41 .... 195 F1
　Locks Heath SO31 .... 129 C2
Montfort Cl SO51 .... 53 E4
Montfort College SO51 .... 53 E4
Montfort Hts SO51 .... 53 E4
Montfort Rd SO51 .... 53 E4
Montgomerie Rd PO5 .... 182 B1
Montgomery Ave
　Bournemouth BH11 .... 189 D4
　Totton SO40 .... 100 B4
Montgomery Rd Gosport PO13 .. 155 E2
　Havant PO9 .... 136 A4
　Southampton SO18 .... 104 A4
Montgomery Way SO53 .... 55 D3
Montgomery Wlk PO7 .... 134 B3
Montpelier Cl SO31 .... 129 E3
Montrose Ave PO16 .... 132 C1
Montrose Cl Hedge End SO30 .. 105 F2
　2 Verwood BH31 .... 114 C2
Montrose Dr BH10 .... 189 D4
Montserrat Rd PO13 .... 179 F1
Monument La Boldre SO41 .. 198 A4
　Southwick PO17 .... 132 B3
　Walderton PO17 .... 137 F
Monxton Gn 11 PO9 .... 136 A3
Moody Rd PO14 .... 179 E1
Moody's Hill SP5 .... 3 E
Moonhills La SO42 .... 149 D.
Moonrakers BH13 .... 214 C
Moonrakers Way BH23 ...... 193 F
Moonscross Ave SO40 .... 100 C
Moor La PO7 .... 48 B
Moor Park PO7 .... 112 A.
Moor Rd BH18 .... 187 D
Moor View Rd BH15 .... 202 C
Moorcroft La BH23 .... 192 B:
Moordown Cl BH9 .... 190 A:
Moordown St John's
　CE Prim Sch BH9 .... 189 F
Moore Ave BH11 .... 189 D:
Moore Cl BH25 .... 194 C
Moore Cres SO31 .... 127 E
Moore Gdns PO12 .... 180 C:
Moorfield Gr BH9 .... 189 F
Moorfields Rd BH13 .... 214 C
Moorgreen Hospl SO30 .... 80 C:
Moorgreen Rd Havant PO9 .. 136 A:
　West End SO30 .... 80 C
Moorhaven BH22 .... 165 E:
Moorhead Ct SO14 .... 103 E
Moorhill Gdns SO18 .... 104 C:
Moorhill Rd Burley BH24 .... 143 D:
　West End SO30 .... 104 B:
Moorhills 13 BH21 .... 163 E:
Moorings The
　7 Christchurch BH23 .... 207 D:
　Fareham PO16 .... 155 D
Moorings Way PO4 .... 183 E:
Moorings Way Inf Sch PO4 .. 183 E:
Moorland Ave BH25 .... 209 F.
Moorland Cl Hythe SO45 .... 125 E:
　Locks Heath SO31 .... 129 D:
Moorland Cres BH16 .... 201 D.
Moorland Gate BH24 .... 141 D:
Moorland Par BH16 .... 201 D.
Moorland Rd
　Bournemouth BH1 .... 205 E:
　Portsmouth PO3 .... 182 C:
Moorland Way BH16 .... 201 D.
Moorlands Cl SO42 .... 145 E
Moorlands Coll BH23 .... 192 A:
Moorlands Cres SO18 .... 104 A.
Moorlands Inf Sch SO18 ...... 80 A
Moorlands Rd
　Swanmore SO32 .... 84 A.
　Verwood BH31 .... 114 C
　West Moors BH22 .... 138 C:
Moorlands Rise BH22 .... 138 C:
Moorlea 11 BH8 .... 205 D:
Moors Cl
　Colden Common SO21 .... 31 F.
　Hurn BH23 .... 191 D.
Moors Valley Ctry Pk BH24 .. 139 E.
Moorside Cl BH11 .... 189 D:
Moorside Rd
　Bournemouth BH11 .... 189 D:
　Corfe Mullen BH21 .... 186 B:
　West Moors BH22 .... 138 C:
　Winchester SO23 .... 2 B
Moortown Ave PO6 .... 134 B.
Moortown Dr BH21 .... 188 A.
Moortown House BH24 ...... 141 D:
Moortown La BH24 .... 141 E:
Moorvale Rd BH9 .... 190 A.
Moot Cl SP5 .... 47 D.
Moot Gdns SP5 .... 46 C.
Moot La Downton SP5 .... 46 C:
　Redlynch SP5 .... 46 C:
Mopley SO45 .... 177 F.
Mopley Cl SO45 .... 177 F.
Morant Ct 14 BH25 .... 195 D:
Morant Rd BH24 .... 117 D.
Morant Ct PO12 .... 181 D.
Morant Dr PO16 .... 156 A.
Moray Ct 10 BH21 .... 163 D.
Mordaunt Rd SO14 .... 103 D.
Morden Ave BH22 .... 165 E.
Morden Rd BH9 .... 189 F.
Morecombe Ct 10 PO5 ...... 182 B:
Moreland Rd PO12 .... 181 D:

orelands Ct PO7 .... 134 C2
orelands Prim Sch PO7 .... 134 C1
orelands Rd PO7 .... 134 C2
orestead Rd Chilcomb SO21 .... 11 F2
Winchester SO21 .... 11 D2
Winchester SO21 .... 11 F2
oreton Rd BH9 .... 190 A2
organ Rd Hedge End SO30 .... 105 E3
Portsmouth PO4 .... 183 E2
organ's La SP5 .... 42 A1
organ's Vale & Woodfall's
Prim Sch SP5 .... 47 E4
organs Dr PO14 .... 154 B3
organs Rise Rd SP5 .... 47 E4
organs Vale Rd SP5 .... 47 E4
oriconium Quay BH15 .... 201 E1
orington Ct **8** BH8 .... 205 D3
orland Rd SO15 .... 78 B1
orley Cl Bournemouth BH5 .... 206 A3
Burton BH23 .... 192 B2
Southampton SO19 .... 103 F3
orley Cres PO8 .... 112 A2
orley Dr SO32 .... 83 E4
orley Rd Bournemouth BH5 .... 206 A3
Portsmouth PO4 .... 183 D1
orningside Ave PO16 .... 132 C1
ornington Dr SO22 .... 1 B1
ornish Rd BH13 .... 203 F1
orpeth Ave SO40 .... 100 C4
orris Cl PO13 .... 155 D3
orris Rd Poole BH17 .... 202 B4
Southampton SO15 .... 102 C3
orrison Ave BH12 .... 203 F3
orse Cl SO31 .... 127 D3
orshead Cres PO16 .... 130 C2
ortimer Cl
Christchurch BH23 .... 208 A3
Kings Worthy SO23 .... 2 A3
10 Netley SO31 .... 127 D3
Totton SO40 .... 76 B1
ortimer Lawn PO9 .... 135 E4
ortimer Rd Botley SO30 .... 106 A3
Bournemouth BH8 .... 190 A1
Cosham PO6 .... 133 E1
Southampton SO19 .... 103 F2
ortimer Way SO52 .... 53 F2
ortimer's Ind Units SO40 .... 75 F3
ortimers Dr **10** SO50 .... 57 E1
ortimers La SO32 .... 58 A2
ortimers Rd PO12 .... 180 C3
osaic Cl SO19 .... 104 C2
osdell Rd PO10 .... 161 F4
osedale Wlk SO16 .... 101 F4
oselle Cl SO15 .... 102 B3
oss Cl GU33 .... 21 D2
oss Dr SO40 .... 101 F1
oss Rd SO23 .... 11 D4
ossleigh Ave SO16 .... 77 F3
ossley Ave BH12 .... 189 D1
otcombe Rd BH13 .... 204 A1
osaic Cl SO19 .... 104 C2

Mountbatten Sports Ctr PO2 .. 157 E2
Mountbatten Sq PO4 .... 183 D1
Mountbatten Way
Romsey SO51 .... 52 C4
Southampton SO15 .... 102 B3
Mountfield SO45 .... 125 F2
Mountjoy Cl BH21 .... 163 F1
Mountview Ave PO16 .... 132 C1
Mountwood Rd PO10 .... 137 E1
Mousehole La Hythe SO45 .... 126 A2
Southampton SO18 .... 103 F4
Mousehole Rd PO6 .... 132 C1
Mowbray Rd SO19 .... 104 A2
Moxhams SP6 .... 69 F1
Moyles Court Sch BH24 .... 117 E3
Mt Pleasant Dr BH23 .... 169 E1
Mt Pleasant Rd BH15 .... 202 B2
Muccleshell Cl PO9 .... 136 A2
Muddyford Rd SP5 .... 47 E4
Mude Gdns BH23 .... 208 A3
Mudeford BH23 .... 208 A3
Mudeford Cty Inf Sch BH23 .. 207 F3
Mudeford Cty Jun Sch BH23 .. 207 F3
Mudeford Green Cl BH23 .... 207 F3
Mudeford La BH23 .... 207 F3
Muir House SO45 .... 125 F1
Muira Est SO14 .... 103 E3
Mulberry Ave Cosham PO6 .... 158 A4
Stubbington SO14 .... 179 E3
Mulberry Cl PO12 .... 181 D2
Mulberry Ct **4** BH23 .... 207 D4
Mulberry Gdns SP6 .... 93 F4
Mulberry Gr SO41 .... 211 E4
Mulberry La PO6 .... 158 A4
Mulberry Mews SP6 .... 93 F4
Mulberry Rd SO40 .... 101 F1
Mulberry Wlk SO15 .... 102 B4
Mullen Cl SO19 .... 103 F2
Mullins Cl BH12 .... 204 B4
Mullion Cl PO6 .... 157 D4
Mumby Rd PO12 .... 181 E3
Mundays Row PO8 .... 88 B1
Munro Cres SO15 .... 101 F4
Munster Rd Poole BH14 .... 203 E2
Portsmouth PO2 .... 157 E1
Murefield Rd PO1 .... 182 B3
Muriel Rd PO7 .... 134 C4
Murley Rd BH9 .... 205 D4
Murray Cl Fareham PO15 .... 130 C1
Southampton SO19 .... 104 C3
Murray Cotts SO32 .... 107 E4
Murray Rd PO8 .... 112 A3
Murray's La PO1 .... 181 F3
Murrills Est PO16 .... 156 C4
Muscliff Prim Sch BH9 .... 190 B2
Muscliffe **21** PO9 .... 136 A3
Muscliffe La BH9 .... 190 A2
Muscliffe Rd BH9 .... 189 F1
Museum Rd PO1 .... 182 A2
Mussett Cl SO40 .... 100 C4
Mustang Ave PO15 .... 129 E4
My Lords La PO11 .... 185 D2
Myers Cl SO32 .... 84 A3
Myrtle Ave Portchester PO16 .. 156 B4
Totton SO40 .... 100 B3
Myrtle Cl Gosport PO13 .... 155 D2
Hordle SO41 .... 195 F2
Myrtle Gr PO3 .... 183 D4
Myrtle Rd
Bournemouth BH8 .... 205 D4
Southampton SO16 .... 78 A2
Myvern Cl SO45 .... 150 B2

Nada Rd BH23 .... 193 E1
Nailsworth Rd PO6 .... 133 D1
Nairn Rd
Bournemouth BH3 .... 204 C3
Poole BH13 .... 214 C4
Naish Ct PO9 .... 135 E4
Naish Dr PO12 .... 156 A1
Naish Holiday Village BH25 .. 209 E4
Naish Rd BH25 .... 209 F4
Naked Man SO42 .... 171 D4
Namu Rd BH9 .... 189 F1
Nansen Ave BH15 .... 202 B3
Napier Cl PO13 .... 180 B3
Napier Cres PO15 .... 130 B1
Napier Rd Hamworthy BH15 .. 201 E2
Horndean PO8 .... 112 B3
Portsmouth PO5 .... 182 B1
Southampton SO19 .... 104 C3
Narrow La Ringwood BH24 .... 117 E1
10 Romsey SO51 .... 52 C4
Narvik Rd PO2 .... 157 E2
Naseby Cl PO6 .... 133 D1
Naseby Rd BH9 .... 190 A1
Nash Cl SO45 .... 125 E1
Nash Rd SO45 .... 125 E1
Nashe Cl PO15 .... 130 B2
Nashe House PO15 .... 130 B2
Nashe Way PO15 .... 130 B2
Nasmith Cl PO12 .... 180 B2
Nat Gonella Sq **21** PO12 .. 181 D2
National Motor Mus The
SO42 .... 148 C1
Nations Hill SO23 .... 2 B3
Nature Quest SO40 .... 123 F4
Navarac Ct BH14 .... 203 E2
Navigator's Way SO30 .... 105 E4
Navy Rd PO1 .... 182 A3
Nea Cl BH23 .... 208 B4
Nea Dr BH24 .... 116 A3
Nea Rd BH23 .... 208 C4
Neacroft Cl BH25 .... 209 E4
Neath Way SO53 .... 55 D3
Needles Ct **11** SO41 .... 211 E4
Needles House PO14 .... 155 D4
Needles Point SO41 .... 211 E2

Neelands Gr PO6 .... 156 C4
Neighbourhood Ctr BH17 .... 187 F1
Neilson Cl SO53 .... 55 E4
Nelson Ave Portchester PO16 .. 156 A4
Portsmouth PO2 .... 157 E1
Nelson Cl Holbury SO45 .... 150 B2
New Milton BH25 .... 194 C2
Romsey SO51 .... 52 C4
Nelson Cres PO8 .... 112 B4
Nelson Ct Fareham PO14 .... 154 C3
Hythe SO45 .... 126 A1
11 Poole BH15 .... 202 B1
Nelson Dr BH23 .... 207 F3
Nelson House PO12 .... 181 E2
Nelson Ind Pk SO30 .... 81 D1
Nelson La PO16 .... 132 B1
Nelson Pl SO41 .... 197 F2
Nelson Rd Bishopstoke SO50 .. 56 B2
Bournemouth BH4 .... 204 A2
Gosport PO12 .... 181 D2
Poole BH12 .... 204 A2
Portsmouth PO5 .... 182 B2
Portsmouth PO1 .... 182 B4
Southampton SO15 .... 102 B3
Winchester SO23 .... 11 C3
Nelson's Gdns SO30 .... 81 E2
Nepean Ct SO16 .... 77 F2
Neptune House **4** PO6 .... 157 F4
Neptune Rd Fareham PO15 .. 130 B1
Gosport PO14 .... 154 C3
Neptune Way SO14 .... 103 D1
Nerissa Ct PO7 .... 135 D4
Nerquis Cl SO51 .... 53 D4
Nesbitt Cl PO13 .... 155 D2
Nessus St PO2 .... 182 B4
Netherliffe Sch SO22 .... 1 C1
Nepean Ct SO16 .... 77 F2
Netherfield Cl PO9 .... 136 A1
Netherhall Gdns BH4 .... 204 B2
Netherhill La Curdridge SO32 .. 82 A1
Durley SO32 .... 82 A1
Netherton Rd PO12 .... 180 C4
Netherwood Pl BH21 .... 163 D3
Netley Abbey Inf Sch SO31 .. 127 D4
Netley Abbey Jun Sch SO31 .. 127 D4
Netley Cliff SO31 .... 127 D3
Netley Court SO31 .... 127 D3
Netley Firs Cl SO19 .... 104 C3
Netley Firs Rd SO30 .... 105 D3
Netley Hill Est SO19 .... 104 C2
Netley Lodge Cl SO31 .... 127 E3
Netley Marsh CE Inf Sch
SO40 .... 100 A4
Netley **21** Portsmouth PO5 .. 182 B1
Titchfield PO14 .... 129 E1
Netley Sta SO31 .... 127 E3
Netley Terr **20** PO5 .... 182 B1
Nettlecombe Ave PO4 .... 182 C1
Nettlestone SO31 .... 127 E4
Nettlestone Rd PO4 .... 183 D1
Nettleton Cl BH17 .... 202 C4
Netton Cl SP5 .... 22 A4
Netton St SP5 .... 22 B4
Neva Rd SO18 .... 103 F4
Nevil Shute Rd PO3 .... 158 A2
Neville Ave PO16 .... 156 B3
Neville Ct PO12 .... 181 D2
Neville Gdns PO10 .... 136 C2
Neville Lovett Com Sch PO14 154 C4
Neville Rd PO3 .... 183 D4
New Borough Rd BH21 .... 163 E2
New Brighton Rd PO10 .... 136 C1
New Cliff House SO19 .... 103 F1
New Cliffe Gdns SO30 .... 105 D3
New Coll (Univ of
Southampton) SO15 .... 102 C4
New Cotts Ashurst SO40 .... 123 F4
Boldre SO41 .... 199 D3
Exbury SO45 .... 177 D3
Fareham PO16 .... 155 D4
Ferndown BH21 .... 164 C1
Nursling SO16 .... 77 E1
New Ct BH24 .... 140 C4
New Cut PO11 .... 159 F2
New Down La Cosham PO6 .... 134 A1
Southwick PO7 .... 134 A1
New Fields Bsns Pk BH17 .... 202 B4
New Forest Dr SO42 .... 145 E1
New Forest Ent Ctr SO40 .... 100 C3
New Harbour Rd BH15 .... 202 A1
New Harbour Rd S BH15 .... 213 D4
New Harbour Rd W BH15 .... 202 A1
New Inn Cotts SO42 .... 175 E3
New Inn La Cadnam SO40 .... 99 D3
East Boldre SO42 .... 175 E3
New Inn Rd SO40 .... 99 D4
New La Havant PO9 .... 136 A2
Milford on Sea SO41 .... 211 F2
New Milton BH25 .... 194 C3
New Marsh House SO45 .... 126 A2
New Merrifield BH21 .... 163 F4
New Milton Inf Sch BH25 .... 195 D1
New Milton Jun Sch BH25 .... 195 D1
New Milton Sta BH25 .... 195 D2
New Orchard BH15 .... 202 A1
New Par Bournemouth BH10 .. 189 F2
Portchester PO16 .... 156 B4
New Park Rd BH6 .... 206 B2
New Quay Rd BH15 .... 202 A1
New Rd Ashurst SO40 .... 100 B1
Bishop's Waltham SO32 .... 59 E1
Blackfield SO45 .... 150 C1
Bournemouth BH10 .... 189 F3
Clanfield PO8 .... 88 B3
Colden Common SO21 .... 31 F1

New Rd Continued
Fair Oak SO50 .... 57 D1
Fareham PO16 .... 131 D1
Ferndown BH22 .... 165 F2
Havant PO9 .... 135 F1
Horndean PO8 .... 111 F3
Hythe SO45 .... 126 A2
Ibsley BH24 .... 117 D4
Landford SP5 .... 49 F1
Littleton SO22 1
Locks Heath SO31 .... 152 C4
Meonstoke SO32 .... 61 E2
Michelmersh SO51 .... 27 E4
Milford on Sea SO41 .... 212 A2
Netley SO31 .... 127 D3
Poole BH15 .... 203 E2
Portsmouth PO2 .... 182 C4
Ringwood BH24 .... 141 D2
Rockbourne SP6 .... 44 C1
Romsey SO51 .... 53 D4
Southampton SO14 .... 103 D3
Southbourne PO10 .... 161 F4
Swanmore SO32 .... 84 A3
Swanwick SO31 .... 128 C4
Westbourne PO10 .... 137 D2
Woodlands BH21 .... 114 A3
New Rd E PO2 .... 182 C4
New St Lymington SO41 .... 197 F2
9 Poole BH15 .... 202 A1
Ringwood BH24 .... 141 D3
New Street Mews SO41 .... 197 F2
New Town SO16 .... 156 B4
New Valley Rd SO41 .... 211 E3
Newbarn La PO10, PO18 .... 137 F4
Newbarn Rd PO9 .... 135 E2
Newbolt Cl PO8 .... 111 F2
Newbolt Rd **13** Cosham PO6 .. 133 D1
Portchester PO6 .... 132 C1
Newbridge BH23 .... 127 E3
Newbridge Jun Sch PO1 .... 182 C4
Newbridge Rd SO40 .... 75 D1
Newbridge Way SO41 .... 197 F1
Newbroke Rd PO13 .... 180 C4
Newburgh St SO23 .... 10 C4
Newbury Cl SO50 .... 57 D1
Newbury Dr BH10 .... 189 E1
Newbury Rd SO15 .... 78 B1
Newcastle Ct PO13 .... 180 B3
Newcombe Rd
Bournemouth BH6 .... 206 C3
Southampton SO15 .... 102 C3
West Moors BH22 .... 138 B1
Newcome Rd PO1 .... 182 C3
Newcomen Ct **8** PO2 .... 157 E1
Newcomen Rd PO2 .... 157 E1
Newcroft Gdns BH23 .... 207 D4
Newenham Rd SO41 .... 197 F1
Newfield Rd GU33 .... 21 D3
Newfoundland Dr BH15 .... 202 B1
Newgate La Fareham PO14 .. 155 D2
Gosport PO14 .... 155 D2
Stubbington PO14 .... 155 D3
Newgate Lane Ind Est PO14 .. 155 D3
Newland Ave PO12 .... 181 D2
Newlands PO15 .... 130 B1
Newlands Ave SO15 .... 102 B4
Newlands Cl SO45 .... 150 C1
Newlands Copse SO45 .... 150 C1
Newlands Inf Sch SO16 .... 77 F1
Newlands Jun Sch SO16 .... 77 F1
Newlands Manor SO41 .... 211 E4
Newlands Rd
Bournemouth BH7 .... 206 A3
Christchurch BH23 .... 207 F4
Fawley SO45 .... 150 C1
New Milton BH25 .... 195 D1
Waterlooville PO7 .... 134 B3
Newlands The **2** SO17 .... 79 E1
Newlands Way BH18 .... 186 B2
Newlease Rd PO7 .... 134 C3
Newlyn Way Poole BH12 .... 203 F4
Portsmouth PO6 .... 157 D4
Newlyn Wlk SO51 .... 28 A1
Newman St SO16 .... 102 A4
Newman's La BH22 .... 138 B2
Newmans Cl BH22 .... 138 C3
Newmans Hill Shedfield PO17 .. 84 B1
Swanmore PO17 .... 84 B1
Newmarket Cl SO50 .... 81 E4
Newmer Ct PO9 .... 135 E3
Newmorton Rd BH9 .... 190 A2
Newney Cl PO12 .... 157 F2
Newnham Ct **40** PO9 .... 136 A3
Newport Cl SO53 .... 55 D2
Newport La SO51 .... 28 B3
Newport Rd PO12 .... 180 C3
Newstead Rd BH6 .... 206 B2
Newton Bglws SP5 .... 24 A2
Newton CE Prim Sch PO12 .. 181 E3
Newton Cl Stubbington PO14 .. 154 B2
Whiteparish SP5 .... 24 A2
Newton La Romsey SO51 .... 52 C3
Whiteparish SP5 .... 24 A2
Newton Morrell BH14 .... 203 E2
Newton Pl PO13 .... 179 F2
Newton Rd
Barton on Sea BH25 .... 210 A4
Poole BH13 .... 214 C4
Southampton SO18 .... 79 F1
Twyford SO21 .... 32 A4
Newtown Bsns Ctr BH12 .... 203 D4
Newtown Cl SO31 .... 128 B1
Newtown La
Corfe Mullen BH21 .... 186 A4
South Hayling PO11 .... 184 C2
Verwood BH31 .... 115 D3

Newtown Rd Eastleigh SO50 .. 56 A2
Locks Heath SO31 .... 152 B4
Sherfield English SO51 .... 26 A2
Southampton SO19 .... 104 A1
Verwood BH31 .... 115 D3
Newtown Soberton Inf Sch
PO17 .... 109 E3
Nichol Rd SO53 .... 30 B1
Nicholas Cl BH23 .... 194 A1
Nicholas Cres PO15 .... 130 C1
Nicholas Ct
10 Lee-on-the-Solent PO13 .. 179 F1
South Hayling PO11 .... 184 C1
Nicholas Gdns BH10 .... 189 E1
Nicholas Rd SO45 .... 177 F4
Nichole Ct BH12 .... 203 D4
Nicholl Pl PO13 .... 155 E1
Nichols Rd SO14 .... 103 D3
Nicholson Cl BH17 .... 202 C4
Nicholson Gdns **38** PO1 .... 182 B3
Nicholson Way PO9 .... 135 F2
Nicholson Wlk SO16 .... 77 E3
Nickel Cl SO23 .... 11 D4
Nickel St PO5 .... 182 A2
Nickleby Gdns SO40 .... 100 A4
Nickleby House **10** PO1 .. 182 B4
Nickleby Rd PO8 .... 88 A3
Nickson Cl SO53 .... 55 D4
Nightingale Ave SO50 .... 55 E1
Nightingale Cl
Bursledon SO31 .... 127 F4
Gosport PO12 .... 180 C3
Romsey SO51 .... 53 D4
Rowland's Castle PO9 .... 113 D1
Verwood BH31 .... 115 D3
West Wellow SO51 .... 50 B2
Winchester SO22 .... 10 B3
Nightingale Cres SO32 .... 107 F4
Nightingale Ct SO16 .... 78 A2
Nightingale Dr SO40 .... 100 B4
Nightingale Gr SO15 .... 102 B4
Nightingale House SO51 .... 53 D4
Nightingale La BH15 .... 202 B1
Nightingale Mews
Locks Heath SO31 .... 129 D2
Netley SO31 .... 127 E3
Nightingale Pk PO9 .... 136 A1
Nightingale Prim Sch SO50 .. 55 E1
Nightingale Rd
Petersfield GU32 .... 40 B1
Portsmouth PO5 .... 182 A1
Southampton SO15 .... 102 B4
Nightingale Wlk SO31 .... 127 D3
Nightingdale Ct **9** SO51 .. 102 B3
Nightjar Cl Broadstone BH17 .. 201 F4
Horndean PO8 .... 112 A3
Nile Rd SO17 .... 79 D1
Nile St PO10 .... 160 C4
Nimrod Dr PO13 .... 180 B3
Nine Acres GU32 .... 20 A1
Nine Elms La PO16 .... 131 F2
Ninian Cl SO50 .... 57 D1
Ninian Park Rd PO3 .... 158 A1
Niton Cl PO13 .... 155 E1
Noads Cl SO45 .... 125 F1
Noads Way SO45 .... 125 F1
Noadswood Sec Sch SO45 .... 125 F1
Nobbs La PO1 .... 182 A2
Nobes Ave PO13 .... 155 E2
Nobes Cl PO13 .... 155 E1
Noble Cl BH11 .... 188 C1
Noble Rd SO30 .... 105 D4
Nobs Crook SO21 .... 57 D4
Noel Cl SO42 .... 146 A1
Noel Rd BH10 .... 189 D1
Noel The BH25 .... 195 E2
Nomansland & Hamptworth
CE Sch SP5 .... 73 E4
Nook The Eastleigh SO50 .... 56 A3
Gosport PO12 .... 155 F1
Noon Gdns BH31 .... 115 D3
Noon Hill Dr BH31 .... 115 D3
Noon Hill Rd BH31 .... 115 D3
Norbury Cl SO53 .... 55 D4
Norbury Gdns SO31 .... 127 D1
Norcliffe Cl BH11 .... 189 D2
Norcliffe Rd SO17 .... 103 D4
Norcroft Ct SO15 .... 78 B1
Nordik Gdns SO30 .... 105 D3
Nore Cres PO10 .... 136 B1
Nore Farm Ave PO10 .... 136 B1
Noreuil Rd GU32 .... 40 B2
Norfolk Ave BH23 .... 191 F1
Norfolk Cres PO11 .... 184 C1
Norfolk Cl SO53 .... 55 E2
Norfolk House PO11 .... 136 A1
Norfolk Mews PO11 .... 184 C1
Norfolk Rd Gosport PO12 .... 180 C4
Southampton SO15 .... 102 B4
Norfolk St PO5 .... 182 B2
Norgett Way PO16 .... 156 A4
Norham Ave SO16 .... 78 B1
Norham Cl SO16 .... 78 B1
Norland Rd **5** PO4 .... 182 C2
Norlands Dr SO21 .... 31 E2
Norley Cl PO9 .... 135 F2
Norleywood BH23 .... 208 C4
Norleywood Rd SO41 .... 198 C4
Norman Ave BH12 .... 204 A3
Norman Ct PO16 .... 156 B3
Norman Ct **6** PO4 .... 182 C1
Norman Gdns
Hedge End SO30 .... 105 D3
Poole BH12 .... 204 A3
Norman House **16** SO14 .... 103 E3

Norman Rd Blackfield SO45 .... 177 F4
  Gosport PO12 .... 181 D3
  Portsmouth PO4 .... 182 C2
  South Hayling PO11 .... 185 D1
  Southampton SO15 .... 102 B3
  Winchester SO23 .... 10 C3
Norman Way PO9 .... 135 E1
Normandy Cl Rownhams SO16 ...... 77 F3
  Sway SO41 .... 172 A1
Normandy Ct
  Locks Heath SO31 .... 128 B1
  Wickham PO17 .... 108 A2
Normandy Dr BH23 .... 207 E4
Normandy Gdns PO12 .... 180 C2
Normandy House SO51 .... 53 D4
Normandy La SO41 .... 197 F1
Normandy Rd PO2 .... 157 F2
Normandy Way
  Fordingbridge SP6 .... 69 F1
  Hamworthy BH15 .... 201 E1
  Marchwood SO40 .... 102 A1
Normanhurst Ave BH8 .... 190 C1
Normans SO22 .... 10 C3
Normanton Cl BH23 .... 191 F1
  St Leonards BH24 .... 139 F2
Norris Cl Romsey SO51 .... 28 B1
  St Leonards BH24 .... 139 F2
Norris Gdns Havant PO9 .... 160 A4
  New Milton BH25 .... 195 D1
Norris Hill SO18 .... 79 F1
Norrish Rd BH12 .... 203 E3
Norset Rd PO15 .... 130 B1
North Ave
  Bournemouth BH10 .... 189 E3
  Portsmouth PO2 .... 157 F3
North Baddesley
  Inf Sch SO52 .... 54 A2
North Baddesley
  Jun Sch SO52 .... 54 A2
North Battery Rd PO2 .... 157 D1
North Bay PO10 .... 161 D2
North Block SO15 .... 102 B3
North Cl Gosport PO12 .... 180 C2
  Havant PO9 .... 160 A4
  Lymington SO41 .... 197 F2
  Romsey SO51 .... 28 B1
North Common La
  Landford SP5 .... 49 D3
  Sway SO41 .... 196 C4
North Cres PO11 .... 185 D2
North Cross St PO12 .... 181 E2
North Ct PO1 .... 182 C4
North Dr Littleton SO22 .... 1 A3
  New Milton BH25 .... 170 C1
North East Cl SO19 .... 104 B3
North East Rd SO19 .... 104 A2
North End Ave PO2 .... 157 E1
North End Cl SO53 .... 55 E2
North End Farm Cotts SO24 ... 14 B4
North End Gr PO2 .... 157 E1
North End La SP6, BH24 .... 93 E2
North Fields Cotts SO21 .... 32 A4
North Front SO14 .... 103 D3
North Greenlands SO41 .... 197 E1
North Head SO41 .... 211 D3
North Hill PO16 .... 131 D2
North Hill Cl SO22 .... 1 C1
North Hill Ct SO22 .... 1 C1
North La Beaulieu SO42 .... 148 C3
  Buriton GU31 .... 65 F3
  Clanfield PO8 .... 88 B4
  East Meon PO8 .... 64 B1
  Nomansland SP5 .... 73 E4
  West Tytherley SP5 .... 4 A4
North Lodge Rd BH14 .... 203 F2
North Millers Dale SO53 .... 55 D4
North Path PO13 .... 180 B3
North Poulner Rd BH24 .... 117 D1
North Rd Bournemouth BH7 .... 205 F3
  Brockenhurst SO42 .... 146 A1
  Horndean PO8 .... 88 B1
  Hythe SO45 .... 125 F1
  Kings Worthy SO23 .... 2 A4
  Petersfield GU32 .... 40 C2
  Poole BH14 .... 203 D2
  Southampton SO17 .... 103 E4
North Rd E PO17 .... 133 D3
North Shore Rd PO11 .... 184 B2
North Solent Nature Reserve
  SO45 .... 178 A4
North St Emsworth PO10 .... 136 C1
  Gosport PO12 .... 181 E2
  Havant PO9 .... 135 F1
  Havant, Bedhampton PO9 .... 135 E1
  Lymington SO41 .... 197 E1
  Poole BH15 .... 202 B1
  Portsmouth PO1 .... 182 A3
  Portsmouth PO1 .... 182 B3
  Westbourne PO10 .... 137 D2
North Street Arc PO9 .... 135 F1
North Stroud La GU32 .... 39 F2
North Town SP5 .... 32 A4
North Trestle Rd SO45 .... 151 E3
North View SO22 .... 10 C4
North Wallington PO16 .... 131 E1
North Walls SO23 .... 11 D4
North Way Gosport PO13 .... 155 E2
  Havant PO9 .... 135 F1
  Locks Heath SO31 .... 129 F2
North Weirs SO42 .... 145 E1
Northam Bsns Ctr SO14 ...... 103 E3
Northam Prim Sch SO14 .... 103 D3
Northam Rd SO14 .... 103 D3
Northam St PO1 .... 182 B3
Northampton La SO45 .... 177 F4
Northarbour Rd PO6 .... 157 E4

Northarbour Spur PO6 .... 157 E4
Northbourne Ave BH10 .... 189 E3
Northbourne Cl SO45 .... 126 A1
Northbourne Gdns BH10 .... 189 F3
Northbourne Pl BH10 .... 189 E3
Northbourne Rdbt BH10 .... 189 F3
Northbrook Ave SO23 .... 11 E4
Northbrook Cl PO1 .... 182 B4
Northbrook Ct SO23 .... 11 E4
Northbrook Ind Est SO16 ...... 78 B1
Northbrook Rd
  Broadstone BH18 .... 187 D1
  Southampton SO14 .... 103 D3
Northcote Rd
  Bournemouth BH1 .... 205 D2
  Portsmouth PO4 .... 182 C2
  Southampton SO17 .... 79 E1
Northcott Cl PO12 .... 180 C2
Northcroft Rd PO12 .... 180 C3
Northdene Rd SO53 .... 55 E3
Northend La SO32 .... 61 D1
Northern Access Rd SO15 ...... 151 E1
Northern Anchorage SO19 ...... 103 E2
Northern Bldgs PO6 .... 157 F4
Northern Inf Sch PO16 .... 132 B1
Northern Jun Sch PO16 .... 132 B1
Northern Par PO2 .... 157 F2
Northern Parade Inf Sch PO2 157 F2
Northern Parade Mid
  Sch PO2 .... 157 F2
Northern Rd Cosham PO6 ...... 157 F4
  Fawley SO45 .... 151 F1
Northerwood Ave SO43 .... 121 F3
Northerwood Cl SO52 .... 53 F2
Northerwood House SO43 ...... 121 F3
Northey Rd BH6 .... 206 C3
Northfield Ave PO14 .... 154 C4
Northfield Cl
  Bishop's Waltham SO32 .... 59 D1
  Horndean PO8 .... 88 B1
Northfield Park PO16 .... 132 A1
Northfield Rd
  Milford on Sea SO41 .... 211 F2
  Ringwood BH24 .... 117 D1
  Southampton SO18 .... 79 F1
Northfields Farm La PO17 ...... 108 A3
Northgate Ave PO2 .... 182 C4
Northlands Cl SO40 .... 100 B4
Northlands Dr SO23 .... 2 A1
Northlands Gdns SO15 .... 102 C4
Northlands Rd Eastleigh SO50 .... 56 A2
  Romsey SO51 .... 53 E3
  Southampton SO15, SO40 ...... 102 C4
  Totton SO40 .... 100 C4
Northleigh Cnr SO18 .... 79 F3
Northleigh La BH21 .... 163 F3
Northmead Dr BH17 .... 201 F4
Northmere Dr BH12 .... 203 F4
Northmere Rd BH12 .... 203 F4
Northmore Cl SO31 .... 129 D3
Northmore Rd SO31 .... 129 D3
Northney La PO11 .... 160 B2
Northney Rd PO11 .... 160 A4
Northolt Gdns SO16 .... 78 A3
Northover Rd
  Lymington SO41 .... 197 D3
  Portsmouth PO3 .... 183 D4
Northover La SO41 .... 195 F4
Northumberland Ct BH24 ...... 140 C4
Northumberland Rd
  Portsmouth PO1 .... 182 C3
  Southampton SO14 .... 103 D3
Northways PO14 .... 179 E3
Northwood Cl SO23 .... 79 D3
Northwood La PO11 .... 160 A1
Northwood Rd PO2 .... 157 F3
Northwood Sq PO16 .... 131 D1
Nortoft Rd BH8 .... 205 D3
Norton Cl Christchurch BH23 ... 207 E4
  Southampton SO19 .... 103 F2
  Southwick PO17 .... 132 C3
  Waterlooville PO7 .... 134 B4
Norton Dr PO16 .... 131 D2
Norton Rd Bournemouth BH9 ... 204 C4
  Southwick PO17 .... 132 C3
Norton Welch Cl SO52 .... 54 A2
Norway Rd PO3 .... 158 A2
Norwich Ave BH2 .... 204 B2
Norwich Ave W BH2 .... 204 B2
Norwich Cl SO31 .... 128 C2
Norwich Ct BH2 .... 204 C2
Norwich Mansions BH2 ...... 204 B2
Norwich Pl PO13 .... 179 F2
Norwich Rd
  Bournemouth BH2 .... 204 C2
  Cosham PO6 .... 133 E1
  Southampton SO18 .... 79 F1
Norwood Cty Prim Sch SO50 .... 56 B1
Norwood Pl BH5 .... 206 A3
Nottingham Pl PO13 .... 179 F2
Nouale La BH24 .... 141 E4
Novello Gdns PO7 .... 134 C3
Noyce Dr SO50 .... 57 E1
Noyce Gdns BH8 .... 191 D1
Nuffield Hospl BH5 .... 205 F2
Nuffield Ind Est BH17 .... 202 B4
Nuffield Rd BH17 .... 202 B4
Nugent Rd BH6 .... 207 D2
Nunns Park SP5 .... 24 A1
Nuns Rd SO23 .... 2 A1
Nurse's Path SO21 .... 32 A3
Nursery Cl Emsworth PO10 ...... 136 C2
  Gosport PO13 .... 155 D2
Nursery Field GU33 .... 20 C1
Nursery Gdns
  Chandler's Ford SO53 .... 55 E2
  Romsey SO51 .... 53 D4

Nursery Gdns Continued
  Southampton SO19 .... 104 A3
  Waterlooville PO8 .... 112 A3
  Winchester SO22 .... 10 B4
Nursery Gr SO30 .... 105 E3
Nursery La PO14 .... 179 E3
Nursery Rd
  Bournemouth BH9 .... 190 A2
  Havant PO9 .... 135 E1
  Ringwood BH24 .... 141 D3
  Southampton SO18 .... 79 E1
Nursling CE Prim Sch SO16 ...... 77 E3
Nursling Cres PO9 .... 136 A3
Nursling Gr BH8 .... 190 B1
Nursling Ind Est SO16 .... 77 D2
Nursling St SO16 .... 77 E3
Nutash PO14 .... 129 E2
Nutbeem Rd SO50 .... 56 A1
Nutbourne House PO6 .... 158 B4
Nutbourne Rd Cosham PO6 ...... 158 B4
  South Hayling PO11 .... 185 F1
Nutburn Rd SO52 .... 54 A3
Nutfield Ct SO16 .... 77 F2
Nutfield Pl PO1 .... 182 B3
Nutfield Rd SO16 .... 77 F3
Nuthatch Cl Broadstone BH17 ... 201 F4
  Ferndown BH22 .... 165 D4
  Rowland's Castle PO9 .... 113 C3
Nutley Cl BH11 .... 188 C2
Nutley Rd PO9 .... 135 E3
Nutley Way BH11 .... 188 C2
Nutsey Ave SO40 .... 76 B1
Nutsey Cl SO40 .... 76 C2
Nutsey La SO40 .... 76 C1
Nutshalling Ave SO16 .... 77 F3
Nutshalling Cl SO40 .... 76 B1
Nutwick Rd PO9 .... 136 A2
Nutwood Way SO40 .... 76 C1
Nyewood Ave PO16 .... 132 B1
Nyria Way PO12 .... 181 E2

O' Jays Ind Pk PO3 .... 158 A1
O'Connell Rd SO50 .... 55 F1
Oak Ave BH23 .... 206 B4
Oak Cl Corfe Mullen BH21 ...... 186 B3
  Ferndown BH22 .... 165 F1
  Hythe SO45 .... 125 F1
  Lyndhurst SO43 .... 121 F2
  Southampton SO15 .... 101 E4
  Upham SO32 .... 58 C3
  Waterlooville PO8 .... 111 F1
Oak Coppice Cl SO50 .... 57 D1
Oak Ct Fareham PO15 .... 130 B1
  Lymington SO41 .... 197 E1
Oak Dr SO50 .... 57 E1
Oak Gdns SO41 .... 211 D4
Oak Green Way SO18 .... 104 A4
Oak La BH24 .... 141 D4
Oak Lodge PO2 .... 157 E1
Oak Lodge Specl Sch SO45 .... 125 E2
Oak Mews BH12 .... 203 E3
Oak Park Dr PO9 .... 136 A2
Oak Rd Alderholt SP6 .... 92 C3
  Bishop's Waltham SO32 .... 83 F4
  Bournemouth BH8 .... 205 E3
  Bursledon SO31 .... 127 F4
  Clanfield PO8 .... 88 B3
Oak St PO12 .... 181 E2
Oak Tree Cl SO21 .... 56 C4
Oak Tree Dr Emsworth PO10 .... 136 C2
  Liss GU33 .... 21 D2
Oak Tree Gdns SO30 .... 105 D3
Oak Tree Rd SO18 .... 79 F1
Oak Tree Way SO50 .... 56 A3
Oak Vale SO30 .... 80 A2
Oak Wlk SO50 .... 57 E1
Oakapple Gdns PO6 .... 158 C4
Oakbank Rd Bishopstoke SO50 .... 56 B2
  Southampton SO19 .... 103 E2
Oakcroft La PO14 .... 154 B3
Oakdale Mid Sch BH15 .... 202 B3
Oakdale Rd BH15 .... 202 C3
Oakdale South Road
  Mid Sch BH15 .... 202 B3
Oakdene Gosport PO13 .... 155 E1
  Southampton SO17 .... 79 D1
  Totton SO40 .... 100 B4
Oakdene Cl BH21 .... 163 E3
Oakdene Gdns SO50 .... 57 E1
Oakdown Rd PO14 .... 154 B2
Oakenbrow Hythe SO45 .... 125 E1
  Sway SO41 .... 172 A1
Oakes The PO14 .... 154 A2
Oakfield Ct PO9 .... 136 A3
Oakfield Prim Sch SO40 .... 76 C1
Oakfield Rd Cadnam SO40 ...... 99 D4
  Poole BH15 .... 202 B3
  Totton SO40 .... 100 C4
Oakfields SO50 .... 56 A4
Oakford Ct BH8 .... 190 B2
Oakgrove Gdns SO50 .... 56 C1
Oakgrove Rd SO50 .... 56 C1
Oakham Grange BH22 .... 165 F3
Oakhill SO31 .... 105 D1
Oakhill Cl Bursledon SO31 ...... 105 D1
  Chandler's Ford SO53 .... 55 F3
Oakhill Ct SO53 .... 55 F3
Oakhill Terr SO31 .... 105 D1
Oakhurst Netley SO31 .... 127 E3
  West Moors BH22 .... 138 C1
Oakhurst Dr PO7 .... 135 D4
Oakhurst Gdns PO7 .... 134 A1
Oakhurst La BH22 .... 138 C1

Oakhurst Rd
  Southampton SO17 .... 79 D2
  West Moors BH22 .... 138 C1
Oakhurst Way SO31 .... 127 E3
Oakland Dr SO40 .... 101 F1
Oakland Wlk SO41 .... 165 F1
Oaklands Lymington SO41 ...... 197 F1
  Waterlooville PO7 .... 135 D3
Oaklands Ave SO40 .... 100 C4
Oaklands Cl Fordingbridge SP6 ... 69 F1
  Verwood BH31 .... 114 C3
  Winchester SO22, SO23 .... 10 B3
Oaklands Com Sch SO16 ...... 77 F3
Oaklands Gdns PO14 .... 129 E1
Oaklands Gr PO8 .... 111 F2
Oaklands House PO6 .... 132 C1
Oaklands RC Sec Sch PO7 ...... 134 C3
Oaklands The SO53 .... 55 E2
Oaklands Way Hythe SO45 ...... 125 E1
  Southampton SO16 .... 78 C2
  Titchfield PO14 .... 129 E1
Oaklea Cl PO7 .... 134 A1
Oakleaf Cl SO40 .... 124 C4
Oakleigh Cres SO40 .... 100 C3
Oakleigh Dr SP5 .... 73 E4
Oakleigh Gdns SO51 .... 53 D4
Oakleigh Way BH23 .... 208 C4
Oakley Cl SO45 .... 150 B2
Oakley Gdns BH16 .... 201 D4
Oakley Hill SO53 .... 163 E4
Oakley House
  Southampton,
  Banister's Pk SO15 .... 102 C4
  Southampton, Shirley SO16 ... 102 A4
Oakley La BH21 .... 163 F1
Oakley Rd Havant PO9 .... 135 E3
  Mottisfont SO51 .... 5 F2
  Oakley BH21 .... 163 E1
  Southampton SO16 .... 102 A4
Oakley Straight BH21 .... 163 F1
Oakmead Gdns BH11 .... 188 C2
Oakmead Rd BH17 .... 201 F4
Oakmead Sec Sch BH11 ...... 188 C2
Oakmeadow Cl PO10 .... 137 D2
Oakmount Ave
  Chandler's Ford SO53 .... 55 E2
  Southampton SO17 .... 79 D1
  Totton SO40 .... 100 C4
Oakmount Dr PO8 .... 111 F1
Oakmount Mansions SO15 ...... 78 C1
Oakmount Rd SO53 .... 55 F3
Oakridge Rd SO15 .... 101 E4
Oaks Coppice PO8 .... 112 A3
Oaks Dr BH24 .... 139 E2
Oaks The Bursledon SO31 ...... 127 F4
  Southampton SO19 .... 103 F3
  Verwood BH31 .... 114 C4
Oakshott Dr PO9 .... 136 A3
Oakthorn Cl PO13 .... 180 B3
Oaktree Ct Milford on Sea SO41 211 E2
  Southampton SO18 .... 78 C2
Oaktree Cvn Pk SO30 .... 80 B2
Oaktree Par BH23 .... 169 D1
Oakum House PO3 .... 183 D3
Oakville Mansions SO15 ...... 102 C3
Oakwood Ave Havant PO9 ...... 135 D2
  New Milton BH25 .... 195 E2
  Otterbourne SO21 .... 31 E2
Oakwood Cl
  Bournemouth BH9 .... 190 A1
  Chandler's Ford SO53 .... 30 B1
  Locks Heath SO31 .... 152 B4
  Otterbourne SO21 .... 31 E2
  Romsey SO51 .... 28 B1
Oakwood Ct
  Chandler's Ford SO53 .... 30 B1
  New Milton BH25 .... 195 D2
Oakwood Ctr The PO9 .... 136 A2
Oakwood Dr SO16 .... 78 B3
Oakwood House SO21 .... 31 E2
Oakwood Inf Sch SO16 .... 78 A3
Oakwood Jun Sch SO16 .... 78 A3
Oakwood Lodge SO21 .... 31 E2
Oakwood Rd
  Bournemouth BH9 .... 190 A1
  Chandler's Ford SO53 .... 55 E4
  Christchurch BH23 .... 193 F1
  Portsmouth PO2 .... 157 F2
  South Hayling PO11 .... 184 C2
Oakwood Way SO31 .... 128 A2
Oasis Mews BH16 .... 201 D4
Oasis The BH12 .... 204 A4
Oates Rd BH9 .... 189 F1
Oatfield Gdns SO40 .... 76 B1
Oatlands SO51 .... 52 C4
Oatlands Cl SO32 .... 81 E1
Oatlands Rd SO32 .... 81 F1
Oban Rd BH3 .... 204 C4
Obelisk Rd SO19 .... 103 E1
Obelisk Rd SO19 .... 103 E1
Ober Rd SO42 .... 145 F1
Oberfield Rd SO42 .... 145 E1
Oberland Ct SO41 .... 197 E2
Oberon Cl PO7 .... 135 D4
Occupation La PO14 .... 153 F4
Ocean Cl PO15 .... 130 B1
Ocean Ct PO11 .... 184 C2
Ocean Heights BH5 .... 205 F2
Ocean Pk PO3 .... 158 A1
Ocean Rd Gosport PO14 .... 154 C3
  Southampton SO14 .... 103 D1
Ocean Village SO14 .... 103 D1
Ocean Way SO14 .... 103 D1
Ockendon Cl PO5 .... 182 B2
Ocknell Gr SO45 .... 125 E2

Octavia Hill SO22 .... 10 B
Octavia Rd SO18 .... 79 F
Octavius Ct PO7 .... 112 A
Odell Cl PO13 .... 130 C
Odeon Bldgs PO6 .... 157 F
Odiham Cl
  Chandler's Ford SO53 .... 55 D
  Southampton SO16 .... 77 F
Oelander Cl SO31 .... 129 C
Oglander Rd SO23 .... 2 A
Ogle Rd SO14 .... 102 C
Okeford Rd BH18 .... 187 D
Okement Cl SO18 .... 80 A
Old Agwi Rd SO45 .... 151 E
Old Bakery Ct BH15 .... 202 B
Old Barn Cl Christchurch BH23 .. 191 E
  Ringwood BH24 .... 141 E
Old Barn Cres PO7 .... 86 B
Old Barn Farm Rd BH21 ...... 139 D
Old Barn Gdns PO8 .... 111 F
Old Barn Rd BH23 .... 191 E
Old Bound Rd BH16 .... 201 E
Old Brickyard Rd SP6 .... 69 D
Old Bridge Cl SO31 .... 128 A
Old Bridge House Rd SO31 ... 128 A
Old Bridge Rd
  Bournemouth BH6 .... 206 B
  Portsmouth PO4 .... 182 C
Old Canal PO4 .... 183 D
Old Christchurch La BH1 ...... 204 C
Old Christchurch Rd
  Bournemouth BH1, BH2 ...... 204 C
  Hordle SO41 .... 196 B
Old Coastguard Rd BH13 ...... 214 A
Old Commercial Rd PO1 ...... 182 B
Old Common SO31 .... 129 D
Old Common Gdns SO31 ...... 129 D
Old Copse Rd PO9 .... 136 A
Old Cottage Cl SO51 .... 50 C
Old Courts The SO16 .... 79 D
Old Cracknore Ct SO40 .... 102 A
Old Down La GU32 .... 18 A
Old Farm Cl BH24 .... 117 E
Old Farm Copse SO51 .... 50 C
Old Farm Dr SO18 .... 79 F
Old Farm La Stubbington PO14 . 179 E
  Westbourne PO10 .... 137 E
Old Farm Rd BH15 .... 202 C
Old Farm Way PO6 .... 158 C
Old Farm Wlk SO41 .... 197 E
Old Farmhouse Mews SO41 ... 197 E
Old Forge Cl SP6 .... 92 C
Old Forge Ct SO41 .... 197 E
Old Forge Rd BH21 .... 164 C
Old Forge The SO32 .... 107 E
Old Garden Cl SO31 .... 129 E
Old Gdns SO22 .... 1 C
Old Gosport Rd PO16 .... 155 D
Old Granary The SP5 .... 46 C
Old Highway Mews BH21 ...... 163 E
Old Hillside Rd SO22 .... 1 B
Old Ivy La SO18 .... 80 A
Old Kennels Cl SO22 .... 10 A
Old Kennels La SO22 .... 10 A
Old Kiln Rd Hamworthy BH16 ... 201 E
  Upton BH16 .... 201 E
Old Litten La GU32 .... 19 E
Old London Rd PO2 .... 157 F
Old Lyndhurst Rd SO40 .... 98 C
Old Magazine Cl SO40 .... 101 F
Old Maltings The SO41 .... 197 E
Old Manor Cl BH21 .... 163 E
Old Manor Farm PO9 .... 135 D
Old Manor Way PO6 .... 158 A
Old Market Rd BH21 .... 186 A
Old Mill House BH24 .... 140 C
Old Mill La Hambledon PO8 ...... 87 E
  Petersfield GU31 .... 41 D
Old Mill Way SO16 .... 78 A
Old Milton Gn BH25 .... 194 C
Old Milton Rd BH25 .... 195 D
Old Orchard BH15 .... 202 B
Old Orchards SO41 .... 197 F
Old Parsonage Ct SO21 .... 31 E
Old Pines Cl BH22 .... 165 F
Old Priory Cl SO31 .... 128 A
Old Priory Rd BH6 .... 206 C
Old Rd Gosport PO12 .... 181 E
  Romsey SO51 .... 53 D
  Southampton SO14 .... 103 D
  Wimborne Minster BH21 ...... 163 D
Old Rectory Cl
  Corfe Mullen BH21 .... 186 B
  Westbourne PO10 .... 137 D
Old Rectory Ct SO40 .... 101 D
Old Rectory Gdns SO21 .... 2 B
Old Rectory La SO21 .... 32 A
Old Rectory Rd PO6 .... 158 C
Old Redbridge Rd SO15 .... 101 E
Old Reservoir Rd PO6 .... 158 B
Old River PO7 .... 110 C
Old Road The PO6 .... 157 F
Old Romsey Rd SO40 .... 98 C
Old Rope Wlk The BH15 ...... 201 F
Old Ropewalk BH15 .... 202 A
Old Salisbury La SO51 .... 27 D
Old Salisbury Rd SO51 .... 75 F
Old School Cl Ferndown BH22 .. 165 E
  Netley SO31 .... 127 E
  Poole BH14 .... 203 D
Old School Dr PO11 .... 185 D
Old School Gdns SO30 .... 80 C
Old School Rd GU33 .... 20 C
Old School The SO32 .... 83 D
Old Shamblehurst La SO30 ...... 81 E
Old Spring La SO32 .... 84 A
Old St PO14 .... 154 A
Old St John's Mews BH9 ...... 189 F

ld Stacks Gdns BH24 141 E3
ld Star Pl 3 PO1 182 A3
ld Station App SO23 11 D4
ld Swanwick La SO31 128 B4
ld Timbers PO11 184 C2
ld Town Mews 5 BH15 202 B1
ld Turnpike PO16 131 D2
ld Turnpike Bsns Pk PO16 131 D1
ld Van Diemans Rd PO7 134 B3
ld Vicarage Cl BH10 189 F3
ld Vicarage La SO41 196 B4
ld Vineries The SP6 69 E1
ld Wareham Rd
Poole BH12 203 D4
Upton BH16 186 A1
ld Well Cl The SO19 104 B2
ld Winchester Hill La
Warnford SO32, GU32 37 D1
West Meon GU32 37 E1
ld Wymering La PO6 157 F4
ldbarn Cl SO40 76 B1
ldbury Ct SO16 77 E1
ldbury House 49 PO5 182 B2
ldbury Way PO14 154 B4
ldenburg SO31 129 D4
ldgate Gdns 8 PO2 157 F2
linda St PO1 182 C3
live Cres PO16 156 B3
live Rd SO16 78 A2
liver Rd Lymington SO41 197 E2
Portsmouth PO4 183 D2
Southampton SO18 79 E2
liver's Battery Cres SO22 10 A2
liver's Battery Gdns SO22 10 A2
liver's Battery Rd N SO22 10 A3
liver's Battery Rd S SO22 10 A2
livers Cl SO40 100 A4
livers Rd BH21 164 A3
livers Way BH21 164 A3
livia Cl PO7 112 A1
lympic Way SO50 57 D1
mdurman Ct 2 SO17 79 D1
mdurman Rd SO17 79 D1
mega House 21 PO1 182 B3
mega St PO1 182 B3
nibury Cl SO18 80 A1
nibury Rd SO18 80 A1
nslow Gdns BH21 163 E3
nslow House BH21 163 E3
nslow Rd Portsmouth PO5 182 B1
Southampton SO14 103 D3
phir Gdns 1 BH8 205 E3
phir Rd Bournemouth BH8 205 D3
Portsmouth PO2 157 F2
racle Dr PO7 134 C2
range Gr PO13 155 E1
range Row PO10 160 C4
ratory Gdns BH13 214 C4
rchard Ave
Bishopstoke SO50 56 C1
Poole BH14 202 C1
rchard Bglws PO17 109 D1
rchard Cl Christchurch BH23 207 D3
Colden Common SO21 31 F1
Corfe Mullen BH21 186 B4
Edmondsham BH21 91 D2
Fawley SO45 151 D2
Ferndown BH22 165 F3
Fordingbridge SP6 69 F1
Gosport PO12 156 A1
Horndean PO8 112 B3
North Baddesley SO52 53 F3
Ringwood BH24 141 D4
South Hayling PO11 184 C1
Totton SO40 100 C3
rchard Ct Cadnam SO40 98 C4
Hedge End SO30 105 F4
10 New Milton BH25 195 D2
Verwood BH31 115 D3
rchard Cvn Pk The SO40 99 E3
rchard Gdns SP6 69 F1
rchard Gr New Milton BH25 195 D1
Portchester PO16 156 A4
Waterlooville PO8 111 F2
rchard House 13 SO14 103 D2
rchard Inf Sch SO45 125 F1
rchard Jun Sch SO45 125 F1
rchard La Corfe Mullen BH21 186 B4
Hermitage PO10 161 D4
Romsey SO51 52 C4
Southampton SO14 103 D2
rchard Lea Inf Sch PO15 130 C2
rchard Lea Jun Sch PO15 130 C2
rchard Leigh 6 BH25 195 D1
rchard Mead 5 BH24 141 D4
rchard Mews 2 BH23 207 D3
rchard Mount 6 BH24 141 D4
rchard Pl SO14 103 D2
rchard Rd Fair Oak SO50 57 E1
Gosport PO12 181 E3
Havant PO9 159 F4
Locks Heath SO31 128 C1
Portsmouth PO4 182 C2
Redlynch SP5 47 E3
South Hayling PO11 185 D1
rchard St BH2 204 C2
rchard The
Bournemouth BH11 188 B3
Bransgore BH23 193 E4
Chilworth SO16 54 C1
Cosham PO6 157 F4
Denmead PO7 110 C2
Milford on Sea SO41 211 E2
Southampton SO16 79 D3
rchard Way SO45 125 F1
rchard Wlk
22 Bournemouth BH2 204 C2
Winchester SO22 1 B1
Orchardlea SO32 84 B2
Orchards Way
Southampton SO17 79 D1
West End SO30 80 B1
Orcheston Rd BH8 205 E3
Orchid Way BH23 207 E4
Ordnance Ct PO3 158 A3
Ordnance Rd Gosport PO12 181 E2
Southampton SO15 103 D3
Ordnance Row PO1 182 A3
Ordnance Way SO40 102 A2
Oregon Cl SO19 104 A2
Orestes Gate BH23 208 A3
Orford Cl BH23 191 E2
Orford Ct 16 PO6 157 F4
Oriana Way SO16 77 D2
Oriel Dr PO14 129 D1
Oriel Rd PO2 157 E1
Orient Dr SO22 1 B2
Oriental Terr SO14 103 D2
Orion Cl Southampton SO16 77 F2
Stubbington PO14 179 E3
Orion Ind Ctr SO18 79 F3
Orkney Cl SO16 77 F2
Orkney Rd PO6 133 F1
Ormesby Dr SO53 30 A1
Ormond Cl SO50 57 D1
Ormonde Rd BH13 204 A1
Ormsby Rd PO5 182 B2
Orpen Rd SO19 104 B2
Ormond Cl PO7 134 C3
Orwell Cl SO16 77 F1
Orwell Cres PO14 129 E1
Orwell Rd GU32 40 C1
Osborn Cres PO13 155 D2
Osborn Ct PO3 158 A2
Osborn Mall 6 PO16 131 E1
Osborn Rd PO16 131 D1
Osborn Sq 5 PO16 131 E1
Osborne Cl Netley SO31 127 E3
Waterlooville PO7 135 D4
Osborne Ct
7 Milford on Sea SO41 211 E2
Southampton SO17 79 E1
Osborne Dr SO53 55 F3
Osborne Gdns Fair Oak SO50 57 F1
Southampton SO17 79 E1
Osborne House SO51 50 C2
Osborne Rd
Bournemouth BH9 204 C4
Lee-on-the-Solent PO13 179 F1
Locks Heath SO31 152 B4
New Milton BH25 195 D2
Petersfield GU32 40 C2
Poole BH14 203 D2
Portsmouth PO5 182 B1
Totton SO40 101 D4
Wimborne Minster BH21 163 E2
Osborne Rd N SO17 79 E1
Osborne Rd S Fareham PO16 131 D1
Southampton SO17 103 E4
Osborne View Rd PO14 179 D3
Osbourne House 4 BH25 195 D2
Osbourne Rd PO12 181 E3
Osier Cl PO2 157 E2
Oslands La SO31 128 B4
Oslo Towers 6 SO19 126 C4
Osprey Cl Christchurch BH23 208 A3
Cosham PO6 158 C4
Marchwood SO40 101 F1
Southampton SO16 78 A3
Osprey Ct PO16 155 F4
Osprey Dr PO11 185 D2
Osprey Gdns PO13 179 F1
Osprey Quay PO10 161 D4
Ossemsley Manor House
BH23 194 B3
Ossemsley South Dr BH25 194 C4
Osterley Cl SO30 105 F3
Osterly Rd SO19 103 F3
Oswald Cl BH9 189 F1
Oswald Rd BH9 189 F1
Othello Dr PO7 135 D4
Otter Cl Bishopstoke SO50 57 D1
Gosport PO13 180 B3
Upton BH16 201 D3
Verwood BH31 115 D3
Otter Rd BH15 202 C3
Otterbourne BH2 204 B2
Otterbourne CE Prim Sch
SO21 31 D1
Otterbourne Cres PO9 135 E3
Otterbourne Hill SO21 31 E2
Otterbourne House SO21 31 D1
Otterbourne House Gdns
SO21 31 D1
Otterbourne Rd SO21 31 E3
Otters Wlk BH25 195 E3
Ouse Cl SO53 55 D4
Outer Circ SO16 78 A2
Outlands La SO30 106 B4
Outram Rd PO5 182 B2
Outwick Cross SP6 69 F4
Oval Gdns PO12 180 C2
Oval Rd SO51 5 D1
Oval The GU33 20 C2
Over Links Dr BH14 203 E1
Overbrook SO45 125 F2
Overbrook Way SO52 53 F3
Overbury Rd BH14 203 E2
Overcliff Rise SO16 78 C2
Overcliffe Mansions BH1 205 E2
Overcombe Cl BH17 187 F1
Overdell Ct 25 SO15 102 C4
Overstrand Cres SO41 211 E2
Overton Cres PO9 135 E3
Overton Rd PO10 137 F1
Oviat Cl SO40 100 A4
Ovington Ave BH7 206 B4
Ovington Ct SO18 104 B4
Ovington Gdns BH7 206 B4
Ovington Rd SO50 56 A1
Owen Cl PO13 180 B4
Owen Rd SO50 55 F1
Owen St PO4 183 D1
Owen's Rd SO22 1 C1
Ower La SO45 178 C4
Owls Rd Bournemouth BH5 205 F2
Verwood BH31 115 D3
Owlshotts BH13 214 C4
Owslebury Bottom SO21 33 D3
Owslebury Gr PO9 135 F3
Owslebury Prim Sch SO21 33 D2
Oxburgh Cl SO50 55 F3
Oxenwood Gn 8 PO9 135 E3
Oxey Cl BH25 195 D1
Oxford Ave Bournemouth BH6 206 A3
Southampton SO14 103 D3
Oxford Cl PO16 131 D1
Oxford La Bournemouth BH11 189 D3
Swanmore SO32 84 C4
Oxford Rd Bournemouth BH1 205 D2
Gosport PO12 180 C3
Portsmouth PO5 182 C2
Southampton SO14 103 D4
Oxford St SO14 103 D2
Oxford Terr SO41 172 A1
Oxlease Cl SO51 28 A1
Oxleys Cl PO14 154 A4
Oxted Ct PO4 183 D3
Oyster Est The PO6 158 B3
Oyster Mews
5 Emsworth PO10 160 C4
Portsmouth PO1 182 A2
Oyster Quay PO6 157 D4
Oyster St PO1 182 A2
Ozier Rd SO18 80 A1

P.L.P.H. Rd SO45 151 D3
Packridge La SO51 53 F1
Padbury Cl PO2 157 F2
Paddington Cl BH11 188 B2
Paddington Gr BH11 188 B2
Paddington Rd PO2 157 F1
Paddock Cl Ferndown BH21 165 D3
St Leonards BH24 139 F2
Paddock End PO7 110 C2
Paddock Gdns SO41 197 E3
Paddock Gr BH31 115 D3
Paddock The
Brockenhurst SO42 145 F1
Eastleigh SO50 56 A3
Fordingbridge SP6 94 C3
Gosport PO12 181 D2
Kings Worthy SO23 2 B3
Stubbington PO14 154 B2
Totton SO40 76 B1
Paddock Way GU32 40 B1
Paddock Wlk 1 PO6 157 D4
Paddocks Cl BH12 203 D4
Paddocks The
Bournemouth BH10 189 E2
Fawley SO45 151 D2
Padfield Cl BH6 206 C3
Padget Rd BH24 117 E1
Padnell Ave PO8 112 A1
Padnell Inf Sch PO8 112 A1
Padnell Jun Sch PO8 112 A2
Padnell Pl PO8 112 A1
Padnell Rd PO8 112 A2
Padstow Pl SP6 93 F4
Padwell Rd SO14 103 D4
Padwick Ave PO6 158 A4
Padwick Ct PO11 184 C2
Paffard Cl PO13 180 B4
Pages La SO42 175 E3
Paget Cl BH21 164 A4
Paget Rd Bournemouth BH11 189 D2
Gosport PO12 181 D1
Paget St SO14 103 D2
Pagham Cl PO10 161 D4
Pagham Gdns PO11 185 F1
Paignton Ave PO3 183 D4
Paignton Rd SO16 77 F1
Paimpol Pl SO51 52 C3
Pain's Rd PO5 182 B2
Painswick Cl Cosham PO6 157 E4
Locks Heath SO31 128 C3
Painter Cl PO3 158 A2
Painters Field SO23 10 C2
Paisley Rd BH6 206 B3
Palace House SO42 148 C1
Palace La SO42 148 C1
Palace Mews SO32 83 E4
Palfrey Rd BH10 189 E3
Palk Rd PO9 135 E1
Pallant Gdns PO16 131 E1
Pallant The PO9 135 F1
Pallet Cl SO21 56 C4
Pallot Cl SO31 104 C1
Palm Ct 16 PO5 182 B1
Palm Hall Cl SO23 11 E4
Palm Rd SO16 78 A2
Palma Ct BH23 209 D4
Palmer Pl BH25 195 D2
Palmer Rd BH15 202 B3
Palmer's Rd PO10 136 C1
Palmers Cl SO50 57 E1
Palmerston Ave
Christchurch BH23 207 E3
Fareham PO16 131 D1
Palmerston Bsns Pk PO14 155 D4
Palmerston Cl BH16 201 E4
Palmerston Ct 2 SO22 10 C3
Palmerston Dr PO14 155 D4
Palmerston Mans 28 PO5 182 B1
Palmerston Rd
Bournemouth BH1 205 F3
Poole BH14 203 E2
Portsmouth PO5 182 B1
South Hayling PO11 185 D2
Southampton SO14 103 D2
Upton BH16 201 E4
Palmerston Rd Prec 29 PO5 182 B1
Palmerston St SO51 52 C4
Palmerston Way PO12 180 C1
Palmyra Rd PO12 181 D4
Palomino Dr PO15 129 D4
Pamphill CE Fst Sch BH21 162 C3
Pamplyn Cl SO41 197 E2
Pan St 7 PO1 182 B3
Pangbourne Ave PO6 158 A4
Pangbourne Cl SO19 104 A2
Pannall Rd PO12 181 D4
Panorama Rd BH13 214 A2
Pansy Rd SO16 79 D2
Pantheon Rd SO53 55 F4
Pantiles The SP6 69 E1
Panton Cl PO10 136 C2
Panwell Rd SO18 104 A4
Parade Ct PO2 157 F3
Parade The
Barton on Sea BH25 194 C1
5 Bournemouth BH6 206 C2
Broadstone BH17 187 D1
Cadnam SO40 98 C4
Gosport PO13 155 D2
New Milton BH25 195 E2
Portsmouth PO1 182 A3
Paradise La
Bishop's Waltham SO32 83 F3
Netley Marsh SO40 99 E3
Portchester PO16 131 F1
Westbourne PO10 137 D2
Paradise St 17 Poole BH15 202 A1
Portsmouth PO1 182 B3
Parchment St SO23 11 D4
Parchment The PO9 135 F1
Pardoe Cl SO30 105 E3
Pardys Hill BH21 186 B4
Parham Cl BH25 194 C2
Parham Dr SO50 55 F2
Parham Rd
Bournemouth BH10 189 E1
Gosport PO12 181 E3
Parish Ct SO41 197 F2
Parish Rd BH15 202 C2
Park Ave Bournemouth BH10 189 E3
Lymington SO41 197 E2
Waterlooville PO7 134 B2
Winchester SO23 11 D4
Park Cl Brockenhurst SO42 146 A1
Burton BH23 192 B2
Gosport PO12 180 C3
Hythe SO45 126 A2
Lyndhurst SO43 122 A2
Marchwood SO40 101 E1
Milford on Sea SO41 211 F2
New Milton BH25 195 E3
Winchester SO23 2 A1
Park Com Sch PO9 135 E3
Park Cotts PO17 108 A2
Park Court Flats 3 SO15 102 B3
Park Cres PO10 136 B1
Park Ct 14 Milford on Sea SO41 211 E2
North Baddesley SO51 53 E3
12 Petersfield GU32 40 C2
37 Portsmouth PO5 182 B2
1 Winchester SO23 2 A1
Park Dr BH31 114 C4
Park Farm Ave PO15 130 B2
Park Farm Cl PO15 130 B2
Park Farm Rd PO7 134 B2
Park Gate Bsns Ctr SO31 129 D3
Park Gate Cty Prim Sch SO31 129 D2
Park Gate Mews 14 BH2 204 C2
Park Gdns BH23 207 F4
Park Glen SO31 129 E2
Park Gr PO6 157 F4
Park Hill Cl SO45 150 B2
Park House
22 Portsmouth PO5 182 B1
8 Winchester SO23 11 D4
Park Homer Rd BH21 163 F3
Park House Farm Way PO9 135 E3
Park House Prim Sch PO9 135 E3
Park La Alderholt SP6 92 C3
Beaulieu SO41 200 A4
Bournemouth BH10 189 F2
Cosham PO6 158 A4
Droxford SO32 61 D1
Fareham PO14, PO16 131 D1
Havant PO9 135 E2
Havant PO9 135 E4
Holbury SO45 150 A2
Kings Worthy SO21 2 B3
Marchwood SO40 101 E1
Milford on Sea SO41 211 E2
Otterbourne SO21 31 D1
Rowland's Castle PO10 137 E4
Stubbington PO14 154 B2
Swanmore SO32 60 B1
Twyford SO21 32 A3
Wimborne Minster BH21 163 E2
Park Lane Rd BH15 202 C1
Park Mansions 3 PO6 158 A4
Park Par PO9 135 F2
Park Pl BH14 202 C2
Park Rd Barton on Sea BH25 194 C1
Bishop's Waltham SO32 83 D4
Bournemouth BH8 205 D3
Chandler's Ford SO53 55 E4
Denmead PO7 110 C3
Fordingbridge SP6 69 F1
Park Rd Continued
Gosport PO12 181 D2
Lymington SO41 197 E2
Milford on Sea SO41 211 F2
New Milton BH25 195 E3
Poole BH14 202 C2
Portsmouth PO1 182 A3
South Hayling PO11 184 B2
Southampton SO15 102 B3
Southbourne PO10 137 E1
Waterlooville PO7 134 B2
Winchester SO22, SO23 1 C1
Park Rd N PO9 135 F1
Park Rd S PO9 135 F1
Park Royal 17 PO2 157 F2
Park St Gosport PO12 181 D3
Portsmouth PO5 182 A2
Southampton SO15, SO16 102 A4
Park Terr 10 PO12 181 E2
Park The Barton on Sea BH25 209 E4
Droxford SO32 61 D1
Park View Botley SO30 106 A4
Compton(Hants) SO21 31 F3
Hedge End SO30 105 D4
Lockerley SO21 4 C2
Otterbourne SO50 31 D1
9 Poole BH15 202 C2
Portsmouth PO2 157 E2
Rowland's Castle PO9 136 A4
Park View Mews BH25 195 D1
Park Villas SO32 61 D1
Park Vista GU32 38 B1
Park Way Fair Oak SO50 57 F1
Havant PO9 135 F1
West Moors BH22 138 C1
Park Wlk Fareham PO15 130 B2
Southampton SO14 103 D3
Parker Cl PO12 156 A1
Parker Gdns PO7 134 B1
Parker Rd BH9 204 C4
Parkfield House 11 PO6 132 C1
Parkland Cl BH31 115 E2
Parkland Dr BH25 209 F4
Parkland Pl 13 SO17 103 D4
Parklands Locks Heath SO31 129 D2
6 Southampton SO18 79 F1
Totton SO40 101 D4
Parklands Ave PO8 112 A3
Parklands Bsns Pk PO7 110 C2
Parklands Cl
Chandler's Ford SO53 55 E4
Gosport PO12 181 D3
Parkside Christchurch BH23 193 E1
Havant PO9 135 E1
Ringwood BH24 141 D3
Totton SO40 100 C3
Parkside Ave SO16 101 E4
Parkside Gdns BH10 189 F1
Parkside Rd BH14 203 E2
Parkside The SO15 102 A4
Parkstone Ave Poole BH14 203 E2
Portsmouth PO4 182 C1
Parkstone Gram Sch BH17 187 D1
Parkstone Hts Poole BH14 202 C3
Poole BH14 203 D3
Parkstone Rd BH15 202 C2
Parkstone Sta BH14 203 D2
Parkview BH2 204 C2
Parkville Rd SO16 79 E2
Parkway Swanwick PO15 129 F3
Swanwick PO15 129 F4
Parkway Dr BH8 205 F4
Parkway Gdns SO53 55 E4
Parkway The Gosport PO13 155 D1
Southampton SO16 79 D3
Parkwood Cl SO30 105 E4
Parkwood Ctr PO7 134 C4
Parkwood La 14 BH5 206 A3
Parkwood Rd
Bournemouth BH5 206 A2
Wimborne Minster BH21 163 E2
Parley Cl BH22 165 F1
Parley Cty Fst Sch BH22 165 E2
Parley La BH23 190 B4
Parley Rd BH9 190 A1
Parliament Pl SO22 10 B2
Parmiter Dr BH21 163 F2
Parmiter House 45 SO23 11 D4
Parmiter Rd BH21 163 F2
Parmiter Way BH21 163 F2
Parnell Rd SO50 55 F1
Parnholt Rd SO51 7 F2
Parr House 5 BH14 203 D2
Parr Rd PO6 157 E4
Parr St BH14 203 D2
Parry Cl PO6 156 C4
Parry Rd SO19 104 B2
Parsonage Barn La BH24 141 D4
Parsonage Cl
Fordingbridge SP6 69 F1
Petersfield GU32 41 D3
Parsonage Ct 9 BH8 205 D3
Parsonage La SO32 82 A3
Parsonage Park Dr SP6 69 F1
Parsonage Rd
Bournemouth BH1 205 D2
Southampton SO14 103 E3
Parsons Cl PO3 157 F2
Partridge Cl
Christchurch BH23 208 A3
Portchester PO16 155 F4
Partridge Down SO22 10 A2
Partridge Dr BH14 203 E1
Partridge Gdns PO8 111 E2
Partridge Gr BH25 195 D3

Partridge Rd
  Brockenhurst SO42 ....172 C4
  Hythe SO45 ....125 F1
Partridge Wlk BH14 ....203 D1
Partry Cl SO53 ....55 D4
Pascoe Cl BH14 ....203 D2
Passage La SO31 ....128 A1
Passfield Ave SO50 ....55 F1
Passfield Cl SO50 ....55 F1
Passfield Wlk 55 P09 ....136 A3
Passford Hill 197 E4
Passingham Wlk P08 ....112 A2
Pastures The Cheriton SO24 ....14 B3
  Denmead P07 ....110 C2
  Locks Heath P014 ....129 E2
Pat Bear Cl SO15 ....101 E4
Patchins Rd BH16 ....201 D2
Patchins The BH14 ....214 B4
Patchway Dr P014 ....154 B4
Paternoster House 31 SO23 ....11 D4
Paternoster Row 30 SO23 ....11 D4
Patricia Cl SO30 ....80 B1
Patricia Dr SO30 ....105 E4
Patrick Howard-Dobson Ct
  5 P08 ....111 F2
Patrick's Cl GU33 ....21 D2
Patrick's Copse Rd GU33 ....21 D2
Paulet Cl SO18 ....80 A1
Paulet Pl SO22 ....10 C3
Pauletts La Ower SO40 ....76 A2
  Totton SO40 ....76 A2
Pauls La SO41 ....196 C4
Paulsgrove Cty Prim Sch
  P06 ....157 E4
Paulsgrove Ent Ctr 6 P06 ....157 D4
Paulsgrove Ind Ctr P06 ....157 D4
Paulsgrove Prim Sch P06 ....157 E4
Paulsgrove Rd P02 ....182 C4
Paulson Cl SO53 ....55 E4
Paultons Park SO51 ....75 E3
Pauncefoot Hill SO51 ....52 B3
Pauncefote Rd BH5 ....206 A3
Pauntley Rd BH23 ....207 F3
Pavan Gdns BH10 ....189 E1
Pavilion Cl SO50 ....81 E4
Pavilion Ct 20 SO15 ....102 C4
Pavilion Rd SO30 ....105 E4
Paxton Cl SO30 ....105 E3
Paxton Rd P014 ....155 D4
Payne Cl BH22 ....138 C3
Payne's La SO50 ....57 E2
Payne's Rd SO15 ....102 B3
Paynes Hay Rd SO51 ....28 B4
Peace Cl BH23 ....193 D4
Peach Rd SO16 ....78 A2
Peacock Cl P016 ....155 F4
Peacock La P01 ....182 A2
Peacock Pl 5 SO23 ....11 E4
Peak Cl SO16 ....101 F4
Peak Dr P014 ....154 B4
Peak La
  Bishop's Waltham SO32 ....59 D2
  Fareham P014 ....154 B4
Peak Rd P08 ....88 A3
Peak The P09 ....113 E1
Peake New Rd SO32 ....61 F4
Peakfield P07 ....110 C2
Pealsham Gdns SP6 ....69 F1
Pear Tree Cl Alderholt SP6 ....92 C3
  Botley SO32 ....81 F1
  Bransgore BH23 ....193 D4
Pear Tree Dr SP5 ....73 E4
Pearce Ave BH14 ....203 D1
Pearce Ct P012 ....181 E3
Pearce Gdns BH14 ....203 D1
Pearce Rd BH16 ....201 D3
Pearce-Smith Ct BH25 ....209 F4
Pearl Gdns BH10 ....189 E2
Pearl Rd BH10 ....189 E2
Pearmain Dr 4 SO41 ....197 F1
Pearman Cl SO41 ....197 E1
Pearson Ave BH14 ....203 D1
Pearson Gdns BH10 ....189 E3
Peartree Ave SO19 ....103 F3
Peartree Cl
  Southampton SO19 ....103 E4
  Stubbington P014 ....154 B2
  West Wellow SO51 ....50 B2
Peartree Ct
  5 Lymington SO41 ....197 F1
  Southampton SO19 ....103 F2
Peartree Rd Hythe SO45 ....125 F1
  Southampton SO19 ....103 E4
Pebble Cl P011 ....185 D1
Pebble Ct SO40 ....101 F1
Pebmarsh Rd 8 P06 ....157 E4
Peckham Ave SO15 ....195 D1
Pedham Cl P04 ....183 D2
Pedlars Wlk BH24 ....140 C4
Pedula Way SO50 ....56 C3
Peel Cl Poole BH12 ....203 E3
  Romsey SO51 ....28 B1
Peel Common Jun &
  Inf Sch P013 ....155 D1
Peel Rd P012 ....181 E2
Peel St SO14 ....103 E3
Peewit Hill SO31 ....105 D2
Peewit Hill Cl SO31 ....105 D2
Pegasus Ave SO41 ....196 A1
Pegasus Cl Gosport P013 ....180 B3
  Hamble-le-Rice SO31 ....127 F1
  Southampton SO16 ....77 F2
Pegasus Ct Bournemouth BH1 ....205 D3
  8 New Milton BH25 ....195 D2
Peggotty House 17 P01 ....182 B4

Pegham Ind Pk P015 ....130 A3
Pelham Cl BH23 ....207 E3
Pelham Rd Gosport P012 ....181 D3
  Portsmouth P05 ....182 B2
Pelham Terr 2 P010 ....161 D4
Pelican Cl P015 ....130 B1
Pelican Ct SO21 ....30 A4
Pelican Mead BH24 ....141 E3
Pelican Rd P014 ....154 C3
Pembers Cl SO50 ....57 E1
Pemberton Rd SO43 ....122 A3
Pembrey Cl SO16 ....78 A3
Pembridge Rd BH23 ....70 A1
Pembroke Cl Eastleigh SO50 ....55 F3
  Portsmouth P01 ....182 A2
  Romsey SO51 ....52 C4
  Totton SO40 ....101 D4
Pembroke Cres P014 ....179 D3
Pembroke Ct
  11 Christchurch BH23 ....209 D4
  Gosport P013 ....155 E1
  Southampton SO17 ....79 D1
Pembroke Rd
  Bournemouth BH4 ....204 A1
  Poole BH12 ....203 E4
  Portsmouth P01 ....182 A2
  Southampton SO19 ....104 A2
Pembury Rd Havant P09 ....160 A4
  Stubbington P014 ....154 B2
Pemerton Rd SO22 ....1 B2
Penarth Ave P06 ....158 A4
Pencraig BH13 ....204 A2
Pendennis Rd P06 ....132 C1
Pendle Cl SO16 ....101 F4
Pendle Gn SO51 ....4 C1
Pendleton Gdns SO45 ....150 C1
Penelope Ct 18 BH23 ....209 D4
Penelope Gdns SO31 ....104 C1
Penfords Paddock SO32 ....83 E4
Pengelly Ave BH10 ....189 F3
Penhale Gdns P014 ....129 D1
Penhale Inf Sch P01 ....182 C3
Penhale Rd P01 ....182 C3
Penhale Way SO40 ....100 C3
Penhurst Rd P09 ....135 D1
Peninsula Rd SO22 ....10 C4
Peninsula Sq 25 SO22 ....10 C4
Penistone Cl SO19 ....104 A1
Penjar Ave P07 ....134 B2
Penk Ridge P09 ....158 C4
Penn Cl BH25 ....194 C1
Penn Ct BH22 ....138 B1
Penn Hill Ave BH14 ....203 E2
Penn Way P012 ....180 C2
Pennant Hills P09 ....135 D1
Pennant Park P016 ....131 E2
Pennant Way BH23 ....207 F4
Pennard Way SO53 ....55 D2
Penner Rd P09 ....159 F4
Pennerley Ct P09 ....135 E4
Pennine Ct 8 BH23 ....207 F4
Pennine Gdns SO45 ....125 E1
Pennine House SO16 ....101 F4
Pennine Rd SO16 ....101 F4
Pennine Way
  Chandler's Ford SO53 ....55 E2
  Lee-on-the-Solent P013 ....180 A2
  Verwood BH31 ....114 C3
Pennine Wlk P014 ....154 C4
Pennington CE Jun Sch
  SO41 ....197 E2
Pennington Cl
  Colden Common SO21 ....56 C4
  Lymington SO41 ....197 E1
  West Moors BH22 ....138 B1
Pennington Cres BH22 ....138 B1
Pennington Cross SO41 ....197 E1
Pennington Inf Sch SO41 ....197 E2
Pennington Oval SO41 ....197 D1
Pennington Rd BH22 ....138 B1
Pennington Way P015 ....130 B2
Penns Rd GU32 ....40 C2
Penny Hedge BH25 ....210 A4
Penny La
  6 Bournemouth BH7 ....205 F2
  Hermitage P010 ....161 D4
Penny Pl P07 ....134 C2
Penny St P01 ....182 A2
Penny's Cl SP6 ....69 F2
Penny's Cnr SO41 ....195 F2
Penny's Cres SP6 ....69 F2
Penny's Ct BH22 ....165 E3
Penny's La SP6 ....69 F2
Penny's Wlk BH22 ....165 E3
Pennycress SO31 ....128 C1
Pennywell Gdns BH25 ....195 E2
Penrhyn Ave P06 ....158 A4
Penrhyn Cl SO50 ....55 F3
Penrith Cl BH31 ....114 C3
Penrith Ct SO16 ....101 F4
Penrith Rd BH5 ....206 A2
Penrose Cl 11 P012 ....157 E1
Penrose Rd BH22 ....165 E3
Penshurst Way SO50 ....56 A3
Pentagon BH15 ....202 B3
Pentagon The SO45 ....151 D1
Pentere Rd SO31 ....112 A3
Pentire Ave SO15 ....78 B1
Pentire Way SO15 ....78 B1
Pentland Cl SO45 ....125 E1
Pentland Rise P016 ....132 B1
Penton Ct P09 ....136 A3
Penton Pl 8 SO23 ....11 E4
Penton Rd SO21 ....32 A4
Pentons Hill SP6 ....94 B3
Pentridge Way SO40 ....100 C3
Penwood Gn 44 P09 ....136 A3
Peper Harow P08 ....112 A3

Peppard Cl SO18 ....104 A4
Peppercorn Way SO30 ....81 E2
Pepys Ave SO19 ....104 B3
Pepys Cl Gosport P012 ....181 D1
  Portsmouth P04 ....182 C2
Percival Rd P02 ....182 C4
Percy Cl SO45 ....125 F3
Percy Rd Bournemouth BH5 ....205 F2
  Gosport P012 ....181 E2
  Portsmouth P04 ....182 C2
  Southampton SO16 ....102 A4
Peregrine Cl SO40 ....100 B3
Peregrine Rd BH23 ....208 A3
Peregrines The P016 ....155 F4
Pergin Cres BH17 ....202 A4
Pergin Way BH17 ....202 A4
Pern Dr SO30 ....106 A4
Peronne Cl P03 ....157 F3
Peronne Rd P03 ....157 F3
Perran Rd SO40 ....77 E1
Perry Gdns BH15 ....202 B1
Perry's Ct SO40 ....102 A1
Perryfield Gdns BH7 ....206 A4
Perrywood Cl SO45 ....150 B2
Perrywood Gdns SO40 ....100 A4
Perseus Pl P07 ....134 C2
Pershore Cl SO31 ....129 D2
Persian Dr P015 ....129 D4
Persley Rd BH10 ....189 F2
Perth Cl BH23 ....191 F1
Perth House 31 P01 ....182 B3
Perth Rd Gosport P013 ....155 E2
  Portsmouth P04 ....183 D2
Pervin Rd P06 ....157 F4
Pestead La SO32 ....85 E2
Peter Ashley Activity Ctr
  P07 ....134 B1
Peter Ashley Rd BH23 ....134 B1
Peter Grant Way BH22 ....165 E4
Peter Symonds' Coll SO22 ....1 C1
Peterborough Ct P013 ....180 B3
Peterborough Rd Cosham P06 ....133 F1
  Southampton SO14 ....103 D4
Peters Cl Locks Heath SO31 ....128 C2
  Upton BH16 ....201 E3
Peters Rd SO31 ....128 C2
Peterscroft Ave SO40 ....100 A1
Petersfield Bsns Pk GU32 ....40 B2
Petersfield House 41 P01 ....182 B3
Petersfield Hospl GU32 ....40 C2
Petersfield Inf Sch GU32 ....40 C2
Petersfield La P08 ....88 B4
Petersfield Pl BH7 ....206 A4
Petersfield Rd
  Bournemouth BH7 ....206 A4
  Buriton GU31 ....65 D3
  Cheriton SO24 ....14 B2
  Havant P09 ....136 A3
  Winchester SO21, SO23 ....11 E4
Petersfield Sch The GU32 ....40 C1
Petersfield Sta GU32 ....40 C2
Petersgate Inf Sch P08 ....88 B2
Petersham Rd BH17 ....202 A4
Petit Rd BH9 ....190 A2
Petrie Rd P013 ....179 F1
Petrel Wlk P013 ....155 D1
Petticoat La SP5 ....47 F4
Pettinger Gdns SO17 ....103 E4
Petty Cl SO51 ....53 D3
Pettycot Cres P013 ....155 D2
Petworth Gdns
  Eastleigh SO50 ....56 A3
  Southampton SO16 ....78 B3
Petworth Rd P03 ....183 D2
Petwyn Cl BH22 ....166 A3
Pevensey Cl SO16 ....77 E1
Peverell Rd BH16 ....201 D2
Peverells Rd SO53 ....55 F4
Peverells Wood Ave SO53 ....55 F4
Peverells Wood Cl SO53 ....55 F3
Peveril Ct BH24 ....139 F3
Peveril Rd SO19 ....103 F2
Pewsey Pl SO15 ....78 B1
Phelipps Rd BH21 ....186 C3
Philip Rd P07 ....134 C3
Phillimore Rd SO16 ....79 E2
Phillips Cl SO16 ....77 F3
Philpott Dr SO40 ....101 F1
Phoenix Bldgs P03 ....158 A1
Phoenix Cl SO31 ....105 D1
Phoenix Park SO50 ....56 B1
Phoenix Pru SO45 ....149 F4
Phoenix Sq P02 ....157 F2
Phoenix Way P013 ....155 E1
Phyldon Cl BH12 ....203 D3
Phyldon Rd BH12 ....203 D3
Pickard Rd BH22 ....165 F4
Pickering Cl BH18 ....187 D1
Picket Cl SP6 ....69 F1
Pickford Rd BH9 ....189 F1
Pickwick Cl SO40 ....100 A4
Pickwick House 13 P01 ....182 B4
Picton House 53 P05 ....182 B2
Pier Head Rd P02 ....157 D1
Pier Rd P01 ....182 A2
Pier St P013 ....179 F1
Pig Shoot La BH23 ....190 C3
Pigeon House La P07 ....133 E2
Pikes Hill SO43 ....121 F3
Pikes Hill Ave SO43 ....121 F3
Pilands Wood Rd SO31 ....127 F4
Pilchards Ave SO50 ....57 D2
Pilford Heath Rd BH21 ....164 A4
Pilgrim Park Homes Cvn Pk
  BH24 ....141 E4
Pilgrim Pl SO18 ....79 F2
Pilgrim's Cl BH25 ....195 E2
Pilgrims Cl SO53 ....55 D3

Pilgrims Gate SO22 ....1 C1
Pilgrims Sch The SO23 ....11 D4
Pilgrims Way
  Broadstone BH17 ....202 A4
  Stubbington P014 ....179 D3
Pill Hill SP5 ....24 A2
Pilley Bailey SO41 ....174 A1
Pilley Gn SO41 ....174 A1
Pilley Hill SO41 ....173 F1
Pilley St SO41 ....174 A1
Pilning Cl P014 ....154 B4
Pilot Hight Rd BH11 ....189 D2
Pilsdon Dr BH17 ....187 F2
Pimpern Cl BH17 ....187 F1
Pimpernel Cl SO31 ....128 C1
Pine Ave Bournemouth BH6 ....206 B2
  Poole BH12 ....203 F3
Pine Cl Ashurst SO40 ....100 B2
  Barton on Sea BH25 ....209 F4
  Ferndown BH22 ....165 E4
  Hythe SO45 ....125 F1
  Landford SP5 ....49 E1
  North Baddesley SO52 ....53 F3
  Winchester SO21, SO22 ....10 A2
Pine Cotts GU33 ....21 D4
Pine Cres
  Chandler's Ford SO53 ....30 B1
  Christchurch BH23 ....208 C4
Pine Ct P010 ....136 C2
Pine Dr Clanfield P08 ....88 B3
  Poole BH13 ....203 F2
  Southampton SO18 ....104 B4
  St Leonards BH24 ....139 F2
Pine Dr E SO18 ....104 C4
Pine Glen Ave BH22 ....165 E4
Pine Gr P09 ....136 A1
Pine Grange 4 BH1 ....205 D2
Pine House SO16 ....78 C4
Pine Lodge 15 BH13 ....214 C4
Pine Manor Rd BH24 ....139 E3
Pine Mansions 3 BH1 ....205 E2
Pine Park Mans 16 BH13 ....204 A2
Pine Rd Alderholt SP6 ....92 C3
  Bishop's Waltham SO32 ....83 E4
  Bournemouth BH9 ....205 D4
  Broadstone BH17 ....162 C1
  Chandler's Ford SO53 ....55 E4
  Romsey SO51 ....53 E3
Pine Tree Cl BH21 ....163 E3
Pine Tree Gdns P08 ....112 A1
Pine Tree Glen BH4 ....204 B2
Pine Trees Cl P014 ....154 B4
Pine View Cl Redlynch SP5 ....47 E2
  Upton BH16 ....201 E3
Pine View Rd BH31 ....114 B4
Pine Way SO16 ....78 C4
Pine Wlk Chilworth SO16 ....78 C4
  Liss GU33 ....21 D3
  Locks Heath SO31 ....129 D3
  Verwood BH31 ....115 D3
Pinebeach Ct BH13 ....214 D4
Pinecliff Rd BH13 ....214 D4
Pinecliffe Ave BH6 ....206 B2
Pinecliffe Rd BH25 ....209 E4
Pinefield Rd SO18 ....79 F1
Pinegrove Rd SO19 ....103 F2
Pineholt Cl BH24 ....140 A3
Pinehurst
  10 Milford on Sea SO41 ....211 E2
  13 Southampton SO17 ....79 D1
Pinehurst Ave BH23 ....207 F3
Pinehurst Cl P07 ....112 B1
Pinehurst Rd
  Southampton SO16 ....78 C4
  West Moors BH22 ....138 C1
Pinelands Ct SO16 ....78 B2
Pinelands Rd SO16 ....78 C4
Pines The Fordingbridge SP6 ....70 B1
  Poole BH13 ....204 A1
  Portchester P016 ....132 A1
  Southampton SO16 ....78 A2
Pineside BH9 ....205 D4
Pinesprings Dr BH18 ....186 C1
Pinetops Cl SO41 ....197 D2
Pinetree Wlk BH17 ....201 E4
Pineview Cl SO31 ....105 D1
Pinewood Gosport P013 ....155 F1
  Southampton SO16 ....78 C3
Pinewood Ave
  Bournemouth BH10 ....189 E3
  Havant P09 ....135 D2
Pinewood Cl
  Bournemouth BH10 ....189 E3
  Christchurch BH23 ....194 A1
  Romsey SO51 ....28 B1
  Stubbington P014 ....154 B2
  Upton BH16 ....201 D4
Pinewood Cres SO45 ....126 A1
Pinewood Dr SO45 ....126 A1
Pinewood Gdns BH25 ....165 E4
Pinewood Lodge 5 P016 ....131 D1
Pinewood Park SO19 ....104 C3
Pinewood Rd
  Christchurch BH23 ....193 F1
  Ferndown BH22 ....165 E4
  Hordle SO41 ....195 F2
  Poole BH13, BH16 ....204 A1
  St Leonards BH24 ....139 F2
  Upton BH16 ....201 D4
Pink Rd P02 ....182 C4
Pinkney La SO43 ....121 F2
Pinks Hill P016 ....131 E1
Pinsley Dr P017 ....133 D3
Pinto Cl P015 ....129 E4
Pipers Ash BH24 ....141 E4
Pipers Cl SO40 ....100 B3
Pipers Dr BH23 ....208 A4

Pipers Mead P08 ....88 A4
Pipers Wood Ind Est P07 ....134 C4
Piping Cl SO21 ....56 C4
Piping Gr 6 SO21 ....56 C4
Piping Rd SO21 ....56 C4
Pipit Cl Gosport P012 ....181 D1
  Horndean P08 ....112 A4
Pippin Cl Christchurch BH23 ....191 F1
  6 Lymington SO41 ....197 E1
Pirelli St SO15 ....102 C4
Pirrie Cl SO15 ....78 B1
Pit Hill La P07 ....86 C4
Pitcairn Mews P04 ....183 D2
Pitchponds Rd SO31 ....152 B1
Pitcroft La GU31 ....65 D3
Pitcroft Rd P02 ....157 F3
Pitmore Cl SO50 ....56 A4
Pitmore La SO41 ....172 E4
Pitmore Rd SO50 ....56 A4
Pitmore Spcl Sch SO53 ....55 D4
Pitreavie Rd P014 ....157 F1
Pitt Rd SO15 ....102 B3
Pitt Rdbt SO22 ....10 A2
Pitter Cl SO22 ....1 A2
Pittmore Rd BH23 ....192 B1
Pitts Deep La SO41 ....199 E3
Pitts Pl BH25 ....195 E1
Pitwines Cl BH15 ....202 B3
Pitymoor La P017 ....133 C1
Place Cres P07 ....134 C4
Place House Cl P015 ....130 B1
Place La SO21 ....31 F4
Plaitford Gr P09 ....135 E4
Plaitford Wlk SO16 ....77 F1
Plant Park Rd BH24 ....140 B4
Plantaganet Cres BH11 ....188 B4
Plantation SO41 ....211 D3
Plantation Ct
  Broadstone BH17 ....187 E4
  Lymington SO41 ....197 E1
Plantation Dr
  Christchurch BH23 ....194 A1
  Marchwood SO40 ....101 F4
Plantation Rd
  Broadstone BH17 ....187 E4
  Hill Brow GU33 ....21 D4
  West Wellow SO51 ....74 A4
Plantation The SO32 ....82 C4
Plants Cl SO51 ....51 D4
Plassey Cres BH10 ....189 E4
Platform Rd SO14 ....103 C2
Platoff Rd SO41 ....212 C3
Player Ct SP6 ....69 F2
Players Cres SO40 ....100 C4
Playfair Rd P05 ....182 B2
Playfields Dr BH12 ....203 F3
Plaza Par 14 SO51 ....52 C4
Pleasance Way BH25 ....194 C1
Pleasant La P010 ....161 B4
Pleasant Rd P04 ....183 D1
Plecy Cl BH22 ....165 E3
Plemont Cl BH12 ....188 C1
Pless Rd SO41 ....211 D3
Plough La SO32 ....85 E2
Plough Way SO22 ....10 A3
Plover Cl Southampton SO16 ....78 A4
  Stubbington P014 ....179 D3
Plover Dr SO41 ....211 D4
Plover Rd SO40 ....100 B3
Plover Reach P04 ....183 D2
Plovers Down SO22 ....10 A3
Plovers Pl P08 ....112 A4
Plumer Rd BH17 ....187 D2
Plumley Wlk P09 ....135 E4
Plumpton Gdns P03 ....158 A4
Plumpton Gr P07 ....112 A1
Plymouth Dr P014 ....154 A4
Plymouth St P01 ....182 B3
Pococks La GU33 ....19 D2
Poets Way SO22 ....10 B3
Pointout Cl SO16 ....78 C4
Pointout Rd SO16 ....78 C4
Pokesdown Prim Sch BH5 ....206 A2
Pokesdown Sta BH7 ....206 A3
Poles La Hursley SO21 ....30 B1
  Lymington SO41 ....197 E4
  Otterbourne SO21 ....31 C1
Police Station La SO32 ....61 D4
Police Training Ctr SO31 ....127 F3
Pollards Moor Rd SO40 ....75 D2
Pollesden Cl SO53 ....55 D4
Polygon Ct SO15 ....102 C4
Polygon Sch (Annexe) The
  SO16 ....78 A2
Polygon Special Sch The
  SO15 ....102 C4
Polygon The SO15 ....102 C4
Pomona Cl BH22 ....165 E4
Pompey's La BH22 ....165 D4
Pond Cl Marchwood SO40 ....101 F4
  New Milton BH25 ....195 D2
Pond Cotts GU32 ....39 D1
Pond La P08 ....88 A4
Pond Piece P07 ....110 C2
Pond Rd SO31 ....128 C1
Pondhead Cl SO45 ....150 B2
Pondside Flats SO42 ....148 C3
Pondside La
  Bishop's Waltham SO32 ....59 E4
  Bishop's Waltham SO32 ....83 E1
Ponsonby House 54 P05 ....182 B2
Ponsonby Rd BH14 ....203 E2
Pony Dr BH16 ....201 E4
Pook La Fareham P017 ....131 E2
  Havant P09 ....160 A4
Pooksgreen SO40 ....101 E4
Poole Commerce Ctr BH12 ....203 F3
Poole Gram Sch BH17 ....187 E1

ole High Sch BH15 .... 202 B2
ole Hill BH2 .... 204 C2
ole Hospl BH15 .... 202 B2
ole La BH11 .... 189 D3
ole Rd
  Bournemouth BH2, BH4 .... 204 B2
  Poole BH12 .... 204 A2
Southampton SO19 .... 103 F2
Jpton BH16, BH17 .... 201 E4
Wimborne Minster BH21 .... 163 E2
ole Sta BH15 .... 202 B2
pes La Totton SO40 .... 100 C4
Jpham SO32 .... 58 B2
pes Rd BH15 .... 202 B3
pham Ct PO9 .... 135 E3
plar Cl Bransgore BH23 .... 193 E4
  Christchurch BH23 .... 209 D4
6 Poole BH15 .... 202 A1
Wimborne Minster BH21 .... 163 E3
plar Cres BH24 .... 141 D4
plar Dr Fareham PO14 .... 154 C4
Marchwood SO40 .... 101 E1
plar Gr PO11 .... 185 D2
plar La BH23 .... 193 E4
plar Rd New Milton BH25 .... 195 E2
Southampton SO19 .... 103 F3
plar Way Hedge End SO30 .... 105 E3
North Baddesley SO52 .... 53 F3
Ringwood BH24 .... 141 D4
plars The SO32 .... 83 E2
ppy Cl Christchurch BH23 .... 208 B4
Locks Heath SO31 .... 128 C1
ppy Rd SO16 .... 79 E3
ppyfields SO53 .... 55 D3
orchester Ct 12 BH1 .... 205 D3
orchester Pl BH8 .... 205 D3
orchester Rd
  Bournemouth BH8 .... 205 D3
  Southampton SO19 .... 103 F2
orlock Rd SO16 .... 77 E1
ort La Hursley SO21 .... 30 B4
Winchester SO21 .... 10 A1
ort Royal St PO1 .... 182 B3
ort Way PO6 .... 157 D4
ortal Rd Bishopstoke SO50 .... 56 B2
Gosport PO13 .... 155 E2
Southampton SO19 .... 104 A2
otton SO40 .... 100 B4
Winchester SO23 .... 11 D3
ortarlington Cl BH2 .... 204 B1
ortarlington Rd BH4 .... 204 B1
ortchester Castle PO16 .... 156 C3
ortchester Com Sch PO16 .... 156 B4
ortchester La PO17 .... 132 B2
ortchester Rd
  Portchester PO16 .... 156 A4
  Portsmouth PO2 .... 182 C4
ortchester Rise SO50 .... 56 A4
ortchester Sch BH7 .... 206 A4
ortchester Sta PO16 .... 156 B4
ortcreek Cotts PO6 .... 158 A3
ortelet Cl BH12 .... 188 B1
ortelet House SO16 .... 77 E2
ortelet Pl SO30 .... 105 E3
orter Rd BH17 .... 202 A4
orter's La SO14 .... 102 C2
orters La BH21 .... 164 B3
ortersbridge St SO51 .... 52 C4
ortesham Gdns BH9 .... 190 A2
ortesham Way BH17 .... 187 F2
orteus Cres SO53 .... 55 F3
ortfield Cl BH23 .... 207 D4
ortfield Rd
  Christchurch BH23 .... 207 D4
  Portsmouth PO3 .... 158 A2
ortfield Sch
  Christchurch BH23 .... 207 D3
  Christchurch BH23 .... 207 D4
ortland Bldgs 5 PO12 .... 181 E2
ortland Dr BH23 .... 180 B2
ortland House 24 PO12 .... 181 E2
ortland Rd
  Bournemouth BH9 .... 205 D4
  Portsmouth PO5 .... 182 B1
Waterlooville PO7 .... 134 C4
ortland Sq 5 GU33 .... 20 C2
ortland St Fareham PO16 .... 131 D1
Portsmouth PO1 .... 182 A3
Southampton SO14 .... 102 C2
ortland Terr
27 Portsmouth PO5 .... 182 B1
Southampton SO14 .... 102 C2
ortland's Cl GU31 .... 41 D3
ortman Cres BH5 .... 206 A2
ortman Rd BH7 .... 205 F3
ortman Terr BH5 .... 206 A2
ortobello Gr PO16 .... 132 C3
ortsdown Ave PO6 .... 158 B4
ortsdown Cty Prim
  Sch PO6 .... 157 F4
ortsdown Hill Rd
  Cosham PO6 .... 133 D1
  Havant PO9 .... 135 D1
Portchester PO17 .... 132 B1
ortsdown Prim Sch PO6 .... 157 F4
ortsdown Rd PO16 .... 156 C4
ortsmouth Cath (CE) PO1 .... 182 A3
ortsmouth Cath(RC) PO1 .... 182 A2
ortsmouth Coll PO3 .... 183 E4
ortsmouth Gram Sch PO1 .... 182 A2
ortsmouth Harbour
  Sta PO1 .... 181 F2
ortsmouth High Sch for
  Girls PO5 .... 182 A1
ortsmouth High Sch for
  Girls(Juns) PO5 .... 182 B1
ortsmouth Print Workshop
  PO1 .... 182 B4

Portsmouth Rd
  Bursledon SO31 .... 105 D1
  Colden Common SO50, SO21 .... 57 E3
  Cosham PO6 .... 157 F4
  Horndean PO8 .... 112 A3
  Lee-on-the-Solent PO13 .... 180 A2
  Southampton SO19, SO31 .... 104 B1
  Waterlooville PO8 .... 112 A3
Portsmouth & Southsea
  Sta PO1 .... 182 B3
Portsview Ave PO16 .... 132 C1
Portsview Gdns PO16 .... 132 B1
Portswood Ave SO17 .... 103 D4
Portswood Ctr 36 SO17 .... 79 D1
Portswood Dr BH9 .... 190 A2
Portswood Pk SO17 .... 103 D4
Portswood Prim Sch SO17 .... 79 E1
Portswood Rd Havant PO9 .... 135 D3
  Portsmouth PO2 .... 157 F3
  Southampton SO17 .... 79 E1
Portuguese Fireplace SO43 .... 120 C2
Portview Rd SO18 .... 79 F1
Portway Cl SO18 .... 104 A4
Posbrook La PO14 .... 153 F3
Posbrooke Rd PO4 .... 183 D2
Post Office Bldgs BH9 .... 204 C4
Post Office La 6 Poole BH15 .... 202 B1
  St Leonards BH24 .... 140 A3
Post Office Rd
  41 Bournemouth BH1 .... 204 C2
  Waterlooville PO7 .... 134 B3
Postern Cl PO16 .... 156 B4
Postern Ct 14 SO14 .... 102 C2
Potash Terr 6 PO9 .... 135 F1
Potterdale House 17 PO6 .... 133 D1
Potteries The PO16 .... 131 D2
Potterne Way BH21 .... 115 D2
Potters Ave PO16 .... 131 D2
Potters Field GU33 .... 21 D2
Potters Heron Cl SO51 .... 29 F2
Potters Heron La SO51 .... 29 F2
Potters Way PO14 .... 203 E1
Pottery Rd BH14 .... 203 D1
Poulner Cl SO19 .... 104 A1
Poulner Ct PO9 .... 135 E3
Poulner Hill BH24 .... 141 F4
Poulner Inf & Jun Schs
  BH24 .... 117 E1
Poulner Mobile Home Pk
  BH24 .... 117 E1
Poulner Pk BH24 .... 117 E1
Pound Cl Gosport PO13 .... 180 B4
  Poole BH15 .... 202 C3
  Ringwood BH24 .... 141 D4
Pound Cotts SO32 .... 61 E3
Pound Ct SO18 .... 104 A4
Pound Gate Dr PO14 .... 153 E4
Pound La Ampfield SO51 .... 29 D1
  Ashurst SO40 .... 100 C2
  Bournemouth BH10 .... 189 D3
  Burley BH24 .... 142 C1
  Cadnam SO40 .... 75 E1
  3 Christchurch BH23 .... 207 D3
  Damerham SP6 .... 68 A3
  Meonstoke SO32 .... 61 E3
  North Baddesley SO51 .... 29 D1
  Plaitford SO51 .... 50 B3
  Poole BH15 .... 202 C3
  Sherfield English SO51 .... 25 F1
Pound Lea PO11 .... 185 D3
Pound Rd Bursledon SO31 .... 104 C1
  Kings Worthy SO23 .... 2 B4
  Lymington SO41 .... 197 D1
Pound St SO18 .... 104 A4
Pound Tree Rd SO14 .... 103 D2
Pounds Terr PO1 .... 182 A3
Powell Cres SO40 .... 100 C3
Powell Rd BH14 .... 203 D2
Powell Sq 11 PO1 .... 182 A3
Power Rd PO1 .... 182 C3
Powerscourt Rd
  Barton on Sea BH25 .... 209 F4
  Portsmouth PO2 .... 182 C4
Powis Cl BH25 .... 195 D2
Powlett Rd SO41 .... 197 F2
Poyner Cl PO16 .... 131 D1
Poynings Pl PO1 .... 182 A2
Precosa Rd SO30 .... 105 F3
Precinct The 10 PO7 .... 134 C4
Prelate Way PO14 .... 129 E1
Premier Ctr The SO51 .... 53 E3
Premier Par SO18 .... 79 F2
Premier Way SO51 .... 53 E3
Preshaw Cl SO16 .... 78 B2
Preshaw Est SO32 .... 35 D2
Presseys Cnr SP6 .... 93 D4
Preston Cl BH16 .... 201 E4
Preston La BH23 .... 192 B2
Preston Rd Poole BH15 .... 202 B3
  Portsmouth PO2 .... 182 C4
Preston Way BH23 .... 208 B4
Prestwood Cl BH25 .... 194 C1
Prestwood Rd SO30 .... 105 E3
Pretoria Rd Hedge End SO30 .... 105 D3
  Portsmouth PO4 .... 182 C2
Prettyjohn House PO4 .... 183 D1
Pricketts Hill PO17 .... 108 A3
Prideaux-Brune Ave PO13 .... 155 E2
Priest Croft SO45 .... 150 C1
Priest Croft Dr SO45 .... 150 C1
Priest La SO41 .... 192 A4
Priestlands SO51 .... 52 C4
Priestlands Cl SO40 .... 100 A3
Priestlands La SO41 .... 197 E2
Priestlands Pl SO41 .... 197 E2
Priestlands Rd SO41 .... 197 E2
Priestlands Sec Sch SO41 .... 197 E1
Priestley Cl SO40 .... 100 B4

Priestley Rd BH10 .... 189 D1
Priestwood Cl SO18 .... 104 B4
Primate Rd PO14 .... 129 E1
Primrose Cl Gosport PO13 .... 155 E3
  Hedge End SO30 .... 105 E3
  North Baddesley SO52 .... 54 C2
Primrose Ct PO7 .... 135 D3
Primrose Gdns BH17 .... 186 C1
Primrose La Rake GU33 .... 21 E2
  Redlynch SP5 .... 47 E3
Primrose Rd SO16 .... 79 D2
Primrose Terr SO32 .... 59 E1
Primrose Way
  Christchurch BH23 .... 208 B4
  Corfe Mullen BH21 .... 186 C4
  Locks Heath SO31 .... 128 C1
  Romsey SO51 .... 28 B1
Prince Albert Rd PO4 .... 183 D2
Prince Alfred St PO12 .... 181 D2
Prince George St PO1 .... 182 A3
Prince George's St PO9 .... 135 F1
Prince of Wales Ave SO15 .... 102 A4
Prince of Wales Cl PO7 .... 135 D4
Prince of Wales Rd
  Bournemouth BH4 .... 204 B2
  3 Gosport PO12 .... 181 E2
Prince Rd Gosport PO14 .... 154 C3
  Rownhams SO16 .... 77 F3
Prince Regent 45 PO5 .... 182 B2
Prince William Ct 8 SO50 .... 56 C1
Prince's Bldgs PO5 .... 11 D4
Prince's Mead Sch SO22 .... 10 C3
Prince's Pl New Milton BH25 .... 195 E2
  Portsmouth PO1 .... 182 B4
Prince's Rd SO51 .... 52 C4
Prince's St Portsmouth PO1 .... 182 B4
  Southampton SO14 .... 103 E3
Princes Cl
  Bishop's Waltham SO32 .... 83 D4
  Redlynch SP5 .... 47 F4
Princes Cotts GU32 .... 63 E4
Princes Cres SO43 .... 122 A3
Princes Ct Lyndhurst SO43 .... 122 A3
  6 Poole BH12 .... 204 A2
  2 Southampton SO14 .... 103 E3
Princes Dr PO7 .... 112 A1
Princes Hill SP5 .... 47 F4
Princes House 3 SO14 .... 103 E3
Princes Pl SO22 .... 10 C3
Princes Rd Ferndown BH22 .... 165 F3
  Petersfield GU32 .... 40 B2
Princess Anne Hospl SO16 .... 78 A2
Princess Ave BH23 .... 207 D3
Princess Cl SO30 .... 80 C1
Princess Ct 7 SO23 .... 11 D4
Princess Gdns PO8 .... 112 B4
Princess Rd Ashurst SO40 .... 100 A1
  Bournemouth BH4 .... 204 A2
  Poole BH12 .... 204 A2
Pringles Cl PO12 .... 165 F3
Pringles Dr BH22 .... 165 F3
Prinstead Cl 7 SO23 .... 11 D3
Prinstead Cres PO6 .... 158 B4
Prinstead La PO10 .... 161 E4
Prinstead Wlk PO14 .... 154 B4
Priors Barton SO23 .... 10 C3
Priors Cl Christchurch BH23 .... 208 B4
  Southbourne PO10 .... 137 F1
Priors Dean Rd SO22 .... 1 B2
Priors Hill La SO31 .... 127 F4
Priors Leaze La PO18 .... 137 F1
Priors Rd BH17 .... 202 A4
Priors Way SO22 .... 10 A2
Priors Wlk 6 BH21 .... 163 D3
Priorsdean Ave PO3 .... 183 D3
Priorsdean Cres PO9 .... 135 E2
Priory Ave SO17 .... 79 E1
Priory CE Prim Sch
  The BH23 .... 207 D3
Priory Cl
  Bishop's Waltham SO32 .... 83 D4
  Southampton SO17 .... 79 E1
Priory Cres PO4 .... 183 D2
Priory Ct
  Bishop's Waltham SO32 .... 83 D4
  Portchester PO16 .... 156 C4
  2 Portsmouth PO5 .... 182 C2
Priory Gdns Portchester PO16 .... 156 B4
  Waterlooville PO7 .... 111 F1
  West Moors BH22 .... 166 A4
Priory House
  Christchurch BH23 .... 207 E3
  18 Southampton SO17 .... 103 D3
Priory Ind Pk BH23 .... 208 A4
Priory Quay BH23 .... 207 E3
Priory Rd Bournemouth BH2 .... 204 C1
  Eastleigh SO50 .... 55 F1
  Fareham PO15, PO17 .... 130 B1
  Gosport PO12 .... 181 D4
  Netley SO31 .... 127 D3
  Portsmouth PO4 .... 183 D1
  Southampton SO17 .... 103 E4
  West Moors BH22 .... 166 A4
Priory Sec Sch PO5 .... 182 C2
Priory View Ct 5 BH23 .... 207 D3
Priory View Pl BH9 .... 190 A2
Priory View Rd
  Bournemouth BH9 .... 190 A2
  Burton BH23 .... 192 B1
Private Rd SO41 .... 197 F3
Privet Rd BH9 .... 204 C4
Privett House PO1 .... 182 A3
Privett Pl PO12 .... 180 C2
Privett Rd Fareham PO15 .... 130 B1
  Froxfield GU32 .... 18 C1
  Gosport PO12 .... 180 C2
  Waterlooville PO7 .... 134 B2

Prochurch Rd PO8 .... 112 A2
Proctor Cl SO19 .... 104 B3
Proctor Dr SO52 .... 53 F2
Proctor La PO1 .... 182 C3
Promenade BH23 .... 208 A3
Promenade Ct 4 PO13 .... 179 F1
Promenade The
  Emsworth PO10 .... 160 C4
  Hythe SO45 .... 126 A3
  19 Portsmouth PO2 .... 157 E1
Prospect La PO9 .... 136 A3
Prospect Pl
  Chandler's Ford SO50 .... 55 E3
  Hythe SO45 .... 126 A3
Prospect Rd PO1 .... 182 B4
Prosperous St 15 BH15 .... 202 B1
Provene Cl SO32 .... 83 F2
Provene Gdns SO32 .... 83 F2
Providence Ct 8 PO1 .... 182 B4
Providence Hill SO31 .... 105 D1
Provost St SP6 .... 69 F1
Pruetts La GU31 .... 20 C1
Prunus Cl Ferndown BH22 .... 165 D4
  Southampton SO16 .... 78 B3
Prunus Dr BH22 .... 165 D4
Pudbrook House SO30 .... 106 A3
Pudbrooke Gdns SO30 .... 105 D4
Pudding La SO23 .... 2 A3
Puddletown Cres PO7 .... 187 F1
Puffin Cl SO16 .... 78 A3
Puffin Cres PO14 .... 154 A2
Puffin Gdns PO13 .... 155 D2
Puffin Wlk PO8 .... 111 E2
Pug's Hole SP5 .... 4 A3
Pulens Cres GU31 .... 41 E2
Pulens La GU31 .... 41 D2
Pullman Ct BH22 .... 138 B1
Pullman Way BH24 .... 141 D3
Pump La PO13 .... 155 E1
Pundle Green Est SO40 .... 99 D3
Punshott La SO24 .... 16 C3
Purbeck Ave BH15 .... 201 F1
Purbeck Cl BH16 .... 201 D4
Purbeck Ct
  Bournemouth BH5 .... 206 A2
  3 Christchurch BH23 .... 207 F4
Purbeck Dr Fareham PO14 .... 154 B4
  Verwood BH31 .... 114 C3
Purbeck Hts BH14 .... 203 D3
Purbeck Rd
  Barton on Sea BH25 .... 209 F4
  Bournemouth BH20 .... 204 C1
Purbeck St PO1 .... 182 A3
Purbeck Wlk PO14 .... 154 B4
Purbrook Chase Prec PO7 .... 134 C2
Purbrook Cl SO16 .... 78 B2
Purbrook Gdns PO7 .... 134 B3
Purbrook Heath Rd PO7 .... 134 A3
Purbrook House PO7 .... 134 B3
Purbrook Inf Sch PO7 .... 134 B3
Purbrook Jun Sch PO7 .... 134 B3
Purbrook Park Sec Sch PO7 .... 134 B2
Purbrook Rd PO1 .... 182 C3
Purbrook Way PO9 .... 135 E2
Purcell Cl PO7 .... 134 C3
Purcell Rd SO19 .... 104 B2
Purchase Rd BH12 .... 204 B4
Purewell BH23 .... 207 E3
Purewell BH23 .... 207 F3
Purewell Cross BH23 .... 207 F3
Purewell Cross Rd BH23 .... 207 E4
Purewell Ct 11 BH23 .... 207 E4
Purkess Cl SO53 .... 55 E4
Purkiss Cl SO40 .... 99 E3
Purley Way SO51 .... 50 A2
Purrocks The GU32 .... 40 C3
Purvis Gdns SO19 .... 104 A1
Pussex La BH23 .... 191 D4
Putmans La GU31 .... 66 C4
Pycroft Cl
  North Hayling PO11 .... 160 B2
  Southampton SO19 .... 104 A3
Pye Cl BH21 .... 186 C4
Pye Cnr BH21 .... 163 D2
Pye La BH21 .... 91 F3
Pye St PO1 .... 182 B3
Pylands La SO31 .... 105 D2
Pyle Cl PO8 .... 112 A2
Pylewell Rd SO45 .... 126 A2
Pyramid Ctr PO3 .... 158 A2
Pyramids L Ctr The PO5 .... 182 B1
Pyrford Cl Gosport PO12 .... 180 C2
  Waterlooville PO7 .... 111 F1
Pyrford Gdns 1 SO41 .... 197 F1
Pyrford Mews SO41 .... 197 F1
Pytchley Cl PO14 .... 179 D3

Quadra Point PO3 .... 158 A2
Quadrangle The
  Eastleigh SO50 .... 56 A2
  North Baddesley SO51 .... 53 E3
Quadrant SP6 .... 93 F4
Quail Way PO8 .... 112 A3
Quaker Ct BH24 .... 140 C3
Quantock Ct 7 BH23 .... 207 F4
Quantock Rd SO16 .... 101 F4
Quantocks The SO45 .... 125 E1
Quarely Rd PO9 .... 135 E3
Quarr House SO41 .... 172 A2
Quarry Chase 7 BH4 .... 204 B2
Quarry Cl BH21 .... 164 A4
Quarry Dr BH21 .... 164 A4
Quarry Rd
  Wimborne Minster BH21 .... 164 A4
  Winchester SO23 .... 11 E4
Quarterdeck Ave PO2 .... 157 D4
Quarterjack Mews 2 BH21 .... 163 E2
Quartremaine Rd PO3 .... 158 A2

Quavey Rd SP5 .... 47 F3
Quay Haven SO31 .... 128 B4
Quay Hill SO41 .... 197 E2
Quay House SO31 .... 128 A1
Quay La Gosport PO12 .... 181 F2
  Gosport, Elson PO12 .... 156 A1
Quay Point 20 BH15 .... 202 B1
Quay Rd Christchurch BH23 .... 207 D3
  Lymington SO41 .... 197 F2
Quay St Fareham PO16 .... 131 E1
  Fareham PO16 .... 155 E4
  Lymington SO41 .... 197 F2
Quay The Hamble-le-Rice SO31 .... 128 A1
  Poole BH15 .... 202 B1
Quayle Dr BH11 .... 188 B3
Quayside SO30 .... 106 A3
Quayside Commerce Ctr
  PO16 .... 155 D4
Quayside Rd Fawley SO45 .... 151 F1
  Southampton SO18 .... 103 E4
Quayside Wlk SO40 .... 101 F2
Quebec Gdns SO31 .... 104 C1
Queen Anne Dr PO9 .... 135 E1
Queen Anne's Dr PO9 .... 135 E1
Queen Elizabeth Ct
  Southampton SO17 .... 79 E2
  Wimborne Minster BH21 .... 163 E3
Queen Elizabeth Cty Pk GU31 .... 65 D2
Queen Elizabeth's Sch BH21 .... 162 C3
Queen Katherine Rd SO41 .... 197 F2
Queen Mary Ave BH9 .... 189 F1
Queen Mary Rd PO16 .... 156 B4
Queen Rd PO14 .... 154 C3
Queen St Emsworth PO10 .... 161 D4
  Lymington SO41 .... 197 E2
  Portsmouth PO1 .... 182 A3
  Twyford SO21 .... 31 F3
  Woodgreen SP6 .... 47 D1
Queen's Ave BH23 .... 207 D3
Queen's Cl SO51 .... 53 D4
Queen's Cres PO5 .... 182 B2
Queen's Ct SO15 .... 102 C3
Queen's Gr PO5 .... 182 B2
Queen's Inclosure
  Prim Sch PO8 .... 112 A1
Queen's Par Lyndhurst SO43 .... 121 F3
  8 Waterlooville PO7 .... 134 C4
Queen's Park Ave BH8 .... 205 E4
Queen's Park Gdns BH8 .... 205 E4
Queen's Park Rd BH8 .... 205 E4
Queen's Park S Dr BH8 .... 205 E4
Queen's Park W Dr BH8 .... 205 E4
Queen's Pl 32 PO5 .... 182 B2
Queen's Rd
  Bournemouth BH4 .... 204 B2
  Chandler's Ford SO53 .... 30 B1
  Christchurch BH23 .... 207 E3
  Corfe Mullen BH21 .... 186 B3
  Fareham PO16 .... 131 D1
  Gosport PO12 .... 181 E2
  Locks Heath SO31 .... 152 B4
  Poole BH14 .... 203 E2
  Portsmouth PO5 .... 181 F3
  Portsmouth, Buckland PO2 .... 182 C4
  Southampton SO15 .... 78 B1
  Waterlooville PO7 .... 111 F1
  Winchester SO22 .... 10 B4
Queen's Terr SO14 .... 103 D2
Queen's Way Portsmouth PO5 .... 182 B2
  Southampton SO14 .... 103 D2
Queens Cl Hythe SO45 .... 126 A2
  Lee-on-the-Solent PO13 .... 179 F1
  West Moors BH22 .... 138 B1
Queens Cres Horndean PO8 .... 112 B4
  Stubbington PO14 .... 154 B2
Queens Ct
  5 Bournemouth BH4 .... 204 B2
  Bournemouth,
    Charminster BH9 .... 205 D4
  New Milton BH25 .... 195 E2
Queens Gdns
  Bournemouth BH4 .... 204 B2
  Fordingbridge SP6 .... 69 F1
Queens Gr New Milton BH25 .... 195 E2
  Waterlooville PO7 .... 134 B3
Queens House 15 SO14 .... 103 D2
Queens Keep 17 PO5 .... 182 B1
Queens Mead SO22 .... 10 B3
Queens Par PO12 .... 180 C2
Queens Rd Ferndown BH22 .... 165 E2
  Lee-on-the-Solent PO13 .... 179 F1
  Lyndhurst SO43 .... 122 A3
  Petersfield GU32 .... 40 B2
Queens Ride SO52 .... 53 F2
Queens View SO31 .... 127 D3
Queens Wa BH24 .... 141 D4
Queensbury
  Mansions 7 BH1 .... 205 D2
Queensland Rd BH5 .... 206 A3
Queensmead 8 BH21 .... 163 E3
Queenstown Rd SO15 .... 102 B3
Queensway
  New Milton BH25 .... 194 C2
  North Hayling PO11 .... 160 A2
Queensway The PO16 .... 156 A4
Queenswood Ave BH23 .... 190 C1
Queenswood Dr BH22 .... 165 E4
Querida Cl SO31 .... 128 B4
Quilter Cl SO19 .... 104 B2
Quince La BH21 .... 164 A4
Quinton Cl Christchurch BH23 .... 208 C4
  Portsmouth PO5 .... 182 B2
Quintrell Ave PO16 .... 156 A4

Quob La SO30 .... 80 C2
Quomp The BH24 .... 141 D4

R L Stevenson Ave BH4 .... 204 A2
Racecourse View SO43 .... 121 F3
Rachel CI SO50 .... 57 D1
Rachel Madocks Sch PO8 ..... 111 E2
Racton Ave PO6 .... 158 A4
Racton Rd PO10 .... 136 C2
Radcliffe Ct 9 SO14 .... 103 D3
Radcliffe Rd SO14 .... 103 D3
Radclyffe Rd PO16 .... 131 E1
Radipole Rd BH17 .... 188 A1
Radley CI SO30 .... 81 E1
Radnor St PO5 .... 182 B2
Radstock Rd SO19 .... 103 F2
Radway Cres SO15 .... 102 B4
Radway Rd SO15 .... 78 C1
Raeburn CI SO24 .... 14 B3
Raeburn Dr SO30 .... 105 E4
Raglan CI SO53 .... 55 D2
Raglan Ct 3 Eastleigh SO50 ... 56 A3
Gosport PO12 .... 181 D2
Locks Heath SO31 .... 129 D3
Raglan Gdns BH11 .... 189 D1
Raglan St PO1 .... 182 B3
Raglan Terr PO10 .... 137 D1
Ragmore La GU32 .... 18 C3
Rails La PO11 .... 185 E1
Railway Cotts
   Southampton SO15 .... 101 E4
   West Meon GU32 .... 37 E2
   West Tisted GU34 .... 17 E3
Railway Flats SO15 .... 182 C3
Railway Terr SO42 .... 172 C4
Railway Triangle Ind Est PO6 158 A4
Railway View PO1 .... 182 B3
Railway View Rd SO17 .... 103 E4
Rainbow PI SO15 .... 102 B3
Rake Bsns Pk GU33 .... 21 F2
Rake CE Prim Sch GU33 .... 21 F3
Rake Rd GU33 .... 21 D2
Raleigh CI Christchurch BH23 .. 207 F4
   New Milton BH25 .... 194 C2
   Ringwood BH24 .... 141 E4
Raleigh House 25 PO1 .... 182 A3
Raleigh Rd BH12 .... 188 C1
Raleigh Wlk PO13 .... 180 B3
Raley Rd SO31 .... 129 D1
Ralph La SO51 .... 28 A1
Ralph Rd BH21 .... 186 C4
Ramalley La SO53 .... 55 D4
Rambler Dr PO13 .... 180 B3
Ramblers Way PO7 .... 112 B1
Ramillies House
   11 Fareham PO14 .... 154 C4
   15 Gosport PO12 .... 181 E2
Ramley Rd SO41 .... 197 D2
Rampart Gdns PO3 .... 157 F3
Rampart Rd SO18 .... 103 E4
Rampart Row PO12 .... 181 F2
Rampart The SO41 .... 197 E3
Rams Wlk GU32 .... 40 C2
Ramsay PI PO13 .... 155 E1
Ramsay Rd Kings Worthy SO23 ... 2 B4
   South Hayling PO11 .... 185 D2
Ramsdale Ave PO9 .... 135 E3
Ramsdean Rd GU32 .... 39 F1
Ramshill GU31 .... 41 D2
Rances Way SO22 .... 10 C3
Randall CI SO40 .... 76 B1
Randall Rd SO53 .... 30 B1
Randall's La BH24 .... 142 C3
Randalls Hill BH16 .... 186 A1
Randolph Rd
   2 Bournemouth BH1 .... 205 F2
   Poole BH14 .... 203 E3
   Portsmouth PO2 .... 157 F1
Randolph St SO15 .... 102 B4
Ranelagh Ct
   Christchurch BH23 .... 208 C4
   8 Southampton SO17 .... 103 D4
Ranelagh Gdns SO15 .... 102 C4
Ranelagh Rd
   Christchurch BH23 .... 208 C4
   Havant PO9 .... 135 E1
   Portsmouth PO2 .... 157 E1
Range Gdns SO19 .... 104 A2
Range Gn PO2 .... 157 E2
Ranmore Ct SO45 .... 125 C2
Rannoch CI PO15 .... 130 C2
Ransome CI PO14 .... 153 F4
Ranvilles Jun & Inf
   Schs PO14 .... 154 B4
Ranvilles La PO14 .... 154 A4
Rapson CI PO6 .... 133 E1
Rareridge La SO32 .... 83 F4
Ratcliffe Rd Hedge End SO30 105 E4
   Hythe SO45 .... 125 F1
Rattigan Gdns PO15 .... 129 E4
Ravana Ct 4 BH8 .... 205 F4
Raven CI PO13 .... 180 B3
Raven Croft 38 PO5 .... 182 B2
Raven Rd SO14 .... 103 D3
Raven Sq SO51 .... 55 E1
Raven Way BH23 .... 208 A3
Ravens CI PO14 .... 179 E3
Ravens Way SO41 .... 211 E2
Ravenscourt Rd
   Bournemouth BH6 .... 206 B3
   Lymington SO41 .... 197 E1
Ravenscroft CI SO31 .... 104 C1
Ravenscroft Way SO32 .... 81 F1
Ravensdale CI BH12 .... 203 E3
Ravenshall BH2 .... 204 B1

Ravenswood PO14 .... 129 E2
Ravenswood Gdns 6 PO5 ... 182 B1
Ravine Ct BH13 .... 214 C4
Ravine Gdns 5 BH13 .... 214 C4
Ravine Rd Bournemouth BH5 .. 206 A2
   Poole BH13 .... 214 C4
Raymond CI Holbury SO45 ... 150 B2
   Verwood BH31 .... 115 D3
   West End SO30 .... 80 C2
Raymond Rd Portchester PO6 .. 132 C1
   Southampton SO15 .... 102 B4
Rayners Gdns SO16 .... 79 E2
Raynes Rd PO13 .... 180 A2
Reading Room La SO32 .... 106 B4
Readon CI GU31 .... 41 D2
Readon House GU31 .... 41 D2
Rebbeck Rd BH7 .... 206 A3
Recess The SO50 .... 56 A3
Record Rd PO10 .... 136 C1
Recreation Cotts SO51 .... 50 C2
Recreation Rd BH12 .... 203 F3
Rectory Ave BH21 .... 162 B1
Rectory Ct Gosport PO12 ...... 181 D1
   Stubbington SO19 .... 154 B2
Rectory Ct SO30 .... 105 F4
Rectory Hill SP5 .... 3 E2
Rectory La Breamore SP6 ...... 46 A1
   Meonstoke SO32 .... 61 E3
Rectory Rd Havant PO9 .... 159 F4
   Poole BH15 .... 202 B3
Red Barn Ave PO17 .... 132 B1
Red Barn Cty Prim Sch PO16 156 B4
Red Barn La PO15, PO16 ..... 130 C2
Red Hill Cres SO16 .... 78 C2
Red Hill Way SO16 .... 78 C2
Red Horn CI BH16 .... 201 E2
Red House Mews SO41 .... 197 F2
Red La
   Compton(Hants) SO21 .... 31 F4
   Corfe Mullen BH21 .... 186 A4
   Owslebury SO21 .... 58 A3
   West Tytherley SP5 .... 4 A4
Red Leaves SO32 .... 83 F1
Red Lodge SO53 .... 55 D2
Red Lodge SO16 .... 78 C2
Red Oaks CI BH22 .... 165 D4
Red Roofs BH22 .... 165 F2
Redan CI BH23 .... 208 C4
Redan The PO12 .... 181 E1
Redbreast Rd BH9 .... 190 A2
Redbreast Rd N BH9 .... 190 A2
Redbridge Cswy SO15, SO40 . 101 D4
Redbridge Com Sch SO16 ..... 101 E4
Redbridge Flyover SO15 ..... 101 E4
Redbridge Gr PO9 .... 135 E2
Redbridge Hill SO16 .... 77 F1
Redbridge La SO16 .... 77 E2
Redbridge Prim Sch SO16 .... 101 E4
Redbridge Rd SO15 .... 101 E4
Redbridge Sta SO15 .... 101 E4
Redbridge Towers SO16 ..... 101 E4
Redbrook Cotts SP6 .... 94 A4
Redcar Ave PO3 .... 158 A1
Redcar St SO15 .... 102 A4
Redcliffe CI BH23 .... 192 B2
Redcote CI SO18 .... 104 A4
Redcotts La BH21 .... 163 D3
Redcotts Rd BH21 .... 163 D3
Redcroft La SO31 .... 105 D1
Redfords The SO40 .... 76 C1
Redhill SO16 .... 78 C2
Redhill Ave BH9 .... 189 F2
Redhill CI
   Bournemouth BH10 .... 189 F2
   Southampton SO16 .... 78 C2
Redhill Cres BH9 .... 189 F2
Redhill Ct
   Bournemouth BH10 .... 189 F2
   Bournemouth BH9 .... 190 A2
Redhill Dr BH10 .... 189 F2
Redhill House 55 PO1 .... 182 B3
Redhill Rd PO9 .... 113 D1
Redhill Rdbt BH10 .... 189 F2
Redhoave Rd BH17 .... 187 F1
Redhouse Park Gdns PO12 .. 180 C4
Redlands BH21 .... 203 F3
Redlands Dr SO19 .... 103 F3
Redlands Gr PO4 .... 183 E2
Redlands La Emsworth PO10 .. 136 C2
   Fareham PO14, PO16 .... 154 C4
Redlands Prim Sch SO16 ..... 155 D4
Redlynch CE Sch SP5 .... 48 A3
Redmans View BH31 .... 114 C3
Redmoor CI SO19 .... 103 F3
Rednal House 23 PO1 .... 182 B3
Redoubt Ct PO14 .... 154 C3
Redrise CI SO45 .... 150 B2
Redsails BH13 .... 214 C4
Redshank CI BH17 .... 186 C1
Redshank Rd PO4 .... 112 A4
Redvers CI SO41 .... 197 E1
Redvers Rd BH23 .... 207 F4
Redward Rd SO16 .... 77 F3
Redwing Ct PO4 .... 183 E3
Redwing Gdns SO40 .... 100 B4
Redwing Rd PO8 .... 88 B2
Redwood CI Hythe SO45 ..... 125 C2
   Lymington SO41 .... 197 E3
   Ringwood BH24 .... 141 D4
   West End SO30 .... 80 B1
Redwood Dr 3 PO7 .... 134 C4
Redwood Dr Ferndown PO22 . 165 E4
   Portchester PO16 .... 156 A4
Redwood Gdns SO40 .... 100 B4
Redwood Gr PO9 .... 136 A2
Redwood Lodge 4 PO16 .... 131 D1

Redwood Rd BH16 .... 201 D4
Redwood Way SO16 .... 79 D3
Reed Dr SO40 .... 101 F1
Reedmace CI PO7 .... 135 D3
Reeds La Liss GU33 .... 21 E3
   Rake GU33 .... 21 E3
Reeds Meadow GU32 .... 39 E2
Reeds PI PO12 .... 181 D3
Reeds Rd PO12 .... 181 D4
Reeves CI SO51 .... 50 C2
Reeves Way SO31 .... 104 C1
Regal CI PO6 .... 157 F4
Regency Ct PO9 .... 159 F4
Regency Gdns PO7 .... 134 B3
Regency PI BH24 .... 141 D4
Regent CI SO21 .... 31 E2
Regent Ct
   24 Southampton SO17 .... 79 D1
   17 Winchester SO23 .... 2 A1
Regent Dr BH7 .... 205 F4
Regent House SO30 .... 81 E2
Regent Mews GU32 .... 40 B2
Regent PI PO5 .... 182 A2
Regent Rd SO53 .... 55 E3
Regent St Portsmouth PO1 ... 182 B4
   Southampton SO14 .... 102 C2
Regent Way BH23 .... 207 D3
Regent's Gr 1 SO15 .... 102 A4
Regent's Park Gdns SO15 .... 102 A4
Regent's Park Rd SO15 .... 102 A4
Regents Ct 6 SO16 .... 102 A4
Regents Gate SO31 .... 128 C3
Regents Park Girls
   Sch SO15 .... 102 A4
Reginald Rd PO4 .... 183 D2
Reid St BH23 .... 207 D4
Reigate House 54 PO1 .... 182 B3
Relay Rd PO7 .... 134 B4
Reldas The PO1 .... 182 A2
Reliant CI SO53 .... 55 D3
Rempstone Rd BH21 .... 187 E4
Renault Dr BH18 .... 187 D1
Renda Rd SO45 .... 150 B2
Renny Rd PO1 .... 182 C3
Renouf CI SO41 .... 197 E2
Renown CI SO53 .... 55 D3
Renown Gdns PO8 .... 111 F3
Renown House 14 PO12 .... 181 E2
Repton CI PO12 .... 180 C2
Repton Gdns SO30 .... 81 E1
Reservoir La
   Hedge End SO30 .... 105 D3
   Petersfield GU32 .... 40 C3
Resolution House 13 PO12 .. 181 E2
Rest-a-Wyle Ave PO11 .... 185 D3
Restharrow BH1 .... 205 D2
Retreat Rd BH1 .... 163 E2
Retreat The Eastleigh SO50 .. 56 A2
   Portsmouth PO5 .... 182 B2
   Totton SO40 .... 101 D3
Revenge CI PO4 .... 183 E3
Revenge House 12 PO12 .... 181 E2
Rewlands Dr SO22 .... 1 B2
Rex Est SO53 .... 55 E3
Reynard CI BH15 .... 202 C2
Reynolds CI SO51 .... 53 D3
Reynolds Dale SO40 .... 100 B3
Reynolds Rd Fair Oak SO50 .. 57 E1
   Gosport PO12 .... 181 E1
   Southampton SO15 .... 102 B4
Rhinefield CI
   Bishopstoke SO50 .... 56 C1
   Brockenhurst SO42 .... 145 F1
   Havant PO9 .... 135 E2
Rhinefield Ornamental Dr
   SO42 .... 144 C3
Rhinefield Rd
   Brockenhurst SO42 .... 145 E1
   New Milton BH25 .... 170 C1
Rhiners CI SO41 .... 172 A1
Rhyme Hall Mews SO45 ...... 151 D2
Rhys Ct PO4 .... 183 D2
Ribble CI Broadstone BH18 .. 187 D1
   Chandler's Ford SO53 .... 55 E3
Ribble CI SO16 .... 77 F1
Ricardo Cres BH23 .... 208 A3
Rice Gdns BH16 .... 201 E2
Rice Terr BH16 .... 201 E2
Richard CI BH16 .... 201 D4
Richard Gr PO12 .... 156 A1
Richard Moss House 6 SO23 .. 11 D4
Richards CI SO31 .... 129 D2
Richards Ct 13 SO15 .... 78 A1
Richlans Rd SO30 .... 105 E3
Richmond CI
   Chandler's Ford SO53 .... 30 B1
   South Hayling PO11 .... 184 C2
   Totton SO40 .... 76 A1
Richmond Ct
   15 Bournemouth BH5 .... 205 F2
   12 Milford on Sea SO41 .... 211 E2
   7 New Milton BH25 .... 195 D2
Richmond Dr PO11 .... 184 C2
Richmond Gdns
   Bournemouth BH1 .... 204 C2
   Southampton SO17 .... 79 D1
   Waterlooville PO7 .... 134 B3
Richmond Hall 6 SO17 .... 79 E1
Richmond Hill BH1, BH2 .... 204 C2
Richmond Hill Dr BH2 .... 204 C2
Richmond House
   34 Portsmouth PO1 .... 182 A3
   5 Southampton SO15 .... 102 B3
Richmond La SO51 .... 28 A1
Richmond Park Ave BH8 .... 205 E4
Richmond Park CI BH8 ...... 205 E4
Richmond Park Cres BH8 ... 205 E4
Richmond Park Rd BH8 ..... 205 E4

Richmond PI PO1 .... 182 A3
Richmond Rd Gosport PO12 . 181 D2
   Lee-on-the-Solent PO13 .... 179 F1
   Poole BH14 .... 203 E2
   Portsmouth PO5 .... 182 B1
   Southampton SO15 .... 102 B3
   Wimborne Minster BH21 ... 163 E2
Richmond Rise
   Bournemouth BH8 .... 205 E3
   Portchester PO16 .... 132 B1
Richmond St SO14 .... 103 D2
Richmond Wood Rd BH8 .... 205 E4
Richville Rd SO16 .... 102 A4
Ridding CI SO15 .... 78 B1
Riders Inf Sch PO9 .... 135 F3
Riders Jun Sch PO9 .... 135 F3
Ridge CI PO8 .... 88 B2
Ridge Common La GU32 .... 40 B3
Ridge La Botley SO30 .... 106 B2
   Romsey SO51 .... 76 B4
Ridge The SP5 .... 47 E3
Ridge Top La GU32 .... 39 F3
Ridgefield Gdns BH23 .... 208 B4
Ridgemede Cty Jun
   Sch SO32 .... 83 E4
Ridgemount Ave SO16 .... 78 C3
Ridgemount Gdns BH15 .... 201 F2
Ridgemount La SO16 .... 78 C3
Ridgeway Broadstone BH18 . 187 D2
   Corfe Mullen BH18 .... 186 B4
   Ferndown BH22 .... 189 F4
   Winchester SO22 .... 10 B3
Ridgeway CI
   Chandler's Ford SO53 .... 55 F3
   Cosham PO6 .... 132 C1
   Fair Oak SO50 .... 57 E2
Ridgeway House Sch SO19 .. 103 F3
Ridgeway La SO41 .... 197 E1
Ridgeway The PO16 .... 131 F1
Ridgeway Wlk SO53 .... 55 F3
Ridgewood CI SO45 .... 125 E2
Ridings The Fair Oak SO50 ... 57 D1
   Liss GU33 .... 21 D2
   Portsmouth PO2 .... 157 F2
   Shedfield SO32 .... 83 F2
Ridley CI SO45 .... 150 B2
Ridley Rd BH9 .... 204 C4
Ridout CI BH10 .... 189 D1
Rigby Rd SO17 .... 103 D4
Riggs Gdns BH11 .... 188 C1
Rigler Rd BH15 .... 202 A1
Rimbury Way BH23 .... 207 D4
Rimington Gdns 1 SO51 .... 28 A1
Rimington Rd PO8 .... 111 F2
Ring The SO16 .... 78 C4
Ringbury SO41 .... 197 E3
Ringlet Way 6 SO23 .... 11 E4
Ringwood CE Inf Sch
   BH24 .... 141 D4
Ringwood Dr SO52 .... 53 F3
Ringwood House PO9 .... 135 F3
Ringwood Jun Sch BH24 .... 141 D4
Ringwood Rd Alderholt SP6 .. 93 D2
   Bournemouth BH11 .... 188 C2
   Bransgore BH23 .... 193 E3
   Burley BH24 .... 142 C3
   Christchurch BH23 .... 194 A1
   Ferndown BH22 .... 165 E2
   Fordingbridge SP6 .... 94 A2
   Fordingbridge SP6 .... 94 B2
   Netley Marsh SO40 .... 100 B4
   Poole BH12,BH14 .... 203 D4
   Portsmouth PO4 .... 183 D2
   Sopley BH23 .... 192 A4
   St Leonards BH24 .... 139 E1
   Three Legged Cross BH22 . 138 C4
   Totton SO40 .... 100 B4
   Verwood BH31 .... 115 D3
Ringwood Terr SO42 .... 146 A1
Ringwood Waldorf Sch BH24 140 B3
Ripley Gr PO3 .... 183 D4
Ripon Rd BH9 .... 190 A1
Ripplewood SO40 .... 102 A1
Ripstone Gdns SO17 .... 79 D2
Rise The Brockenhurst SO42 . 145 F1
   Waterlooville PO7 .... 134 B1
Ritchie CI PO11 .... 185 D2
Ritchie Ct SO19 .... 104 A2
Ritchie PI BH22 .... 138 B2
Ritchie Rd BH11 .... 189 D2
Rival Moor Rd GU31 .... 41 E1
River CI BH21 .... 163 E3
River Ct SO41 .... 197 F2
River Gr SO31 .... 128 A1
River La PO15 .... 130 B3
River Mews SO50 .... 56 B2
River Park L Ctr SO23 .... 2 A1
River Pk BH6 .... 206 C3
River St PO10 .... 137 D2
River View House SO19 .... 103 E2
River View Rd SO18 .... 79 E1
River Way Christchurch BH23 191 E1
   Havant PO9 .... 136 A2
River Wlk SO18 .... 79 F2
River's St PO5 .... 182 B2
Riverbourne Ct SO18 .... 103 E4
Riverdale Ave PO7 .... 135 D4
Riverdale CI SP6 .... 69 F1
Riverdale Cotts PO16 .... 131 E2
Riverdale La BH23 .... 207 D3
Riverdene PI SO18 .... 103 E4
Riverhead CI PO4 .... 183 D3
Riverlea Rd BH23 .... 207 D3
Rivermead CI SO51 .... 52 B4
Rivermead Ct PO10 .... 137 D2

Rivermead Gdns BH23 191
Riverpark Ct SO18 79
Rivers Reach SO41 197
Riversdale 9 BH21 163
Riversdale CI SO19 126
Riversdale Gdns PO9 135
Riversdale Rd BH6 207
Riverside Bishopstoke SO50 .. 56
   Bournemouth BH10 189
   Ringwood BH24 140
Riverside Ave
   Bournemouth BH7 191
   Fareham PO16 131
Riverside Bsns Pk SO41 197
Riverside CI Cadnam SO40 ... 99
   Liss GU33 20
Riverside Cotts SO21 31
Riverside Ct SO18 103
Riverside Gdns SO51 52
Riverside House 44 SO23 11
Riverside La BH6 206
Riverside Mews PO17 108
Riverside Park BH23 207
Riverside Pk BH21 163
Riverside Rd
   Bournemouth BH6 206
   West Moors BH22 138
Riverside Sch PO7 134
Riverside Terr PO16 131
Riverside Wlk GU31 41
Riverslea Mews BH23 207
Riverview SO40 100
Riverview Terr SO31 128
Riviera Ct
   3 Bournemouth BH2 204
   3 Poole BH13 214
Rivirea 22 BH1 205
Road View PO2 182
Roads Hill PO8 88
Robere House SO19 103
Robert Cecil Ave SO18 79
Robert Mack Ct 32 PO1 182
Robert Whitworth Dr
   1 SO51 52
Roberts CI Hordle SO41 196
   Wickham PO17 108
Roberts La BH17 202
Roberts Rd
   Bournemouth BH7 206
   Broadstone BH17 187
   Gosport PO12 180
   Hythe SO45 125
   Southampton SO15 102
Robertshaw House SO43 121
Robin Cres BH25 194
Robin Ct SO15 102
Robin Gdns Totton SO40 100
   Waterlooville PO8 111
Robin Gr BH25 194
Robin Sq SO50 55
Robina CI PO7 135
Robinia Gn SO16 78
Robins CI PO14 154
Robins Ct 8 BH21 163
Robins Meadow PO14 129
Robins Way BH23 208
Robinson Ct PO16 132
Robinson Rd PO14 179
Robinson Way PO3 158
Robinswood Dr BH22 165
Robsall CI BH12 203
Robville St BH6 206
Roche Court (Boundary
   Oak Prep Sch) PO17 131
Rochester Ct PO13 180
Rochester Rd
   Bournemouth BH11 189
   Portsmouth PO4 182
Rochester St SO14 103
Rochford Rd PO6 157
Rockall CI SO16 77
Rockbourne Ct PO9 135
Rockbourne Gdns BH25 209
Rockbourne La
   Damerham SP6 68
   Rockbourne SP6 68
Rockbourne Rd SO22 1
Rockery CI SO45 125
Rockford CI BH6 206
Rockford House SO50 57
Rockingham Way PO16 156
Rockleigh Dr SO40 100
Rockleigh Rd SO16 78
Rockley Rd BH15 201
Rockpit Cotts GU33 21
Rockram CI SO40 99
Rockram Gdns SO45 125
Rockstone La SO14 103
Rockstone PI SO15 102
Rockville Dr PO7 134
Rodbard House SO31 104
Rodbourne CI SO41 211
Rodfield La SO24 13
Rodlease La SO41 173
Rodney CI Gosport PO13 180
   Poole BH12 204
Rodney Ct Christchurch BH23 208
   Poole BH12 202
   Southampton SO14 104
Rodney Dr BH23 207
Rodney House 27 PO12 181
Rodney Rd PO4 183
Rodney Way PO8 112
Rodway Rd BH21 163
Rodwell CI BH10 189
Roebuck CI Cosham PO6 157
   New Milton BH25 195

Roeshot Cres BH23 .... 193 F1
Roeshot Hill BH23 .... 193 F1
Roewood Cl SO45 .... 150 B2
Roewood Rd SO45 .... 150 B2
Rogate Gdns PO16 .... 132 B1
Rogate House 48 SO14 .... 182 B3
Roger Penny Way
  Brook SO43, SP6 .... 73 E1
  Fordingbridge, Bramshaw SP6 .... 72 B3
  Fordingbridge, Godshill SP6 .... 71 D3
Rogers Cl Bishopstoke SO50 ...... 56 C2
  Gosport PO12 .... 181 D3
Rogers House PO13 .... 179 F1
Rogers Mead PO11 .... 159 F2
Rogers Rd SO50 .... 56 C2
Roker Way SO50 .... 57 D1
Roland Cl PO8 .... 112 A3
Rolleston Rd SO45 .... 150 B1
Rolls Dr BH6 .... 207 D2
Roman Ct SO53 .... 55 F4
Roman Ct PO10 .... 137 E1
Roman Dr SO18 .... 78 C4
Roman Gdns SO45 .... 125 C1
Roman Gr PO16 .... 156 B3
Roman House SO18 .... 103 E4
Roman Hts BH21 .... 186 C4
Roman Meadow SP5 .... 46 C4
Roman Quay SP6 .... 69 F1
Roman Rd Chilworth SO16 .... 78 C4
  Corfe Mullen BH18 .... 186 C3
  Havant PO10 .... 136 B1
  Holbury SO45 .... 150 A3
  Hythe SO45 .... 125 E1
  Twyford SO21 .... 32 A3
Roman Row SO32 .... 83 E4
Roman Way Havant PO9 .... 135 E1
  Hythe SO45 .... 125 E1
  Pamphill BH21 .... 162 B3
Romans' Rd 1 SO23 .... 11 D3
Romford Rd SO31 .... 152 B4
Romill Cl SO30 .... 80 A2
Romney Cl BH10 .... 189 F2
Romney Rd BH10 .... 189 F2
Romsey Abbey CE Prim Sch
  SO51 .... 52 C4
Romsey Ave Portchester PO16 .. 156 A4
  Portsmouth PO3 .... 183 D3
Romsey Cl SO50 .... 56 A2
Romsey Ct
  10 Southampton SO15 ...... 102 B3
  New Milton BH25 .... 194 C2
Romsey Hospl SO51 .... 53 D4
Romsey Ind Est SO51 .... 52 C4
Romsey Inf Sch SO51 .... 52 C4
Romsey Jun Sch SO51 .... 53 D4
Romsey Lodge 7 SO15 .... 78 A1
Romsey Rd Cadnam SO40 .... 75 F3
  Eastleigh SO50 .... 56 A2
  Horndean PO8 .... 88 B1
  King's Somborne SO51 .... 6 B4
  Lyndhurst SO43 .... 121 F3
  Ower SO40 .... 75 E2
  Rownhams SO16 .... 77 F2
  Southampton SO16 .... 77 F2
  West Wellow SO51 .... 51 D2
  Whiteparish SP5 .... 24 C2
  Winchester SO22, SO23 .... 10 B3
Romsey Sch The SO51 .... 52 C4
Romsey Sta SO51 .... 52 C4
Romyns Ct PO14 .... 130 C1
Ronald Bowker Ct 1 SO22 .. 10 C4
Ronald Pugh Ct SO18 .... 79 F1
Rook Hill Rd BH23 .... 208 B3
Rookcliff 13 SO41 .... 211 E2
Rookcliff Way SO41 .... 211 E2
Rookery Ave Swanwick SO31 ... 129 D4
  Swanwick PO15 .... 129 E4
Rookery Cotts SP5 .... 3 E2
Rookery La SP6 .... 45 F1
Rookery The PO10 .... 137 D1
Rookes Cl PO8 .... 112 A3
Rookes La SO41 .... 197 E1
Rookesbury Park Sch PO17 .. 108 B2
Rookley SO31 .... 127 E4
Rooks Down Rd SO22 .... 10 B3
Rooksbridge SO45 .... 125 D2
Rooksbury Croft PO9 .... 136 A3
Rooksway Gr PO16 .... 155 F4
Rookwood 3 SO41 .... 211 E2
Rookwood Cl SO50 .... 56 A3
Rookwood View PO7 .... 110 C3
Roosevelt Cres BH11 .... 189 D3
Rope Hill SO41 .... 173 E1
Rope Wlk SO31 .... 128 A1
Ropers La BH16 .... 201 E4
Ropley Cl SO19 .... 127 D4
Ropley Ct PO11 .... 184 C2
Ropley Rd Bournemouth BH7 .. 206 B4
47 Havant PO9 .... 136 A3
Rosamund Ave BH21 .... 163 F1
Roscrea Cl BH6 .... 207 D2
Roscrea Dr BH6 .... 207 D2
Rose Cl Hedge End SO30 ...... 105 E4
  Hythe SO45 .... 126 A1
Rose Cott PO8 .... 112 B4
Rose Cres BH15 .... 202 C3
Rose Ct BH15 .... 202 C2
Rose Gdn The BH23 .... 191 E1
Rose Gdns BH9 .... 190 A2
Rose Hill PO8 .... 112 A3
Rose Rd Southampton SO14 .. 103 D4
  Totton SO40 .... 101 D3
Rosebank Cl SO16 .... 77 F3
Rosebank Lodge SO16 .... 77 F3
Rosebay Cl SO50 .... 81 E3
Rosebay Ct 4 PO7 .... 134 C3
Rosebery Ave Cosham PO6 .. 158 A4
  Hythe SO45 .... 126 A1

Rosebery Cl BH31 .... 115 E3
Rosebery Cres SO50 .... 56 A3
Rosebery Rd BH5 .... 206 A3
Rosebrook Ct 16 SO18 ...... 103 F4
Rosebud Ct BH9 .... 190 A1
Rosedale Ave SO51 .... 53 D4
Rosedale Cl
  3 Christchurch BH23 .... 207 F3
  Titchfield PO14 .... 153 F4
Rosehill Cl BH23 .... 169 D1
Rosehill Dr BH23 .... 169 D1
Roselands Waterlooville PO8 .. 112 A3
  West End SO30 .... 104 B4
Roselands Cl SO50 .... 57 D2
Roselands Gdns SO17 .... 79 D1
Roseleigh Dr SO40 .... 100 C3
Rosemary Ct 14 BH23 .... 209 D4
Rosemary Gdns
  Hedge End SO30 .... 105 E3
  Poole BH15 .... 203 D4
Rosemary La 18 PO1 .... 182 A3
Rosemary Rd BH12 .... 203 E4
Rosemary Way PO8 .... 112 A3
Rosemary Wlk 17 PO13 .... 179 F1
Rosemoor Gr SO53 .... 30 A1
Rosemount Rd BH4 .... 204 A1
Rosendale Rd SO53 .... 55 E2
Rosery The PO12 .... 181 D1
Rosetta Rd PO4 .... 183 D2
Rosewall Rd SO16 .... 77 F2
Rosewarne Ct 28 SO23 .... 2 A1
Rosewood PO13 .... 155 F1
Rosewood Gdns
  Clanfield PO8 .... 88 B3
  Marchwood SO40 .... 102 A1
  New Milton BH25 .... 194 C2
Rosina Cl PO7 .... 135 D4
Roslin Gdns BH3 .... 204 B4
Roslin Rd BH3 .... 204 C4
Roslin Rd S BH3 .... 204 C4
Roslyn House 19 PO5 .... 182 B2
Rosoman Ct SO19 .... 103 F2
Rosoman Rd SO19 .... 103 F2
Ross Gdns
  Bournemouth BH11 .... 188 B3
  Southampton SO16 .... 78 A1
Ross Glades BH3 .... 204 C3
Ross Mews 2 SO31 .... 127 D3
Ross Rd BH24 .... 117 E1
Ross Way PO13 .... 179 F2
Rossan Ave SO31 .... 152 B4
Rossington Ave SO18 .... 103 F4
Rossington Way SO18 .... 103 F4
Rossiters La SO40 .... 99 F3
Rossley Cl BH23 .... 193 F1
Rosslyn Cl SO52 .... 54 A2
Rossmore Rd BH12 .... 203 E4
Rossmore Sh Par BH12 ...... 203 D4
Rostrevor La 3 PO4 .... 182 C1
Rostron Cl SO18 .... 80 A1
Rosyth Rd SO18 .... 103 F4
Rotary Cl BH21 .... 163 F4
Rotary Ct SO31 .... 127 D3
Rotary House SO15 .... 102 B4
Rothbury Cl
  Southampton SO19 .... 104 A2
  Totton SO40 .... 76 B1
Rothbury Park BH25 .... 195 D1
Rother Cl Petersfield GU31 ... 41 E2
  West End SO30 .... 80 A1
Rother Dale SO19 .... 104 C2
Rother House GU33 .... 20 C2
Rotherbank Farm La GU33 .... 21 D3
Rothercombe La GU32 .... 40 A2
Rotherfield Rd
  Bournemouth BH5 .... 206 A2
  Christchurch BH23 .... 194 A1
Rotherley La GU32 .... 40 C2
Rotherwick Cl PO9 .... 136 A3
Rothesay Dr BH23 .... 208 C4
Rothesay Rd
  Bournemouth BH4 .... 204 B3
  Gosport PO12 .... 181 D4
Rothsbury Dr SO53 .... 55 D3
Rothschild Cl SO19 .... 103 F1
Rothville Pl SO53 .... 30 A1
Rothwell Cl PO6 .... 133 D1
Rotterdam Dr BH23 .... 207 F3
Rotterdam Towers 8 SO19 .. 126 C4
Roughdown La SO45 .... 150 B1
Roumelia La BH5 .... 205 F2
Round Hill SP5 .... 69 F1
Roundabouts The GU33 ...... 21 D3
Roundcopse SO45 .... 125 E2
Roundhaye Rd BH11 .... 188 C3
Roundhill Cl SO18 .... 80 A1
Roundhouse Ct PO11 .... 185 D1
Roundhouse Dr SO40 .... 100 A3
Roundhouse Meadow PO10 .. 161 D4
Roundhuts Rise 4 SO23 ..... 11 E4
Roundway PO7 .... 134 C4
Roundways BH11 .... 188 C2
Routs Way SO16 .... 77 F4
Row The SP5 .... 47 E4
Row Wood La PO13 .... 155 D1
Rowallan Ave PO13 .... 180 B4
Rowan Ave PO8 .... 112 A4
Rowan Cl Bursledon SO31 .. 127 F4
  Christchurch BH23 .... 208 B4
  Lee-on-the-Solent PO13 .... 179 F1
  Romsey SO51 .... 53 E2
  Southampton SO16 .... 78 A4
  St Leonards BH24 .... 139 E2
  Swanmore SO32 .... 84 A2
  Sway SO41 .... 172 A1
  Totton SO40 .... 100 B3
Rowan Ct Portsmouth PO4 .. 182 C2
  Southampton SO19 .... 103 F2

Rowan Dr Broadstone BH17 .. 186 C1
  Christchurch BH23 .... 208 B4
  Verwood BH31 .... 115 D2
Rowan Gdns SO30 .... 105 E3
Rowan Rd PO9 .... 136 A2
Rowan Tree Cl GU33 .... 21 D2
Rowan Way PO14 .... 154 B4
Rowans Pk SO41 .... 197 E2
Rowans The SO40 .... 101 F1
Rowbarrow Cl BH17 .... 187 E1
Rowborough Rd SO18 ...... 103 F4
Rowbury Rd PO9 .... 135 E3
Rowden Cl SO51 .... 50 C1
Rowe Asheway SO31 .... 128 C2
Rowena Rd BH6 .... 206 C3
Rowes Alley PO1 .... 181 F2
Rowes La SO41 .... 199 D4
Rowhay La SO32 .... 58 B3
Rowhill Dr SO45 .... 125 E2
Rowin Cl PO14 .... 185 E1
Rowland Ave BH15 .... 202 C3
Rowland Ct PO15 .... 130 C1
Rowland Rd PO6 .... 132 C1
Rowlands Castle Rd PO8 .. 112 C3
Rowlands Castle CE Prim Sch
  PO9 .... 136 A4
Rowlands Castle Sta PO9 .. 113 E1
Rowlands Cl SO53 .... 55 D2
Rowlands Hill BH21 .... 163 E3
Rowlands Wlk 2 SO18 .... 80 A1
Rowley Cl SO30 .... 105 F4
Rowley Ct SO30 .... 105 F4
Rowley Dr SO30 .... 105 F4
Rowlings Rd SO22 .... 1 B2
Rowner Cl PO13 .... 155 E1
Rowner Jun & Inf Schs PO13 .. 155 E1
Rowner La Gosport PO13 .... 155 E1
  Gosport, Rowner PO13 ...... 180 B4
Rowner Rd Gosport PO13 .. 155 D1
  Stubbington PO13 .... 155 D1
Rownhams CE Prim Sch SO16 .. 77 F3
Rownhams Cl SO16 .... 77 F3
Rownhams La SO52 .... 53 F1
Rownhams Rd
  Bournemouth BH8 .... 190 B2
  Havant PO9 .... 135 E3
  North Baddesley SO52 .... 54 A2
  Southampton SO16 .... 77 F2
Rownhams Rd N SO16 .... 77 F3
Rownhams Way SO16 .... 77 F3
Roxan Ct 9 SO15 .... 102 C4
Roxburgh House SO31 ...... 129 D2
Royal Arc 5 BH7 .... 205 F2
Royal Bournemouth
  Gen Hospl The BH23 .... 191 D1
Royal Crescent Rd SO14 .. 103 D2
Royal Ct Chandler's Ford SO53 .. 55 E3
  Southampton SO17 .... 79 E1
Royal Gate PO4 .... 183 D1
Royal Gdns PO9 .... 113 D1
Royal Greenjackets
  Mus The SO22 .... 10 C4
Royal Hampshire Cty Hospl
  SO22 .... 10 B4
Royal Hampshire
  Regiment Mus SO22 .... 10 C4
Royal London Pk SO30 ...... 105 D4
Royal Marines Mus PO4 .... 183 D1
Royal Naval Cotts PO17 .... 132 C3
Royal Naval Hospl Haslar
  PO12 .... 181 E1
Royal Oak Rd BH10 .... 189 E3
Royal South Hants Hospl
  SO14 .... 103 D3
Royal Sovereign Ave PO14 .. 155 D3
Royal Victoria Ctry Pk SO31 .. 127 E2
Royal Victoria Hospl BH2 .. 204 B2
Royal Way PO7 .... 135 D4
Royden La SO41 .... 173 E2
Roydon Cl SO22 .... 10 C3
Royster Cl BH17 .... 187 E1
Royston Ave SO50 .... 56 A3
Royston Cl SO17 .... 79 D1
Royston Ct SO50 .... 76 C1
Royston Dr BH21 .... 163 E3
Royston Pl BH25 .... 210 A4
Rozel Ct SO16 .... 77 F2
Rozel Manor BH13 .... 204 A1
Rozelle Cl SO22 .... 1 A3
Rozelle Rd BH14 .... 203 E2
Rubens Ct BH25 .... 195 D2
Ruby Rd SO19 .... 104 A3
Rudd Lane SO51 .... 27 F4
Rudgewick Cl PO16 .... 156 A4
Rudmore Rd PO2 .... 182 B4
Rudmore Sq PO2 .... 182 B4
Ruffield Cl SO22 .... 1 B1
Rufford Gdns BH6 .... 206 C3
Rufus Cl
  Chandler's Ford SO53 .... 55 F4
  Rownhams SO16 .... 77 E3
Rufus Ct SO43 .... 122 A3
Rufus Gdns SO40 .... 100 B4
Rufus Stone SO43 .... 98 A3
Rugby Rd Broadstone BH17 .. 187 D1
  Portsmouth PO5 .... 182 C2
Rumbridge Gdns SO40 ...... 101 D4
Rumbridge St SO40 .... 101 D3
Runnymede Fareham PO15 .. 130 B2
  West End SO30 .... 80 B1
Runnymede Ave BH11 ...... 188 C3
Runton Rd BH12 .... 203 F3
Runway The PO8 .... 208 A4
Rushall La BH21 .... 186 A3
Rushcombe Cty Fst
  Sch BH21 .... 186 B3

Rushcombe Way BH21 ...... 186 C3
Rushes Farm GU32 .... 40 C2
Rushes Rd GU32 .... 40 C2
Rushes The SO40 .... 101 F1
Rushford Warren BH23 ..... 207 F2
Rushington Bsns Pk SO40 .. 100 C3
Rushington Ave SO40 ...... 100 C3
Rushington La SO40 .... 100 C3
Rushmere Gate PO7 .... 86 B1
Rushmere La SO18 .... 79 F1
Rushmere Rd BH6 .... 206 B4
Rushmere Wlk 3 PO9 .... 135 E3
Rushpole Ct SO45 .... 125 E2
Rushton Cres BH3 .... 204 C3
Ruskin Ave BH9 .... 190 A2
Ruskin Rd Eastleigh SO50 .... 56 A3
  Portsmouth PO4 .... 183 D2
Ruskin Way PO8 .... 111 F2
Rusland Cl SO53 .... 55 D4
Russel Rd BH10 .... 189 E3
Russell Bldgs PO16 .... 156 B4
Russell Churcher Ct PO12 .. 180 C4
Russell Cl PO13 .... 179 F1
Russell Cotes Art Gall & Mus
  BH1 .... 205 D1
Russell Cotes Rd BH1 .... 205 D1
Russell Ct 3 BH25 .... 195 D2
Russell Dr BH23 .... 207 E3
Russell Gdns
  Hamworthy BH16 .... 201 E2
  St Leonards BH24 .... 140 A3
Russell Pl Fareham PO16 .... 131 D1
  Southampton SO17 .... 79 D1
Russell Rd Havant PO9 ..... 135 F2
  Lee-on-the-Solent PO13 .... 179 F1
  Winchester SO23 .... 2 A1
Russell St Gosport PO12 .... 181 D3
  21 Southampton SO14 ..... 103 D2
Russell Way GU31 .... 41 D1
Russet Cl Ferndown BH22 .. 165 E3
  9 Lymington SO41 .... 197 F1
Russet House SO30 .... 105 D3
Russett Cl SO32 .... 84 A2
Rustan Cl Fair Oak SO50 .... 57 E1
  Hedge End SO30 .... 105 D3
Rutland Cl SO18 .... 104 A4
Rutland Gdns SO31 .... 105 D1
Rutland Manor 9 BH12 .... 204 A2
Rutland Rd
  Bournemouth BH9 .... 205 D4
  Christchurch BH23 .... 191 F1
Rutland Way SO18 .... 80 A1
Ruxley Cl SO45 .... 150 B2
Ryall Rd BH17 .... 187 E1
Ryan Cl BH22 .... 165 E4
Ryan Gdns
  Bournemouth BH11 .... 189 D3
  Ferndown BH22 .... 165 E4
Rydal Cl Christchurch BH23 .. 191 E2
  20 Cosham PO6 .... 133 D1
Rydal House 22 PO6 .... 133 D1
Rydal Mews BH21 .... 163 E3
Rydal Rd PO12 .... 181 D3
Ryde Pl PO13 .... 180 A2
Ryde Terr SO14 .... 103 D2
Rye Dale SO40 .... 100 B2
Rye Paddock La SO45 ...... 151 D2
Ryecroft Havant PO9 .... 136 A1
  Titchfield PO14 .... 129 E1
Ryecroft Ave BH11 .... 188 C3
Ryedown La SO51 .... 51 F2
Ryefield Cl GU31 .... 41 E2
Ryefield Cotts GU31 .... 41 F1
Rylands Cl SO16 .... 77 F2

Sabre Rd PO10 .... 161 D2
Sackville St PO5 .... 182 B2
Saddle Cl BH21 .... 164 B3
Saddlers Cl SO50 .... 56 A3
Saddlers La SO45 .... 126 A1
Sadlers Wlk PO10 .... 161 D4
Saffron Ct SO31 .... 128 C1
Saffron Dr BH23 .... 208 A4
Sage Cl PO7 .... 135 D4
Sages La GU34 .... 17 E3
Sailors La SO32 .... 60 B4
Sainsbury Lodge PO1 ...... 182 C3
Saints Cl BH21 .... 138 C4
St Adlem's CE Comb Sch
  BH12 .... 204 A3
St Agatha's Rd SO31 .... 128 A2
St Agathas Way 10 PO1 .... 182 B3
St Alban's Ave SO40 .... 205 E4
St Alban's CE Prim Sch PO9 .. 136 A2
St Alban's Cres BH8 .... 205 D4
St Alban's Rd
  Bournemouth BH8 .... 205 D4
  Havant PO9 .... 136 A2
  Portsmouth PO4 .... 182 C2
  Southampton SO14 .... 103 D3
St Albans Ct SO13 .... 180 B3
St Aldhelm's BH14 .... 203 E2
St Aldhelm's Cl BH13 .... 203 F2
St Aldhelm's Rd BH13 ...... 203 F2
St Andrew Cl PO8 .... 88 B1
St Andrew's Bldgs SO31 .. 128 A1
St Andrew's Rd
  Cosham PO6 .... 158 C4
  Gosport PO12 .... 181 D3
  Portsmouth PO5 .... 182 B2
  South Hayling PO11 .... 185 D1
St Andrews BH23 .... 207 D3
St Andrews Cl
  Michelmersh SO51 .... 27 C3
  North Baddesley SO52 ...... 53 F3
St Andrews Gn SO32 .... 61 E3
St Andrews House 18 SO17 .. 103 D4
St Andrews Park SO50 .... 81 D4

St Andrews Rd
  Broadstone BH18 .... 187 D3
  Southampton SO17 .... 103 D3
St Ann's Cres PO12 .... 181 D3
St Ann's Ct 1 BH1, ... 205 F3
St Ann's Hospl BH13 .... 214 C3
St Ann's Rd PO8 .... 112 B4
St Ann's Ave BH6 .... 206 C3
St Anne's Convent RC
  Girls Sch
  SO15 .... 102 C3
St Anne's Gdns SO19 ...... 103 F1
St Anne's Gr PO14 .... 154 C4
St Anne's Rd Portsmouth PO4 .. 182 C2
  Southampton SO19 .... 103 F1
  Upton BH16 .... 201 D4
St Annes Cl SO22 .... 10 B2
St Annes Gdns SO41 .... 197 E3
St Annes House SO51 .... 52 C3
St Annes La SO32 .... 107 F4
St Annes Mews 16 SO14 .. 103 D4
St Anns Ct 7 SO17 .... 79 D1
St Anthony's RC Prim Sch
  PO14 .... 129 E1
St Anthony's Rd BH2 ...... 204 C3
St Aubin's Ave SO19 .... 104 A3
St Aubin's Park PO11 ...... 184 B2
St Aubyns Ct 3 BH15 ...... 202 A1
St Aubyns La PO14 .... 117 F1
St Augustin's Rd BH2 ...... 204 C3
St Augustine Gdns SO17 .... 79 E1
St Augustine Rd PO4 .... 182 C2
St Austell Cl SO50 .... 56 C2
St Barbara Way PO2 .... 157 F2
St Barbe Cl SO51 .... 53 D3
St Bartholomew's Gdns PO5 .. 182 B2
St Bede CE Prim Sch SO23 .. 11 D4
St Bede's Ct 28 SO23 .... 2 A1
St Bernard House 24 SO14 .. 103 D2
St Birinus Rd SP5 .... 47 E3
St Blaize Rd SO51 .... 53 E4
St Boniface Ct SO52 .... 54 A2
St Bonnet Dr SO32 .... 83 E4
St Brelade Pl SO16 .... 77 E2
St Brelades BH14 .... 203 E1
St Brelades Ave BH12 ...... 188 B1
St Catherine St PO5 .... 182 B1
St Catherine's Par BH23 .. 191 F1
St Catherine's RC Prim Sch
  BH21 .... 164 A3
St Catherine's Rd
  Bournemouth BH6 .... 206 C2
  South Hayling PO11 .... 184 B2
  Southampton SO18 .... 79 F1
  Winchester SO23 .... 11 D3
St Catherine's Way BH23 .. 191 E2
St Catherines Ct SO23 ...... 163 E2
St Catherines Ct PO11 ...... 184 B2
St Catherines Rd SO50 ...... 56 A3
St Catherines View SO30 .. 105 D3
St Catherines Way
  Portchester PO16 .... 131 E2
  Winchester SO23 .... 11 E3
St Chad's Ave PO2 .... 157 F1
St Christopher Ave PO16 .. 131 E2
St Christopher's Rd PO9 .. 135 E2
St Christophers Cl SO52 .... 54 A2
St Christophers Gdns PO13 .. 155 E1
St Christophers Hospl PO16 .. 131 E2
St Christophers Rd SO18 .. 103 F4
St Clair Rd BH13 .... 214 C4
St Clares Ave PO9 .... 135 E2
St Clement St
  Winchester SO22 .... 10 C4
  28 Winchester SO23 .... 11 D4
St Clement & St John
  CE First Sch BH8 .... 205 E3
St Clement's Gdns BH1 .... 205 E3
St Clement's Rd BH8 .... 205 E3
St Clements Cl SO51 .... 52 C4
St Clements La BH15 .... 202 A1
St Clements Rd BH15 ...... 203 D4
St Colman's Ave PO6 .... 158 A4
St Cross Ct 4 SO22 .... 10 C3
St Cross Mede SO22 .... 10 C2
St Cross Rd SO22 .... 10 C3
St Cuthberts Cl SO31 ...... 129 D2
St Cuthberts La SO31 ...... 129 D2
St Cyres Meml Cotts SO41 .. 197 F3
St David's Cl SO40 .... 76 B1
St David's Ct
  3 Bournemouth BH1, ... 205 F3
  Gosport PO13 .... 180 B3
  North Baddesley SO52 ...... 54 A2
St David's Rd Clanfield PO8 .. 88 B3
  Portsmouth PO5 .... 182 B2
  Upton BH16 .... 201 D4
St Davids Rd SO31 .... 128 C2
St Denys 28 BH25 .... 195 D1
St Denys Ind Pk SO17 ...... 103 E4
St Denys Prim Sch SO17 .... 79 E1
St Denys Rd SO17, SO18 .... 79 E1
St Denys' Sta SO17 .... 103 E4
St Denys Wlk 6 PO9 .... 135 E3
St Edmonsbury Ct PO13 .. 180 B3
St Edmund Cl PO14 .... 129 D1
St Edmund's Rd SO16 ...... 102 A4
St Edmunds RC Sch PO1 .. 182 B3
St Edward's RC/CE
  Comp Sch BH15 .... 202 C4
St Edward's Rd
  Gosport PO12 .... 181 D2
  Portsmouth PO5 .... 182 B2
St Edward's Ter 3 PO12 .. 181 D3
St Edwards Rd SO31 .... 127 D4

St Elizabeth's Ave SO18 104 A4
St Evox Cl SO16 77 F3
St Faith's CE Prim Sch SO22 10 C3
St Faith's Cl PO12 181 D3
St Faith's Rd
Portsmouth PO1 182 B3
Winchester SO22 10 C3
St Francis Ave SO18 104 A4
St Francis CE Prim Sch SO53 55 D3
St Francis Cl SO45 177 F4
St Francis Ct 2 PO2 157 F2
St Francis Pl PO9 135 F2
St Francis Rd Blackfield SO45 177 F4
Gosport PO12 181 E1
St Francis Specl Sch PO14 154 B4
St Gabriel's Rd SO18 104 A4
St George Cl SO31 104 C1
St George RC Sch (Boys) SO17 79 E3
St George's Almshouses 11 BH15 202 A1
St George's Ave
Bournemouth BH8 205 E4
Havant PO9 136 A1
Poole BH12 203 D4
St George's Beneficial CE Prim Sch PO1 182 A3
St George's Bsns Ctr 28 PO1 182 A3
St George's Cl
Bournemouth BH8 205 E4
Christchurch BH23 208 B4
St George's Cotts SP6 47 E2
St George's Cres SP6 69 F1
St George's Ct
2 Bournemouth BH1, 205 F3
North Baddesley SO52 54 A2
Portsmouth PO5 182 A2
St George's Dr BH22 165 E2
St George's Rd Cosham PO6 157 F4
Portsmouth PO1 182 A2
Portsmouth, Southsea PO4 183 D1
South Hayling PO11 184 B2
St George's Sq SO32 83 E4
St George's St
Southampton SO14 103 D2
Winchester SO23 11 D4
St George's Way PO1 182 A3
St George's Wlk 11 PO7 134 C4
St Georges Cl BH23 193 D4
St Georges Cotts Martin SP6 43 E2
Woodgreen SP6 70 C4
St Georges Ct PO16 155 D4
St Georges House 20 SO17 103 D4
St Georges Mans 18 BH5 205 F2
St Georges Rd
Fordingbridge SP6 69 F1
Locks Heath SO31 128 C2
St Georges Sq PO1 182 A3
St Giles Cl SO23 11 D4
St Giles Way PO8 88 B1
St Helen's Cl PO4 182 C1
St Helen's Par PO4 182 C1
St Helen's Rd Gosport PO12 180 C2
South Hayling PO11 184 B2
St Helena Gdns SO18 79 F2
St Helena Way PO16 156 B4
St Helens Mews 8 SO50 57 E1
St Helier Pl SO16 77 F2
St Helier Rd BH12 188 B1
St Hellen's Rd PO6 158 B4
St Hermans Mans PO11 185 E1
St Hermans Rd PO11 185 E1
St Hilda Ave PO8 88 B1
St Hubert Rd PO8 88 B1
St Ives Cty Fst Sch BH24 140 A3
St Ives End Rd BH24 140 A2
St Ives Gdns BH2 204 C3
St Ives Park BH24 140 A3
St Ives Wood BH24 140 A3
St James CE Fst Sch SP6 93 D3
St James CE Prim Sch
Bournemouth BH7 206 A3
Emsworth PO10 136 C1
West End SO30 80 C1
St James Cl Clanfield PO8 88 B2
7 Poole BH15 202 A1
St James House 23 SO14 103 D2
St James Hospl PO4 183 E3
St James' La SO22 10 C4
St James Pk (Cvn Pk) SO53 55 D4
St James' Rd PO10 136 C1
St James Rd
Ferndown BH21 165 D3
Sway SO41 172 B1
West End SO30 80 B1
St James' Terr SO22 10 C4
St James' Villas SO22 10 C4
St James Way PO16 156 B4
St James's 20 BH5 205 F2
St James's Cl SO15 78 B1
St James's Park Rd SO16 78 B1
St James's Rd
Portsmouth PO5 182 B2
Southampton SO15 102 B4
St James's Sq BH5 206 A3
St James's St PO1 182 A3
St John the Baptist CE Inf Sch PO14 129 E1
St John The Baptist CE Prim Sch SO32 83 F1
St John's Ave PO7 134 C2
St John's Cl Gosport PO12 181 D3
Wimborne Minster BH21 163 E2
St John's Coll PO5 182 B2
St John's Ctr SO30 105 D3
St John's Ct
4 Bournemouth BH1, 205 F3
North Baddesley SO52 54 A2
16 Portsmouth PO2 157 E1
St John's Gdns BH9 189 F1
St John's Hill BH21 163 E3
St John's Hospl (N) 21 SO23 11 D4
St John's Hospl (S) 32 SO23 11 D4
St John's Rd
Bournemouth BH5 205 F2
Christchurch BH23 207 D3
Cosham PO6 158 A4
Eastleigh SO50 56 A2
Havant PO9 135 E2
Hedge End SO30 105 D3
Locks Heath SO31 129 D1
Poole BH15 202 B2
Southbourne PO10 137 E1
Winchester SO23 11 D4
St John's St Hythe SO45 126 A2
Winchester SO23 11 D4
St Johns CE Fst Sch BH21 163 E2
St Johns CE Prim Sch PO12 181 D4
St Johns Cl
Rownhams SO16 77 F4
South Hayling PO11 184 C1
St Johns Ct SO40 101 F1
St Johns Dr SO40 101 F1
St Johns Gdns SO51 52 C4
St Johns Glebe SO16 77 F3
St Johns Inf Sch SO14 102 C2
St Johns La SO32 107 F4
St Johns Mews SO31 129 E2
St Johns RC Prim Sch PO1 182 B3
St Johns Rd BH25 195 D4
St Johns Sq 19 PO12 181 D3
St Joseph Cl SO31 129 D2
St Joseph's Mews PO5 182 B2
St Joseph's RC Prim Sch BH23 208 A4
St Joseph's RC Sch BH12 203 F4
St Jude's CE Prim Sch PO1 182 A2
St Jude's RC Prim Sch PO14 130 C1
St Julien's Hospl Almshouses SO14 103 D1
St Just Cl BH22 165 E2
St Katharine's CE Prim Sch BH6 207 D2
St Katherine's CE Prim Sch BH6 206 A2
St Kitts House 4 PO6 132 C1
St Lawrence Cl SO30 81 E1
St Lawrence Rd
Eastleigh SO50 56 A2
31 Southampton SO14 103 D2
St Ledger's Pl BH1 205 E3
St Ledger's Rd BH8 205 E3
St Leonard's Ave PO11 185 D2
St Leonard's Rd
Bournemouth BH8 205 D3
Winchester SO23 11 E3
St Leonards Cl PO15 129 F2
St Leonards Hospl BH24 139 E1
St Leonards Way BH24 139 E2
St Lucia House 2 PO6 132 C1
St Luke's CE Prim Sch BH9 204 C4
St Luke's CE Sec Sch PO1 182 B3
St Luke's Rd
Bournemouth BH3 204 C4
Gosport PO12 181 D3
St Lukes Cl SO30 81 E1
St Margaret's Almshouses BH21 163 D3
St Margaret's Ave BH23 207 D3
St Margaret's Cl SO18 104 A4
St Margaret's Cotts SO32 59 E1
St Margaret's Rd
Bishopstoke SO50 56 B2
Bournemouth BH10 189 E1
Poole BH15 202 B2
St Margarets BH2 204 C3
St Margarets Cl BH21 163 D3
St Margarets Hill BH21 163 D3
St Margarets House 6 SO16 102 C4
St Margarets La PO14 129 F1
St Margarets Rd PO11 185 D2
St Mark's CE Jun Sch SO15 102 B4
St Mark's Cl PO12 181 D1
St Mark's Pl PO12 181 D1
St Mark's Prim Sch BH10 189 E1
St Mark's Rd
Bournemouth BH11 189 D2
Gosport PO12 181 D1
Portsmouth PO2 157 E1
St Marks Cl SO53 30 C1
St Marks Ct 11 PO12 181 D3
St Marks Rd SO41 197 D2
St Martin Cl SO23 11 D4
St Martin's Cl
Bishopstoke SO50 56 B2
Southampton SO16 77 F2
St Martin's House 15 PO5 182 B1
St Martins Ind Est SO23 11 D4
St Martins Rd BH16 201 D4
St Mary Gr SO41 196 A1
St Mary Magdalen Almshouses 35 SO23 11 D4
St Mary St SO22 10 B3
St Mary's SO51 52 C3
St Mary's Ave PO12 181 D1
St Mary's Church Cl SO18 79 E2
St Mary's Cl
Droxford SO32 61 D1
Kings Worthy SO21 2 B3
Redlynch SP5 47 F2
St Mary's Coll
Southampton SO18 103 F4
Winchester SO23 11 D3
St Mary's Ct BH6 206 C2
St Mary's House PO1 182 C3
St Mary's Hospl East Wing PO3 183 D3
St Mary's Hospl West Wing PO1 182 C3
St Mary's Maternity Hospl BH15 202 B2
St Mary's Mews BH22 165 E2
St Mary's Pl SO14 103 D2
St Mary's Prim Sch SO14 103 D2
St Mary's RC Prim Sch PO12 181 D3
St Mary's Rd
Bishopstoke SO50 56 B2
Bournemouth BH1 205 E3
Ferndown BH22 165 E3
Liss GU33 20 C2
Netley SO31 127 E3
Poole BH15 202 C2
Portsmouth PO1 182 C3
South Hayling PO11 184 C2
Southampton SO14 103 D3
Stubbington PO14 154 B2
St Mary's St SO14 103 D2
St Mary's Terr SO21 32 A3
St Marys Cl BH23 193 E4
St Matthew's Rd PO6 157 F4
St Matthews Cl 20 SO14 103 D3
St Matthews Ct PO12 181 E3
St Matthews Rd SO22 1 B1
St Merrin's Cl BH10 189 E2
St Michael's 2 BH2 204 B2
St Michael's CE Mid Sch BH21 163 F4
St Michael's CE Prim Sch BH2 204 B2
St Michael's Ct 27 PO6 133 D1
St Michael's Gdns 20 SO22 10 C4
St Michael's Gr PO14 154 C4
St Michael's House 8 PO14 154 C4
St Michael's Mews 6 BH2 204 C2
St Michael's Pass SO23 11 D3
St Michael's Pl 18 BH2 204 C2
St Michael's Rd
Bournemouth BH2 204 C1
Havant PO9 135 E2
Portsmouth PO1 182 A2
Winchester SO22 10 C3
St Michael's Sq 16 SO14 102 C2
St Michael's St 18 SO14 102 C2
St Michaels Cl Blackfield SO45 150 C1
Verwood BH31 114 C3
St Michaels Ct 1 BH6 206 B2
St Michaels Rd
Locks Heath SO31 129 D1
Totton SO40 100 C4
Verwood BH31 114 C2
St Michaels Way PO8 88 B1
St Monica Inf Sch SO19 104 A2
St Monica Jun Sch SO19 104 A2
St Monica Rd SO19 104 A2
St Nicholas Ave PO13 180 B4
St Nicholas Flats 17 PO2 157 E1
St Nicholas' Rd PO9 135 E2
St Nicholas Rise SO23 2 A3
St Nicholas Row PO17 108 A2
St Nicholas St PO1 182 A2
St Osmund's Rd BH14 203 E2
St Patrick's Ct SO52 54 A2
St Patrick's La Liss GU33 21 E3
Rake GU33 21 E3
St Patrick's RC Prim Sch SO19 103 F2
St Paul's Hill SO22 10 C4
St Paul's Hospl SO22 10 C4
St Paul's La BH1 205 D2
St Paul's Pl BH1 205 D2
St Paul's Rd
Bournemouth BH1 205 D2
Locks Heath SO31 128 C3
Portsmouth PO5 182 A2
St Paul's Sq PO5 182 A2
St Pauls Pl 11 SO22 10 C4
St Pauls RC Prim Sch PO6 157 D4
St Peter St SO23 11 D4
St Peter's Ave PO11 160 B1
St Peter's Cres 33 BH1 204 C2
St Peter's Ct
17 Petersfield GU32 40 C2
7 Poole BH14 203 D2
St Peter's Gr PO5 182 B2
St Peter's RC Prim Sch PO7 134 C4
St Peter's RC Sch BH7 206 A4
St Peter's RC Sec Sch BH6 206 C2
St Peter's Rd
Bournemouth BH1 205 D2
Petersfield GU32 40 C2
Poole BH14 203 D2
St Peter's Sq 6 PO10 160 C4
St Peter's St SO32 83 E4
St Peter's Wlk 38 BH1 204 C2
St Peters Cl SO32 106 B4
St Peters Ct
Bournemouth BH1 205 D2
4 Emsworth PO10 161 D4
St Peters Rd PO11 160 B2
St Philip's Way SO18 104 A4
St Piran's Ave PO3 183 D4
St Quentin House 12 PO14 154 C4
St Richards Gdns PO7 134 B3
St Ronan's Ave PO4 182 C1
St Ronan's Rd PO4 182 C1
St Saviors Cl BH7 206 B4
St Sebastian Cres PO16 131 D2
St Simon Cl SO31 129 D2
St Simon's Rd PO5 182 B1
St Stephen's Ct 6 BH2 204 C2
St Stephen's Rd
Bournemouth BH2 204 C2
Portsmouth PO2 182 C4
Winchester SO22 1 B1
St Stephen's Way 27 BH2 204 C2
St Stephens La BH31 115 D4
St Swithun Cl SO32 83 D4
St Swithun St SO23 11 D4
St Swithun Wells (RC) Prim Sc SO53 55 F3
St Swithun's Cl SO51 28 B1
St Swithun's RC Prim Sch PO5 182 B1
St Swithun's Rd
Bournemouth BH1 205 D2
Portsmouth PO2 157 F1
St Swithun's Rd S BH1 205 D2
St Swithun's Sch SO23 11 E4
St Swithuns Ct 5 SO14 103 D3
St Theresas Cl PO9 135 E2
St Thomas Ave PO11 184 B2
St Thomas Cl PO16 131 E2
St Thomas Ct 7 SO50 57 E1
St Thomas Garnet's RC Sch BH5 206 A3
St Thomas More's RC Prim Sch PO9 135 E2
St Thomas' Pas 24 SO22 10 C4
St Thomas Pk SO41 197 E2
St Thomas St
Winchester SO22 10 C4
24 Winchester SO23 11 D4
St Thomas's Cl BH10 189 F1
St Thomas's Ct PO1 182 A2
St Thomas's Rd PO12 181 D4
St Thomas's St
Lymington SO41 197 F2
Portsmouth PO1 182 A2
St Tristan Cl SO31 129 D1
St Ursula Gr PO5 182 B2
St Valerie Rd
Bournemouth BH2 204 C3
Gosport PO12 181 D2
St Vigor Way
Colden Common SO21 31 F1
Colden Common SO21 57 D4
St Vincent Coll PO12 181 D3
St Vincent Cres PO8 112 A3
St Vincent L Ctr PO12 181 E3
St Vincent Rd Gosport PO12 181 D3
Portsmouth PO5 182 B1
St Vincent St PO5 182 A2
St Walburga's RC Prim Sch BH9 190 A1
St Winifred's Rd
Bournemouth BH2 204 C3
Southampton SO16 78 B1
St Winifred's Sch SO17 79 D1
Salcombe Ave PO3 158 A1
Salcombe Cl SO53 55 D2
Salcombe Cres SO40 100 C3
Salcombe Rd
Southampton SO15 102 B4
Totton SO40 100 C3
Salcot Rd SO23 2 A1
Salem St SO15 78 B1
Salerno Dr PO12 180 C2
Salerno House
Fareham PO14 154 C4
Romsey SO51 53 D4
Salerno Pl BH15 201 E1
Salerno Rd Portsmouth PO2 157 E2
Southampton SO16 78 B2
Salet Way PO7 112 A1
Salisbury Cl SO50 56 A2
Salisbury Ct 2 SO50 56 A2
Salisbury Rd Awbridge SO51 52 A3
Bournemouth BH1 205 F2
Breamore SP6 70 A3
Burton BH23 192 A3
Cosham PO6 158 A4
Fordingbridge SP6 70 A1
Fordingbridge SP6 70 A3
Fordingbridge, Ibsley SP6 94 A1
Ibsley BH24 116 C3
Ower SO40 76 B2
Poole BH14 203 E3
Portsmouth PO4 182 C1
Ringwood BH24 116 C3
Sopley, Burton BH23 192 B2
Sopley, Winkton BH23 192 A3
Southampton SO17 79 D2
Totton SO40 76 B2
West Wellow SO51 50 B2
Salisbury Road Arc SO40 100 C4
Salisbury St
Fordingbridge SP6 69 F1
6 Southampton SO15 102 C3
Salisbury Terr PO13 179 F1
Salmon Dr SO50 56 C1
Salt La Upham SO32 & SO24 34 C2
Upham SO32 & SO24 34 C2
Salt Meat La PO12 181 E3
Salter Rd BH13 214 B2
Salterns Ave PO4 183 D3
Salterns Cl PO11 185 E2
Salterns Ct BH14 214 A4
Salterns Est PO16 155 D4
Salterns La Bursledon SO31 128 A4
Fareham PO16 155 D4
South Hayling PO11 185 E2
Salterns Point BH14 214 A4
Salterns Rd Poole BH14 203 D2
Stubbington PO14 179 D2
Salterns Specl Sch SO40 101 D4
Salterns Way BH14 214 A4
Salters Acres SO22 1 B
Salters La SO22 1 A
Saltgrass La SO41 212 A
Saltings Rd BH16 201 D
Saltings The Cosham PO6 158 C
Havant PO9 159 F
Saltmarsh La PO11 184 C
Saltmarsh Rd SO14 103 D
Saltmead SO17 79 E
Salvia Cl PO7 135 D
Salwey Rd SO30 105 E
Samber Cl SO41 197 E
Sampan Cl SO31 128 C
Samphire Cl SO41 197 F
Samples Way BH17 202 C
Sampson Rd Gosport PO14 154 C
Portsmouth PO1 181 F
Samson Cl PO13 180 B
Samson Rd BH15 201 E
Samuel Rd PO1 182 C
San Diego Rd PO12 181 D
San Remo Towers 23 BH5 205 F
Sancreed Rd BH12 203 F
Sancroft BH21 164 A
Sand Cl SO51 50 C
Sandbanks Bsns Ctr BH13 214 A
Sandbanks Rd BH14 203 D
Sandbourne Rd
Bournemouth BH4 204 B
Poole BH15 202 B
Sandcroft Cl PO12 180 C
Sandecotes Rd BH14 203 E
Sandell Ct SO16 79 D
Sanderling Rd PO4 183 E
Sanderlings BH24 141 E
Sanderlings The PO11 185 D
Sandford Ave PO12 180 B
Sandford Cl BH9 190 B
Sandford Way BH18 186 C
Sandhill Way PO13 180 A
Sandhills Cl BH17 187 E
Sandhurst Dr BH21 139 D
Sandhurst Rd SO15 102 C
Sandilands Way SO45 126 A
Sandisplatt PO14 154 E
Sandle Copse SP6 69 D
Sandleford Rd PO9 135 E
Sandleheath Ind Est SP6 69 D
Sandleheath Rd SP6 92 C
Sandlewood Cl Clanfield PO8 88 E
Totton SO40 100 B
Sandmartin Cl BH25 209 F
Sandown Cl PO12 180 B
Sandown Rd
Christchurch BH23 207 F
Cosham PO6 157 F
Southampton SO15 78 A
Sandpiper Cl
Broadstone BH17 186 C
Horndean PO8 112 A
Marchwood SO40 101 F
Sandpiper Rd SO16 78 A
Sandpipers PO3 158 C
Sandpit La Beaulieu SO41 199 E
Poole BH15 202 E
Sandport Gr PO16 156 A
Sandringham Cl
Bournemouth BH9 190 A
North Baddesley SO52 54 C
Sandringham Ct
Bournemouth BH8 205 E
Southampton, Millbrook SO15 102 A
21 Southampton, Westwood Pk SO17 79 D
Sandringham Gdns BH9 190 A
Sandringham House 2 PO7 134 C
Sandringham La PO1 182
Sandringham Rd
Fareham PO14 154
Petersfield GU32 40
Poole BH14 203
Portsmouth PO1 182
Southampton SO18 79
Sandsbury La GU32 40
Sandy Beach Est PO11 185
Sandy Brow PO7 134
Sandy Cl Petersfield GU31 41
Wimborne Minster BH21 164
Sandy Down SO41 173
Sandy La Abbotswood SO51 28
Bournemouth BH6 206
Christchurch BH23 191
Fair Oak SO50 57
Lyndhurst SO43 121
North Baddesley SO52 54
Pamphill BH21 162
Rake GU33 21
Redlynch SP5 47
Shedfield SO32 83
St Leonards BH24 140
Three Legged Cross BH21 114
Titchfield PO14 153
Upton BH16 201
Verwood BH31 115
Wimborne Minster BH21 164
Sandy Mead Rd BH8 190
Sandy Plot BH23 207
Sandy Point Rd PO11 185
Sandy Way BH10 189
Sandycroft SO31 152
Sandyfield Cres PO8 111
Sandyhurst Cl BH17 187
Sanross Cl PO14 179
Santoy BH13 214
Sapphire Ridge PO7 135
Saracen Cl SO41 197
Saracens Rd SO53 55
Sarah Cl BH7 206

arah Robinson House 38 PO1 .... 182 A3
arah Sands Cl BH23 .... 207 E4
arisbury CE Jun Sch SO31 .... 128 C3
arisbury Gate SO31 .... 129 D3
arisbury Inf Sch SO31 .... 128 C2
ark Rd BH12 .... 203 E4
arnia Cl SO16 .... 77 F2
arum Ave BH22 .... 138 C2
arum Cl SO22 .... 10 B4
arum Ct BH14 .... 203 E2
arum Rd
  Chandler's Ford SO53 .... 55 F3
  Winchester SO22 .... 10 A4
arum Road Hospl SO22 .... 10 B4
arum St 14 BH15 .... 202 A1
arum View SO22 .... 10 A4
arum Wlk SO41 .... 197 E3
atchell La SO31 .... 128 A2
aturn Cl SO16 .... 77 F2
aulfand House BH23 .... 208 B4
aulfand Pl BH23 .... 208 B4
aulford Dr BH23 .... 208 B4
aunders House PO16 .... 132 C1
aunders La SO51 .... 26 C3
aunders Mews PO4 .... 183 D1
avernake Cl Gosport PO13 .... 155 E1
  9 Romsey SO51 .... 28 A1
aville Cl Bishopstoke SO50 .... 56 B3
  Gosport PO12 .... 180 C2
aville Ct 17 BH21 .... 163 E2
aville Gdns PO16 .... 131 D2
avoy Bldgs 20 PO16 .... 131 D1
awyer Cl SO22 .... 1 A1
axholm Cl SO16 .... 78 C3
axholm Dale SO16 .... 78 C3
axholm Way SO16 .... 78 C3
axley Ct PO9 .... 135 E3
axon Cl Horndean PO8 .... 88 B2
  Locks Heath SO31 .... 128 C1
  Portchester PO16 .... 132 A1
axon Gdns SO30 .... 105 D3
axon House 17 SO14 .... 103 E3
axon King Gdns BH6 .... 207 D2
axon Meadow SP5 .... 46 C4
axon Pl SO41 .... 197 E3
axon Rd Blackfield SO45 .... 150 C1
  Southampton SO15 .... 102 B3
  Winchester SO23 .... 2 A1
axon Shore Inf Sch PO6 .... 156 C4
axon Sq Sh Ctr 4 BH21 .... 207 D3
axon Way Alderholt SP6 .... 93 D3
  Romsey SO51 .... 53 D4
axon Wlk SO53 .... 55 F3
axonbury BH6 .... 206 C3
axonford Rd BH23 .... 208 B4
axonhurst SP5 .... 47 D4
axonhurst Cl BH10 .... 189 F2
axonhurst Gdns BH10 .... 189 F2
axonhurst Rd BH10 .... 189 F2
ayers Rd SO50 .... 56 C2
cafell Ave SO14 .... 154 B4
callops La SO51 .... 50 C3
cantabout Ave SO53 .... 55 F4
cantabout Prim Sch SO53 .... 55 F4
carf BH17 .... 202 C4
carff Ct PO15 .... 185 D1
cholars' Wlk PO6 .... 158 B4
chool Cl SO53 .... 55 D3
chool Hill SO32 .... 85 E3
chool La Boldre SO41 .... 197 F4
  Bournemouth BH11 .... 189 D3
  Bransgore BH23 .... 169 F2
  Chandler's Ford SO53 .... 55 D3
  Compt(Sussex) PO18 .... 90 C1
  Denmead PO7 .... 110 B3
  Emsworth PO10 .... 160 C4
  Hamble-le-Rice SO31 .... 128 A1
  Kings Worthy SO23 .... 2 A3
  3 Liss GU33 .... 20 C2
  Lymington SO41 .... 197 F2
  Michelmersh SO51 .... 6 B1
  Milford on Sea SO41 .... 211 F3
  Petersfield GU32 .... 41 D3
  Poole BH15 .... 202 B3
  Ringwood BH24 .... 141 D4
  Southbourne PO18 .... 161 F4
  St Leonards BH24 .... 140 A2
  Three Legged Cross BH21 .... 138 C4
  Westbourne SO32 .... 137 D3
  Wimborne Minster BH21 .... 163 D3
chool Pl SO19 .... 103 F2
chool Rd Bransgore BH23 .... 169 F2
  Burslendon SO31 .... 128 A4
  Fawley SO45 .... 151 D2
  Havant PO9 .... 155 F1
  Hythe SO45 .... 126 A2
  Nomansland SP5 .... 73 E4
  Redlynch SP5 .... 48 A3
  Romsey SO51 .... 28 B1
  Totton SO40 .... 101 D3
  Twyford SO21 .... 31 F3
  West Wellow SO51 .... 50 C1
  Wickham PO17 .... 108 A2
chooner Way
  Locks Heath SO31 .... 128 C1
  Portsmouth PO4 .... 183 E3
cimitars The PO14 .... 154 A2
civier's La SO32 .... 58 B1
cotland Cl SO51 .... 57 F1
cotney Ct 8 PO9 .... 136 A3
cott Cl Poole BH12 .... 188 C1
  Stubbington PO14 .... 154 B2
cott House 2 PO14 .... 157 E1
cott Rd Eastleigh SO50 .... 55 F1
  Poole BH12 .... 188 C1
  Portsmouth PO1 .... 181 F3

Scott Rd Continued
  Portsmouth PO1 .... 182 A2
  Portsmouth, Hilsea PO3 .... 157 F3
  Southampton SO19 .... 103 F1
Scott's Gn BH23 .... 207 F4
Scotter Rd Bishopstoke SO50 .... 56 B2
Scotter Sq SO50 .... 56 B2
Scotts Cl SO21 .... 57 D4
Scotts Hill La BH23 .... 207 E4
Scratchface La Havant PO9 .... 135 D1
  Waterlooville PO7 .... 134 C2
Scullards La 1 SO14 .... 102 C2
Sea Crest Rd PO13 .... 179 F1
Sea Front PO11 .... 184 C2
Sea Front Est PO11 .... 185 D1
Sea Grove Ave PO11 .... 185 D1
Sea Kings PO14 .... 179 D3
Sea La PO13 .... 179 E2
Sea Life Ctr PO5 .... 182 B1
Sea Mill Gdns 24 PO1 .... 182 A3
Sea Pines 9 SO41 .... 211 E2
Sea Point 8 BH13 .... 214 C4
Sea Rd
  Barton on Sea BH25 .... 209 F4
  Bournemouth, Boscombe BH5, BH6 .... 205 F2
  Bournemouth,Southbourne BH6 .... 206 C2
  Milford on Sea SO41 .... 211 F2
  Southampton SO19 .... 103 E2
Sea View Cotts PO10 .... 160 C4
Sea View Est SO31 .... 127 D3
Sea View Rd Cosham PO6 .... 134 B1
  Poole BH12 .... 203 D3
  South Hayling PO11 .... 185 E2
  Upton BH16 .... 201 D4
Sea Vixen Ind Est BH23 .... 208 A4
Seabank Cl BH16 .... 201 D4
Seabird Way PO16 .... 155 D4
Seabourne Pl 12 BH5 .... 206 A3
Seabourne Rd BH5 .... 206 A3
Seacombe Gn SO16 .... 77 E1
Seacombe Rd BH13 .... 214 A2
Seacroft Ave BH25 .... 209 F4
Seafarers Wlk PO11 .... 185 F1
Seafield Cl BH25 .... 209 F4
Seafield Dr BH6 .... 206 C3
Seafield Park Rd PO14 .... 179 D3
Seafield Rd
  Barton on Sea BH25 .... 209 F4
  Bournemouth BH6 .... 206 B2
  Christchurch BH23 .... 208 B4
  Portchester PO16 .... 156 A4
  Portsmouth PO3 .... 158 A1
  Southampton SO16 .... 77 F2
Seafield Terr PO12 .... 181 E2
Seafields PO10 .... 160 C4
Seaford Cl SO31 .... 104 C1
Seagarth Cl SO16 .... 78 B2
Seagarth La SO16 .... 78 B2
Seager's Ct PO1 .... 181 F2
Seagrove Rd PO2 .... 157 E1
Seagull Cl PO4 .... 183 E3
Seagull La PO10 .... 136 C1
Seagull Rd BH8 .... 190 B1
Seagulls The PO13 .... 180 A2
Seahorse Wlk PO12 .... 181 E3
Seamans La SO43 .... 98 B2
Seamead PO14 .... 179 E2
Seamoor La BH4 .... 204 A4
Seamoor Rd BH4 .... 204 A4
Searles Hill SO21 .... 32 A4
Seathwaite House 26 PO6 .... 133 D1
Seaton Ave PO3 .... 183 D4
Seaton Cl Christchurch BH23 .... 209 D4
  Lymington SO41 .... 197 F3
  Stubbington PO14 .... 179 E3
  West End SO18 .... 80 B1
Seaton Rd BH23 .... 209 D4
Seatown Cl PO17 .... 188 A1
Seaview Ave PO16 .... 132 C1
Seaview Ct Gosport PO12 .... 180 B2
  14 Lee-on-the-Solent PO13 .... 179 F1
Seaview Rd
  Barton on Sea BH25 .... 209 E4
  Christchurch BH23 .... 194 B1
Seaward Ave BH25 .... 209 F4
Seaward Gdns SO19 .... 103 F2
Seaward Rd Hythe SO45 .... 126 A2
  Southampton SO19 .... 103 F2
Seaward Tower PO12 .... 181 F2
Seaway BH25 .... 210 A4
Seaway Ave BH23 .... 208 B4
Seaway Cres PO4 .... 183 E2
Seaway Gr PO12 .... 156 B3
Seawinds SO41 .... 211 D3
Sebastian Gr PO7 .... 135 D4
Second Ave Cosham PO6 .... 157 F4
  Cosham, Farlington PO6 .... 158 C4
  Emsworth PO9 .... 136 A1
  Southampton SO15 .... 101 E4
  Southbourne PO10 .... 161 E4
Second Marine Ave BH25 .... 210 A3
Second St SO45 .... 150 C4
Sedberg House SO16 .... 77 E1
Sedbergh Rd SO16 .... 77 E1
Seddul-Bahr SO30 .... 80 C3
Sedgefield Cl
  Portchester PO6 .... 156 C4
  Totton SO40 .... 100 B4
Sedgeley Gr PO12 .... 181 D4
Sedgemead SO31 .... 127 D3
Sedgemead Ct SO31 .... 127 D3
Sedgewick Cl PO13 .... 180 A4
Sedgewick Rd
  Bishopstoke SO50 .... 56 B2
  Southampton SO19 .... 104 B3

Sedgley Cl PO5 .... 182 B2
Sedgley Rd BH9 .... 204 C4
Seed Warehouse The
  16 BH15 .... 202 B1
Segars La SO21 .... 31 F3
Segensworth East (Ind Est)
  PO15 .... 129 E3
Segensworth Rd PO15 .... 129 F2
Segensworth West (Ind Est)
  PO15 .... 129 E3
Selangor Ave PO10 .... 136 B1
Selborne Ave Havant PO9 .... 135 E3
  Southampton SO18 .... 104 B4
Selborne Ct 3 SO51 .... 28 A1
Selborne Pl SO51 .... 10 B3
Selborne Rd SO40 .... 100 B4
Selborne Wlk SO18 .... 104 B4
Selbourne Dr SO50 .... 56 A2
Selbourne Gdns PO12 .... 180 C2
Selbourne Pl PO9 .... 135 F1
Selbourne Terr PO1 .... 182 C3
Seldon Cl SO22 .... 10 A2
Seldown BH15 .... 202 B2
Seldown Bridge BH15 .... 202 B2
Seldown La BH15 .... 202 B2
Seldown Rd BH15 .... 202 B2
Self Rd BH15 .... 202 A1
Selfridge Ave BH6 .... 207 D2
Selfridge Cl BH6 .... 207 D2
Selhurst House 53 PO1 .... 182 B3
Selhurst Way SO50 .... 57 E1
Seliot Cl BH15 .... 202 B3
Selkirk Cl PO21 .... 163 F1
Sellwood Rd SO31 .... 127 E3
Sellwood Way BH25 .... 209 E4
Selsdon Ave SO51 .... 53 D4
Selsey Ave Gosport PO12 .... 181 D4
  Portsmouth PO4 .... 183 D1
Selsey Cl South Hayling PO11 .... 185 F1
  Southampton SO16 .... 77 F1
Selsmore Ave PO11 .... 185 E4
Selsmore Rd PO11 .... 185 D2
Selworth La SO32 .... 85 D2
Selworthy Cl BH14 .... 203 D1
Selwyn Ct 20 PO6 .... 157 F4
Selwyn Gdns SO50 .... 56 A3
Sengana Cl SO30 .... 105 F3
Senlac Rd SO51 .... 53 D4
Sennen Pl PO6 .... 157 D4
Sentinal Ct BH15 .... 202 C2
Sentinel Cl PO7 .... 112 A1
Seps 4 Rd SO45 .... 151 E2
September Ct SO30 .... 80 B1
Serle Cl SO40 .... 100 A4
Serle Gdns SO40 .... 100 B3
Sermon Rd SO22 .... 1 A1
Serpentine Rd
  Fareham PO16 .... 131 D1
  Poole BH15 .... 202 B2
  28 Portsmouth PO5 .... 182 B1
  Waterlooville PO7 .... 134 B2
Service Rd PO6 .... 157 E4
Set Thorns Rd SO41 .... 172 B1
Setley Gdns BH8 .... 190 C2
Setters Cl SO21 .... 56 C4
Settle Cl SO16 .... 102 A4
Settlers Cl 34 PO1 .... 182 B3
Sevenoaks Dr BH7 .... 206 A4
Sevenoaks Rd PO6 .... 157 F4
Severn Cl Cosham PO6 .... 133 D1
  Portchester PO16 .... 156 A4
Severn Rd Ferndown BH22 .... 166 A3
  Southampton SO16 .... 101 F4
Severn Way SO30 .... 80 B1
Seward Ave BH6 .... 206 B2
Seward Rise SO51 .... 53 E4
Seymour Cl
  Chandler's Ford SO53 .... 55 F3
  Portsmouth PO2 .... 182 B4
  Southampton SO16 .... 78 B2
  Totton SO40 .... 76 B1
Seymour House SO16 .... 78 B2
Seymour La SO52 .... 53 F2
Seymour Rd
  Lee-on-the-Solent PO13 .... 180 A2
  Ringwood BH24 .... 117 D1
  Southampton SO16 .... 78 B2
Shackleton House 2 PO2 .... 157 F1
Shackleton Rd PO13 .... 180 B4
Shackleton Sq BH23 .... 169 D1
Shadwell Ct 9 PO2 .... 157 F1
Shadwell Rd PO2 .... 157 F1
Shaftesbury Ave
  Chandler's Ford SO53 .... 55 E2
  Southampton SO17 .... 79 D1
  Waterlooville PO7 .... 134 C2
Shaftesbury Ct BH21 .... 138 C1
Shaftesbury Rd Gosport PO12 .... 181 E2
  Poole BH15 .... 202 B2
  West Moors BH22 .... 138 C1
Shaftesbury St SP6 .... 69 F1
Shaftsbury Rd
  Bournemouth BH8 .... 205 E3
  Portsmouth BH5 .... 182 B1
Shaggs Meadow SO43 .... 122 A3
Shakespeare Ave SO17 .... 103 D4
Shakespeare Bsns Ctr 1
  SO50 .... 56 A2
Shakespeare Cty Jun Sch
  SO50 .... 56 A3
Shakespeare Dr SO40 .... 76 B1
Shakespeare Gdns PO8 .... 111 D2
Shakespeare Mews PO14 .... 154 A4
Shakespeare Rd
  Bournemouth BH6 .... 206 B4
  Eastleigh SO50 .... 56 A2

Shakespeare Rd Continued
  Portsmouth PO1 .... 182 B4
  Wimborne Minster BH21 .... 163 D3
Shakespeare Road Cty
  Inf Sc SO50 .... 56 A3
Shalbourne Rd PO12 .... 181 D4
Shalcombe SO31 .... 127 E4
Shalden Cl SO16 .... 78 B2
Shaldon Rd 18 PO9 .... 136 A3
Shales Rd SO18 .... 104 A4
Shallow The SO41 .... 197 F4
Shallows The SP6 .... 70 B4
Shamblehurst La N
  Hedge End SO30 .... 81 E2
  West End SO32 .... 81 E2
Shamblehurst La S SO30 .... 81 E1
Shamblehurst Prim Sch SO30 .... 105 E4
Shamrock Cl PO12 .... 181 D2
Shamrock Ct 3 BH21 .... 163 E2
Shamrock Rd SO19 .... 103 E2
Shamrock Villas 9 SO17 .... 79 E1
Shamrock Way SO45 .... 126 A3
Shanklin Cres SO15 .... 78 B1
Shanklin Rd
  Portsmouth PO4 .... 182 C2
  Southampton SO15 .... 78 B1
Shannon Cl PO15 .... 130 B1
Shannon House 28 SO14 .... 103 E3
Shannon Rd Gosport PO14 .... 155 D3
  Stubbington PO14 .... 154 A2
Shannon Way SO53 .... 55 D3
Shapland Ave BH11 .... 188 C3
Shappen Hill La BH24 .... 142 C1
Shapton Cl SO45 .... 150 A2
Shapwick Rd BH15 .... 202 A1
Shard Cl BH31 .... 115 D3
Sharlands Rd BH18 .... 187 D2
Sharon Ct PO12 .... 181 E3
Sharon Rd SO30 .... 80 B1
Sharp Rd BH12 .... 204 A4
Sharp's Copse Inf Sch PO9 .... 136 A3
Sharp's Copse Jun Sch PO9 .... 136 A3
Sharp's Rd PO9 .... 136 A3
Sharpley Cl SP6 .... 69 F2
Sharpness Ct PO14 .... 154 B4
Sharps Cl PO3 .... 158 A3
Sharvells Rd SO41 .... 211 E3
Shavard La SO32 .... 61 E3
Shaves La BH25 .... 195 D3
Shaw Cl Totton SO40 .... 100 B4
  West End SO18 .... 80 A1
Shaw Rd BH24 .... 117 E1
Shawcross Ind Pk PO3 .... 158 A3
Shawfield Rd PO9 .... 160 A4
Shawford Cl SO16 .... 78 C2
Shawford Gdns BH8 .... 190 B1
Shawford Gr PO9 .... 135 E3
Shawford Rd BH8 .... 190 B2
Shawford Sta SO21 .... 31 F3
Shayer Rd SO15 .... 78 B1
Shear Hill GU31 .... 41 D3
Sheardley La SO32 .... 62 A1
Shearer Rd PO1 .... 182 C4
Shears Brook Cl BH23 .... 169 D1
Shears Rd SO50 .... 56 C2
Shearwater Ave PO16 .... 155 F4
Shearwater Cl PO13 .... 155 D1
Shearwater Ct PO11 .... 185 E1
Shearwater Dr PO6 .... 158 C4
Sheep Pond La SO32 .... 61 D2
Sheep St GU32 .... 40 C2
Sheepwash La PO7 .... 133 F4
Sheet Prim Sch GU32 .... 41 D3
Sheffield Cl SO50 .... 56 B3
Sheffield Ct PO13 .... 180 B3
Sheffield Rd PO1 .... 182 C3
Sheiling Sch The BH24 .... 140 B3
Shelbourne Cl BH8 .... 205 E3
Shelbourne Rd BH8 .... 205 D3
Sheldrake Gdns Hordle SO41 .... 196 A2
  Southampton SO16 .... 78 A3
Sheldrake Rd BH23 .... 208 A3
Shelford Rd PO4 .... 183 D3
Shell Ct SO40 .... 101 F1
Shellcroft SO31 .... 152 B4
Shelley Ave PO6 .... 132 C1
Shelley Cl Bournemouth BH1, ... 205 F3
  Christchurch BH23 .... 208 B4
  St Leonards BH24 .... 139 F3
  Winchester SO21, SO22 .... 10 B4
Shelley Ct Ferndown BH22 .... 165 E2
  Southampton SO16 .... 102 C3
Shelley Gdns
  Bournemouth BH1 .... 205 F3
  Waterlooville PO8 .... 111 F2
Shelley Hamlets BH23 .... 208 B4
Shelley Hill BH23 .... 208 B4
Shelley House 18 BH25 .... 195 D1
Shelley La SO51 .... 75 F4
Shelley Rd
  Bournemouth BH1, BH7 .... 205 F3
  Eastleigh SO50 .... 55 F1
  Poole BH12 .... 203 E3
  Southampton SO19 .... 104 C3
  Totton SO40 .... 76 B1
Shelley Rd E BH7 .... 205 F3
Shelley Way SO41 .... 211 E3
Shelly Park(B'mth & Poole
  Coll of Art & Design) BH5 .... 205 F2
Shelton Rd BH6 .... 206 B3
Shenley Cl PO15 .... 130 B1
Shenstone Ct 18 BH25 .... 195 D1
Shepards Cl PO14 .... 154 B4
Shepheard's Way PO12 .... 181 D3
Shepherd Cl BH23 .... 193 F1
Shepherds Cl Cadnam SO40 .... 99 D3
Shepherds Down Sch SO21 .... 31 E3

Sar – Sho 251
Shepherds Hey Rd SO40 .... 76 A1
Shepherds Hill BH24 .... 116 B3
Shepherds La
  Compton(Hants) SO21 .... 31 E3
  Ibsley BH24 .... 116 A3
Shepherds Purse Cl SO31 .... 128 C1
Shepherds Rd Cadnam SO40 .... 99 E3
  Winchester SO23 .... 11 E4
Shepherds Way
  Bournemouth BH7 .... 206 A4
  Nursling SO16 .... 77 E3
Sheppard Cl PO8 .... 112 A3
Sheppards Field 4 BH21 .... 163 D3
Sherborn Cres BH17 .... 188 A1
Sherborne Cl SO50 .... 56 A3
Sherborne Dr BH22 .... 165 E2
Sherborne House Sch SO53 .... 55 E4
Sherborne Rd SO17 .... 79 D2
Sherborne Way SO30 .... 105 E3
Sherbrooke Cl SO23 .... 2 B4
Sherecroft Gdns SO30 .... 106 A4
Sherfield Ave PO9 .... 136 A3
Sherfield Cl BH8 .... 190 B1
Sherfield English La SO51 .... 50 B3
Sherfield House 26 SO15 .... 102 C4
Sheridan Cl
  Southampton SO19 .... 104 B3
  Winchester SO22 .... 10 B3
Sheridan Gdns
  Swanwick PO15 .... 129 E4
  Totton SO40 .... 100 B4
Sheringham Rd Cosham PO6 .... 133 E1
  Poole BH12 .... 203 F3
Sherley Gn SO31 .... 105 E3
Sherrin Cl PO15 .... 202 B3
Sherringham Cl SO45 .... 151 D2
Sherwin Wlk PO12 .... 181 D2
Sherwood Ave Ferndown BH22 .... 165 E2
  Hedge End SO30 .... 105 E2
  Poole BH12 .... 203 D2
Sherwood Cl Liss GU33 .... 21 D4
  Southampton SO16 .... 78 C2
Sherwood Dr BH31 .... 115 D3
Sherwood Gdns SO31 .... 128 C2
Sherwood Rd
  Chandler's Ford SO53 .... 30 C1
  Gosport PO12 .... 181 D2
Sherwood Way SO45 .... 177 E2
Shetland Cl Cosham PO6 .... 133 F1
  Totton SO40 .... 100 A4
Shillinglee PO7 .... 134 C2
Shillingstone Dr BH9 .... 190 A2
Shillito Rd BH12 .... 203 F3
Shingle Bank Dr SO41 .... 211 E2
Shinwell Ct 14 SO15 .... 78 A1
Ship Leopard St 12 PO1 .... 182 A3
Shipbuilding Rd PO1 .... 181 F4
Shipcote La SO32 .... 59 E1
Shipley Rd SO21 .... 32 A4
Shipstal Cl BH16 .... 201 E2
Shipton Gn PO9 .... 135 E3
Shire Cl Swanwick PO15 .... 129 D4
  Waterlooville PO7 .... 112 B1
Shires Copse BH6 .... 206 C2
Shires The SO30 .... 105 D3
Shires Wlk SO40 .... 100 A4
Shirley Ave Portsmouth PO4 .... 183 E2
  Southampton SO15 .... 102 B4
Shirley Cl Bransgore BH23 .... 169 D1
  West Moors BH22 .... 138 C1
Shirley High St SO15, SO16 .... 102 A4
Shirley Holms Boldre SO41 .... 173 D1
  Sway SO41 .... 173 D1
Shirley Inf Sch SO15 .... 78 B1
Shirley Park Rd SO16 .... 102 A4
Shirley Rd
  Bournemouth BH9 .... 190 A1
  Poole BH12 .... 203 D3
  Portsmouth PO5 .... 182 C1
  Southampton SO15 .... 102 B4
  Upton BH16 .... 201 E4
Shirley Towers SO15 .... 102 B4
Shirley Warren Prim
  Sch SO16 .... 78 A1
Shirrel Ct PO12 .... 180 B2
Shoblands Way SO45 .... 126 A1
Shoe La SO32 .... 58 C3
Sholing Ct PO9 .... 135 E3
Sholing Inf Sch SO19 .... 104 A3
Sholing Jun Sch SO19 .... 104 A3
Sholing Rd SO19 .... 103 F2
Sholing Sec Sch (Girls)
  SO19 .... 104 A2
Sholing Sta SO19 .... 103 F1
Shoot Hill Denmead PO17 .... 109 E2
  Southwick PO17 .... 109 E2
Shoot La Gosport PO13 .... 180 A4
  Lee-on-the-Solent PO13 .... 180 A4
Shooters Hill Cl SO19 .... 104 A2
Shop La SO31 .... 104 C1
Shore Ave Portsmouth PO4 .... 183 D3
  Upton BH16 .... 201 E1
Shore Cl Milford on Sea SO41 .... 211 D3
  Upton BH16 .... 201 E1
Shore Cres SO32 .... 83 E4
Shore Gdns BH16 .... 201 D3
Shore La
  Bishop's Waltham SO32 .... 83 E4
  Upton BH16 .... 201 E1
Shore Rd Hythe SO45 .... 126 A2
  Locks Heath SO31 .... 128 B1
  Poole BH13 .... 214 B3
Shoreacres BH13 .... 214 B2
Shorefield Cres SO41 .... 211 E3
Shorefield Cvn Pk SO41 .... 211 D3

Shorefield Rd
Marchwood SO40 .... **101** F1
Milford on Sea SO41 .... **211** D3
Shorefield Way SO41 .... **211** E3
Shorehaven PO6 .... **156** C4
Shorewell SO31 .... **127** E4
Shorewood CI SO31 .... **128** C1
Short CI BH12 .... **204** A4
Short Hill Nomansland SP5 ...... **73** D4
Romsey SO51 .... **28** B1
Short Rd PO14 .... **179** D3
Short Row PO1 .... **182** A3
Shorts CI BH23 .... **192** B1
Shorts Rd SO50 .... **57** E1
Shotterfield Terr GU33 .... **20** C2
Shotters Hill CI SO30 .... **80** B1
Shotts La SO41 .... **198** C2
Shottsford Rd BH15 .... **202** B3
Shraveshill CI SO40 .... **76** B1
Shrubb's Ave SO41 .... **197** F2
Shrubbery CI PO16 .... **156** B4
Shrubbery The PO12 .... **180** C4
Shrubbs Hill Gdns SO43 .... **121** F2
Shrubbs Hill Rd SO43 .... **121** F2
Shrubland CI SO18 .... **104** A4
Sibland CI PO14 .... **154** B4
Sicily House [15] PO14 .... **154** C4
Sidings The Downton SP5 .... **47** D4
Netley SO31 .... **127** E3
Sidlesham CI PO11 .... **185** F1
Sidmouth Ave PO3 .... **183** D4
Sidney Gdns BH9 .... **190** A2
Sidney Smith Ct BH17 .... **187** F1
Silchester CI BH2 .... **204** C3
Silchester Rd PO3 .... **183** D4
Silhouette Ct PO11 .... **185** E1
Silkin Gdns SO40 .... **100** B3
Silkstead Ave PO9 .... **135** F3
Silkstead La SO21 .... **30** C4
Sillen La SP6 .... **43** D2
Silver Birch Ave PO14 .... **154** C4
Silver Birch CI Liss GU33 .... **21** D2
Poole BH12 .... **204** A2
Southampton SO19 .... **104** B2
Silver Birches SO31 .... **127** F4
Silver Bsns Pk BH23 .... **207** F4
Silver Hill SO23 .... **2 B4**
Silver St Christchurch BH23 ..... **207** D3
Hordle SO41 .... **196** B3
Lyndhurst SO43 .... **121** E3
Portsmouth PO5 .... **182** A2
Silver Way BH23 .... **208** C4
Silverdale CI BH18 .... **186** C2
Silverdale Cres SP6 .... **93** D3
Silverdale CI [22] SO15 .... **102** C4
Silverdale Rd SO15 .... **102** C4
Silverlock CI [1] PO2 .... **182** B4
Silverlock PI PO10 .... **137** D3
Silvers End SO45 .... **126** A1
Silvers Wood SO40 .... **76** B1
Silversands Gdns PO11 .... **185** D1
Silverthorne Way PO7 .... **134** B4
Silvertrees PO10 .... **136** C1
Silverwood CI Oakley BH21 ..... **163** E1
Winchester SO22, SO23 .... **10** B3
Silvester Rd PO8 .... **111** F1
Silwood CI SO22 .... **1** B1
Simmonds Gr PO11 .... **185** E2
Simmonds Rd BH15 .... **202** B3
Simmons CI SO30 .... **105** E4
Simnel St [13] SO14 .... **102** C2
Simon CI SO14 .... **104** C4
Simon Way SO19 .... **104** C3
Simonds Ct [5] SO23 .... **2** A1
Simpson CI PO16 .... **156** B4
Simpson Rd PO2 .... **157** E1
Sinah La PO11 .... **184** B2
Sinclair Ct [8] BH14 .... **203** D2
Sinclair Inf Sch SO16 .... **78** A3
Sinclair Jun Sch SO16 .... **78** A3
Sinclair Rd SO16 .... **78** A3
Singleton Dr BH10 .... **189** E1
Singleton Gdns PO8 .... **88** B2
Sir George's Rd SO15 .... **102** B3
Sir Harold Hillier Gardens
 & Arboretum SO51 .... **28** B2
Sirdar House SO17 .... **79** E2
Sirdar Rd SO17 .... **79** E2
Siskin CI
 Bishop's Waltham SO32 .... **83** D4
 Ferndown BH22 .... **165** D4
 Southampton SO16 .... **78** A3
Siskin Gr PO7 .... **135** D3
Siskin Inf Sch PO13 .... **180** B3
Siskin Jun Sch PO13 .... **180** B3
Sissinghurst CI SO19 .... **104** A1
Sissinghurst Rd PO16 .... **156** A4
Siverdale Dr PO7 .... **111** E2
Siward House [20] GU32 .... **40** C2
Six Dials SO14 .... **103** D3
Six Oaks Rd SO52 .... **54** A2
Sixpenny CI
 Locks Heath PO14 .... **129** D1
 Poole BH12 .... **203** F4
Sixth Ave PO6 .... **157** F4
Sizer Way SO45 .... **125** D2
Skew Rd PO17 .... **132** B1
Skinner St BH15 .... **202** B1
Skintle Gr [5] SO21 .... **56** C4
Skipper Way PO13 .... **180** A3
Skipton CI BH18 .... **187** D1
Skipton Rd SO53 .... **55** E2
Sky End La SO41 .... **196** A1
Skys Wood Rd SO52 .... **54** C3

Slab La Redlynch SP5 .... **47** E3
 West Wellow SO51 .... **50** C2
Slade CI SO41 .... **196** A2
Slade's La BH10 .... **204** B4
Slades Farm Hostel BH11 ...... **189** E1
Slades Farm Rd BH10 .... **189** E1
Slades Farm Specl Sch
 BH10 .... **189** E1
Slades Hill SO45 .... **150** C1
Slater App PO2 .... **157** D1
Sleepbrook CI BH31 .... **114** C3
Sleeper's Hill SO22 .... **10** B3
Sleeper's Hill Rd SO22 .... **10** B3
Sleepers Delle Gdns SO22 ...... **10** C3
Sleepers Hill Gdns SO22 .... **10** B3
Sleight La BH21 .... **186** B4
Slepe Cres BH12 .... **203** F4
Slindon CI PO8 .... **88** B3
Slindon Gdns [18] PO9 .... **135** F1
Slindon St PO1 .... **182** B3
Slingsby CI PO1 .... **182** A2
Slinn Rd BH23 .... **207** F4
Slip Way BH15 .... **202** A1
Slipper Rd PO10 .... **161** D4
Slipway The PO6 .... **157** D4
Sloane Ave SO45 .... **150** B2
Sloane CI SO45 .... **150** B2
Sloane Park SO32 .... **107** E4
Sloane Stanley Ct PO12 .... **181** D3
Slocum House [17] PO12 .... **181** E2
Sloe Tree CI PO14 .... **129** E1
Slough La BH16 .... **201** D3
Smallcuts Ave PO10 .... **137** E1
Smeaton St [7] PO2 .... **157** E1
Smeeton Rd PO13 .... **179** F1
Smith CI SO45 .... **150** C1
Smith Gr SO30 .... **105** E3
Smith La PO11 .... **161** E1
Smith St PO12 .... **181** D3
Smith's Field SO51 .... **28** A1
Smithe CI SO50 .... **56** A2
Smithfield PI BH9 .... **189** F1
Smiths La SO32 .... **107** F4
Smithson CI BH12 .... **204** B4
Smithy La BH25 .... **194** C3
Smithy The PO7 .... **110** C2
Smugglers La BH21 .... **163** F4
Smugglers La N BH23 .... **193** F1
Smugglers La S BH23 .... **208** C4
Smugglers Reach BH23 .... **208** A3
Smugglers Wood Rd BH23 ..... **193** E1
Smythe Rd SO19 .... **104** B2
Snailing La GU33 .... **20** B4
Snails La BH24 .... **117** D2
Snakemoor La Durley SO32 ..... **81** F3
 Fair Oak SO32 .... **81** F3
Snapdragon CI SO31 .... **128** C1
Snape CI PO13 .... **180** B4
Snellgrove CI SO40 .... **76** B1
Snellgrove PI SO40 .... **76** B1
Snooks La SO41 .... **198** A3
Snowdon Dr PO14 .... **154** C4
Snowdon Rd BH4 .... **204** B2
Snowdrop Gdns BH23 .... **193** D1
Soake Rd PO7 .... **111** D2
Soalwood La GU32 .... **39** F4
Soberton House [34] SO17 ..... **79** D1
Soberton Rd
 Bournemouth BH8 .... **205** E3
 Havant PO9 .... **135** F2
Soberton Towers SO32 .... **85** E3
Soldridge CI PO9 .... **136** A3
Solent Ave Lymington SO41 ..... **198** A2
 Southampton SO19 .... **104** C3
Solent CI Chandler's Ford SO53 .. **55** F3
 Lymington SO41 .... **197** F2
Solent Ct
 [6] Milford on Sea SO41 .... **211** E2
 Southampton SO19 .... **103** F1
Solent Ctr PO15 .... **129** F4
Solent Dr Barton on Sea BH25 ... **210** A4
 Hythe SO45 .... **125** F2
 Locks Heath SO31 .... **152** B3
 South Hayling PO11 .... **184** C1
Solent House Fareham PO14 .... **155** D4
 Havant PO9 .... **136** A2
Solent Homes SO19 .... **104** C3
Solent Hts
 [12] Lee-on-the-Solent PO13 .... **179** F1
 Portsmouth PO4 .... **183** E2
Solent Ind Ctr SO15 .... **102** B3
Solent Ind Est SO30 .... **81** D1
Solent Inf Sch PO6 .... **158** B4
Solent Jun Sch PO6 .... **158** B4
Solent Lodge [21] BH25 .... **195** D1
Solent Meadows SO31 .... **128** A1
Solent Pines [2] SO41 .... **211** D2
Solent Rd
 Barton on Sea BH25 .... **209** E4
 Bournemouth BH6 .... **207** D2
 Christchurch BH23 .... **194** A1
 Cosham PO6 .... **158** B4
 Havant PO9 .... **135** F1
 Hythe SO45 .... **149** F4
 Southampton SO15 .... **102** C2
 Stubbington PO14 .... **179** D3
Solent View Boldre SO41 .... **198** A2
 Bournemouth BH6 .... **207** D2
 Fawley SO45 .... **178** C4
Solent View Sch SO41 .... **197** F4
Solent Village PO15 .... **129** F3
Solent Way Gosport PO12 ...... **180** C2
 Milford on Sea SO41 .... **211** D2
Solihull House PO5 .... **182** A2
Solly CI BH12 .... **203** F4
Solomons La SO32 .... **83** F1
Solona Rd SO53 .... **55** F4

Solway House [10] SO14 .... **103** E3
Somborne Ct [32] SO17 .... **79** D1
Somborne Dr PO9 .... **135** F3
Somborne House SO19 .... **103** F1
Somerby Rd BH15 .... **202** B3
Somerford Ave BH23 .... **208** A4
Somerford Bsns Ctr BH23 ...... **208** A4
Somerford CI SO19 .... **104** A3
Somerford Ct BH23 .... **208** C4
Somerford Cty Inf Sch BH23 .... **207** F4
Somerford Cty Jun Sch BH23 ... **207** F4
Somerford Rd BH23 .... **207** F4
Somerford Way BH23 .... **207** F3
Somerley Rd BH9 .... **205** D4
Somerley View [1] BH24 .... **141** D4
Somers CI SO22 .... **10** B3
Somers Park Prim Sch PO1 ..... **182** B3
Somers Rd Portsmouth PO1 ..... **182** B2
 Portsmouth PO1 .... **182** B3
Somers Rd N PO1 .... **182** C3
Somerset Ave SO18 .... **104** B4
Somerset Cres SO53 .... **55** E2
Somerset Ct [4] SO15 .... **102** B3
Somerset Rd
 Bournemouth BH7 .... **206** A3
 Christchurch BH23 .... **206** C4
 Portsmouth PO5 .... **182** B1
 Southampton SO17 .... **79** E1
Somerset Terr SO15 .... **102** B3
Somerston Flats PO9 .... **136** A1
Somerton Ave SO18 .... **104** A4
Somerton CI BH25 .... **195** E2
Somervell CI PO12 .... **181** D1
Somervell Dr PO16 .... **131** D2
Somerville Ct [12] BH25 .... **194** C2
Somerville PI [1] PO2 .... **157** E1
Somerville Rd
 Bournemouth BH2 .... **204** B2
 Kings Worthy SO23 .... **2** B4
 Ringwood BH24 .... **141** E4
Sommers CI SO19 .... **103** E2
Sonnet Way PO7 .... **135** D4
Sonning Way BH8 .... **190** A1
Soper's La BH23 .... **207** D3
Sopers La BH17 .... **187** D1
Sopley CI BH25 .... **209** E4
Sopley Ct [10] PO9 .... **136** A3
Sopley Farm Bldgs BH23 .... **192** A3
Sopley Prim Sch BH23 .... **168** B1
Sopwith CI BH23 .... **208** A3
Sopwith Cres BH21 .... **163** F1
Sopwith Way SO31 .... **128** C4
Sorrel CI Romsey SO51 .... **28** B1
 Waterlooville PO7 .... **135** D3
Sorrel Dr PO15 .... **129** E4
Sorrel Gdns BH18 .... **186** C1
Sorrell CI SO31 .... **128** C1
Sorrell Ct BH23 .... **208** A4
Sorrell Way BH23 .... **208** A4
South Ave Fawley SO45 .... **150** C2
 New Milton BH25 .... **195** D1
 Portsmouth PO2 .... **157** F2
South Baddesley CE Prim
 Sch SO41 .... **198** C3
South Baddesley Rd SO41 ...... **198** A2
South Bay PO10 .... **161** D2
South CI Gosport PO12 .... **180** C1
 Havant PO9 .... **160** A4
 Romsey SO51 .... **28** B1
South Cliff Rd BH2 .... **204** C1
South Cross St PO12 .... **181** E2
South Ct SO31 .... **127** F1
South Downs Coll PO7 .... **135** D2
South Dr PO21 .... **1** A2
South East Cres SO19 .... **104** A3
South East Rd SO19 .... **104** A2
South End CI SO21 .... **30** A4
South Front [17] Romsey SO51 .. **52** C4
 Southampton SO14 .... **103** D2
South Grove SO41 .... **197** F2
South Hampshire
 Ind Pk SO40 .... **76** B1
South Haven CI BH16 .... **201** D2
South Hill Alderholt SP6 .... **93** D3
 Droxford SO32 .... **85** D4
 Southampton SO16 .... **79** D2
South Kinson Dr BH11 .... **189** D2
South La Buriton GU31 .... **65** E2
 Clanfield PO8 .... **88** A3
 Clanfield, Chalton PO8 .... **89** D2
 Downton SP5 .... **46** C4
 Horndean PO8 .... **89** D2
 Nomansland SP5 .... **73** E4
 Southbourne PO10 .... **137** F1
 Westbourne PO10 .... **137** E2
South Lodge Fareham PO15 ..... **130** A1
 Poole BH13 .... **214** D4
South Mill Rd SO15 .... **102** A4
South Millers Dale SO53 .... **55** D4
South Normandy PO1 .... **182** A2
South Par Portsmouth PO5 ..... **182** B1
 Totton SO40 .... **100** C4
South Park Rd BH12 .... **204** A4
South PI PO13 .... **180** A2
South Rd Bournemouth BH1 .... **205** F3
 Corfe Mullen BH21 .... **186** C3
 Cosham PO6 .... **158** B4
 Poole BH15 .... **202** B1
 Portsmouth PO1 .... **182** C4
 South Hayling PO11 .... **184** C2
 Southampton SO17 .... **103** E4
South Road Comb Sch
 BH15 .... **202** B1

South St Continued
 Hythe SO45 .... **126** A2
 Lymington SO41 .... **197** E1
 [41] Portsmouth PO5 .... **182** B2
 Titchfield PO14 .... **153** F4
South Stoneham House SO18 ... **79** E2
South Sway La SO41 .... **196** B4
South Terr PO1 .... **182** A3
South Trestle Rd SO45 .... **151** E3
South View
 Bournemouth BH2 .... **204** C3
 Winchester SO22 .... **10** C4
South View PI [17] BH2 .... **204** C3
South View Rd
 Christchurch BH23 .... **207** D3
 Southampton SO15 .... **102** A4
 Winchester SO22 .... **10** A2
South Way PO15 .... **129** F2
South Weirs SO42 .... **172** B4
South Western Cres BH14 ..... **203** D1
Southampton
 Airport (Parkway) Sta SO18 .. **79** F3
Southampton Central Sta
 SO15 .... **102** C3
Southampton City Coll SO15 ... **103** D2
Southampton
 (Eastleigh) Airport SO50 ..... **80** A4
Southampton Gen Hospl SO16 .. **78** A1
Southampton Hill SO31 .... **153** D4
Southampton House [28] PO9 .. **136** A3
Southampton Inst
 (City Campus) SO14 .... **103** D3
Southampton Inst of H Ed
 Marine Ops Ctr SO14 .... **102** A1
Southampton Oceanography
 Ctr SO14 .... **103** D1
Southampton Rd
 Cadnam SO40 .... **98** C4
 Cadnam, Bartley SO40 .... **99** D4
 Cosham PO6 .... **157** D4
 Eastleigh SO50 .... **56** A1
 Fareham PO14, PO16 .... **131** D1
 Fareham PO14, PO15 .... **154** A4
 Fordingbridge SP6 .... **70** A4
 Hythe SO45 .... **125** F2
 Locks Heath PO14 .... **129** E2
 Lymington SO41 .... **197** E2
 Lyndhurst SO43 .... **122** A3
 North Baddesley SO51 .... **53** D3
 Ringwood BH24 .... **140** C4
 Romsey SO51 .... **53** D3
Southampton St [3] SO15 ...... **102** C3
Southbourne Ave
 Cosham PO6 .... **158** A4
 Hermitage PO10 .... **161** D4
 Holbury SO45 .... **150** B2
Southbourne Coast Rd BH6 ... **206** C2
Southbourne Cross Roads
 [6] BH6 .... **206** C2
Southbourne Cty Jun &
 Inf Sch PO10 .... **161** F4
Southbourne Gr BH6 .... **206** B2
Southbourne Halt PO10 .... **161** F4
Southbourne Overcliff Dr
 BH6 .... **206** B2
Southbourne Rd
 Bournemouth BH5,BH6 .... **206** B2
 Lymington SO41 .... **197** E2
Southbourne Sands BH6 .... **206** B2
Southbrook CI Havant PO9 ..... **159** F4
 Poole BH13 .... **188** A1
Southbrook Mews SO32 .... **83** E4
Southbrook Rd Havant PO9 ..... **159** F4
 [15] Southampton SO15 .... **102** C3
Southcliff PO13 .... **179** F2
Southcliff Rd SO14 .... **103** D4
Southcliffe House [1] SO14 ..... **103** D3
Southcliffe Rd
 Barton on Sea BH25 .... **209** E4
 Christchurch BH23 .... **208** B3
Southcote Rd BH1 .... **205** E2
Southcroft Rd PO12 .... **180** C3
Southdale CI SO53 .... **55** E3
Southdene Rd SO53 .... **55** E3
Southdown Ct [1] BH23 .... **207** F4
Southdown Rd
 Compton(Hants) SO21 .... **31** E3
 Cosham PO6 .... **158** A4
 Horndean PO8 .... **88** B2
Southdown View PO7 .... **111** E1
Southdown Way BH22 .... **138** C3
Southend La SO32 .... **109** E4
Southern Ave BH22 .... **139** D1
Southern Gdns SO40 .... **100** C4
Southern La BH25 .... **209** F4
Southern Oaks BH25 .... **194** C1
Southern Rd
 Bournemouth BH6 .... **206** B2
 Fawley SO45 .... **151** F1
 Lymington SO41 .... **197** E2
 Southampton SO15 .... **102** C2
 West End SO30 .... **80** C1
Southernhay PO7 .... **110** C2
Southernhay Rd BH31 .... **115** D3
Southey Rd BH23 .... **207** F4
Southfield BH23 .... **141** D3
Southfield La BH24 .... **143** E1
Southfield Mews [5] BH24 ..... **141** D3
Southfield Wlk PO9 .... **135** E4
Southfields CI SO32 .... **83** E4
Southgate St SO23 .... **10** C4
Southgate Villas SO23 .... **10** C4
Southill Ave SO14 .... **203** E3
Southill Gdns BH9 .... **190** A1
Southill Rd Bournemouth BH9 .. **190** A1
 Poole BH12 .... **203** E4
Southlands Cosham PO6 .... **158** A4
 Lymington SO41 .... **197** E1

Southlands Ave
 Bournemouth BH6 .... **206** C
 Corfe Mullen BH21 .... **186** C
Southlands CI BH21 .... **186** B
Southlands Ct BH18 .... **187** E
Southlands Sch SO41 .... **197** F
Southlawns Wlk BH25 .... **194** C
Southlea Ave BH6 .... **206** C
Southleigh Gr PO11 .... **184** C
Southleigh Rd Emsworth PO9 ... **136** B
 Havant PO9 .... **136** B
Southmead Rd PO15 .... **130** C
Southmoor La PO9 .... **159** E
Southsea Castle PO5 .... **182** B
Southsea Inf Sch PO4 .... **182** C
Southsea Terr PO5 .... **182** A
Southview SO32 .... **61** D
Southville Rd BH5 .... **206** A
Southwater [1] PO13 .... **179** F
Southway PO13 .... **155** E
Southways PO14 .... **179** E
Southwick Ave PO16 .... **132** C
Southwick CI SO22 .... **1** B
Southwick Ct PO14 .... **155** D
Southwick Hill Rd PO6 .... **133** F
Southwick PI BH6 .... **206** B
Southwick Rd
 Bournemouth BH6 .... **206** B
 Cosham PO7,PO17 .... **133** E
 Denmead PO7 .... **110** C
 Southwick PO17 .... **108** B
 Wickham PO17 .... **108** B
Southwood Ave
 Bournemouth BH6 .... **206** B
 Christchurch BH23 .... **194** A
Southwood CI
 Christchurch BH23 .... **194** A
 Ferndown BH22 .... **165** E
Southwood Ct BH23 .... **194** A
Southwood Gdns SO31 .... **128** C
Southwood Rd
 Portsmouth PO2 .... **157** F
 South Hayling PO11 .... **185** E
Sovereign Bsns Ctr BH15 ...... **202** A
Sovereign CI
 Bournemouth BH7 .... **205** F
 Portsmouth PO4 .... **183** E
Sovereign Cres PO14 .... **129** D
Sovereign Ct [20] SO17 .... **79** D
Sovereign Ctr BH1 .... **205** F
Sovereign Dr
 Hedge End SO30 .... **105** E
 Portsmouth PO4 .... **183** E
Sovereign La PO7 .... **134** C
Sovereign Sq [8] BH7 .... **205** F
Sovereign Way SO50 .... **55** F
Soverign Dr SO30 .... **105** F
Sowden CI SO30 .... **105** D
Sowley La SO41 .... **199** E
Spa Rd SO14 .... **102** C
Spain Bldgs [18] GU32 .... **40** C
Spain The GU32 .... **40** C
Spalding Rd SO19 .... **104** C
Spaniard's La SO51 .... **53** D
Sparkford CI
 Bournemouth BH7 .... **206** A
 Winchester SO22 .... **10** C
Sparkford Rd SO22 .... **10** C
Sparrow CI PO8 .... **111** F
Sparrow Ct PO13 .... **179** F
Sparrow Sq SO50 .... **55** E
Sparrowgrove SO21 .... **31** E
Sparsholt CI PO9 .... **135** D
Sparsholt Rd
 Southampton SO19 .... **126** C
 Winchester SO21 .... **9** E
Spartan CI Stubbington PO14 ... **154** B
 Thorney Island PO10 .... **161** D
Spartina Dr SO41 .... **197** F
Spear Rd SO14 .... **103** D
Specks La PO4 .... **183** D
Speedwell CI
 Chandler's Ford SO53 .... **55** D
 Locks Heath SO31 .... **128** C
Speedwell Dr BH23 .... **208** A
Speggs Wlk SO30 .... **105** E
Speltham Hill PO7 .... **86** B
Spencer CI PO11 .... **185** D
Spencer Ct
 [5] New Milton BH25 .... **195** D
 Stubbington PO14 .... **154** C
Spencer Dr PO13 .... **179** F
Spencer Gdns PO8 .... **111** F
Spencer Rd
 Bournemouth BH1 .... **205** E
 Eastleigh SO50 .... **55** F
 Emsworth PO10 .... **136** C
 New Milton BH25 .... **195** D
 Poole BH13 .... **214** C
 Portsmouth PO4 .... **182** C
 Southampton SO19 .... **104** B
Spenlow CI PO2 .... **182** B
Spenser CI SO31 .... **152** B
Spetisbury CI BH9 .... **190** A
Spice Quay PO1 .... **182** A
Spicer CI [4] SO22 .... **10** C
Spicer La BH11 .... **188** C
Spicer St [43] PO1 .... **182** B
Spicer's Hill SO40 .... **100** C
Spicer's Way SO40 .... **100** C
Spicewood PO15 .... **130** C
Spinacre BH25 .... **210** A
Spindle CI Broadstone BH18 .... **186** C
 Havant PO9 .... **136** B
Spindle Warren PO9 .... **136** B
Spindlewood CI [26]
 Barton on Sea BH25 .... **195** D
 Southampton SO16 .... **79** D

Spindlewood Way SO40 124 C4
Spinnaker Cl Gosport PO13 180 B4
South Hayling PO11 184 C2
Spinnaker Grange PO11 160 B2
Spinnaker View PO9 135 D1
Spinners Cl BH22 138 C1
Spinney Cl St Leonards BH24 139 E2
Waterlooville PO8 111 F2
Spinney Dale SO45 126 A1
Spinney Gdns SO45 126 A1
Spinney The
Compton(Hants) SO21 31 E3
Denmead PO7 110 C2
Fair Oak SO50 57 D1
Gosport PO13 155 E1
Portchester PO16 131 F1
Southampton SO16 79 D3
St Leonards BH24 139 F3
Totton SO40 76 B1
Waterlooville PO8 112 A3
Spinney Way BH25 195 D3
Spinney Wlk SO18 79 F2
Spinneys La BH22 165 E3
Spinningfield House 4 GU32 40 C2
Spitfire Ct SO19 103 E2
Spitfire End 7 SO23 11 E4
Spitfire Link SO23 11 E4
Spitfire Loop SO50 80 A4
Spitfire Rdbt SO23 11 E4
Spitfire Way SO31 127 F1
Spithead Ave PO12 181 E1
Spithead House PO14 155 D4
Spithead Hts PO4 183 E2
Spittlefields BH24 141 D4
Spouts La SO51 50 B3
Spring Cl Fair Oak SO50 57 E1
Southampton SO19 103 F2
Spring Cres SO17 103 D4
Spring Ct Poole BH12 203 E3
17 Southampton SO15 102 C3
Spring Firs SO19 103 F2
Spring Garden La PO12 181 E3
Spring Gdns
1 Emsworth PO10 161 D4
North Baddesley SO52 54 A2
Poole BH12 203 E3
Portsmouth PO1 182 A3
Spring Gr SO31 105 D1
Spring House Cl SO21 32 A1
Spring La Bishopstoke SO50 56 B2
Colden Common SO21 31 F1
New Milton BH25 195 E1
Swanmore SO32 84 A3
Spring Pl 5 SO51 52 C4
Spring Rd
Bournemouth BH1 205 E3
2 Hythe SO45 126 A2
Locks Heath SO31 128 C3
Lymington SO41 198 A2
Southampton SO19 103 F2
Waterlooville PO8 112 A2
Spring St PO1 182 B3
Spring The PO7 110 C2
Spring Vale Swanmore SO32 84 A2
Waterlooville PO8 112 A2
Spring Wlk 12 PO1 182 B3
Springbank Rd BH7 205 F4
Springbourne Ct BH1 205 E3
Springbourne Mews BH1 205 E3
Springcroft PO13 155 D3
Springdale Ave BH18 186 C3
Springdale Ct SO40 100 C4
Springdale Fst Sch BH18 186 C2
Springdale Gr BH18 186 C2
Springdale Rd BH18 186 C2
Springfield 2 GU33 20 C2
Springfield Ave
Bournemouth BH6 207 D2
Christchurch BH23 191 E1
Holbury SO45 150 B2
Springfield Cl Havant PO9 135 D1
Lymington SO41 198 A2
Verwood BH31 114 C3
Springfield Cres
Poole BH14 203 D2
Redlynch SP5 47 E3
Springfield Ct SO19 103 F1
Springfield Dr SO40 100 C3
Springfield Gdns BH25 195 E1
Springfield Gr SO45 150 B2
Springfield Rd Poole BH14 203 D2
Verwood BH31 114 C3
Springfield Sch PO6 158 B4
Springfield Way PO14 179 E3
Springfields Cl 3 SO21 31 F1
Springford Cl SO16 78 A2
Springford Cres SO16 78 A2
Springford Gdns SO16 78 A2
Springford Rd SO16 78 A2
Springhill RC Prim Sch SO15 102 C3
Springhill Rd SO53 55 E3
Springles La PO15 130 A3
Springvale Ave
Bournemouth BH7 206 A4
Kings Worthy SO23 2 A3
Springvale Rd SO23 2 A4
Springwater Cl BH11 189 D2
Springwater Rd BH11 189 D2
Springwood Ave PO7 134 C3
Spruce Ave PO7 135 D4
Spruce Cl Broadstone BH17 186 C1
Locks Heath SO31 152 B4
Spruce Dr
Southampton SO19 104 C3
Totton SO40 100 A4
Spruce Wlk 22 PO13 179 F1
Spur Cl BH21 164 B3
Spur Hill Ave BH14 203 E2
Spur Rd Cosham PO6 157 F4
Poole BH14 203 E2
Waterlooville PO7 134 C4
Spur The Gosport PO12 180 C1
Wickham PO17 108 A2
Spurgeon Rd BH7 206 A3
Spurlings Rd PO17 131 E2
Square The
Bournemouth BH2 204 C2
Compt(Sussex) PO18 90 C1
Fawley SO45 151 D2
Gosport PO12 181 E4
Hamble-le-Rice SO31 128 A1
Lymington SO41 197 E2
Petersfield GU32 40 C2
Sherfield English SO51 26 A2
Southbourne PO10 161 E4
Titchfield PO14 153 F4
Westbourne PO10 137 D2
Wickham PO17 108 A2
Wimborne Minster BH21 163 D3
Winchester SO23 11 D4
Squarey Cl SP5 46 C3
Squires Wlk
Southampton SO19 103 F1
3 Southampton SO19 126 C4
Squirrel Cl 7 SO50 56 C1
Squirrel Dr SO19 104 A2
Squirrel Wlk BH31 114 C3
Squirrel's Cl BH23 191 E1
Squirrels Wlk SO45 125 F1
Stable Cl PO14 129 E1
Stables The SO31 129 D1
Stacey Cl BH12 203 E4
Stacey Ct PO9 135 E4
Stacey Gdns BH8 190 C1
Staff Rd SO51 6 A1
Stafford Rd
Bournemouth BH1 205 D2
Petersfield GU32 40 C3
Portsmouth PO5 182 B2
Southampton SO15 102 B3
Stag Bsns Pk BH24 141 D3
Stag Cl Bishopstoke SO50 56 C1
New Milton BH25 194 C2
Stag Gates SO45 150 C1
Stagbrake Cl SO45 150 A2
Stags La SO21 33 D3
Stagshorn Rd PO8 112 B4
Stainer Cl SO19 104 B2
Staith Cl SO19 104 B3
Stake's La SO32 59 F4
Stakes Hill Inf Sch PO7 134 C3
Stakes Hill Rd PO7 134 C3
Stakes La SO32 58 C2
Stakes Rd PO7 134 B2
Stalbridge Dr BH22 165 E2
Stalbridge Rd BH17 202 A4
Stalham Rd BH12 203 F3
Stallards La BH24 140 C4
Stalybridge Cl SO31 129 D3
Stamford Ave PO11 184 C2
Stamford Lodge PO11 184 C2
Stamford Rd BH6 206 B3
Stamford St PO1 182 C3
Stamford Way SO50 57 E1
Stampsey Ct 5 PO2 157 E1
Stamshaw Ct 14 PO2 157 E1
Stamshaw Inf Sch PO2 157 E1
Stamshaw Jun Sch PO2 157 E1
Stamshaw Rd PO2 157 E1
Stanbridge Earls Sch SO51 27 D2
Stanbridge La SO51 27 D2
Stanbridge Rd PO9 136 A2
Standard Way PO16 131 F2
Standford St SO14 103 D2
Standing Hill SP5 3 F4
Stanfield Cl BH12 203 E4
Stanfield Rd
Bournemouth BH9 204 C4
Ferndown BH22 165 E3
Poole BH12 203 E4
Stanford Cl PO6 157 E4
Stanford Ct 51 Havant PO9 136 A3
Southampton SO19 104 B2
Stanford Hill SO41 197 E2
Stanford Rd SO41 197 E2
Stanford Rise SO41 172 A1
Stanhope Rd PO1 182 B3
Stanier Way SO30 81 E1
Staniforth Ct BH23 207 E3
Stanley Ave PO3 183 D4
Stanley Cl Croucheston SP5 22 A4
Fareham PO15 130 C1
Gosport PO12 156 A1
Verwood BH31 115 D3
Stanley Ct Bournemouth BH1 205 E3
Poole BH15 202 B3
Stanley Green Cres Ind Est
BH15 202 B3
Stanley Green Fst Sch BH15 202 B3
Stanley Green Rd BH15 202 B3
Stanley La PO5 182 B1
Stanley Pearce House BH17 187 E1
Stanley Rd
Bournemouth BH1 205 E3
Christchurch BH23 209 D4
Emsworth PO10 161 D4
Holbury SO45 150 B2
Lymington SO41 198 A1
Poole BH15 202 B1
Portsmouth PO2 157 E1
Southampton SO17 79 E1
Totton SO40 76 B1
Stanley St PO5 182 B1
Stanmore La SO22 10 B3
Stanmore Prim Sch SO22 10 C3
Stannington Cl BH25 195 D1
Stannington Cres SO40 100 C4
Stannington Way SO40 100 C4
Stanpit BH23 207 F3
Stanstead Rd SO50 55 F2
Stansted Cl PO9 113 E1
Stansted Cres PO9 136 A3
Stansted Ct PO9 113 E1
Stansted Rd PO5 182 C2
Stanswood Rd
Blackfield SO45 178 B3
Fawley SO45 178 B3
Havant PO9 135 E3
Stanton Bldgs 20 SO15 102 A4
Stanton Lacy 17 BH13 214 C4
Stanton Rd
Bournemouth BH10 189 E1
Petersfield GU32 40 C2
Southampton SO15 102 A4
Stanton Road Ind
Est 21 SO15 102 A4
Stapehill Abbey Gdns BH21 164 C3
Stapehill Cres BH21 164 B3
Stapehill Rd BH21 164 C2
Staple Ash La GU32 39 E4
Staple Cl PO7 111 E1
Staple Close La BH15 202 B3
Staple Cross Burton BH23 207 F4
Southwick PO17 132 A4
Staple Gdns SO23 10 C4
Staplecross La BH23 207 E4
Stapleford Ave BH22 165 F3
Stapleford Cl SO51 28 A1
Stapleford La SO32 81 F3
Staplehurst Cl SO19 104 A1
Staplers Reach PO13 155 D1
Stapleton Rd PO3 183 D4
Staplewood La Ashurst SO40 124 B4
Marchwood SO40 124 B4
Star Cotts PO17 108 A2
Star La BH24 140 C4
Stares Cl PO13 180 B4
Starina Gdns PO7 135 D4
Starling Sq SO50 55 E1
Station App Broadstone BH18 187 D2
1 Portsmouth PO1 182 A3
Station Cl PO17 108 A2
Station Cotts SO42 123 E1
Station Hill Bursledon SO31 128 A4
Curdridge SO30 106 B4
Eastleigh SO50 56 A2
Winchester SO21, SO23 10 C4
Station La SO53 55 E3
Station Rd Alderholt SP6 92 C3
Bishop's Waltham SO32 83 E4
Burley BH24 170 B4
Bursledon SO31 128 A4
Christchurch BH23 207 D4
Christchurch, Highcliffe BH23 193 F1
Cosham PO6 158 B4
Fordingbridge SP6 69 E1
Gosport PO12 180 C4
Hamworthy BH15 202 A1
Liss GU33 20 C2
Locks Heath SO31 129 D3
Netley SO31 127 E3
New Milton BH25 195 D1
Nursling SO16 77 D3
Petersfield GU31, GU32 40 C2
Poole BH14 203 D2
Portchester PO16 156 B4
Portsmouth PO3 183 D4
Romsey SO51 52 C4
Soberton SO32 85 E4
South Hayling PO11 184 C2
Southampton, Redbridge SO15 101 E4
Southampton, Sholing SO19 103 F2
Sway SO41 172 A1
Verwood BH31 114 C4
West Meon GU32 37 E2
West Moors BH22 138 B1
Wickham PO17 108 A2
Wimborne Minster BH21 163 E2
Station Rd N SO40 101 D4
Station Rd S SO40 101 D4
Station St Lymington SO41 197 F2
Portsmouth PO1 182 B3
Station Terr BH21 163 E2
Staunton BH2 204 C1
Staunton Ave PO11 184 B2
Staunton Ctry Pk Havant PO9 135 F4
Rowland's Castle PO9 136 A4
Staunton Park Sec Sch PO9 136 A4
Staunton Rd PO9 135 F1
Staunton St PO1 182 B3
Stead Cl PO11 185 D2
Stedman Rd BH5 206 A3
Steel St PO5 182 A2
Steele Cl SO53 55 E2
Steels Dro SP6 70 C4
Steels La SP6 68 B2
Steep CE Prim Sch GU32 40 C4
Steep Cl Portchester PO16 132 B1
Southampton SO18 104 B4
Steepdene BH14 203 D2
Steeple Cl BH17 187 E2
Steeple Way PO14 129 E2
Steepleton Rd BH18 187 E2
Steerforth Cl PO2 182 B4
Stein Rd PO10 137 E1
Steinbeck Cl PO15 129 E4
Stella Ct
19 Christchurch BH23 209 D4
Southampton SO16 78 B2
Stem La BH25 194 C2
Stenbury Way SO31 127 E4
Stenhurst Rd BH15 202 C3
Step Terr SO22 10 C4
Stephen Cl PO8 112 A1
Stephen Langton Dr BH11 188 B3
Stephen Martin Gdns SP6 69 F1
Stephen Rd PO15 130 C1
Stephens Ct SO51 52 C3
Stephens Wlk BH24 140 C4
Stephenson Cl PO12 181 D1
Stephenson Rd SO40 76 B1
Stephenson Way SO30 81 D2
Steplake La SO51 25 E1
Steplake Rd SO51 50 B4
Stepnell Reach BH16 201 E3
Sterte Ave BH15 202 A2
Sterte Ave W BH15 202 A2
Sterte Cl BH15 202 B2
Sterte Ct BH15 202 A2
Sterte Espl BH15 202 B2
Sterte Ind Est BH15 202 A2
Sterte Rd BH15 202 B2
Steuart Rd SO18 103 E4
Stevenson Cres BH14 203 F2
Stevenson Rd BH6 207 D2
Stevensons Cl 4 BH21 163 E2
Steventon Rd SO18 104 B4
Stewart Cl 5 BH8 205 E3
Stewart House SO53 30 B1
Stewart Pl PO1 182 C4
Stewart Rd BH8 205 D3
Stewarts Gn PO7 86 B2
Stewarts Way BH22 165 F4
Stibbs Way BH23 169 E1
Stillmore Rd BH11 188 B2
Stinchar Dr SO53 55 D3
Stinsford Cl BH9 190 A2
Stinsford La BH17 202 B4
Stinsford Rd BH17 187 E1
Stirling Ave PO7 134 C4
Stirling Cl New Milton BH25 195 D2
Totton SO40 77 D1
Stirling Cres Hedge End SO30 81 E1
Totton SO40 101 D4
Stirling Ct
Bournemouth BH4 204 B1
Fareham PO15 130 C2
21 New Milton BH25 195 D2
Stirling Rd BH3 204 C4
Stirling St PO2 182 B4
Stirling Way BH23 208 A3
Stirling Wlk SO51 52 C4
Stirrup Cl Upton BH16 201 E4
Wimborne Minster BH21 164 B3
Stoborough Dr BH18 187 D1
Stock La SP5 49 E3
Stock's Cross SO43 73 F2
Stock's La SO32 61 F3
Stockbridge Cl Havant PO9 136 A3
Poole BH17 188 A1
Stockbridge Rd SO21, 22, 23 1 B1
Stocker Pl PO13 155 E1
Stockers Ave SO22 1 B1
Stockheath La PO9 135 F2
Stockheath Rd PO9 135 F2
Stockheath Way PO9 135 F2
Stockholm Dr SO30 105 E3
Stockley Cl SO45 150 B2
Stocks Heath La PO9 135 F2
Stockton Cl SO30 105 E4
Stoddart Ave SO19 103 F3
Stodham La GU33 20 C1
Stoke Common Rd SO50 56 C3
Stoke Gdns PO12 181 E2
Stoke Hts SO50 57 D2
Stoke Park Dr SO50 56 B2
Stoke Park Inf Sch SO50 56 C1
Stoke Park Jun Sch SO50 56 C1
Stoke Park Rd SO50 56 B2
Stoke Rd Gosport PO12 181 E2
Southampton SO16 78 A1
Winchester SO23 2 A2
Stoke Wood Cl SO50 57 D1
Stoke Wood Rd BH3 204 C3
Stokes Ave BH15 202 B2
Stokes Bay Rd PO12 180 C1
Stokesay Cl SO45 150 A4
Stokeway 4 PO12 181 E2
Stone Gdns BH8 191 D1
Stone La 5 Gosport PO12 181 D2
Wimborne Minster BH21 163 D3
Stone Lane Ind Est BH21 163 D3
Stone Sq PO9 135 F2
Stone St PO5 182 A2
Stone Terr SO50 31 D1
Stonechat Cl Ferndown BH22 165 D4
Petersfield GU31 41 E1
Stonechat Ct BH23 207 F4
Stonechat Dr SO40 100 B4
Stonechat Rd PO8 112 A4
Stonecrop Cl
Broadstone BH18 186 C1
Locks Heath SO31 128 C1
Stoneham Cemetery Rd SO18 79 F2
Stoneham Cl Petersfield GU32 40 B2
Southampton SO16 79 E3
Stoneham Ct SO16 79 D3
Stoneham Gdns SO31 104 C1
Stoneham La Chilworth SO50 79 F4
Southampton SO16 79 E3
Stoneham Pk GU32 40 B2
Stoneham Way SO16, SO18 79 F3
Stonehills SO45 151 E2
Stoneleigh 13 BH13 214 C4
Stoneleigh Ave SO41 195 F2
Stoneleigh Cl PO16 156 A4
Stoner Hill Rd GU32 19 D2
Stoners Cl PO13 155 D2
Stoney La SO22 1 B1
Stony La Burton BH23 192 B1
Froxfield GU32 18 C1
Portsmouth PO1 182 A3
Stony La S BH23 207 E3
Stonymoor Cl SO45 150 B2
Stopples La SO41 195 F2
Storrington Rd PO8 88 B3
Story La BH18 187 D2
Stour Cl Ferndown BH21 164 B2
West End SO18 80 A2
West Wellow SO51 50 B2
Stour Rd Bournemouth BH8 205 E3
Christchurch BH23 207 D3
Stour View Gdns BH21 162 C1
Stour Way BH23 191 E1
Stour Wlk Bournemouth BH8 190 B2
18 Wimborne Minster BH21 163 E2
Stourbank Rd BH23 207 D3
Stourcliffe Ave BH6 206 B2
Stourcroft Dr BH23 191 F1
Stourfield Fst & Jun Schs
BH6 206 B3
Stourfield Rd BH5 206 A2
Stourpaine Rd BH17 187 E1
Stourton Ct 17 BH4 204 B2
Stourvale Ave BH23 206 B4
Stourvale Gdns SO53 55 E3
Stourvale Pl 10 BH5 206 A3
Stourvale Rd BH5,BH6 206 B3
Stourwood Ave BH6 206 B2
Stourwood Mans 4 BH6 206 B2
Stourwood Rd BH6 206 B2
Stouts La BH23 169 D1
Stow Cres PO15 130 B1
Stowe Rd PO4 183 D2
Stradbrook PO13 155 D1
Stragwyne Cl SO52 53 F3
Straight Mile The
Ampfield SO51 28 C1
North Baddesley SO51 28 C1
Strand SO14 103 D2
Strand St BH15 202 B1
Strand The PO11 185 E1
Stratfield Dr SO53 30 A1
Stratfield Gdns PO9 135 E4
Stratfield Pk PO7 134 B4
Stratfield Pl BH25 194 C2
Stratford Ct 9 SO23 2 A1
Stratford House 47 PO5 182 B2
Stratford Pl Eastleigh SO50 56 A2
Lymington SO41 197 E3
Stratford Rd PO7 135 D4
Strathmore Dr BH31 115 D3
Strathmore Rd
Bournemouth BH9 190 A2
Gosport PO12 181 E2
Stratton Cl PO6 157 E4
Stratton Rd Bournemouth BH9 190 B2
Southampton SO15 78 B1
Winchester SO23 11 E4
Strawberry Fields
East Boldre SO42 175 E3
Hedge End SO30 105 D3
Strawberry Hill SO31 128 C2
Streamleaze PO14 129 E1
Street End SO52 54 A3
Street The SP5 24 A2
Streets La BH24 141 E2
Strete Mount 10 BH23 207 F4
Stretton Ct BH14 203 D2
Stride Ave PO3 183 D3
Strides La BH24 140 C4
Strides Way SO40 100 A4
Strode Gdns BH24 140 A3
Strode Rd PO2 157 E1
Strongs Cl SO51 53 D4
Stroud Cl BH21 164 A3
Stroud End GU32 40 A2
Stroud Gdns BH23 207 F3
Stroud Green La PO14 154 B3
Stroud La BH23 207 F3
Stroud Park Ave BH23 207 F3
Stroud Sch The SO51 53 F4
Strouden Ave BH8 205 E4
Strouden Court Prec PO9 135 E4
Strouden Ct PO9 135 E4
Strouden Rd BH9 190 A1
Stroudley Ave PO6 158 B3
Stroudley Way SO30 81 E1
Stroudwood Rd Fair Oak SO32 58 A2
Havant PO9 136 A2
Struan Cl BH24 139 F3
Struan Ct BH24 140 A3
Struan Dr BH24 140 A3
Struan Gdns BH24 139 F3
Stuart Bridgewater House
SO18 104 A4
Stuart Cl Stubbington PO14 179 E3
Upton BH16 201 D4
Stuart Cres SO22 10 C3
Stuart Ct 7 PO6 157 F4
Stuart Rd BH23 209 D4
Stubbermere PO10 136 C4
Stubbington Ave PO2 157 F1
Stubbington Gn PO14 154 B2
Stubbington La PO14 179 E3
Stubbington Study Ctr PO14 179 E2
Stubbington Way SO50 57 E1
Stubbs Dro SO30 105 E4
Stubbs Rd SO19 104 B1
Stuckton Rd SP6 94 A4
Student Village BH12 204 B4
Studland Cl SO16 77 E1
Studland Dr SO41 211 E3
Studland Rd
Bournemouth BH4 204 B1
Lee-on-the-Solent PO13 179 F1
Southampton SO16 77 E1

Studley Ave SO45 .... 150 B2
Studley Cl BH23 .... 209 E4
Studley Ct BH25 .... 209 E4
Sturminster House 2 SO16 .... 78 A1
Sturminster Rd BH9 .... 190 A2
Styles The SP5 .... 22 B4
Submarine Mus PO12 .... 181 F2
Sudbury Rd PO6 .... 157 E4
Suetts La SO32 .... 83 F4
Suffolk Ave Christchurch BH23 .... 191 F1
  Southampton SO15 .... 102 B4
Suffolk Cl
  Chandler's Ford SO53 .... 55 E1
  Wimborne Minster BH21 .... 164 B3
Suffolk Dr
  Chandler's Ford SO53 .... 55 E1
  Swanwick PO15 .... 129 D4
Suffolk Gr SO53 .... 55 E1
Suffolk Rd Bournemouth BH2 .... 204 B2
  Bournemouth BH2 .... 204 C2
  Portsmouth PO4 .... 183 D2
Suffolk Rd S BH2 .... 204 B2
Sullivan Cl PO6 .... 156 C4
Sullivan Rd SO19 .... 104 B2
Sullivan Way PO7 .... 134 C3
Sultan Rd Emsworth PO10 .... 136 C1
  Portsmouth PO1, PO2 .... 182 B4
Sumar Cl PO14 .... 154 B3
Summer Field Cl BH21 .... 164 A2
Summerbee First Sch BH8 .... 190 B1
Summerbee Jun Sch BH8 .... 190 B1
Summerbee Sec Sch BH8 .... 190 B1
Summercroft Way BH22 .... 138 C2
Summerfield Cl BH23 .... 192 B1
Summerfield Ct PO3 .... 158 A2
Summerfield Gdns SO16 .... 79 E3
Summerfields
  Bournemouth BH7 .... 205 F4
  Locks Heath SO31 .... 129 D1
Summerhill Rd PO8 .... 112 A2
Summerlands BH22 .... 165 E3
Summerlands Rd SO50 .... 57 E1
Summerlands Wlk 42 PO9 .... 136 A3
Summers Ave BH11 .... 189 D3
Summers La BH23 .... 192 B1
Summers St SO14 .... 103 E1
Summersfield GU33 .... 20 C2
Summertrees Ct BH25 .... 195 E2
Summit Way SO18 .... 79 F1
Sumner Rd GU31 .... 65 F3
Sun St PO1 .... 182 A3
Sunbeam Way PO12 .... 181 D2
Sunbury Cl BH11 .... 189 D3
Sunbury Ct
  8 Bournemouth BH2 .... 204 C2
  Fareham PO15 .... 130 C2
Suncourt Villas PO12 .... 180 C4
Sunderland Dr BH23 .... 208 A4
Sunderton La PO8 .... 88 B3
Sundew Cl BH25 .... 195 E2
Sundew Rd BH18 .... 186 C1
Sundridge Cl PO6 .... 157 F4
Sunningdale
  Christchurch BH23 .... 206 C3
  Hythe SO45 .... 125 F2
  7 Poole BH15 .... 202 C2
Sunningdale Cl
  6 Bishopstoke SO50 .... 56 C1
  Gosport PO13 .... 155 E1
Sunningdale Cres BH10 .... 189 E2
Sunningdale Gdns
  Broadstone BH18 .... 187 D3
  Southampton SO18 .... 104 A4
Sunningdale Rd
  Portchester PO16 .... 156 B4
  Portsmouth PO3 .... 183 D4
Sunny Hill Ct BH12 .... 203 E3
Sunny Hill Rd BH12 .... 203 E3
Sunny Way SO40 .... 100 C4
Sunny Wlk PO1 .... 182 A3
Sunnybank Dr BH21 .... 164 A3
Sunnybank Rd BH21 .... 164 A3
Sunnybank Way BH21 .... 164 A3
Sunnydown Rd SO22 .... 10 A2
Sunnyfield Rd BH25 .... 210 A4
Sunnyheath PO9 .... 135 F2
Sunnyhill Rd BH6 .... 206 B3
Sunnylands Ave BH6 .... 206 C2
Sunnymead Dr PO7 .... 111 E1
Sunnymoor Rd BH11 .... 189 D1
Sunnyside Rd BH12 .... 203 E3
Sunnyside Wlk PO9 .... 135 E4
Sunridge Cl BH12 .... 204 A3
Sunset Ave SO40 .... 100 C4
Sunset Lodge BH13 .... 204 A1
Sunset Rd SO40 .... 100 C4
Sunshine Ave PO11 .... 185 D1
Suntrap Gdns PO11 .... 185 D1
Sunvale Cl SO19 .... 104 A2
Sunwood Rd PO9 .... 135 E3
Surbiton Rd SO50 .... 56 A3
Surrey Cl Christchurch BH23 .... 191 F1
  Totton SO40 .... 100 B3
Surrey Ct SO15 .... 102 B3
Surrey Gdns BH4 .... 204 B2
Surrey House SO53 .... 55 E2
Surrey House Inf Sch SO19 .... 104 B2
Surrey Rd
  Bournemouth BH2, BH4 .... 204 A2
  Chandler's Ford SO53 .... 55 E2
  Poole BH12 .... 204 A2
  Southampton SO19 .... 103 E1
Surrey Rd S BH4 .... 204 B2
Surrey St PO1 .... 182 B3
Sussex Cl BH9 .... 190 A2

Sussex Gdns GU31 .... 40 C1
Sussex Pl
  34 Portsmouth PO5 .... 182 B2
  4 Portsmouth PO1 .... 182 B2
Sussex Rd
  Chandler's Ford SO53 .... 55 E2
  Petersfield GU31 .... 41 D1
  Portsmouth PO5 .... 182 B2
  Southampton SO14 .... 103 D2
Sussex St SO23 .... 10 C4
Sussex Terr 33 PO5 .... 182 B2
Sutherland Ave BH18 .... 186 C3
Sutherland Cl 6 SO51 .... 28 A1
Sutherland Ct SO53 .... 55 E3
Sutherland Rd
  Portsmouth PO4 .... 182 C2
  Southampton SO16 .... 77 F3
Sutherlands Way SO53 .... 55 D4
Sutton Cl Poole BH17 .... 188 A1
  Portsmouth PO3 .... 158 A2
  Waterlooville PO8 .... 111 E2
Sutton Gdns SO23 .... 11 C4
Sutton Pl SO42 .... 146 A1
Sutton Rd Bournemouth BH9 .... 190 A1
  Totton SO40 .... 76 C1
  Waterlooville PO8 .... 111 E2
Swale Dr SO45 .... 55 D4
Swallow Cl Broadstone BH17 .... 201 E4
  Havant PO9 .... 136 A1
  Totton SO40 .... 100 A3
Swallow Ct Clanfield PO8 .... 88 A3
  Lee-on-the-Solent PO13 .... 179 F2
Swallow Dr BH21 .... 211 F2
Swallow Sq SO50 .... 55 E1
Swallow Way BH21 .... 164 A4
Swallow Wood PO16 .... 131 D2
Swan Cl Emsworth SO31 .... 161 D4
  Swanwick SO31 .... 128 A4
Swan Ct Burslesdon SO31 .... 128 B4
  Gosport PO13 .... 155 D2
Swan Ctr The SO50 .... 56 A1
Swan Gn 8 BH23 .... 207 D3
Swan La SO23 .... 10 C4
Swan Mead BH24 .... 141 E3
Swan Quay Portchester PO16 .... 155 E4
  Southampton SO18 .... 103 E4
Swan St GU32 .... 40 C2
Swanage Cl SO19 .... 103 F2
Swanage Rd PO13 .... 179 F1
Swancote PO16 .... 155 F4
Swanley Cl SO50 .... 56 A3
Swanmore Ave SO19 .... 104 B2
Swanmore Bsns Pk SO32 .... 83 F3
Swanmore CE Prim Sch SO32 .... 84 A3
Swanmore Cl
  Bournemouth BH7 .... 206 A4
  Winchester SO22 .... 1 B2
Swanmore Park House SO32 .... 84 B4
Swanmore Rd
  Bournemouth BH7 .... 206 A4
  Droxford SO32 .... 84 C4
  Havant PO9 .... 135 E4
  Swanmore SO32 .... 84 A3
  Swanmore, Droxford SO32 .... 84 C4
Swanmore Sec Sch SO32 .... 84 A2
Swans Wlk PO11 .... 185 D2
Swansbury Dr BH8 .... 191 D1
Swanton Gdns SO53 .... 55 D4
Swanwick Bsns Ctr SO31 .... 128 B4
Swanwick La SO31 .... 128 C4
Swanwick Shore Rd SO31 .... 128 B4
Swanwick Sta SO31 .... 129 D3
Swarraton Rd PO9 .... 136 A2
Sway Ct Havant PO13 .... 136 A3
  Sway SO41 .... 196 B4
Sway Gdns BH8 .... 190 B1
Sway Park Ind Est SO41 .... 172 A1
Sway Rd Brockenhurst SO42 .... 172 C4
  Hordle SO41 .... 197 D3
  Lymington SO41 .... 197 D3
  New Milton BH25 .... 195 E3
Sway St Luke's CE Prim Sch
  SO41 .... 172 A1
Sway Sta SO41 .... 172 A1
Swaythling Prim Sch SO17 .... 79 D2
Swaythling Rd Havant PO9 .... 135 E3
  West End SO18,SO30 .... 80 A1
Swaythling Sta SO18 .... 79 E2
Swedish Houses SO41 .... 198 C4
Sweep The BH24 .... 140 C4
Sweetbriar Gdns PO7 .... 134 C3
Sweethills Cres PO15 .... 129 E4
Sweyns Lease SO42 .... 175 E3
Swift Cl Broadstone BH17 .... 201 F4
  Eastleigh SO50 .... 55 E1
  Horndean PO8 .... 112 A4
  Lee-on-the-Solent PO13 .... 179 F2
  Winchester SO23 .... 10 B3
Swift Gdns SO19 .... 103 E1
Swift Hollow SO19 .... 103 E1
Swift Rd Southampton SO19 .... 103 E1
  Thorney Island PO10 .... 161 D2
Swinburn Gdns PO8 .... 111 F2
Swincombe Rise SO18 .... 80 A1
Swiss Rd PO7 .... 134 C4
Switch House Rd SO45 .... 151 F1
Swivelton La PO17 .... 132 A2
Sword Cl Clanfield PO8 .... 88 A3
  Gosport PO12 .... 180 C1
Sword Sands Rd PO3 .... 183 E4
Swordfish Dr BH23 .... 208 A4
Sycamore Ave SO53 .... 30 B1
Sycamore Cl
  Broadstone BH17 .... 186 C1
  Burslesdon SO31 .... 127 F4
  Christchurch BH23 .... 206 B4
  Clanfield PO8 .... 88 B3
  Gosport PO13 .... 155 F1

Sycamore Cl Continued
  Milford on Sea SO41 .... 211 E3
  North Baddesley SO52 .... 53 F3
  Romsey SO51 .... 53 E3
  Titchfield PO14 .... 129 E1
  Waterlooville PO8 .... 111 F2
Sycamore Ct BH24 .... 117 C1
Sycamore Dr Holbury SO45 .... 150 A3
  Kings Worthy SO23 .... 2 A4
  South Hayling PO11 .... 184 C2
Sycamore Rd
  Bishop's Waltham SO32 .... 83 F4
  Hordle SO41 .... 195 F2
  Hythe SO45 .... 125 F2
  Southampton SO16 .... 78 A1
Sycamore Wlk SO30 .... 105 F4
Sycamores The 4 SO45 .... 126 A2
Sydenham Cl PO1 .... 182 C3
Sydenham Terr
  Portsmouth PO1 .... 182 C3
  Westbourne PO10 .... 137 D3
Sydling Cl BH7 .... 188 A1
Sydmanton Cl SO51 .... 53 D3
Sydmonton Ct 2 PO9 .... 136 A3
Sydney Ave SO31 .... 127 F2
Sydney House 33 PO1 .... 182 B3
Sydney Rd Bishopstoke SO50 .... 56 B2
  Broadstone BH18 .... 187 D2
  Christchurch BH23 .... 191 F1
  Gosport PO12 .... 181 D2
  Southampton SO15 .... 78 A1
Syers Cl GU33 .... 20 C2
Syers Rd GU33 .... 20 C2
Sylmor Gdns BH9 .... 190 A1
Sylvan Ave SO19 .... 104 B3
Sylvan Cl Hordle SO41 .... 196 A1
  St Leonards BH24 .... 139 E2
Sylvan Dr SO52 .... 53 F2
Sylvan Fst Sch BH12 .... 203 D3
Sylvan La SO31 .... 128 A1
Sylvan Rd BH12 .... 203 D3
Sylvan View PO7 .... 134 C3
Sylvans The SO45 .... 125 E2
Sylvia Cres SO40 .... 76 C1
Symes Rd Hamworthy BH15 .... 201 F2
  Romsey SO51 .... 53 D4
Symonds Cl SO53 .... 55 E2
Symonds St SO23 .... 11 D4
Sywell Cres PO3 .... 158 B2

Tadburn Cl
  Chandler's Ford SO53 .... 55 E3
  Romsey SO51 .... 53 D4
Tadburn Gn SO51 .... 52 C3
Tadburn Rd SO51 .... 53 D3
Tadden Cotts BH21 .... 162 B4
Tadden Wlk BH18 .... 186 C1
Tadfield Cres SO51 .... 53 D4
Tadfield Rd SO51 .... 53 D4
Tadhurst House 24 PO1 .... 182 B3
Tait Cl BH17 .... 202 C4
Tait Pl PO13 .... 155 E1
Talbot Ave BH3 .... 204 C4
Talbot Cl Havant PO9 .... 135 E2
  Southampton SO16 .... 78 C2
Talbot Comb Sch BH12 .... 204 A4
Talbot Dr Christchurch BH23 .... 193 F1
  Poole BH12 .... 204 A4
Talbot Heath Sch BH4 .... 204 B3
Talbot Hill Rd BH9 .... 204 B4
Talbot House Prep Sch BH9 .... 204 C4
Talbot Meadows BH12 .... 204 A4
Talbot Mews BH10 .... 189 D1
Talbot Rd Bournemouth BH9 .... 204 B4
  Bournemouth BH9 .... 204 C4
  Havant PO9 .... 135 E2
  Hythe SO45 .... 125 F1
  Portsmouth PO4 .... 182 C2
Talbot Rdbt BH3 .... 204 B4
Talbot Rise BH10 .... 189 E1
Talisman Bsns Ctr SO31 .... 129 D3
Tall Trees BH14 .... 203 D3
Talland Rd PO14 .... 129 D1
Tallywater Hill GU32 .... 18 B2
Tamar Cl Ferndown BH22 .... 166 A3
  Portchester PO16 .... 132 A1
Tamar Down PO7 .... 135 D4
Tamar Gdns SO18 .... 80 A1
Tamar Gr SO45 .... 125 F2
Tamarisk Cl Portsmouth PO4 .... 183 E2
  Stubbington PO14 .... 179 E3
  Waterlooville PO7 .... 135 D3
Tamarisk Gdns SO18 .... 103 F4
Tamarisk Rd SO30 .... 105 D3
Tamella Rd SO30 .... 105 F3
Tammys Turn PO14 .... 154 A4
Tamorisk Dr SO40 .... 100 B3
Tamworth Ct 10 PO12 .... 181 D2
Tamworth Rd
  Bournemouth BH7 .... 205 F3
  Portsmouth PO3 .... 183 D3
Tan Howse Cl BH7 .... 206 A4
Tanfield La PO17 .... 108 A3
Tanfield Pk PO17 .... 108 A2
Tangier La SO32 .... 83 D4
Tangier Rd PO3 .... 183 D4
Tanglewood Fareham PO16 .... 131 D2
  Marchwood SO40 .... 102 A1
Tanglewood Cl PO7 .... 134 B2
Tanglewood Ct 11 BH25 .... 195 D2
Tanglewood Lodge BH17 .... 201 F4
Tangley Wlk PO9 .... 136 A3
Tangmere Cl BH23 .... 208 A3
Tangmere Dr SO16 .... 78 A2
Tangmere Pl BH17 .... 202 C4
Tangyes Cl PO14 .... 154 B2

Tanhouse Cl SO30 .... 105 E3
Tanhouse La Botley SO30 .... 105 E2
  Hedge End SO30 .... 105 E2
Tankerdale La GU33 .... 41 E4
Tankerton Ct 2 PO6 .... 157 F4
Tankerville Rd SO19 .... 103 E2
Tankerville Sch SO50 .... 56 A3
Tanner St 20 SO23 .... 11 D4
Tanner's Brook Way SO15 .... 101 F3
Tanner's La PO7 .... 111 D3
Tanner's Ridge PO7 .... 134 C2
Tanneries Ind Est The PO9 .... 135 F1
Tanners Brook Inf Sch SO15 .... 101 F3
Tanners Brook Jun Sch SO15 .... 101 F3
Tanners La Boldre SO41 .... 199 D2
  Gosport PO14 .... 154 C3
  West Wellow SO51 .... 51 E4
Tanners Rd SO52 .... 54 A2
Tanners The PO14 .... 129 E1
Tansy Cl PO7 .... 135 D3
Tansy Meadow SO52 .... 54 C2
Tanyards The SO53 .... 30 A1
Taplin Dr SO30 .... 105 E2
Taplings Cl SO22 .... 1 B2
Taplings Rd SO22 .... 1 B2
Tapper Ct BH21 .... 163 F2
Taranto Rd SO16 .... 78 B2
Tarbery Cres PO8 .... 112 B4
Tardif House SO16 .... 78 A1
Target Rd PO2 .... 157 E1
Tarius Cl PO13 .... 155 E2
Tarleton Rd PO6 .... 133 D1
Tarn Dr BH17 .... 201 F4
Tarn Rise PO8 .... 88 B1
Tarrant Cl BH17 .... 187 F1
Tarrant Gdns PO9 .... 135 E2
Tarrant Rd BH9 .... 190 A2
Tasman Cl
  Christchurch BH23 .... 206 C4
  Southampton SO14 .... 103 D1
Tasman Ct SO14 .... 103 D1
Taswell Rd PO5 .... 182 B1
Tatchbury La SO40 .... 99 F4
Tatchbury Mount Hospl SO40 .... 76 A1
Tate Ct SO15 .... 101 E4
Tate Mews SO15 .... 101 E4
Tate Rd SO15 .... 101 E4
Tates Rd Hythe SO45 .... 126 A1
  Hythe SO45 .... 126 A1
Tatnam Rd BH15 .... 202 B2
Tattenham Rd SO42 .... 172 C4
Tattershall Cres PO16 .... 156 A4
Tatum Cres BH15 .... 202 B2
Tatwin Cl SO19 .... 104 B3
Tatwin Cres SO19 .... 104 B3
Taunton Coll SO15 .... 78 C1
Taunton Dr SO18 .... 104 A4
Taunton Row SO53 .... 55 E2
Tavell's La SO40 .... 101 F1
Tavells Cl SO40 .... 101 F1
Taverner Cl BH15 .... 202 B1
Taverners Cl SO19 .... 104 B2
Tavistock Cl 4 SO51 .... 28 A1
Tavistock Gdns PO9 .... 136 A1
Tavy Cl SO53 .... 55 D3
Taw Dr SO53 .... 55 D3
Tawny Owl Cl PO14 .... 154 A2
Taylor Cl SO19 .... 103 E1
Taylor Dr BH8 .... 190 B2
Taylor Rd PO12 .... 181 E1
Taylor's Bldgs 22 BH15 .... 202 B1
Taylors Cnr SO23 .... 2 A3
Teachers Way SO45 .... 150 A2
Teak Cl BH13 .... 214 D4
Teal Cl Portchester PO16 .... 155 E4
  South Hayling PO11 .... 185 D2
  Totton SO40 .... 100 A4
Teal Wlk PO13 .... 155 D2
Teapot Row PO4 .... 183 D1
Teasel Way BH22 .... 138 C1
Teazle Cl GU31 .... 41 E1
Tebourba Cotts SO41 .... 172 A1
Tebourba Dr PO12 .... 181 D2
Tebourba House 6 PO14 .... 154 C4
Tebourba Way
  Curdridge SO30 .... 106 B4
  Southampton SO16 .... 101 F4
  Southampton SO15 .... 102 A4
Ted Kelly Ct 28 PO1 .... 182 A3
Tedder Cl BH11 .... 189 D2
Tedder Gdns BH11 .... 189 D2
Tedder Rd
  Bournemouth BH11 .... 189 D2
  Gosport PO13 .... 155 E2
  Southampton SO18 .... 104 A4
Tedder Way SO40 .... 100 B4
Teddington Rd PO4 .... 183 D2
Tees Cl SO53 .... 55 D4
Tees Farm Rd SO21 .... 56 C4
Tees Gr 2 SO21 .... 56 C4
Teg Down GU31 .... 41 D2
Teg Down Meads SO22 .... 1 B1
Teglease Gn PO9 .... 135 E4
Teignmouth Rd
  Gosport PO12 .... 180 C4
  Portsmouth PO3 .... 183 D4
Telegraph Rd SO30 .... 80 C1
Telephone Rd PO4 .... 182 C2
Telford Rd Ferndown BH21 .... 165 D4
  Portsmouth PO2 .... 157 D2
Teme Cres SO16 .... 101 F4
Teme Rd SO16 .... 101 F4
Tempest Ave PO7 .... 135 D4
Templar Ct 27 SO14 .... 103 D4
Templars Mede SO53 .... 55 D2
Templars Way SO53 .... 55 D2
Temple Gdns SO19 .... 103 E2
Temple La GU32 .... 63 F4

Temple Rd Liss GU33 .... 21 D3
  Southampton SO19 .... 103 F1
Temple St PO1 .... 182 B3
Templecombe Rd SO50 .... 56 C1
Templemere PO14 .... 154 A4
Templer Cl BH11 .... 188 C1
Templeton Cl PO2 .... 157 F2
Tenby Cl SO18 .... 104 A4
Tenby Dr SO53 .... 55 D2
Tench Way SO51 .... 52 C4
Tennyson Ct
  27 Southampton SO17 .... 79 D1
  37 Southampton SO17 .... 79 D1
Tennyson Gdns PO16 .... 131 D1
Tennyson Rd
  Bournemouth BH9 .... 189 F1
  Eastleigh SO50 .... 55 F1
  1 Poole BH14 .... 203 D2
  Portsmouth PO2 .... 182 C4
  Southampton SO17 .... 79 D1
  Totton SO40 .... 76 B1
  Wimborne Minster BH21 .... 163 E3
Tensing Cl PO16 .... 131 D2
Tensing Rd BH23 .... 207 F4
Tenterton Ave SO19 .... 104 A1
Terence Ave BH17 .... 187 E1
Terence Rd BH21 .... 186 B3
Terminus Terr SO14 .... 103 D2
Tern Cl SO45 .... 126 A1
Tern Ct BH6 .... 206 B3
Tern Wlk PO13 .... 155 D2
Terrace Rd BH2 .... 204 C2
Terrace The
  Damerham SP6 .... 68 B3
  Rockbourne SP6 .... 68 C4
Terrier Cl SO30 .... 81 E2
Terrington Ave BH23 .... 193 F1
Terriote Cl SO53 .... 55 E4
Test Cl GU32 .... 40 C1
Test House SO51 .... 52 B4
Test La Nursling SO16 .... 77 D1
  Southampton SO16 .... 77 D1
Test Rd SO14 .... 126 A4
Test Valley Bsns Ctr SO51 .... 77 E1
Test Valley Bsns Pk SO52 .... 54 A3
Testbourne Ave SO40 .... 100 B4
Testbourne Cl SO40 .... 100 B4
Testbourne Rd SO40 .... 100 B3
Testcombe Rd PO12 .... 181 D2
Testlands Ave SO16 .... 77 E3
Testwood Ave SO40 .... 76 C1
Testwood Cres SO40 .... 76 B1
Testwood La SO40 .... 101 D4
Testwood Pl SO40 .... 101 D4
Testwood Rd Havant PO9 .... 135 E3
  Southampton SO15 .... 102 A3
Testwood Sch SO40 .... 76 C1
Tethering Dro SP6 .... 47 E2
Tetney Cl SO16 .... 77 F2
Tetsome Cotts PO17 .... 130 C4
Teviot House 9 SO14 .... 103 E3
Teviot Rd SO53 .... 55 D3
Tewkesbury Ave
  Fareham PO15 .... 130 B2
  Gosport PO13 .... 181 D4
Tewkesbury Cl PO6 .... 157 E4
Texas Dr SO22 .... 10 A2
Thackeray Mall 24 PO16 .... 131 D1
Thackeray Rd SO17 .... 103 D4
Thackeray Sq 4 PO16 .... 131 E1
Thacking Gr 3 SO21 .... 56 C4
Thames Alley 13 BH15 .... 202 A1
Thames Cl
  Ferndown BH22 .... 166 A3
  West End SO18 .... 80 A1
Thames Ct 1 PO8 .... 111 F2
Thames Dr PO15 .... 130 B2
Thames Mews 12 BH15 .... 202 A1
Thames St BH15 .... 202 A1
Thamesmead Cl PO12 .... 180 C4
Thatchers La Boldre SO41 .... 198 C4
  Sopley BH23 .... 168 C2
Theatre Mews 2 PO5 .... 182 B1
Theobold Rd BH23 .... 191 D4
Theseus Rd PO13 .... 179 E2
Thessaly St 17 BH5 .... 205 F2
Thetchers Cl BH25 .... 195 D3
Thetford Gdns SO53 .... 55 D4
Thetford Rd Gosport PO12 .... 180 C4
  Poole BH12 .... 203 F3
Thicket The Gosport PO13 .... 155 F1
  Portchester PO16 .... 131 F1
  Portsmouth PO5 .... 182 B2
  Romsey SO51 .... 53 E3
  Waterlooville PO7 .... 134 B2
Third Ave Cosham PO6 .... 157 F4
  Havant PO9 .... 136 A1
  Southampton SO15 .... 101 F3
Thirlmere SO50 .... 55 F1
Thirlmere Cl PO14 .... 154 B2
Thirlmere House 23 PO6 .... 133 D1
Thirlmere Rd SO16 .... 77 F1
Thirlstane Firs SO53 .... 55 D2
Thistle Rd SO30 .... 105 D3
Thistlebarrow Rd BH7 .... 205 F3
Thistledown PO8 .... 112 A3
Thistledowne Gdns PO10 .... 161 D4
Thomas Cl SO40 .... 100 B3
Thomas Lewis Way SO17 .... 79 F3
Thomas Lockyer Cl BH31 .... 115 D3
Thomas Rd SO52 .... 54 A2
Thomas St 9 PO1 .... 182 B3
Thompson's La SO21 .... 57 E4
Thoresby Ct BH25 .... 194 C2

Thorn Cl Eastleigh SO50 .... 56 A3
  Petersfield GU31 .... 41 E1
Thorn Rd BH17 .... 187 E2
Thornbrake Rd PO12 .... 181 E2
Thornbury **15** BH4 .... 204 B2
Thornbury Ave SO15 .... 102 C4
Thornbury Cl PO14 .... 154 B4
Thornbury House **16** PO6 .... 132 C1
Thornbury Hts SO53 .... 30 C1
Thornbury Rd BH6 .... 207 D2
Thornbury Wood SO53 .... 30 C1
Thornby Ct PO3 .... 158 A2
Thorncliffe Cl PO2 .... 157 F2
Thorncombe Cl
  Bournemouth BH9 .... 190 A2
  Broadstone BH17 .... 187 F1
Thorncroft Rd PO1 .... 182 C3
Thornden Sec Sch SO53 .... 55 F4
Thorndike Cl SO16 .... 78 A1
Thorndike Rd SO16 .... 77 F1
Thorne Cl BH31 .... 114 C3
Thorne Way BH21 .... 139 D3
Thorner's Homes,
  Centre Ct **10** SO15 .... 102 A4
Thorner's Homes,
  North Ct **9** SO15 .... 102 A4
Thorner's Homes,
  South Ct **11** SO15 .... 102 A4
Thorner's Homes,
  West Ct **12** SO15 .... 102 A4
Thorners Ct **8** SO15 .... 102 C3
Thorness Cl SO16 .... 77 E1
Thorney Cl PO14 .... 154 B4
Thorney Island Cty Prim Sch
  PO10 .... 161 D2
Thorney Old Park PO10 .... 161 E1
Thorney Rd Hermitage PO10 .... 161 D3
  Thorney Island PO10 .... 161 D3
Thorney View PO11 .... 160 B1
Thornfield Cl PO8 .... 88 B1
Thornfield Dr BH23 .... 193 F1
Thorngate Ct **7** PO12 .... 181 D3
Thorngate Way **22** PO12 .... 181 E2
Thornham Rd BH25 .... 195 E2
Thornham La PO10 .... 161 E3
Thornhill Ave SO19 .... 104 B3
Thornhill Cl SO45 .... 150 C1
  Thornhill Inf Sch SO19 .... 104 B3
Thornhill Jun Sch SO19 .... 104 B3
Thornhill Park Rd SO18 .... 104 C4
Thornhill Rd Blackfield SO45 .... 150 C1
  Southampton SO16 .... 78 B2
Thorni Ave PO15 .... 130 B2
Thornleigh Rd SO19 .... 103 F1
Thornley Rd BH10 .... 189 E2
Thorns La SO41 .... 199 F3
Thornton Ave SO31 .... 128 B1
Thornton Cl Corfe Mullen BH21 .. 186 B3
  Waterlooville PO7 .... 134 A1
Thornton Rd PO12 .... 181 D4
Thornycroft Ave SO19 .... 103 E1
Thorogood Ct **4** BH15 .... 202 C2
Thorold Ct SO18 .... 79 F1
Thorold Rd
  Chandler's Ford SO53 .... 30 C1
  Southampton SO18 .... 79 F1
Three Acre Dr BH25 .... 209 F4
Three Acres PO7 .... 111 D2
Three Cross Rd BH21, BH22 .... 138 C3
Three Horse Shoes La GU34 .. 16 C1
Three Legged Cross
  Cty First Sch BH21 .... 114 C1
Three Oaks SO19 .... 104 C3
Three Tun Cl **21** PO1 .... 182 A3
Threefield La SO14 .... 103 D2
Thresher Cl PO7 .... 112 B1
Throop Cl BH8 .... 191 D1
Throop Rd BH8 .... 190 C2
Throopside Ave BH9 .... 190 B2
Thrush Rd PO12 .... 188 B1
Thrush Wlk PO8 .... 111 F2
Thruxton Ct SO19 .... 103 F3
Thruxton Rd PO9 .... 135 E3
Thurbern Rd PO2 .... 157 F1
Thurmell Cl SO30 .... 105 E2
Thurmell Wlk SO30 .... 105 E2
Thurmond Cres SO22 .... 10 B3
Thurmond Rd SO22 .... 10 B3
Thursby Rd BH23 .... 193 F1
Thurston Cl SO53 .... 55 E4
Thwaite Rd BH12 .... 204 A3
Tichborne Rd Eastleigh SO50 .... 80 A4
  Southampton SO18 .... 104 B4
Tichborne Way PO13 .... 155 E1
Tichbourne House SO30 .... 105 E4
Tickleford Dr SO19 .... 104 A1
Tickner Cl SO30 .... 105 F3
Ticonderoga Gdns SO19 .... 103 F1
Tidcombe Gn PO9 .... 135 E4
Tidemill Cl BH23 .... 207 D4
Tides Reach SO18 .... 103 E4
Tides Way SO40 .... 101 F1
Tideway Gdns PO4 .... 183 E2
Tidworth Rd PO9 .... 135 F2
Tiffany Cl SO41 .... 195 F2
Tiffield Cl PO3 .... 158 B2
Tilbrook Rd SO15 .... 102 A4
Tilburg Rd BH23 .... 207 E4
Tilden Rd SO21 .... 31 E3
Tilebarn La SO42 .... 173 D3
Tilford Rd PO8 .... 111 F3
Tillingbourn PO14 .... 129 E2
Tillinton Gdns PO8 .... 88 B2
Tilmore Gdns GU32 .... 40 C3
Tilmore Rd GU32 .... 40 C3
Timberlane PO7 .... 134 B2
Timberley La SP5 .... 48 A3
Timberly SO45 .... 150 B2

Timbers The PO15 .... 130 B1
Timor Cl PO15 .... 129 E4
Timothy Cl BH10 .... 189 E3
Timpson Rd PO1 .... 182 C3
Timsbury Cres PO9 .... 135 F1
Timsbury Ct SO19 .... 103 F2
Timsbury Dr SO16 .... 77 F1
Timson Cl SO40 .... 100 B3
Tincleton Gdns BH9 .... 190 A2
Tindale Rd SO16 .... 77 F1
Tinker Alley SP5 .... 80 A4
Tinkers Cross SP6 .... 69 F2
Tinneys SP5 .... 47 E2
Tintagel Cl SO16 .... 78 B3
Tintagel Way PO6 .... 157 D4
Tintern Cl PO6 .... 133 D1
Tintern Gr **18** SO15 .... 102 C3
Tintern Rd PO12 .... 181 D2
Tiptoe Gn **9** PO9 .... 136 A3
Tiptoe Prim Sch SO41 .... 195 E4
Tiptoe Rd BH25 .... 171 D1
Tipton House **12** PO5 .... 182 B2
Tiptree Cl SO50 .... 56 A3
Tisted Ct **34** PO9 .... 136 A3
Titchborne Cl PO9 .... 135 E3
Titchfield Hill PO14 .... 154 A4
Titchfield House **45** PO1 .... 182 B3
Titchfield Industries PO14 .... 154 A4
Titchfield La PO15, PO17 .... 107 E2
Titchfield Park Rd PO15 .... 129 E2
Titchfield Prim Sch PO14 .... 129 F1
Titchfield Rd PO14 .... 154 A3
Tithe Barn SO41 .... 197 F3
Tithe The PO7 .... 110 C2
Tithelands La SO24 .... 15 F2
Tithewood Cl SO53 .... 30 A1
Titus Gdns PO7 .... 135 D4
Tiverton Ct
  24 Bournemouth BH4 .... 204 B2
  1 Fareham PO16 .... 131 E1
Tivoli Cl SO53 .... 55 F4
Toby St **9** PO1 .... 182 B3
Todber Ct BH11 .... 188 C2
Tokar St PO4 .... 183 D1
Tokio Rd PO3 .... 158 A1
Tollard Cl PO12 .... 203 F4
Tollbar Way SO30 .... 81 D1
Tollerford Rd BH17 .... 187 E1
Tollgate SO53 .... 55 E1
Tollgate Rd SO31 .... 128 B4
Tollgate The **20** SO23 .... 2 A1
Tolpuddle Gdns BH9 .... 190 A2
Tolstoi Rd BH14 .... 203 D3
Toms La BH24 .... 118 A4
Tonbridge St PO5 .... 182 B1
Tonge Rd BH11 .... 189 D3
Tonnant Cl PO14 .... 179 E3
Toogoods Way SO16 .... 77 E3
Toomer Cl SO45 .... 150 C1
Toothill Rd SO51 .... 53 E1
Top La BH24 .... 141 D4
Topaz Gr PO7 .... 135 D4
Topiary Gdns SO31 .... 129 D2
Tor Cl Portchester PO16 .... 131 F1
  Waterlooville PO7 .... 134 C2
Tor Way GU31 .... 41 D2
Torbay Rd BH14 .... 203 E2
Torberry Dr GU31 .... 41 D1
Torch Cl SO50 .... 57 D1
Torcross Cl SO19 .... 103 F1
Torfrida Ct PO4 .... 183 E2
Tormead SO45 .... 125 F2
Tornay Gr SO52 .... 53 F2
Toronto Pl PO12 .... 181 D3
Toronto Rd PO2 .... 182 C4
Torquay Ave Gosport PO12 .... 181 D4
  Southampton SO15 .... 102 B4
Torque Cl SO19 .... 104 C2
Torre Cl SO50 .... 56 A3
Torridge Gdns SO18 .... 80 A2
Torrington Cl SO19 .... 104 A2
Torrington Rd PO2 .... 157 F2
Tortworth Ct PO14 .... 154 B4
Torwood Gdns SO50 .... 56 C1
Tosson Cl SO16 .... 101 F4
Totland Cl SO16 .... 101 F4
Totland Ct **8** SO41 .... 211 E2
Totland Rd Cosham PO6 .... 157 F4
  Gosport PO13 .... 155 E1
Totmel Rd BH17 .... 188 A1
Totnes Cl SO50 .... 55 F3
Tottehale Cl SO52 .... 53 F2
Tottenham Rd PO1 .... 182 C3
Totton By Pass SO40 .... 101 D4
Totton Coll SO40 .... 100 B4
Totton Recn Ctr SO40 .... 100 B4
Totton Sta SO40 .... 101 D4
Totton Western By-Pass
  SO40 .... 100 B3
Totton Wlk **5** PO9 .... 135 E3
Tournerbury La PO11 .... 185 D2
Tourney Rd BH11 .... 188 C3
Tovey Pl SO23 .... 2 B4
Towans The BH13 .... 214 B2
Tower Cl PO12 .... 180 B2
Tower Ct Bournemouth BH2 .... 204 C1
  Locks Heath SO31 .... 128 B1
  6 Winchester SO22 .... 10 C4
Tower Gdns SO16 .... 78 C2
Tower House SO19 .... 103 F1
  Tower Ind Est The SO50 .... 56 B1
Tower La Eastleigh SO50 .... 56 B1
  Wimborne Minster BH21 .... 163 E3
Tower Pl SO30 .... 80 B1

Tower Rd Bournemouth BH1 .... 205 D2
  Poole BH13 .... 204 A1
  Portsmouth PO4 .... 182 C2
  Winchester SO22 .... 10 C4
Tower Rd W BH13 .... 204 A1
Tower St Emsworth PO10 .... 161 D4
  Portsmouth PO1 .... 181 F2
  Southampton SO23 .... 10 C4
Tower The **16** PO12 .... 181 D3
Towers Farm BH21 .... 186 B4
Towers Gdn PO9 .... 159 F3
Towers Way BH21 .... 186 B4
Town Hall Rd PO9 .... 135 F1
Town La GU32 .... 41 D3
Town Quay Portsmouth PO1 .... 181 F2
  Southampton SO14 .... 102 C1
Town St PO1 .... 182 B3
Towngate Bridge BH15 .... 202 B2
Towngate Sh Ctr **1** BH15 .... 202 B1
Townhill Inf Sch SO18 .... 80 A1
Townhill Jun Sch SO18 .... 80 A1
Townhill Park House (The
  Gregg Sch) SO18 .... 80 A2
Townhill Way
  Southampton SO18 .... 80 A1
  West End SO18 .... 80 A1
Townsend Cl BH11 .... 189 D3
Townsend Prim Sch BH8 .... 191 D1
Townsville Rd BH9 .... 190 A1
Towpath Mead PO4 .... 183 E2
Toynbee Cl SO50 .... 56 A2
Toynbee Rd SO50 .... 56 A2
Toynbee Sec Sch SO53 .... 55 F3
Tozer Cl BH11 .... 188 C1
Tracey Ct BH23 .... 209 D4
Trafalgar Cl SO53 .... 55 D3
Trafalgar Ct Christchurch BH23 .. 207 F3
  Fareham PO14 .... 154 C4
  33 Portsmouth PO5 .... 182 B1
Trafalgar Pl Lymington SO41 .... 197 F2
  Portsmouth PO1 .... 182 C3
Trafalgar Rd Bournemouth BH9 .. 204 C4
  Southampton SO15 .... 102 B3
Trafalgar Sq PO12 .... 181 D3
Trafalgar St SO23 .... 10 C4
Trafalgar Way SO45 .... 126 A1
Trafford Way SO50 .... 57 E1
Trampers La PO17 .... 109 D2
Tranby Rd SO19 .... 103 F2
Tranmere Cl SO41 .... 197 F1
Tranmere Rd PO4 .... 183 D2
Treadwheel Rd PO8 .... 113 D3
Treagore Rd SO40 .... 76 B1
Trearnan Cl SO16 .... 101 F4
Treble Cl SO22 .... 10 A2
Tredegar Rd PO4 .... 183 D2
Tree Hamlets BH16 .... 201 E3
Tree Side Way PO7 .... 111 F1
Treebys Cl BH23 .... 192 B1
Treeside SO17 .... 79 D1
Treeside Ave SO40 .... 101 D4
Treeside Rd SO15 .... 102 B4
Treetops **9** BH13 .... 214 C4
Trefoil Cl PO7 .... 135 D4
Trefoil Way BH23 .... 208 B4
Tregaron Ave PO6 .... 158 A4
Tregonwell Rd BH2 .... 204 C1
Treloar Rd PO11 .... 185 F1
Treloen Ct **3** BH8 .... 205 D3
Treloyhan Cl SO53 .... 55 E2
Tremona Ct SO16 .... 78 A1
Tremona Rd SO16 .... 78 A1
Trenley Cl SO45 .... 150 B2
Trent Cl SO18 .... 79 F1
Trent House **25** SO14 .... 103 E3
Trent Rd SO18 .... 79 F1
Trent Way Ferndown BH22 .... 166 A3
  Lee-on-the-Solent PO13 .... 179 F1
  West End SO30 .... 80 B1
Trent Wlk PO16 .... 156 A4
Trentham Ave BH7 .... 206 A4
Trentham Rd BH7 .... 206 A4
Tresillian Cl BH23 .... 194 A1
Tresillian Gdns SO18 .... 80 A1
Tresillian Way BH23 .... 194 A1
Trevis Rd PO4 .... 183 E2
Trevone BH25 .... 195 D2
Trevone Cl SO40 .... 100 C3
Trevor Rd PO4 .... 182 C2
Trevose Cl
  Chandler's Ford SO53 .... 55 E2
  Gosport PO13 .... 155 E1
Trevose Cres SO53 .... 55 E3
Trevose Way PO14 .... 129 D1
Triangle Gdns SO16 .... 77 E2
Triangle La PO14 .... 153 F3
Triangle The
  Bournemouth BH2 .... 204 C2
  Upton BH16 .... 201 D4
  Whiteparish SP5 .... 24 A2
Tribe Rd PO12 .... 181 D3
Tricketts La BH22 .... 165 F3
Tricorn The PO1 .... 182 B3
Trigon Rd BH15 .... 202 B4
Trimaran Rd SO31 .... 128 C1
Trimm's Dro SP6 .... 70 C4
Trimmer's Ct PO1 .... 181 F2
Trinidad House **1** PO6 .... 132 C1
Trinidad Cres PO4 .... 203 E4
Trinidad Fst Sch BH12 .... 203 E4
Trinidad House BH12 .... 203 E4
Trinity **2** BH1 .... 205 D2
Trinity Cl PO12 .... 181 F2
Trinity Ct Chandler's Ford SO53 .. 55 E3
  2 Southampton SO15 .... 102 B3
  Totton SO40 .... 76 C1
Trinity Gdns PO16 .... 131 D1
Trinity Gr PO12 .... 181 F2

Trinity Ind Est SO15 .... 101 F4
  Southampton SO14 .... 103 D3
Trinity St PO16 .... 131 D1
Tripps End Cvn Site SO30 .... 105 E4
Tristan Cl SO45 .... 178 C4
Triton Ctr The SO51 .... 53 E3
Triumph Cl PO15 .... 130 B1
Triumph Rd PO14 .... 154 C4
Troak Cl BH23 .... 207 F4
Trojan Way PO7 .... 134 C2
Troon Cres PO6 .... 134 B1
Troon Rd BH18 .... 187 D3
Trooper Bottom GU32 .... 19 D2
Trosnant Inf Sch PO9 .... 135 F2
Trosnant Jun Sch PO9 .... 135 F2
Trosnant Rd PO9 .... 135 F1
Trotters La BH21 .... 164 A3
Trowbridge Cl SO16 .... 77 F3
Truman Rd BH11 .... 189 D3
Truro Cl PO13 .... 180 B3
Truro Rd PO6 .... 132 C1
Truro Rise SO50 .... 56 C2
Truscott Ave BH9 .... 205 D4
Trussell Cl SO22 .... 1 B2
Trussell Cres SO22 .... 1 B2
Trystworthy **10** BH2 .... 204 C2
Tuckers Cl BH15 .... 201 F1
Tucks Cl BH23 .... 193 D4
Tuckton Cl BH6 .... 206 B2
Tuckton Rd BH6 .... 206 C2
Tudor Ave PO10 .... 136 C2
Tudor Cl Alderholt SP6 .... 93 D3
  Gosport PO13 .... 180 B4
  Portchester PO16 .... 132 A1
  South Hayling PO11 .... 184 C1
  Totton SO40 .... 100 B4
Tudor Cres PO6 .... 157 F3
Tudor Ct Bournemouth BH1 .... 205 D3
  8 Cosham PO6 .... 157 F4
  18 Fareham PO14 .... 154 C4
  Poole BH15 .... 202 C3
  8 Portsmouth PO5 .... 182 B1
Tudor Gdns SO30 .... 105 D3
Tudor House (Mus) SO14 .... 102 C2
Tudor Rd BH18 .... 187 D2
Tudor Way SO23 .... 2 A4
Tudor Wood Cl SO16 .... 78 C2
Tuffin Cl SO16 .... 77 E3
Tukes Ave PO13 .... 155 D2
Tulip Gdns Havant PO9 .... 135 E1
  Locks Heath SO31 .... 128 C2
Tulip Rd SO16 .... 79 E2
Tumulus Cl SO19 .... 104 C3
Tunstall Rd SO19 .... 104 C2
Tunworth Ct PO9 .... 136 A3
Tupman Rd **18** PO1 .... 182 B4
Tuppenny La PO10 .... 161 E4
Turbary Ct
  Bournemouth BH11 .... 189 D1
  Ferndown BH22 .... 165 F3
  Upton BH16 .... 201 E4
Turbary Hts BH11 .... 188 C1
Turbary Park Ave BH11 .... 189 D1
Turbary Rd BH22 .... 165 F3
Turbary Ret Pk BH11 .... 188 C2
Turbury Cl BH12 .... 203 E4
Turbury Rd BH12 .... 203 E4
Turf Croft BH23 .... 194 A1
Turk's La BH14 .... 203 D1
Turlin Moor Fst Sch SO16 .... 201 E2
Turlin Moor Mid Sch SO16 .... 201 E2
Turlin Rd BH16 .... 201 E2
Turner Ave PO13 .... 180 C4
Turner Rd PO1 .... 182 B4
Turners Farm Cres SO41 .... 196 A1
Turners Oak Ct SO15 .... 78 B1
Turnpike Way SO30 .... 105 D4
Turnstone Gdns SO16 .... 78 A3
Turnworth Cl BH18 .... 187 E2
Turtle Cl PO14 .... 154 A2
Turvy King Ct PO7 .... 110 C2
Tuscan Wlk SO53 .... 55 F3
Tuscany Way PO7 .... 135 D4
Tussocks The SO40 .... 101 F1
Tutland Rd SO52 .... 53 F2
Tutt's La SO51 .... 50 C2
Tweed Cl SO53 .... 55 D4
Tweed La SO41 .... 197 E4
Tweedale Rd BH9 .... 190 B2
Twemlow Ave BH14 .... 202 C2
Twiggs End Cl SO31 .... 128 C2
Twiggs La SO40 .... 124 C4
Twiggs Lane End SO40 .... 124 B3
Twin Oaks SO19 .... 103 F2
Twin Oaks Cl BH18 .... 187 D2
Twittens Way **13** PO9 .... 135 F1
Twyford Ave
  Portsmouth PO2 .... 157 E1
  Southampton SO15 .... 78 B1
Twyford CE Prim Sch SO21 .. 31 F3
Twyford Ct **15** SO23 .... 2 A1
Twyford Dr PO13 .... 179 F1
Twyford Rd SO50 .... 56 B3
Twyford Sch SO21 .... 32 A3
Twyford Way PO14 .... 188 A1
Twynham Ave BH23 .... 207 D4
Twynham Cl SP5 .... 46 C3
Twynham Comp Sch BH23 .... 207 D3
Twynham Rd BH6 .... 206 C2
Twynhams Hill SO32 .... 108 A4
Tyler Ct PO9 .... 135 F3
Tylers Cl SO41 .... 197 E4
Tyleshades The SO51 .... 53 D3
Tyne Cl SO53 .... 55 D3

Tynedale Cl Bournemouth BH9 .. 190 A2
  Gosport PO12 .... 180 C4
Tyneham Ave BH12 .... 203 E4
Tyrell Lawn PO9 .... 135 E4
Tyrel Rd SO53 .... 55 E4
Tyrrell Gdns BH8 .... 191 D1
Tyrrells Ct BH23 .... 169 D1
Tyseley Rd PO1 .... 182 B2
Tytherley Gn **18** PO9 .... 136 A3
Tytherley Gr BH8 .... 190 B1
Tytherley Rd SO18 .... 104 B4

Uddens Dr BH21 .... 164 B4
Uddens Trad Est BH21 .... 164 C3
Ullswater SO50 .... 56 A1
Ullswater Ave SO18 .... 80 A1
Ullswater House **15** PO6 .... 133 D1
Ullswater Rd Oakley BH21 .... 163 E1
  Southampton SO16 .... 77 F1
Undercliff Dr BH1, BH5 .... 205 E1
Undercliff Gdns SO16 .... 78 C2
Undercliff Rd BH5 .... 205 F2
Underdown Ave PO7 .... 134 B1
Undershore SO41 .... 197 F3
Undershore Rd SO41 .... 198 A2
Underwood Cl
  Broadstone BH17 .... 187 D1
  Southampton SO16 .... 78 C2
Underwood Rd
  Bishopstoke SO50 .... 56 C2
  Southampton SO16 .... 78 C2
Unicorn Rd
  Lee-on-the-Solent PO13 .... 179 E2
  Portsmouth PO1 .... 182 A3
Union La SO32 .... 61 D1
Union Pl PO1 .... 182 B3
Union Rd Havant PO9 .... 135 F1
  Southampton SO14 .... 103 D3
Union St
  Fareham PO16 .... 131 E1
  8 Portsmouth PO1 .... 182 A3
  Winchester SO23 .... 11 D4
Univ of Portsmouth PO1 .... 182 A3
Univ of Portsmouth
  (Langstone Campus) PO4 .... 183 E3
Univ of Portsmouth
  (Milton Campus) PO4 .... 183 D2
University Cres SO17 .... 79 D2
University Parkway SO16 .... 54 B3
University Rd SO17 .... 79 D2
Unwin Cl SO19 .... 103 E1
Upham CE Prim Sch SO32 .... 58 C3
Upham St SO32 .... 58 B3
Uphill Rd SO22 .... 1 B3
Upland La GU33 .... 20 A4
Uplands Ave BH25 .... 210 A4
Uplands Cl BH22 .... 166 A4
Uplands Cres PO16 .... 131 D1
Uplands Prim Sch PO16 .... 131 D2
Uplands Rd
  Bournemouth BH8 .... 190 B1
  Cosham PO6 .... 158 B4
  Denmead PO7 .... 110 B3
  Rowland's Castle PO9 .... 113 A3
  West Moors BH22 .... 139 D1
  Winchester SO22 .... 1 C2
Uplands Sch BH14 .... 203 E2
Uplands Way SO17 .... 79 D1
Uplyme Cl BH17 .... 188 A1
Uppark (NT) GU31 .... 90 C4
Upper Arundel St PO1 .... 182 B3
Upper Banister St **1** SO15 .. 102 C3
Upper Barn Copse SO50 .... 57 D2
Upper Bere Wood PO7 .... 134 C4
Upper Brook Dr SO31 .... 128 C1
Upper Brook St SO23 .... 11 D4
Upper Brownhill Rd SO16 .... 77 F1
Upper Bugle St SO14 .... 102 C2
Upper Church Rd SO32 .... 107 F4
Upper Common Rd SO41 .... 196 A3
Upper Crabbick La PO7 .... 110 B3
Upper Crescent Rd SO52 .... 53 F3
Upper Deacon Rd SO19 .... 104 B3
Upper Golf Links Rd BH18 .... 187 D3
Upper Gordon Rd BH23 .... 194 A1
Upper Heyshott GU31 .... 41 D2
Upper High St SO23 .... 10 C4
Upper Hinton Rd BH1 .... 204 C2
Upper House Ct PO17 .... 108 A2
Upper Market St SO50 .... 56 A2
Upper Mead Cl **9** SO50 .... 57 E1
Upper Moors Rd SO21 .... 56 C4
Upper Mount GU33 .... 20 C2
Upper Mullins La SO45 .... 125 E2
Upper New Rd SO30 .... 80 B1
Upper Northam Cl SO30 .... 105 D3
Upper Northam Rd
  Hedge End SO30 .... 104 C3
  Hedge End SO30 .... 105 D3
Upper Norwich Rd **13** BH2 .. 204 C2
Upper Old St PO14 .... 154 A2
Upper Piece PO7 .... 111 D2
Upper Rd BH12 .... 203 D2
Upper Shaftesbury Ave SO17 .. 79 D1
Upper Shirley Ave SO15 .... 78 B1
Upper Spinney SO31 .... 152 B4
Upper St Helens Rd SO30 .... 105 D3
Upper Terrace Rd BH2 .... 204 C2
Upper Toothill Rd SO16 .... 77 D4
Upper Wardown GU31 .... 41 D2
Upper Weston La SO19 .... 104 A1
Upper Wharf PO16 .... 155 E4
Uppleby Rd BH12 .... 203 E3

Upton Cl Havant PO9 .... 135 E4
Upton BH16 .... 201 D4
Upton Cres SO16 .... 77 E4
Upton Cross Mobile
Home Pk BH16 .... 201 E4
Upton Ct BH16 .... 201 E4
Upton Ctry Pk BH17 .... 201 F3
Upton Cty Inf Sch BH16 .... 201 D4
Upton Cty Jun Sch BH16 .... 201 D4
Upton Grey Cl SO22 .... 1 B2
Upton Heath Est BH16 .... 201 E4
Upton House 1 SO16 .... 78 A1
Upton La SO16 .... 77 E3
Upton Rd Broadstone BH17 .... 202 A4
Poole BH17 .... 201 F4
Upton Way BH18 .... 186 C2
Upwey Ave BH15 .... 201 F2
Utrecht Ct BH23 .... 207 E4

Vadne Gdns PO12 .... 181 D3
Vaggs La Hordle SO41 .... 195 F3
New Milton SO41 .... 195 E4
Vale Cl BH14 .... 203 F2
Vale Dr SO18 .... 79 F1
Vale Gr PO12 .... 181 D4
Vale Lodge BH1 .... 205 E3
Vale Mansions 4 BH1 .... 205 E2
Vale Rd Bournemouth BH1 .... 205 E2
Poole BH14 .... 203 F2
Redlynch SP5 .... 47 E3
Winchester SO23 .... 11 E3
Vale The Horndean PO8 .... 88 B1
Hythe SO45 .... 125 F2
Locks Heath SO31 .... 129 D1
Petersfield GU32 .... 41 D3
Portsmouth PO5 .... 182 B1
Valencia Cl BH23 .... 191 E2
Valentine Ave SO19 .... 104 B2
Valentine Cl PO15 .... 130 B1
Valentine Ct
Southampton SO19 .... 104 B2
Waterlooville PO7 .... 135 D4
Valerian Cl SO50 .... 81 E3
Valerian Rd SO30 .... 105 E3
Valetta Park PO10 .... 160 C4
Valette Rd BH9 .... 190 A2
Valiant Rd PO10 .... 161 E1
Valiant Way BH23 .... 208 A4
Valley Cl Blackfield SO45 .... 150 C1
Christchurch BH23 .... 191 F2
Colden Common SO21 .... 56 C4
Redlynch SP5 .... 47 E3
Waterlooville PO7 .... 134 B2
Valley Ct The 4 SO22 .... 10 B3
Valley La BH23 .... 169 F2
Valley Park Dr PO8 .... 88 B2
Valley Rd Bournemouth BH8 .... 190 C2
Chandler's Ford SO53 .... 55 E4
Littleton SO22 .... 1 A3
Totton SO40 .... 100 C3
Valley Rise SO31 .... 128 C2
Valley The SO22 .... 10 B3
Valley View Poole BH12 .... 204 A4
Southampton SO19 .... 104 A2
Southampton SO19 .... 104 A3
Valleydene SO45 .... 125 F1
Vallis Cl BH13 .... 202 B1
Valsheba Dr PO14 .... 179 D3
Valview Mobile Home Pk
SO41 .... 195 E4
Vanburgh Way SO53 .... 30 A1
Vanguard Rd
Bournemouth BH8 .... 190 C1
Poole BH15 .... 202 B1
Southampton SO18 .... 104 A4
Vanstone Rd PO13 .... 180 B4
Vardy Cl SO19 .... 104 B2
Varna Rd SO15 .... 102 B3
Varsity Rd PO10 .... 161 E1
Vaudrey Cl SO15 .... 78 B1
Vaughan Cl SO19 .... 104 C3
Vaughan Rd SO45 .... 125 E2
Vauxhall Way GU32 .... 40 C2
Veal's La SO40 .... 125 D4
Vear's La SO21 .... 57 D4
Vecta Cl BH23 .... 208 B3
Vectis Ct SO16 .... 78 C2
Vectis Rd
Barton on Sea BH25 .... 209 E4
Gosport PO12 .... 180 C2
Vectis Way PO6 .... 157 F4
Velder Ave PO4 .... 183 D3
Vellan Ct SO16 .... 77 E1
Velmore Rd SO53 .... 55 D2
Velsheda Ct 2 SO45 .... 126 A3
Velvet Lawn Rd BH25 .... 194 C2
Venator Pl BH21 .... 163 E3
Venerable Rd PO14 .... 155 D3
Vengeance Rd PO13 .... 179 F2
Venice Cl PO7 .... 135 D4
Venning Ave BH11 .... 188 C3
Ventnor Ct SO16 .... 79 E3
Ventnor Rd Gosport PO13 .... 155 D2
Portsmouth PO4 .... 182 C2
Ventnor Way PO16 .... 131 F1
Ventry Cl BH13 .... 203 F2
Ventura Ctr The BH16 .... 201 E3
Ventura Pl BH16 .... 201 E3
Venture Ind Pk PO3 .... 158 A3
Venture Rd PO3 .... 158 A3
Venture Rd SO16 .... 54 B1
Verbena Cres PO8 .... 112 A2
Verbena Way SO30 .... 105 E3
Verdon Ave SO31 .... 127 F2

Verger Cl PO14 .... 129 E2
Verity Cres BH17 .... 188 A1
Vermont Cl SO16 .... 78 C2
Vermont Sch SO16 .... 78 C2
Vernalls Cl BH10 .... 189 E3
Vernalls Gdns BH10 .... 189 E3
Verne Rd BH31 .... 115 D3
Verney Cl BH11 .... 189 D2
Verney Rd BH11 .... 189 D2
Vernham Rd SO22 .... 1 C1
Vernon La BH23 .... 193 E1
Vernon Ave PO4 .... 183 D3
Vernon Cl
Bishop's Waltham SO32 .... 59 E1
Gosport PO12 .... 181 D3
Vernon Ct 3 PO2 .... 157 F1
Vernon Hill SO32 .... 59 E1
Vernon Mews PO4 .... 183 D3
Vernon Rd Gosport PO12 .... 181 D3
Portsmouth PO3 .... 158 A1
Vernon Wlk 5 SO15 .... 102 C3
Verona Ave BH6 .... 206 B3
Verona Rd SO53 .... 55 F3
Verwood Cres BH6 .... 207 D2
Verwood First Sch BH31 .... 114 C3
Verwood Ind Est BH31 .... 115 D3
Verwood Rd Havant PO9 .... 136 A3
Ibsley BH24 .... 116 A1
St Leonards BH24 .... 140 B4
Three Legged Cross BH21 .... 114 C1
Verwood BH31 .... 114 A4
Woodlands BH21 .... 114 A4
Veryan PO15 .... 130 C1
Vespasian Ct SO18 .... 103 E4
Vespasian Rd SO18 .... 103 E4
Vespasian Way SO53 .... 55 F4
Vesta Way SO53 .... 55 F4
Vetch Cl BH23 .... 208 B4
Vian Cl PO13 .... 155 E2
Vian Ct 14 BH25 .... 194 C2
Vian Pl SO53 .... 2 B4
Vian Rd PO7 .... 134 C3
Vicarage Cotts BH8 .... 190 C2
Vicarage Dr SO30 .... 105 D3
Vicarage Farm SO50 .... 57 E3
Vicarage Gdns SO41 .... 196 A1
Vicarage La Cadnam SO40 .... 75 D1
Curdridge SO32 .... 106 B4
Hambledon PO7 .... 86 B2
Hordle SO41 .... 196 A1
Stubbington PO14 .... 154 B2
Swanmore SO32 .... 84 B3
Vicarage Park SP5 .... 47 E3
Vicarage Rd
Bournemouth BH9 .... 189 F1
Marchwood SO40 .... 101 F1
Poole BH15 .... 202 B3
Redlynch SP5 .... 48 A3
Verwood BH31 .... 114 C3
Vicarage Way BH23 .... 192 B1
Vice La SO51 .... 74 A2
Viceroy Rd SO19 .... 104 A2
Vickers Cl BH8 .... 191 D1
Vickery Way BH23 .... 207 E4
Victena Rd SO50 .... 57 E1
Victor Ct SO19 .... 104 B3
Victor Rd Portsmouth PO1 .... 182 C4
Thorney Island PO10 .... 161 E1
Victor St SO14 .... 78 A1
Victoria Ave
Bournemouth BH9 .... 189 F1
South Hayling PO11 .... 184 C2
Waterlooville PO7 .... 134 A2
Victoria Bldgs SO32 .... 83 D4
Victoria Cl
Corfe Mullen BH21 .... 186 B3
Locks Heath PO14 .... 129 D1
Victoria Cottage Hospl PO10 . 160 C4
Victoria Cres BH12 .... 203 E3
Victoria Ct Durley SO32 .... 82 B4
South Hayling PO11 .... 184 C2
Victoria Gdns
Ferndown BH22 .... 165 E3
Fordingbridge SP6 .... 69 E1
Ringwood BH24 .... 141 D3
Victoria Glade SO31 .... 127 E3
Victoria Gr PO5 .... 182 B2
Victoria House 11 PO16 .... 131 D1
Victoria Hospl BH23 .... 163 D3
Victoria Park Rd BH9 .... 189 F1
Victoria Pl
Bournemouth BH1 .... 205 E3
6 Gosport PO12 .... 181 D2
2 Lymington SO41 .... 197 F1
Romsey SO51 .... 52 C4
Wimborne Minster BH21 .... 163 D3
Victoria Rd
Bishop's Waltham SO32 .... 83 D4
Bournemouth BH1 .... 205 E3
Christchurch BH23 .... 207 F3
Eastleigh SO50 .... 56 A3
Emsworth PO10 .... 136 C1
Ferndown BH22 .... 165 E3
Fordingbridge SP6 .... 69 E1
Milford on Sea SO41 .... 211 E2
Netley SO31 .... 127 D3
North Hayling PO11 .... 159 F1
Poole BH12 .... 203 E3
Portsmouth PO1 .... 182 A3
Southampton SO19 .... 103 E1
Waterlooville PO7 .... 134 C4
Wimborne Minster BH21 .... 163 D3
Winchester SO23 .... 1 C1
Victoria Rd N PO5 .... 182 B2
Victoria Rd S PO5 .... 182 B1

Victoria Sch BH13 .... 203 F2
Victoria Sq PO13 .... 179 F1
Victoria St Gosport PO12 .... 181 E3
Portsmouth PO1 .... 182 B4
Southampton SO14 .... 103 E3
Victoria Terr Hermitage PO10 .. 137 D1
Southbourne PO10 .... 161 E4
Westbourne BH10 .... 137 D2
Victoria Wlk SO30 .... 80 C1
Victory Cl
Chandler's Ford SO53 .... 55 D3
West Moors BH21 .... 139 D3
Victory Cotts SO31 .... 128 B4
Victory Cres SO15 .... 102 A3
Victory Ct Gosport PO13 .... 155 E1
3 Lee-on-the-Solent PO13 .... 179 F1
Victory Gn PO2 .... 157 E1
Victory Rd
17 Portsmouth PO1 .... 182 A3
Southampton SO15 .... 102 A3
Stubbington PO14 .... 179 E3
Victory Sq SO15 .... 102 A3
Victory Trad Est PO3 .... 158 A1
Victory Way SO16 .... 77 F4
Viewside Cl BH21 .... 186 B3
Viking Cl Blackfield SO45 .... 177 F4
Bournemouth BH6 .... 207 D2
Southampton SO16 .... 77 F2
Stubbington PO14 .... 154 A2
Viking Way
Bournemouth BH6 .... 207 D2
Christchurch BH23 .... 208 A3
Horndean PO8 .... 88 B2
Vikings The SO51 .... 53 D4
Villa Gdns PO7 .... 134 C4
Village Ctr SO40 .... 101 F1
Village Gate PO14 .... 153 F4
Village Rd PO12 .... 180 C1
Village St GU31 .... 41 D3
Ville de Paris Rd PO14 .... 155 D3
Villette Cl BH23 .... 192 A1
Villiers Rd Hythe SO45 .... 149 F4
Portsmouth PO5 .... 182 B1
Southampton SO15 .... 102 B4
Vimoutiers Ct SP6 .... 69 F1
Vimy House 3 PO14 .... 154 C4
Vince Cl BH11 .... 189 D3
Vincent Ave SO16 .... 78 B1
Vincent Cl 2 BH25 .... 195 D1
Vincent Gr PO16 .... 156 B4
Vincent Rd 1 BH25 .... 195 D1
Vincent St SO15 .... 102 B4
Vincent's Gr SO15 .... 102 A4
Vincent's Wlk SO14 .... 103 D2
Vine Bank SO18 .... 104 A4
Vine Cl Bournemouth BH7 .... 206 A4
Locks Heath SO31 .... 128 B2
Vine Coppice PO7 .... 134 C2
Vine Ct 21 PO6 .... 157 F4
Vine Farm Cl BH12 .... 204 B4
Vine Farm Rd BH12 .... 204 A4
Vine Hill BH21 .... 162 C3
Vine House SO31 .... 129 D3
Vine Rd SO16 .... 78 A2
Vinegar Hill SO41 .... 211 E3
Vineries Cl BH21 .... 163 F3
Vineries The BH21 .... 163 F3
Vinery Gdns SO16 .... 78 B1
Vinery Rd SO16 .... 78 B1
Vinery The BH25 .... 195 D1
Vineside PO13 .... 155 F1
Viney Ave SO51 .... 53 D4
Viney Rd SO41 .... 197 F1
Vineyard Cl SO19 .... 103 E2
Vineyards The SO52 .... 54 A2
Vinnells La GU32 .... 37 E3
Vinneys Cl BH23 .... 192 B1
Vinson Rd GU33 .... 21 D2
Violet Ave PO14 .... 179 D3
Violet Cl SO53 .... 55 D3
Violet Farm Cl BH21 .... 186 B4
Violet La BH25 .... 195 D2
Violet Rd SO16 .... 79 D2
Virginia Cl BH12 .... 203 E4
Virginia Park Rd PO12 .... 180 C3
Viscount Ct BH11 .... 188 B3
Viscount Dr BH23 .... 208 A3
Viscount Wlk BH11 .... 188 B3
Vista Marina BH13 .... 214 B3
Vita Rd PO2 .... 157 F2
Vitre Gdns SO41 .... 197 F1
Vivash Rd PO1 .... 182 C3
Vixen Cl PO14 .... 179 D3
Vixen Wlk BH25 .... 195 D3
Vokes Cl SO19 .... 104 A3
Vulcan Cl SO15 .... 101 F3
Vulcan Rd Portsmouth PO1 .... 182 A2
Southampton SO15 .... 101 F3
Thorney Island PO10 .... 161 E1
Vulcan Way BH23 .... 208 A4
Vyse La 20 SO14 .... 102 C2

Wade Court Rd PO9 .... 160 A4
Wade La PO9 .... 160 A4
Wadham Rd PO2 .... 157 E1
Wadhurst Gdns SO19 .... 127 D4
Wadhurst Rd SO30 .... 105 E3
Wagtail Dr BH25 .... 194 C1
Wagtail Way PO16 .... 155 F4
Wainscot Rd PO4 .... 183 D1
Wainsford Cl SO41 .... 197 D1
Wainsford Rd Hordle SO41 .... 196 C1
Lymington SO41 .... 196 C1
Wainwright Cl PO6 .... 158 B3
Wainwright Gdns SO30 .... 81 D2
Wait End Rd PO7 .... 134 C2
Waite End Prim Sch PO7 .... 134 C3
Wake Lawn PO4 .... 183 D2

Wakefield Ave
Bournemouth BH10 .... 189 F3
Fareham PO16 .... 130 C2
Wakefield Ct 6 SO18 .... 80 A1
Wakefield Rd SO18 .... 80 A1
Wakeford Cl 16 SO51 .... 52 C4
Wakefords Way PO9 .... 136 A3
Wakely Gdns BH11 .... 189 D3
Wakely Rd BH11 .... 189 D3
Walberant Bldgs 9 PO2 .... 157 F2
Walberton Ave PO6 .... 158 A4
Walberton Ct 1 PO6 .... 158 A4
Walcheren Pl BH15 .... 201 E2
Walcott Ave BH23 .... 191 F1
Waldegrave Cl SO19 .... 103 E1
Walden Gdns PO8 .... 112 A4
Walden Rd PO2 .... 157 E1
Walditch Gdns BH17 .... 187 F1
Waldren Cl BH15 .... 202 C1
Wales St SO23 .... 11 D4
Walford Cl BH21 .... 163 E3
Walford Gdns BH21 .... 163 E3
Walford Mill Craft Ctr BH21 .. 163 D3
Walford Rd PO6 .... 133 E1
Walhampton Hill SO41 .... 198 A3
Walhampton Sch SO41 .... 198 A3
Walker Gdns SO30 .... 81 E1
Walker Pl PO13 .... 155 E1
Walker Rd PO2 .... 157 E1
Walker's Lane S SO45 .... 177 F4
Walkers Cl SO50 .... 57 E1
Walkers La N SO45 .... 150 C1
Walkford La BH25 .... 194 B2
Walkford Rd BH23 .... 194 B1
Walkford Way BH23 .... 194 A1
Walkwood Ave BH7 .... 206 A4
Wallace La SO42 .... 175 E3
Wallace Rd Broadstone BH18 .. 187 D2
Portsmouth PO2 .... 182 C4
Southampton SO19 .... 103 F1
Wallington Ct PO14 .... 154 C3
Wallington Dr SO53 .... 55 D4
Wallington Hill 3 PO16 .... 131 E1
Wallington Rd PO2 .... 157 F1
Wallington Shore Rd
Fareham PO16 .... 131 E1
14 Portchester PO16 .... 131 E1
Wallington Way PO16 .... 131 E1
Wallis Bglws PO12 .... 180 C2
Wallis Gdns PO7 .... 111 F1
Wallis Rd
Bournemouth BH10 .... 189 D1
Waterlooville PO7 .... 111 F1
Walliscott Rd BH11 .... 189 D1
Wallisdean Ave PO14 .... 154 C4
Wallisdean Jun & Inf Schs
PO14 .... 154 C4
Wallisdean Rd PO3 .... 183 D4
Wallisdown Rd BH10, BH11 .. 204 B4
Wallrock Wlk PO10 .... 136 C2
Walmer Cl SO50 .... 56 A4
Walmer Rd PO1 .... 182 C3
Walnut Ave SO18 .... 79 F3
Walnut Cl
Chandler's Ford SO53 .... 30 B1
16 New Milton BH25 .... 194 C2
Southampton SO16 .... 77 F1
Walnut Dr PO14 .... 154 C4
Walnut Gr SO16 .... 77 F1
Walnut Tree Cl PO11 .... 184 C2
Walnut Tree Dr PO10 .... 137 C2
Walpole La SO31 .... 128 C4
Walpole Rd
Bournemouth BH1 .... 205 F3
Gosport PO12 .... 181 E2
Winchester SO22 .... 10 B3
Walpole Terr 9 PO12 .... 181 D2
Walsall Rd PO3 .... 183 D3
Walsford Rd BH4 .... 204 B3
Walsingham Cl PO6 .... 133 E1
Walsingham Dene BH7 .... 205 F4
Walsingham Gdns SO18 .... 79 F2
Waltham Cl Droxford SO32 .... 61 D1
Portchester PO16 .... 132 B1
Waltham Cres SO16 .... 78 B2
Waltham Dr BH7 .... 206 A3
Waltham St PO5 .... 182 A2
Walton Cl Gosport PO12 .... 181 D2
Waterlooville PO7 .... 134 C3
Walton Ct Fareham PO15 .... 130 B2
Portsmouth PO1 .... 182 A2
Walton Pl SO22 .... 10 B3
Walton Rd
Bournemouth BH10 .... 189 E1
Cosham PO6 .... 158 B3
Gosport PO12 .... 181 D2
Poole BH15 .... 203 D3
Southampton SO19 .... 104 B2
Waltons Ave SO45 .... 150 B2
Wandesford Pl PO12 .... 156 A1
Wangfield La SO32 .... 82 B1
Wansbeck Cl SO53 .... 55 D3
Wanstead Cl BH24 .... 117 D1
War Meml Hospl
Gosport PO12 .... 181 D2
Milford on Sea SO41 .... 211 E2
Warbler Cl Hamworthy BH16 .. 201 D4
Horndean PO8 .... 112 A4
Southampton SO16 .... 78 A3
Warblington Ave PO9 .... 136 A1
Warblington Cl SO53 .... 55 D3
Warblington Ct PO1 .... 182 A2
Warblington Halt PO9 .... 136 A1
Warblington Rd PO10 .... 160 C4
Warblington Sch PO9 .... 136 A1
Warblington St PO1 .... 182 A2
Warborne La SO41 .... 198 A4

Warbrook Ct 22 PO9 .... 136 A3
Warburton Cl SO19 .... 104 C1
Warburton Rd Poole BH17 .... 202 C4
Southampton SO19 .... 104 C2
Ward Cres PO10 .... 137 D2
Ward Ct PO11 .... 184 C1
Ward House 38 PO1 .... 182 A3
Ward Rd PO4 .... 183 D1
Warden Cl SO30 .... 80 B1
Wardens Cl PO11 .... 184 C3
Warders Ct 15 PO12 .... 181 D3
Wardle Rd SO50 .... 56 B4
Wardroom Rd PO2 .... 157 D1
Wareham Ct PO7 .... 134 C4
Wareham Rd Broadstone BH21 . 186 B2
Upton BH21 .... 186 B2
Warfield Ave PO7 .... 134 C4
Warfield Cres PO7 .... 134 C4
Warland Way BH21 .... 186 C4
Warlock Cl SO19 .... 104 B2
Warmwell Cl
Bournemouth BH9 .... 190 A2
Poole BH17 .... 187 F1
Warnborough Ct 6 PO9 .... 136 A3
Warner Ct 11 SO23 .... 2 A1
Warnes La BH24 .... 142 C1
Warnford Cl PO12 .... 180 C2
Warnford Cres PO9 .... 135 E3
Warnford Rd BH6, BH7 .... 206 B4
Warren Ave
Chandler's Ford SO53 .... 55 F3
Christchurch BH23 .... 207 F3
Portsmouth PO4 .... 183 D3
Southampton SO16 .... 78 A1
Warren Cl Chandler's Ford SO53 . 55 F3
South Hayling PO11 .... 184 B2
Southampton SO16 .... 78 A1
St Leonards BH24 .... 140 B3
Warren Cres SO16 .... 78 A1
Warren Dr BH24 .... 140 B3
Warren Edge Cl BH6 .... 206 C2
Warren Edge Ct BH6 .... 206 C2
Warren Edge Rd BH6 .... 206 C2
Warren Gdns SO51 .... 28 A1
Warren La Beaulieu SO42 .... 200 C4
Colemore GU32 .... 19 D3
Froxfield GU32 .... 19 D3
Owslebury SO21 .... 33 F4
St Leonards BH24 .... 140 B3
Warren Park Prim Sch PO9 .. 135 E4
Warren Pk SO41 .... 211 D3
Warren Pl SO40 .... 76 B1
Warren Rd
Bournemouth BH4 .... 204 A1
Liss GU33 .... 21 D4
Poole BH14 .... 203 E2
Winchester SO23 .... 11 E4
Warren The SO45 .... 150 A3
Warren Wlk BH22 .... 165 D4
Warrior Bsns Ctr The PO6 .. 158 C4
Warrior Cl SO53 .... 55 D2
Warrior Pk SO53 .... 55 D2
Warrys Cl SO45 .... 150 A4
Warsash Cl PO9 .... 135 F3
Warsash Ct SO31 .... 128 B1
Warsash Gr PO13 .... 155 D1
Warsash Maritime
Ctr (Soton Inst) SO31 .... 152 B4
Warsash Rd SO31 .... 129 D1
Warton Cl SO42 .... 175 E3
Warwick Ave BH25 .... 195 D2
Warwick Cl
Chandler's Ford SO53 .... 55 D2
Lee-on-the-Solent PO13 .... 180 A2
13 Winchester SO23 .... 2 A1
Warwick Cres PO5 .... 182 B2
Warwick Ct
14 Bournemouth BH5 .... 205 F2
4 Emsworth PO10 .... 160 C4
14 Winchester SO23 .... 2 A1
Warwick House 21 SO14 .... 103 E3
Warwick Pl
3 Bournemouth BH7 .... 206 A3
West Wellow SO51 .... 50 C2
Warwick Rd
Bournemouth BH7 .... 206 A3
Poole BH14 .... 203 E2
Southampton SO15 .... 78 B1
Totton SO40 .... 100 C4
Warwick Way PO17 .... 108 A2
Wasdale Cl PO8 .... 88 B1
Washbrook Rd PO6 .... 133 E1
Washington Ave BH8 .... 205 E3
Washington Ct PO4 .... 183 D3
Washington Rd
Emsworth PO10 .... 136 C1
Portsmouth PO2 .... 182 B4
Wastwater House 25 PO6 .... 133 D1
Watcombe Rd BH6 .... 206 B3
Water Cl SO23 .... 11 D4
Water La
Bournemouth BH6 .... 206 B4
Hythe SO45 .... 125 F1
Totton SO40 .... 100 C4
Winchester SO23 .... 11 D4
Water Lane Farm BH10 .... 189 F3
Water Tower Rd BH18 .... 187 E2
Water's Edge SO30 .... 105 D3
Waterbeech Dr SO30 .... 105 E4
Waterberry Dr PO7 .... 111 E1
Waterditch Rd
Bransgore BH23 .... 193 D2
Burton BH23 .... 193 D2
Waterford Cl Lymington SO41 .. 197 F2
Poole BH14 .... 203 D1
Waterford Ct SO41 .... 197 E1
Waterford Gdns BH23 .... 209 D4

Waterford La SO41 .... 197 F1
Waterford Lodge BH23 ...... 208 A3
Waterford Pl BH23 .... 209 D4
Waterford Rd
Christchurch BH23 .... 209 D4
New Milton BH25 .... 195 E2
Watergate PO12 .... 181 F2
Waterhouse La SO15 .... 102 A4
Waterhouse Way SO15 ...... 102 A4
Waterlock Gdns PO4 .... 183 E2
Waterloo Cl PO8 .... 111 E2
Waterloo House BH17 ...... 187 D1
Waterloo Ind Est SO30 ...... 81 D1
Waterloo Rd
Bournemouth BH9 .... 204 C4
Broadstone BH17 .... 202 B4
Corfe Mullen BH21 .... 186 A3
Gosport PO12 .... 181 E1
Havant PO9 .... 135 F1
Lymington SO41 .... 197 F2
Southampton SO15 .... 102 B3
Waterloo Spcl Sch PO7 .... 134 C4
Waterloo St PO5 .... 182 B2
Waterloo Terr SO15 .... 102 C3
Waterloo Way BH24 .... 141 D3
Watermans La SO45 .... 207 D3
Watermead GU21 .... 206 A2
Watermead Rd PO6 .... 158 C4
Watermill Rd BH23 .... 207 D4
Waters Edge
Lee-on-the-Solent PO13 ...... 179 F1
Poole BH13 .... 214 B3
Waters Edge Gdns PO10 ...... 160 C4
Waters Gn SO42 .... 146 A1
Waters Green Ct SO42 ...... 146 A1
Waters The PO17 .... 130 C3
Watersedge Rd PO6 .... 157 D4
Watershed Ct PO6 .... 133 D1
Watership Dr BH24 .... 141 E1
Waterside Christchurch BH23 ... 207 F2
Hythe SO45 .... 126 A3
Waterside Cl BH24 .... 117 D1
Waterside Gdns PO16 .... 131 E1
Waterside La PO16 .... 156 C3
Waterside Rd SO51 .... 28 A1
Waterside Sch
Portsmouth, Milton PO4 .... 183 E2
Portsmouth, Tipner PO2 .... 157 D2
Waterside Sq SO45 .... 125 F3
Waterston Cl BH17 .... 187 E1
Waterworks Rd Cosham PO6 ... 158 B4
Otterbourne SO21 .... 31 E2
Petersfield GU32 .... 41 D3
Watery La
Christchurch BH23 .... 208 A4
Upton BH16 .... 201 D4
Watkin Rd
19 Bournemouth BH5 ...... 205 F2
Hedge End SO30 .... 81 E1
Watley Cl SO16 .... 77 E3
Watley La SO21 .... 32 A3
Watson Wlk SO40 .... 100 B4
Watton Cl BH8 .... 191 D1
Watton La SO32 .... 61 F1
Watton Rd SO45 .... 150 B2
Watts Cl SO16 .... 77 F2
Watts Rd Hedge End SO30 ... 105 E4
Portsmouth PO1 .... 182 B4
Wavell Ave BH17 .... 187 D1
Wavell Rd Bournemouth BH11 ... 189 D4
Gosport PO13 .... 155 E2
Southampton SO18 .... 104 A4
Wavell Way SO22 .... 10 B3
Wavendon Ave BH25 .... 209 F4
Waveney Cl PO13 .... 179 F1
Waveney Gn SO16 .... 77 F1
Waverley Ave SO31 .... 127 E3
Waverley Cl
Fordingbridge SP6 .... 69 F2
Romsey SO51 .... 28 A1
Waverley Cres BH15 .... 202 B3
Waverley Ct SO31 .... 127 E3
Waverley Gr PO4 .... 182 C1
Waverley House **12** BH25 ... 195 D1
Waverley Path PO12 .... 180 C2
Waverley Rd
Bournemouth BH1 .... 205 D2
Cosham PO6 .... 158 B4
Fordingbridge SP6 .... 69 F2
New Milton BH25 .... 195 D1
Portsmouth PO4 .... 182 C1
Southampton SO15 .... 102 B3
Wayfarer Cl
Locks Heath SO31 .... 128 C1
Portsmouth PO4 .... 183 E4
Wayfarers PO13 .... 180 B4
Wayground Rd BH21 .... 162 C1
Waylands Pl SO30 .... 105 D2
Wayman Rd BH21 .... 186 C3
Wayne Rd BH12 .... 203 D1
Waynflete Cl SO32 .... 83 E4
Waynflete Pl SO22 .... 10 B3
Wayside Cl SO41 .... 211 E3
Wayside Rd
Bournemouth BH6 .... 206 C2
St Leonards BH24 .... 166 C4
Wayte St PO6 .... 157 F4
Waytown BH17 .... 187 E1
Weald Cl SO31 .... 129 D2
Weardale Rd SO53 .... 55 E2
Weavers Cl SO50 .... 57 D1
Weavers Cl PO11 .... 185 D1
Weavers Gn PO9 .... 136 B2
Weavers Pl SO53 .... 55 D4
Weavills Rd SO50 .... 57 D1
Webb Cl PO11 .... 185 D1
Webb La PO11 .... 185 D1

Webb Rd PO16 .... 156 B3
Webb's Way BH11 .... 188 C1
Webbers Way PO12 .... 181 E1
Webbs Cl BH24 .... 139 E3
Webbs Way BH24 .... 139 F3
Webburn Gdns SO18 .... 80 A2
Webster Rd
Bournemouth BH9 .... 190 A2
Winchester SO22 .... 1 A1
Wedgewood Cl
Holbury SO45 .... 150 B2
Stubbington PO14 .... 179 D3
Wedgewood Way PO8 ...... 111 F1
Wedgwood Dr BH14 .... 203 D1
Wedgwood Gdns BH23 ...... 169 E1
Wedmore Cl SO22 .... 10 A2
Weeke Manor Cl SO22 ...... 1 B1
Weeke Prim Sch SO22 ...... 1 B1
Weevil La PO12 .... 181 E3
Weirs The **4** SO23 .... 11 D3
Welbeck Ave SO17 .... 79 D1
Welburn Ct SO18 .... 80 A1
Welch Rd Gosport PO12 .... 181 D4
Portsmouth PO4 .... 182 C1
Welch Way SO16 .... 77 F3
Welchwood Cl PO8 .... 111 F3
Weldon Ave BH11 .... 188 C3
Well Cl BH25 .... 194 C1
Well Copse Cl PO8 .... 88 B1
Well Hill PO7 .... 110 B4
Well House La SP6 .... 45 D2
Well House La SO22 .... 1 C3
Well La Hamble-le-Rice SO31 ... 128 A1
Poole BH15 .... 202 B2
Swanmore SO32 .... 84 A4
Well Meadow PO9 .... 135 F3
Welland Gdns SO18 .... 80 A1
Welland Gn SO16 .... 101 F4
Welland Rd BH21 .... 163 E2
Wellands Rd SO43 .... 122 A3
Wellbrook Gdns SO53 ...... 55 D4
Weller House **16** PO1 ...... 182 B4
Wellers Cl SO40 .... 100 A4
Welles Rd SO53 .... 55 E3
Wellesley Ave BH23 .... 208 B4
Wellesley Cl PO7 .... 134 C4
Wellington Ave
Christchurch BH23 .... 208 B4
Southampton SO18 .... 104 A4
Wellington Cl Horndean PO8 ... 112 B3
Hythe SO45 .... 125 E1
Wellington Ct
7 Bournemouth, Deane Pk BH8 ... 205 D3
Bournemouth, Westbourne BH2 ... 204 B2
7 Havant PO9 .... 135 F1
New Milton BH25 .... 195 D2
Southampton SO15 .... 102 B3
West End SO30 .... 80 B1
Wellington Gr PO16 .... 156 B4
Wellington Pk SO30 .... 81 D1
Wellington Pl SO40 .... 98 C4
Wellington Rd
Bournemouth BH1, BH8 ...... 205 D3
Poole BH14 .... 203 E2
Southampton SO18 .... 79 E1
Wellington St PO5 .... 182 B2
Wellington Way **9** PO7 ...... 134 C4
Wellman Ct SO16 .... 78 C2
Wellow Cl Havant PO9 .... 135 E2
Southampton SO18 .... 104 B4
Wellow Cl **11** BH8 .... 205 E3
Wellow Cty Prim Sch SO51 ... 50 C2
Wellow Dro SO51 .... 50 C4
Wellow Gdns PO14 .... 129 E1
Wellow Wood Rd SO51 ...... 50 B4
Wellowbrook Cl SO53 .... 55 D3
Wells Cl PO15 .... 129 E4
Wells Pl SO50 .... 56 A1
Wells Rd SO50 .... 56 A1
Wellsmoor PO14 .... 129 E1
Wellspring Gdns PO9 .... 113 E2
Wellsworth La PO9 .... 113 E2
Wembley Gr PO6 .... 158 A3
Wembley Way SO50 .... 57 E1
Wendleholme Nature
Reserve SO31 .... 128 B2
Wendover Ct BH25 .... 194 C1
Wendover Rd PO9 .... 135 F1
Wenlock Ct **9** BH23 .... 207 F4
Wensley Gdns PO10 .... 136 C2
Wentwood Gdns BH25 ...... 195 E1
Wentworth BH14 .... 214 B4
Wentworth Ave BH5 .... 206 A2
Wentworth Coll BH5 .... 206 A2
Wentworth Dr
Broadstone BH18 .... 187 D3
Christchurch BH23 .... 206 C3
Horndean PO8 .... 112 A4
Wentworth Gdns
Holbury SO45 .... 150 B2
Southampton SO19 .... 104 A1
Wentworth Gr **14** SO45 ...... 150 B2
Wentworth Grange SO22 .... 10 C3
Wescott Way BH11 .... 188 C2
Wesley Cl
8 Bournemouth BH8 ...... 205 E3
Southampton SO19 .... 104 B2
Wesley Ct PO1 .... 182 C1
Wesley Gr PO3 .... 158 A2
Wesley Grange **33** BH4 ...... 204 B2
Wesley Rd
Kings Worthy SO23 .... 2 B4
Poole BH12 .... 203 E3
Wimborne Minster BH21 .... 163 F3
West Station Terr BH4 .... 204 B2
West Tytherley CE Prim Sch
SP5 .... 4 A4
West View Cotts PO10 ...... 137 D1

Wessex Ct
Southampton, Sholing SO19 ... 104 A2
7 Southampton, Westwood Pk
SO17 .... 103 D4
Wessex Dr SO22 .... 1 C1
Wessex Est BH24 .... 141 D4
Wessex Gate Ind Est PO8 ... 112 B3
Wessex Gdns Portchester PO16 ... 156 A4
Romsey SO51 .... 53 D4
Wessex La SO18 .... 79 E2
Wessex Nuffield Hospl SO53 ... 31 C1
Wessex Rd Horndean PO8 ... 88 B2
Poole BH14 .... 203 D2
Ringwood BH24 .... 141 D4
Wessex Trad Ctr BH12 ...... 203 D4
Wessex Way
Bournemouth BH8 .... 205 E3
Colden Common SO21 ...... 57 D4
West Ave BH21 .... 138 C4
West Bargate **2** SO14 ...... 102 C2
West Battery Rd PO2 .... 157 D1
West Bay Rd SO15 .... 102 B3
West Block SO15 .... 102 B3
West Borough BH21 .... 163 D3
West Butts St **1** BH15 ...... 202 A1
West Cl Lymington SO41 .... 197 D1
Verwood BH31 .... 114 B3
West Cliff Cotts BH2 .... 204 C1
West Cliff Gdns BH2 .... 204 C1
West Cliff Mews BH2 .... 204 C1
West Cliff Rd BH2, BH4 ...... 204 B1
West Close Ct BH6 .... 207 D2
West Close House BH6 ...... 207 D2
West Common SO45 .... 177 F3
West Ct Portsmouth PO1 .... 182 C1
Portsmouth, Southsea PO4 .. 183 D2
Southampton SO19 .... 103 D4
West Downs Cl PO16 .... 131 D2
West Dr SO50 .... 56 B2
West End Cl SO14 .... 10 C4
West End Cotts **18** PO16 ...... 131 D1
West End Rd Hedge End SO31 ... 104 C2
Southampton SO18 .... 104 A4
West End Terr SO22 .... 10 C4
West Gr SP6 .... 69 F1
West Haye Rd PO11 .... 185 E1
West Hayes Lymington SO41 ... 197 F2
Winchester SO22 .... 10 B4
West Hill Ct SO15 .... 102 C3
West Hill Dr Hythe SO45 .... 125 F3
Winchester SO22 .... 10 C4
West Hill Park Sch PO14 .... 153 F4
West Hill Pk SO22 .... 10 B4
West Hill Pl BH2 .... 204 C2
West Hill Rd BH2 .... 204 C1
West Hoe La SO32 .... 83 F4
West Horton Cl SO50 .... 56 C1
West Horton La SO50 .... 56 C1
West Howe Cl BH11 .... 189 D2
West Howe Ind Est BH11 ... 188 C2
West La Hordle SO41 .... 196 C1
North Baddesley SO52 ...... 53 F3
North Hayling PO11 .... 184 C3
South Hayling PO11 .... 184 C3
West Links SO53 .... 55 E1
West Lodge SO19 .... 179 E2
West Mansions **8** BH4 ...... 204 B2
West Marlands Rd SO14 .... 102 C3
West Meon CE
Prim Sch GU32 .... 37 E3
West Moors Mid Sch BH22 ... 138 C1
West Moors Oakhurst
Fst Sch SO22 .... 138 C1
West Moors Rd
Ferndown BH22 .... 165 E4
Three Legged Cross BH21 .. 138 C3
West Moors BH22 .... 138 B3
West Moors St Mary's CE
Fst Sch BH22 .... 138 B2
West Overcliff Dr BH4 ...... 204 B1
West Park La SP6 .... 68 B3
West Park Rd SO15 .... 102 C3
West Point PO13 .... 179 F1
West Quay Rd
Poole BH15 .... 202 A1
Southampton SO15 .... 102 C2
West Rd
Bournemouth BH5 .... 206 A2
Bransgore BH23 .... 193 D4
Emsworth PO10 .... 160 C4
Fawley SO45 .... 150 B4
Hedge End SO30 .... 104 C3
Hythe SO45 .... 125 E1
Milford on Sea SO41 .... 211 D3
Southampton, Old Docks SO14 ... 103 D1
Southampton, Woolston SO19 ... 103 F1
West Row BH21 .... 163 D4
West Row Mews BH21 ...... 163 D2
West St
Emsworth PO10 .... 160 C4
Fareham PO16, PO17 ...... 131 D1
Fordingbridge SP6 .... 69 F1
Hambledon PO7 .... 86 B1
Havant PO9 .... 135 F1
Hythe SO45 .... 125 F3
Poole BH15 .... 202 A1
Portchester PO16 .... 156 B4
Portsmouth PO1 .... 181 F2
Ringwood BH24 .... 140 C4
Soberton SO32 .... 85 E3
Southampton SO14 .... 102 C2
Southwick PO17 .... 132 C3
Titchfield PO14 .... 153 F4

West View Rd
Christchurch BH23 .... 207 F3
Poole BH15 .... 202 B2
West Way Bournemouth BH9 ... 190 A1
Broadstone BH18 .... 187 D2
Locks Heath PO15 .... 129 F2
Lymington SO41 .... 197 E1
West Way SO41 BH9 .... 190 A1
West Wing SO31 .... 127 D4
Westbeams Rd SO41 .... 172 A1
Westborn Rd PO16 .... 131 D1
Westbourne Ave
Emsworth PO10 .... 137 D1
Holbury SO45 .... 150 B2
Westbourne Cl
Bournemouth BH4 .... 204 B2
Emsworth PO10 .... 137 D1
Westbourne Cres SO17 ...... 79 D1
Westbourne Ct BH23 .... 193 D4
Westbourne Cty Prim Sch
PO10 .... 137 D2
Westbourne Mans **9** SO17 ... 79 D1
Westbourne Park Rd BH4 ... 204 A1
Westbourne Rd
Emsworth PO10 .... 137 A2
Portsmouth PO2 .... 182 C4
Westbourne PO10 .... 137 D1
Westbroke Gdns SO51 ...... 27 F1
Westbrook Cl SO31 .... 129 D3
Westbrook Ctr The PO7 .... 112 A1
Westbrook Gr PO7 .... 134 B2
Westbrook Rd PO16 .... 156 B3
Westbrooke Cl PO8 .... 112 A3
Westbury C **30** PO6 .... 133 D1
Westbury Cl
Barton on Sea BH25 .... 210 A4
Bransgore BH23 .... 193 D4
Christchurch BH23 .... 193 E1
Cosham PO6 .... 133 D1
Westbury Ct Hedge End SO30 ... 105 E3
10 Poole BH14 .... 203 D2
Westbury Mall **22** PO16 .... 131 D1
Westbury Rd Fareham PO16 ... 131 D1
Ringwood BH24 .... 141 D4
Southampton SO15 .... 101 F4
Westbury Sq **3** PO16 .... 131 D1
Westby Rd BH5 .... 205 F2
Westcliff PO13 .... 179 F2
Westcliff Mews SO19 .... 103 E2
Westcliff Wlk SO45 .... 125 F3
Westcot Sch SO45 .... 150 A2
Westcroft Par **10** BH25 ...... 195 D1
Westcroft Park BH18 .... 187 E2
Westcroft Rd PO12 .... 180 C3
Westdown Rd BH11 .... 189 D3
Westdown Rd BH11 .... 189 D3
Westerham Cl PO6 .... 157 F4
Westerham Rd BH4 .... 204 A2
Westering PO6 .... 157 F4
Westerleigh BH4 .... 204 B1
Westerley Cl SO31 .... 128 C1
Western Ave
Barton on Sea BH25 .... 209 E4
Bournemouth BH10 .... 189 E4
Emsworth PO10 .... 160 B4
Poole BH13 .... 203 F1
Southampton SO15 .... 102 A3
Western CE Prim Sch SO22 ... 10 B4
Western Cl BH10 .... 189 D4
Western Com Hospl SO16 ... 77 F1
Western Ct **14** PO6 .... 131 D1
Western District Cut SO15 ... 102 B4
Western Downland CE
Prim Sch
Damerham SP6 .... 68 B2
Rockbourne SP6 .... 44 C1
Western Espl SO14 .... 102 C2
Western Par Emsworth PO10 ... 160 C4
Portsmouth PO5 .... 182 A1
Western Rd
Chandler's Ford SO53 .... 30 C1
Cosham PO6 .... 157 E4
Fareham PO16 .... 131 D1
Fawley SO45 .... 151 F1
Havant PO9 .... 135 F1
Liss GU33 .... 20 C2
Lymington SO41 .... 197 E2
Poole, Branksome Pk BH13 ... 204 A1
Poole, Canford Cliffs BH13 ... 214 C4
West End SO30 .... 80 B1
Winchester SO22 .... 10 C4
Western Terr PO2 .... 157 E1
Western Way Fareham PO16 ... 131 D1
Gosport PO12 .... 180 C1
Westerngate BH13 .... 204 A2
Westfield **11** BH21 .... 163 D3
Westfield Ave Fareham PO14 ... 154 C4
South Hayling PO11 .... 184 C2
Westfield Cl Fair Oak SO50 ... 81 E4
Hamble-le-Rice SO31 .... 127 F1
Wimborne Minster BH21 .... 163 D3
Westfield Cnr SO18 .... 79 F3
Westfield Comm SO31 ...... 127 F1
Westfield Cres SO53 .... 55 E2
Westfield Dro SO24 .... 34 C4
Westfield Gdns BH23 .... 193 D4
Westfield House SO18 ...... 79 F2
Westfield Ind Est
Gosport PO12 .... 181 D2
Hordean PO8 .... 112 B4
Westfield Jun Sch PO6 ...... 156 C4
Westfield Oaks PO11 .... 184 C2
Westfield Rd
Bournemouth BH6 .... 206 C2
Chandler's Ford SO53 .... 55 E2
Gosport PO12 .... 181 D2
Littleton SO22 .... 1 A3
Lymington SO41 .... 198 A1

Westfield Rd Continued
Portsmouth PO4 .... 183 D2
Southampton SO15 .... 102 A4
Totton SO40 .... 100 C4
Westgate SO22 .... 179 E3
Westgate Mews SO30 .... 80 C1
Westgate Park BH4 .... 204 A2
Westgate Sec Sch SO22 .... 1 C1
Westgate St **15** SO14 .... 102 C2
Westgrove Gdns PO10 ...... 160 C4
Westham BH17 .... 187 F2
Westheath Rd BH18 .... 187 D2
Westland Dr PO7 .... 134 C2
Westland Gdns PO12 .... 181 D2
Westlands Ct BH23 .... 193 D4
Westlands Gr PO16 .... 156 B4
Westley SO22 .... 1 B1
Westley Gr PO14 .... 154 C4
Westmarch Ct **1** SO17 ...... 79 E1
Westmead PO11 .... 184 C2
Westminster Ct BH25 .... 209 F4
Westminster Gate SO22 .... 10 A3
Westminster Gdns PO14 .... 129 E2
Westminster Pl PO1 .... 182 B4
Westminster Rd
Milford on Sea SO41 .... 211 E2
Poole BH13 .... 204 A1
Westminster Rd E BH13 .... 204 A1
Westmoreland Ct SO41 ...... 195 F2
Westmorland Way SO53 .... 55 F3
Weston Ave PO4 .... 183 D2
Weston Cl SO19 .... 103 F1
Weston Cres SO18 .... 104 B4
Weston Dr BH1 .... 205 D2
Weston Grove Rd SO19 .... 103 E1
Weston Homes **11** SO19 .... 126 C4
Weston House BH32 .... 40 C2
Weston La Buriton GU32 .... 65 E4
Nursling SO16 .... 77 D2
Southampton SO19 .... 103 F1
Weston Par SO19 .... 126 C4
Weston Park Inf Sch SO19 ... 104 A1
Weston Park Jun Sch SO19 ... 104 A1
Weston Park Sec Sch (Boys)
SO19 .... 104 A1
Weston Rd Eastleigh SO50 ... 56 A2
Petersfield GU31 .... 41 D2
Weston Shore Inf Sch SO19 ... 126 C4
Westons La **9** BH15 .... 202 B1
Westover Rd BH7 .... 140 B3
Westover Prim Sch PO3 .... 183 D4
Westover Rd
Bournemouth BH1 .... 204 C2
Milford on Sea SO41 .... 211 D2
Portsmouth PO3 .... 183 D4
Southampton SO16 .... 101 E4
Westquay House **8** PO16 ... 131 E1
Westray Hall BH4 .... 204 B1
Westridge Ct **39** SO17 ...... 79 D1
Westridge Rd SO17 .... 103 D4
Westrow Gdns SO15 .... 102 C4
Westrow Rd SO15 .... 102 C4
Westside View PO7 .... 111 E4
Westview Rd SO22 .... 1 A1
Westward Rd SO30 .... 105 E4
Westways Cosham PO6 ...... 158 C4
Stubbington BH23 .... 179 E3
Westways Cl SO16 .... 77 E3
Westwood Ave BH22 .... 165 E3
Westwood Cl PO10 .... 137 D1
Westwood Ct
11 Southampton SO17 .... 103 D4
Totton SO40 .... 76 C1
Westwood Gdns SO53 ...... 55 F4
Westwood Mansions
28 SO17 .... 79 D1
Westwood Rd
Lyndhurst SO43 .... 121 F3
Netley SO31 .... 127 D4
Portsmouth PO2 .... 157 F2
Southampton SO17 .... 103 D4
Westwood View SO24 ...... 14 C1
Westwoods & Glendene Pk
BH25 .... 194 B3
Wetherby Cl BH18 .... 187 D1
Wetherby Ct SO40 .... 100 B4
Wetherby Gdns SO40 .... 100 B4
Weyhill Cl Havant PO9 ...... 135 E2
Portchester PO16 .... 132 B1
Weyman's Ave BH10 .... 189 D4
Weymans Dr BH10 .... 189 D4
Weymouth Ave PO12 .... 180 C4
Weymouth Rd Poole BH14 ... 203 D2
13 Portsmouth PO2 .... 157 E1
Whaddon Chase PO14 ...... 179 D3
Whaddon Ct PO9 .... 135 D2
Whaddon La
Colden Common SO21 ...... 58 A4
Owslebury SO21 .... 33 D2
Whale Island Way PO2 ...... 157 E1
Whalesmead Cl SO50 .... 56 C1
Whalesmead Rd SO50 ...... 56 C1
Whaley Rd PO2 .... 157 D1
Wharf Cl BH12 .... 203 F3
Wharf Hill SO23 .... 11 D3
Wharf Ind **2** SO23 .... 11 D3
Wharf Rd Portsmouth PO2 ... 182 B4
Southampton SO19 .... 103 E2
Wharfdale Rd
Bournemouth BH4 .... 204 B2
Poole BH12 .... 203 F3
Wharncliffe Ct BH23 .... 208 C4
Wharncliffe Gdns BH23 .... 209 D4
Wharncliffe House SO19 .... 103 E2

Wharncliffe Rd
Bournemouth BH5 .... 205 E2
Christchurch BH23 .... 209 D4
Southampton SO19 .... 103 E2
Whartons Cl SO40 .... 100 B2
Whartons La SO40 .... 100 B2
Whatleigh Cl BH15 .... 202 B1
Wheatcroft Dr SO18 .... 80 A1
Wheatcroft Rd PO13 .... 179 F1
Wheatear Dr GU31 .... 41 E1
Wheatears Dr SO51 .... 50 C2
Wheatland Cl SO22 .... 10 B3
Wheatlands PO14 .... 129 C2
Wheatlands Ave PO11 .... 185 F1
Wheatlands Cres PO11 .... 185 F1
Wheatley La PO9 .... 135 E3
Wheaton Grange BH4 .... 204 B2
Wheaton Rd BH7 .... 206 A3
Wheatsheaf Ct SO30 .... 105 D3
Wheatsheaf Dr PO8 .... 111 E2
Wheatstone Rd PO4 .... 182 C2
Wheeler Cl PO12 .... 181 D3
Wheelers La BH11 .... 188 B3
Wheelers Wlk SO45 .... 177 F4
Wheelwright Mews SP5 .... 46 C4
Wherneside Cl SO16 .... 101 F4
Wherwell Ct 43 PO9 .... 136 A3
Whichers Cl PO9 .... 136 A4
Whichers Gate Rd PO9 .... 136 A4
Whiitemoor La SO40 .... 75 F2
Whimbrel Cl PO4 .... 183 E3
Whimbrel Ct BH23 .... 208 A3
Whinchat Cl Fareham PO15 .. 130 B2
Southampton SO16 .... 78 A3
Whincroft Cl BH23 .... 165 F4
Whincroft Dr BH22 .... 165 F3
Whinfield Rd SO45 .... 149 F4
Whinwhistle Rd SO51 .... 51 D1
Whippingham Cl PO6 .... 157 E4
Whistler Cl SO19 .... 104 B2
Whistler Rd SO19 .... 104 B2
Whitaker Cres SO41 .... 197 E2
Whitby Ave BH18 .... 187 D1
Whitby Cl BH23 .... 191 E2
Whitby Cres BH18 .... 187 D1
Whitby Cl 4 SO41 .... 211 D2
Whitby Rd SO41 .... 211 D2
Whitchurch Ave BH18 .... 187 E2
Whitchurch Ct SO19 .... 103 F2
Whitcombe Cl SO40 .... 100 C4
Whitcombe Gdns PO1 .... 182 C3
White Barn Cres SO41 .... 196 A2
White Beam Rise PO8 .... 88 B3
White Cl BH15 .... 203 D4
White Cloud Pk 7 PO4 .... 182 C2
White Cloud Pl 8 PO4 .... 182 C2
White Dirt La PO8 .... 88 B2
White Farm Cl BH10 .... 204 B4
White Gates SO32 .... 82 A3
White Harmony Acres Ind Est
SO30 .... 80 C3
White Hart La Cadnam SO40 .. 98 C4
Portchester PO16 .... 156 B4
White Hart Rd Fair Oak SO50 .. 57 E1
4 Gosport PO12 .... 181 D2
Portsmouth PO1 .... 182 A2
White Heather Ct 1 SO45 .. 126 A3
White Horse Crossroads
GU32 .... 18 C3
White Horse Dr BH15 .... 202 B3
White Horse La PO7 .... 111 D3
White Horses BH25 .... 209 F4
White House Gdns
Petersfield GU32 .... 40 C3
Southampton SO15 .... 102 A4
White Knights BH25 .... 209 F4
White La SO21 .... 32 A4
White Ladies Cl PO9 .... 136 A1
White Lion Ctyd BH24 .... 140 C4
White Lion Wlk PO12 .... 181 E3
White Lodge BH15 .... 202 C2
White Lodge Gdns PO16 .... 130 C2
White Oak Wlk 38 PO9 .... 136 A3
White Rd SO50 .... 56 B2
White Row SP5 .... 46 B4
White Swan Rd PO1 .... 182 A3
White Way SO32 .... 61 D4
White Wings House PO7 .... 110 C2
White's Rd SO19 .... 104 A3
Whiteacres Cl 17 PO12 .... 181 D3
Whitebeam Cl
Colden Common SO21 .... 57 D4
2 Fareham PO14 .... 154 C4
Waterlooville PO8 .... 112 B3
Whitebeam Rd SO30 .... 105 E3
Whitebeam Way
North Baddesley SO52 .... 54 A3
Verwood BH31 .... 115 D3
Whitechimney Row PO10 .... 137 D2
Whitecliff Cres BH14 .... 203 D1
Whitecliff Rd BH14 .... 202 C1
Whitecliffe Ave PO3 .... 183 D4
Whitecliffe Ct PO12 .... 180 B2
Whitecroft SO45 .... 126 A1
Whitecross Cl BH17 .... 187 F2
Whitecross Gdns 14 PO2 .... 157 F2
Whitefield Lodge 1 BH25 .. 195 D2
Whitefield Rd Holbury SO45 .. 150 B2
New Milton BH25 .... 195 D1
Poole BH14 .... 203 D1
Whitehall BH23 .... 207 D3
Whitehart Fields BH24 .... 141 E4
Whitehaugh Cl 1 SO50 .... 56 B2
Whitehaven Horndean PO8 .. 112 B3
Portchester PO16 .... 156 A4

Whitehaven Home Pk SO45 ... 177 F4
Whitehayes Cl BH23 .... 192 B1
Whitehayes Rd BH23 .... 192 B1
Whitehill Cl SO18 .... 104 B4
Whitehorn Dr SP5 .... 73 E4
Whitehouse Rd PO13 .... 163 E1
Whitelands Brangore BH23 .. 169 E2
Droxford SO32 .... 85 D4
Whitelaw Rd SO15 .... 102 A4
Whiteleaf La PO7 .... 86 B4
Whitelegg Way PO10 .... 189 F3
Whiteley La
Locks Heath PO15 .... 129 F3
Swanwick SO31 .... 106 B1
Whiteley Way PO15 .... 129 E3
Whitemoor Rd SO42 .... 145 E1
Whitenap Cl SO51 .... 53 D3
Whitenap La SO51 .... 53 E3
Whiteparish All Saints
CE Prim Sch SP5 .... 24 A2
Whites Ct 18 PO2 .... 157 E1
Whites Hill SO21 .... 33 D2
Whites La SO45 .... 151 D2
Whiteshoot SP5 .... 47 F2
Whiteshoot Hill SP5 .... 47 F2
Whiteshute La SO23 .... 10 C3
Whitestone Cl SO16 .... 101 F4
Whitethorn Rd PO11 .... 185 D2
Whitewater Rise SO45 .... 125 F1
Whiteways SO21 .... 163 F3
Whitfield Park BH24 .... 140 A3
Whitingham Ct 8 BH5 .... 206 A3
Whitley Cl PO10 .... 137 D3
Whitley Way BH25 .... 195 D3
Whitmore La BH21 .... 114 A4
Whitsbury Cl BH8 .... 190 B1
Whitsbury Cross SP6 .... 69 E4
Whitsbury Rd
Fordingbridge SP6 .... 69 F2
Havant PO9 .... 136 A3
Whitstable Rd PO6 .... 157 F4
Whittington Cl SO45 .... 125 F2
Whittington Ct PO10 .... 160 C4
Whittle Ave PO15 .... 129 E3
Whittle Rd BH21 .... 164 C4
Whittles Way BH15 .... 202 A1
Whitwell SO31 .... 127 E4
Whitwell Rd PO4 .... 182 C1
Whitworth Cl PO12 .... 181 D2
Whitworth Cres SO18 .... 103 E4
Whitworth Ct SO18 .... 103 E4
Whitworth Rd
Gosport PO12 .... 181 D3
Portsmouth PO2 .... 182 C4
Southampton SO18 .... 103 E4
Whyke Ct 2 PO9 .... 135 F1
Whyte Cl SO45 .... 150 A2
Whyteways SO50 .... 56 A2
Wick 1 Ind Est BH25 .... 194 C1
Wick 2 Ind Est BH25 .... 194 C1
Wick Cl BH25 .... 194 C1
Wick Dr BH25 .... 194 C1
Wick Farm BH6 .... 207 D3
Wick La
Bournemouth BH6 .... 207 D3
Christchurch BH23 .... 207 D3
Downton SP5 .... 46 A4
Wicket Rd BH10 .... 189 E3
Wicket The SO45 .... 125 F1
Wickford Ave BH23 .... 207 D3
Wickford Cl BH23 .... 207 D3
Wickford House BH23 .... 207 D3
Wickham CE Prim Sch PO17 .. 108 A2
Wickham Croft PO17 .... 108 A2
Wickham Ct Ferndown BH22 .. 165 F3
Gosport PO12 .... 180 B2
Wickham Dr BH21 .... 186 B2
Wickham House
17 Southampton SO17 .... 79 D1
38 Southampton SO17 .... 79 D1
Wickham Rd
Bournemouth BH7 .... 206 A3
Droxford SO32 .... 85 D3
Fareham PO16, PO17 .... 131 D3
Wickham St PO1 .... 182 A3
Wicklea Rd BH6 .... 207 D2
Wicklow Dr SO53 .... 55 D3
Wickmeads Rd BH6 .... 207 D3
Wickor Cl PO10 .... 137 D1
Wickor Way PO10 .... 137 D1
Wicor Mill La PO16 .... 156 A4
Wicor Path PO16 .... 156 B3
Wicor Prim Sch PO16 .... 156 A4
Widbury Rd SO41 .... 197 E1
Widden Cl SO41 .... 172 A1
Widdicombe Ave BH14 .... 203 F1
Wide La SO18 .... 79 F3
Wide Lane Cl SO42 .... 145 F1
Widecombe Dr SO45 .... 125 F2
Widgeon Cl SO16 .... 155 F4
Widget Cl BH11 .... 189 D1
Widlers La SO32 .... 58 C3
Widley Court Dr PO6 .... 158 A4
Widley Ct 4 Cosham PO6 .. 158 A4
Fareham PO14 .... 155 D3
Widley Gdns PO7 .... 134 B2
Widley Rd Cosham PO6 .. 158 A4
Portsmouth PO2 .... 157 E1
Widley Wlk PO7 .... 133 F2
Widworthy Dr BH18 .... 186 C3
Wield Cl PO7 .... 135 E2
Wigan Cres PO9 .... 135 D1
Wight View PO11 .... 185 E1
Wight Wlk BH22 .... 165 F1
Wightway Mews SO31 .... 128 B1
Wigmore House 24 PO1 .... 182 B3

Wilberforce Cl 2 SO22 .... 10 B3
Wilberforce Rd Gosport PO12 .. 181 E1
38 Portsmouth PO5 .... 182 B2
Wilby La PO3 .... 158 B2
Wild Arum Way SO52 .... 54 C3
Wild Cherry Way SO53 .... 55 D3
Wild Grounds Nature
Reserve PO13 .... 180 B3
Wild Ridings PO14 .... 154 B4
Wild Rose Cres SO31 .... 128 C1
Wildburn Cl SO40 .... 76 B1
Wilde Cl SO40 .... 100 B4
Wildern Cl SO31 .... 128 C2
Wildern La SO30 .... 105 E4
Wildern Sec Sch SO30 .... 105 E4
Wilderness Hts SO18 .... 80 B1
Wilderton Rd BH13 .... 203 F2
Wilderton Rd W BH13 .... 204 A2
Wildfell Cl BH23 .... 192 A1
Wildground Inf Sch SO45 .. 125 F1
Wildground Jun Sch SO45 .. 125 F1
Wildmoor Wlk PO9 .... 136 A3
Wildown Gdns BH6 .... 207 D2
Wildown Rd BH6 .... 207 D2
Wilfred Rd BH5 .... 205 F2
Wilkins Cl PO8 .... 88 A3
Wilkins Way SO15 .... 202 A1
Wilkinson Dr BH8 .... 191 D1
Wilkinson House PO4 .... 183 D1
Wilks Cl SO16 .... 77 E3
Willersley Cl PO6 .... 133 E1
Willett Rd BH21 .... 163 E1
William Booth House 37 PO1 . 182 A3
William The
Christchurch BH23 .... 194 A1
Stubbington PO14 .... 179 E3
William Ct 17 BH23 .... 209 D4
William George Ct 9 PO12 .. 179 F1
William Gilpin CE Prim Sch
SO41 .... 173 F1
William Macleod Way SO16 .. 78 A1
William Price Gdns PO16 .. 131 D1
William Rd
Bournemouth BH7 .... 205 F4
Lymington SO41 .... 197 F3
Southampton SO14 .... 103 E3
William's Ind Pk BH25 .... 194 C1
Williams Cl Gosport PO13 .. 180 B4
Holbury SO45 .... 150 B2
Williams Rd PO3 .... 158 A2
Willis Ave SO52 .... 54 A2
Willis Rd Gosport PO12 .... 181 E2
Portsmouth PO1 .... 182 B3
Southampton SO16 .... 79 E3
Willis Way BH15 .... 202 A3
Willis Waye SO23 .... 2 B3
Willow Ave SP6 .... 69 F1
Willow Cl
Bournemouth BH4 .... 204 A3
Havant PO9 .... 136 A1
Hedge End SO30 .... 105 E3
St Leonards BH24 .... 139 E2
Upton BH16 .... 201 E3
West End SO30 .... 80 C2
Willow Ct
Bournemouth BH7 .... 206 B3
Fareham PO14 .... 130 B1
Southampton SO16 .... 78 A2
Willow Dr Christchurch BH23 .... 207 D3
Marchwood SO40 .... 124 C4
Ringwood BH24 .... 141 D3
Wimborne Minster BH21 .... 164 B3
Willow Gdns
North Baddesley SO52 .... 53 F3
Westbourne PO10 .... 137 D2
Willow Gn SO21 .... 57 D4
Willow Gr 11 SO50 .... 57 E1
Willow Herb Cl SO31 .... 128 C1
Willow La BH23 .... 169 E2
Willow Lodge 1 BH1 .... 205 E2
Willow Mead
Bournemouth BH8 .... 190 B2
Hedge End SO30 .... 105 D4
Willow Pk BH14 .... 203 D2
Willow Pl
Christchurch BH23 .... 207 E3
Gosport PO12 .... 181 D3
Willow Rd
Bishop's Waltham SO32 .... 83 F4
Liss GU33 .... 21 D2
Willow Tree Ave PO8 .... 112 A1
Willow Tree Gdns PO14 .... 154 C4
Willow Tree House SO41 .... 197 E1
Willow Tree Rise BH11 .... 189 D2
Willow Tree Wlk SO19 .... 104 A2
Willow Way
Christchurch BH23 .... 207 D3
Ferndown BH22 .... 165 E4
Willow Wood Rd PO11 .... 185 D2
Willowdale Cl GU32 .... 40 A2
Willowdene Cl Havant PO9 ..... 135 D2
New Milton BH25 .... 195 D2
Willows The
Barton on Sea BH25 .... 210 A4
Chandler's Ford SO53 .... 55 E2
Denmead PO7 .... 110 C2
Wills Cl BH21 .... 186 B2
Wills Rd BH12 .... 203 F2
Wills Way SO51 .... 53 D3
Willwood Cl BH17 .... 187 F2
Wilmcote Gdns 20 PO1 .... 182 B3
Wilmcote House 19 PO1 .... 182 B3
Wilmer Rd SO50 .... 56 A1
Wilmington Cl SO18 .... 79 F2
Wilmot Cl SO50 .... 56 C3
Wilmott Cl PO12 .... 180 C3
Wilmott La PO12 .... 180 C3
Wilson Cres BH15 .... 202 C3

Wilson Ct Fair Oak SO50 .... 81 E4
Fordingbridge SP6 .... 69 F1
Wilson Gr PO5 .... 182 C2
Wilson Rd Bournemouth BH1 .. 205 F3
Poole BH14 .... 203 D2
Portsmouth PO2 .... 157 E1
Wilson St SO14 .... 103 E3
Wilton Ave SO15 .... 102 C3
Wilton Cl
Christchurch BH23 .... 191 E1
Gosport PO12 .... 180 C2
Wilton Cres SO15 .... 78 B1
Wilton Ct SO15 .... 102 B4
Wilton Dr PO8 .... 112 A3
Wilton Gdns
New Milton BH25 .... 194 C2
Southampton SO15 .... 78 B1
Wilton Pl PO5 .... 182 B1
Wilton Rd
Bournemouth BH7 .... 205 F3
Southampton SO15 .... 78 B1
Wilton Terr PO5 .... 182 B1
Wiltshire Gdns BH23 .... 192 C4
Wiltshire Rd Brangore BH23 .. 192 C4
Chandler's Ford SO53 .... 55 E2
Wiltshire St PO5 .... 182 A2
Wilverley Ave
Bournemouth BH8 .... 190 C1
Havant PO9 .... 136 A2
Wilverley Cl SO41 .... 197 D1
Wilverley Pl SO45 .... 150 C1
Wilverley Rd
Brockenhurst SO42 .... 145 F1
Brockenhurst, Wootton BH25 . 170 C2
Christchurch BH23 .... 208 A4
Wimbledon Park Rd PO5 .. 182 B1
Wimborne Cty Fst Sch BH21 . 163 D2
Wimborne House SO16 .... 77 F1
Wimborne Inf & Jun Schs
PO4 .... 183 D2
Wimborne Rd
Bournemouth BH10,11,2,3,9 .. 204 C3
Bournemouth, Kinson
BH10,11,2,3,9 .... 189 E3
Broadstone BH21 .... 162 C1
Poole BH15 .... 202 B3
Portsmouth PO4 .... 183 D2
Wimborne Minster BH21 .... 163 D3
Wimborne Minster BH21 .... 163 F3
Wimborne Rd E BH21 .... 165 E3
Wimborne Rd W
Ferndown BH21 .... 164 B3
Wimborne Minster BH21 .... 164 B3
Wimpole Ct 63 PO1 .... 182 B3
Wimpole St PO1 .... 182 B3
Wimpson Gdns SO16 .... 77 F1
Wimpson La SO16 .... 101 F4
Wincanton Way PO7 .... 112 A3
Winchcombe Rd PO6 .... 133 D1
Winchelsea Sch BH12 .... 188 B1
Winchester 4 SO31 .... 127 D3
Winchester Coll SO23 .... 10 C3
Winchester Coll (New Hall)
SO23 .... 11 D3
Winchester Ct Gosport PO13 .. 180 B3
5 Romsey SO51 .... 28 A1
Southampton SO15 .... 78 B1
Winchester Hill SO51 .... 53 D4
Winchester House 30 PO9 .. 136 A3
Winchester Pl 3 BH15 .... 202 B1
Winchester Rd
Bishop's Waltham SO32 .... 83 D4
Botley SO32 .... 81 F2
Chandler's Ford SO53 .... 55 F2
Durley SO32 .... 81 D2
Fair Oak SO32,SO50 .... 81 F2
Langrish GU32 .... 39 F2
New Milton BH25 .... 195 E2
North Baddesley SO51 .... 28 B1
Owslebury SO21, SO32 .... 58 B2
Petersfield GU32 .... 39 F2
Portsmouth PO2 .... 182 C4
Romsey SO51 .... 28 B1
Romsey SO51 .... 52 C4
Shedfield SO32 .... 83 F1
Southampton SO16 .... 78 B1
Upham SO32 .... 58 B2
Winchester Sch of Art SO23 .... 11 D4
Winchester St
Botley SO30 .... 106 A4
4 Southampton SO15 .... 102 C3
Winchester Sta SO22 .... 10 C4
Winchester Way SO40 .... 100 B4
Winchfield Cl SO19 .... 104 A1
Winchfield Cres PO9 .... 135 E2
Winchfield House PO12 .... 181 F2
Wincombe Cl BH22 .... 165 E2
Wincombe Dr BH22 .... 165 E2
Windbury Rd SO16 .... 77 F1
Windermere Ave
Southampton SO16 .... 77 F1
Stubbington PO14 .... 154 B2
Windermere Gdns SO40 .... 100 C4
Windermere House 5 PO6 .. 157 D4
Windermere Rd
Bournemouth BH3 .... 205 D4
Portsmouth PO2 .... 157 F2
West End SO18 .... 80 A1
Windgreen Est BH21 .... 186 C4
Windham Mews BH1 .... 205 E3
Windham Rd BH1 .... 205 E3
Windhill Field PO7 .... 111 D2
Windmill Clanfield PO8 .... 88 B3
5 Milford on Sea SO41 .... 211 E3
St Leonards BH24 .... 140 B2
Windmill Copse SO45 .... 125 F1
Windmill Gr PO16 .... 156 B3

Windmill La
Bursledon SO31 .... 105 D4
St Leonards BH24 .... 140 B4
Windover SO19 .... 104 B4
Windrush Gdns PO7 .... 134 B4
Windrush Rd SO16 .... 101 F4
Windrush Way SO45 .... 126 A4
Windsor Cl Hordle SO41 .... 195 F4
St Leonards BH24 .... 139 F4
Windsor Ct
5 Christchurch BH23 .... 209 D4
9 Cosham PO6 .... 157 F4
Poole BH14 .... 203 D2
13 Southampton, Bitterne SO18 103 F4
Southampton, Millbrook SO15 .. 102 A4
5 Southampton, Westwood Pk
SO17 .... 103 D4
Windsor Gate SO50 .... 56 A4
Windsor House
25 Portsmouth PO1 .... 182 B4
18 Winchester SO23 .... 11 D3
Windsor La 24 PO5 .... 182 B1
Windsor Rd
Bournemouth BH5 .... 205 F1
Christchurch BH23 .... 206 C3
Cosham PO6 .... 157 F4
Gosport PO12 .... 181 D2
Petersfield GU32 .... 40 C1
Poole BH14 .... 203 D2
Portchester PO16 .... 156 B4
Windsor Way SO41 .... 93 D3
Windward Dr 11 PO12 .... 181 E1
Wine Cross PO17 .... 109 D2
Winecross PO17 .... 109 D1
Winfield Way PO10 .... 136 C3
Winfrid House SO40 .... 100 B4
Winfrith Cres BH12 .... 203 F1
Winfrith Way SO16 .... 77 E3
Wingate Dr SO19 .... 104 A3
Wingate Rd
Gosport PO12 .... 155 F2
Totton SO40 .... 100 B4
Wingfield Ave
Christchurch BH23 .... 193 E1
Poole BH15 .... 202 B3
Wingfield Ct BH1 .... 205 E2
Wingfield St PO1 .... 182 B4
Wingrove Rd SO40 .... 100 B3
Winifred Cl SO50 .... 57 E2
Winifred Rd Poole BH15 .... 202 C3
Waterlooville PO7 .... 134 C4
Winkfield Row PO8 .... 112 A3
Winkle St SO14 .... 103 D1
Winkton Cl Burton BH23 .... 192 B2
Havant PO9 .... 135 E2
Winkton House BH23 .... 192 B2
Winn Ct SO17 .... 102 C4
Winn Mansions 25 SO17 .... 79 D1
Winn Rd SO17 .... 79 D1
Winnal Ind Est 9 SO23 .... 11 D3
Winnall Cl SO23 .... 2 B1
Winnall Manor Rd SO23 .... 11 E4
Winnall Prim Sch SO23 .... 11 E4
Winnall Trad Est SO23 .... 11 E4
Winnall Valley Rd SO23 .... 11 E4
Winnards Cl BH22 .... 165 F1
Winnards Pk SO31 .... 128 B2
Winnham Dr PO16 .... 132 A1
Winnington PO15 .... 130 B2
Winnington Cl PO15 .... 130 B2
Winscombe Ave PO8 .... 112 A1
Winsford Ave SO50 .... 57 D1
Winsford Cl Bishopstoke SO50 .. 57 D1
Christchurch BH23 .... 193 E1
Winsford Gdns SO50 .... 57 D1
Winslade Rd Havant PO9 .... 135 E3
Winchester SO22 .... 1 B2
Winsley Ave BH6 .... 206 B2
Winslow Ct PO6 .... 158 B4
Winsor Cl PO11 .... 185 E1
Winsor Ct SO50 .... 56 B2
Winsor La SO40 .... 99 F4
Winsor Rd Cadnam SO40 .... 75 E1
Totton SO40 .... 101 D3
Waterlooville PO7 .... 111 E1
Winspit Cl BH15 .... 201 F2
Winstanley Rd Nursling SO16 .. 77 E3
Portsmouth PO2 .... 157 E1
Winston Ave BH12 .... 204 A3
Winston Churchill Ave PO5 .. 182 B2
Winston Cl
Eastleigh SO50 .... 56 A2
South Hayling SO11 .... 184 C2
Winston Ct
1 Christchurch BH23 .... 207 D4
20 New Milton BH25 .... 195 D1
Winston Gdns BH12 .... 204 A3
Winston Par 22 BH25 .... 195 D1
Winston Pk BH12 .... 204 A3
Winston Rd BH9 .... 190 A2
Winston Way BH24 .... 141 D4
Winstone Bldgs SO16 .... 78 C2
Winstone Cres SO52 .... 54 A2
Winter Rd PO4 .... 183 D2
Winterbourne Cl BH15 .... 202 B2
Winterbourne Rd
Cosham PO6 .... 132 C1
Poole BH15 .... 202 B3
Romsey SO51 .... 28 A1
Winterhayes Cl BH17 .... 187 F2
Winterhill Rd PO6 .... 157 E4
Winters Cl SO45 .... 150 B2
Winters Hill
Bishop's Waltham SO32 .... 82 C4
Durley SO32 .... 82 C4
Winters Rd SO32 .... 84 A1
Winterslow Dr PO9 .... 135 F3
Winton Cl SO41 .... 197 F2

Winton Ct
[11] Petersfield GU32 .... 40 C2
West End SO30 .... 80 B1
Winton Prim Sch BH9 .... 189 F1
Winton Rd Petersfield GU32 .... 40 C2
  Portsmouth PO2 .... 157 F1
Winton Sch for Boys (Annex)
  BH9 .... 189 F1
Winton Sec Sch BH10 .... 189 E1
Winton St [12] SO14 .... 103 D3
Winton Way
  Bournemouth BH10 .... 189 E1
  New Milton BH25 .... 195 D3
Wisbech Way SO41 .... 195 F2
Wisborough Rd PO5 .... 182 C1
Wisbro Ct PO12 .... 181 F2
Wish Pl PO5 .... 182 C2
Wishart Gdns BH9 .... 190 A3
Wistaria House BH10 .... 189 F2
Wisteria Dr BH12 .... 115 E2
Witchampton Cl PO9 .... 136 A3
Witchampton Rd BH18 .... 186 C1
Witham Cl SO53 .... 55 D3
Withedwood Ave SO15 .... 102 B4
Witherbed La
  Locks Heath PO15 .... 129 E2
  Locks Heath PO15 .... 129 F3
Withermoor Rd BH9 .... 204 C4
Withers La SO42 .... 175 E4
Withewood Mans [2] SO15 .... 102 B4
Withies Rd PO13 .... 180 B4
Withingham Rd BH13 .... 203 F2
Withington Cl PO6 .... 133 D1
Withy Cl SO51 .... 52 C4
Witley BH14 .... 214 B4
Witley Rd PO8 .... 111 F3
Witney Rd BH17 .... 187 E1
Witt Rd SO50 .... 57 E1
Wittensford La SO43 .... 98 B4
Wittering Rd
  South Hayling PO11 .... 185 F1
  Southampton SO16 .... 78 A2
Witts Hill SO18 .... 79 F1
Woburn Cl SO50 .... 56 A3
Woburn Ct PO13 .... 179 F1
Woburn Rd SO16 .... 78 B3
Wode Cl PO8 .... 88 B2
Wodehouse Rd SO19 .... 103 F2
Woking Rd BH14 .... 203 E2
Wolfe Cl Christchurch BH23 .... 207 E4
  Winchester SO22 .... 10 B3
Wollaston Rd BH6 .... 206 C2
Wollaton Cres BH22 .... 165 E2
Wollaton Rd BH22 .... 165 E2
Wollstonecraft Rd [25] BH5 .... 205 F2
Wolseley Rd Poole BH12 .... 203 E3
  Southampton SO15 .... 102 B4
Wolsey Way SO41 .... 211 E3
Wolterton Rd BH12 .... 204 A3
Wolverley Ct
[16] Bournemouth BH4 .... 204 B2
  Southampton SO16 .... 78 B2
Wolverton Rd
  Bournemouth BH7 .... 205 F3
  Havant PO9 .... 135 F3
  Southampton SO14 .... 103 D3
Wolvesey Pl SO53 .... 55 D2
Wolvesey Terr [3] SO23 .... 11 D3
Wonderholm Par BH11 .... 189 D1
Wonston Ct PO9 .... 136 A3
Wonston Rd SO16 .... 78 A2
Wood Cl SO19 .... 104 B2
Wood End Rd BH24 .... 141 F3
Wood End Way SO53 .... 55 D3
Wood Glade Cl SO40 .... 101 F1
Wood House La SO41 .... 174 A1
Wood La
  Bournemouth BH11 .... 188 C3
  Bramdean SO24 .... 15 F3
  Milford on Sea SO41 .... 211 E2
  Southwick PO17 .... 133 D3
Wood Lark Gdns GU31 .... 41 E2
Wood Lawn Cl BH25 .... 209 F4
Wood Lodge SO40 .... 76 A1
Wood Rd SO40 .... 100 A1
Wood View BH21 .... 164 A4
Wood's Cnr BH24 .... 143 E3
Woodacre Gdns BH22 .... 165 F2
Woodberry La PO9 .... 136 C4
Woodbourne Cl
  Fareham PO15 .... 130 B1
  Liss GU33 .... 21 D2
Woodbury BH1 .... 205 D1
Woodbury Ave
  Bournemouth BH8 .... 190 C1
  Havant PO9 .... 159 F4
  Petersfield GU32 .... 40 C2
Woodbury Cl BH23 .... 191 F2
Woodcock La SO41 .... 196 A2
Woodcocks Cres BH7 .... 206 A4
Woodcot Cres PO9 .... 136 A3
Woodcot Prim Sch PO13 .... 155 D2
Woodcote Cotts SO24 .... 15 E2
Woodcote Dr BH16 .... 201 D3

Woodcote La PO14 .... 155 D2
Woodcote Rd SO17 .... 79 E2
Woodcroft La PO8 .... 111 F3
Woodend Rd BH9 .... 204 C4
Wooderson Cl SO50 .... 57 D2
Woodfern SP6 .... 70 B1
Woodfield Ave PO6 .... 134 C1
Woodfield Cotts GU32 .... 19 D2
Woodfield Dr SO22 .... 10 A3
Woodfield Gdns BH23 .... 193 E1
Woodfield Park Rd PO10 .... 161 D4
Woodfield Rd BH11 .... 189 D3
Woodford Cl BH24 .... 141 E4
Woodford House PO15 .... 130 B1
Woodford Rd BH11 .... 205 E2
Woodgason La PO11 .... 160 B1
Woodgreen Ave PO9 .... 135 E2
Woodgreen Dr BH11 .... 188 B2
Woodgreen Rd SO22 .... 1 B2
Woodgreen Wlk SO40 .... 76 A1
Woodhall Way PO15 .... 130 C2
Woodhay Wlk [13] PO9 .... 136 A3
Woodhayes Ave BH23 .... 193 F1
Woodhill Prep Sch SO30 .... 105 F4
Woodhill Sch SO53 .... 55 E4
Woodhouse La
  Hedge End SO30 .... 105 F4
  Rowland's Castle PO8,PO9 .... 113 E2
Woodington Cl PO9 .... 136 A3
Woodington Rd SO51 .... 51 E3
Woodlake SO17 .... 187 E1
Woodland Ave BH5 .... 206 A2
Woodland Cl
  Southampton SO18 .... 104 B4
  West Wellow SO51 .... 51 D1
Woodland Ct BH7 .... 205 F3
Woodland Drove SO21 .... 32 A3
Woodland Mans BH14 .... 203 D3
Woodland Mews SO30 .... 80 B1
Woodland Pl [18] SO15 .... 102 C4
Woodland St PO1 .... 182 C3
Woodland Vale SO19 .... 104 A2
Woodland View
  Bursledon SO31 .... 127 F4
  Horndean PO8 .... 111 F3
Woodland Way
  Christchurch BH23 .... 208 B4
  Milford on Sea SO41 .... 211 E2
Woodland Wlk
  Bournemouth BH5 .... 206 A2
  Ferndown BH22 .... 165 F4
Woodlands PO16 .... 131 E1
Woodlands Ave
  Emsworth PO10 .... 136 C2
  Hamworthy BH15 .... 201 F2
Woodlands Cl
  Bransgore BH23 .... 193 D4
  Chandler's Ford SO53 .... 30 B1
  Gosport PO13 .... 180 B3
  Hythe SO45 .... 125 F1
  Locks Heath SO31 .... 128 C3
Woodlands Com Sch SO18 .... 104 B4
Woodlands Cres BH15 .... 201 F3
Woodlands Ct Hythe SO45 .... 125 F1
[18] Winchester SO23 .... 2 A1
Woodlands Dr SO31 .... 127 E3
Woodlands Dro SO40 .... 99 F2
Woodlands Gdns [8] SO51 .... 28 A1
Woodlands Gr PO7 .... 134 B3
Woodlands La Liss GU33 .... 21 D2
  South Hayling PO11 .... 184 C3
Woodlands Prim Sch PO8 .... 111 E2
Woodlands Rd Ashurst SO40 .... 99 F2
  Barton on Sea BH25 .... 209 F4
  Brockenhurst SO42 .... 172 C4
  Netley Marsh SO40 .... 99 F2
Woodlands The
  Chandler's Ford SO53 .... 30 A1
  Kings Worthy SO23 .... 2 B3
Woodlands Way
  Bursledon SO31 .... 127 F4
  Havant PO9 .... 135 F2
  New Milton BH25 .... 195 D3
  North Baddesley SO52 .... 53 F2
  Southampton SO15 .... 102 C4
  St Leonards BH24 .... 139 F2
Woodlane SO24 .... 15 E3
Woodlea Cl SO22 .... 1 C1
Woodlea Gdns SO30 .... 80 C1
Woodlea House SO53 .... 55 E2
Woodlea Way SO51 .... 29 F1
Woodleaze Cl BH18 .... 187 D3
Woodleigh Cl PO9 .... 136 B2
Woodley Cl SO51 .... 28 B1
Woodley Close Flats SO51 .... 28 B1
Woodley Gdns SO41 .... 197 E3
Woodley La SO51 .... 28 A1
Woodley Rd Gosport PO12 .... 181 E2
  Southampton SO19 .... 103 E2
Woodley Way SO51 .... 28 B1
Woodling Cres SP6 .... 70 B1
Woodlinken Cl BH31 .... 115 D2
Woodlinken Dr BH31 .... 115 D3
Woodlinken Way BH31 .... 115 E2

Woodmancote La PO10 .... 137 F2
Woodmancote Rd PO4 .... 183 D2
Woodmill La SO18 .... 79 F1
Woodmoor Cl SO40 .... 102 A1
Woodpath PO5 .... 182 B2
Woodpath House [35] PO5 .... 182 B2
Woodpecker Cl Havant PO9 .... 136 A1
  Verwood BH31 .... 114 C3
Woodpecker Copse SO31 .... 129 D2
Woodpecker Dr
  Broadstone BH17 .... 201 F4
  Marchwood SO40 .... 101 F1
  Winchester SO22 .... 1 B1
Woodpecker Way SO50 .... 55 E1
Woodrising BH13 .... 214 A2
Woodrisings The BH2 .... 204 B2
Woodroffe Wlk PO10 .... 136 C2
Woodrow PO7 .... 110 C2
Woodrush Cres SO31 .... 128 C1
Woods House [3] GU32 .... 40 C2
Woods View Rd BH9 .... 204 B4
Woodsedge PO7 .... 135 D3
Woodside
  Brockenhurst SO42 .... 173 D4
  Chilworth SO16 .... 54 C1
  Gosport PO13 .... 155 D3
Woodside Ave Eastleigh SO50 .... 56 A3
  Lymington SO41 .... 197 F1
Woodside Cl Ferndown BH22 .... 165 F3
[13] Lymington SO41 .... 197 F1
  Marchwood SO40 .... 101 F1
Woodside Cres SO16 .... 54 C1
Woodside Ct [21] SO17 .... 103 D4
Woodside Gdns SO40 .... 100 B2
Woodside La SO41 .... 197 F1
Woodside Rd
  Bournemouth BH5 .... 206 A2
  Eastleigh SO50 .... 55 F2
  Ferndown BH22 .... 165 F3
  North Baddesley SO52 .... 53 F2
  Poole BH14 .... 203 E2
  Southampton SO17 .... 103 D4
  West Moors BH22 .... 138 B2
Woodside Way SO30 .... 105 D3
Woodstock Ave BH25 .... 112 A3
Woodstock Cl Fareham PO15 .... 130 C1
  Hedge End SO30 .... 105 E3
  Poole BH14 .... 203 D1
Woodstock Dr SO17 .... 79 D1
Woodstock La BH24 .... 141 D3
Woodstock Rd
  Burton BH23 .... 192 B1
  Gosport PO12 .... 181 E2
  Havant PO9 .... 135 E1
  Poole BH14 .... 203 D1
Woodthorpe Gdns SO31 .... 128 C3
Woodvale PO15 .... 130 B1
Woodvale Gdns BH25 .... 195 E2
Woodview SO16 .... 79 D3
Woodville Dr PO1 .... 182 A2
Woodville Rd Fawley SO45 .... 151 D2
  Havant PO9 .... 135 D1
Woodward Cl PO12 .... 180 C2
Woofferton Rd PO6 .... 133 D1
Wool Rd BH12 .... 203 D4
Woolfield La GU34 .... 18 A2
Woolford Cl [1] SO22 .... 10 B3
Woolley House [15] SO14 .... 103 D3
Woolmer Ct [35] PO9 .... 136 A3
Woolmer La BH24 .... 117 D1
Woolmer St PO10 .... 136 C2
Woolner Ave Cosham PO6 .... 158 A4
  Petersfield GU32 .... 40 C2
Woolsbridge Ind Est BH21 .... 139 D3
Woolsbridge Rd BH24 .... 139 F3
Woolslope Cl BH22 .... 138 C1
Woolslope Gdns BH22 .... 138 C1
Woolslope Rd BH22 .... 138 C1
Woolston Ct PO12 .... 180 B2
Woolston Inf Sch SO19 .... 103 F1
Woolston Rd Havant PO9 .... 135 E3
  Netley SO31 .... 127 E4
Woolston Sch (Annexe) SO19 .... 103 F2
Woolston Sec Sch SO19 .... 103 F1
Woolston Sta SO19 .... 103 E2
Woolven Cl BH14 .... 203 D3
Woolwich Cl SO31 .... 104 C1
Wootton SO31 .... 127 E4
Wootton Farm Rd BH25 .... 170 C1
Wootton Gdns BH1 .... 205 D2
Wootton Mount BH1 .... 205 D2
Wootton Rd
  Lee-on-the-Solent PO13 .... 180 A2
  New Milton BH25 .... 195 E4
Wootton Rough BH25 .... 195 D3
Wootton Sta PO6 .... 157 F4
Worbarrow Gdns BH12 .... 203 E4
Worcester Ct PO13 .... 180 B3
Worcester Pl
[7] Lymington SO41 .... 197 F1
  Southampton SO19 .... 104 A1
Wordsworth Ave
  Bournemouth BH8 .... 190 C1
  Portchester PO6 .... 132 C1

Wordsworth Cl
  Bishop's Waltham SO32 .... 83 F4
  Winchester SO22 .... 10 B4
Wordsworth Inf Sch SO15 .... 78 A1
Wordsworth Rd SO15 .... 78 B1
Worgret Rd BH15 .... 202 B4
Workhouse La GU32 .... 38 B1
Worldham Rd PO9 .... 136 A3
Worrell Dr BH12 .... 203 E4
Worsley Rd PO5 .... 182 B2
Worsley St PO4 .... 183 D1
Worthing Ave PO12 .... 180 C4
Worthing Rd PO5 .... 182 B1
Worthington Cres BH14 .... 203 D2
Worthy Ct [46] PO9 .... 136 A3
Worthy House SO16 .... 78 A1
Worthy La SO23 .... 1 C1
Worthy Rd
  New Milton BH25 .... 195 D1
  Winchester SO22 .... 2 A1
Wortley Rd BH23 .... 209 D4
Wraxall Ct PO4 .... 187 E1
Wraysbury Park Rd PO10 .... 136 C2
Wren Cl
  Christchurch BH23 .... 208 A3
  New Milton BH25 .... 194 C1
  Ringwood BH24 .... 141 E3
  Winchester SO22 .... 10 B3
Wren Cres BH12 .... 204 A3
Wren Gdns SP6 .... 93 D3
Wren Rd SO50 .... 55 F1
Wrenway PO16 .... 155 F4
Wrexham Gr PO8 .... 88 A1
Wright Way SO45 .... 151 F1
Wright's Hill SO19 .... 104 A1
Wrights Wlk SO31 .... 104 C1
Wroxham Rd BH12 .... 203 F3
Wryneck Cl SO16 .... 78 A3
Wuthering Hghts SO22 .... 10 C3
Wyatts Cl BH21 .... 186 B3
Wyatts La BH21 .... 186 B3
Wyborn Cl PO11 .... 185 D1
Wych La BH21 .... 155 D2
Wychwood Cl BH2 .... 204 C2
Wychwood Dr
  Blackfield SO45 .... 177 F4
  Bournemouth BH2 .... 204 C2
Wychwood Gr SO53 .... 55 F4
Wychwood Grange [1] BH2 .... 204 C2
Wycliffe Rd
  Bournemouth BH9 .... 204 C4
  Southampton SO18 .... 80 A1
Wycote Rd PO13 .... 155 D2
Wyeford Cl [4] PO9 .... 136 A3
Wyelands Ave BH21 .... 164 B3
Wykeham Ave PO2 .... 157 F1
Wykeham Cl Netley SO31 .... 127 E3
  Poole BH17 .... 202 C4
  Southampton SO16 .... 78 C2
Wykeham Field PO17 .... 108 A2
Wykeham House Sch PO16 .... 131 E1
Wykeham Ind Est The SO23 .... 2 B2
Wykeham Lodge BH13 .... 214 C3
Wykeham Pl
  Lymington SO41 .... 197 F2
  Winchester SO22 .... 10 B3
Wykeham Rd
[3] Netley SO31 .... 127 D3
  Portsmouth PO2 .... 157 F1
Wyld Green La GU33 .... 21 D3
Wylds La GU32 .... 65 E4
Wyllie Rd PO2 .... 157 F2
Wylye Cl SO18 .... 80 A2
Wymering La PO6 .... 133 F1
Wymering Manor Cl [9] PO6 .... 157 E4
Wymering Rd PO2 .... 182 C4
Wyn Sutcliffe Ct PO4 .... 183 D2
Wyncombe Rd BH5 .... 206 A3
Wyndcliffe Rd PO4 .... 182 C2
Wyndham Cl
  Christchurch BH23 .... 194 A1
  Waterlooville PO8 .... 112 A2
Wyndham Ct SO15 .... 102 C3
Wyndham Mews PO1 .... 182 A2
Wyndham Pl [14] SO15 .... 102 C3
Wyndham Rd
  Christchurch BH23 .... 194 A1
  Poole BH14 .... 203 D2
Wynford Ind Est
  Abbotswood SO51 .... 27 F2
  Michelmersh SO51 .... 27 F2
Wynford Rd
  Bournemouth BH9 .... 190 A2
  Poole BH14 .... 203 E2
Wynne Cl BH18 .... 186 C2
Wynter Cl BH7 .... 205 F4
Wynter Rd SO18 .... 104 A4
Wynton Way PO15 .... 130 B2
Wynyards Gap SO52 .... 53 F2
Wyre Cl SO53 .... 55 D3
Wyvern Cl
  Chandler's Ford SO53 .... 55 E3
  Poole BH12 .... 203 E4
Wyvern Sch The SO50 .... 57 E1

Yaldhurst Ct [12] PO9 .... 136 A3
Yaldhurst La SO41 .... 197 D2
Yapton St PO1 .... 182 B3
Yarborough Rd PO5 .... 182 B2
Yardlea Cl PO9 .... 113 D1
Yardley Cl PO3 .... 158 B2
Yardley Rd SO30 .... 105 E3
Yarmouth Cl BH12 .... 204 A3
Yarmouth Gdns [11] SO15 .... 78 A1
Yarmouth Rd BH12 .... 203 F3
Yarrell Mead SO41 .... 197 D2
Yarrells Cl BH16 .... 201 E3
Yarrells Dr BH16 .... 201 E3
Yarrells La BH16 .... 201 E3
Yarrells Sch BH16 .... 201 D4
Yarrow Cl BH23 .... 208 A4
Yarrow Rd BH12 .... 203 D4
Yarrow Way SO31 .... 128 C1
Yateley Cl PO9 .... 135 E3
Yaverland SO31 .... 127 E3
Yeatminster Rd BH17 .... 187 F1
Yeatton House SO41 .... 196 A1
Yelverton Ave SO45 .... 150 A4
Yelverton Rd [33] BH1 .... 204 C2
Yeo Ct PO4 .... 183 E2
Yeoman Pk BH8 .... 77 E1
Yeomans Ind Pk BH8 .... 190 C1
Yeomans Rd BH8 .... 190 C2
Yeomans Way
  Bournemouth BH8 .... 190 C1
  Totton SO40 .... 100 C4
Yeovil Chase SO18 .... 104 A4
Yeovilton Cl SO41 .... 196 C1
Yerville Gdns SO41 .... 195 F2
Yew La BH25 .... 195 E2
Yew Rd SO18 .... 104 A4
Yew Tree Ave PO8 .... 112 A1
Yew Tree Cl Fair Oak SO50 .... 57 E3
  Hedge End SO30 .... 105 D3
  Wimborne Minster BH21 .... 163 E3
Yew Tree Ct
  Fordingbridge SP6 .... 93 F4
  Locks Heath SO31 .... 129 D4
[30] New Milton BH25 .... 195 D1
Yew Tree Dr PO15 .... 129 D4
Yew Tree Gdns PO7 .... 110 C2
Yew Tree Pl GU33 .... 21 D2
Yew Tree Rd PO11 .... 185 D4
Yews The PO8 .... 112 B4
Yewside PO13 .... 155 F1
Yewtree La SO16 .... 77 E2
Yoells Cres PO8 .... 111 F3
Yoells La PO8 .... 111 F3
Yokesford Hill SO51 .... 27 F2
Yokesford Hill Est SO51 .... 27 F3
Yonge Cl SO50 .... 56 A2
York Ave BH25 .... 195 D4
York Bldgs SO14 .... 103 D2
York Cl
  Broadstone BH18 .... 187 D1
  Christchurch BH23 .... 206 C4
  Fair Oak SO50 .... 81 E4
  North Baddesley SO52 .... 54 C2
  Petersfield GU32 .... 40 B2
  Southampton SO14 .... 103 E3
  Totton SO40 .... 101 D4
York Cres PO13 .... 180 A2
York Dro
  Nomansland SP5 .... 73 E4
  Southampton SO18 .... 104 A4
York Gdns SO16 .... 156 C3
York House
[26] Gosport PO12 .... 181 E2
[7] Southampton SO14 .... 103 E3
[32] Winchester SO23 .... 2 A1
York Pl
  Bournemouth BH7 .... 206 A3
[17] New Milton BH25 .... 195 D3
  Portsmouth PO1 .... 182 A3
York Rd
  Bournemouth BH1 .... 205 D2
  Broadstone BH18 .... 187 D1
  Eastleigh SO50 .... 80 A4
  Netley SO31 .... 127 D3
  Southampton SO15 .... 102 B4
York Terr PO3 .... 157 F3
Yorke St PO5 .... 182 B2
Yorke Way SO31 .... 127 F2
Yorkwood GU33 .... 20 C2
Youngbridge Ct PO14 .... 155 D4
Youngs Rd BH11 .... 189 D3
Yves Mews PO5 .... 182 B1

Zamek Cl BH11 .... 189 D3
Zetland Ct BH4 .... 204 A1
Zetland Rd
  Cosham PO6 .... 158 B4
  Gosport PO12 .... 181 D3
Zeus La PO7 .... 134 C2
Zinnia Cl BH10 .... 189 F1

STREET ATLASES ORDER FORM

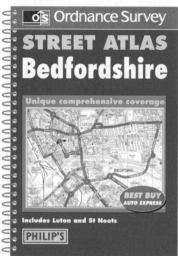

PHILIP'S

The Street Atlases are available from all good bookshops or by mail order dire from the publisher. Orders can be made in the following ways. **By phone** Ring our speci Credit Card Hotline on **01933 443863** during office hours (9am to 5pm) or leave a message on the answering machine, quoting your full credit card number plus expiry date and your full name and address. **By post or fax** Fill out the order form below (you may photocopy it) and post it to: **Philip's Direct, 27 Sanders Road, Wellingborough, Northants NN8 4NL** or fax it to: **01933 443849**. Before placing an order by post, by fax or on the answering machine, please telephone to check availability and prices.

COLOUR LOCAL ATLASES	PAPERBACK	Quantity @ £3.50 each	£ Total
CANNOCK, LICHFIELD, RUGELEY		☐ 0 540 07625 2 ➤	
DERBY AND BELPER		☐ 0 540 07608 2 ➤	
NORTHWICH, WINSFORD, MIDDLEWICH		☐ 0 540 07589 2 ➤	
PEAK DISTRICT TOWNS		☐ 0 540 07609 0 ➤	
STAFFORD, STONE, UTTOXETER		☐ 0 540 07626 0 ➤	
WARRINGTON, WIDNES, RUNCORN		☐ 0 540 07588 4 ➤	

COLOUR REGIONAL ATLASES				
	HARDBACK	SPIRAL	POCKET	
	Quantity @ £10.99 each	Quantity @ £8.99 each	Quantity @ £4.99 each	£ Total
MERSEYSIDE	☐ 0 540 06480 7	☐ 0 540 06481 5	☐ 0 540 06482 3 ➤	
	Quantity @ £12.99 each	Quantity @ £8.99 each	Quantity @ £5.99 each	£ Total
BERKSHIRE	☐ 0 540 06170 0	☐ 0 540 06172 7	☐ 0 540 06173 5 ➤	
	Quantity @ £12.99 each	Quantity @ £9.99 each	Quantity @ £4.99 each	£ Total
DURHAM	☐ 0 540 06365 7	☐ 0 540 06366 5	☐ 0 540 06367 3 ➤	
	Quantity @ £12.99 each	Quantity @ £9.99 each	Quantity @ £5.50 each	£ Total
GREATER MANCHESTER	☐ 0 540 06485 8	☐ 0 540 06486 6	☐ 0 540 06487 4 ➤	
TYNE AND WEAR	☐ 0 540 06370 3	☐ 0 540 06371 1	☐ 0 540 06372 X ➤	
	Quantity @ £12.99 each	Quantity @ £9.99 each	Quantity @ £5.99 each	£ Total
BEDFORDSHIRE	☐ 0 540 07801 8	☐ 0 540 07802 6	☐ 0 540 07803 4 ➤	
BIRMINGHAM & WEST MIDLANDS	☐ 0 540 07603 1	☐ 0 540 07604 X	☐ 0 540 07605 8 ➤	
BUCKINGHAMSHIRE	☐ 0 540 07466 7	☐ 0 540 07467 5	☐ 0 540 07468 3 ➤	
CHESHIRE	☐ 0 540 07507 8	☐ 0 540 07508 6	☐ 0 540 07509 4 ➤	
DERBYSHIRE	☐ 0 540 07531 0	☐ 0 540 07532 9	☐ 0 540 07533 7 ➤	
EDINBURGH & East Central Scotland	☐ 0 540 07653 8	☐ 0 540 07654 6	☐ 0 540 07656 2 ➤	
NORTH ESSEX	☐ 0 540 07289 3	☐ 0 540 07290 7	☐ 0 540 07292 3 ➤	
SOUTH ESSEX	☐ 0 540 07294 X	☐ 0 540 07295 8	☐ 0 540 07297 4 ➤	
GLASGOW & West Central Scotland	☐ 0 540 07648 1	☐ 0 540 07649 X	☐ 0 540 07651 1 ➤	
NORTH HAMPSHIRE	☐ 0 540 07471 3	☐ 0 540 07472 1	☐ 0 540 07473 X ➤	

Registered Office: 2-4 Heron Quays, London E14 4JP
Registered in England number: 3597451

COLOUR REGIONAL ATLASES

	HARDBACK	SPIRAL	POCKET	£ Total
	Quantity @ £12.99 each	Quantity @ £9.99 each	Quantity @ £5.99 each	
SOUTH HAMPSHIRE	☐ 0 540 07476 4	☐ 0 540 07477 2	☐ 0 540 07478 0	➤ ☐
HERTFORDSHIRE	☐ 0 540 06174 3	☐ 0 540 06175 1	☐ 0 540 06176 X	➤ ☐
EAST KENT	☐ 0 540 07483 7	☐ 0 540 07276 1	☐ 0 540 07287 7	➤ ☐
WEST KENT	☐ 0 540 07366 0	☐ 0 540 07367 9	☐ 0 540 07369 5	➤ ☐
LEICESTERSHIRE	☐ 0 540 07854 9	☐ 0 540 07855 7	☐ 0 540 07856 5	➤ ☐
NORTHAMPTONSHIRE	☐ 0 540 07745 3	☐ 0 540 07746 1	☐ 0 540 07748 8	➤ ☐
OXFORDSHIRE	☐ 0 540 07512 4	☐ 0 540 07513 2	☐ 0 540 07514 0	➤ ☐
SURREY	☐ 0 540 07794 1	☐ 0 540 07795 X	☐ 0 540 07796 8	➤ ☐
EAST SUSSEX	☐ 0 540 07306 7	☐ 0 540 07307 5	☐ 0 540 07312 1	➤ ☐
WEST SUSSEX	☐ 0 540 07319 9	☐ 0 540 07323 7	☐ 0 540 07327 X	➤ ☐
WARWICKSHIRE	☐ 0 540 07560 4	☐ 0 540 07561 2	☐ 0 540 07562 0	➤ ☐
SOUTH YORKSHIRE	☐ 0 540 06330 4	☐ 0 540 07667 8	☐ 0 540 07669 4	➤ ☐
WEST YORKSHIRE	☐ 0 540 07671 6	☐ 0 540 07672 4	☐ 0 540 07674 0	➤ ☐
	Quantity @ £14.99 each	Quantity @ £9.99 each	Quantity @ £5.99 each	£ Total
LANCASHIRE	☐ 0 540 06440 8	☐ 0 540 06441 6	☐ 0 540 06443 2	➤ ☐
NOTTINGHAMSHIRE	☐ 0 540 07541 8	☐ 0 540 07542 6	☐ 0 540 07543 4	➤ ☐
	Quantity @ £14.99 each	Quantity @ £10.99 each	Quantity @ £5.99 each	£ Total
STAFFORDSHIRE	☐ 0 540 07549 3	☐ 0 540 07550 7	☐ 0 540 07551 5	➤ ☐

BLACK AND WHITE REGIONAL ATLASES

	HARDBACK	SOFTBACK	POCKET	£ Total
	Quantity @ £11.99 each	Quantity @ £8.99 each	Quantity @ £3.99 each	
BRISTOL & AVON	☐ 0 540 06140 9	☐ 0 540 06141 7	☐ 0 540 06142 5	➤ ☐
	Quantity @ £12.99 each	Quantity @ £9.99 each	Quantity @ £4.99 each	£ Total
CARDIFF, SWANSEA & GLAMORGAN	☐ 0 540 06186 7	☐ 0 540 06187 5	☐ 0 540 06207 3	➤ ☐

Name..

Address..

....

....

....

....Postcode.....................

➤ **Add £2 postage and packing per order**

➤ All available titles will normally be dispatched within 5 working days of receipt of order but please allow up to 28 days for delivery

☐ Please tick this box if you do not wish your name to be used by other carefully selected organisations that may wish to send you information about other products and services

Total price of order   £ ☐

(including postage and packing at £2 per order)

I enclose a cheque/postal order, for   £ ☐

made payable to *Octopus Publishing Group Ltd*,

or please debit my ☐ Mastercard ☐ American Express

☐ Visa   account by £ ☐

Account no

☐☐☐☐ ☐☐☐☐ ☐☐☐☐ ☐☐☐☐

Expiry date ☐☐ ☐☐

Signature..

Post to: Philip's Direct, 27 Sanders Road, Wellingborough, Northants NN8 4NL

o|s Ordnance Survey

STREET ATLASES ORDER FORM

o|s Ordnance Survey

STREET ATLAS
Leicestershire and Rutland
LEICESTER CITY CENTRE AT EXTRA-LARGE SCALE
Plus town maps of Corby, Grantham, Nuneaton and Rugby
Unique comprehensive coverage
BEST BUY AUTO EXPRESS
Includes Stamford and Swadlincote
PHILIP'S

o|s Ordnance Survey
STREET ATLAS
Tyne and Wear
COMPLETE COUNTY...

o|s Ordnance Survey
STREET ATLAS
Glasgow
and West Central Scotland
Comprehensive coverage from Stirling to Ayr and Greenock to Lanark
PHILIP'S

o|s Ordnance Survey
STREET ATLAS
North Essex
BEST BUY AUTO EXPRESS
Unique comprehensive coverage
Plus Bishop's Stortford, Felixstowe, Ipswich
PHILIP'S

PHILIP'S

Ordnance Survey

Updated annually

MOTORING ATLAS
Britain

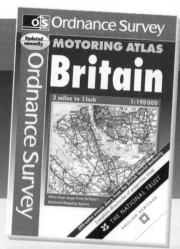

The best-selling *OS Motoring Atlas Britain* uses unrivalled and up-to-date mapping from the Ordnance Survey digital database. The exceptionally clear mapping is at a large scale of 3 miles to 1 inch (Orkney/Shetland Islands at 5 miles to 1 inch).

A special feature of the atlas is its wealth of tourist and leisure information. It contains comprehensive directories, including descriptions and location details, of the properties of the National Trust in England and Wales, the National Trust for Scotland, English Heritage and Historic Scotland. There is also a useful diary of British Tourist Authority Events listing more than 300 days out around Britain during the year.

Available from all good bookshops or direct from the publisher:
Tel: 01933 443863

The atlas includes:

- 112 pages of fully updated mapp
- 45 city and town plans
- 8 extra-detailed city approach me
- route-planning maps
- restricted motorway junctions
- local radio information
- distances chart
- county boundaries map
- multi-language legend